Recent Progress in Digital Video Processing

Recent Progress in Digital Video Processing

Edited by **Anna Sanders**

New York

Published by Willford Press,
118-35 Queens Blvd., Suite 400,
Forest Hills, NY 11375, USA
www.willfordpress.com

Recent Progress in Digital Video Processing
Edited by Anna Sanders

International Standard Book Number: 978-1-68285-312-2 (Hardback)

Contents

Preface

Digital video processing has revolutionised the field of video recording and processing. The applications of digital video processing have found its way across different sectors like multimedia, communications, security, etc. The topics covered in this extensive book deal with core subjects such as video compression and restoration, video coding, different techniques for video processing, etc. As this field is emerging at a rapid pace, the contents of this book will help the readers understand the modern concepts and applications of the subject.

The information shared in this book is based on empirical researches made by veterans in this field of study. The elaborative information provided in this book will help the readers further their scope of knowledge leading to advancements in this field.

Finally, I would like to thank my fellow researchers who gave constructive feedback and my family members who supported me at every step of my research.

Editor

Full-reference video quality metric assisted the development of no-reference bitstream video quality metrics for real-time network monitoring

Iñigo Sedano[1*], Kjell Brunnström[2,4], Maria Kihl[3] and Andreas Aurelius[2,3]

Abstract

High-quality video is being increasingly delivered over Internet Protocol networks, which means that network operators and service providers need methods to measure the quality of experience (QoE) of the video services. In this paper, we propose a method to speed up the development of no-reference bitstream objective metrics for estimating QoE. This method uses full-reference objective metrics, which makes the process significantly faster and more convenient than using subjective tests. In this process, we have evaluated six publicly available full-reference objective metrics in three different databases, the EPFL-PoliMI database, the HDTV database, and the Live Video Wireless database, all containing transmission distortions in H.264 coded video. The objective metrics could be used to speed up the development process of no-reference real-time video QoE monitoring methods that are receiving great interest from the research community. We show statistically that the full-reference metric Video Quality Metric (VQM) performs best considering all the databases. In the EPFL-PoliMI database, SPATIAL MOVIE performed best and TEMPORAL MOVIE performed worst. When transmission distortions are evaluated, using the compressed video as the reference provides greater accuracy than using the uncompressed original video as the reference, at least for the studied metrics. Further, we use VQM to train a lightweight no-reference bitstream model, which uses the packet loss rate and the interval between instantaneous decoder refresh frames, both easily accessible in a video quality monitoring system.

Keywords: H.264; Full reference; Objective metrics; Video quality; Transmission distortions

1. Introduction

Streaming high-quality digital video over Internet Protocol (IP)-based networks is increasing in popularity both among users and operators. Two examples of these applications are *IPTV* and *Over The Top (OTT) Video* [1]. IPTV systems are managed by one operator, from video head-end to the user, and are based on ordinary broadcast television, using IP multicast. OTT Video is used to describe the delivery of TV over the public Internet, using unicast.

In order to ensure a high Quality of Experience (QoE), the network operators and service providers need methods to monitor the quality of the video services [2]. The monitoring and prediction should be performed in real-time and in different parts of the network. Since

* Correspondence: inigo.sedano@tecnalia.com
[1]TECNALIA, ICT - European Software Institute, Parque Tecnológico de Bizkaia, Edificio 202, Zamudio E-48170, Spain
Full list of author information is available at the end of the article

users' experienced quality is not easily understood and depends on many aspects [3], subjective assessments involving a panel of observers constitutes the most accurate method to measure the video QoE. However, in a monitoring situation, subjective assessments are very hard to perform and therefore objective measurement methods are desirable. Even for the development of these measurement methods subjective data is usually required, which may be cumbersome and time consuming to obtain when developing real-time monitoring systems. Furthermore, for subjective testing to be accurate, it requires careful planning, preparation and involvement of a number of viewers. This makes it costly to conduct.

Instead, objective metrics, which accurately characterize the video quality and predict viewer quality of experience, have evolved for some time now, but there is still a long way to go before they, in general, can accurately predict the results of subjective measurements [4]. The objective metrics can be classified as no reference, reduced reference, and full reference [5]. Traditionally, in the full-reference scenario, an original undistorted high-quality video is compared to a degraded version of the same video, for example, pixel by pixel or block based. Reduced-reference methods require partial or parameterized information about the original video sequence. No-reference methods rely only on the degraded video. Here, we generalize the concept of FR, RR, and NR by also including packet header models, bitstream models, and hybrid models together with the pure video-based models based on the amount of reference information used by the models, as suggested in Barkowsky et al. [6].

Objective video quality metrics are usually argued to be useful because subjective quality assessment is expensive and time consuming to perform. However, in the development of the objective metrics, subjective data is essential to train, optimize, and evaluate these metrics. Therefore, it would be advantageous and shorten the development time, if it was possible to use well performing objective quality metrics in the development process of new video quality metrics. The purpose of this paper is to show a cost- and time-effective development strategy for computationally efficient light weight no-reference bitstream video quality metrics. Here, the scope of model, meaning the area in which it is valid, is an additional important parameter, for example, see [6]. This is especially true for NR models where it is harder to develop good performing models with broad scopes. Therefore, by limiting the scope of a NR video quality metric, it is possible to achieve high prediction performance using a limited number of parameters. The drawback is that the usage should be within the scope that it was designed for. However, the strategy is then to redesign the model using the same method again to tailor it for the new application area. Specifically, the proposed method is to first find a full-reference metric that performs well for the types of distortions we are interested

in, and then we use this metric to develop a no-reference metric. This could be summarized in a four step procedure as shown in the Figure 1 in a bit more detail.

1. Definition of scope
2. Find FR model for the scope
3. Train NR mode using FR model
4. Evaluate the performance of NR model

To illustrate the methodology, we have selected a concrete example, where we perform all the necessary steps for the procedure described above. This does not mean that we claim that this is the first time FR models are evaluated for packet loss, but to our knowledge, it has not been done for this particular scope, i.e., packet loss combined with coded reference. Still, it is presented for illustrating the methodology. In case it is already known which FR model that is best for a particular scope, then this step can be omitted. There may also be better NR models also for this scope, but it should be taken into account the relatively high performance combined with its simplicity of model and most importantly the low development effort.

As an example in this paper, see Figure 2, we first evaluate and select the best full-reference metric for transmission distortions in the case of compressed reference, which is a very specific scope. Then, we create a training database and we execute on it the selected full-reference metric. Finally, we model and validate the no-reference bitstream model. The created model will therefore be valid only in the scope of evaluating only transmission distortions. However, it can be redesigned following the same procedure in order to take into account other types of distortions, such as compression distortions. Here, we show the necessary steps in order to extend the model that we present in this paper. It would be necessary first to find the most suitable already existing objective metric to measure compression distortions, create a new training

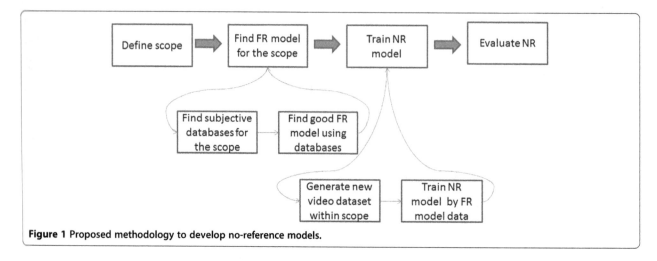

Figure 1 Proposed methodology to develop no-reference models.

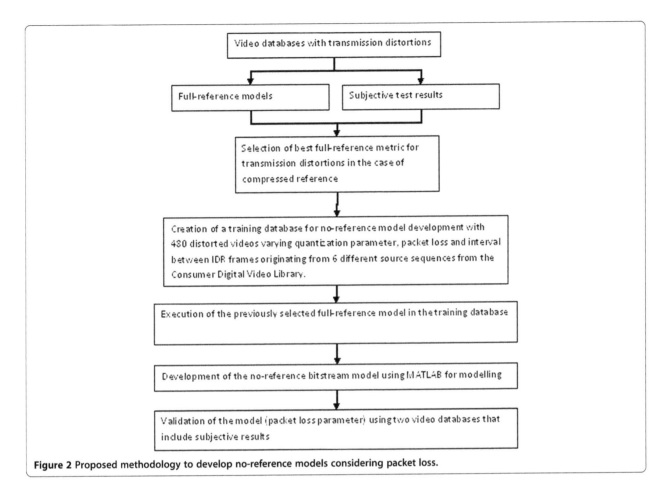

Figure 2 Proposed methodology to develop no-reference models considering packet loss.

database varying all the parameters of the extended model (model with compression and transmission distortions), execute the selected full-reference metric for compression distortions on the training database, and finally redesign the model incorporating the compression dependent parameters.

2. Background

Traditionally, video quality metrics make predictions on computations on the video data itself. Nowadays, there are emerging models also utilizing network information either by itself, i.e., bitstream models or in combination with the video data, i.e., hybrid models. A review of no-reference video quality estimators can be found in [7].

Most of the objective metrics have been developed and tested to estimate the perceived quality when the video is only compression degraded, for example, see [8,9]. However, video delivered over Internet will be degraded by transmission distortions, for example, packet loss. Several studies have shown that even a low packet loss rate can and most often will affect the video quality, for example, see [10].

Also, for objective quality monitoring, there are two other aspects of performance apart from prediction accuracy that are important: computational requirements and run time [11]. To be used in a real-time monitoring and prediction system, the objective quality methods must be lightweight and cannot require the original video reference [12,13]. Independent evaluations are scarce with the notable exception of the work by the Video Quality Experts Group (VQEG) [14]. One of the problems a developer or a tester must face is the unavailability of video databases, especially if they contain videos subject to packet losses. Also, in real network deployments, the uncompressed original sequence is usually not available. Therefore, we believe that it is important to evaluate the performance of the metrics when a compressed reference is used instead. For example, the video quality degradation introduced by a network node could be evaluated applying a full-reference metric such as VQM comparing the compressed reference that is available before the video enters the network node and the degraded video due to transmission distortions that is available after the video exits the network node.

The paper starts by describing the publicly available video databases that have been used for the development work. The details about the video sequences and how they have been compressed and distorted are described.

Also, the subjective tests that have been performed with the aforementioned video sequences are described in terms of number of viewers, viewing conditions, etc.

In the following section, the objective full-reference assessment algorithms are reviewed, and the scenarios in which they are used are outlined.

The following section contains the results of the evaluation of the objective full-reference assessment algorithms against the databases with subjective test data. The means of evaluation are the Spearman Rank Order Correlation Coefficient (SROCC), the Pearson correlation coefficient, the Root Mean Square Error (RMSE), and the Outlier Ratio (OR).

In the last section of the paper, we show how a no-reference objective model can be developed by training it against a full-reference objective metric. Naturally, we choose the metric with the best performance, as evaluated in the previous section.

3. Video databases

In the paper, we evaluate some full-reference objective metrics against three different publicly available databases with subjective quality ratings, based on H.264 coded videos that also contained transmission distortions. The transmission in the databases was handled by RTP over UDP (Real-time Transport Protocol over User Datagram Protocol), and the distortions were in the form of packet losses. This means that the work in this paper is applicable to cases with these conditions, such as, e.g.,

IPTV cases. This is an extention of the study done in [15]. The databases considered are EPFL-PoliMI (Ecole Polytechnique Fédérale de Lausanne and Politecnico di Milano) video quality assessment database [16-18], an HDTV video database made available by IRCCyN [19] and the LIVE Wireless Video Quality Assessment database [20]. In addition to the following descriptions, Table 1 summarizes the parameters corresponding to the three databases.

3.1 EPFL-PoliMI video database
3.1.1 Description
The freely available EPFL-PoliMI (Ecole Polytechnique Fédérale de Lausanne and Politecnico di Milano) video quality assessment database [16-18] was specifically designed for the evaluation of transmission distortions. The database contains 78 video sequences at 4CIF spatial resolution (704 × 576 pixels). The distorted videos were created from five 10-s-long and one 8-s-long uncompressed video sequences in planar I420 raw progressive format [21].

The reference videos were lightly compressed to ensure high video quality in the absence of packet losses. Therefore, a fixed Quantization Parameter between 28 and 32 was selected for each sequence. The Quantization Parameter regulates how much spatial detail is saved. The sequences were encoded and decoded in H.264/AVC [22] High Profile in the H.264/AVC reference software. B-pictures and Context-adaptive binary arithmetic coding (CABAC) were enabled for coding efficiency. Each frame

Table 1 Summary of conditions of all databases

	EPFL-PoliMI	HDTV video database	LIVE Wireless video database
Number of sequences	Total 78, 6 different source sequences	Total 45, 9 different source sequences in compressed and uncompressed formats	Total 170, 10 different source sequences
Resolution	4CIF (704 × 576)	1,920 × 1,080	768 × 480
Duration	10 and 8 s	10 s	10 s
Reference	Compressed (with high quality)	Compressed (with high quality) and uncompressed	Compressed (with high quality)
Compression parameter	Fixed QP between 28 and 32	Fixed QP value 26	Reference video: Fixed QP value 18; Degraded videos: bitrates 500 kbps, 1 Mbps, 1.5 Mbps and 2 Mbps
I-frame period	Not available	24 frames	Reference video: 14 frames; Degraded videos: 96
Frame rate	25 and 30 fps	59,94 (interlaced) fps	30 fps
Transmission distortions	PLR 0.1%, 0.4%, 1%, 3%, 5%, 10%. Two different channel realizations for each PLR	PLR 0.7% (from 42% to 56% of the way), 4.2% (from 21% to 64% of the way), 4.2% (from 42% to 56% of the way).	PLR 0.5%, 2%, 5% and 17%
Encoder/decoder	H.264/AVC JM reference software	Not available	H.264/AVC JM reference software
Number of subjects	21 at PoliMI lab and 19 at EPFL lab	24	31
Processing of subjective scores	Difference scores → Z-scores (with outliers detection) → re-scaling to range [0,5] → DMOS	Difference scores → Z-scores (with outliers detection) → re-scaling to range [0,5] → DMOS both for compressed and uncompressed reference	Difference scores → DMOS → re-scaling to range [0,5]

was divided into a fixed number of slices, where each slice consists of a full row of macroblocks.

The compressed videos in the absence of packet losses were used as the reference for the computation of the DMOS (Differential Mean Opinion Score) values. Three of the reference videos have a frame rate of 25 frames per second (fps). This was accomplished by cropping HD resolution video sequences down to 4CIF resolution and reducing the frame rate from 50 to 25 fps. The other three videos have a frame rate of 30 fps.

The transmission distortions were simulated at different packet loss rates (PLR) (0.1%, 0.4%, 1%, 3%, 5%, 10%). The packet loss was generated using a two-state Gilbert's model with an average burst length of three packets and two different channel realizations were selected for each PLR.

Forty naive subjects took part in the subjective tests. The subjective evaluation was done using the ITU continuous scale in the range [0–5] [23]. Twenty-one subjects participated in the evaluation at the PoliMI lab and 19 at the EPFL lab. More details about the subjective evaluation can be found in [16-18].

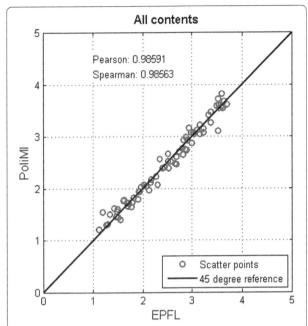

Figure 3 Scatter plot showing the correlation between the DMOS values obtained in the EPFL lab and in the PoliMI lab.

3.1.2 Processing of subjective scores
Although the raw subjective scores were already processed in the EPFL-PoliMI database, we processed them in a different way in order to merge the data from the two labs.

A Student T test considering the overall mean and standard deviation of the raw MOS individual scores of each lab showed that at 95% confidence level the data from the two labs were not significantly different, and therefore, we decided that they could be merged. As an additional verification, the DMOS and confidence interval values (in this case after normalization, screening, and re-scaling) were calculated for each content and distortion type and compared between the two labs, confirming that the data from the two labs were sufficiently similar to be merged. Seventy-two PVS were checked corresponding to six different packet loss rate, two different channel realizations for each PLR, for each of the six source sequences. In the scatter plot in Figure 3, it can be seen that the linear correlation between the DMOS values obtained in the PoliMI lab and the EPFL lab is high (0.986).

First of all, we calculated the difference scores by subtracting the scores of the degraded videos to the score of the reference videos. The difference scores for the reference videos were set to 0 and were removed. Accordingly, a lower difference score indicates a higher quality.

Each subject may have used the rating scale differently and with different offset. In order to account for this, the Z-scores were computed for each subject separately by means of the Matlab zscore function. The Z-scores

transform the original distribution to one in which the mean becomes zero and the standard deviation becomes one. Indeed, this normalization procedure reduces the gain and offset between the subjects. Subsequently, the outliers were detected according to the guidelines described in ITU-T Rec 910 Annex 2 Section 2.3.1 [23] and removed.

Next, the Z-scores were re-scaled to the range [0,5]. The Z-scores are assumed to be distributed as a standard Gaussian. Consequently, 99% of the scores will be in the range [−3,3]. In our study, 100% of the scores were placed in that range. All the data was in fact in the range [−3,3] so no clipping was done. The re-scaling was performed by linearly mapping the data range [−3,3] to the range [0,5] using the following formula:

$$z' = \frac{5.(z+3)}{6}$$

Finally, the Difference Mean Opinion Score (DMOS) of each video was computed as the mean of the re-scaled Z-scores from the 36 subjects that remained after rejection. Additionally, the confidence intervals were also computed. The methodology for the processing of the scores shown in this paper has been applied by many authors. For example, see [24].

3.2 HDTV video database
The HDTV video database was made freely available by Barkowsky et al. [19]. The video database contains nine different source video sequences, and we selected three

different conditions corresponding only to transmission distortions. In [19], these are referred to as the Hypothetical Reference Circuit (HRC) 5, 6, and 7. HRCs 5 to 7 are coded with high quality (QP26) and contain simulated transmission errors, mainly blurriness and motion artifacts. The errors were inserted in the middle of the video sequence. In HRC 5, from 42% to 56% of the way through the 14-s sequence's bitstream (before removing the beginning and end of the sequence), 0.7% of packets were randomly lost. HRC 6 contained 4.2% of packets randomly lost from 21% to 64% of the way through the bitstream. HRC 7 contained 4.2% of packets randomly lost from 42% to 56% of the way through the bitstream.

The encoder always used two interlaced slice groups of two macroblock lines. For error recovery, an intra image was forced every 24 frames and the ratio of intra macroblock refresh was 5%. The video resolution was 1,920 × 1,080 pixels at 59.94 fields-per-second in interlaced format. The sequences have a duration of 10 s. In total, 24 naive observers viewed the content. The Absolute Category Rating with Hidden Reference (ACR-HR) conforming to ITU-T P.910 with a five-point rating scale was used. The subjects viewed the content at a distance of 1.5 m corresponding to three times the picture height. More details about the subjective experiment can be found in [19].

The processing of the subjective scores was performed in the same way as for the EPFL-PoliMI video database. The DMOS values were calculated both for the scenario with compressed reference (QP26, HRC1) and with uncompressed reference (HRC0). Two outliers were found in the case of compressed reference and no outliers in the case of uncompressed reference.

3.3 LIVE Wireless video database

Moorthy et al. [20] evaluated publicly available full-reference video quality assessment algorithms on the LIVE Wireless Video Quality Assessment database. The LIVE Wireless video database contains ten source sequences, each 10 s long at a rate of 30 frames per second. The source videos are in RAW uncompressed progressive scan YUV420 format with a resolution of 768 × 480. However, the videos used as reference were already compressed with high quality (average PSNR > 45 dB). For the reference sequences, the Quantization Parameter was set to 18 and the I-frame period to 14. One-hundred sixty distorted videos were created (4 bitrates × 4 packet loss rates = 16 distorted videos per reference sequence). The simulated wireless transmission errors were inserted to the H.264 compressed videos, which were generated with the JM reference software (Version 13.1). The source videos were encoded using different bitrates: 500 kbps, 1 Mbps, 1.5 Mbps, and 2 Mbps with three different slice groups and an I-frame period of 96. The RD Optimization was

enabled, and the baseline profile was used for encoding and hence did not include B-frames. The packet size was set to between 100 and 300 bytes. The Flexible Macroblock Ordering (FMO) mode was set as 'dispersed'.

Packet loss rates of 0%, 5%, 2%, 5%, and 17% were simulated using bit-error patterns captured from different real or emulated mobile radio channels. The JM reference software was used to decode the compressed video stream.

For the subjective test, the Single Stimulus Continuous Quality Evaluation with hidden reference was used. A total of thirty-one subjects participated in the study. The difference scores were calculated by subtracting the score that the subject assigned to the distorted sequence to the score that the subject assigned to the reference sequence. One subject was rejected. The scores from the remaining subjects were then averaged to form a Differential Mean Opinion Score (DMOS) for each sequence. No Z-scores were used. Finally, we re-scaled the DMOS values to the range [0–5]. More details on the subjective study can be found on [20]. The LIVE Wireless video database is no longer publicly available because of the uniformity and simplicity of the content. However, we use this database because our study involves various video databases.

4. Objective assessment algorithms

The video quality metrics that were evaluated are the following well-known publicly available algorithms: Peak Signal-to-Noise Ratio (PSNR) [4], Structural SIMilarity (SSIM) index [25], Multi-scale SSIM (MS-SSIM) [26], Video Quality Metric (VQM) [27], Visual Signal to Noise Ratio (VSNR) [28], and MOtion-based Video Integrity Evaluation (MOVIE) [29]. The performance of the objective models is evaluated using the Spearman Rank Order Correlation Coefficient, the Pearson Linear Correlation Coefficient, the Root-Mean-Square Error (RMSE) and the Outlier Ratio. A non-linear regression was done using a monotonic function. The performance of the different metrics was compared by means of a statistical significance analysis based on the Pearson, RMSE, and Outlier Ratio coefficients.

4.1 Scenarios

The typical full-reference scenario is shown in Figure 4. The original uncompressed video is compared to the uncompressed video that contains the compression and transmission distortions.

In this paper, we also consider the scenario shown in Figure 5 that corresponds to compressed reference. The reference videos are lightly compressed to ensure high video quality in the absence of packet losses. The references are thus similar in quality to the uncompressed original. Therefore, in the compressed reference scenario, the video is first compressed before being used in the evaluation.

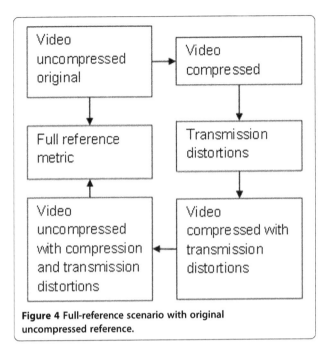

Figure 4 Full-reference scenario with original uncompressed reference.

The decompressed video with compression distortions is compared to the decompressed video with compression and transmission distortions.

4.2 Video quality algorithms

We have evaluated and compared several well-known objective video quality algorithms using the videos and

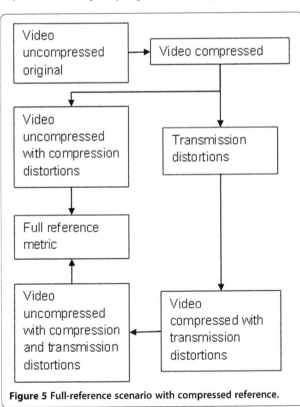

Figure 5 Full-reference scenario with compressed reference.

subjective results in the three databases. The objective algorithms are described below. The default values of the metrics were used for all the metrics. No registration problems, i.e., a misalignment between the reference and degraded videos due to the loss of entire frames, occurred in the dataset.

4.2.1 Peak Signal-to-Noise Ratio

PSNR is computed using the mean of the MSE vector (contains the Mean Square Error of each frame). The MSE is computed per frame. The implementation used is based on the 'PSNR of YUV videos' program (yuvpsnr. m) by Dima Pröfrock available in the MATLAB Central file repository [30]. Only the luminance values were considered.

4.2.2 Structural SIMilarity

SSIM [25] is computed for each frame. After that an average value is produced. The implementation used is an improved version of the original version [25] in which the scale parameter of SSIM is estimated. The implementation, named ssim.m, can be downloaded in the author's implementation home page [31]. Only the luminance values were considered.

4.2.3 Multi-scale SSIM

MS-SSIM [26] is computed for each frame. Afterwards, an average value is produced. The implementation used was downloaded from the Laboratory for Image & Video Engineering (LIVE) at the University Of Texas at Austin [32]. Only the luminance values were considered.

4.2.4 Video Quality Metric

For VQM, we used the software version 2.2 for Linux that was downloaded from the author's implementation home page [27]. We used the following parameters: parsing type none, spatial, valid, gain and temporal calibration automatic, temporal algorithm sequence, temporal valid uncertainty false, alignment uncertainty 15, calibration frequency 15, and video model general model. The files were converted from planar 4:2:0 to the format required by VQM (Big-YUV file format, 4:2:2) using ffmpeg.

4.2.5 Visual Signal-to-Noise Ratio

VSNR [28] is computed using the total signal and noise values of the sequence. We modified the authors' implementation available at [33] to extract the signal and noise values in order to sum them separately. Only the luminance values were considered. The VSNR was obtained dividing the total amount of signal by the total amount of noise.

Table 2 EPFL-POLIMI video database

	Pearson	Spearman	RMSE	Outlier ratio
PSNR	0.958	0.961	0.219	0.625
SSIM	0.959	0.969	0.217	0.597
MS-SSIM	0.964	0.978	0.204	0.597
VSNR	0.974	0.973	0.173	0.472
VQM	0.961	0.960	0.210	0.541
MOVIE	0.965	0.962	0.202	0.625
SPATIAL MOVIE	0.981	0.978	0.148	0.458
TEMPORAL MOVIE	0.924	0.914	0.294	0.611

4.2.6 MOtion-based Video Integrity Evaluation

MOVIE [29] includes three different versions: the Spatial MOVIE index, the Temporal MOVIE index and the MOVIE index. The MOVIE Index version 1.0 for Linux was used and can be downloaded from [32]. The optional parameters framestart, frameend, or frameint were not used. Only EPFL-PoliMI was analyzed with MOVIE.

4.3 Statistical analysis

In order to test the performance of the objective algorithms, we computed the Spearman Rank Order Correlation Coefficient (SROCC), the Pearson correlation coefficient, the RMSE, and the Outlier Ratio (OR) [34]. The Spearman coefficient assesses how well the relationship between two variables can be described using a monotonic function. The Pearson coefficient measures the linear relationship between a model's performance and the subjective data. The RMSE provides a measure of the prediction accuracy. Finally, the consistency attribute of the objective metric is evaluated by the Outlier Ratio.

The Pearson, RMSE, and Outlier Ratio were computed after a non-linear regression. In the analysis of the EPFL-PoliMI video database, the regression was performed using a monotonic cubic polynomial function with four parameters. The function is constrained to be monotonic:

$$DMOSp = a \cdot x^3 + b \cdot x^2 + c \cdot x + d.$$

In the above equation, the DMOSp is the predicted value. The four parameters were obtained using the MATLAB function 'nlinfit'.

In the analysis of the other two databases, a monotonic logistic function with four parameters was used instead:

$$DMOSp = \frac{\beta_1 - \beta_2}{1 + \exp\left(-\frac{x - \beta_3}{|\beta_4|}\right)} + \beta_2$$

In each of the databases, we used the function providing the best fitting. The performance of the metrics is compared by means of a statistical significance analysis

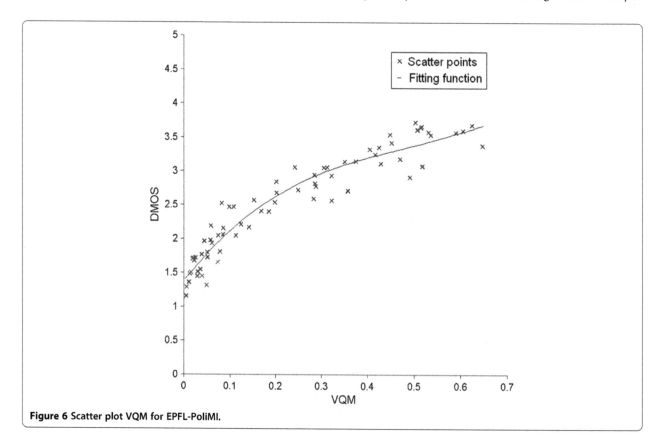

Figure 6 Scatter plot VQM for EPFL-PoliMI.

Table 3 HDTV video database compressed reference

	Pearson	Spearman	RMSE	Outlier ratio
PSNR	0.817	0.804	0.346	0.296
SSIM	0.871	0.856	0.295	0.370
MS-SSIM	0.891	0.884	0.273	0.296
VSNR	0.837	0.774	0.328	0.444
VQM	0.887	0.860	0.277	0.333

based on the Pearson, RMSE, and Outlier Ratio coefficients [34].

5. Evaluation of full-reference objective metrics

In this section, we present the results of the statistical analysis. Also, in several figures, the scatter plots of the VQM objective metric scores vs. DMOS for the different databases are shown. We show the plots of the VQM objective metric because the VQM metric performs very well in all the video databases. The fitting function is also plotted.

5.1 EPFL-PoliMI

In Table 2, the values of the coefficients corresponding to all the metrics for the EPFL-PoliMI video database are shown. The meaning of each coefficient was explained in the previous section. The values for the Pearson correlation coefficient ranged from 0.92 (for TEMPORAL MOVIE) to 0.98 (for SPATIAL MOVIE). The values for

the Spearman rank order correlation coefficient were confined within 0.91 (TEMPORAL MOVIE) and 0.98 (SPATIAL MOVIE). Looking also at the RMSE, we can see that the TEMPORAL MOVIE performed significantly worse than the other methods. In general, the magnitude of the coefficients was high and the differences between them were small. The statistical significance analysis based on Pearson and RMSE confirms that at 95% confidence level MS-SSIM, VSNR, VQM, MOVIE, and SPATIAL MOVIE performed better than TEMPORAL MOVIE, being SPATIAL MOVIE the best performing metric.

Further, in Figure 6, the scatter plot of VQM is shown including the fitting function. The horizontal axis corresponds to the values of the VQM metric. The vertical axis corresponds to the DMOS values. A lower DMOS means higher video quality. The fitting function is plotted in circles (one circle per VQM value). In the scatter plot, we can see that the correlation between VQM and DMOS is not linear and that the correlation is very high.

5.2 HDTV video database

In Table 3, the values of the coefficients corresponding to all the metrics for the HDTV video database when the reference is lightly compressed can be observed. It can be seen in the table that the values for the Pearson correlation coefficient were distributed within 0.82 (for PSNR) and 0.89 (for MS-SSIM). The values for the

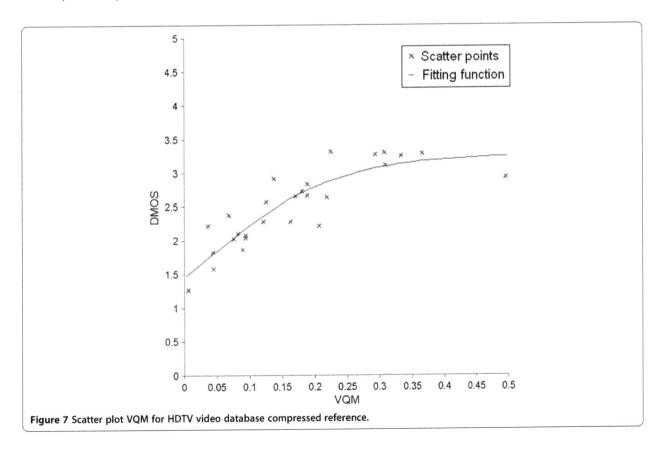

Figure 7 Scatter plot VQM for HDTV video database compressed reference.

Table 4 HDTV video database uncompressed reference

	Pearson	Spearman	RMSE	Outlier ratio
PSNR	0.661	0.600	0.422	0.555
SSIM	0.720	0.653	0.391	0.518
MS-SSIM	0.727	0.664	0.386	0.518
VSNR	0.629	0.511	0.438	0.592
VQM	0.840	0.782	0.305	0.370

Spearman rank order correlation coefficient were confined within 0.80 (for PSNR) and 0.88 (for MS-SSIM). The general magnitude of the coefficients was high. The statistical significance analysis based on Pearson and RMSE shows that at 95% confidence level, there were no significant differences between the studied metrics.

Further, in Figure 7, the scatter plot of VQM using compressed reference is shown including the fitting function. In the scatter plot, we can see that the correlation between VQM and DMOS is not linear and that the correlation is high.

In Table 4, the values of the coefficients corresponding to all the metrics for the HDTV video database when the reference is uncompressed are presented. The values for the Pearson correlation coefficient ranged from 0.63 (for VSNR) to 0.84 (for VQM). The values for the Spearman rank order correlation coefficient had the lowest value at 0.51 (VSNR) and the highest at 0.78 (VQM). The general

magnitude of the coefficients was low. The statistical significance analysis based on RMSE shows that at 95% confidence level, VQM performed better than VSNR.

Further, in Figure 8, the scatter plot of VQM using uncompressed reference is shown including the fitting function. The correlation between VQM and DMOS is high and not linear.

5.3 Live Wireless database

The coefficients corresponding to the LIVE Wireless database are shown in Table 5. The values for the Pearson correlation coefficient are distributed within 0.93 (for VSNR) and 0.97 (for VQM). The values for the Spearman rank order correlation coefficient are confined within 0.95 (VSNR) and 0.97 (VQM). The general magnitude of the coefficients is very high and the differences between them are small. The statistical significance analysis based on Pearson and RMSE shows that at 95% confidence level VQM performed better than all the other metrics.

Further, in Figure 9, the scatter plot of VQM is shown including the fitting function. In this case, the correlation between VQM and DMOS is approximately linear and very high.

5.4 Discussion

Our results show that VQM has a very good performance in all the databases, being the best metric among

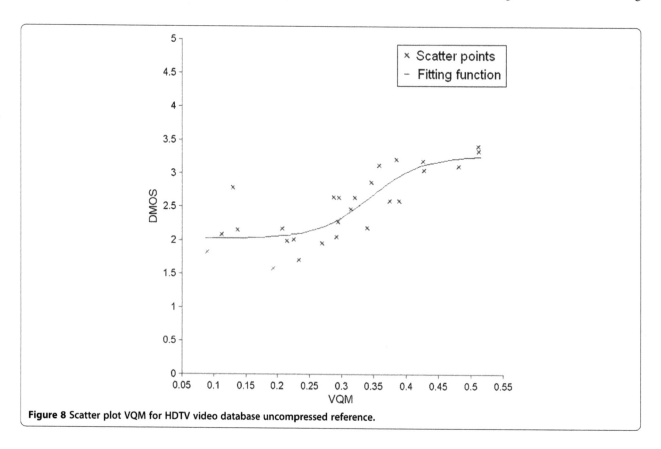

Figure 8 Scatter plot VQM for HDTV video database uncompressed reference.

Table 5 Live Wireless video database

	Pearson	Spearman	RMSE
PSNR	0.959	0.960	0.365
SSIM	0.954	0.954	0.386
MS-SSIM	0.96	0.963	0.364
VSNR	0.949	0.946	0.409
VQM	0.974	0.974	0.294

the studied in the HDTV video database (uncompressed reference) and in the LIVE Wireless video database. In the EPFL-PoliMI video database, SPATIAL MOVIE performed better than the other metrics. On the other hand, the performance of TEMPORAL MOVIE was lower than the other metrics, at least for the EPFL-PoliMI video database.

The performance of MOVIE, SPATIAL MOVIE, and TEMPORAL MOVIE was not evaluated in HDTV video databases and in the LIVE Wireless video database because the execution of the metric requires a very significant amount of time (many days) in comparison with the other metrics. This fact decreases the usability of these metrics considerably. It may be argued that for development purposes, it is less important, but with computation times of several hours, this is a problem also for this usage.

In the results from the HDTV video database, we can appreciate that the accuracy in the prediction can be increased if the reference is compressed, compared to the case where the reference is uncompressed.

6. No-reference bitstream model development

In this section, we demonstrate how the full-reference objective metrics can be used to speed up the development process of no-reference bitstream real-time video QoE monitoring methods. In particular, we develop a no-reference bitstream model using the VQM full-reference metric, and we validate it using the subjective databases EPFL-PoliMI and LIVE Wireless Video Quality Assessment database.

We present a lightweight no-reference bitstream method that uses the packet loss rate and the interval between instantaneous decoder refresh frames (IDR frames) to estimate the video quality. IDR frames are 'delimiters' in the stream. After receiving an IDR frame, frames prior to the IDR frame can no longer be used for prediction. As well as this, IDR frames are also I-frames, so they do not reference data from any other frame. This means they can be used as seek points in a video. The no-reference bitstream model was fitted using several videos from the Consumer Digital Video Library (CDVL) database [35] and the VQM metric. Then, it was validated with the video databases EPFL-PoliMI and LIVE Wireless Video Quality Assessment database. The VQM metric has been used to train the no-reference bitstream

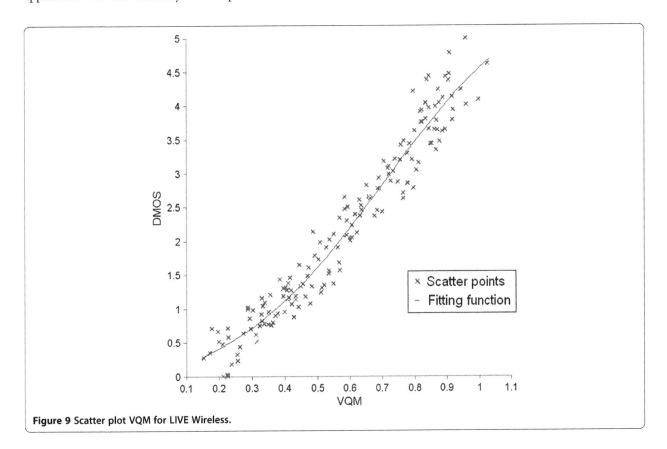

Figure 9 Scatter plot VQM for LIVE Wireless.

model regarding only the transmission distortions, and no compression distortions such as QP have been taken into consideration because it has been shown that VQM is very accurate when only transmission distortions are considered using a compressed reference. The case where VQM is used to measure a combination of compression and transmission distortions (for example, different QP and packet loss rate with uncompressed reference) is not evaluated in this paper.

6.1 Framework for model development

We selected the VQM metric to develop a no-reference bitstream model because of the very good performance shown in the previous section.

Six sequences with resolution $1,920 \times 1,080$ pixels were downloaded from the Consumer Digital Video Library (CDVL) database [35], with different characteristics. In five of the videos, the final part was removed to generate videos of a total length of 17 s at 30 fps. One of the sequences had a total length of 14 s at 25 fps. The SRC, listed in Table 6, were selected to spread a large variety of different content in Full-HD $1,920 \times 1,080$ format.

The videos were converted from YUV packed 4:2:2 to YUV planar 4:2:0. The videos were compressed with the Quantization Parameter set to 26, 32, 38 and 44. In order to make sure the no-reference model is valid for the different compression qualities the QP has been set to 26, 32, 38 and 44. However the performance of VQM in the case of compressed reference has been only tested in the case of compressed reference of high quality, which may not correspond to a QP value of 44. This causes a small degree of uncertainty in the obtained results because the scenario in which the compressed reference has low quality remains to be verified. The parameter keyint in the x264 encoder, corresponding to the interval between IDR frames, was set to 12, 36, 60 and 84. The maximum slice size was set to 1400 bytes. We consider that the keyint parameter is important since the distortion due to a packet loss propagates until the next IDR frame. Thus a higher value implies more error propagation and lower video quality. Finally the packet loss rate was set to 0.1%, 1%, 3%, 5%, and 10%. In total, $6 \times 4 \times 4 \times 5 = 480$ distorted videos were evaluated using the VQM metric.

Table 6 List of SRCs used in model development

SRC	Thumbnail	Description	Name of the sequence in CDVL
1		Woman smoking and people on a street, high contrast in the rock	NTIA outdoor mall with tulips (3e)
2		Kayaking, scene changes, fast moving water	NTIA Red Kayak
3		Trees, leaves, short and numerous movements in most of the image, scene changes	NTIA Aspen Trees in Fall Color, Slow Scene Cuts
4		Mountain with snow and moving fog in a sunny day, high brightness, scene changes	NTIA Snow Mountain
5		Global view of a city, buildings, scene changes, rather static	NTIA Denver Skyscrapers
6		Two people speaking in a table and showing an electronic device	NTIA Front End (Part of a Longer Talk)

The videos were encoded with the x264 encoder [36], random packet losses were inserted using a packet loss simulator [37] and the videos were decoded with the ffmpeg decoder. The ffmpeg decoder produces incomplete video files when random packet losses are inserted. To be able to apply the VQM metric, the videos were reconstructed so that they have the same length as the original. The reconstruction was done in two steps. First, the frame numbers were inserted into the luminance information of the uncompressed original sequence. After decoding the videos, the frame numbers were read and used to identify the missing frames and reconstruct the decoded video. The reconstruction method is explained in detail in [38].

The framework is described in Figure 10. As it can be seen in the figure, the VQM metric was applied (after conversion to packed 4:2:2 format) between the compressed reference (video compressed and uncompressed) and the reconstructed video. We used the same version of VQM than in the previous sections (described in Section 4.2). The same parameters as in Section 4.2 were used for VQM.

6.2 Model development

In this case, our objective was to develop a lightweight model to predict the quality of the video as a function of two parameters: packet loss rate in percentage, denoted p, and interval between IDR frames in number of frames, denoted I. The MATLAB function nlinfit was used to calculate the coefficients of the following equation:

$$VQM = b_0 + b_1 \cdot I^3 + b_2 \cdot I^2 + b_3 \cdot I + b_4 \cdot p^3 + b_5 \cdot p^2 + b_6 \cdot p.$$

With the non-linear fit, we obtained the following no-reference bitstream model for the predicted quality, $f(I,p)$:

$$f(I, p) = -0.16 - 0.0001 \cdot I^2 + 0.0064 \cdot I + 0.0003 \cdot p^3 - 0.0092 \cdot p^2 + 0.1106 \cdot p.$$

The three-dimensional plot in Figure 11 shows the VQM values as a function of packet loss rate and interval between IDR frames together with the developed model (surface).

6.3 Validation of the model

To validate the no-reference bitstream model, we applied the model to the EPFL-PoliMI and LIVE Wireless Video Quality Assessment databases, and we calculated the linear correlation coefficient with the subjective values. The model was not checked on the HDTV database because the HDTV database was done applying a packet loss rate to a percentage of the way through the

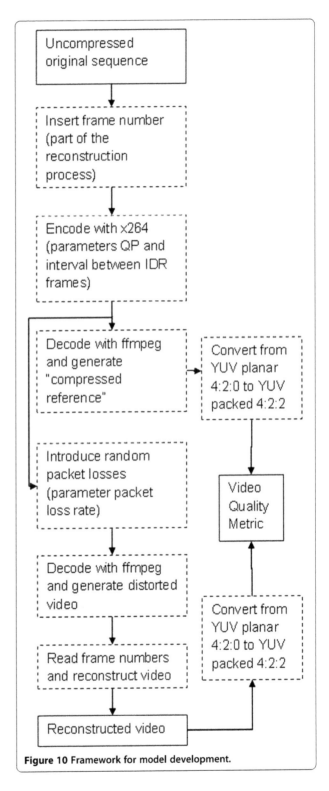

Figure 10 Framework for model development.

sequence. In order to apply our model, we expect a constant packet loss rate along all the sequence. As the interval between IDR frames is fixed in all the databases used, we are only able to verify the part of the equation related to the packet loss rate. For the EPFL-PoliMI, we

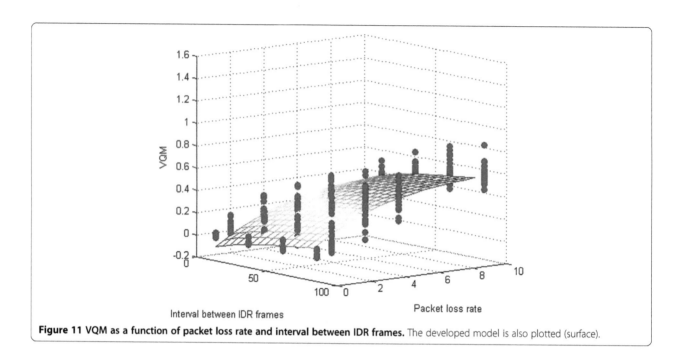

Figure 11 VQM as a function of packet loss rate and interval between IDR frames. The developed model is also plotted (surface).

obtained a linear correlation coefficient of 0.945, and for the LIVE Wireless Video Quality Assessment database, we obtained a linear correlation coefficient of 0.903. We believe that the model can be improved by adding new parameters and improving the fitting function used. The important fact is that these results validate the methodology followed in order to develop a no-reference bitstream model.

7. Conclusions

High-quality video streaming services over the Internet are increasing in popularity, and as people start to pay for the services, the quality must be guaranteed. Therefore, video quality monitoring and prediction become important in the development of Internet service management systems. Numerous objective assessment methods have been proposed; however, independent comparisons are scarce. Also, real-time monitoring requires lightweight no-reference bitstream models that perform accurately enough.

In this paper, we propose a strategy for developing new no-reference objective video quality metrics by using well performing full-reference video objective quality metrics to reduce the development time. The starting point is to define a relatively narrow scope. Find a FR model to create a big training database by varying the parameters that will be present. Train the NR model on this database. The NR model can then be validated using a smaller subjective test. In case there is a need for the use of the model outside the scope, the strategy is to retrain the model for the new scope.

This strategy is illustrated on the scope of transmission distortions in the case of compressed reference. As a first step, we have evaluated six publicly available full-reference metrics using three freely available video databases. The main objective of the evaluation was to compare the performance of the metrics when transmission distortions in the form of packet loss were introduced. The results show that VQM performs very well in all the video databases, being the best metric among the studied in the HDTV video database (uncompressed reference) and in the LIVE Wireless video database. In the EPFL-PoliMI database, SPATIAL MOVIE performed best and TEMPORAL MOVIE performed worst. When transmission distortions are evaluated, using the compressed video as the reference provides greater accuracy than using the uncompressed original video as the reference, at least for the studied metrics.

We believe that the correlation values obtained would be lower if registration problems occurred and different error concealment strategies were applied.

Further, to demonstrate the suggested strategy of model development, we present a no-reference bitstream model trained and optimized using full-reference model evaluation. The objective of the model is to accurately enough predict the video quality when transmission distortions are introduced. We fit the model using videos from the Consumer Digital Video Library (CDVL) database and the VQM metric. Then, the model is validated using the video databases EPFL-PoliMI and LIVE Wireless Video Quality Assessment database with reasonable performance.

Competing interests
The authors declare that they have no competing interests.

Acknowledgements
This work was developed inside the Future Internet project supported by the Basque Government within the ETORTEK Programme and the FuSeN project supported by the Spanish Ministerio de Ciencia e Innovación, under grant from Fundación Centros Tecnológicos - Iñaki Goenaga and Tecnalia Research & Innovation. The work was also partly financed by the CELTIC project IPNQ-SIS, and the national project EFRAIM, with the Swedish Governmental Agency for Innovation Systems (VINNOVA) supporting the Swedish contribution.

Author details
[1]TECNALIA, ICT - European Software Institute, Parque Tecnológico de Bizkaia, Edificio 202, Zamudio E-48170, Spain. [2]Acreo Swedish ICT AB, NETLAB: Visual Media Quality, Box 1070, Kista SE-164 25, Sweden. [3]Deptartment of Electrical and Information Technology, Lund University, Box 117, Lund SE-221 00, Sweden. [4]Department of Information Technology and Media, Mid Sweden, University, Holmgatan 10, Sundsvall SE-851 70, Sweden.

References
1. K Ahmad, A Begen, IPTV and video networks in the 2015 timeframe: The evolution to medianets. IEEE. Commun. Mag. **47**, 68–74 (2009)
2. A Takahashi, D Hands, V Barriac, Standardization activities in the ITU for a QoE assessment of IPTV. IEEE. Commun. Mag. **46**, 78–84 (2008)
3. F Kuipers, R Kooij, DD Vleeschauwer, K Brunnström, *Techniques for measuring quality of experience.* Lecture notes in computer science 6074/2010 (Springer Berlin, Heidelberg, 2010)
4. S Winkler, P Mohandas, The evolution of video quality measurements: from PSNR to Hybrid metrics. IEEE. Trans. Broadcast. **54**, 660–668 (2008)
5. AR Reibman, VA Vaishampayan, Y Sermadevi, Quality monitoring of video over a packet network. IEEE. Trans. Multimed. **6**, 327–334 (2004)
6. M Barkowsky, I Sedano, K Brunnström, M Leszczuk, N Staelens, Hybrid video quality prediction: re-viewing video quality measurement for widening application scope. Multimed Tool Appl. in press
7. S Hemami, A Reibman, No-reference image and video quality estimation: applications and human-motivated design. Signal Process. Image Commun. Elsevier. **25**, 469–481 (2010)
8. M Pinson, S Wolf, A new standardized method for objectively measuring video quality. IEEE. Trans. Broadcast. **50**(3), 312–322 (2004)
9. C Lee, S Cho, J Choe, T Jeong, W Ahn, E Lee, Objective video quality assessment. Optic. Engineer. **45**(1), 017004 (2006)
10. J Greengrass, J Evans, A Begen, Not all packets are equal, part 2: the impact of network packet loss on video quality. IEEE. Int. Comput. **13**, 74–82 (2009)
11. K Brunnström, D Hands, F Speranza, A Webster, VQEG validation and ITU standardization of objective perceptual video quality metrics. IEEE. Signal. Process. Mag. **26**, 96–101 (2009)
12. M Naccari, M Tagliasacchi, S Tubaro, No-reference video quality monitoring for H.264/AVC coded video. IEEE. Trans. Multimed. **11**, 932–946 (2009)
13. M Garcia, A Raake, P List, Towards content-related features for parametric video quality prediction of IPTV services, in *Proceedings of the IEEE International Conference on Acoustic, Speech and Signal Processes* (, Las Vegas, NV, 2008)
14. Video quality experts group page. http://www.its.bldrdoc.gov/vqeg. Accessed 07 Jan 2014
15. I Sedano, M Kihl, K Brunnstrom, A Aurelius, Evaluation of video quality metrics on transmission distortions in H.264 coded videos, in *Proceedings of the IEEE International Symposium on Broadband Multimedia Systems and Broadcasting (BMSB)* (Nuremberg, 2011)
16. F De Simone, M Naccari, M Tagliasacchi, F Dufaux, S Tubaro, T Ebrahimi, Subjective assessment of H.264/AVC video sequences transmitted over a noisy channel, in *Proceedings of the International Workshop on Quality of Multimedia Experience (QoMEX)* (San Diego, CA, 2009)
17. F De Simone, M Tagliasacchi, M Naccari, S Tubaro, T Ebrahimi, A H264/AVC video database for the evaluation of quality metrics, in *Proceedings of the IEEE International Conference on Acoustics, Speech, and Signal Processing (ICASSP)* (Dallas, TX, 2010)
18. EPFL-PoliMI video quality assessment database [Online]. Available: http://vqa.como.polimi.it. Accessed 07 Jan 2014
19. M Barkowsky, M Pinson, R Pépion, P Le Callet, Analysis of freely available subjective dataset for HDTV including coding and transmission distortions, in *Proceedings of the Fifth International Workshop on Video Processing and Quality Metrics for Consumer Electronics (VPQM)* (Scottsdale, AZ, 2010)
20. AK Moorthy, K Seshadrinathan, R Soundararajan, AC Bovik, Wireless video quality assessment: a study of subjective scores and objective algorithms. IEEE. Transact. Circ. Syst. Video Technol. **20**(4), 513–516 (2010)
21. FOURCC, YUV formats [Online]. Available: http://www.fourcc.org/yuv.php. Accessed 07 Jan 2014
22. H.264/AVC reference software version JM14.2, Tech. Rep., Joint Video Team (JVT) [Online]. Available: http://iphome.hhi.de/suehring/tml/download/old_jm/. Accessed 07 Jan 2014
23. ITU-T, *Recommendation ITU-T P 910, September 1999, Subjective video quality assessment methods for multimedia applications* (ITU-T, Geneva)
24. K Seshadrinathan, R Soundararajan, AC Bovik, LK Cormack, Study of subjective and objective quality assessment of video. IEEE. Trans. Image Process. **19**, 1427–1441 (2010)
25. Z Wang, AC Bovik, HR Sheikh, EP Simoncelli, Image quality assessment: from error visibility to structural similarity. IEEE. Trans. Image Process. **13**(4), 600–612 (2004)
26. Z Wang, EP Simoncelli, AC Bovik, Multi-scale structural similarity for image quality assessment, in *Proceedings of the IEEE Asilomar Conference Signals, Systems and Computers* (Pacific Grove, CA, 2003)
27. Video Quality Metric (VQM) software [online]. Available: http://www.its.bldrdoc.gov/vqm/. Accessed 07 Jan 2014
28. DM Chandler, SS Hemami, VSNR: a wavelet-based visual signal-to-noise ratio for natural images. IEEE. Trans. Image Process. **16**(9), 2284–2298 (2007)
29. K Seshadrinathan, AC Bovik, Motion tuned spatio-temporal quality assessment of natural videos. IEEE. Trans. Image Process. **19**(2), 335–350 (2010)
30. MATLAB Central File Exchange [Online]. Available: http://www.mathworks.com/matlabcentral/fileexchange/. Accessed 07 Jan 2014
31. The Structural SIMilarity (SSIM) index author's home page [Online]. Available: http://www.ece.uwaterloo.ca/~z70wang/research/ssim/. Accessed 07 Jan 2014
32. Laboratory for image & video engineering [online]. Available: http://live.ece.utexas.edu/research/Quality/index.htm. Accessed 07 Jan 2014
33. VSNR implementation from the authors [Online]. Available: http://foulard.ece.cornell.edu/dmc27/vsnr/vsnr.html. Accessed 07 Jan 2014
34. Final report from the video quality experts group on the validation of objective models of multimedia quality assessment, phase I [Online]. Available: ftp://vqeg.its.bldrdoc.gov/Documents/VQEG_Approved_Final_Reports/VQEG_MM_Report_Final_v2.6.pdf. Accessed 07 Jan 2014
35. The consumer digital video library [online]. Available: http://www.cdvl.org/about/index.php. Accessed 07 Jan 2014
36. x264 software [Online]. Available: http://www.videolan.org/developers/x264.html. Accessed 07 Jan 2014
37. JVT-Q069 [Y. Guo, H. Li, Y.-K. Wang] SVC/AVC loss simulator [Online]. Available: http://wftp3.itu.int/av-arch/jvt-site/2005_10_Nice/. Accessed 07 Jan 2014
38. I Sedano, M Kihl, K Brunnstrom, A Aurelius, Reconstruction of incomplete decoded videos for use in objective quality metrics, in *Proceedings of the 19th Int. Conf. Syst. Signals Image Process (IWSSIP)* (s, Vienna, 2012), pp. 376–379

2

Implementation of fast HEVC encoder based on SIMD and data-level parallelism

Yong-Jo Ahn[1], Tae-Jin Hwang[1], Dong-Gyu Sim[1*] and Woo-Jin Han[2]

Abstract

This paper presents several optimization algorithms for a High Efficiency Video Coding (HEVC) encoder based on single instruction multiple data (SIMD) operations and data-level parallelism. Based on the analysis of the computational complexity of HEVC encoder, we found that interpolation filter, cost function, and transform take around 68% of the total computation, on average. In this paper, several software optimization techniques, including frame-level interpolation filter and SIMD implementation for those computationally intensive parts, are presented for a fast HEVC encoder. In addition, we propose a slice-level parallelization and its load-balancing algorithm on multi-core platforms from the estimated computational load of each slice during the encoding process. The encoding speed of the proposed parallelized HEVC encoder is accelerated by approximately ten times compared to the HEVC reference model (HM) software, with minimal loss of coding efficiency.

Keywords: HEVC; HEVC encoder; SIMD implementation; Slice-level parallelism; Load balancing

1 Introduction

Along with the development of multimedia and hardware technologies, the demand for high-resolution video services with better quality has been increasing. These days, the demand for ultrahigh definition (UHD) video services is emerging, and its resolution is higher than that of full high definition (FHD), by a factor of 4 or more. Based on the market demands, ISO/IEC Moving Picture Experts Group (MPEG) and ITU-T Video Coding Experts Group (VCEG) have organized Joint Collaborative Team on Video Coding (JCT-VC) and standardized High Efficiency Video Coding (HEVC), whose target coding efficiency was twice better than that of H.264/AVC [1]. In the near future, HEVC is expected to be employed for many video applications, such as video broadcasting and video communications.

Historically, MPEG-x and H.26x video compression standards employ the macro-block (MB) as one basic processing unit [2], and its size is 16×16. However, HEVC supports larger sizes of the basic processing unit, called coding tree unit (CTU), from 8×8 to 64×64. A CTU is split into multiple coding units (CU), in a quad-

tree fashion [3]. Along with the CU, the prediction unit (PU) and transform unit (TU) are defined, and their sizes and shapes are more diverse than the prior standard technologies [4,5]. On top of them, many advanced coding tools that improve prediction, transform, and loop filtering are employed to double the compression performance compared with H.264/AVC. However, the computation requirement of HEVC is known to be significantly higher than that of H.264/AVC because HEVC has more prediction modes, larger block size, longer interpolation filter, and so forth.

Typically, a huge number of rate-distortion (RD) cost computations are required to find the best mode from 64×64 to 8×8 block sizes in the encoder side for HEVC. With respect to applications, HEVC would be employed for ultrahigh-resolution video services. For such cases, fast video coders are required to process more data with a given processing power. Thus, parallelization techniques would be crucial, with multiple low-power processors or platforms. The single instruction multiple data (SIMD) implementation of the most time-consuming modules on HM 6.2 encoders was proposed [6]. This work implemented the cost functions, transformation, and interpolation filter with SIMD, and it reported that the average time saving obtained is approximately 50% to 80%, depending on the modules. Wavefront parallel

* Correspondence: dgsim@kw.ac.kr
[1]Department of Computer Engineering, Kwangwoon University, Wolgye-dong, Nowon-gu, Seoul 447-1, South Korea
Full list of author information is available at the end of the article

processing (WPP) for HEVC encoders and decoders was introduced [7]. For the decoder case, they achieved parallel speed-up by a factor of 3. The acceleration factor of the wavefront parallelism is in general saturated into 2 or 3 due to data communication overhead, epilog, and prolog parts. There are no works that incorporate all the parallel algorithms, with maximum harmonization for fast HEVC encoders. In this paper, we focus on load-balanced slice parallelization, with optimization implementation of HEVC. This paper presents several optimization techniques using SIMD operations for the RD cost computations and transforms for variable block sizes. In addition, motion estimation is also efficiently implemented with a frame-based processing to reduce the number of redundant filtering. For data-level parallelization, this paper demonstrates how to allocate encoding jobs to all the available cores through the use of complexity estimation. As a result, it is possible to achieve load-balanced slice parallelism in HEVC encoders to significantly reduce the average encoding time. With all the proposed techniques, the optimized HEVC encoder achieves a 90.1% average time saving within 3.0% Bjontegaard distortion (BD) rate increases compared to HM 9.0 reference software.

The paper is organized as follows. Section 2 presents a complexity analysis of HEVC encoder, and Section 3 introduces basic data-level parallelisms for video encoders. In Section 4, the SIMD optimization for cost functions and transform, as well as frame-level implementation of interpolation filter, is explained in detail. A slice-level parallelization technique with a load-balancing property is proposed in Section 5. Section 6 shows the performance and numerical analysis of the proposed techniques.

Finally, Section 7 concludes the work, with further research topics.

2 HEVC and its complexity analysis

Figure 1 shows a block diagram of HM encoder [8]. The HEVC encoder consists of prediction, transformation, loop filters, and entropy coder, which are the same cores as the prior hybrid video coders. However, HEVC employs more diverse block sizes and types, named CU, PU, and TU. The CU sizes range from 8×8 to 64×64, when the CTU is set to 64×64. The CU structure is partitioned in a quad-tree fashion, and each CU can have one of several PU types inside it. This allows each CU to be predicted with diverse block sizes and shapes. In addition, advanced motion vector prediction (AMVP) [9] and block merging techniques [10,11] are adopted to effectively represent the estimated motion vectors. For residual coding, the transform block sizes and shapes are determined based on a rate-distortion optimization (RDO). The quad-tree transform is used for each CU, and it is independent of the PU type. Transform coefficients are quantized with a scalar quantizer. To improve coding efficiency, the rate-distortion optimized quantization (RDOQ) is often employed, during the quantization process. Finally, the reconstructed blocks are filtered with two-stage loop filters: the de-blocking filter (DBF) and sample adaptive offset (SAO).

As mentioned before, HEVC supports hierarchical block partitioning. Figure 2 shows an example of diverse CU and PU realizations in a slice, when the CTU size is set to 64×64. A slice is divided into multiple CTUs, and each CTU is again partitioned into multiple CUs. The quad-tree structure is effectively represented by

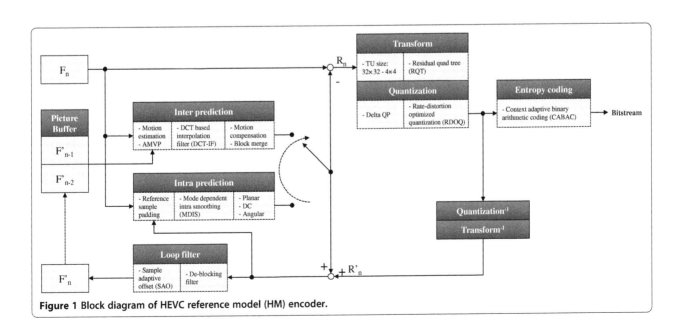

Figure 1 Block diagram of HEVC reference model (HM) encoder.

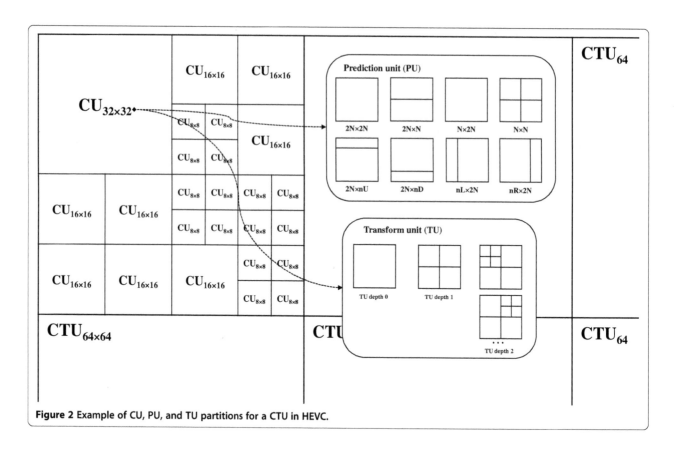

Figure 2 Example of CU, PU, and TU partitions for a CTU in HEVC.

hierarchical flag syntaxes. HEVC has one identical syntax for diverse CU block sizes. The size of a CU block can be derived with quad-tree split flags. In addition, one CU can be coded with one of the several PUs. For a current CU of 2 N × 2 N, the CU can have one of seven PU splitting types: 2 N × 2 N, 2 N × N, N × 2 N, or four asymmetric shapes (2 N × nU, 2 N × nD, nL × 2 N, and nR × 2 N) [12]. The residual signal is transformed in TU, which can be recursively split into multiple level quadrants. HEVC supports diverse TU sizes, from 4 × 4 up to 32 × 32, and the maximum TU size depends on the CU size. However, quadtree-based TU partitioning is conducted independent of PU partitioning.

In this section, the complexity of HEVC encoder is investigated, and critical modules can be identified based on the complexity analysis. In this work, HM 9.0 reference software [13] was used for HEVC encoder analysis. Note that it was used as the base software for our optimization. A HEVC encoder can be mainly modularized into five parts: entropy coding, intra prediction, inter prediction, transform quantization, and loop filter. The cycle analyzer, Intel® VTune™ Amplifier XE 2013 [14] on Intel® Core™ i7-3960 K processor, was employed to measure the number of cycles for each module, in cases of the random access (RA) and low-delay (LD) test configurations, under the common test conditions [15]. Note that class B (1,920 × 1,080) and class C (832 × 480) sequences were used.

Table 1 shows the percentages of computation cycles of all the key modules, for two configurations, RA and LD. We found that the inter prediction takes around 68.4% to 89.1% of the total cycles, whereas the intra prediction takes only 1.2% to 3.3%. For the transform quantization and entropy coding, the percentages of cycles are counted as 10.1% to 20.7% and 0.3% to 6.6%, respectively. Note that quantization is one of the key modules in terms of functionality, but its computational cycle is not significant for measuring it independently. In this paper, the total computational cycles of transform and quantization were measured. As shown in Table 1, the inter prediction, which consists of motion estimation and compensation, is the dominant module

Table 1 Percentages of computational cycles of HM 9.0 encoder

Module	RA (%)	LD (%)	Average (%)
Entropy coding	2.98	2.40	2.69
Intra prediction	2.25	1.95	2.10
Inter prediction	79.03	82.23	80.63
Transform quantization	14.48	12.50	13.49
In-loop filter (de-blocking filter)	0.08	0.08	0.08
In-loop filter (sample adaptive offset)	0.10	0.10	0.10
Others	1.28	0.93	1.10

in computational complexity. For HEVC inter prediction coding, a large number of coding modes for various size blocks are evaluated and coded by computing rate-distortion costs. In addition, the hierarchical block partition is traversed in a recursive fashion in HM.

Table 2 shows percentages of the cycles for intra prediction, inter prediction, and skip modes, depending on the CU sizes. Regardless of the CU sizes, the percentage of inter prediction coding is about 73.7% to 83.4%. For the CU of 8 × 8, the cycle percentage of the intra prediction coding is approximately 2 to 3 times higher than the others, because 4 × 4 and 8 × 8 intra prediction modes are tested for RDO.

Table 3 shows the percentiles of the numbers of cycles for the top four functions. The interpolation filter, sum of absolute differences (SAD), sum of absolute transformed differences (SATD), and discrete cosine transform (DCT)/ inverse DCT (IDCT) take approximately 67% to 71% in the total cycles. The interpolation filter is the most complex function of HEVC encoders and is used for motion estimation and motion compensation. SAD and SATD are cost functions to calculate distortions between original and prediction blocks. In particular, SAD and SATD are the metrics for motion estimation of integer-pels and fractional-pels, respectively. In addition, SATD is also used for intra prediction. DCT/IDCT is applied to the residual signal from intra or inter prediction for data compaction in the DCT domain. We can say that optimization of the four functions is inevitable in order to accelerate HEVC encoder.

3 Data-level parallelization of video encoders

Data-level and function-level parallelization approaches are widely used for high-speed video codecs. In particular, function-level parallel processing is frequently used for

Table 2 Percentages of computational cycles, depending on CU sizes and modes

Size	Mode	RA (%)	LD (%)	Average (%)	Ratio in each CU size (%)
64 × 64	Intra	2.1	1.0	1.6	5.6
	Inter	19.0	31.9	25.5	82.3
	Skip	3.9	3.4	3.7	12.1
32 × 32	Intra	1.9	0.7	1.3	4.5
	Inter	25.0	27.4	26.2	83.4
	Skip	4.5	3.2	3.9	12.2
16 × 16	Intra	2.3	0.2	1.3	4.4
	Inter	17.0	12.5	14.8	82.9
	Skip	3.2	1.7	2.5	12.7
8 × 8	Intra	2.4	0.4	1.4	13.5
	Inter	8.7	4.9	6.8	73.7
	Skip	1.7	0.6	1.2	12.8

Table 3 Percentages of computational cycles of top four functions

Module	RA (%)	LD (%)	Average (%)
Interpolation filter	35.74	36.00	35.87
SATD	12.99	18.57	15.78
SAD	15.33	13.26	14.30
Transform/inverse transform	3.52	3.08	3.30
Total (%)	67.58	70.91	69.25

hard-wired implementations. Note that function-level parallel processing is not easily implemented mainly due to difficulties of load balancing and longer development period. Data-level parallel processing is relatively easy to be employed for video encoders because the data processing flows are the same for all the data. The data-level parallelism for HEVC can be conducted in terms of CU-, slice-, and frame-level ones. In addition, HEVC contains a parallel tool, called tile, which divides a picture into multiple rectangles [16]. In tile partitioning, the number of CTUs adjacent to boundaries of tile partitions is less than that of slices. From this fact, tile partitioning can yield slightly lower coding loss in compression efficiency compared to an implementation with the same number of slices [17].

For parallel implementations, we need to consider several factors, such as throughput and core scalability, as well as coding efficiency. Note that the core scalability means how much we need to change an implementation, depending on an increasing or decreasing number of cores. In addition, the throughput can be improved with parallel processing as compared with the single processing unit. However, many video coding algorithms, in general, have dependencies among neighboring coding units, neighboring frame, earlier-coded syntaxes, and so on. At the same time, we need to consider the coding efficiency degradation from the parallelization. Even though the throughput can be improved with parallel processing, it is not desirable that the coding efficiency is significantly degraded. Regarding the core scalability, it is better to employ a scalable parallelization method that can be easily extended for an increasing number of cores. If not, we are required to change the implementation, depending on the number of cores.

The 2D wavefront algorithm [18] has been used for the parallelization of video coding in CTU level. This coding tool does not impact the coding gain, but there is a limitation in the parallelization factor, even with many cores, due to coding dependence. Frame-level parallelization can be also used for non-reference bidirectional pictures; however, it depends on the encoding of reference structures.

The slice-level parallelism is widely used because we can assume any dependencies among multiple slices. However, we need to realize that the coding gain can be degraded with increased number of slices. In this paper, we evaluated bitrate increases in terms of the number of slices in the HM encoder software. Figure 3 shows the bitrate increases in terms of the number of slices, for four sequence classes. In our evaluation, class A (2,560 × 1,600), class B (1,920 × 1,080), class C (832 × 480), and class D (416 × 240) of the HEVC common test sequences [15] were used, under HEVC common test conditions. As shown in Figure 3, we can see the bitrate increases in terms of the number of slices. The bitrate increase becomes less significant as video resolution increases. In general, multiple slices are widely used for larger sequences due to parallel processing and error resilience. Regarding many commercial applications, the slice-level parallel processing is one of the good approaches for such large resolution videos.

As mentioned before, the slice-level parallelism has relatively high coding losses of around 2% to 4% compared to tile-level parallelism and wavefront processing [19]. However, slice-level parallelism has an advantage that the slice partitioning is more flexible and accurate for picture partitioning, by adjusting the number of CTUs, compared to the tile partitioning. Note that the tiles within the same row and column should use the same tile width and height, respectively. Slice-level parallelism of a fine-grained load balancing can yield additional encoding speed-up compared to the tile levels. WPP has the advantage that the loss of parallelization is relatively small compared to other parallelization methods. However, the acceleration factor of WPP is not so high compared to slice- or tile-level parallelism because WPP has prolog and epilog so that parts of the cores are inactivated. It is not easy to utilize all the cores with WPP on average. In our work, slice-level parallelism was chosen for the acceleration of parallelization. In addition, slice partitioning is widely used for the packetizing of bitstreams for error resiliencies, in practical video encoders and services.

There are two main criteria to divide a picture into multiple slices. One is an equal bitrate, and the other is the same number of CTUs for all the slices. The first one cannot be easily employed for parallel encoding because we cannot define the target bit prior to actual encoding. For the second method, we can easily use the same number of CTUs at a time.

4 Optimization for fast HEVC encoder

In this section, two software optimization methods, frame-level processing and SIMD implementation, for three most complex functions at the function-level are presented. The proposed software optimization methods have several advantages to accelerate HEVC encoders without any bitrate increase.

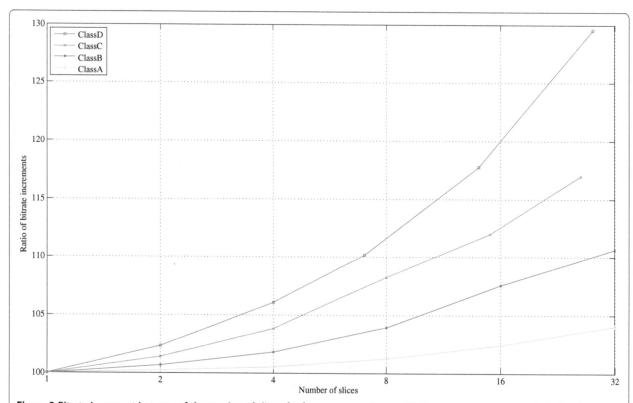

Figure 3 Bitrate increment in terms of the number of slices, for four sequence classes. HEVC common test sequences [15]; class A, 2,560 × 1,600; class B, 1,920 × 1,080; class C, 832 × 480; class D, 416 × 240.

4.1 Frame-level interpolation filter in HEVC encoder

The HEVC DCT-based interpolation filter (DCT-IF), which is used for obtaining fractional sample positions, is the most complex function, especially with motion estimation in encoders. Instead of using 6-tap and bilinear interpolation filters of H.264/AVC, HEVC adopts 8(7)-tap DCT-IF for luminance components, and 4-tap DCT-IF for chrominance components [20]. Furthermore, all of the fractional position samples are derived by increasing the number of filter taps without intermediate rounding operations which can reduce potential rounding errors compared to H.264/AVC. In order to determine the optimal CU size and coding modes, HM encoder uses a recursive scheme for the RD optimization process. In particular, the PU-level interpolation filter causes iterative memory accesses for the same positions redundantly. Excessive memory accesses significantly increase encoding time due to the limit of memory bandwidth. Actually, the DCT-IF occupies approximately 30% to 35% of the total cycles in the HM encoder. We adopt a frame-level interpolation filter to reduce redundant memory accesses. The frame-level interpolation filter avoids redundant execution that occurs in the RD optimization process and enables parallel process with independency among neighboring blocks. However, it requires the additional amount of memory for 15 factional samples per

integer sample in an entire frame. In addition, SIMD instructions and multi-thread processes using OpenMP and GPU can be easily used for fast encoding.

4.2 SIMD implementation of cost function and transformation

SAD, SATD, and DCT are the most complex functions in the HEVC encoder, except for DCT-IF. Several cost functions are used to decide the best coding mode and its associated parameters. SAD and SATD are the two main metrics to find integer and quarter-pel motion vectors in the motion estimation process, respectively. SAD takes around 10% to 12% of the total cycles in HEVC encoder, and SATD takes 15% to 16%. These two cost functions are defined by

$$\text{SAD} = \sum_{i,j}^{I,J} ||O(i,j) - P(i,j)|| \tag{1}$$

$$\text{SATD} = \left(\sum_{i,j}^{I,J} ||H(i,j)|| \right) / 2 \tag{2}$$

where i and j are the pixel indices, and their ranges are determined by a block size. $O(i,j)$ and $P(i,j)$ are the original and predicted pixel values, respectively. Note that

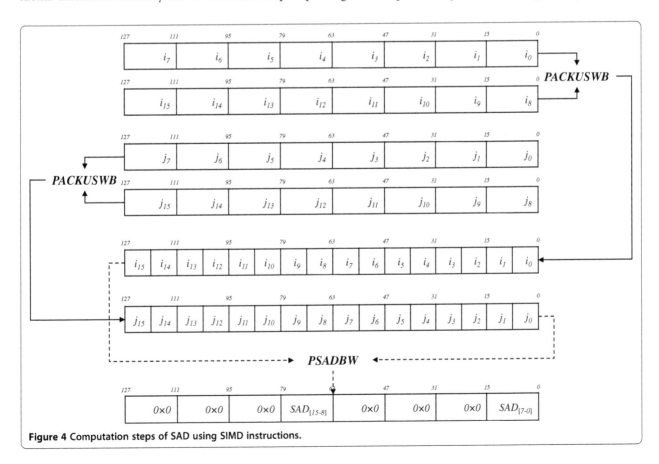

Figure 4 Computation steps of SAD using SIMD instructions.

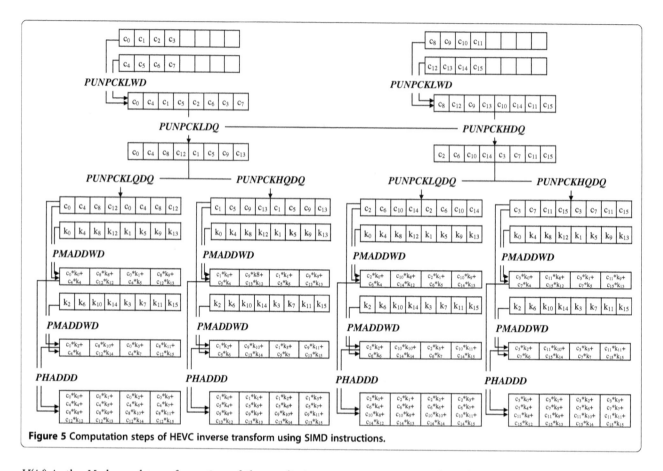

Figure 5 Computation steps of HEVC inverse transform using SIMD instructions.

$H(i,j)$ is the Hadamard transformation of the prediction error, $O(i,j) - P(i,j)$ [8]. Because only addition and subtraction operations are involved for the cost functions, SATD can yield an accurate cost in the transform domain with relatively small complexity compared to DCT. Since both apply the same operations on multiple data, vector instructions are quite useful to reduce the required clock cycles. This work uses SSE2 and SSE3 instructions defined in Intel SIMD architecture, which are widely employed for many DSP processors [21]. In the case of the SAD operation, we employed *PSADBW* (packed sum of absolute differences), *PACKUSWB* (packed with unsigned saturation), and *PADDD* (add packed double word integers) instructions. Sixteen SAD values can be computed by *PSADBW* instruction at once. Figure 4 shows how to compute SAD with SIMD instructions. Data packing is conducted with sixteen 16-bit original pixels (i_x) and sixteen 16-bit reference pixels (j_x) using *PACKUSWB* instruction. For 8-bit internal bit depth, the data packing is conducted to form 16-bit short data. For 10-bit internal bit depth, the data packing process is not required. Sixteen original pixels and reference pixels are packed into two 128-bit registers, and *PSADBW* is performed. The computed SAD from i_0-j_0 to i_7-j_7 is stored in the lower 16 bits, and the SAD from i_8-j_8 to i_{15}-j_{15} is stored at bit position 64 to 79. Acceleration of 4×4 to 64×64 SAD

computations can be achieved using the aforementioned instructions based on instruction-level parallelism. The 4×4 and 8×8 SATD operations are implemented using interleaving instructions, such as *PUNPCKLQDQ* (unpack low-order quad-words), *PUNPCKHWD* (unpack high-order words), *PUNPCKLWD* (unpack low-order words), and arithmetic instructions, such as *PADDW* (add packed word integers), *PSUBW* (subtract packed word integers), and *PABSW* (packed absolute value).

Not only the cost function but also the forward transform and inverse transform can be implemented with SIMD instructions. The forward transform and inverse transform in HEVC are implemented by partial butterfly or matrix multiplication. In this paper, the matrix multiplication is chosen due to its simplicity and regularity. Transform and inverse transform are accelerated using interleaving instructions such as *PUNPCKLDQ* (unpack

Table 4 Normalized complexity for variable CU size and mode

CU size	Skip	Inter	Intra
64×64	109	760	52
32×32	42	280	16
16×16	9	71	3
8×8	2	19	1

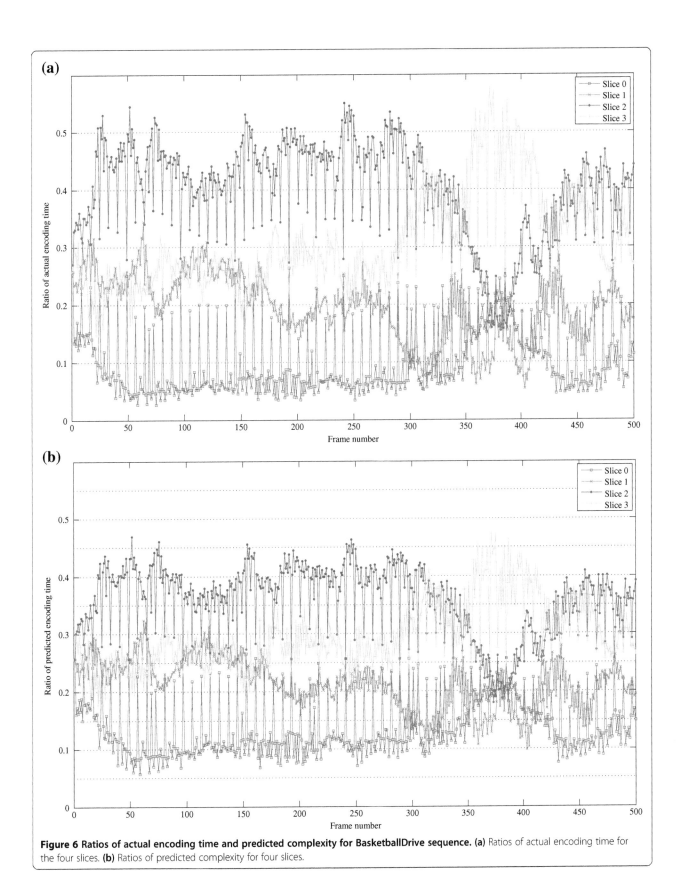

Figure 6 Ratios of actual encoding time and predicted complexity for BasketballDrive sequence. (a) Ratios of actual encoding time for the four slices. **(b)** Ratios of predicted complexity for four slices.

low-order double words), *PUNPCKHDQ* (unpack high-order double words), *PUNPCKLQDQ*, *PUNPCKHQDQ* (unpack high-order quad words), and arithmetic instructions such as *PMADDWD* (packed multiply and add), *PADDD*, and shift instruction such as *PSRAD* (packed shift right arithmetic). For HEVC forward and backward transformation, we need to consider the data range and the center value in computing matrix multiplications, unlike SAD and SATD implementations. Figure 5 shows how to compute the HEVC inverse transform using SIMD instructions. Data packing is conducted with sixteen 16-bit coefficients (c_x) using *PUNPCKLWD* instruction. The 16 coefficients are packed into two 128-bit registers. For reordering coefficients, the packed coefficient signals are repacked using *PUNPCKLQDQ and PUNPCKHQDQ* instructions. Repacked coefficients and the kernel (k_x) of the inverse transform are multiplied for eight 16-bit data in 128-bit registers. Then, the results of multiplications are added into 128-bit registers using *PMADDWD* instruction. Finally, the results of *PMADDWD* are added into the 128-bit destination register to compute inverse-transformed residuals using *PHADD* instruction. Input data for transformation range from −255 to 255. As a result, the data should be represented by at least 9 bits. Data ranges of coefficients of HEVC transform kernels depend on the size of the transform kernels. However, they can be represented in 8 bits for the 32×32 kernel because they range from −90 to 90 [22]. For computation of one transform coefficient, the required number of addition and multiplication operations is as many as the size of the transform kernel along the horizontal and vertical directions. A downscale should be employed to keep 16 bits in every operation for each direction. To avoid overflow and underflow, four 32-bit data should be packed into the 128-bit integer register of SSE2. In addition, the transform matrix is transposed in advance to reduce memory read/write operations.

5 Proposed slice-level parallelism with load balance

To reduce the computational load of the RD optimization, early termination and mode competition algorithms have been adopted in HM reference software [23-25]. However, these fast encoding algorithms cause different encoding complexities among different slices. To maximize parallelism of the data-level task partition, an accurate load balance for slice parallelization is required. Several works [26,27] have been conducted to achieve accurate load balance for slice parallelization. In Zhang's algorithm [26], the adaptive data partitioning for MPEG-2 video encoders was proposed by adjusting computational loads based on the complexity of a previously encoded frame of the same picture type. In Jung's algorithm [27], the adaptive slice

partition algorithm was proposed to use early-decided coding mode for macro-blocks in H.264/AVC. In the conventional algorithm, a quantitative model was designed to estimate the computational load associated with each candidate MB mode group. However, in order to apply slice-level parallelism to a HEVC encoder, we need to focus on CTU structures, variable block sizes, and coding modes. In this section, a complexity estimation model and adaptive slice partition algorithm to achieve load-balanced slice parallelization are proposed.

5.1 Complexity estimation model

In this section, a load-balancing technique for a slice parallelization is proposed by allocating the proper number of CTUs for each core after estimating the computational load for one slice. For this purpose, this work introduces a model of computational load for CU-level RD optimization process, in terms of diverse coding tools such as CU size, skip mode, AMVP, and many intra prediction directions. Table 4 shows normalized computational complexities by setting the complexity of 8×8 intra prediction to 1, as shown in Table 2. The normalized computational complexities for variable CU sizes and modes are computed by

$$R(s, m) = r(s, m) \times 2^{w(\text{CTU})/w(s)} \tag{3}$$

$$\text{CEM}(s, m) = R(s, m) \times \text{NF} \tag{4}$$

where $R(s,m)$ and $r(s,m)$ represent the complexity per unit and the complexity ratio of each CU size and mode, respectively. $w(s)$ and $\text{CEM}(s,m)$ are the width of CU size and the complexity estimation model in Table 4, respectively. Note that NF is a normalization factor for

Table 5 Pearson product moment correlations of the actual and predicted times

Class	Sequence name	Pearson product moment correlation
Class A (2,560 × 1,600)	Traffic	0.9495
	PeopleOnStreet	0.9083
Class B (1,920 × 1,080)	Kimono	0.9859
	ParkScene	0.9689
	Cactus	0.9382
	BasketballDrive	0.9456
	BQTerrace	0.9093
Class C (832 × 480)	BasketballDrill	0.9568
	BQMall	0.9723
	PartyScene	0.9326
	RaceHorses	0.9484
Average		0.9469

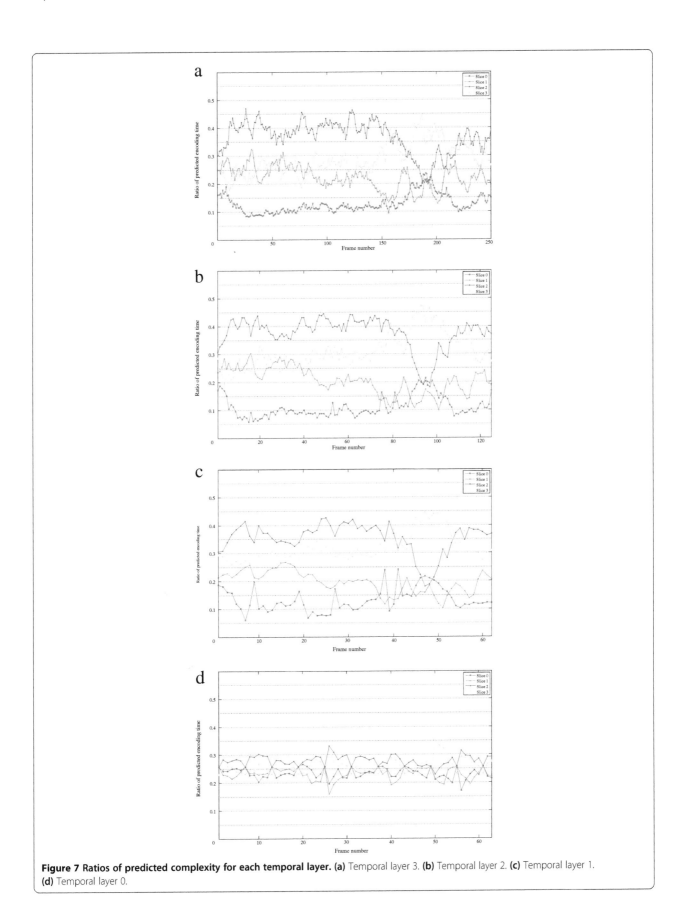

Figure 7 Ratios of predicted complexity for each temporal layer. (a) Temporal layer 3. **(b)** Temporal layer 2. **(c)** Temporal layer 1.
(d) Temporal layer 0.

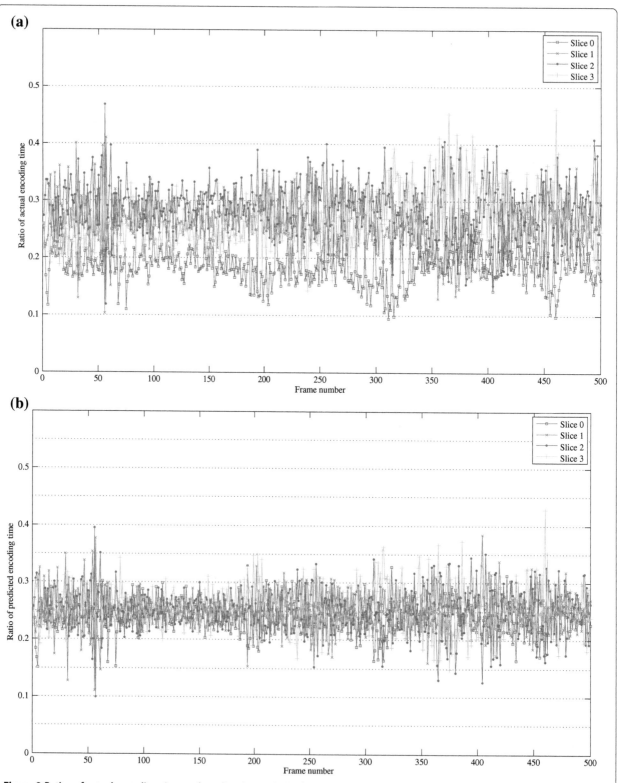

Figure 8 Ratios of actual encoding time and predicted complexity for BasketballDrive sequence. (a) Ratios of actual encoding time for the four slices. **(b)** Ratios of predicted complexity for the four slices.

fixed-point operation. The complexity of the lth CTU is defined by

$$CC_i(l) = \sum_{s \in S} \sum_{m \in M} CEM(s, m) \times CHK(s, m|l) \qquad (5)$$

$$CHK(s, m|l) = \begin{cases} 1, \text{if selected}(s, m|l) \\ 0, \text{otherwise} \end{cases} \qquad (6)$$

where $CHK(s, m|l)$ represents the selected mode for the CTU. S and M are defined by $\{64 \times 64, 32 \times 32, 16 \times 16, 8 \times 8\}$ and $\{Skip, Inter, Intra\}$, respectively. The predicted complexity for each slice is computed by summation of complexity for CTU and is defined by

$$SC_i(k) = \sum_{l=0}^{L(k)-l} CC_i(l) \qquad (7)$$

The proposed estimated complexity for a slice is evaluated with the Pearson product moment correlation with HEVC common test sequences [15]. The HEVC common test sequences are the most widely used video sequences for tool experiments of HEVC standard. In our evaluation, we used three classes of sequences (class A, class B, and class C). The size of class A is 2,560 × 1,600, and it consists of two sequences (Traffic and PeopleOnStreet). The sequences are formed by cropping 4 K videos for storage and evaluation time. Class B (1,920 × 1,080) is for full HD sequences and class C (832 × 480) is widely used for mobile devices. For this evaluation, we employed these sequences, and they are coded with multiple quantization parameters (QPs) of 22, 27, 32, and 37, under the HEVC common test condition [15]. The QP values were selected to cover many video applications, such as broadcasting, video communication, and high-quality media players, by considering the quality of reconstructed videos and bitrates. Figure 6 shows the ratio of an actual encoding time and the

Table 6 Test sequences

Class	Sequence number	Sequence name	Frame count	Frame rate
Class B (1,920 × 1,080)	S01	Kimono	240	24
	S02	ParkScene	240	24
	S03	Cactus	500	50
	S04	BasketballDrive	500	50
	S05	BQTerrace	600	60
Class C (832 × 480)	S06	BasketballDrill	500	50
	S07	BQMall	600	60
	S08	PartyScene	500	50
	S09	RaceHorses	300	30

predicted complexity for the 'BasketballDrive' sequence under random access setting with the proposed model for four slices. Table 5 shows the Pearson product moment correlation of the actual and predicted times for the test sequences. Note that the correlation coefficients can vary, depending on the coding parameters. In this paper, the correlation coefficients are computed from HM software under the common test conditions that are widely used for practical HEVC encoder. As shown in Table 5, the correlation coefficient is about 0.95, and it is quite high in predicting computational complexity, in the case of slice partitioning.

5.2 Adaptive slice partitioning using characteristics of temporal layers

In the current frame, the number of CTU for each slice is adaptively determined based on the complexity of the co-located slice in previously coded frames. In the proposed algorithm, the hierarchical temporal coding structure is considered to select the coded frame for the complexity prediction of each slice. Figure 7 shows the ratio of the predicted complexity of each slice in terms of temporal layers for the BasketballDrive sequence. In this evaluation, four temporal layers are used for the hierarchical coding structure, with four reference frames, based on the common test conditions. HEVC adopts a temporal layer coding structure to improve coding efficiency and temporal scalability, and each temporal layer has a different quantization parameter. The ratio of skip mode and the characteristics of CU split appear differently over the different temporal layers, and the same temporal layer has a high similarity of the actual encoding time and the predicted encoding time. As shown in Figures 6 and 7, the complexity of each slice, without considering the temporal layers, has a large fluctuation compared to that with considered temporal layers. In order to compare the complexity fluctuation of each slice, the statistical variance of complexities of each slice was measured. In the case in Figure 6, the variances of the complexity ratio of each slice are 29.23, 27.83, 61.25, and 57.87, respectively. The cases classified by the temporal layer, as shown in Figure 7, have the low variances of the complexity ratio of each slice of (a) 10.74, 17.85, 33.80, and 31.10; (b) 13.45, 23.85, 33.34, and 38.89; (c) 18.02, 16.29, 30.51, and 25.62; and (d) 3.78, 4.61, 3.30, and 6.61. The number of CTU in each slice is adjusted by an offset based on the predicted complexity of the slice in the same temporal layer of the hierarchical structure. The number of CTU in a slice, $L(k)$, and the offset to control the number of CTU in a slice, $offset(k)$, are defined by

$$L_i^j(k) = \frac{CTU_{inFrame}}{N} + offset_i^j(k) \qquad (8)$$

Table 7 HM 9.0 vs. optimized HEVC encoder software

	Sequence	RA			LD		
		SIMD (A)	Frame-level IF (B)	A + B	SIMD (A)	Frame-level IF (B)	A + B
B	S01	14.13	17.79	31.92	15.74	19.44	35.18
	S02	12.38	20.18	32.56	14.78	21.10	35.88
	S03	14.09	19.56	33.65	16.23	20.26	36.49
	S04	15.16	16.85	32.01	17.62	17.12	34.74
	S05	11.93	20.35	32.28	13.59	21.58	35.17
C	S06	14.33	18.51	32.84	16.49	19.60	35.99
	S07	13.84	20.90	34.74	16.02	20.95	36.97
	S08	11.88	18.49	30.37	13.44	19.94	33.38
	S09	14.67	15.03	29.70	17.23	15.54	32.77
	Average (B)	13.54	18.95	32.48	15.59	19.90	35.49
	Average (C)	13.68	18.23	31.91	15.80	18.98	34.78

$$\text{offset}_i^j(k) = \text{offset}_{i-1}^j(k) + \left(\frac{1}{N} - \frac{SC_{i-1}^j(k)}{\sum_{n=0}^{N-1} SC_{i-1}^j(n)} \right) \times \text{CTU}_{\text{inFrame}} \quad (9)$$

where $L(k)$ is the number of CTU in the kth slice, i is the frame index, j is the temporal layer index, and k is the slice index. Also, N is the number of slices in a frame, and $\text{CTU}_{\text{inFrame}}$ is the number of CTUs in the frame. In Equation 9, the CTU offset for each slice is set to the additional number of CTUs. The proposed algorithm adopts the adaptive slice partitioning method, with the difference between the ideal complexity for each slice, and the ratio of predicted complexity, which achieves the speed-up of slice-level parallelism. Figure 8 shows the actual encoding time and predicted encoding time using the proposed load-balanced slice parallelization. This shows

that the complexity load is quite well balanced compared to that shown in Figure 6. In addition, the maximum difference between the ratios of actual encoding time and the predicted one is 0.09363, and the minimum difference is 4×10^{-5}.

6 Experimental results

In this section, we show the performance of the proposed optimization techniques for HEVC encoder in terms of Bjontegaard distortion-bitrate (BD-BR) [28], Bjontegaard distortion peak signal-to-noise ratio (BD-PSNR) [28], and average time saving (ATS). In order to evaluate the efficiency of the proposed methods, HM 9.0 reference software was utilized. A PC equipped with an Intel® Core™ i7-3930 K CPU (six cores, 12 threads are supported with hyper-threading) and 16 GB memory was used for this evaluation. Intel® C++ 64-bit compiler XE 13.0 and VTune analyzer (performance monitoring tool) were used in a

Table 8 HM 9.0 vs. slice parallelization using OpenMP

	Sequence	RA			LD		
		BD-BR (%)	BD-PSNR (dB)	ATS (%)	BD-BR (%)	BD-PSNR (dB)	ATS (%)
B	S01	1.79	−0.05	70.25	1.49	−0.05	70.60
	S02	1.00	−0.03	71.53	0.89	−0.03	70.61
	S03	1.38	−0.03	71.08	1.29	−0.03	71.60
	S04	2.06	−0.05	68.03	1.53	−0.04	68.65
	S05	1.39	−0.02	70.27	1.35	−0.03	70.23
C	S06	3.41	−0.14	68.95	2.60	−0.10	69.26
	S07	3.78	−0.14	66.98	2.89	−0.11	66.98
	S08	1.58	−0.07	68.04	1.45	−0.06	69.61
	S09	2.96	−0.11	68.53	2.03	−0.08	68.75
	Average (B)	1.52	−0.04	70.23	1.31	−0.03	70.34
	Average (C)	2.93	−0.12	68.13	2.24	−0.09	68.65

Windows 7 64-bit operating system. The encoding configuration of this evaluation is set as follows:

(a) According to HEVC common test condition [15]
(b) Profile: HEVC main profile (MP) [1]

(c) Level: Level 4.1 [1]
(d) Encoding structure: RA and LD
(e) QP value: 22, 27, 32, 37
(f) Test sequences: HEVC common test sequences
    (classes B and C) in Table 6

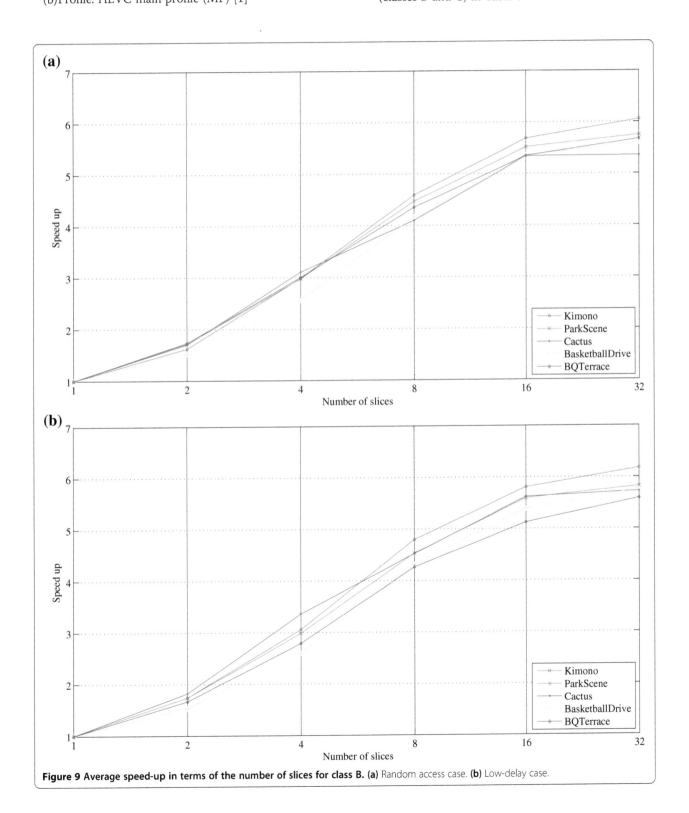

Figure 9 Average speed-up in terms of the number of slices for class B. **(a)** Random access case. **(b)** Low-delay case.

In this work, we define the average load balance saving (ALS) to measure the prediction accuracy of the proposed load balance performance against an anchor. ALS is calculated by

$$ALS(\%) = \frac{AML_{anchor} - AML_{proposed}}{AML_{anchor}} \times 100(\%) \qquad (10)$$

where AML_{anchor} is the average of the maximum ratio of complexity load over all the slices for the anchor, and $AML_{proposed}$ is the average of the maximum ratio of complexity load over all the slices for the proposed algorithm. In addition, BD-BR (%) for bitrate increase, BD-PSNR (dB) for objective quality decrease, and ATS (%) for average time saving were evaluated. Note that the ATS is defined by

$$ATS(\%) = \frac{Etime_{anchor} - Etime_{proposed}}{Etime_{anchor}} \times 100(\%) \qquad (11)$$

where $Etime_{anchor}$ is the encoding time of the anchor encoder and $Etime_{proposed}$ is the proposed method.

Firstly, the ATS comparison between the anchor and the proposed software optimizations will be shown. Secondly, the coding efficiency of the slice parallelism using OpenMP will be presented for the four-slice case. Thirdly, the coding efficiency of the proposed load-balanced slice parallelism will be presented. Finally, the coding efficiency of the overall proposed encoder based on software optimization and parallelization will be evaluated, comparing to the HM 9.0 reference encoder.

Table 7 shows ATS performances of SIMD implementation for cost functions and the frame-level interpolation filter on HM 9.0. As mentioned in Section 2, interpolation filter, SAD, SATD, transform, and inverse-transform are the main sources of computation load of HEVC encoder, and they take 35.87%, 14.30%, 15.78%, and 3.30% of the overall encoder time, respectively. In Table 7, the ATS gain

of the developed SIMD implementations is found to be from 13.54% to 15.80%; and the ATS gain of frame-level interpolation is from 18.23% to 19.90%. With the optimized SIMD implementation, the computational complexities of SAD, SATD, and transform/inverse-transform reduce by approximately up to 50%. In addition, the amount of complexity reduction with the frame-level interpolation filter is about 60% to 70%. Through software optimization, the total ATS gain of the developed optimization method is 31.91% to 35.49%, without any loss in coding efficiency.

Table 8 shows performance evaluation results of the slice parallelization using OpenMP for the four slices. Compared to cases without parallelization, four-slice parallelization for an entire frame with HM 9.0 encoder yields an ATS gain of 70.06% with only 1.52% BD-BR increase and 0.037 dB BD-PSNR reduction for class B and an ATS gain of 69.21% with only 3.36% BD-BR increase and 0.128 dB BD-PSNR reduction for class C, respectively.

Figure 9 illustrates average speed-up factors of the slice parallelization, in terms of the number of slices (2, 4, 8, 16, and 32). As shown in Figure 9, the speed-up also increases up to 6, as the number of slices increases. We can see that the increasing trend becomes slow, from the eight-slice case. The speed-up factor according to the number of slices does not linearly increase due to data communication; memory accesses; context switching overhead; complexity imbalance over the slices; and frame-level sequential processes, such as DBF, SAO, and entropy coding. Note that we used an Intel processor that has six cores, with hyper-threading technology. The hyper-threading technology can somehow reduce the context switching overhead to improve parallel performance. However, the speed-up factor is saturated to nearby 5.5 to 6.0 due to the communication and other overheads [29,30]. For class B sequence, the speed-up factors are

Table 9 BD-BR, ATS, and ALS for slice and load-balanced slice parallelization

	Sequence	RA			LD		
		BD-BR (%)	ATS (%)	ALS (%)	BD-BR (%)	ATS (%)	ALS (%)
B	S01	−0.01	13.44	16.33	−0.04	12.03	11.72
	S02	0.01	11.31	14.94	−0.02	12.44	13.25
	S03	0.05	0.46	2.95	−0.01	−0.16	14.86
	S04	0.16	18.05	22.58	0.05	17.82	20.83
	S05	−0.01	10.90	11.16	−0.08	14.63	16.18
C	S06	0.16	5.64	6.29	0.10	6.50	7.88
	S07	0.33	17.71	15.99	0.23	19.13	18.55
	S08	0.18	8.01	10.17	0.08	8.02	8.89
	S09	−0.01	8.72	10.62	0.02	8.90	9.65
	Average (B)	0.04	10.83	13.59	−0.02	11.35	15.37
	Average (C)	0.17	10.02	10.77	0.11	10.64	11.24

Table 10 HM 9.0 vs. the proposed accelerated and parallelized HEVC encoder

	Sequence	RA			LD		
		BD-BR (%)	BD-PSNR (dB)	ATS (%)	BD-BR (%)	BD-PSNR (dB)	ATS (%)
B	S01	3.88	−0.12	90.13	3.29	−0.10	89.34
	S02	3.45	−0.11	91.33	3.56	−0.11	90.47
	S03	4.81	−0.10	89.12	3.96	−0.09	88.77
	S04	4.34	−0.10	88.26	3.08	−0.07	87.93
	S05	4.52	−0.07	91.28	3.32	−0.06	90.19
C	S06	5.44	−0.22	86.86	3.84	−0.15	86.72
	S07	7.46	−0.28	88.92	5.41	−0.21	88.31
	S08	4.30	−0.18	86.75	3.65	−0.15	86.10
	S09	6.10	−0.23	85.44	3.76	−0.15	85.46
	Average (B)	4.20	−0.10	90.02	3.44	−0.09	89.34
	Average (C)	5.83	−0.23	86.99	4.17	−0.17	86.65

higher than those for any other sequences, in cases of four to eight slices parallelization. Based on the speed-up factors for Class B, we can predict that speed-up factors with eight or more slice parallelization for ultrahigh-resolution sequences such as 4 K (3,840 × 2,160) can be higher than those for lower resolution videos.

Table 9 shows the performance comparison between slice parallelism with OpenMP and the proposed load-balanced slice parallelism. A frame is partitioned into four slices for fair evaluation; and two fast encoding algorithms, CFM [23] and ECU [24], adopted for HM, are employed for the evaluation of the proposed load-balanced parallelization. In Table 9, the proposed load-balanced algorithm achieves 10.5% ATS gain, on average (minimum −0.16% and maximum 19.13%), by adaptively controlling the number of CTUs in a slice. Moreover, the ratio of the maximum complexity load is highly reduced in ALS gain by 12.89% to 14.94%. Note that the bottleneck of parallelization is the maximum computational load for one, over all the slices, and it is crucial to reduce the ratio of the maximum complexity load for overall performance. In our implementation, we found that the ALS reduces by load balancing; as a result, the overall encoding speed is moderately improved. The average ratio of encoding time saving is 0.15%, which is relatively small, for sequences whose complexity load gap over multiple slices, for example, 'Cactus' sequence,

is small before the load balancing. However, the amount of encoding time saving is about 12% to 18% for sequences whose complexity load gap among slices, such as Basket-ballDrive and 'Kimono' sequences, is large, without load balancing. In terms of coding gain, it is confirmed that BD-BR and BD-PSNR losses are quite small compared to uniform slice partition.

BD-BR, BD-PSNR, and ATS of the proposed fast HEVC encoder against HM 9.0 encoder are shown in Table 10. A frame is partitioned into four slices. The proposed fast HEVC encoder yields 89.34% to 90.02% in ATS compared to HM 9.0 encoder with only 3.44% to 4.20% BD-BR increase and 0.09 to 0.10 dB BD-PSNR decrease for class B sequences. For class C sequences, we found that BD-BR increases by 4.17% to 5.83% and BD-PSNR decreases by 0.17 to 0.23 dB. We found that coding loss for lower resolution videos is moderate higher than that for higher resolution ones. In addition, we evaluated BD-BR, DB-PSNR, and ATS of the proposed HEVC encoder, on top of HM9.0, for class A (2,560 × 1,600). Note that class A consists of two sequences (Traffic and PeopleOnStreet). As shown in Table 11, we found that BD-BR increases by 2.29% to 3.72%, and BD-PSNR decreases by 0.09 to 0.17 dB, on top of HM9.0, with ATS gains of 85.48% to 91.14%. Figure 10 illustrates the RD comparison of HM 9.0 and the proposed accelerated and parallelized HEVC encoder. Thinking about the

Table 11 BD-BR, BD-PSNR, and ATS of the proposed HEVC encoder for class A (2,560 × 1,600)

Sequence	RA			LD		
	BD-BR (%)	BD-PSNR (dB)	ATS (%)	BD-BR (%)	BD-PSNR (dB)	ATS (%)
Traffic	3.66	−0.12	91.14	3.72	−0.17	85.48
PeopleOnStreet	2.80	−0.09	90.43	2.29	−0.11	85.80
Average	3.23	−0.11	90.79	3.01	−0.14	85.64

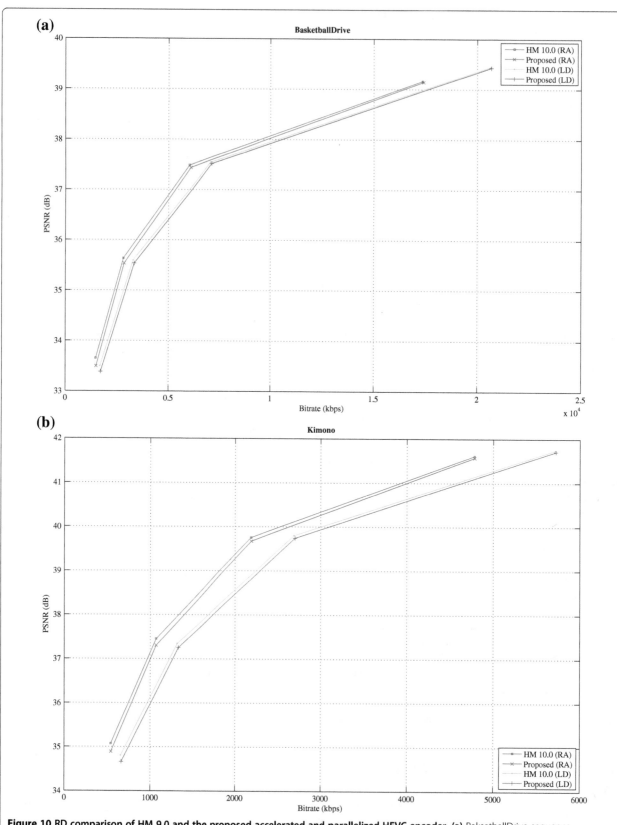

Figure 10 RD comparison of HM 9.0 and the proposed accelerated and parallelized HEVC encoder. **(a)** BaksetballDrive sequence. **(b)** Kimono sequence.

90.0% ATS performance gain, the RD performance loss, as shown in Table 10, is quite negligible, even containing the loss from the fast encoding algorithm and slice partitioning.

7 Conclusions

In this paper, the computational complexity of the HM 9.0 encoder was analyzed for acceleration and parallelization of the HEVC encoder. We identified five key modules for the HM 9.0 encoder, requiring dominant computing cycles. Based on the complexity analysis, two software optimization methods were used for acceleration: the frame-level interpolation filter and SIMD implementation. In addition, load-balanced slice parallelization is proposed. Software optimization methods achieve 33.56% of the average time saving, with any coding loss. In addition, load balancing for the slice parallelization method achieves about 10% of average time saving compared to uniform slice partition. The overall average time saving of the proposed HEVC encoder yields approximately 90% compared to HM 9.0 with acceptable coding loss. HEVC encoder with the proposed methods can compress full HD videos at approximately 1 fps speed in a commercial PC environment, without any hardware acceleration.

Further study will be focused on additional software optimization, fast encoding algorithm, and tile-level parallel processing for real-time encoder of HEVC.

Competing interests
The authors declare that they have no competing interests.

Acknowledgements
This research was partly supported by the IT R&D program of MSIP/KEIT [10039199, A Study on Core Technologies of Perceptual Quality based Scalable 3D Video Codecs], the MSIP (Ministry of Science, ICT & Future Planning), Korea, under the ITRC (Information Technology Research Center) support program (NIPA-2013-H0301-13-1011) supervised by the NIPA (National IT Industry Promotion Agency), and the grant from the Seoul R&BD Programs (SS110004M0229111).

Author details
[1]Department of Computer Engineering, Kwangwoon University, Wolgye-dong, Nowon-gu, Seoul 447-1, South Korea. [2]Department of Software Design and Management, Gachon University, Seongnam, Gyeonggi 461-701, South Korea.

References
1. B Bross, W-J Han, GJ Sullivan, JR Ohm, T Wiegand, *High Efficiency Video Coding (HEVC) text specification draft 9*, ITU-T/ISO/IEC Joint Collaborative Team on Video Coding (JCT-VC) document JCTVC-K1003, 2012
2. ITU-T and ISO/IEC JTC 1, Advanced video coding for generic audiovisual services, ITU-T Rec. H.264/and ISO/IEC 14496–10 (MPEG-4 AVC), versions 1–16, 2003-2012
3. H Samet, The quadtree and related hierarchical data structures. ACM Comput Surv (CSUR) **16**(2), 187–260 (1984)
4. W-J Han, J Min, I-K Kim, E Alshina, A Alshin, T Lee, J Chen, V Seregin, S Lee, YM Hong, MS Cheon, N Shlyakhov, K McCann, T Davies, JH Park, Improved video compression efficiency through flexible unit representation and corresponding extension of coding tools. Circuits Syst Video Technol, IEEE Trans **20**(12), 1709–1720 (2010)
5. T Wiegand, J-R Ohm, GJ Sullivan, W-J Han, R Joshi, TK Tan, K Ugur, Special section on the joint call for proposals on High Efficiency Video Coding (HEVC) standardization. Circuits Syst Video Technol, IEEE Trans **20**(12), 1661–1666 (2010)
6. K Chen, Y Duan, L Yan, J Sun, Z Guo, *Efficient SIMD optimization of HEVC encoder over X86 processors*, in Signal & Information Processing Association Annual Summit and Conference (APSIPA ASC) (Asia-Pacific, Hollywood, CA, 2012), pp. 1–4
7. G Clare, F Henry, S Pateux, *Wavefront parallel processing for HEVC encoding and decoding*, ITU-T/ISO/IEC Joint Collaborative Team on Video Coding (JCT-VC) document JCTVC-F274, 2011
8. I-K Kim, K McCann, K Sugimoto, B Bross, W-J Han, *HM9: High Efficiency Video Coding (HEVC) test model 9 encoder Description*, ITU-T/ISO/IEC Joint Collaborative Team on Video Coding (JCT-VC) document JCTVC-K1002, 2012
9. K McCann, WJ Han, IK Kim, JH Min, E Alshina, A Alshin, T Lee, J Chen, V Seregin, S Lee, YM Hong, MS Cheon, N Shlyakhov, Samsung's response to the call for proposals on video compression technology, ITU-T/ISO/IEC Joint Collaborative Team on Video Coding (JCT-VC) document JCTVC-A124. (2010)
10. R De Forni, D Taubman, On the benefits of leaf merging in quad-tree motion models. IEEE Int Conf Image Process **2005**, 858–861 (2005)
11. J Jung, B Bross, P Chen, W-J Han, *Description of core experiment 9: MV coding and skip/merge operations*, ITU-T/ISO/IEC Joint Collaborative Team on Video Coding (JCT-VC) document JCTVC-D609, 2011
12. Y Yuan, X Zheng, X Peng, J Xu, IK Kim, L Liu, Y Wang, X Cao, C Lai, J Zheng, Y He, H Yu, CE2: non-square quadtree transform for symmetric and asymmetric motion partition, ITU-T/ISO/IEC Joint Collaborative Team on Video Coding (JCT-VC) document JCTVC-F412. (2011)
13. Joint Collaborative Team on Video Coding, (JCT-VC) of ITU-T SG 16 WP 3 and ISO/IEC JTC 1/SC 29/WG 11, HM-9.0 reference software. (2014)
14. VTune™Amplifier XE 2013 from Intel. (2014). http://software.intel.com/en-us/articles/intel-vtune-amplifier-xe/
15. F Bossen, *Common HM test conditions and software reference configuration*, ITU-T/ISO/IEC Joint Collaborative Team on Video Coding (JCT-VC) document JCTVC-K1100, 2012
16. GJ Sullivan, JR Ohm, WJ Han, T Wiegand, Overview of the High Efficiency Video Coding (HEVC) standard. IEEE Transactions on Circuits and Systems for Video Technology **22**(12), 1649–1668 (2012)
17. A Fuldseth, M Horowitz, S Xu, A Segall, M Zhou, *Tiles*, ITU-T/ISO/IEC Joint Collaborative Team on Video Coding (JCT-VC) document JCTVC-F335, 2011
18. F Henry, S Pateux, *Wavefront parallel processing*, ITU-T/ISO/IEC Joint Collaborative Team on Video Coding (JCT-VC) document JCTVC-E196, 2011
19. CC Chi, M Alvarez-Mesa, B Juurlink, G Clare, F Henry, S Pateux, T Schierl, Parallel scalability and efficiency of HEVC parallelization approaches. IEEE Transactions on Circuits and Systems for Video Technology **22**(12), 1827–1838 (2012)
20. A Alshin, E Alshina, JH Park, WJ Han, *DCT based interpolation filter for motion compensation in HEVC*, in Proceedings of the SPIE 8499 Applications of Digital Image Processing XXXV (San Diego, CA, 2012)
21. Intel, Intel 64 and IA-32 architectures software developer manuals. (2014). http://www.intel.com/content/www/us/en/processors/architectures-software-developer-manuals.html
22. M Budagavi, V Sze, *Unified forward + inverse transform architecture for HEVC*, in 19th IEEE International Conference on Image Processing (ICIP), 30 September 30 2012 to 3 October (Orlando, Florida, USA, 2012), pp. 209–212
23. RH Gweon, Y-L Lee, J Lim, *Early termination of CU encoding to reduce HEVC complexity*, ITU-T/ISO/IEC Joint Collaborative Team on Video Coding (JCT-VC) document JCTVC-F045, 2011
24. K Choi, ES Jang, *Coding tree pruning based CU early termination*, ITU-T/ISO/IEC Joint Collaborative Team on Video Coding (JCT-VC) document JCTVC-F092, 2011
25. J Yang, J Kim, K Won, H Lee, B Jeon, *Early skip detection for HEVC*, ITU-T/ISO/IEC Joint Collaborative Team on Video Coding (JCT-VC) document JCTVC-G543, 2011
26. N Zhang, C-H Wu, Study on adaptive job assignment for multiprocessor implementation of MPEG2 video encoding. IEEE Trans. Ind. Electron **44**(5), 726–734 (1997)
27. B Jung, B Jeon, Adaptive slice-level parallelism for H.264/AVC encoding using pre macroblock mode selection. J Vis Commun Image. Representation **19**(8), 558–572 (2008)
28. G Bjontegaard, *Document VCEG-M33: calculation of average PSNR differences between RD-curves*, ITU-T VCEG Meeting (Austin, Texas, USA, 2001)

29. X Tian, Y-K Chen, M Girkar, S Ge, R Lienhart, S Shah, *Exploring the use of hyper-threading technology for multimedia applications with Intel® OpenMP compiler, in Proceedings of International Symposium on Parallel and Distributed Processing 2003* (Nice, France, 2003)
30. S Sankaraiah, LH Shuan, C Eswaran, J Abdullah, Performance optimization of video coding process on multi-core platform using GOP level parallelism. Int J Parallel Program Springer , 1–17 (2013)

3

A robust adaptive algorithm of moving object detection for video surveillance

Elham Kermani and Davud Asemani[*]

Abstract

In visual surveillance of both humans and vehicles, a video stream is processed to characterize the events of interest through the detection of moving objects in each frame. The majority of errors in higher-level tasks such as tracking are often due to false detection. In this paper, a novel method is introduced for the detection of moving objects in surveillance applications which combines adaptive filtering technique with the Bayesian change detection algorithm. In proposed method, an adaptive structure firstly detects the edges of motion objects. Then, Bayesian algorithm corrects the shape of detected objects. The proposed method exhibits considerable robustness against noise, shadows, illumination changes, and repeated motions in the background compared to earlier works. In the proposed algorithm, no prior information about foreground and background is required and the motion detection is performed in an adaptive scheme. Besides, it is shown that the proposed algorithm is computationally efficient so that it can be easily implemented for online surveillance systems as well as similar applications.

Keywords: Moving object detection; Adaptive noise cancellation; Bayesian; Maximum *a posteriori*, Video stream; Background subtraction; Surveillance

1 Introduction

Today, stationary cameras are extensively used for video surveillance systems [1]. Visual surveillance is employed in many applications, such as car and pedestrian traffic monitoring, human activity surveillance for unusual activity detection, people counting, etc. A typical surveillance system consists of three building blocks: moving object detection, object tracking and higher-level motion analysis [2]. The detection of regions corresponding to moving objects (people and vehicles) in video is the first processing step of almost every vision system because the rest of processing stages including tracking and activity analysis are locally applied to the regions of moving objects [3]. Thus, the identification of moving objects from a video sequence plays an important role in the performance of vision systems [2].

Numerous algorithms of motion detection have been presented up to now. The simplest ones mostly use a thresholding operation on the intensity difference (e.g., between consecutive video frames or between the current and background frames). These basic algorithms often yield a poor performance [1]. To improve the performance, other proposed methods employ probabilistic models [4-7] and statistical tests [8,9]. So probabilistic models and statistical tests are used to model and extract the background. The performance of these detection algorithms would be largely influenced by the choice of threshold. Higher performance can theoretically be obtained by adaptively modifying threshold value. Up to now, several threshold adaptation methods have been proposed [1]. The most successful algorithms of detection are those which exploit frame differencing and modelling of change labels using Markov random field (MRF) in Bayesian framework [10].

On parallel, the change detection methods have been developed based on the maximum *a posteriori* (MAP) probability criterion which use MRFs as *a priori* models [11-13]. MAP-inspired change detection algorithms result in better performance. However, they are computationally complex, because MAP estimation is an optimization problem requiring special algorithms such as simulated annealing or graph-cuts [14].

To reduce the complexity of MAP estimation, it can be formulated as a likelihood test called local MAP estimation. Local MAP estimation coupled with MRF as

* Correspondence: Asemani@eetd.kntu.ac.ir
Electrical Engineering Faculty, K.N. Toosi University of Technology, Tehran 1431714191, Iran

a priori probability has been widely used for moving object detection. These algorithms generally use one of the current background subtraction methods in MAP-MRF framework [1,10,15-18].

In this work, a new structure of detection is proposed in which adaptive noise cancellation (ANC) algorithm is utilized along with local MAP estimation. Adaptive noise cancellation basically is an alternative technique for estimating the original signals corrupted by additive noise or interference. In the context of signal and image processing, ANC has been already used in works which mostly estimate an image from a version of itself contaminated with additive noise [19-22]. In other words, it only removes the effect of noise. In this paper, ANC is exploited for moving object detection in video surveillance applications so that it eliminates noise, repeated motions of background, illumination changes, and shadows. Then, MAP estimation renders the regions corresponding to moving objects more compact and smooth. Proposed ANC-MAP method suffers no longer from heavy computational complexity required in global MAP estimation. Also, it is adequately robust and efficient.

The organization of this paper is as follows. Section 2 provides a review on the basic Bayesian algorithm of change detection. Section 3 describes the principles of ANC algorithm. The proposed combinational method is presented in Section 4. Simulation results are discussed in Section 5. Finally, Section 6 summarizes the results as conclusion.

2 Bayesian change detection algorithm

The goal of a motion detection system is to divide each image frame into moving and still segments. It is realized through generating a mask Q consisting of binary labels q(m) for each pixel m on the image grid. The labels take either the label 'u' (unchanged) or 'c' (changed). In order to determine the label q(m = i) of pixel i, it may be started from the gray-level difference D = {d(m)} between two successive frames and then looking for a change mask which maximizes P(Q|D) (MAP estimate). Assuming that d(m) values are conditionally independent and the labels q(m) are known for all picture elements except i, the estimation of Q reduces to the determination of q(i) [u or c]. Depending on the choice of q(i), there would be two possible change masks of Q_u^i, Q_c^i. According to the Bayes' theorem, it may be deduced that [10]:

$$\frac{P(d(i)|Q_u^i)}{P(d(i)|Q_c^i)} \underset{c}{\overset{u}{\underset{<}{>}}} t \frac{P(Q_c^i)}{P(Q_u^i)} \tag{1}$$

where t represents a threshold value for decision.

To make the detection more reliable, the decision should be taken based on the gray-level difference at pixel i and its neighboring pixels. Supposing a zero-mean Gaussian distribution for the difference values and applying the inequality (1) to the pixels around pixel i, a decision rule may be obtained as follows [10]:

$$\overline{\Delta_i^2} = \frac{1}{\sigma_u^2} \sum_{m \in w_i} d^2(m) \underset{u}{\overset{c}{\underset{<}{>}}} T \tag{2}$$

σ_u represents the noise standard deviation of the gray-level differences in the stationary areas assuming to be constant over space. $\overline{\Delta_i^2}$ is the sum of squared differences within a small sliding window w_i having center i. T is an adaptive threshold derived from modelling *a priori* knowledge by MRF. This adaptive threshold varies with the label values in the pixel's neighborhood, i.e., decreases inside changed areas and increases outside [9]. T is defined as following:

$$T = T_0 + (4 - n_i) \times B \tag{3}$$

where T_0 stands for a constant threshold and B is a positive-valued potential. n_i is the number of changed pixels in 3×3 neighborhood of each pixel. The higher the number n_i of changed pixels found in this neighborhood, the lower the threshold is [10].

Figure 1 shows the general flowchart of basic Bayesian change detection algorithm.

Though this method performs well, the interior parts of the foregrounds are not detected in the case of big, uniform, or slow objects. This originates from differencing two successive frames. Moreover, it has significant difficulties with changing illumination conditions. In practice, every change causing $\overline{\Delta_i^2}$ to become larger than T would be considered as a motion event.

3 Adaptive noise cancellation

Adaptive noise cancellation is a method for estimating signals corrupted by additive noise or interference. Though the concept of ANC is based on using only an adaptive filter, the structure of ANC would appear so helpful in the proposed algorithm. According to Figure 2, it comprises two available inputs: a primary input d(n) and a reference input $N_1(n)$. The first one represents the main signal s[n] corrupted by noise $N_0(n)$. The reference input $N_1(n)$ provides a filtered form of main noise $N_0(n)$. In ANC, the reference input is adaptively filtered and subtracted from the primary input to obtain the original signal (removing the noise). The output will be an error signal (difference between d[n], y[n]), which is used through a feedback path to adjust the adaptive filter. The adaptive

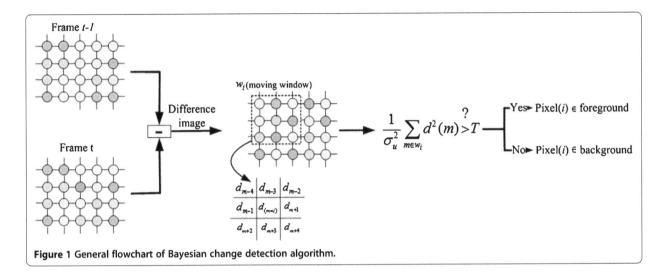

Figure 1 General flowchart of Bayesian change detection algorithm.

filter continuously readjusts its coefficients to minimize the energy of the error signal [23].

The adaptive filter can effectively work in unknown environments and can track the input signal with time-varying characteristics [24]. Several algorithms have been proposed to optimally adjust the filter coefficients, such as least mean square (LMS) algorithm and recursive least square (RLS) algorithm [25]. Here, LMS algorithm has been used because of its simplicity and fast convergence. Basically, LMS algorithm tries to minimize the energy (or mean square) of error signal, i.e., $E[e^2]$ [25]. The LMS algorithm leads to a recursive update relation for filter coefficients $W(n)$ as follows [26]:

$$w(n+1) = w(n) + \mu.e(n).x(n) \qquad (4)$$

where the parameters are as follows: n, iteration number; W, the vector of adaptive filter coefficients; X, the input vector entering adaptive filter; μ, a positive scalar called the step size.

4 Proposed algorithm for motion detection

In this section, a new algorithm is proposed that uses the ANC technique in a Bayesian framework to detect moving parts of each frame in a video sequence. To better follow up the concept of proposed algorithm, the basic idea of detection using ANC is firstly described.

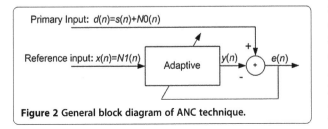

Figure 2 General block diagram of ANC technique.

Then, it will be combined with local MAP estimation so that an integrated ANC-MAP algorithm is obtained for optimally detecting moving objects.

4.1 Basic idea

In video surveillance applications, the camera is often located at a fixed position. This enables us to assume a rather stationary background. Since the areas related to moving objects are relatively small, the background information of two frames, whether successive or not, is highly correlated. This correlation will be used to separate background from foreground in an adaptive scheme.

As previously mentioned, the ANC algorithm requires two signals as inputs: a primary corrupted signal and a reference input containing noise. To apply this algorithm for motion detection, two possible situations may be imagined in terms of input signals. The input signals of ANC may be defined as following choices:

- One background frame (processed frame) and one original frame
- Two successive original frames without any processing

The two possible solutions above have been implemented and examined. In practice, the second solution is preferred because of the simplicity (no need of background extraction). The related procedure is implemented as following. First of all, two original frames are considered (containing unknown moving objects). The normalized gray levels of these two frames are put into column vectors X and Y and utilized as the inputs of the ANC algorithm (Figure 3). The vectors X and Y are supposed to represent the reference N_1 and primary $N_0 + s[n]$ signals (refer to Section 3). $s[n]$ is here assumed as the change caused by motion in the second frame.

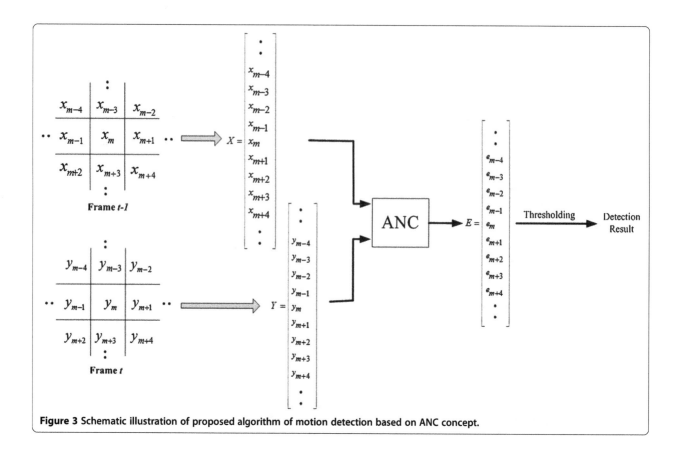

Figure 3 Schematic illustration of proposed algorithm of motion detection based on ANC concept.

Since the ANC algorithm suppresses any correlation (mostly due to background information), it is normally expected that the motion part remains at the output. By a simple thresholding on the absolute error and reshaping the vector, the output signal can be realized as an image including only moving objects. The proposed algorithm can detect the moving object being present either at both frames or at only one frame (entrance of the person). Figure 4 demonstrates the algorithm performance in two cases. Figure 4b represents the output (error signal $e[n]$) of detection result when only one frame contains moving objects. Figure 4c is the result of applying the ANC algorithm on two successive frames both including moving objects.

4.2 Proposed ANC-MAP detection algorithm

Having some primary frames with no moving object, a background model may be available. In this case, the proposed ANC method would have an almost perfect performance (as shown in Figure 4b). However, a scene with no moving object may be at times impossible or very restrictive on the system such as traffic surveillance system. Moreover, a robust method of moving object detection should discriminate nonstationary background objects such as moving leaves and rain. Also, it should

be able to quickly adapt to background changes (for example starting and stopping of vehicles). To cope with these problems, successive frames are selected to be applied to the proposed ANC-based algorithm in spite of better performance when a background model is used.

If two successive frames are applied to ANC-based algorithm, the inner parts of moving foreground objects are not detected and classified as the background. It is due to the large correlation of inner regions which are omitted by the ANC algorithm supposed as background segment. To overcome this problem, the proposed ANC system is followed by a Bayesian stage to detect changes (refer to Section 2).

To integrate Bayesian motion detection framework with mentioned ANC detection, the error signal which has turned back to an image is applied to the Bayesian algorithm as an input image (Figure 5). *A priori* probability function is selected so that smooth regions appear more probable than irregular ones. This procedure renders the output of detection algorithm more realistic (i.e., detected moving areas are made uniformly connected). *A priori* probability is here modeled by MRF. MRF estimation increases the probability of being a foreground pixel in the proximity of a pixel detected by ANC method and provides a context-dependent variable threshold. So detected objects would become more

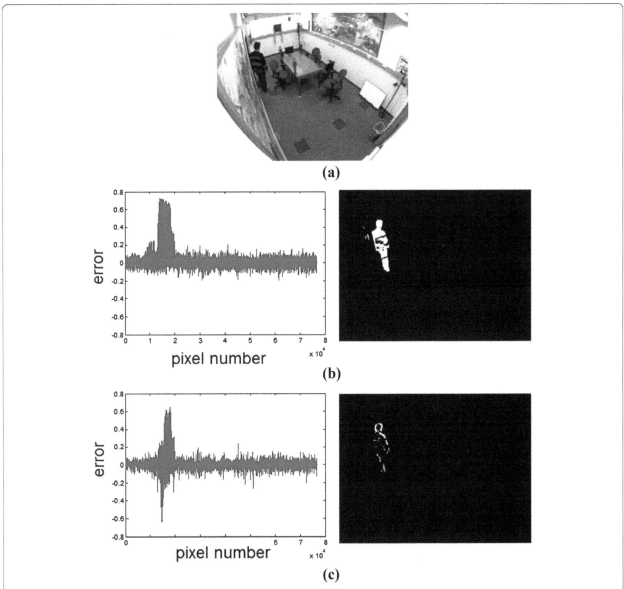

Figure 4 ANC-based motion detection. (a) One frame of an indoor video sequence. **(b)** The output of algorithm using one background frame and a frame including moving object. **(c)** Output of ANC algorithm using two consecutive frames both containing moving objects.

accurate and compact. The procedure finally results in the following equation:

$$\overline{\mathrm{err}_i^2} \overset{c}{\underset{u}{\gtrless}} t_s + 16B - 4n_c B \qquad (5)$$

where t_s is a constant threshold. $\overline{\mathrm{err}_i^2}$ stands for the sum of square errors in a window around pixel i. The parameter B is a positive-valued potential and n_c is the number of changed pixels in 3×3 neighborhood of each pixel. Since the output error is an estimation of the original image with background elimination, the original image

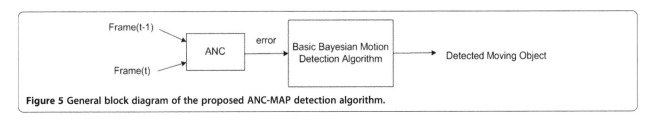

Figure 5 General block diagram of the proposed ANC-MAP detection algorithm.

should be normalized in order to have a normalized error. So, the threshold t_s will not be very sensitive to error value and can have a rather fixed value for different sequences.

5 Experimental results

To date, many motion detection algorithms have been developed that perform well in some types of videos but not in others. There is a list of challenging problems in the video surveillance applications addressed including illumination changes, repeated motions of background, bootstrapping, and shadows [17]. To show the ability of the proposed method to handle key challenges of real-world videos, it has been implemented and applied to several indoor and outdoor sequences with different frame rates and detection challenges. Regarding each motion detection challenge, two or more videos have been selected. Selected sequences are related to Visor dataset, Caviar dataset, and videos referenced in [7]. All videos are accessible at [27-29].

To evaluate the performance, earlier works [5,7,17] have been simulated and compared with the proposed algorithm. In all experimentations, the parameters are set as follows: the step size is chosen as 10^{-6}, filter length is equal to 8, and the parameter B is set to $0.5t_s$.

t_s is a fixed threshold which is selected experimentally and has a value between 0 and 1.

5.1 Simulation results

The proposed ANC-MAP detection algorithm has been tested on a variety of environments. The results which are shown in Figure 6 have been compared with other methods. The compared algorithms are as follows. The first comparison is made with mixture of Gaussian (MOG) algorithm [5] being a widely used adaptive background subtraction method. It performs well for both stationary and nonstationary backgrounds [7]. Another compared algorithm is the robust method of [7] which incorporates spectral, spatial, and temporal features to characterize the background appearance in a Bayesian framework. The proposed method has been also compared with the algorithm presented in [17] being a combination of MOG and local MAP estimation.

Detection results have been compared for the case where rival methods exhibit the best possible performance as the results of other methods have been collected from [7,17] (Figures 6, 7, and 8 of [7] and Figure 2 of [17]). The results shown for the algorithms of [5] and [7] have gained after a level of post-processing [7].

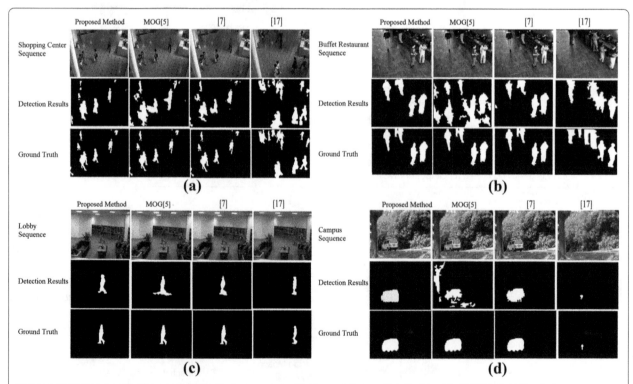

Figure 6 Detection results of proposed algorithm compared with three earlier works introduced in [5,7,17]. (a,b) Two indoor sequences with shadows and bootstrapping. **(c)** An office building with switching on/off light. **(d)** An environment containing repeated motions in the background due to waving trees.

Figure 7 Detection results of proposed algorithm. (a,b) Two indoor sequences with shadows. **(c)** A sequence with varying illumination. **(d,e)** Two environments containing repeated motions in the background.

5.1.1 Indoor environments and shadow

Figure 6a,b shows the results of two indoor test sequences including 'Shopping Center and Buffet Restaurant'. It may be seen that the proposed algorithm can detect and separate the moving objects and eliminate the shadows of walking persons almost perfectly.

5.1.2 Bootstrapping

Figure 6a,b is the two examples of bootstrapping too, in which no training period (i.e., no frame without foreground objects) is available. In spite of background subtraction algorithms, the proposed method needs no primary training frame without foreground.

5.1.3 Illumination variations

Figure 6c shows the results for a sequence (Lobby) with sudden illumination changes caused by switching on or off lights.

5.1.4 Repeated changes in the background

Campus is a sequence with changes in background. Results show that the proposed algorithm can easily omit the repeated motions in background (waving trees) (Figure 6d).

Figure 7 shows the performance of the proposed method on five other videos with the same challenges discussed above.

5.2 Quantitative evaluation

To quantitatively evaluate the proposed algorithm versus earlier works, the similarity measure can be used as introduced in [7]. The similarity measure is defined as follows:

$$S(A, B) = \frac{N(A \cap B)}{N(A \cup B)} \tag{6}$$

where A is the foreground region detected by the proposed algorithm; B, ideal foreground (ground truth); $N(x)$, number of pixels in the region x.

$S(A,B)$ approaches to a maximum value of 1 if A and B are the same. Five video sequences (Shopping center, Buffet Restaurant, Lobby, Fountain, and Campus) were selected to evaluate algorithms based on manually produced ground truth. Each of these videos is about one or two leading challenges in motion detection. Twenty frames of each sequence was randomly selected and used for making a comparison between the proposed method and other algorithms. This method of sampling frames is just like what is used in [7].

The averaging values of similarity measures for mentioned video sequences are shown in Table 1. Columns 1, 2, and 3 are the similarity measure values clearly expressed in [7,17]. The last row shows the average of results for five sequences. Quantitative evaluation and comparison with the existing methods show that the proposed method provides better performance.

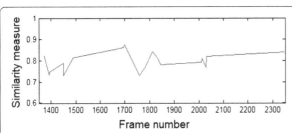

Figure 8 Similarity measure plot of sequence Campus for the proposed method.

Table 1 Quantitative evaluation: $S(A,B)$ values from the test sequences

	MOG [5]	[7]	[17]	Proposed method
Shopping center	0.42	0.64	0.74	0.79
Buffet restaurant	0.35	0.56	0.53	0.58
Lobby	0.42	0.70	0.69	0.67
Fountain	0.66	0.67	0.70	0.68
Campus	0.48	0.68	0.71	0.80
Average	0.466	0.65	0.674	0.704

Figure 8 is a plot of similarity measure for the sampled frames of sequence 'Campus.'

5.3 Limitations of the method

Since background and foreground are not *a priori* modeled in the proposed method, some restrictions appear at the results. A problem occurs when a foreground moving object stops suddenly or remains still for a period of time. The algorithm is not able to recognize a motionless foreground unless it starts moving again. Another problem arises when a color similarity exists between foreground and background. In this case, many foreground pixels are misclassified. However, the moving object is detected.

5.4 Complexity and computational cost analysis

To evaluate the computational load of proposed algorithm, it is supposed that the length of adaptive filter of ANC algorithm and the size of sliding window in Bayesian method are L and W respectively. In this case, the proposed algorithm will comprise of $W + L + 2$ addition and $W + 2L + 5$ multiplication operation for each pixel. Table 2 is a comparison of complexity in terms of the required additions and multiplications per pixel in each algorithm. The number of operations needed in each method is dependent on its parameters. The letters used in Table 2 refer to the following parameters:

- k, number of Gaussian distributions in each pixel
- m, number of matched distributions in each pixel ($m \leq k$)
- L, length of adaptive filter of ANC algorithm

- W, size of sliding window in Bayesian method
- $N(\nu)$, number of principle features of the background at 1 pixel

Assuming $k = 3$, $W = 9$, $L = 8$, and $N(\nu) = 15$, the operations required per pixel for each algorithm would be as follows:

- MOG, 27 additions and 39 multiplications
- [7], 74 additions and 43 multiplications
- [17], 40 additions and 52 multiplications
- Proposed method, 19 additions and 30 additions

According to Table 2, the proposed ANC-MAP detection algorithm needs slightly low computational complexity compared to the real-time algorithm of [7] which requires a large amount of memory (1.78 KB memory) for calculations of each pixel [7]. Although the computational cost of MOG or [17] is relatively comparable with proposed method, the latter proposes a superior performance as stated in Table 1.

6 Conclusions

A new algorithm was proposed in this paper for the detection of moving objects using the structure of adaptive noise cancellation. The proposed detection algorithm is integrated with Bayesian-MRF algorithm to improve the performance in terms of the shape continuity of detected objects. This algorithm benefits from the correlation of background pixels on the successive frames and removes the background. What is left at the output would be an approximation of moving areas. The shape of moving objects is then improved using Bayesian algorithm. The algorithm appears to be very efficient in eliminating noise, shadows, illumination variations, and repeated motions in the background. Experiments on different environments have shown the effectiveness of the proposed method. Despite earlier adaptive detection algorithms, the proposed method tries to directly detect moving objects using adaptive filtering. The promising detection results and simplicity of algorithm make the proposed method to be a suitable candidate for real-time practical implementations.

Table 2 Complexity and computational cost comparison

	MOG [5]	[7]	[17]	Proposed method
Additions (per pixel)	$3k + 6m$	$4N(\nu) + 14$	$W + 3k + 6m + 4$	$W + L + 2$
Multiplications (per pixel)	$5k + 8m$	$2N(\nu) + 13$	$W + 5k + 8m + 4$	$W + 2L + 5$
Other requirements	Initialization of Gaussian functions and parameters	Estimating seven probability functions using histograms	-	-
	Post processing	Post processing		

Abbreviations
ANC: adaptive noise cancellation; MAP: maximum *a posteriori*; MRF: Markov random field.

Competing interests
The authors declare that they have no competing interests.

Authors' information
EK was born in Iran in 1986. She received the B.Sc. and M.Sc. degrees in electronic engineering from K.N. Toosi University of Technology, Tehran, Iran, in 2008 and 2011, respectively. She is currently a teacher of digital logic laboratory at K.N. Toosi University of Technology. Her main interests are design of digital electronic circuits and signal and image processing. DA received the B.Sc. and M.Sc. degrees in electronics and bioelectric engineering from Sharif University of Technology, Tehran, Iran, in 1996 and 1998, respectively, and the Ph.D. degree in electronics engineering from SUPELEC, Gif-Sur-Yvette, France, in 2007. He is now with the Department of Electrical Engineering, K.N. Toosi University of Technology in Tehran, Iran. His research interests include blind signal processing, particularly applied to electronic systems and design of analog and digital electronic circuits.

References
1. JM McHugh, J Konrad, V Saligrama, P Jodoin, Foreground-adaptive background subtraction. IEEE Signal. Process Lett. **16**, 390–393 (2009)
2. L Ovsenik, AK Kolesarova, J Turan, Video surveillance systems. Acta Electrotechnica et Informatica **10**(4), 46–53 (2010)
3. HR Shayegh, N Moghadam, A new background subtraction method in video sequences based on temporal motion windows, in *International Conference on IT* (Thailand, 2009). March
4. CR Wren, A Azarbayejani, T Darrell, A Pentland, Pfinder: real-time tracking of the human body. IEEE Trans. Pattern Anal. Mach. Intell. **18**(7), 780–785 (1997)
5. C Stauffer, W Grimson, Adaptive background mixture models for real-time tracking. IEEE Conf. Comp. Vision Pattern Recog. **2**, 246–252 (1999)
6. A Elgammal, R Duraiswami, D Harwood, L Davis, Background and foreground modelling using nonparametric kernel density for visual surveillance. Proc. IEEE **90**(7), 1151–1163 (2002)
7. L Li, W Huang, IY Gu, Q Tian, Statistical modelling of complex backgrounds for foreground object detection. IEEE Trans. Image Process. **13**(11), 1459–1472 (2004)
8. YZ Hsu, HH Nagel, G Refers, New likelihood test method for change detection in image sequences. Comput. Vision Graph Image Process. **26**, 73–106 (1984)
9. T Aach, A Kaup, R Mester, Statistical model-based change detection in moving video. Signal Process. **31**, 165–180 (1993)
10. T Aach, A Kaup, Bayesian algorithms for adaptive change detection in image sequences using Markov random fields. Signal Process Image Comm. **7**(2), 147–160 (1995)
11. J Migdal, EL Grimson, Background subtraction using Markov thresholds. IEEE Workshop Motion Video Computing **2**, 58–65 (2005)
12. Y Sheikh, M Shah, Bayesian modelling of dynamic scenes for object detection. IEEE Trans. Pattern Anal. Mach. Intell. **27**(11), 1778–1792 (2005)
13. SY Yu, F Wang, YF Xue, J Yang, Bayesian moving object detection in dynamic scenes using an adaptive foreground model. J. Zhejiang Univ. (Sci.) **10**(12), 1750–1758 (2009)
14. Z Kato, *Multiresolution Markovian models in computer vision*. Application on segmentation of SPOT images, PhD Thesis (INRIA, Sophia Antipolis, France, 1994)
15. T Aach, L Dumbgen, R Mester, D Toth, Bayesian illumination-invariant motion detection, in *IEEE International Conference on Image Processing, Thessaloniki, 7–10 October*, 2001, pp. 640–643
16. Q Liu, M Sun, RJ Sclabassi, Illumination-invariant change detection model for patient monitoring video, in *26th Annual International Conference of the IEEE Engineering in Medicine and Biology Society, 2004* (IEMBS 04, San Francisco, 2004), pp. 1782–1785
17. TH Tsai, CY Lin, Markov random field based background subtraction method for foreground detection under moving background scene, in *Conference on Genetic and Evolutionary Computing* (Shenzhen, 2010), pp. 691–694
18. E Kermani, D Asemani, A new illumination-invariant method of moving object detection for video surveillance systems, in *Conference on Machine Vision and Image Processing* (Tehran, 2011), pp. 1–5
19. M Das, An improved adaptive wiener filter for de-noising and signal detection, in *Proceedings of IASTED International Conference on Signal and Image Processing* (Hawaii, 2005), pp. 226–230
20. CY Chen, CW Hsia, Image noise cancellation by adaptive filter with weight-training mechanism (AFWTM), in *Information, Decision, and Control Conference* (Adelaide, 2007), pp. 332–335
21. S Sudha, GR Suresh, R Sukanesh, Speckle noise reduction in ultrasound images by wavelet thresholding based on weighted variance. IJCTE **1**(1), 1793–8201 (2009)
22. VJ Naveen, T Prabakar, JV Suman, PD Pradeep, Noise suppression in speech signals using adaptive algorithms. Int J Signal Process. Image Process. **3**(3), 87–96 (2010)
23. A Singh, *Adaptive noise cancellation, undergraduate B.E. project report* (Netaji Subhas Institute of Technology, 2001)
24. Y He, H He, L Li, Y Wu, H Pan, The applications and simulation of adaptive filter in noise canceling, in *Conference on Computer Science and Software Engineering* (Hubei, 2008), pp. 1–4
25. A. Singh, *Adaptive noise cancellation (2001)*. Available at www.cs.cmu.edu/~aarti/pubs/ANC.pdf. Accessed 21 January 2012
26. Z Ramadan, Error vector normalized adaptive algorithm applied to adaptive noise canceller and system identification. J. Eng. Appl. Sci. **3**(4), 710–717 (2010)
27. Visor dataset, http://imagelab.ing.unimore.it/visor/. Accessed 15 August 2011
28. *CAVIAR test case scenarios (2003–2004)*, http://homepages.inf.ed.ac.uk/rbf/CAVIARDATA1/. Accessed 10 October 2011
29. *Background modeling dataset*, http://perception.i2r.a-star.edu.sg/bk_model/bk_index.html. Accessed 19 January 2012

4

Classification of extreme facial events in sign language videos

Epameinondas Antonakos[1,2]*, Vassilis Pitsikalis[1] and Petros Maragos[1]

Abstract

We propose a new approach for Extreme States Classification (ESC) on feature spaces of facial cues in sign language (SL) videos. The method is built upon Active Appearance Model (AAM) face tracking and feature extraction of global and local AAMs. ESC is applied on various facial cues - as, for instance, pose rotations, head movements and eye blinking - leading to the detection of extreme states such as left/right, up/down and open/closed. Given the importance of such facial events in SL analysis, we apply ESC to detect visual events on SL videos, including both American (ASL) and Greek (GSL) corpora, yielding promising qualitative and quantitative results. Further, we show the potential of ESC for assistive annotation tools and demonstrate a link of the detections with indicative higher-level linguistic events. Given the lack of facial annotated data and the fact that manual annotations are highly time-consuming, ESC results indicate that the framework can have significant impact on SL processing and analysis.

Keywords: Sign language; Active appearance models; Semi-supervised classification/annotation; Linguistic events

1 Introduction

Facial events are inevitably linked with human communication and are more than essential for gesture and sign language (SL) comprehension. Nevertheless, both from the automatic visual processing and the recognition viewpoint, facial events are difficult to detect, describe and model. In the context of SL, this gets more complex given the diverse range of potential facial events, such as head movements, head pose, mouthings and local actions of the eyes and brows, which could carry valuable information in parallel with the manual cues. Moreover, the above visual phenomena can occur in multiple ways and at different timescales, either at the sign or the sentence level, and are related to the meaning of a sign, the syntax or the prosody [1-4]. Thus, we focus on the detection of such low-level visual events in video sequences which can be proved important both for SL analysis and for automatic SL recognition (ASLR) [5,6].

SL video corpora are widely employed by linguists, annotators and computer scientists for the study of SL

*Correspondence: e.antonakos@imperial.ac.uk
[1] Department of Electrical and Computer Engineering, National Technical University of Athens, Athens 15773, Greece
[2] Department of Computing, Imperial College London, 180 Queen's Gate, London SW7 2AZ, UK

and the training of ASLR systems. All the above require manual annotation of facial events, either for linguistic analysis or for ground truth transcriptions. However, manual annotation is conducted by experts and is a highly time-consuming task (in [7] is described as 'enormous', resulting on annotations of 'only a small proportion of data'), justifying their general lack. Simultaneously, more SL data, many of which lack facial annotations, are built or accumulated on the web [8-11]. All the above led on efforts towards the development of automatic or semi-automatic annotation tools [12-14] for the processing of corpora.

Let us consider a case that highlights the visual events as well as our motivation. Figure 1 shows an example from Greek sign language (GSL) [8,15], where the signer signs in a continuous manner the following phrases as could be freely translated in English: 'I walked to the line - it was long - and waited there. (This was until) ticket, and passport or id-card, were checked (referring to the control procedure), depending on whether they were going inside EU or abroad (respectively)'[a]. By examining facial events, we notice the following relation between the visual level and the sentence level regarding *alternative construction*: during this event, a phrase has two conjunctive parts linked with a - not always articulated - 'or'. This is observed to be synchronized with

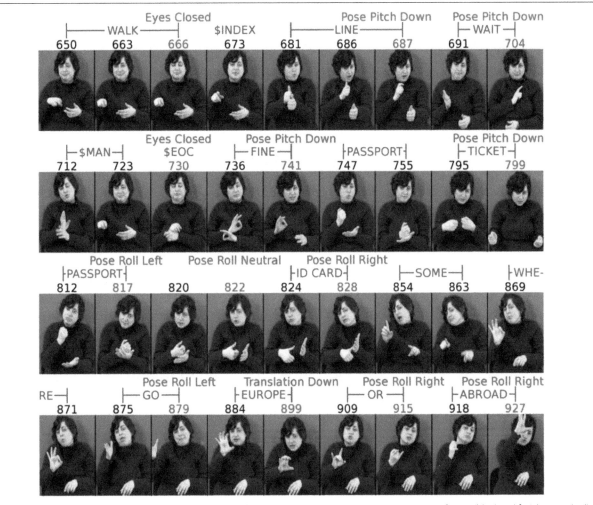

Figure 1 GSL continuous signing example. On frames' top: frame number (black), gloss transcriptions across frames (blue) and facial events (red). Concerning sentence structure, the linguistic event of alternative construction consists of two conjunctive parts: PASSPORT or ID-CARD. Notice how the visual event of pose over roll extreme angles marks these two parts. Such visual events of extreme states we aim to detect. For more details, see in text.

the extreme bounds (right, left) of the pose over the roll angle. The first part of the alternative construction 'PASSPORT' (812 to 817) is synchronized with a head tilt at the one extreme (left), whereas at the second part 'ID-CARD' (824 to 828), the roll angle is at the other extreme (right). The low-level visual events serve as time markers concerning sentence-level linguistic structure. The conjunctive parts are marked by a head's rotation over the roll angle. The same is repeated with the alternative construction 'GO EUROPE OR ABROAD' (875 to 927). Further, note (Figure 1) the signer's blinks (e.g. 666, 730) and nods (e.g. 704, 799): some of them are synchronized with the corresponding sentence or sign boundaries. Such issues are under linguistic research too [1-4,16,17].

In this article, we focus on the low-level visual detection of facial events in videos within what we call *extreme*

states framework. Our contributions start with the low-level detection of events - as the head pose over yaw, pitch and roll angles, the opening/closing of the eyes and local cues of the eyebrows and the mouth; see also the example in Figure 1. This list only demonstrates indicative cases. For instance, in the case of head turn over the yaw angle, we detect the extreme states of the rotation (left/right), and for the eyes, the closed/open states. The proposed approach, referred to as the *Extreme States Classification* (ESC), is formulated to detect and classify in a simple but effective and unified way the extreme states of various facial events. We build on the exploitation of global and local Active Appearance Models (AAMs), trained in facial regions of interest, to track and model the face and its components. After appropriate feature selection, ESC over-partitions the feature space of a referred cue and applies maximum-distance hierarchical clustering, resulting on extreme clusters - and the corresponding statistically trained models - for each cue. The framework is applied successfully on videos from *different* SLs, American sign language (ASL) and GSL corpora, showing promising results. In the case of existing facial-level annotations, we quantitatively evaluate the method. ESC is also applied on a multi-person still images database, showing its *person-independent* generalization. Finally, the potential impact of the low-level facial events detection is further explored: We highlight the *link* of the detections with higher-level linguistic events. Based on low-level visual detections, we detect linguistic phenomena related to the sign and sentence boundaries or the sentence structure. We also show the incorporation of ESC in assistive annotation, e.g. within environments as ELAN [18]. The presented evidence renders ESC a candidate expected to have practical impact in the analysis and processing of SL data.

2 Relative literature

Given the importance of facial cues, the incorporation and the engineering or linguistic interest of facial features and head gestures have recently received attention. This interest is manifested through different aspects with respect to (w.r.t.) visual processing, detection and recognition. There are methods related to non-manual linguistic markers direct recognition [19-21] as applied to negations, conditional clauses, syntactic boundaries, topic/focus and wh-, yes/no questions. Moreover, there are methods for the detection of important facial events such as head gestures [20,22,23], eyebrows movement and eyes blinking/squint [20], along with facial expressions recognition [22,24,25] within the context of SL. The authors in [20] employ a two-layer Conditional Random Field for recognizing continuously signed grammatical markers related to facial features and head movements. Metaxas et al. [21] employ geometric and Local Binary pattern (LBP) features on a combined 2D and 3D face tracking framework to automatically recognize linguistically significant non-manual expressions in continuous ASL videos. The challenging task of fusion of manuals and non-manuals for ASLR has also received attention [5,6,26,27]. Due to the cost - timewise - and the lack of annotations, recently, there is a more explicit trend by works towards preliminary tools for semi-automatic annotation via a recognition and a translation component [12] at the sign level concerning manuals, by categorizing manual/non-manual components [13], providing information on lexical signs and assisting sign searching. Early enough, Vogler and Goldenstein [24,25] have contributed in this direction. Such works clearly mention the need for further work on facial cues.

More generally, unsupervised and semi-supervised approaches for facial feature extraction, event detection and classification have dragged interest [28]. Aligned Cluster Analysis (ACA) [29] and Hierarchical ACA (HACA) [30] apply temporal clustering of naturally occurring facial behaviour that solves for correspondences between dynamic events. Specifically, ACA is a temporal segmentation method that combines kernel k-means with a dynamic time warping kernel, and HACA is its extension that employs an hierarchical bottom-up framework. Consequently, these methods are dynamic which differs from the static nature of our proposed method that detects potential facial events on each frame of a video. Authors in [31] use Locally Linear Embedding to detect head pose. Hoey [32] aims at the unsupervised classification of expression sequences by employing a hierarchical dynamic Bayesian network. However, the above are applied on domains such as facial expression recognition and action recognition [33].

Facial features are employed in tasks such as facial expression analysis [34] and head pose estimation [35]. A variety of approaches are proposed for tracking and feature extraction. Many are based on deformable models, like Active Appearance Models (AAMs), due to their ability to capture shape and texture variability, providing a compact representation of facial features [5,6,13,29,36]. There is a variety of tracking methods including Active Shape Models with Point Distribution Model [22,37,38], Constrained Local Models [39], deformable part-based models [40], subclass divisions [41] and appearance-based facial features detection [42]. The tracking can also be based on 3D models [24,25] or a combination of models [21]. There are also numerous features employed as SIFT [22], canonical appearance [21,39], LBPs [21] and geometric distances on a face shape graph [21,29]. Authors in [19] recognize grammatical markers by tracking facial features based on probabilistic Principal Components Analysis (PCA)-learned shape constraints. Various pattern recognition techniques are applied for the detection and classification/recognition of facial features in SL tasks, such as Support Vector Machines [22,39], Hidden Markov Models [5,6] and combinations [21].

This work differs from other SL-related works. First, multiple facial events are handled in a *unified way* through a single framework. As shown next, this *unified handling* of ESC along with the extreme-states formulation are suitable for SL analysis in multiple ways. Second, the method detects the facial events in question at each new unseen frame, rather than performing a segmentation procedure given a whole video sequence; thus, it is static. Then, the method is inspired and designed for SL video corpora, and the whole framework is designed having in mind assistive automatic *facial annotation* tools, extending [13]. The detection of even *simple* events can have *drastic* impact, given the lack of annotations. This is strengthened given their relation with linguistic phenomena. From the facial-linguistic aspect, the methods as [21] are aiming on the recognition of linguistic phenomena themselves in a supervised model-based manner, thus requiring linguistic annotations. Herein, we rather focus on visual phenomena for the detection of visual events and provide an interactive assistive annotation tool for their discovery in corpora, while exploring their potential link with higher-level phenomena. Given the difficulty of ASLR in continuous, spontaneous tasks [15], recognition-based annotation tools have still low performance - or rather preliminary for the case of the face [13,25]. Focusing on independent frames, without interest on the dynamics, ESC can be effective on multiple information cues, useful for SL annotation and recognition. Thus, our results could feed with salient detections, higher-level methods such as [20,21] or ASLR systems [5]. Of course, the area would benefit by further incorporation of more unsupervised approaches [29,31,33]. Overall, different methods focus partially on some of the above aspects, and to the best of our knowledge, none of them shares all described issues. In [43], we introduced ESC. Herein, the approach is extensively presented with mature and updated material, including the application to multiple events and more experiments. In addition, there is an updated formulation and rigorous handling of parameters - e.g. event symmetry, SPThresh (see Section 4.2.2) - which allows the user to employ the framework in an unsupervised way. Finally, we further highlight linguistic and assistive annotation perspectives.

3 Visual processing: global and local AAMs for tracking and features

3.1 Active Appearance Model background

Active Appearance Models (AAMs) [44,45] are generative statistical models of an object's shape and texture that recover a parametric description through optimization. Until recently, mainly due to the project-out inverse compositional algorithm [45], AAMs have been widely criticized of being inefficient and unable to generalize well in illumination and facial expression variations. However, recent research has proved that this is far from being true. The employment of more efficient optimization techniques [46-48] as well as robust feature-based appearance representations [47,49] has proved that AAMs are one of the most efficient and robust methodologies for face modelling. In this paper, we take advantage of adaptive, constrained inverse compositional methods [46] for improved performance, applied on pixel intensities. Even though other proposed AAM variations may be more successful, the main focus of this paper is the facial events detection in SL videos and the proposed method is independent of the AAM optimization technique in use.

In brief, following the notation in [46], we express a *shape instance* as $\mathbf{s} = [x_1, y_1, \ldots, x_N, y_N]$, a $2N \times$ 1 vector consisting of N landmark points' coordinates (x_i, y_i), $\forall i = 1, \ldots, N$ and a *texture instance* as an $M \times 1$ vector A consisting of the greyscale values of the M column-wise pixels inside the shape graph. The shape model is trained employing Principal Components Analysis (PCA) on the aligned training shapes to find the eigenshapes of maximum variance and the mean shape $\mathbf{s}_0$. The texture model is trained similarly in order to find the corresponding eigentextures and mean texture A_0. Additionally, we employ the *similarity transformation* $S(\mathbf{t}) = \begin{bmatrix} 1+t_1 & -t_2 \\ t_2 & 1+t_1 \end{bmatrix} \begin{bmatrix} x_i \\ y_i \end{bmatrix} + \begin{bmatrix} t_3 \\ t_4 \end{bmatrix}$, $\forall i = 1, \ldots, N$ that controls the face's global rotation, translation and scaling and the *global affine texture transform* $T_\mathbf{u} = (u_1 + 1)I + u_2$, used for lighting invariance. $\mathbf{t} = [t_1, \ldots, t_4]$ and $\mathbf{u} = [u_1, u_2]$ are the corresponding parameter vectors.

Synthesis is achieved via linear combination of eigenvectors weighted with the according parameters, as $\mathbf{s_p} = \mathbf{s}_0 + \sum_{i=1}^{N_s} p_i \mathbf{s}_i$ (shape) and $A_\lambda = A_0 + \sum_{i=1}^{N_t} \lambda_i A_i$ (texture). We denote by $\tilde{\mathbf{p}} = [\mathbf{t}_{1:4}, \mathbf{p}_{1:N_s}]^T$ the *concatenated shape parameters* vector consisting of the similarity $\mathbf{t}$ and shape parameters $\mathbf{p} = [p_1, \ldots, p_{N_s}]$. Similarly, we denote by $\tilde{\lambda} = [\mathbf{u}_{1:2}, \lambda_{1:N_t}]^T$ the *concatenated texture parameters* consisting of the affine texture transform $\mathbf{u}$ and the texture parameters $\lambda = [\lambda_1, \ldots, \lambda_{N_t}]$. The *piecewise affine warp function* $\mathbf{W}(\mathbf{s}; \tilde{\mathbf{p}})$ maps pixels inside the source shape $\mathbf{s}$ into the mean shape $\mathbf{s}_0$ using the barycentric coordinates of Delaunay triangulation. Next, we employ both global and local AAMs denoted with a 'G' or 'L' exponent. For more details, see the relative literature as in [45,46]. Finally, the complexity of the employed AAM fitting algorithm is $\mathcal{O}((N_s + N_t)M + N_s^2 N_t^2)$ per iteration which results in a close to real-time performance of 15 fps.

3.2 Initialization using face and skin detection

AAMs are effective on the fitting of high-variation deformations of facial parts but are inefficient within large pose variation of SL videos due to the gradient-based optimization criterion rendering the fitting sensitive to initial parameters. Various methods deal with the *initialization issue*, such as landmark localization using deformable part-based models [40], facial point detection using Gabor feature boosted classifiers [50] or boosted regression with Markov Random Fields [51]. Next, we rely on skin detection, morphological processing and face detection, for robust initialization. Our goal is to align facial parts between the target image and the mean shape by initializing the similarity parameters $\mathbf{t}_{1:4}$ (rotation θ, scaling s, translation (x, y)) (Figure 2). Firstly, we find a *symmetric head mask*, by training two Gaussian mixture models (GMMs) on the human skin/non-skin, based on the chrominance YCbCr colourspace channels. The hair colour is included in the skin GMM in order to preserve head symmetry. We fit an ellipsis on the

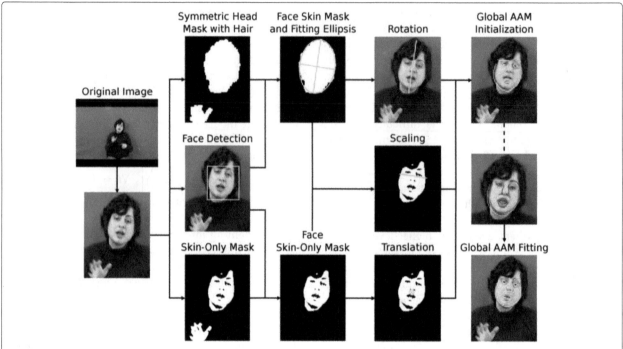

Figure 2 GAAM fitting initialization. GAAM fitting initialization framework for estimation of initial similarity transform parameters (rotation, translation, scaling).

resulting head mask, which has the same normalized second central moments as the mask region. We then use the major axis' orientation to initialize pose over the roll angle (similarity transform's *rotation* parameter). Secondly, we find a *compact skin-only mask* expanding at the face edges, by computing the intersection of a skin-only GMM-based result with a threshold-based skin detection on HSV colourspace - due to colour perception [52]. Then, we apply morphological operators for hole filling and expansion to find all skin pixels. The initial face *scaling* is estimated via the skin mask's width on the previous fitting ellipse' minor axis direction. The initial *translation* is defined by aligning the skin mask's and the global AAM (GAAM) mean shape's centroids. In all steps, the selection of facial skin mask vs. the hand skin regions is achieved via Viola-Jones face detection with Kalman filtering, which guarantees robustness [53]. The similarity parameters are re-initialized per frame, allowing failure recovery and preventing error accumulation. In this work, we do not address fitting on occlusions, by first applying an algorithm for occlusion detection [54].

3.2.1 *Global AAM fitting results*

We show a fitting experiment comparing the proposed initialization framework with the Viola-Jones face detection framework. As shown in the histograms (Figure 3), the mean MSE decreases by 76.7% and the high-MSE cases are eliminated, resulting in accurate fitting and

tracking (Figure 4), especially on regions with intense texture differences. This is because the proposed initialization method also estimates the initial rotation apart from scaling and translation that can be extracted from the Viola-Jones bounding box. The difficulty of GAAM fitting on SL videos, caused by extreme mouthings or poses, highlights the need for robust initialization. Note that the two databases in Figure 4 have different landmark points configurations adapted to each signer's face. However, ESC is independent of this configuration, as it simply needs correspondence labels between landmarks and facial areas.

3.3 Projection from global to local AAMs

Local AAMs (LAAMs) are trained to model a specific facial area and decompose its variance from the rest of the facial variance. LAAM fitting is achieved by projecting

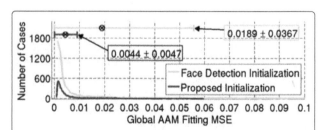

Figure 3 GAAM fitting initialization experiment. Histogram comparison of GAAM fitting MSE between the proposed and the Viola-Jones face detection initialization frameworks on GSL video.

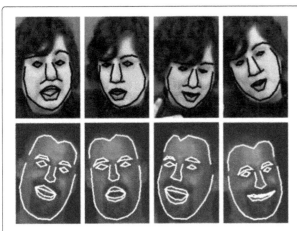

Figure 4 GAAM fitting results. GAAM fitting results on GSL (top) and BU (bottom) video frames.

the shape and texture parameters from the GAAM to the LAAM eigenvectors. Figure 5 shows a projection of GAAM to eyes, brows, mouth, nose and jaw LAAMs. Following notations in Section 3.1, we describe the GAAM with $\{N^G, \mathbf{s}_0^G, N_s^G, \tilde{p}_i^G, \mathbf{s}_i^G\}$ and the LAAM by $\{N^L, \mathbf{s}_0^L, N_s^L, \tilde{p}_i^L, \mathbf{s}_i^L\}$. We then compute the parameters $\tilde{\mathbf{p}}^L$ given the GAAM parameters $\tilde{\mathbf{p}}^G$. The GAAM fitting shape result is synthesized by $\mathbf{s}_{\tilde{\mathbf{p}}^G} = S\left(\mathbf{t}^G, \mathbf{s}_{\mathbf{p}^G}\right)$. We form the respective $\mathbf{s}_{\tilde{\mathbf{p}}^L}$ shape vector keeping N^L LAAM's landmark points - a subset of the N^G landmarks. Then, we align the $\mathbf{s}_{\tilde{\mathbf{p}}^L}$ and $\mathbf{s}_0^L$ shape vectors using Procrustes Analysis to find the similarity parameters $\mathbf{t}_{1:4}^L$. The resulting aligned vector $\mathbf{s}_{\mathbf{p}^L}$ is used to compute the projection to the LAAM eigenshapes by $p_i^L = \left(\mathbf{s}_{\mathbf{p}^L} - \mathbf{s}_0^L\right)^T \mathbf{s}_i^L$, $\forall i = 1, \ldots, N_s^L$. Similarly, we project the fitted GAAM texture of $\{N^G, A_0^G, N_t^G, \tilde{\lambda}_i^G, A_i^G\}$ to LAAM $\{N^L, A_0^L, N_t^L, \tilde{\lambda}_i^L, A_i^L\}$. The difference is that we warp the texture from the GAAM's shape subgraph defined by the N^L landmarks to the LAAM's mean shape;

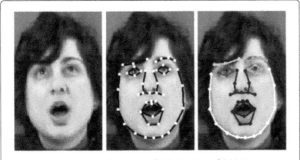

Figure 5 LAAM projection example. Projection of GAAM to left/right eye, brow, nose, mouth and jaw LAAMs. Left: original image. Middle: GAAM. Right: LAAMs.

thus, $A_\lambda^L = A_\lambda^G\left(\mathbf{W}\left(\mathbf{x}; \tilde{\mathbf{p}}^L\right)\right)$, where $\mathbf{x}$ are the pixels in the LAAM's shape graph. The projection is then $\lambda_i^L = \left(A_{\lambda^L} - A_0^L\right)^T A_i^L, \forall i = 1, \ldots, N_t^L$.

3.4 Features and dimensionality

AAMs provide a wide range of features suitable for a variety of facial events. The designer selects the feature that best describes an event from three categories: (1) a single GAAM parameter out of $\mathbf{q}^G = [\tilde{\mathbf{p}}^G, \tilde{\boldsymbol{\lambda}}^G]^T$, (2) a single LAAM parameter out of $\mathbf{q}^L = [\tilde{\mathbf{p}}^L, \tilde{\boldsymbol{\lambda}}^L]^T$, and (3) a *geometrical measure* such as the Euclidean distance $d = \sqrt{(x_i - x_j)^2 + (y_i - y_j)^2}$ between (x_i, y_i) and (x_j, y_j) landmarks, or the vertical displacement $d = y_i^{(f)} - y_i^{(f-1)}$ of a landmark i over frame number f or the angle of the similarity transform $d = \arctan\frac{t_2}{t_1+1}$. The above results in *single-dimensional* (1D) features, which is an important advantage of ESC. 1D features make the method easy to use in terms of their clustering, whilst the combination of multiple 1D-based facial events leads to more complex ones. AAM synthesis is a linear combination of the eigenvectors weighted with the parameters. Hence, there is *continuity* in the model deformation instances and in the facial event variation, as the 1D feature value increases from minimum to maximum in a constant step. Figure 6 shows examples of 1D spaces of various features and their relation with the continuity of the AAM instance's deformation or alteration. In all cases, the mean instance is placed in the middle. As the feature value varies over/under the mean position, the model's deformation converges towards two *extreme* and *opposing* model states, respectively.

4 Extreme States Classification of facial events

We highlight the ESC concept with an example showing a frame sequence from GSL (Figure 7). We aim to detect the change in facial pose over the yaw angle from right to left. For this, we focus on detecting the extreme states of pose in terms of assignment of a right or left label and not computing the precise angle. These extreme states are observed on the very first and last frames of the video segment. Apart from SL tasks, which are the aim of this paper, ESC can be used as is for various facial gesture-related tasks.

4.1 Event symmetry and feature spaces

Next, we take advantage of the characteristics of 1D features and the continuity of the model's deformation (Section 3.4). Since the feature values' variation causes the respective facial event to smoothly alternate between two extreme instances, ESC aims to automatically detect these extreme states, the *upper* and the *lower* one. The instances located between the extremes are labelled as *undefined* or *neutral* depending on the event.

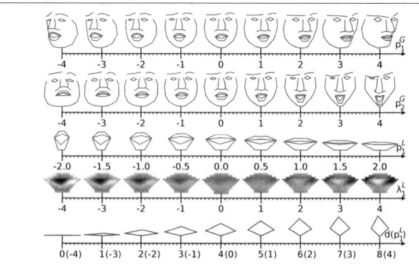

Figure 6 1D feature types. First row: GAAM's first shape parameter. Second row: GAAM's second shape parameter. Third row: mouth LAAM's first shape parameter. Fourth row: mouth LAAM's first texture parameter. Fifth row: Euclidean distance between the eye's upper/lower landmarks.

The facial events are categorized into two groups in terms of symmetry between the extreme states: *symmetric* and *asymmetric*. For example, the face pose is a symmetric facial cue since there is a balance between the left and right pose w.r.t. the neutral. In contrast, the eyes or mouth opening/closing is asymmetric, because unlike the closed label that is unique with very small differentiation, the open label has many possible states with variable distance between the eyelids or lips and different labels such as widely open and slightly open. Asymmetric facial cues are further separated in upper and lower ones depending on whether the upper or lower extreme has a unique instance describing it. Figure 8 shows an example of a facial event's feature space per category.

4.2 Training

Given a training feature space, once the designer selects the feature best describing the event, ESC performs an unsupervised training of probabilistic models. The 1D features provide simplicity in the automatic cluster selection and real-time complexity. See Figure 7 for an example employing the GAAM's first eigenshape parameter symmetric feature.

4.2.1 Hierarchical breakdown

ESC automatically selects *representative* clusters that will be used to train Gaussian distributions. These clusters must be positioned on the two *edges* and the *centre* of the 1D feature space, as shown in Figure 8. We apply agglomerative hierarchical clustering resulting in a large number of clusters, approximately half the number of the training observations. This hierarchical over-clustering eliminates the possible bias of the training feature space. It neutralizes its density differences, creating small groups that decrease the number of considered observations. In case we have a significant density imbalance between the feature's edges of our training set, the over-clustering equalizes the observations at each edge.

Direct application of a clustering method for the automatic selection of representative clusters would take into account the inter-distances of data points resulting in biased large surface clusters that spread towards the centre of the feature space. If the two edges of the feature space were not equalized w.r.t. the data points' density, then we would risk one of the two clusters to capture intermediate states. Consequently, the models corresponding to the extreme states would also include some unde-

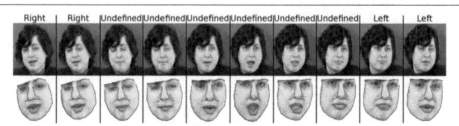

Figure 7 Pose over the yaw angle detection. Pose over the yaw angle detection (labels on top) with ESC application (GSL). First row: original images. Second row: reconstructed shape and texture global AAM.

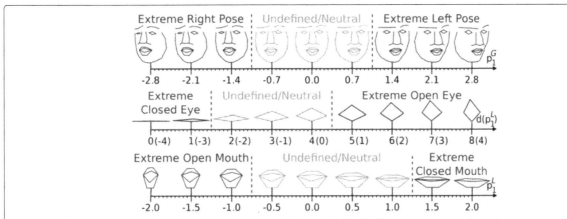

Figure 8 Facial event symmetry. First row: symmetric; pose over the yaw with GAAM's first shape parameter. Second row: upper-asymmetric; eye opening/closing with Euclidean distance. Third row: lower-asymmetric; mouth opening/closing with LAAM's first shape parameter.

fined/neutral cases from the centre of the feature space, increasing the percentage of false-positive detections.

4.2.2 Cluster selection

Another reason not applying a direct clustering method for the automatic selection of three representative clusters - two on the edges, one in the centre - is that the trained distributions for each cluster would intersect and share data points, leading to false-positive detections. We tackle this issue with a cluster selection procedure based on *maximum-distance* criterion. We take advantage of the 1D feature space continuous geometry, according to which the extreme states are the ones with maximum distance. Thus, we automatically select appropriate clusters on the edges of the feature space and a central cluster at half the distance between them.

The cluster selection employed here selects certain observations for inclusion in a cluster and rejects the rest. Additionally, all clusters should be equalized w.r.t. the number of observations. The determination of the spreading of each edge cluster towards the central part of the feature space depending on the facial event type that

we aim to detect has a key role for ESC efficiency. This spreading is controlled through a parameter that we call *Subjective Perceived Threshold* (SPThres). In our previous work [43], we formed clusters by selecting pairs of data points that have maximum distance until reaching each time the selected scalar SPThres value. In this work, the SPThres value is determined depending on the introduced facial event symmetry. SPThres is expressed as three percentages: SPThres = [SPThres$_L$, SPThres$_C$, SPThres$_U$], one for each cluster - (L)ower, (C)entral and (U)pper - that control the spread thresholds $[T_L, T_C, T_U]$ of each cluster. The central threshold T_C has two values $[T_{CL}, T_{CU}]$ corresponding to the lower and upper bounds. Spread thresholds are calculated as follows:

$$T_L = \min_{\mathcal{F}} + \text{SPThres}_L \, |\text{med}_{\mathcal{F}} - \min_{\mathcal{F}}| \qquad (1)$$

$$\left.\begin{array}{l} T_{CL} = \text{med}_{\mathcal{F}} - \text{SPThres}_C \, |\text{med}_{\mathcal{F}} - \min_{\mathcal{F}}| \\ T_{CU} = \text{med}_{\mathcal{F}} + \text{SPThres}_C \, |\max_{\mathcal{F}} - \text{med}_{\mathcal{F}}| \end{array}\right\} \Rightarrow T_C = [T_{CL}, T_{CU}]$$

$$(2)$$

$$T_U = \max_{\mathcal{F}} - \text{SPThres}_U \, |\max_{\mathcal{F}} - \text{med}_{\mathcal{F}}| \qquad (3)$$

Table 1 Facial event default configuration

Facial event	Feature		Symmetry	SPThres	Figure
Pose yaw	GAAM	p_1^G	Symmetric	[30, 10, 30]	7
Pose pitch	GAAM	p_2^G	Symmetric	[30, 10, 30]	11
Pose roll	GAAM	θ	Symmetric	[30, 10, 30]	11
Vertical translation	Geometrical	Nosetip	Symmetric	[30, 10, 30]	12
Eye open/close	Geometrical	Eyelids	Upper-asymmetric	[20, 10, 40]	12
Brow up/down	Brow LAAM	p_1^L	Symmetric	[30, 10, 30]	13
Mouth open/close	Mouth LAAM	p_1^L	Lower-asymmetric	[40, 10, 20]	13
Teeth in/out	Mouth LAAM	λ_1^L	Symmetric	[30, 10, 30]	13
Tongue in/out	Mouth LAAM	λ_2^L	Symmetric	[30, 10, 30]	13

Correspondence among facial events, feature type, symmetry/asymmetry and SPThres$_{(L,C,U)}$ default values. The presented SPThres values correspond to ESC's default configuration.

where $\mathcal{F}$ is the 1D feature space of the training set and $\min_{\mathcal{F}}$, $\mathrm{med}_{\mathcal{F}}$ and $\max_{\mathcal{F}}$ are its minimum, median and maximum, respectively. The SPThres configuration depends on the symmetry of the facial event presented in Section 4.1. If the event is *symmetric*, then the edge SPThres values are set to be equal: $\mathrm{SPThres}_U = \mathrm{SPThres}_L$. On the contrary, if the event is *asymmetric*, then the edge values are unequal and we set $\mathrm{SPThres}_U > \mathrm{SPThres}_L$ and $\mathrm{SPThres}_U < \mathrm{SPThres}_L$ in the case of upper and lower asymmetric events, respectively. Additionally, as shown in Section 6.2, the SPThres value configuration depends on our need on high precision or recall percentages. Thus, SPThres is a *performance refinement parameter*. Its *default values* are constant and ensure a balanced performance of ESC with high *F*-score, which is sufficient for most applications of ESC. However, its potential manual refinement can adjust the tightness/looseness of the Gaussian distributions, resulting in higher precision or recall percentages that could be useful in other applications. Table 1 shows the correspondence among facial events, appropriate features and default SPThres values.

4.2.3 Final clusters interpretation and training feature space

The utility of a central cluster is to represent intermediate-state facial events labelled as undefined/neutral. If the intermediate state lacks physical interpretation, then the central cluster represents the two extremes' transition, labelled as *undefined*. For instance, in Figure 7, if the extreme states of right/left pose are detected correctly, then it is concluded that the in-between frames portray the transition from right to left pose, and thus, the central cluster has the role of a non-extreme sink. However, if we are interested in meaningfully labelling the intermediate states as *neutral*, then we automatically select five clusters: three for the representative states and two in between the extreme and central clusters functioning as non-extreme/non-neutral sinks (Figure 9).

After appropriate automatic selection of the representative clusters, the final step is to train a Gaussian distribution per cluster using the Expectation Maximization (EM) algorithm. The number of observations of the final clusters is equalized by applying a uniform random

sampling on the data points, so that the training is balanced. This ensures that the final clusters include points covering the whole allowed spreading region. Algorithm 1 summarizes the ESC training procedure, and Figure 10 illustrates the cluster selection training steps concerning the facial event of Figure 7.

Algorithm 1 ESC training

Require: 1D feature space $\mathcal{F}$ and corresponding $\mathrm{SPThres} = [\mathrm{SPThres}_L, \mathrm{SPThres}_C, \mathrm{SPThres}_U]$ (Table 1)

1: **Compute:** Number of training observations: $K = \mathrm{length}(\mathcal{F})$
2: **Compute:** Feature space $\mathcal{K}$ with $K \leftarrow \frac{K}{2}$ observations by agglomerative hierarchical clustering on $\mathcal{F}$
3: **Compute:** Sorted feature space: $\mathcal{K} \leftarrow \mathrm{sort}(\mathcal{K})$
4: **Compute:** Spreading thresholds T_L, T_C, T_U on feature space $\mathcal{K}$ using Equations 1 to 3
5: Initialize clusters: $Low \leftarrow \{\}, Cen \leftarrow \{\}, Upp \leftarrow \{\}$
6: **for all** $i \in [1, K]$ **do**
7:     **if** $\mathcal{K}(i) \leq T_L$ **then**
8:         $Low \leftarrow Low \cup \{i\}$
9:     **else if** $T_{CL} \leq \mathcal{K}(i) \leq T_{CU}$ **then**
10:        $Cen \leftarrow Cen \cup \{i\}$
11:    **else if** $\mathcal{K}(i) \geq T_U$ **then**
12:        $Upp \leftarrow Upp \cup \{i\}$
13:    **end if**
14: **end for**
15: **Compute:** Minimum number of observations: $N = \min[\mathrm{length}(Low), \mathrm{length}(Cen), \mathrm{length}(Upp)]$
16: **Compute:** Subsets $Low' \subseteq Low$, $Cen' \subseteq Cen$ and $Upp' \subseteq Upp$ with N observations each with uniform random sampling
17: $Low \leftarrow Low', Cen \leftarrow Cen', Upp \leftarrow Upp'$
18: Train a Gaussian distribution per selected cluster Low, Upp and Cen

---

The above training procedure is applied on a given 1D training feature space $\mathcal{F}$. The designer can choose between two possible types of training feature space after the appropriate feature selection. The first option is to use the feature values from a video's frames. This has the

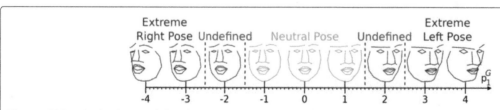

Figure 9 ESC method training with five clusters. The central cluster represents the neutral pose state.

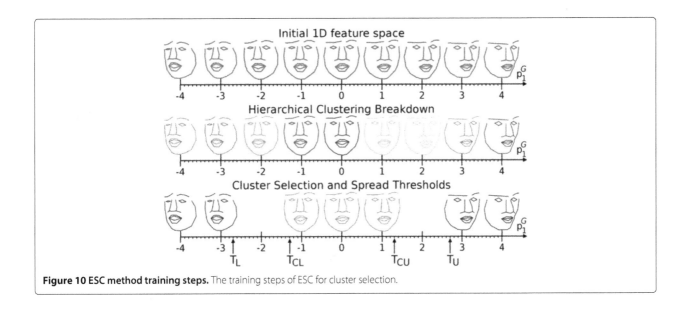

Figure 10 ESC method training steps. The training steps of ESC for cluster selection.

advantage that the training set is adjusted to the facial event's variance within the specific video. The second option is to synthesize the feature space from the AAM, by forming a linear 1D space of the selected feature's values ranging from a minimum to a maximum value. The minimum and maximum values are selected so as to avoid distortion: a safe value range for a parameter is in $[-3\sqrt{m_i}, 3\sqrt{m_i}]$, where m_i is the respective eigenvalue. This scenario forms an unbiased training feature space containing all possible instances with balanced density between the representative clusters.

4.3 Classification and ESC character

Each observation of a testing set is classified in a specific class out of the three, based on maximum likelihood criterion. Following the example of Figure 7, the final extreme pose over the yaw angle detection is summarized in the subcaptions. ESC builds on the AAM fitting results; thus, it is a supervised method w.r.t. the landmark points annotation for AAM training. It also requires the designer's intervention for the selection of the appropriate 1D feature space best describing the facial event, which, by using Table 1, becomes a semi-supervised task. However, given the AAM trained models and the training feature space that corresponds to the facial event, the ESC method requires no further manual intervention. In other words, given a 1D feature space, the ESC method detects extreme states of facial events in an *unsupervised* manner. As explained in Section 4.2.2, the symmetry type of the event leads to a *default* SPThres configuration (Table 1). However, the designer has the option to alter the SPThres defaults to *refine* the ESC performance w.r.t. the difference of precision vs. recall percentages - as further explained in Section 6.2 - which is useful in

certain applications such as assistive annotation. Finally, it is highlighted that ESC does not require any facial event annotations, as opposed to other facial event detection methods.

5 Databases

Next, we employ two databases in different SLs. From the *GSL database* [8,15], we employ Task 4 of Subject 012B. Regarding ASL, we process the story 'Accident' from *RWTH-BOSTON-400 (BU) Database* [9,10]. The low face resolution of both databases makes the tasks more difficult. We also use the Technical University of Denmark's *IMM Face Database* [55]. We train a *subject-specific* GAAM on each signer of GSL and BU databases and a *generic* GAAM on the IMM database. We keep 90% of the total variance, achieving a nearly lossless representation. Frames for GAAM training are selected, considering balance between the extreme pose and mouth instance subsets. The GAAM training configuration is shown in Table 2. We use the same training images to train eye, eyebrow and mouth LAAMs.

Table 2 GAAM training attributes

	BU	GSL	IMM
Number of frames	16,845	8,082	240
Number of train images	44	70	40
Number of landmark points N	82	46	58
Number of eigenshapes N_s	29	41	21
Number of eigentextures N_t	40	63	93
Mean shape resolution M	5,624	2,385	22,477

GAAM training attributes on BU, GSL and IMM databases. The same number of frames is used to train the various LAAMs.

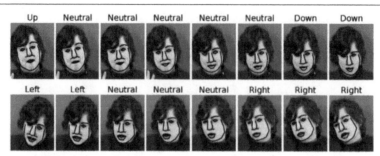

Figure 11 ESC qualitative results on GSL using GAAM features. Top: pose over pitch angle. Bottom: pose over roll angle.

6 Experimental results

Herein, we present qualitative results on GSL (Section 6.1) which lacks annotations, a quantitative comparison between ESC, supervised classification and k-means clustering on ASL (Section 6.2), a quantitative testing of the effect of AAM fitting accuracy on ESC performance (Section 6.3) and a subject-independent application on IMM (Section 6.4). Section 7 provides links with linguistic phenomena (Section 7.1) and demonstrates annotation perspectives (Section 7.2).

6.1 Qualitative results for continuous GSL

The steps presented in Section 4 are not event dependent; ESC can detect extremes on a variety of cues. Figures 11,12,13 present detection results as a *qualitative* evaluation on consecutive GSL video frames - GSL database lacks facial annotations - for facial events using GAAM, LAAM and geometrical features. The link between features and facial events, as listed in Table 1, is of course dependent on the existence of phenomena and data. However, whichever the dataset is, the events of highest variance will be explained by the top eigenvectors, and ESC will be meaningful but on a different set of events. We use the first p_1^G and second p_2^G shape parameters for pose over yaw and pitch angles, respectively, since these cues cause the largest shape deformation in the GSL corpora. In contrast, we employ the similarity transform rotation angle $\tan^{-1}\left(\frac{t_2^G}{t_1^G+1}\right)$ for the pose over roll angle. Figure 11 shows examples with pitch and roll pose detection. Figure 12 shows examples of facial

events using geometrical measures. The first row illustrates the left eye's opening/closing using the Euclidean distance between the eyelids' landmarks, and the second row shows the face's vertical translation using the displacement of the nosetip's landmark. To detect events on specific facial areas, we employ LAAM features. The mouth LAAM produces five eigenshapes: by using the first shape parameter p_1^L, we detect its opening/closing, as shown in Figure 13 (first row). Similarly, by using the left eyebrow's LAAM first shape parameter p_1^L, we detect the brow's up/down (second row). Figure 13 shows the tongue's state (inside/outside, third row) and the teeth's visibility (fourth row), employing the second λ_2^L and first λ_1^L mouth's LAAM texture parameters, respectively.

6.2 Quantitative evaluation of ESC vs. supervised classification vs. k-means on ASL

We conduct experiments to compare ESC with supervised classification and k-means clustering on the BU database, taking advantage of existing annotations. The task includes some indicative facial events from the ones presented in Section 6.1 that have the appropriate annotation labels: yaw and roll pose, left eye opening/closing and left eyebrow up/down movement. Note that we only use the non-occluded annotated frames of the ASL video and aim to compare the individual detections on each frame. We group similar annotations to end up with three labels. For example, we consider the yaw pose annotated labels *right* and *left* to be extreme and the labels *slightly right* and *slightly left* to be neutral.

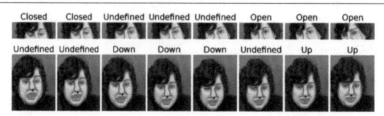

Figure 12 ESC qualitative results on GSL using geometrical features. Top: left eye opening/closing. Bottom: vertical translation.

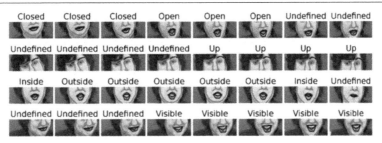

Figure 13 ESC qualitative results on GSL using LAAMs features. First row: mouth opening/closing. Second row: left eyebrow up/down. Third row: tongue in/out mouth. Fourth row: teeth visible/invisible.

ESC We carry out experiments for different values of SPThres (SPThres$_{\{L,C,U\}}$ ∈[0.05, 0.5]), taking into consideration the event symmetry (Section 4.2.2). Based on Equations 1, 2 and 3, this SPThres range guarantees that the edge threshold values T_L and T_U are lower and greater than the central T_{CL} and T_{CU}, respectively. Thus, the three representative clusters do not intersect. Depending on the SPThres value of each experiment, the number of data points N that ESC selects during the *cluster selection* stage to train Gaussian distributions varies (4% ≤ N ≤ 15% of total frames). The rest of the video's frames consist the testing set. By observing the confusion matrices, we notice that via cluster selection, we eliminate the risk to incorrectly classify an extreme observation at the opposite extreme cluster. Table 3 shows such an indicative confusion matrix.

Supervised classification For the supervised classification, we partition the feature space in three clusters following the annotations. Subsequently, we apply uniform random sampling on these annotated sets in order to select $N/3$ points for each and N in total, as chosen by the ESC cluster selection. Again, the rest consist the testing set. These points are then employed to train one Gaussian distribution per cluster.

k-means We employ the k-means algorithm in order to compare with a state-of-the-art unsupervised clustering method. The algorithm is directly applied on the same testing set as in ESC and supervised classification, requiring three clusters.

Table 3 Indicative ESC confusion matrix

		Annotation		
		Left	Neutral	Right
	Left	317	320	0
Detection	**Neutral**	15	679	375
	Right	0	0	226

Indicative confusion matrix of the ESC method for face pose over the yaw angle on the BU database.

Figure 14 shows the precision, recall and F-score percentages of the experiment, averaged between the two extreme states for all facial events. For example, the precision of pose yaw is $P(\%) = \left[P_{\text{left}}(\%) + P_{\text{right}}(\%)\right]/2$. Figure 14 (top) shows the ESC performance using the default SPThres configuration. In Figure 14 (middle), we have selected the SPThres values that maximize the precision performance, which represents whether the decision of the frames classified with the extreme labels is correct. In contrast, Figure 14 (bottom) shows the best recall performance, meaning that most of the frames supposed to contain an extreme state were eventually detected. ESC has in almost all cases better precision percentages than the supervised classification. However, since the precision scores are usually high, the final F-score depends on the recall percentages. This is the reason why the experiments of Figure 14 (bottom) have slightly better or at least similar F-scores compared to the supervised classification. Additionally, depending on the event, ESC outperforms k-means. The fact that ESC has better performance in some cases than the supervised classification is due to the subjectivity/errors on manual annotations (see Section 7.2). Annotation errors along with possible GAAM fitting failures are also responsible for differences in performance between facial cues.

Figure 15 shows the performance surfaces w.r.t. the SPThres value change. The presented surfaces are the averages of the four employed facial cues, after appropriate normalization of the results, so as to eliminate differences between the events. For each SPThres values combination j, the respective precision surface percentage is $P(j) = \frac{1}{L}\sum_{i=1}^{L}\frac{P_i(j)}{\max P_i(j)}$, where $L = 4$ is the number of facial events and $P_i(j)$ is the precision percentage of the ith event with the jth SPThres combination. The precision percentages are at very high level and start dropping after increasing the SPThres of the edge clusters and decreasing the central one. On the other hand, the F-score clearly depends on the recall percentage since the precision surface is approximately flat. The above illustrates the advantage of ESC and simultaneously its usage methodology: ESC scores high precisions, which means that the

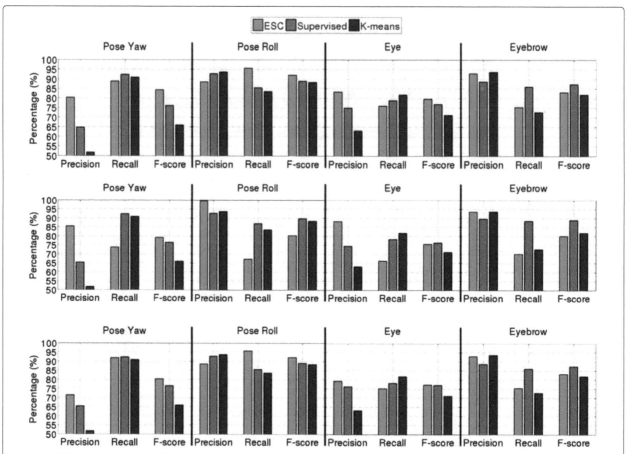

Figure 14 ESC vs. supervised classification vs. *k*-means results on the BU database. ESC vs. supervised classification vs. *k*-means clustering on the BU database for the facial events of pose yaw, pose roll, eye opening/closing and eyebrow up/down. The precision, recall and *F*-score percentages are averaged between the extreme states. Top: ESC performance with default configuration. Middle: ESC configuration for the best precision performance. Bottom: ESC configuration for the best recall performance.

frames labelled as extreme are true positives. This is useful in applications we want the classification decisions to be correct and not to correctly classify all the extreme states. By applying the default SPThres values (Table 1), ESC ensures high *F*-score performance, with precision/recall

balance. However, Figures 14 and 15 also show that we can achieve higher precision or recall percentages with a slight SPThres configuration. Additionally, the above highlight the strength of ESC as a method to classify facial events in the cases at which manual annotations are unavailable.

6.3 ESC dependency on AAM fitting

As previously explained, ESC builds upon the AAM fitting result. Herein, we examine the effect of potential AAM fitting inaccuracy on the final classification result. We aim to detect the pose over the yaw angle on the BU database using noisy AAM fitted shapes. Specifically, we corrupted the AAM fitted shapes of the database with noise randomly sampled from Gaussian distributions with various standard deviations. We retrieve our new feature value $\mathbf{p}_1$ for each image by projecting the noisy shape $\mathbf{s}_n$ in the first shape eigenvector $\mathbf{s}_1$ as $\mathbf{p}_1 = (\mathbf{s}_n - \mathbf{s}_0)^T \mathbf{s}_1$. Figure 16 visualizes the result for small (top) and large (bottom) values of standard deviation. The horizontal axis represents the standard deviation as a percentage of the average face size. This results in $\sigma = [1, 9]$ and $\sigma = [1, 70]$ pixels for the

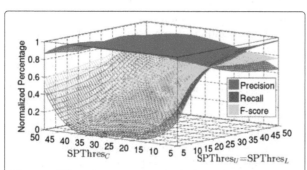

Figure 15 ESC performance w.r.t. the SPThres values on the BU database. ESC performance surfaces w.r.t. the SPThres values on the BU database for the facial events of pose yaw, pose roll, eye opening/closing and eyebrow up/down.

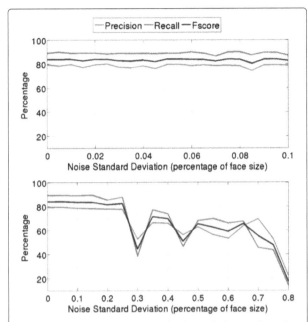

Figure 16 ESC performance w.r.t. the GAAM fitting result on the BU database. Plot of the ESC performance on noisy fitted shapes for the facial event of pose yaw. The horizontal axis shows the noise's standard deviation σ as a percentage of the average face size. Top: small values of σ. Bottom: large values of σ.

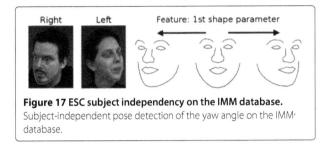

Figure 17 ESC subject independency on the IMM database. Subject-independent pose detection of the yaw angle on the IMM database.

7 Further applications

Next, we examine two practical cases that show the application of the presented approach within tasks related to SL. The first concerns linguistic phenomena as related to facial events, while the second highlights ESC application for assistive annotation of facial events.

7.1 ESC detections and linguistic phenomena

Facial cues are essential in SL articulation and comprehension. Nevertheless, the computational incorporation of information related to facial cues is more complex when compared, for instance, with handshape manual information. This is due to the multiple types of parallel facial cues, the multiple ways each cue is involved each time and the possibly different linguistic levels. Based on existing evidence [1-3,17,56] and observations, we account each time for a facial cue and link it with linguistic phenomena. We construct links of (1) facial cues via the corresponding ESC detections (Section 4), with (2) a few selected indicative linguistic phenomena. The phenomena include (1) sign and sentence boundaries and (2) sentence-level linguistic markers which determine the phrase structure: alternative constructions, which refer to conjunctive sentences and *enumerations*, when the signer enumerates objects (see Section 1 and Figure 1).

7.1.1 Eye blinking

The eyes may take one of the open/closed states. Herein, we are interested on the transient phenomenon of blinking, thus opening/closing transitions which we aim to detect. Figure 18 presents an example of such a detection between neutral-close-neutral - neutral is considered as intermediate. Assuming that eye blinking is related to sentence - and possibly sometimes to sign - boundaries. Figure 18 shows the detection and the annotated sign boundaries. Referring to the whole signing (Figure 1), these blinks fall after the ends of signs WALK and $INDEX. The above does not imply that every boundary is linked with eye blinking nor vice versa.

7.1.2 Pose variation and head movements

We focus on the cases of face translations along the perpendicular axis, pose over the pitch (up/down), yaw (right/left) and roll (right/left) angles. The transient pitch

first and second cases, respectively. ESC's performance remains almost stable for small values of σ and drops for very large ones. Consequently, we reach the conclusion that it is not required to achieve a very accurate fitted shape in order to detect facial events. Even a rough estimate of the landmarks' locations is enough in order for the according parameters to provide the feature space with an indicative feature value.

6.4 ESC subject independency

The above trained AAMs are subject specific. Herein, we indicatively apply ESC on the IMM data for pose detection over the yaw angle. IMM has pose annotations and we train a *generic* GAAM on a set of 17% of the total number of images. For SPThres values in the range 10% to 45%, the precision and recall percentages are between 93.7% to 95.2% and 95.2% to 98.5% for right and left, respectively, and the resulting F-scores are in the range 95.2% to 96.3%. Figure 17 shows examples with the employed 1D feature. Even though the task is easier - IMM data has more clear extreme poses than SL videos - these results indicate that ESC is subject independent. Facial event detection is independent of the subject's appearance as long as there is an eigenvector on the generic AAM describing the event. This reveals the possible extension of the method in multiple-person applications.

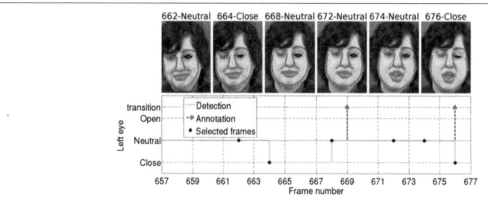

Figure 18 Sign boundary detection. Sign boundary detection based on eye blinking detection on the GSL database. Indicative frames (up) are marked with a black dot in the detection diagram (down).

pose variation is linked to the face vertical translation and corresponds to head nodding. We assume that the pose over the pitch angle could be related to sign and possibly sentence boundaries. For sentence-level linguistic structures, we *assume* that (1) roll pose variation is related to alternative constructions and (2) pitch pose or vertical translation to enumerations. Figure 19 shows an indicative example for the first case superimposing the detection result on a conjunctive sentence annotation. These presented detections w.r.t the whole signing (Figure 1), concern sign PASSPORT, sign ID-CARD and their in-between segment.

7.1.3 Quantitative evaluation

The GSL corpus annotations provide ground-truths for sign/sentence boundaries. The alternative construction and enumeration ground-truths are based on our annotations via ELAN [18] based on descriptions in [56, p. 12]. The cues to test are pose over the yaw, pitch and roll angles, head's vertical translation and eye open/closing.

We build on ESC detections of a facial cue for the detection of the desired transitions. For each event, the dynamic transition's labels are assigned at each frame with a different state (detection change) than the previous frame.

The comparison of detection vs. annotation boundaries cannot be frame specific due to possible asynchronization. This is due to (1) subjective manual annotations and (2) so as to allow for a few frame minor deviations. We apply a window ([1, . . . , 5] samples) aiming on a *relaxed* comparison. For each experiment, we compute the confusion matrix. Nevertheless, we are interested only in the recall percentages since we do not assume that for each positive detection there should be the assumed phenomenon. Figure 20 shows the mean, over windows [1, 5], recall percentages of each phenomenon per cue. We observe that the eye blinking cue could be suitable for sentence and sign boundary phenomena. The next best cues are pitch angle variation and vertical translation. These are related since the up/down pose variation implies head translation over the vertical axis. In addition, the eye's open/close

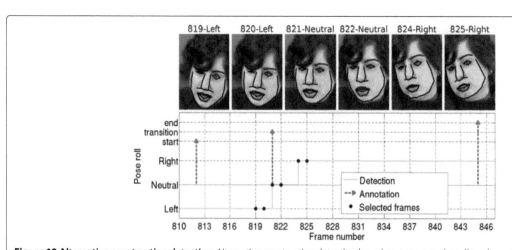

Figure 19 Alternative construction detection. Alternative construction detection based on pose over the roll angle on the GSL database. Indicative frames (up) are marked with a black dot in the detection diagram (down).

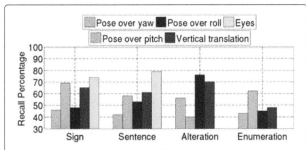

Figure 20 Linguistic phenomena detection results. Mean recall percentages for linguistic phenomena detection w.r.t. facial events.

state is related to the pose variation over the pitch angle, since when the subject is looking down, the state of the eye could be wrongly detected as closed. We do not assume that a single facial cue sufficiently describes an event. We rather observe that the eye's state, the head's vertical translation and the pose variation over pitch and roll are related to the phenomena compared to other cues, following our intuition. Figure 20 shows that alternative constructions are related to the pose over roll angle and the vertical translation. Yaw pose also has fair performance, as opposed to the pitch pose. Second, the *enumerations* are related to the pose variation over pitch angle, following our assumption. Table 4 summarizes each cue's suitability per phenomenon.

7.2 Assistive application to annotation tools
As discussed (Section 1), the need for semi-supervised methods is evident given the general lack of manual annotations. These require many times the real-time duration of a SL video, let alone the required training of an annotator who is subjective and possibly error-prone after many annotation hours. ESC can be potentially employed for the benefit of annotators via assistive or semi-automatic annotation.

7.2.1 Annotator-defined extreme states
ESC can be easily extended for annotator-defined extreme states, instead of the default ones. Instead of detecting the

Table 4 Facial cue suitability for linguistic phenomena detection

| | Linguistic phenomena | | | |
| | Boundaries | | Alternative construction | Enumeration |
Facial event	Sign	Sentence		
Yaw pose			3	
Pitch pose	2	2		1
Roll pose	3	3	1	3
Vertical translation	2	2	1	
Eye blinking	1	1		

Facial cue suitability rating 1 (best) to 3 per linguistic phenomena detection.

right/left extremes of the pose yaw angle, the annotator defines a *specific angle range* via manually selecting appropriate example frames. The selected frames' feature values determine the feature space's value range. Then, ESC detects this event range, in which the extreme cases correspond to the user-defined bounds. Figure 21 shows this higher-precision event annotation where the annotator intends to detect neutral and slightly left pose.

7.2.2 Annotation labels consistency and errors
In some results of Section 6.2, we observe that ESC results in superior performance compared to the supervised method. This is explained given the already mentioned subjectivity of annotations, which results in non-consistent labels and thus has a negative effect on the trained models. The ESC approach could be employed as an assistive annotation tool to discover such inconsistencies. Next, we present an indicative experiment on the BU data in which we have scrambled the annotation labels of pose over yaw and roll angles. In this way, we mimic in a simple way possible annotation errors or inconsistencies. As expected, this results to inferior performance for the supervised case: the more labels are scrambled, the lower the performance gets (Figure 22). In contrast, ESC's performance is invariant of any altered labels.

7.2.3 Incorporation of results into annotation software
Given the importance of annotation environments such as ELAN [18], we note the importance of incorporating annotation results into them, since they allow the time linking of annotations to the media stream, while offering other appealing functionalities too. We show (Figure 23) a low-level annotation tier, i.e. the extreme detection of the roll angle, as a result of ESC incorporated in the ELAN environment. Such annotation tier initializations of linguistically interesting phenomena would be useful for annotators.

8 Discussion and conclusions
We present an efficient approach for the detection of facial events that are of interest within the context of processing and analysis of continuous SL videos. We formulate our framework by introducing the notion of 'extreme states',

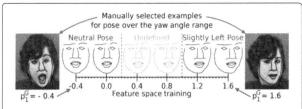

Figure 21 ESC training for annotation. Annotator-defined yaw poses between neutral and slightly left with manual selection of example frames followed by feature space training.

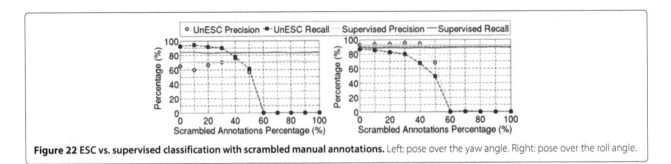

Figure 22 ESC vs. supervised classification with scrambled manual annotations. Left: pose over the yaw angle. Right: pose over the roll angle.

which is intuitive: take, for instance, left/right extremes of yaw head pose angle, up/down extremes of pitch head angle, open/close extremes of the eyes, and so on. Although simple, such events are potentially related with various SL linguistic phenomena, such as sign/sentence boundaries, role playing and dialogues, enumerations and alternative constructions, to name but a few, which are still under research. By applying the proposed approach on SL videos, we are able to detect and classify salient low-level visual events. As explained in Section 4.3, the method builds upon face tracking results and performs an unsupervised classification. Evaluations are conducted on multiple datasets. The detection accuracy is comparable with that of the supervised classification, and *F*-scores range between 77% and 91%, depending on the facial event. These detection results would be of great assistance for annotators, since the analysis and annotation of such events in large SL video corpora consumes many times the real-time duration of the initial videos. Moreover, via the relation with higher-level linguistic events, a few of which have been only indicatively presented, the ESC detections could further assist analysis or assistive consistency tests of existing labels.

Axes of further work concern the automatic adaptation of unknown signers, the incorporation of facial expression events and the incorporation of more linguistic phenomena of multiple levels. Although ongoing research in SL recognition is still far from the development of a complete ASLR system, the integration of facial and linguistic events in such a system is an important future step. The qualitative/quantitative evaluations of the approach on multiple databases and different SLs (GSL, ASL), the evaluation on the multi-subject IMM database, which have all shown promising results, as well as the practical examples and intuitive applications indicate that ESC is in a field that opens perspectives with impact on the analysis, processing and automatic annotation of SL videos.

Endnote

[a]In the parentheses, we have added comments that assist the understanding. The gloss transcriptions are 'WALK $INDEX LINE WAIT $MANUAL' (frames 650 to 723) and 'FINE PASSPORT TICKET PASSPORT ID-CARD SOME WHERE GO EUROPE OR ABROAD' (736 to 927). Gloss: the closest English word transcription corresponding to a sign. $INDEX: variable convention

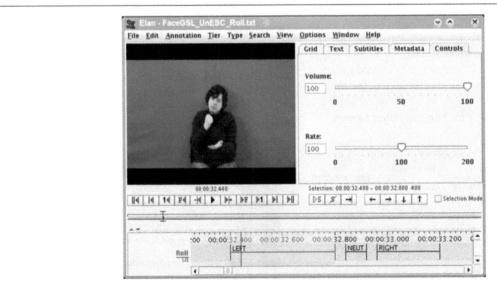

Figure 23 ESC incorporation in ELAN environment. Incorporation of ESC detection for pose roll in ELAN environment for manual annotation.

that refers to previous gloss WALK concerning spatial location. $MANUAL: manual classifier for spatial queue description. $EOC: end-of-clause.

Competing interests
The authors declare that they have no competing interests.

Acknowledgements
This research work was supported by the project 'COGNIMUSE' which is implemented under the ARISTEIA Action of the Operational Program Education and Lifelong Learning and is co-funded by the European Social Fund (ESF) and Greek National Resources. It was also partially supported by the EU research projects Dicta-Sign (FP7-231135) and DIRHA (FP7-288121). The major part of this work was done when the first author was at the National Technical University of Athens, Greece. The authors want to thank I. Rodomagoulakis for his contribution and S. Theodorakis for insightful discussions.

References
1. W Sandler, The medium and the message: prosodic interpretation of linguistic content in Israeli Sign Language. Sign Language & Linguistics John Benjamins Publishing Company. **2**(2), 187–215 (1999)
2. D Brentari, L Crossley, Prosody on the hands and face. Gallaudet University Press, Sign Language & Linguistics, John Benjamins Publishing Company. **5**(2), 105–130 (2002)
3. R Wilbur, Eyeblinks & ASL phrase structure. Sign Language Studies. Gallaudet University Press. **84**(1), 221–240 (1994)
4. R Wilbur, C Patschke, Syntactic correlates of brow raise in ASL. Sign Language & Linguistics. John Benjamins Publishing Company. **2**(1), 3–41 (1999)
5. U Von Agris, J Zieren, U Canzler, B Bauer, K Kraiss, Recent developments in visual sign language recognition. Universal Access in the Information Society, Springer. **6**(4), 323–362 (2008)
6. U von Agris, M Knorr, K Kraiss, The significance of facial features for automatic sign language recognition, in *8th IEEE Int. Conf. on Automatic Face & Gesture Recognition (FG)* (Amsterdam, The Netherlands, 17–19 Sept 2008)
7. T Johnston, A Schembri, Issues in the creation of a digital archive of a signed language, in *Sustainable Data from Digital Fieldwork: Proc. of the Conf., Sydney University Press* (Sydney, Australia, 4–6 Dec 2006)
8. S Matthes, T Hanke, A Regen, J Storz, S Worseck, E Efthimiou, AL Dimou, A Braffort, J Glauert, E Safar, Dicta-Sign – building a multilingual sign language corpus, in *Proc. of the 5th Workshop on the Representation and Processing of Sign Languages: Interactions Between Corpus and Lexicon (LREC), European Language Resources Association* (Istanbul, Turkey, 23–27 May 2012)
9. C Neidle, C Vogler, A new web interface to facilitate access to corpora: development of the ASLLRP data access interface, in *Proc. of the Int. Conf. on Language Resources and Evaluation (LREC), European Language Resources Association* (Istanbul, Turkey, 23–27 May 2012)
10. P Dreuw, C Neidle, V Athitsos, S Sclaroff, H Ney, Benchmark databases for video-based automatic sign language recognition, in *Proc. of the Int. Conf. on Language Resources and Evaluation (LREC), European Language Resources Association* (Marrakech, Morocco, 28–30 May 2008)
11. O Crasborn, E van der Kooij, J Mesch, European cultural heritage online (ECHO): publishing sign language data on the internet, in *8th Conf. on Theoretical Issues in Sign Language Research, John Benjamins Publishing Company* (Barcelona, Spain, 30 Sept–2 Oct 2004)
12. P Dreuw, H Ney, Towards automatic sign language annotation for the elan tool, in *Proc. of Int. Conf. LREC Workshop: Representation and Processing of Sign Languages, European Language Resources Association* (Marrakech, Morocco, 28–30 May 2008)
13. M Hrúz, Z Krňoul, P Campr, L Müller, Towards automatic annotation of sign language dictionary corpora, in *Proc. of Text, speech and dialogue, Springer* (Pilsen, Czech Republic, 1–5 Sept 2011)
14. R Yang, S Sarkar, B Loeding, A Karshmer, Efficient generation of large amounts of training data for sign language recognition: a semi-automatic tool. Comput. Helping People with Special Needs, 635–642 (2006)
15. Dicta-Sign Language Resources, Greek Sign Language Corpus (31 January 2012). http://www.sign-lang.uni-hamburg.de/dicta-sign/portal
16. F Sze, Blinks and intonational phrasing in Hong Kong Sign Language, in *8th Conf. on Theoretical Issues in Sign Language Research, John Benjamins Publishing Company* (Barcelona, Spain, 30 Sept–2 Oct 2004)
17. R Pfau, Visible prosody: spreading and stacking of non-manual markers in sign languages, in *25th West Coast Conf. on Formal Linguistics, Cascadilla Proceedings Project* (Seattle, USA, 28–30 Apr 2006)
18. P Wittenburg, H Brugman, A Russel, A Klassmann, H Sloetjes, ELAN: a professional framework for multimodality research, in *Proc. of the Int. Conf. on Language Resources and Evaluation (LREC), European Language Resources Association* (Genoa, Italy, 24–26 May 2006)
19. T Nguyen, S Ranganath, Facial expressions in american sign language: tracking and recognition. Pattern Recognition Elsevier. **45**(5), 1877–1891 (2012)
20. T Nguyen, S Ranganath, Recognizing continuous grammatical marker facial gestures in sign language video, in *10th Asian Conf. on Computer Vision, Springer* (Queenstown, New Zealand, 8–12 Nov 2010)
21. D Metaxas, B Liu, F Yang, P Yang, N Michael, C Neidle, Recognition of nonmanual markers in ASL using non-parametric adaptive 2D-3D face tracking, in *Proc. of the Int. Conf. on Language Resources and Evaluation (LREC), European Language Resources Association* (Istanbul, Turkey, 23–27 May 2012)
22. C Neidle, N Michael, J Nash, D Metaxas, IE Bahan, L Cook, Q Duffy, R Lee, A method for recognition of grammatically significant head movements and facial expressions, developed through use of a linguistically annotated video corpus, in *Proc. of 21st ESSLLI Workshop on Formal Approaches to Sign Languages* (Bordeaux, France, 27–31 July 2009)
23. U Erdem, S Sclaroff, Automatic detection of relevant head gestures in American Sign Language communication, in *IEEE Proc. of 16th Int. Conf. on Pattern Recognition* (Quebec, Canada, 11–15 Aug 2002)
24. C Vogler, S Goldenstein, Analysis of facial expressions in american sign language, in *Proc, of the 3rd Int. Conf. on Universal Access in Human-Computer Interaction, Springer* (Las Vegas, Nevada, USA, 22–27 July 2005)
25. C Vogler, S Goldenstein, Facial movement analysis in ASL. Universal Access in the Information Society Springer. **6**(4), 363–374 (2008)
26. S Sarkar, B Loeding, A Parashar, Fusion of manual and non-manual information in american sign language recognition. *Handbook of Pattern Recognition and Computer Vision* (CRC, FL, 2010), pp. 1–20
27. O Aran, T Burger, A Caplier, L Akarun, Sequential belief-based fusion of manual and non-manual information for recognizing isolated signs. *Gesture-Based Human-Computer Interaction and Simulation* (Springer, 2009), pp. 134–144
28. MS Bartlett, Face image analysis by unsupervised learning and redundancy reduction. PhD thesis. (University of California, San Diego, 1998)
29. F Zhou, F De la Torre, JF Cohn, Unsupervised discovery of facial events, in *IEEE Conf. on Computer Vision and Pattern Recognition (CVPR)* (San Francisco, CA, USA, 13–18 June 2010)
30. F Zhou, F De la Torre Frade, JK Hodgins, Hierarchical aligned cluster analysis for temporal clustering of human motion. IEEE Trans. on Pattern Analysis and Machine Intelligence. **35**(3), 582–596 (2013)
31. A Hadid, O Kouropteva, M Pietikainen, Unsupervised learning using locally linear embedding: experiments with face pose analysis (Quebec, Canada, 11–15 Aug 2002)
32. J Hoey, Hierarchical unsupervised learning of facial expression categories, in *Proc. of IEEE Workshop on Detection and Recognition of Events in Video* (Vancouver, BC, Canada, 8 July 2001)
33. J Niebles, H Wang, L Fei-Fei, Unsupervised learning of human action categories using spatial-temporal words. International Journal of Computer Vision, Springer. **79**(3), 299–318 (2008)
34. M Pantic, LJ Rothkrantz, Automatic analysis of facial expressions: the state of the art. IEEE Trans. on Pattern Analysis and Machine Intelligence. **22**(12), 1424–1445 (2000)
35. E Murphy-Chutorian, M Trivedi, Head pose estimation in computer vision: a survey. IEEE Trans. on Pattern Analysis and Machine Intelligence. **31**(4), 607–626 (2009)
36. D Lin, Facial expression classification using PCA and hierarchical radial basis function network. Journal of Information Science and Engineering, Citeseer. **22**(5), 1033–1046 (2006)

37. U Canzler, T Dziurzyk, Extraction of non manual features for video based sign language recognition, in *IAPR Workshop on Machine Vision Applications, ACM* (Nara, Japan, 11–13 Dec 2002)

38. N Michael, C Neidle, D Metaxas, Computer-based recognition of facial expressions in ASL: from face tracking to linguistic interpretation, in *Proc. of the Int. Conf. on Language Resources and Evaluation (LREC), European Language Resources Association* (Malta, 17–23 May 2010)

39. A Ryan, J Cohn, S Lucey, J Saragih, P Lucey, F De la Torre, A Rossi, Automated facial expression recognition system, in *IEEE 43rd Int. Carnahan Conference on Security Technology* (Zürich, Switzerland, 5–8 Oct 2009)

40. X Zhu, D Ramanan, Face detection, pose estimation, and landmark localization in the wild, in *IEEE Conf. on Computer Vision and Pattern Recognition (CVPR)* (Providence, RI, USA, 16–21 June 2012)

41. L Ding, A Martinez, Precise detailed detection of faces and facial features, in *IEEE Conf. on Computer Vision and Pattern Recognition (CVPR)* (Anchorage, Alaska, USA, 24–26 June 2008)

42. L Ding, A Martinez, Features versus context: an approach for precise and detailed detection and delineation of faces and facial features. IEEE Trans. on Pattern Analysis and Machine Intelligence. **32**(11), 2022–2038 (2010)

43. E Antonakos, V Pitsikalis, I Rodomagoulakis, P Maragos, Unsupervised classification of extreme facial events using active appearance models tracking for sign language videos, in *IEEE Proc. of Int. Conf. on Image Processing (ICIP)* (Orlando, Florida, USA, 30 Sept–3 Oct 2012)

44. T Cootes, G Edwards, C Taylor, Active appearance models. IEEE Trans. on Pattern Analysis and Machine Intelligence. **23**(6), 681–685 (2001)

45. I Matthews, S Baker, Active appearance models revisited. International Journal of Computer Vision, Springer. **60**(2), 135–164 (2004)

46. G Papandreou, P Maragos, Adaptive and constrained algorithms for inverse compositional active appearance model fitting, in *IEEE Conf. on Computer Vision and Pattern Recognition (CVPR)* (Anchorage, Alaska, USA, 24–26 June 2008)

47. G Tzimiropoulos, Medina Alabort-i J, S Zafeiriou, M Pantic, Generic active appearance models revisited, in *Asian Conf. on Computer Vision, Springer* (Daejeon, Korea, 5–9 Nov 2012)

48. A Batur, M Hayes, Adaptive active appearance models. IEEE Trans. on Image Processing. **14**(11), 1707–1721 (2005)

49. R Navarathna, S Sridharan, S Lucey, Fourier active appearance models, in *IEEE Int. Conf. on Computer Vision (ICCV)* (Barcelona, Spain, 6–13 Nov 2011)

50. D Vukadinovic, M Pantic, Fully automatic facial feature point detection using Gabor feature based boosted classifiers, in *IEEE Int. Conf. on Systems, Man and Cybernetics* (Waikoloa, Hawaii, USA, 10–12 Oct 2005)

51. M Valstar, B Martinez, X Binefa, M Pantic, Facial point detection using boosted regression and graph models, in *IEEE Conf. on Computer Vision and Pattern Recognition (CVPR)* (San Francisco, CA, USA, 13–18 June 2010)

52. V Vezhnevets, V Sazonov, A Andreeva, A survey on pixel-based skin color detection techniques, in *Proc. Graphicon* (Moscow, Russia, 2003)

53. S Tzoumas, Face detection and pose estimation with applications in automatic sign language recognition. Master's thesis, National Technical University of Athens, 2011

54. A Roussos, S Theodorakis, V Pitsikalis, P Maragos, Hand tracking and affine shape-appearance handshape sub-units in continuous sign language recognition, in *11th European Conference on Computer Vision, Workshop on Sign, Gesture and Activity (ECCV), Springer* (Crete, Greece, 5–11 Sept 2010)

55. M Nordstrøm, M Larsen, J Sierakowski, M Stegmann, The IMM face database-an annotated dataset of 240 face images. Inform. Math. Model. **22**(10), 1319–1331 (2004)

56. CNRS-LIMSI, Dicta-Sign Deliverable D4.5: report on the linguistic structures modelled for the Sign Wiki. Techical Report D4.5, CNRS-LIMSI (2012)

5

Real-time video stabilization without phantom movements for micro aerial vehicles

Wilbert G Aguilar* and Cecilio Angulo

Abstract

In recent times, micro aerial vehicles (MAVs) are becoming popular for several applications as rescue, surveillance, mapping, etc. Undesired motion between consecutive frames is a problem in a video recorded by MAVs. There are different approaches, applied in video post-processing, to solve this issue. However, there are only few algorithms able to be applied in real time. An additional and critical problem is the presence of false movements in the stabilized video. In this paper, we present a new approach of video stabilization which can be used in real time without generating false movements. Our proposal uses a combination of a low-pass filter and control action information to estimate the motion intention.

Keywords: Video stabilization; Micro aerial vehicles; Real time; Filter; Motion intention

Introduction

The growing interest in developing unmanned aircraft vehicles (UAVs) is due to their versatility in several applications such as rescue, transport, or surveillance. A particular type of UAV that becomes popular nowadays are micro aerial vehicles (MAVs) by their advantage to fly in closed and reduced spaces.

Robust guidance, navigation, and control systems for MAVs [1] depend on the input information obtained from on-board sensors as cameras. Undesired movements are usually generated during the fly as a result of complex aerodynamic characteristics of the UAV. Unnecessary image rotations and translations appear in the video sequence, increasing the difficulty to control the vehicle.

There are multiple techniques in the literature [2-5] designed to compensate the effects of undesired movements of the camera. Recently, the video stabilization algorithm 'L1 Optimal' provided by the YouTube editor was introduced in [6]. Another interesting proposal is the Parrot's Director Mode, implemented as an iOS application (iPhone operative system) for post-processing of videos captured with Parrot's AR.Drones.

Usually, offline video stabilization techniques are divided in three stages:

- Local motion estimation
- Motion intention estimation
- Motion compensation

Local motion estimation

In this phase, the parameters that relate the uncompensated image and the image defined as reference are determined frame by frame. Optical flow [7,8] and geometric transformation models [9-11] are two common approaches for local motion estimation. Our algorithm uses the latter one.

Geometric transformation models are based on the estimation of the motion parameters. For this estimation, interest points should be detected and described. A list of techniques performing this task can be found in the literature [12-14], but Binary Robust Invariant Scalable Keypoints (BRISK) [15], Fast Retina Keypoint (FREAK) [16], Oriented FAST and Rotated BRIEF (ORB) [17], Scale Invariant Feature Transform [18] (SIFT), and Speeded Up Robust Feature (SURF) [19] are common in solving computer vision problems [20]. We are using SURF in this phase as a state-of-the-art algorithm because our contribution is not focused on reducing delays due to the calculation of interest points, not being significant. The delay due to smoothing techniques is higher.

*Correspondence: wilbert.aguilar@upc.edu
Automatic Control Department, UPC-BarcelonaTech, Pau Gargallo Street 5, 08028 Barcelona, Spain

The second part of the motion estimation process is interest points matching across consecutive frames. This is a critical part because the estimated motion parameters are directly dependent on the reliability of matched points. False correspondences will be removed using an iterative technique called Random Sample Consensus (RANSAC), a widely used technique based on a model from a set of points [21-24]. In our work, RANSAC uses a simple cost function based on gray level difference, minimizing the delay.

Motion intention estimation

In a second phase, for ensuring coherence in the complete motion sequence, the parameters estimated previously are validated in the global and not just in the relative motion between consecutive frames. The main objective of motion intention estimation is to obtain the desired motion in the video sequence suppressing high-frequency jitters from the accumulative global motion estimation.

Several motion smoothing methods are available for motion intention estimation such as particle filter [10], Kalman filter [11], Gaussian filter [25,26], adaptive filter [26,27], spline smoothing [28,29], or point feature trajectory smoothing [30,31]. In our approach, the control signal sent to the MAV is dealt as a known information; hence, a new and different methodology to those in the literature is considered. A combination of a second-order low-pass filter, using as few frames as possible, and action control input is employed to estimate a reliable motion intention. We achieve to reduce the number of frames (time window) required for the smoothing signal using an optimization process.

Most of the techniques cited perform well in video stabilization applications, but there is an additional challenge, not studied in the literature and introduced in this paper, which we have called 'phantom movement'.

Phantom movement

A phantom movement is mainly a false displacement generated in the scale and/or translation parameters due to the compensation of the high-frequency movements in the motion smoothing. Sometimes the motion smoothing process removes real movements and/or introduces a delay in them. Both cases are defined as phantom movements. This phenomenon represents a problem when teleoperating the MAV, and its effects in other state-of-the-art algorithms will be shown in the 'Results and discussion' section.

Additionally, our proposal to solve this problem will be explained in the 'Real-time video stabilization' section.

Motion compensation

Finally, the current frame is warped using parameters obtained from the previous estimation phase to generate a stable video sequence.

This paper is organized as follows: the estimation of local motion parameters in our method is explained in the next section. In addition, we describe the combination of RANSAC and gray level difference-based cost function for robust local motion estimation. In the 'Motion intention estimation' section, we present a motion smoothing based on a low-pass filter. Then, the 'Real-time video stabilization' section focuses on the optimization of the algorithm with minimum number of frames to estimate the motion intention. Furthermore, we propose a novel approach to solve the problem of phantom movement. Experimental results and conclusions are presented in the last section.

Robust local motion estimation

To obtain a stabilized video sequence, we estimate the inter-frame geometric transformation, i.e., the local motion parameters. In this phase, we determine the relationship between the current and the reference frame as a mathematical model. This process can be structurally divided into two parts: (a) interest point detection, description, and matching and (b) inter-frame geometric transformation estimation using matched points. Additionally, an extra process to ensure robustness is (c) robust cumulative motion parameters.

Interest point detection, description, and matching

As mentioned in the latter section, there are several techniques for detecting and matching interest points. According to the results presented in [20], the computational cost of SURF is considerably lower than that of SIFT, with equivalent performance. Using the Hessian matrix and a space-scale function [32], SURF locates way-points and describes their features using a 64-dimensional vector. Once the vector descriptors are obtained, the interest point matching process is based on minimum Euclidian distance in the 64-dimensional feature space.

Inter-frame geometric transform estimation using matched points

From the matched interest points, motion parameters between the current and the reference frame can be estimated. Variations between two specific frames are mathematically expressed by the geometric transformation which relates feature points in the first frame with their correspondences in the second frame [33-35],

$$\mathbf{I}_{\text{sp}} = \mathbf{H}_t \cdot \mathbf{I}_t \qquad (1)$$

where $\mathbf{I}_{\text{sp}} = \left[x_{\text{sp}}, y_{\text{sp}}, 1\right]^T$ and $\mathbf{I}_t = \left[x_t, y_t, 1\right]^T$ are the coordinates of the interest points at the reference image and the uncompensated image, respectively, and $\mathbf{H}_t$ is the 3×3 geometric transformation matrix. How to chose the reference image will be analyzed in the next subsection.

The geometric transformation represented by $\mathbf{H}_t$ can be characterized by different models as appropriate. The most common models are translation, affine, and projective models.

In previous works [36,37], we have found experimentally that in both cases, handheld devices and on-board cameras of flying robots, most of the undesired movements and parasitic vibrations in the image are considered significant only on the plane perpendicular to the roll axis (scale, rotation, and translations). This type of distortion can be modeled by a projective transformation, and we use the affine model in our algorithm as a particular case of the projective one [38]. The benefit is twofold: a lower computation time than for the projective model and its ability for direct extraction of relevant motion parameters (scale, rotation roll, and translations in the xy-plane).

The affine model will determine different roll angles for $\mathbf{H}_t(1,1)$, $\mathbf{H}_t(1,2)$, $\mathbf{H}_t(2,1)$, and $\mathbf{H}_t(2,2)$. However, we estimate the mean angle adjustable to these values. This model is called nonreflective similarity and is a particular case of the affine model,

$$\mathbf{H}_t = \begin{bmatrix} s\cos(\phi) & -s\sin(\phi) & t_x \\ s\sin(\phi) & s\cos(\phi) & t_y \\ 0 & 0 & 1 \end{bmatrix} \quad (2)$$

Robust cumulative motion parameters

Robustness in our algorithm directly depends on the correct matching of interest points in consecutive frames. RANSAC (see Algorithm 1) is a reliable iterative technique for outlier rejection on a mathematical model, in this case, the affine model.

Algorithm 1 RANSAC algorithm based on cost function $\sum_j J_j$

1: **for** $j = 1$ to N **do**
2:    j_{th} affine transform estimation: $\mathbf{H}_j$
3:    j_{th} warping of the i_{th} frame: $\mathbf{Frame}'_j$
4:    j_{th} cost function computation: $J_j = \left| \mathbf{Frame}'_j - \mathbf{Frame}_{sp} \right|$
5: **end for**
6: Selection of parameters of $\mathbf{H}_{opt}$ for cost function minimization: $\arg\min_{(\phi,s,t_x,t_y)} \sum_j \left| \mathbf{Frame}'_j - \mathbf{Frame}_{sp} \right|$

Affine transform can be estimated from three pairs of noncollinear points, but SURF and other techniques obtain hundreds of these pairs of points. RANSAC is performed iteratively N times using three pairs for each $\mathbf{H}_j$,

obtaining N different affine transforms. The value of N is based on the required speed of the algorithm. An alternative is to use an accuracy threshold, but this procedure can be slower.

The cost function of RANSAC algorithm is a key point. In our proposal, we use the absolute intensity difference, pixel by pixel, between the warped and the reference frame. The intensity on a pixel can be affected by common problems such as lighting changes; however, this is not significant in consecutive frames. Therefore, the parameters of the affine model $\mathbf{H}_{opt}$ that minimize the cost function are

$$\arg\min_{(\phi,s,t_x,t_y)} \sum_j \left| \mathbf{Frame}'_j - \mathbf{Frame}_{sp} \right| \quad (3)$$

The affine model has been selected as the geometric transform between two frames, the one to be compensated and another used as reference, and there are several alternatives for selecting the reference frame. An experimental comparative study was carried out in [37] on three candidates to be the reference frame: the initial frame $(\mathbf{Frame}_{sp} = \mathbf{Frame}_0)$, the previous frame $(\mathbf{Frame}_{sp} = \mathbf{Frame}_{i-1})$, and the compensated previous frame $(\mathbf{Frame}_{sp} = \mathbf{Frame}'_{i-1})$. The analysis for the three proposed approaches was performed by using data obtained from an on-board camera of a real micro aerial vehicle. The obtained results show that the approach based on the previous frame is the best candidate to reference.

Finally, the transformation matrix $\mathbf{H}_{opt}$ is calculated and applied on the current frame for obtaining a warped frame similar to the reference frame, i.e., a stable video sequence.

Motion intention estimation

The RANSAC algorithm, based on the minimization of the gray level difference, is enough for obtaining a high accuracy in the image compensation of static scenes (scenes without moving objects) [36,37]. However, our goal is to achieve a robust stabilization of video sequences obtained with on-board cameras in micro-aerial vehicles. Most of the unstable videos captured with either flying robots or handheld devices contain dynamic scenes (scenes with moving objects) mainly due to the camera motion. In this way, some movements of the capture device should not be eliminated, but softly compensated, generating a stable motion video instead of a static scene.

The process of approximating the capture device's movements is known as motion intention. Several video stabilization algorithms use smoothing methods for the motion intention estimation such as Kalman filter, Gaussian filter, and particle filter. Our approach is based on a second-order Butterworth filter, a low-pass filter used for smoothing of signals [39].

Our experimentation platform is a low-cost MAVs, which shows a complex dynamic behavior during indoor flight. Consequently, the videos captured with on-board cameras usually contain significant displacements and high speed movements on the plane perpendicular to the roll axis. Effects of wireless communication problems such as frame-by-frame display, low-frequency videos, and video freezing should be also considered.

Using the low-pass filter as a motion intention estimator, most of the problems associated to indoor flight are avoided. However, freezing effects can eventually still appear by a low communication quality. Motion parameters computed from frozen frames must be discarded before to continue with the estimation process.

Once the affine transformation parameters (scale, rotation, and translations x and y) are extracted, as well as the values of parameters from frozen screens are removed, the low-pass filter computes the motion intention as an output without high-frequency signals. Low frequencies are associated to the intentional motion, and high frequencies are referred to undesired movements, thus the cutting frequency depending on the application and system characteristics. For cutting frequency, a higher value means an output video similar to the original movements, including the undesired movements, while a lower value means that the output video eliminates intentional movements. In our case, we use a second-order filter with the same cutting frequency 66.67 Hz to smooth the signals of the four motion parameters. An alternative option is to use a different filter for each motion parameter.

The undesired movement can be estimated by the subtraction of the motion intention, obtaining a high-frequency signal. This signal is then used in image warping to compensate vibrations and, simultaneously, to keep intentional motions. It can be seen in Figure 1 the motion intention signal estimated with the low-pass filter (top) and the high-frequency signal (warping parameter in the figure) to be compensated (down) for the parameter angle. Similar graphics can be obtained for the scale and translations in the x-axis and y-axis (Figures 2, 3, and 4).

Real-time video stabilization

A robust post-processing algorithm for video stabilization has been detailed; however, the goal is a real-time version. In this context, it is worth noting that there are very few techniques for real-time video stabilization, and the first challenge to be solved being computational cost. Hence, calculation time is minimized in [40] by using efficient algorithms of interest point detection and description. This method reduces time in motion intention estimation by means of a Gaussian filter without accumulative global motion, using the stabilized frames in addition to the original frames. Our proposal uses an off-line optimization process for obtaining the minimum number of frames that can be applied in real time to the system at hands without decrease in initial off-line video stabilization performance. Furthermore, this filter will be combined with the known

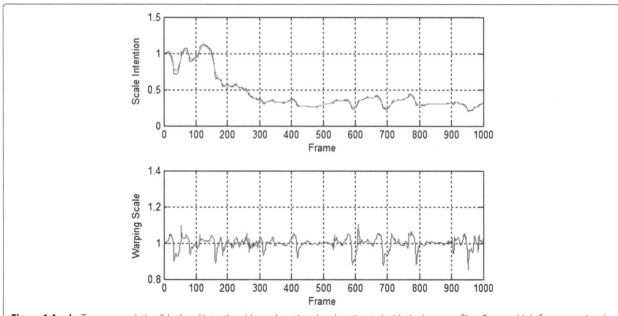

Figure 1 Angle. Top: accumulative (blue) and intentional (green) motion signals estimated with the low-pass filter. Bottom: high-frequency signal to be compensated.

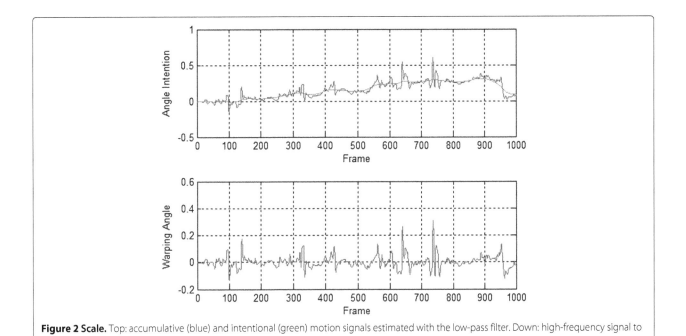

Figure 2 Scale. Top: accumulative (blue) and intentional (green) motion signals estimated with the low-pass filter. Down: high-frequency signal to be compensated.

control action signal in order to eliminate the so-called 'phantom' movements (in fact, a sort of 'freezing') in the compensated video.

Optimized motion intention estimation

To minimize the number of frames required in the video stabilization process, an exhaustive search has been implemented by an algorithm that iteratively increases the number of frames used to estimate the motion intention, whose results are plotted in Figure 5.

For the optimization process, it is necessary to define an evaluation metric of the video stabilization performance. Subjective evaluation metrics can be found in the literature, such as the mean opinion score (MOS), which

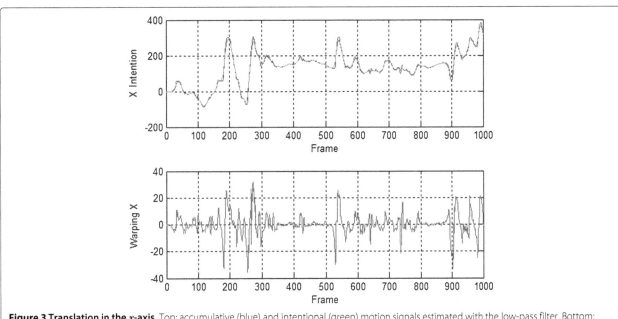

Figure 3 Translation in the x-axis. Top: accumulative (blue) and intentional (green) motion signals estimated with the low-pass filter. Bottom: high-frequency signal to be compensated.

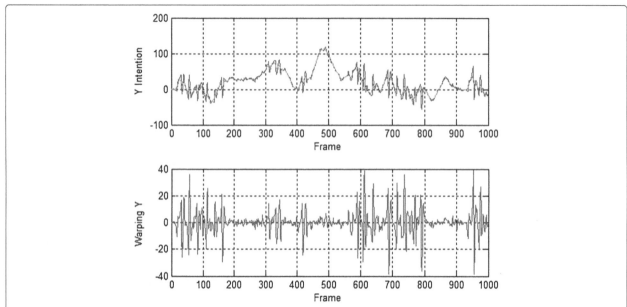

Figure 4 Translation in the *y*-axis. Top: accumulative (blue) and intentional (green) motion signals estimated with the low-pass filter. Bottom: high-frequency signal to be compensated.

is very common in the quality evaluation of the compressed multimedia [41]. The other possibility is to use objective evaluation metrics such as bounding boxes, referencing lines, or synthetic sequences [42]. The advantage of the three referred objective metrics is that estimated motion parameters can be directly compared against real motion. The inter-frame transformation fidelity (ITF) [40]

is a widely used method to measure the effectiveness and performance of video stabilization, whose mathematics expression is

$$\text{ITF} = \frac{1}{N_f - 1} \sum_{k=1}^{N_f - 1} \text{PSNR}(k) \qquad (4)$$

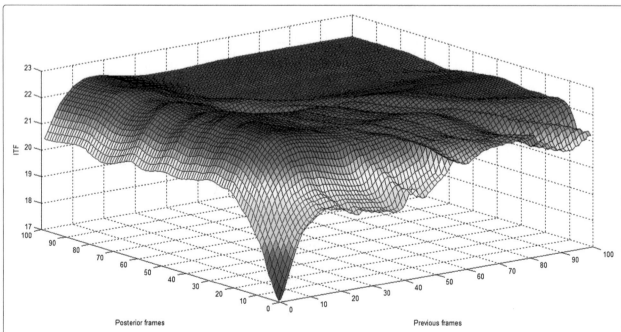

Figure 5 Minimization of inter-frame transformation fidelity (ITF). We obtain, using four (4) previous and four (4) posterior frames or using only six (6) previous frames, a performance as good as using the complete video sequence to estimate the motion intention.

where N_f is the number of video frames and

$$\text{PSNR}(k) = 10\log_{10}\frac{\text{Ip}_{\text{MAX}}}{\text{MSE}(k)} \tag{5}$$

is the peak signal-to-noise ratio between two consecutive frames, with

$$\text{MSE}(k) = \frac{1}{M \cdot N}\sum_{i=0}^{M-1}\sum_{j=0}^{N-1}\|\textbf{Frame}_k(i,j) - \textbf{Frame}_{k-1}(i,j)\|^2 \tag{6}$$

being the mean square error between monochromatic images with size $M \cdot N$ and Ip_{MAX} the maximum pixel intensity in the frame.

Based on the optimization of the objective evaluation metric ITF, two solutions have been obtained with a performance as high as using the complete video sequence to estimate the motion intention: a) using four (4) previous and four (4) posterior frames and b) using only six (6) previous frames.

Our work is focused on the real-time application, so it is important to analyze how this issue is affected for both options: a) For the first case, to use four previous and four posteriors frames means that the algorithm will be launched four frames after the video sequence initialization, and the stabilized sequence will be ready after four frames. b) In the second case, the algorithm starts six frames after the video sequence initialization, two frame later than in the first case, but for the rest of the sequence, it can be applied without added delay. Considering that the sample frequency was 10 Hz for the system at hands, a 0.4-s delay would be introduced in the total computational time when using the first option. Our algorithm uses the second option, which relies only on precedent information.

Phantom movements

Previous video stabilization approaches have obtained good results eliminating undesired movements in images captured with handheld devices and complex systems, but all of them were evaluated using the ITF as cost function. Although the final video has achieved a good ITF performance, i.e., a stable video, the motion smoothing process has generated phantom movements.

For video post-processing applications, the main objective is to stabilize the video; hence, phantom movements do not represent a problem. Notwithstanding, for real-time applications, the objective is to obtain a stable video, but it should be as real as possible. In this sense, it is important to decrease the difference between the real and estimated motion intention, preserving the ITF performance.

The root mean square error (RMSE) [43] is adopted in order to evaluate the reliability of the estimated motion

with respect to the observed motion. A low RMSE means that the estimated motion intention is similar to the real motion intention.

Consequently, the proposed objective evaluation metric to be optimized is the difference between the estimated global motion and the observed motion, measured as RMSE:

$$\text{RMSE} = \frac{1}{2F}\left(\sqrt{\sum_{j=0}^{F}\left(E_{x,j} - T_{x,j}\right)^2} + \sqrt{\sum_{i=0}^{F}\left(E_{y,i} - T_{y,i}\right)^2}\right) \tag{7}$$

where $E_{x,j}$ and $E_{y,i}$ are the estimated global motion of the jth frame in the x-axis and y-axis, respectively, $T_{x,j}$ and $T_{y,i}$ are the observed motions of the jth frame in the x-axis and y-axis, respectively, and F denotes the number of frames in the sequence.

Two alternatives exist to merge information when computing real motion intention ($T_{x,j}$, $T_{y,i}$): information obtained from the on-board inertial measurement unit (IMU) or the control action data. Choice depends on the accuracy of the model. In our algorithm, the control action is employed since IMU information is not very reliable in most of the micro aerial vehicles. In this way, the observed motion is defined as a combination between the control action and the smoothed motion signal.

Our algorithm of motion intention estimation (see Algorithm 2) uses control action as a logical gate allowing the execution of the low-pass filter only when a tele-operated motion intention is present. Additionally, our algorithm inserts a hysteresis after the execution of the action control. The objective of this hysteresis is that the system reaches its maximal (or minimal, according to the control action signal) position before the effect of a new control action.

Algorithm 2 Algorithm of reduction of phantom movements using the control action information

---

1: $\{U_i$ is the current control action, E_{R_i} is the estimated current motion without phantom movements, E_i is the estimated current motion using the filter$\}$
2: **if** $U_i \neq 0$ **then**
3: $\quad E_{R_i} = E_i$
4: **else if** $((U_{i-1} > 0) \wedge (E_i > E_{i-1}) \vee (U_{i-1} < 0) \wedge (E_i < E_{i-1}))$ **then**
5: $\quad E_{R_i} = E_i$
6: **else**
7: $\quad E_{R_i} = R_F \cdot (E_i - E_{i-1}) + E_{i-1}$
8: **end if**

We have defined a reliability parameter $0 < R_F < 1$. A value of R_F close to one leads to achieve a higher ITF value, i.e., a more stable video with phantom movements. On the other hand, using a value of R_F close to zero, we obtain a less stable video without phantom movements. Our complete algorithm is shown in Figure 6.

Results and discussion

This section has been divided into three parts: experimental design, video stabilization performance, and comparison with another algorithm.

The experimental design

The AR.Drone 1.0, a low-cost quadrotor built by the French company Parrot (Paris, France), has been used as experimental platform for several reasons: low cost, energy conservation, safe flight, and vehicle size. The proposed methodology has been implemented in a laptop with the following characteristics: Intel Core i7-2670QM processor, 2.20 GHz with Turbo Boost up to 3.1 GHz and RAM 16.0 Gb. Real images of four different scenarios are obtained with the on-board camera (sample frequency = 10 Hz) and processed. Furthermore, a video has been recorded with a zenith camera to capture the real motion

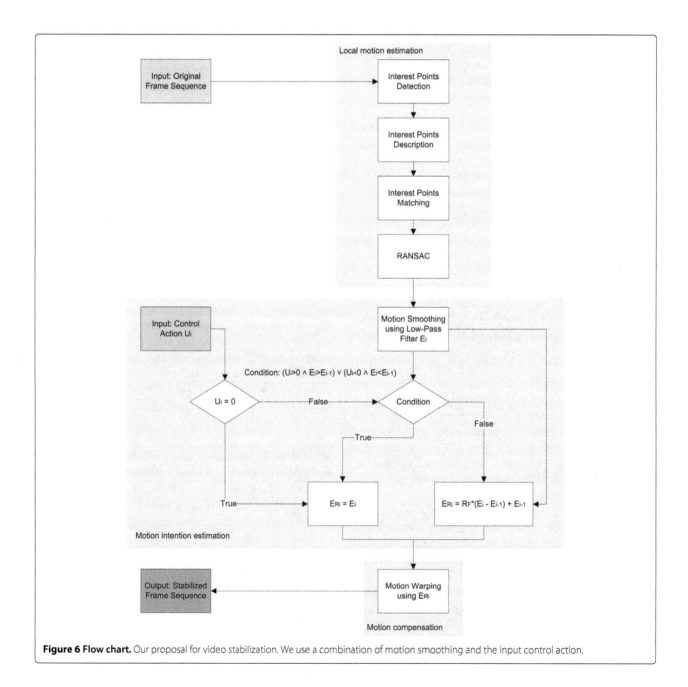

Figure 6 Flow chart. Our proposal for video stabilization. We use a combination of motion smoothing and the input control action.

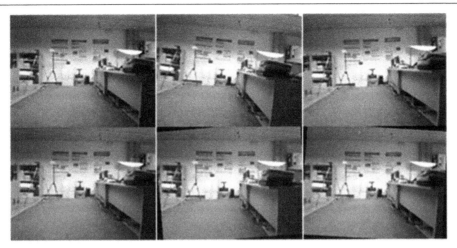

Figure 7 Scene 1. Top: original video. Bottom: stabilized video.

of the flying robot in the xy-plane. RMSE is selected as objective measure of motion reliability, comparing the estimated motion with the observed motion. In order to obtain a position measure, we use a tracker based on optical flow [44] and camera calibration method for radial distortion [45]. Next, the RMSE is computed by comparing the estimate with the observed motion (from the zenith camera).

Video stabilization performance

Now, a visual perception of the results obtained for each experimental environment is shown[a] in Figures 7, 8, 9, and 10. Experiments demonstrate that the approach based on motion intention estimation presented in this paper is robust to the presence of nearby objects, scenes with

moving objects, and common problems described in past sections from on-board cameras for MAVs during indoor flight.

Presence of nearby objects

Nearby objects in the scene represents one of the main problems of video stabilization, because most of interest points are generated in the objects' region. The image compensation is computed using the objects' motion instead of the scene motion. However, our process of matching interest points is based on the RANSAC algorithm and the gray level difference between consecutive frames as cost function. Consequently, the process of motion estimation is not performed on the objects' interest points but on the whole scene.

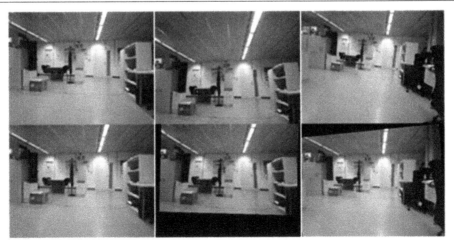

Figure 8 Scene 2. Top: original video. Bottom: stabilized video.

Figure 9 Scene 3. Top: original video. Bottom: stabilized video.

Scenes with moving objects

Moving objects are another common problem. Some objects with many points cause, during the motion estimation, undesirable tracking of these objects. Once more, the RANSAC-based process of matching interest point is not only referenced to moving objects but to the whole image.

Problems from on-board cameras for quadrotors

Scenes frame by frame, significant displacements, low-frequency videos, freezing, and high-speed displacements are frequent problems in images captured with an on-board camera due to the complex dynamic of the quadrotors during indoor flight. In all of them, the change between two consecutive frames could be considerable, producing a critical problem in video stabilization. In

our approach, motion intention estimation solves these problems, and previous rejection of data higher than a threshold provides additional robustness.

Phantom movements

They corresponds to a phenomenon present in previous video stabilization techniques, but not still reported. Independently of which approach is used, video stabilization process depends on a phase of motion intention estimation. The phantom movements are generated during the elimination of the high-frequency movements due to the motion intention estimation which reduces the frequency of the movements and the previous motion intention estimators which are not able to detect or correct these troubles. Our proposal eliminates this phantom movements using a combination of a low-pass filter, as a motion

Figure 10 Scene 4. Top: original video. Bottom: stabilized video.

Table 1 Evaluation metrics

Video name	Evaluation metric	Original	L1-Optimal	Our approach
Video 1	ITF (dB)	14.09	19.62	19.48
	RMSE		0.046	0.028
Video 2	ITF (dB)	13.43	19.57	19.52
	RMSE		0.051	0.023
Video 3	ITF (dB)	14.65	20.16	19.89
	RMSE		0.047	0.029
Video 4	ITF (dB)	16.96	21.24	21.12
	RMSE		0.036	0.017

ITF is the measure of video stability. RMSE is the measure of reliability of the video movements.

intention estimator, with the control action. However, this method slightly decreases the ITF value.

Comparison

Our approach has been compared with the off-line method L1-Optimal [6], which is applied in the YouTube Editor as a video stabilization option. Results on four different scenes are presented in Table 1 using two evaluation metrics: ITF and RMSE.

The obtained results show that our algorithm is comparable with the L1-Optimal method. The performance of our approach with respect to the ITF measure is slightly lower than L1-Optimal, which means that the output video is a little less stable. However, the RMSE value, which represents the similarity between the stabilized

video motion and the intentional motion, is higher in our approach.

It is worth noting that the ITF measure could be increased varying the reliability factor $R_F \in [0,1]$, but the RMSE inevitably would decrease. For post-production applications, the value for R_F can be equal to one, but for applications of motion control based on camera information, the realism of the movement is important, so the reliability factor should decrease to zero. Both, observed and estimated scales are graphically compared in Figure 11 for the technique L1-Optimal and our approach.

Conclusions

After conducting an initial study of motion smoothing methods, it has been experimentally checked that the low-pass filter has a high performance as algorithm for motion intention estimation, eliminating undesired movements.

However, this method can be optimized using a lower number of frames without decreasing the ITF measure, as we have presented in this paper. The cutting frequency depends on the model characteristics; hence, the information about the capture system implicates a considerable contribution in a calibration phase.

The phantom movements are a phenomenon that had not yet been studied in the video stabilization literature, but it is a key point in the control of complex dynamic systems as micro aerial vehicles, where the realism in the movements could mean the difference that prevents an accident.

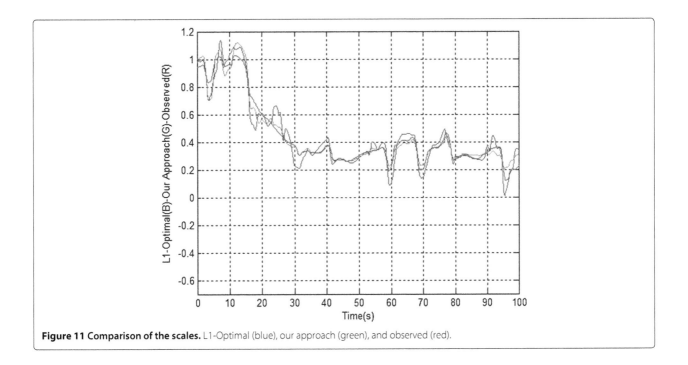

Figure 11 Comparison of the scales. L1-Optimal (blue), our approach (green), and observed (red).

The reliability factor is adapted to the purpose of the application. This application can be a post-production with a high ITF value and a lower realism or the opposite situation, for real-time video stabilization used in tele-operation systems.

As a future work, we will extend our video stabilization method, using the quadrotor model estimated in [46], for aggressive environments with turbulence and communication problems. We will apply it for increasing the performance of detection and tracking algorithms. In [47] we presented a first application for face detection.

Endnote

[a] Video results are provided: www.youtube.com/user/VideoStabilizerMAV/videos.

Competing interests
The authors declare that they have no competing interests.

Acknowledgements
This work has been partially supported by the Spanish Ministry of Economy and Competitiveness, through the PATRICIA project (TIN 2012-38416-C03-01). The research fellow Wilbert G. Aguilar thanks the funding through a grant from the program 'Convocatoria Abierta 2011' issued by the Secretary of Education, Science, Technology and Innovation SENESCYT of the Republic of Ecuador.

References

1. F Kendoul, Survey of advances in guidance, navigation, and control of unmanned rotorcraft systems. J. Field Robot. **29**(2), 315–378 (2012)
2. Z Duric, A Rosenfeld, Shooting a smooth video with a shaky camera. Mach. Vis. Appl. **13**(5–6), 303–313 (2003)
3. S Battiato, G Gallo, G Puglisi, S Scellato, SIFT features tracking for video stabilization, in *14th International Conference on Image Analysis and Processing, 2007. ICIAP 2007* (Modena, 10–14 Sept 2007), pp. 825–830
4. Y-F Hsu, C-C Chou, M-Y Shih, Moving camera video stabilization using homography consistency, in *2012 19th IEEE International Conference on Image Processing (ICIP)* (Lake Buena Vista, 30 Sept–3 Oct 2012), pp. 2761–2764
5. C Song, H Zhao, W Jing, H Zhu, Robust video stabilization based on particle filtering with weighted feature points. Consum. Electron. IEEE Trans. **58**(2), 570–577 (2012)
6. M Grundmann, V Kwatra, I Essa, Auto-directed video stabilization with robust l1 optimal camera paths, in *2011 IEEE Conference on Computer Vision and Pattern Recognition (CVPR)* (Colorado Springs, 20–25 June 2011), pp. 225–232
7. H-C Chang, S-H Lai, K-R Lu, A robust and efficient video stabilization algorithm, in *2004 IEEE International Conference on Multimedia and Expo, 2004. ICME '04*, vol. 1 (Taipei, 27–30 June 2004), pp. 29–321
8. R Strzodka, C Garbe, Real-time motion estimation and visualization on graphics cards. IEEE Vis. **2004**, 545–552 (2004)
9. K-Y Lee, Y-Y Chuang, B-Y Chen, M Ouhyoung, Video stabilization using robust feature trajectories, in *2009 IEEE 12th International Conference on Computer Vision* (Kyoto, 27 Sept–4 Oct 2009), pp. 1397–1404
10. J Yang, D Schonfeld, M Mohamed, Robust video stabilization based on particle filter tracking of projected camera motion. Circuits Syst. Video Technol. IEEE Trans. **19**(7), 945–954 (2009)
11. C Wang, J-H Kim, K-Y Byun, J Ni, S-J Ko, Robust digital image stabilization using the Kalman filter. Consum. Electron. IEEE Trans. **55**(1), 6–14 (2009)
12. J Canny, A computational approach to edge detection. Pattern Anal. Mach. Intell. IEEE Trans. **PAMI-8**(6), 679–698 (1986)
13. C Harris, M Stephens, A combined corner and edge detector, in *Proceedings of The Fourth Alvey Vision Conference*, (31 Aug–2 Sept 1988), pp. 147–151
14. O Miksik, K Mikolajczyk, Evaluation of local detectors and descriptors for fast feature matching, in *2012 21st International Conference on Pattern Recognition (ICPR)* (Tsukuba, 11–15 Nov 2012), pp. 2681–2684
15. S Leutenegger, M Chli, RY Siegwart, BRISK: Binary Robust Invariant Scalable Keypoints, in *2011 IEEE International Conference on Computer Vision (ICCV)* (Barcelona, 6–13 Nov 2011), pp. 2548–2555
16. A Alahi, R Ortiz, P Vandergheynst, Freak: Fast retina keypoint, in *2012 IEEE Conference on Computer Vision and Pattern Recognition (CVPR)* (Providence, 16–21 June 2012), pp. 510–517
17. E Rublee, V Rabaud, K Konolige, G Bradski, ORB: an efficient alternative to SIFT or SURF, in *2011 IEEE International Conference on Computer Vision (ICCV)* (Barcelona, 6–13 Nov 2011), pp. 2564–2571
18. DG Lowe, Object recognition from local scale-invariant features, in *The Proceedings of the Seventh IEEE International Conference on Computer Vision, 1999*, vol. 2 (Kerkyra, 20–25 Sept 1999), pp. 1150–11572
19. H Bay, T Tuytelaars, L Gool, SURF: Speeded Up Robust Features, in *Computer Vision – ECCV 2006*, ed. by A Leonardis, H Bischof, A Pinz, and (eds.) Lecture Notes in Computer Science, vol. 3951 (Springer Berlin, 2006), pp. 404–417
20. J Luo, G Oubong, A Comparison of SIFT, PCA-SIFT and SURF. Int. J. Image Process. (IJIP). **3**(4), 143–152 (2009)
21. MA Fischler, RC Bolles, Random sample consensus: a paradigm for model fitting with applications to image analysis and automated cartography. Commun. ACM. **24**(6), 381–395 (1981)
22. B Tordoff, D Murray, Guided sampling and consensus for motion estimation, in *Computer Vision – ECCV 2002*, ed. by A Heyden, G Sparr, M Nielsen, P Johansen, and (eds.) Lecture Notes in Computer Science, vol. 2350 (Springer Berlin, 2002), pp. 82–96
23. S Choi, T Kim, W Yu, Performance evaluation of RANSAC family, in *Proceedings of the British Machine Vision Conference 2009* (London, 7–10 Sept 2009), pp. 81–18112
24. KG Derpanis, *Overview of the RANSAC algorithm.* (Technical report, Computer Science, York University, 2010)
25. Y Matsushita, E Ofek, W Ge, X Tang, H-Y Shum, Full-frame video stabilization with motion inpainting. Pattern Anal. Mach. Intell. IEEE Trans. **28**(7), 1150–1163 (2006)
26. P Rawat, J Singhai, Adaptive motion smoothening for video stabilization. Int. J. Comput. **72**(20), 14–20 (2013)
27. S Wu, DC Zhang, Y Zhang, J Basso, M Melle, Adaptive smoothing in real-time image stabilization, in *Visual Information Processing XXI* (Baltimore, 24–25 April 2012)
28. Y Wang, Z Hou, K Leman, R Chang, Real-time video stabilization for unmanned aerial vehicles, in *MVA2011 IAPR Conference on Machine Vision Applications* (Nara, 13–15 June 2011), pp. 336–339
29. Y Wang, R Chang, T Chua, Video stabilization based on high degree b-spline smoothing, in *2012 21st Conference on Pattern Recognition (ICPR)* (Tsukuba, 11–15 Nov 2012), pp. 3152–3155
30. YG Ryu, HC Roh, M-J Chung, Long-time video stabilization using point-feature trajectory smoothing, in *2011 IEEE International Conference on Consumer Electronics (ICCE)* (Las Vegas, 9–12 Jan 2011), pp. 189–190
31. D Jing, X Yang, Real-time video stabilization based on smoothing feature trajectories. Appl. Mech. Mater. **519—520**(1662–7482), 640–643 (2014)
32. K Mikolajczyk, C Schmid, Scale & affine invariant interest point detectors. Int. J. Comput. Vis. **60**(1), 63–86 (2004)
33. O Faugeras, Q-T Luong, T Papadopoulou, *The Geometry of Multiple Images: the Laws That Govern the Formation of Images of a Scene and Some of Their Applications.* (MIT Press, Cambridge, 2001)
34. DA Forsyth, J Ponce, *Computer Vision: a Modern Approach.* (Prentice Hall, Upper Saddle River, 2002)
35. R Hartley, A Zisserman, *Multiple View Geometry in Computer Vision*, 2nd edn. (Cambridge University Press, New York, 2003)
36. WG Aguilar, C Angulo, Estabilización robusta de vídeo basada en diferencia de nivel de gris, in *Proceedings of the 8th Congress of Science and Technology ESPE 2013*, (Sangolquí, 5–7 June 2013)
37. WG Aguilar, C Angulo, Robust video stabilization based on motion intention for low-cost micro aerial vehicles, in *2014 11th International Multi-conference on Systems, Signals and Devices (SSD)* (Barcelona, 11–14 Feb 2014), pp. 1–6

38. M Vazquez, C Chang, Real-time video smoothing for small RC helicopters, in *IEEE International Conference on Systems, Man and Cybernetics, 2009. SMC 2009* (San Antonio, 11–14 Oct 2009)

39. SW Bailey, B Bodenheimer, A comparison of motion capture data recorded from a Vicon system and a Microsoft Kinect sensor, in *Proceedings of the ACM Symposium on Applied Perception. SAP '12* (ACM New York, 2012), pp. 121–121

40. J Xu, H-W Chang, S Yang, M Wang, Fast feature-based video stabilization without accumulative global motion estimation. Consum. Electron. IEEE Trans. **58**(3), 993–999 (2012)

41. M Niskanen, O Silven, M Tico, Video stabilization performance assessment, in *2006 IEEE International Conference on Multimedia and Expo* (Toronto, 9–12 July 2006), pp. 405–408

42. S-J Kang, T-S Wang, D-H Kim, A Morales, S-J Ko, Video stabilization based on motion segmentation, in *2012 IEEE International Conference on Consumer Electronics (ICCE)*, (2012), pp. 416–417

43. C-L Fang, T-H Tsai, C-H Chang, Video stabilization with local rotational motion model, in *2012 IEEE Asia Pacific Conference on Circuits and Systems (APCCAS)* (Kaohsiung, 2–5 Dec 2012), pp. 551–554

44. A Yilmaz, O Javed, M Shah, Object tracking: a survey. ACM Comput. Surv. **38**(13) (2006)

45. Z Zhang, A flexible new technique for camera calibration. Pattern Anal. Mach. Intell. IEEE Trans. **22**(11), 1330–1334 (2000)

46. WG Aguilar, R Costa, C Angulo, L Molina, Control autónomo de cuadricópteros para seguimiento de trayectorias, in *Proceedings of the 9th Congress of Science and Technology ESPE 2014* (Sangolquí, 28–30 May 2014)

47. WG Aguilar, C Angulo, Estabilización de vídeo en micro vehículos aéreos y su aplicación en la detección de caras, in *Proceedings of the 9th Congress of Science and Technology ESPE 2014* (Sangolquí, 28–30 May 2014)

6

No-reference image and video quality assessment: a classification and review of recent approaches

Muhammad Shahid*, Andreas Rossholm, Benny Lövström and Hans-Jürgen Zepernick

Abstract

The field of perceptual quality assessment has gone through a wide range of developments and it is still growing. In particular, the area of no-reference (NR) image and video quality assessment has progressed rapidly during the last decade. In this article, we present a classification and review of latest published research work in the area of NR image and video quality assessment. The NR methods of visual quality assessment considered for review are structured into categories and subcategories based on the types of methodologies used for the underlying processing employed for quality estimation. Overall, the classification has been done into three categories, namely, pixel-based methods, bitstream-based methods, and hybrid methods of the aforementioned two categories. We believe that the review presented in this article will be helpful for practitioners as well as for researchers to keep abreast of the recent developments in the area of NR image and video quality assessment. This article can be used for various purposes such as gaining a structured overview of the field and to carry out performance comparisons for the state-of-the-art methods.

Keywords: No-reference; Image quality assessment; Video quality assessment; Perceptual quality

1 Review

1.1 Introduction

There has been a tremendous progress recently in the usage of digital images and videos for an increasing number of applications. Multimedia services that have gained wide interest include digital television broadcasts, video streaming applications, and real-time audio and video services over the Internet. The global mobile data traffic grew by 81% in 2013, and during 2014, the number of mobile-connected devices will exceed the number of people on earth, according to predictions made by Cisco. The video portion of the mobile data traffic was 53% in 2013 and is expected to exceed 67% by 2018 [1]. With this huge increase in the exposure of image and video to the human eye, the interest in delivering quality of experience (QoE) may increase naturally. The quality of visual media can get degraded during capturing, compression, transmission, reproduction, and displaying due to the distortions that might occur at any of these stages.

The legitimate judges of visual quality are humans as end users, the opinions of whom can be obtained by subjective experiments. Subjective experiments involve a panel of participants which are usually non-experts, also referred to as test subjects, to assess the perceptual quality of given test material such as a sequence of images or videos. Subjective experiments are typically conducted in a controlled laboratory environment. Careful planning and several factors including assessment method, selection of test material, viewing conditions, grading scale, and timing of presentation have to be considered prior to a subjective experiment. For example, Recommendation (ITU-R) BT.500 [2] provides detailed guidelines for conducting subjective experiments for the assessment of quality of television pictures. The outcomes of a subjective experiment are the individual scores given by the test subjects, which are used to compute mean opinion score (MOS) and other statistics. The obtained MOS, in particular, represents a ground truth for the development of objective quality metrics. In ITU-R BT.500 and related recommendations, various types of subjective methods have been described. These types include either single

*Correspondence: muhammad.shahid@ieee.org
Blekinge Institute of Technology, Karlskrona SE-37179, Sweden

stimulus or double stimulus-based methods. In single stimulus methods, the subjects are shown variants of the test videos and no reference for comparison is provided. In some situations, a hidden reference can be included but the assessment is based only on a no-reference scoring of the subjects.

Due to the time-consuming nature of executing subjective experiments, large efforts have been made to develop objective quality metrics, alternatively called as objective quality methods. The purpose of such objective quality methods is to automatically predict MOS with high accuracy. Objective quality methods may be classified into psychophysical and engineering approaches [3]. Psychophysical metrics aim at modeling the human visual system (HVS) using aspects such as contrast and orientation sensitivity, frequency selectivity, spatial and temporal pattern, masking, and color perception. These metrics can be used for a wide variety of video degradations but the computation is generally demanding. The engineering approach usually uses simplified metrics based on the extraction and analysis of certain features or artifacts in a video but do not necessarily disregard the attributes of the HVS as they often consider psychophysical effects as well. However, the conceptual basis for their design is to do analysis of video content and distortion rather than fundamental vision modeling.

A set of features or quality-related parameters of an image or video are pooled together to establish an objective quality method which can be mapped to predict MOS. Depending on the degree of information that is available from the original video as a reference in the quality assessment, the objective methods are further divided into full reference (FR), reduced reference (RR), and no-reference (NR) as follows:

- FR methods: With this approach, the entire original image/video is available as a reference. Accordingly, FR methods are based on comparing distorted image/video with the original image/video.
- RR methods: In this case, it is not required to give access to the original image/video but only to provide representative features about texture or other suitable characteristics of the original image/video. The comparison of the reduced information from the original image/video with the corresponding information from the distorted image/video provides the input for RR methods.
- NR methods: This class of objective quality methods does not require access to the original image/video but searches for artifacts with respect to the pixel domain of an image/video, utilizes information embedded in the bitstream of the related image/video format, or performs quality assessment as a hybrid of pixel-based and bitstream-based approaches.

1.2 Applications of no-reference image and video quality assessment

In recent years, there has been increasing interest in the development of NR methods due to the widespread use of multimedia services in the context of wireless communications and telecommunication systems. Applications of NR methods include the following areas:

- Network operators and content providers have a strong interest to objectively quantify the level of service quality delivered to the end user and inside the network nodes. NR methods will provide the data needed to adopt network settings such that customer satisfaction is secured and hence churn can be avoided.
- The involvement of multiple parties between content providers and the end users gives rise to establish service-level agreements (SLA) under which an agreed level of quality has to be guaranteed. In this respect, NR methods are a suitable choice for in-service quality monitoring in live systems.
- In general, NR methods are well suited to perform real-time objective quality assessment where resources are limited such as frequency spectrum in wireless communications. In such cases, RR methods have limited application as an ancillary channel is required to transmit the required features of the original video.
- Real-time communication and streaming services require quality adaptations using NR methods for collecting statistics of the delivered quality.

1.2.1 Related work: published reviews of objective visual quality methods

According to the framework introduced in [4] for NR visual quality estimation, three stages are present in an NR quality estimation approach. These stages are *measurement* of a physical quantity relevant for visual quality, also called as feature, *pooling* the measured data over space and/or time, and *mapping* the pooled data to an estimate of perceived quality. A survey of the measurement stage, which is essentially the main focus in much of the work done in NR quality estimation, has been provided in the same contribution. The survey in [4] divides the literature review into two main categories. In the first category, the methods estimating mean square error (MSE) caused by block-based compression, MSE caused by packet loss errors, and noise estimation methods to compute MSE have been discussed. The second category encompasses the approaches that are termed as feature-based. The feature-based methods are based on either a model developed for particular artifacts related to a visible degradation, or a model developed to quantify the impact of degradations on a specific set of attributes of the original uncorrupted image or video. A brief survey of NR methods of image quality assessment (IQA) based on the notion of quantifying the impact of distortions on natural scene statistics (NSS) is provided in [5]. Some NR methods of visual quality are discussed in [6] also under the categorization of features and artifacts detection. Similarly, a review of the objective methods of video quality assessment (VQA) is provided in [7] including a classification of objective methods in general without specifying it for no-reference methods. In [7], the objective methods are classified as data metrics, pictures metrics, and packet or bitstream-based metrics. The review and performance comparison of video quality assessment methods in [8] present a classification of FR and RR methods only. A survey on visual quality assessment methods that are based on information theory is given in [9]. It was observed that information theory-based research for the development of NR methods is rather limited. The type of NR methods surveyed in [9] relies on an approach that employs Rényi entropy for determining the amount of randomness in the orientation of local structures in an image. NR methods have been reviewed in [10] by classifying them following three approaches. Firstly, a review of NR methods has been performed by classifying them based on the type of distortion that is estimated to formulate a quality value. The second approach used for the classification is based on methods that are designed for quantifying the artifacts produced by a specific compression standard. Lastly, a review of methods that are not designed specifically for a particular distortion has been performed. A broad survey of image and video quality methods, as well as a classification of the methods, was published during 2007 in [11]. This includes both NR and RR methods, and our article focuses on a classification and review of NR methods of IQA and VQA published after [11].

1.2.2 Our proposed classification

The current literature in the area of methods of NR image/video quality assessment is quite diverse. Hence, it is a challenging task to classify these methods into a well-structured and meaningful categorization. A good categorization of such methods should be concise enough to be properly understandable and also comprehensive enough to present most of the relevant methodologies. The aforementioned types of classifications cover a range of NR methods, but there is a need to broaden the categorization approaches in order to review currently existing methods in this area. Reibman et al. [12] classify NR methods as either stemming from statistics derived from pixel-based features and call them NR pixel (NR-P) type or computed directly from the coded bitstream and call them NR bitstream (NR-B) type. We believe that this is a useful classification which can serve as an effective basis for constructing a broader classification.

In the case of NR-P-based methods, one relevant method to classify available approaches is to investigate these in terms of the employment of certain artifacts that are related to a specific kind of degradation of the visual quality. Quantification of such artifacts has been used as a measure for the quality assessment. The quality values may depend only on a single artifact or it may depend upon a combination of many artifacts. It is common that single artifact measure-based methods are developed by considering a given model of degradation, often simulated artifacts, and sometimes their performance remains unknown for realistic or more general scenarios. For example, most of the available blur methods are based on Gaussian or linear blur models, which may not adequately measure the blur produced by a complex relative motion between image capturing device and the object. Moreover, single-artifact-based quality methods may not have satisfactory performance in the assessment of the overall quality, in the presence of other artifacts. Therefore, methods have been introduced where estimation of a combination of artifacts is fused to generate a single quality score. Also, in the domain of NR-P-based methods, there are many methods which work beyond simple artifacts computation and the quality assessment is derived from the impact of distortions upon NSS (referring to statistical characteristics commonly found in natural images). Moreover, some quality-relevant features can be computed from the image/video pixels to formulate an estimation of the perceptual quality.

The NR-B-based methods are relatively simpler to compute than NR-P-based methods, and the quality values can often be computed in the absence of a full decoder. However, such methods can have limited scope of application as they are usually designed for a particular coding technique and bitstream format, e.g., H.264/AVC standard. Such methods are based on either the encoding information derived from the bitstream or the packet header information or a combination of both. These methods are quite suitable for network video applications such IPTV and video conferencing.

Quality assessment performance can be compromised in NR-B-based methods to gain reduction in the computational complexity as compared to the NR-P-based methods. The performance of NR-B-based methods of quality assessment can be improved by adopting an approach of adding some input from NR-P-based quality assessment. Such composites of NR-P- and NR-B-based methods are called hybrid methods. These methods inherit the computational simplicity of NR-B-based methods and depend on NR-P-related data to gain further robustness.

In light of the aforementioned discussion, our approach of a meaningful classification of NR objective visual quality methods is outlined in Figure 1. This classification is formulated by considering the type and granularity of usage of the image or video data for the design of an objective method of quality. Thus, it offers the opportunity to present a discussion of most of recently published techniques of the NR visual quality assessment. It is to be noted that the main focus of this article is to review, in a systematic and structured manner, recent advancements in this area. Hence, a performance comparison of the reviewed methods on a comprehensive test database is out of the scope of this paper.

1.2.3 The preliminaries and organization of this paper

Most of the existing NR quality methods fall into NR-P or NR-B type methods or a hybrid of these two approaches. As shown in Figure 1, the following sections present an overview of the different classes of NR methods of IQA and VQA. In each section, we have presented a general idea used in computation of various types of methods of quality estimation using block diagrams. Summaries of most of the discussed methods are shown in tables throughout the paper and in dedicated discussion sections. Mostly, the performance of an objective quality prediction model is reported by using measure of prediction accuracy, i.e., Pearson's linear correlation coefficient, and measure of monotonicity, i.e., Spearman's rank order correlation coefficient, as recommended by Video Quality Expert Group (VQEG) [13]. These measures have been used to report the performance of the reviewed methods

in the tables. In these tables, some cells have been marked with a hyphen (-) in cases where the corresponding value has not been reported in the reference or some uncommon measure of performance has been used. Other than the explicit numerical values of the number of pixels used for stating the resolution of the test data, the following short forms are used:

- QCIF, Quarter Common Intermediate Format (176×144)
- CIF, Common Intermediate Format (352×288)
- SIF, Standard Interchange Format (320×240)
- SD, Standard Definition (720×480 or 720×576)
- HD, High Definition (1920×1080 or 1280×720)

For validation of the proposed method, some publicly available databases of images and videos have been used in most of the reference papers. In this article, the reference to a public database of test media indicates that either a subset or the complete set of the available media has been used. These sources of the test media include the following:

- Laboratory for Image and Video Engineering (LIVE): LIVE offers databases of compressed images and videos with the corresponding data of the subjective assessment. The images have been encoded using Joint Photographic Experts Group (JPEG) and JPEG2000 standards. Moreover, some images have been generated using simulated conditions of certain artifacts such as Gaussian blur and white noise. The video database contains sets of videos encoded

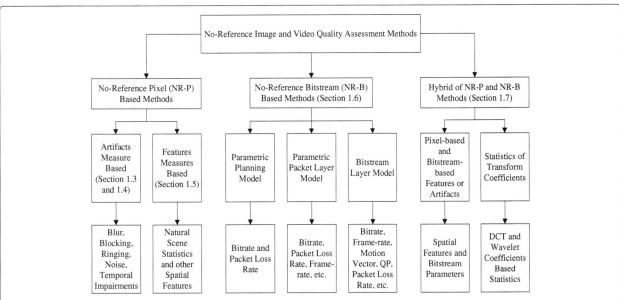

Figure 1 An overview of NR image and video quality assessment methods. The second row of boxes gives a division into three main categories, further divided into subcategories in the next row. The bottom row gives examples of extracted features or information used for processing in each subcategory.

using Moving Picture Experts Group (MPEG)-2 and H.264/AVC. While we refer to the usage of test data from LIVE in the tables, the standard used for encoding shown in the column *Processing* indicates whether the used data is an image or a video. References to the publications based on the use of these databases have been provided at the source website [14].

- Video Quality Experts Group (VQEG): VQEG has released its test data for public use which is available on their website [15]. The data contains standard definition television videos and the corresponding values of the subjective assessment.
- Tampere Image Database 2008 (TID2008): This database contains test data produced from 17 different types of distortion introduced in the given 25 reference images. The test images have been provided with the corresponding subjective assessment scores and values of many objective methods of quality estimation. More information on it is found in [16].
- Images and Video Communications (IVC): The IVC database contains a set of ten original images distorted by four types of processing and is supported by the corresponding quality scores as available in [17].
- Toyoma: This database consists of subjective assessment data and test stimuli generated through processing of 14 reference images using JPEG and JPEG2000 [18].

This article is organized as follows. For the pixel-based approaches, the methods that apply direct estimation of single and multiple artifacts are reviewed in Sections 1.3 and 1.4, respectively. The methods based on computation of various features and an evaluation of impacts of pertinent artifacts upon NSS are discussed in Section 1.5. Bitstream-based NR methods are reviewed in Section 1.6. The methods constructed as hybrids of pixel and bitstream-based approaches are discussed in Section 1.7. Finally, some conclusive remarks and a brief outlook of possible future works in this area are presented in Section 2.

1.3 Single artifact NR-P-based methods

Blurring, blocking, and ringing are considered to be the most commonly found spatial domain artifacts in images/videos compressed by lossy encoders [19]. Moreover, noise is also a common source of annoyance in images and videos. Transmission of videos over lossy networks gives rise to temporal artifacts such as frame freeze. In the following, we examine the recent methods which adopt the approach of quantifying a single artifact for perceptual quality estimation. The section is divided into subsections for each of these artifacts, and an overall discussion is provided at the end.

1.3.1 Blurring

Winkler defines blur as an artifact which appears as a loss of spatial detail and a reduction of edge sharpness [20]. The reasons for the occurrence of blur can be many, originating in the acquisition, processing, or compression [21]. The primary source of blur in compression techniques is the truncation of high-frequency components in the transform domain of an image. Other possible reasons of the blurring of an image or video can be out-of-focus capturing, relative motion between the camera and the object being captured, or limitations in the optical system. Traditional no-reference blur methods usually focus on a particular coding artifact for quality prediction and hence their performance is compromised in circumstances of more general blur. Moreover, there has been little work carried out to build methods which have the capability of assessing blur in natural scenarios, rather, most of the work is focused on the simulated blur. A basic schematic of NR blur assessment is shown by the flowchart given in Figure 2. In many NR methods of estimating the impact of blur on visual quality, the computations begin with measuring the spread of pixels present on the edges in an image. Usually, it involves the application of commonly used edge detectors such as Sobel and/or Canny for finding the edges in the image. The next step is typically the computation of the edge distortion value that can be used towards finding an estimate of the blur. Some methods, however, make use of HVS adaptation to the value of edge distortion to classify it as perceivable or not perceivable by a human subject.

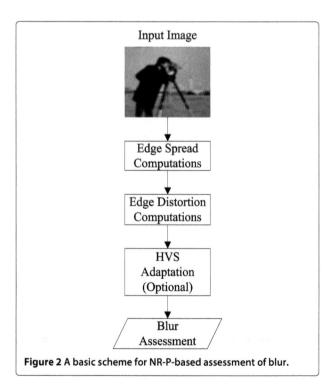

Figure 2 A basic scheme for NR-P-based assessment of blur.

A paradigm for blur evaluation has been presented in [22] that is mainly composed of four methods of blur quantification, given in [23-25] and [26], which have been integrated by an artificial neural network (ANN) powered multifeature classifier. In the method given in [23], an image quality measurement method in terms of global blur has been proposed. The method relies on histograms of discrete cosine transform (DCT) coefficients present in MPEG and JPEG encoded data to qualitatively encompass the distribution of null coefficients, given the fact that blurred images usually end up having a lot of high-frequency coefficients set to zero. This algorithm provides results which align with subjective assessment but it focuses only on out-of-focus blur and it does not perform well when there is a uniform background present or when an image is over-illuminated. The blur assessment algorithm proposed in [24] exploits the ability of the Haar wavelet transform (HWT) to distinguish edge types, and the method works both for out-of-focus and linear-motion blur. This method is however not tested for realistic blur. The method proposed in [25] presents a framework where global blur is measured in terms of averaged edge lengths. The authors considered only a small set of Gaussian blurred images for its evaluation. Nonetheless, the method has good correlation with subjective scores. An improved version of [25] is found in [26] where HVS properties have been added to get weighted edge lengths. It is to be noted that none of these four reference methods quantify realistic blur situations, but Ciancio et al. [22] have shown their method to be useable for measuring naturally occurring blur. Overall, [22] uses local phase coherence, mean brightness level, and variance of the HVS frequency response and contrast as additional inputs, together with the earlier mentioned four methods, to various ANN models designed for quality estimation. For input calibration, a five-parameter nonlinear mapping function was used for the types of blur including simulated Gaussian, simulated linear motion, a combination of both, and real blur. The proposed method outperforms the given four reference methods when tested on a fairly large database of 6,000 images corrupted by blur. Although the proposed method does not correlate so well with subjective scores in realistic blur scenarios, with a Pearson's correlation coefficient of approximately 0.56, it performs better than the reference methods with respect to subjective rating. In an earlier paper, the same authors have used the idea of estimating image blur using local phase coherence [27] and a similar method proposed by Hassen et al. is found in [28].

It has been argued in [29] that blur below a certain threshold value remains unperceived by the HVS and such a threshold value is termed as just noticeable blur (JNB). By incorporating the response of the HVS to sharpness at various contrast levels, the authors have proposed a measure of image sharpness. It is suggested that most of the existing no-reference blur assessment methods do not perform well for a variety of images and are rather limited to assess varying blur in a certain image. They have validated this argument by testing a set of 13 contemporary reference methods, which are based on different techniques of blur assessment used for quality assessment such as pixel-based techniques, statistical properties, edge-detection-based, and derivative-based techniques. The proposed method has higher correlation with subjective MOS than the given 13 objective methods of quality assessment when it has been tested on a public database of test images. In [29], the block size used for finding edge pixels is 64×64, and a similar contribution based on JNB from the same authors is reported in [30] where a block size of 8×8 has been used for finding the edge pixels. The method proposed in [30] has been improved in [31] by adding the impact of saliency-weighting in foveated regions of an image. Specifically, more weighting is given to the local blur estimates that belong to salient regions of an image, while spatial blur values are pooled together to compute an overall value of blur for the whole image.

A similar method found in [21,32] improves [29] by addition of the concept of commutative probability of blur detection (CPBD) so that the method should estimate the quality by including the impact of HVS sensitivity towards blur perception at different contrast levels. Testing the proposed method upon three public image databases having different blur types reveals that the method performance is considerably better than some of the contemporary sharpness/blur methods. However, this method gives a quality index in a continuous range of 0 to 1 and the authors have modified it in [33] where it gives a quality value on a discrete scale of 1 to 5, the usual five quality classes which are described from *Bad* to *Excellent*. Given that blur estimation methods most often work on the idea of measurement of edge-spread and blur manifests itself in smooth or diminished edges, some edges may remain undetected. Varadarajan et al. [34] improved the method proposed in [29] by incorporating an edge refinement method to enhance the edge detection and hence outperformed the blur assessment. The authors achieved as much as 9% increase in Pearson's correlation coefficient.

In contrast to usual schemes of blur detection at the edges, the method proposed in [35] does an estimation of blur at the macroblock (MB) boundaries. The overall blur of an image can be calculated by averaging the block level measure for the whole image. The authors have also used a content-sensitive masking approach to compensate the impact of image texture. As the method was designed for videos encoded following the H.264/AVC standard, it mainly quantifies the blurring effects from quantization and de-blocking filter. This method is essentially based on a method proposed for images [36] where an estimation of the blur in a video is made by taking an average measure of blur values for each frame.

A wavelet-based noise-resilient color image sharpness method is presented in [37]. The procedure is to compute a multiscale wavelet-based structure tensor which represents the multiscale gradient information of local areas in a color image (image gradient is defined as the directional change in the intensity or color in an image). The proposed tensor structure preserves edges even in the presence of noise. Thus, the sharpness method is defined by calculating the eigenvalues of the multiscale tensor once edges have been identified. A competitive correlation with subjective MOS is achieved when the proposed method is tested on LIVE image database [14], in comparison to a similar sharpness method.

Out-of-focus blur estimation without using any reference information has been given in [38] using the point spread function (PSF) which is derived from edge information. As the proposed algorithm works in the spatial domain, avoiding any iterations or involvement of complex frequencies, it is expected to operate fast and possible to be deployed in real-time perceptual applications. Based on the similar approach in [39], the method has been made workable to assess blurriness of conditions like added blur, realistic blur, and noise contamination.

Chen et al. [40] have claimed that their method works for any kind of blurriness, without being sensitive to the source of the blur. A gradient image is calculated from the given image pixel array. A Markov model is used and a transition probability matrix is computed. Finally, a pooling strategy is applied to the probabilistic values to obtain the blurriness measure.

Some of the other recently introduced no-reference blur assessment methods include the following: In [41] a method based on multiscale gradients and wavelet decomposition of images is given, an image sharpness based on Riemannian tensor mapping into a non-Euclidean space has been found in [42], radial analysis of blurred images in frequency domain is done in [43] to set an image quality index for blur estimation, and reference [44] presents a perceptual blur method to assess quality of Gaussian blurred images. A method based on blur measure in salient regions has been presented in [45]. The perceptually relevant areas in an image are identified through elements of visual attention, namely, color contrast, object size, orientation, and eccentricity. Quality values in correlation with subjective scores are produced by localizing the degradation measure in these elements.

1.3.2 Blocking

Blocking is an artifact which manifests itself as a discontinuity between adjacent blocks in images and video

frames [3]. It is a predominant degradation that occurs after employment of block-based processing and compression techniques at high compression ratio conditions. In such techniques, transform is usually followed by quantization of each block individually leading to incoherent block boundaries in the reconstructed images or frames. Blockiness can be estimated in a region of an image, in general, by computing the difference between neighboring blocks and the amount of brightness around those blocks as shown in Figure 3. After the value of blockiness is determined in a certain region, it is important to estimate whether it would be significant for human perception or not by taking into account the impact from masking effects. This way, certain features that represent the input from HVS can be calculated. In general, blocking perception is affected by various factors including the blockiness strength (i.e., the difference between adjacent blocks), the local brightness around the blocks, and the local texture present in an image.

A frequency domain pixel-based bi-directional (horizontal and vertical) measure used to gauge blocking in images is presented in [46]. The authors claim that the proposed method can be used for any image or video format. Unlike the traditional no-reference blocking measures, this method does not require any *a priori* information about block origin, block offset or block-edge detection. The method has been evaluated on a large set of LIVE image and video database available as JPEG encoded images and MPEG-2 encoded videos. It outperforms a set of 13 contemporary blockiness methods in terms of prediction accuracy and monotonicity.

Liu et al. [47] presented an HVS-based blocking method to assess image quality using a grid detector to locate

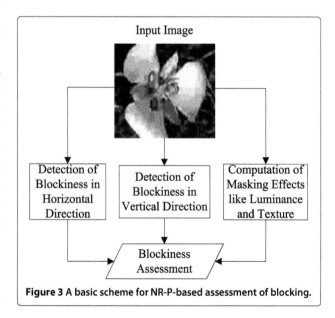

Figure 3 A basic scheme for NR-P-based assessment of blocking.

blocking. A local pixel-based blockiness measure which is calculated on the detected degraded regions is averaged to provide a blockiness value for the whole image. The main strength of this method in terms of computational efficiency and relevance to HVS response lies in the application of visual masking which makes the calculations perform only in the areas of blockiness visible to human perception. The authors took up the same method for further extensive evaluation in [48] under various conditions of comparison of performance where, for example, HVS models and grid detector are omitted or included. The results show that the proposed method performs better than some contemporary methods and can be a good candidate for real-time applications due to its simplified HVS model.

In [49], a blockiness assessment method is presented for block-based discrete cosine transform (BDCT) coded images. It is based on the estimation of noticeable blockiness. The so-called noticeable blockiness map is derived from luminance adaptation and texture masking in line with HVS response combined with a discontinuity map to quantify the visual quality. Along with its validated usability for deblocking of JPEG images, it has the potential of optimizing the codec parameters and similar other post-processing techniques.

Babu et al. presented their HVS related features-based blocking method in [50]. Blockiness as perceived by humans in JPEG encoded images is affected by a number of features such as edge amplitude around the borders of DCT blocks and edge length; the value of these increase in amount as compression rate is increased. It is also affected by the amount of background activity and background luminance as these have masking impact on possible blocking artifacts. The authors have used a sequential learning algorithm in a growing and pruning radial basis function (GAP-RBF) network to estimate the relationship between the mentioned features and the corresponding quality measure. Babu et al. also proposed a method of determining block-edge impairment [51] using the idea that edge gradients of blocks in the regions of low spatial details would contribute towards the overall blocking in an image. The level of spatial details is estimated through edge activity that is computed through standard deviation measurement of each edge.

Other methods in this area include the blind measurement of blocking in low bit rate H.264/AVC encoded videos based on temporal blocking artifact measure between successive frames of a video presented in [52]. A weighted Sobel operator-based blocking method is presented in [53], in which the computation involves luminance gradient matrices of DCT-coded images. A method where a rather simple approach of taking abrupt change in pixel values as a signal of blocking has been proposed in [54] and it can be implemented both in

pixel and DCT domain, and a method of blockiness estimation in natural scene JPEG compressed images has been presented in [55] which was influenced by the impact of multineural channels pattern of HVS for vision sensing.

1.3.3 Ringing

The ringing artifact is associated with Gibbs phenomenon and is observed along edges in otherwise smooth texture areas [20]. It has yet been relatively less investigated for NR perceptual quality measurements. This kind of degradation is caused by rough quantization of the high-frequency transform coefficients and is observed in the form of ripples around high contrast edges. A schematic block diagram of commonly used approaches for the estimation of perceptual ringing is shown in Figure 4. Certain features can be extracted from the edge maps to classify the image areas in terms of relevance towards ringing artifact. Masking effects of textured regions can be examined to check if the ringing would be visible to HVS perception. From the obtained data, a ringing map is generated for various regions and an overall value of perceptual ringing is obtained for the whole image. We have not found any publication on the NR estimation of ringing in videos.

Liu et al. have put forward HVS-based quality assessment methods which quantify ringing in compressed images in [56,57]. The work in [56] does not incorporate the masking effects of HVS properties. However, in [57], Liu et al. have improved the already existing method

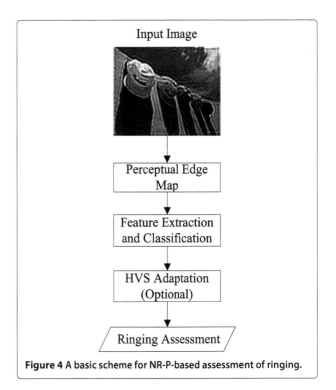

Figure 4 A basic scheme for NR-P-based assessment of ringing.

in multiple aspects. Edge detection is crucial for locating the possible ringing artifact and is used along with consideration of HVS masking in designing of such a method. The HVS masking is integrated by adding human visibility index of ringing nuisance estimate inside the already detected distorted regions. This method has a performance level comparable to a full reference method and it outperforms the two given no-reference methods of ringing assessment while tested on JPEG compressed images. As the method does not use coding parameters like DCT coefficients, the authors argue that a slightly tuned version of the same method should perform similarly well when employed on other types of compressed images, e.g., JPEG2000.

Ringing may occur also as a result of an image restoration process, unlike the other artifacts which usually occur during compression. The ringing that occurs due to image restoration has different characteristics as compared to the one that occurs due to compression. Iterations of blind deconvolution in the image restoration process are likely to result in the generation of ringing [58]. A quality method to assess perceived ringing as a result of application of blind deconvolution methods for image restoration is proposed in [58] and in [59]. The authors claim that these methods evaluate ringing with no sensitivity to the image content type and any specific ringing process. In the method proposed in [58], a 2D Gabor wavelet filter and a line detector were used to quantify ringing in restored images. A similar approach with enhancement is found in [59] where the authors have proposed to assess the degradation on image boundaries and image edges separately and then fuse the weighted results of the two values to have the overall ringing value. A 2D Gabor filter response image is used to calculate the perceived ringing at boundaries, and a Canny edge detector is used for locating ringing around edges in the image. The proposed method was tested on gray scale images restored from simulated blur. It has been found that the reported results are in line with subjective scores of quality assessment.

1.3.4 Noise

Besides the aforementioned unwanted components of an image or video that affect the perceptual quality, there can be other types of spatial noise as well. The mostly occurring types of spatial noise include salt and pepper noise, quantization noise, Gaussian noise, and speckle in coherent light situations. Mostly, the noise is considered to be an additive component, e.g., Gaussian noise, but in some situations the noise component is multiplicative, e.g., speckle noise [60]. Noise can be introduced during the image/video acquisition, recording, processing, and transmission [61]. Estimation of noise is required due to numerous reasons and applications in image processing

such as denoising, image filtering, image segmentation, and feature extraction. For the estimation of noise signal, in most cases, it is assumed to be *independent, identically distributed additive and stationary zero-mean signal*, i.e., white noise [62]. Image noise estimation methods can be categorized into either smoothing-based approaches, where noise is computed using the difference between the input image and a smoothed version of it, or block-based approaches, where block variances of the most homogenous block in a set of image blocks is taken as noise variance [63]. Similar to the approaches used for estimation of other artifacts, computation of noise characteristics depends on the extraction of some features that are affected by noise. Figure 5 shows the basic scheme of a block-based approach of noise estimation where an image is divided into smooth areas. A variance higher than a certain threshold in those areas gives an estimate of the noise.

A block-based approach proposed in [64] uses statistical analysis of a histogram of local signal variances to compute an estimation of image noise variance. However, this method is challenged by high computational requirements due to its iterative processing, and [65] simplifies this technique by taking image structure into consideration. It uses high-pass directional operators to determine the homogeneity of blocks besides using average noise variances. The performance of the improved method has

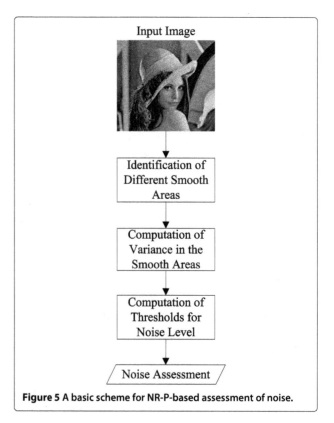

Figure 5 A basic scheme for NR-P-based assessment of noise.

been verified using highly noisy as well as good quality images. This method requires a full search of an image to determine the homogeneous areas in it. At the expense of decreased accuracy, spatial separations between blocks can be used to reduce the computational complexity. This approach has been adopted in [66] where particle filtering techniques have been used in the process of localization of the homogeneous regions. It has been shown that the proposed method reduces the number of required computations for homogeneity measurements while it outperforms [65] in accuracy. More examples of block-based approaches are found in [67-69] where noise level is computed by performing principal component analysis (PCA) of the image blocks.

1.3.5 Temporal impairments

Temporal impairments can be divided into two main categories: impairments caused by the encoding process and impairments caused by network perturbations. The typical temporal impairments caused by the encoding process come from temporal downsampling which can be performed uniformly or non-uniformly, depending on different underlying reasons. The impairments generated by network perturbations come from delay or packet loss [70]. These different impairments can be categorized as the following [3,4,71,72]:

- Jerkiness: non-fluent and non-smooth presentation of frames as a result of temporal downsampling
- Frame freeze: frame halts as a result of unavailability of new frames to present due to network congestion or packet loss etc.
- Jitter: perceived as unnatural motion due to variations in transmission delay as a result of, e.g., fluctuations in the available bandwidth or network congestion
- Flickering: noticeable discontinuity between consecutive frames as a result of a too-low frame rate together with high texture, coding artifacts, or motion content
- Mosquito noise: appears as temporal shimmering seen mostly in smooth textured areas produced by ringing and prediction error due to motion compensation mismatch

Jerkiness is the impairment perceived by the user, while jitter and frame freezes are the technical artifacts which produce jerkiness. Figure 6 presents an overview of how temporal impairments are computed in most of the contemporary methods. Generally, the first step is to compute the inter-frame difference of pixel intensities (usually the luminance channel only) and the obtained value can be used as it is or a mean square value can be calculated. Afterwards, various techniques can be applied to determine the location and possibility of frame freeze or frame drops. Some kind of thresholding is then useful to obtain

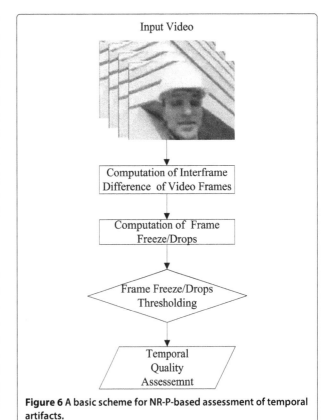

Figure 6 A basic scheme for NR-P-based assessment of temporal artifacts.

more information about the occurrence of a potential temporal artifact. Finally, a suitable pooling mechanism is used to compute an overall value of the artifact under consideration.

Borer [71] presented a model based on the mean square difference (MSD) of frames for measuring jerkiness (both frame jitter and frame freeze) which proved its potential for quality assessment of videos with resolution ranging from QCIF up to HD. This model calculates jerkiness as an accumulative result of multiplication of three functions called relative display time, a monotonic function of display time, and motion intensity of all frames. The display time and motion intensity values are parameterized through a mapping S-shaped function, which is equivalent to a sigmoid function. Besides the fact that the proposed model has reasonable correlation with MOS, it does not take into account the value of the motion intensity at the start of a freezing interval.

An earlier proposed temporal quality method which is centered around measuring the annoyance of frame freeze duration is given in [72]. This method uses MSD value to mark freeze events and builds a mapping function based on such durations of freeze to estimate the subjective MOS. The method is a part of ITU-T Recommendation J.247 Annex C [73] for the objective perceptual quality measurement of video. Although the quality method has not been compared for performance against other methods, it has promising values of correlation with the subjective scores. However, the blind frame freeze detection system proposed in [74] claims to outperform the model [72] in terms of precision of correctly signaling a zero MSD event as a frame freeze event or not. They have presented an algorithm for thresholding such as zero MSD events to be classified as frame freeze events or the absence of it. The proposed method is reported to be equally good in performance for videos encoded using low or high quantization parameter (QP) values.

Wolf proposed an approach to accurately detect video frame dropping in [75]. One of the salient features of this approach is its use in a RR method where an adaptive threshold value is determined to avoid detection of very low amount of motion (e.g., lips movement) as a potential frame drop event. Similar to the temporal-artifact-based methods discussed before, this method also derives its computations from the basic difference in pixel values between frames to check for possible frame drops.

A method for visual quality distortion due to arbitrary frame freeze is discussed in [76]. It recursively aggregates arbitrary freeze distortions in the video under test using a method which they proposed earlier in [77]. Essentially, the approach presented in [77] replaces the sum of various freeze distortions with an equivalent single freeze length for predicting the video quality.

Yang et al. targeted their research to assess both consistent and inconsistent frame drops as a measure of perceptual quality in their contribution found in [78]. The constituents of the quality method are the amount of frame drops, motion of various objects in a video, and localized contrast of temporal quality. Instead of relying on frame rate to be used as a basis for temporal quality method, the event length of frame losses has been used. The proposed method correlates well with subjective MOS for test sequences with a range of frame rates and a variety of motion contents.

A rather general model was proposed in [79] for several fluidity break conditions: isolated, regular, irregular, sporadic, and varying discontinuity durations with different distributions and densities. Similarly, the temporal quality method proposed in [80] accounts for the impact of various frame dropping situations and spatio-temporal luminance variations due to motion.

In [81], the authors have shared their preliminary findings on estimation of the effects of lost frames on visual quality by analyzing the inter-frame correlation present at the output of the rendering application. As the lost frames are replaced by a repetition of the previous frame, this results in high temporal correlation at those locations. Analysis of this correlation results in temporal and distortion maps.

1.3.6 Discussion

Except for temporal impairments, most of the methods reviewed in this section have been proposed and tested for images and not for videos. For example, blockiness is a common artifact at high compression rates and some coding standards such as H.264/AVC include the use of a deblocking filter while the videos are being processed by the codec. The blockiness methods proposed for images can be used in the case of videos as well where a suitable temporal pooling scheme needs to be used. We believe that development and testing of more NR methods of blockiness estimation for videos would be beneficial. For the case of spatial-artifacts-based methods, it is evident that most of the research focus has been aimed at the development of techniques that are based on a specific coding technique or image compression standard. This fact necessitates the focus towards unraveling cross-encoder methodologies. Considering the available methods related to the quantification of perceptual impacts of various temporal artifacts, it is noted that more diverse methods are required in this area that can be applied for a variety of video resolutions and frame rates. It has also been observed that many methods employ some commonly used test database of images and videos which in turn gives an opportunity to compare the performance of competitive methods on the common benchmarks of quality. One important strength of the methods that are tested for the performance using test databases such as LIVE (image or video) is their higher applicability because the media present in such databases have been assessed for overall perceptual quality and not for a particular artifact. However, the test databases should be enriched with new demanding areas such as higher-resolution images and videos (HD and above). Besides declaring the performance of the proposed methods, finding some common approaches for reporting the computational complexity would be interesting. Table 1 presents a summary of the methods discussed in the subsections regarding blurring, blocking, ringing, and temporal artifacts. It is noted that a very low number of methods have been tested for HD resolution images. Competitive methods can be seen at a glance by observing the significantly high values of the performance indicators.

1.4   Multiple artifacts NR-P-based methods

Various artifacts found in images and videos, incurred due to compression or other reasons, can be combined to predict the overall perceived quality. As shown in Figure 7, an image or video can be processed for the extraction of features relevant to different artifacts. A suitable pooling mechanism can be employed to combine the results of different artifact measurements, to make an estimate of overall perceptual quality.

Table 1 Characteristic summary of single-artifact-based metrics

Method	Reference	Processing	Resolution	Test data[a]	Performance[b]
Blurring	Narvekar et al. [21]	JPEG2000	768 × 512	LIVE image, TID2008,	(LIVE) PC = 0.88, SC = 0.88
		Gaussian blur	768 × 512	IVC, Toyoma	(LIVE) PC = 0.91, SC = 0.94
	Ciancio et al. [22]	Multiple	Multiple	6,000 test images	Multiple
	Hassen et al. [28]	Multiple	768 × 512	LIVE image	PC = 0.92, SC = 0.93
	Ferzli et al. [29]	JPEG2000	768 × 512	LIVE image	PC = 0.88, SC = 0.87
		Gaussian blur	768 × 512	LIVE image	PC = 0.93, SC = 0.94
	Varadarajan et al. [34]	Gaussian blur	-	24 test images	PC = 0.75
	Debing et al. [35]	H.264/AVC	HD	1,176 test images	PC = 0.85
	Maaloof et al. [37]	Multiple	768 × 512	LIVE image	PC = 0.96, SC = 0.95
	Chen et al. [41]	Gaussian blur	768 × 512	LIVE image	SC = 0.61
	Chetouani et al. [43]	Gaussian blur	Multiple	LIVE image, IVC	PC = 0.86 (LIVE), 0.94 (IVC)
	Hua et al. [44]	Gaussian blur	768 × 512	LIVE image	PC = 0.96, SC = 0.95
	Oprea et al. [45]	JPEG2000	768 × 512	29 test images	PC = 0.85
Blocking	Chen et al. [46]	JPEG	768 × 512	LIVE image	PC = 0.96, SC = 0.94
		MPEG-2	768 × 512	LIVE video	PC = 0.95, SC = 0.85
	Liu et al. [47]	JPEG	768 × 512	LIVE image	PC = 0.73, SC = 0.91
	Liu et al. [48]	JPEG	768 × 512	LIVE image	PC = 0.79, SC = 0.91
	Zhai et al. [49]	JPEG	768 × 512	LIVE image	PC = 0.96, SC = 0.91
	Babu et al. [50]	JPEG	768 × 512	LIVE image	R-square = 0.95
	Zhang et al. [52]	H.264/AVC	CIF	50 test videos	-
	Hua et al. [53]	JPEG	768 × 512	LIVE image	PC = 0.92, SC = 0.83
	Suthahran et al. [55]	JPEG	768 × 512	LIVE image	PC = 0.94
Ringing	Liu et al. [56]	JPEG	768 × 512	16 test images	-
	Liu et al. [57]	JPEG	768 × 512	55 test images	PC = 0.80, SC = 0.73
	Zuo et al. [59]	-	171 × 256	LIVE image	PC = 0.94
Temporal impairments	Borer [71]	H.264/AVC	CIF, HD	-	-
	Huynh-Thu et al. [72]	-	QCIF	-	PC = 0.95
	Wolf [75]	H.264/AVC	SD	VQEG phase 1	-
	Yang et al. [78]	-	QCIF	6 SRCs	PC = 0.94

[a] The used test database; [b] performance denotes the correlation with subjective assessment, unless stated otherwise; SRC, source sequence; PC, Pearson's correlation coefficient; SC, Spearman's rank order correlation coefficient.

Blurring and ringing are the main associated degradations when JPEG2000 coding is operated at low bitrate conditions. The quality method proposed in [19] predicts quality of JPEG2000 coded images by combining blur and ringing assessment methods. Based on the local image structures, a gradient profile sharpness histogram is calculated for evaluation of a blur estimation method, and a ringing method is generated from regions associated with gradients profiles. Here, a gradient profile is essentially the distribution of the gradient magnitude along the gradient direction. It has been argued that the underlying proposed blur method is insensitive to the inherent blur found in natural images, e.g., out-of-focus blur. The performance of the method is similar to or better than a number of competitive methods while tested on LIVE JPEG2000 and TID2008 datasets.

A rule-based VQA method given in [82] relies on a group of pixel domain features of a video. It includes blockiness and blurriness as well as spatial activity, temporal predictability, edge continuity, motion continuity, and color continuity. The authors have used already available methods to measure the first five features and have

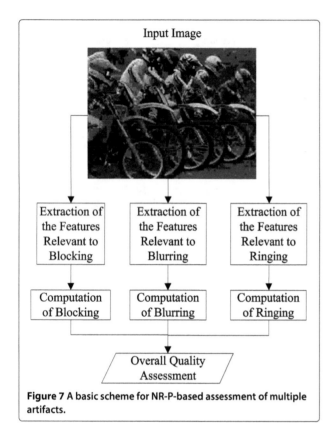

Input Image

Extraction of the Features Relevant to Blocking

Extraction of the Features Relevant to Blurring

Extraction of the Features Relevant to Ringing

Computation of Blocking

Computation of Blurring

Computation of Ringing

Overall Quality Assessment

Figure 7 A basic scheme for NR-P-based assessment of multiple artifacts.

proposed their own methods for the estimation of the motion continuity and color continuity. A multivariate data analysis technique has been used to combine all the features for computing a single quality score. The earliest mentioned three features (blockiness, blurriness, and spatial activity) are measured on a single frame and the rest is calculated on an inter-frame basis. The used approach is to segregate the given set of videos into one of the given feature models and then estimate an initial prediction of the quality measure. After that, using a low-quality version of the video, a correction value is added to the initial quality estimate of the original videos. The authors claim that at the time of publication, this is the first reference-free quality method for H.264/AVC encoded videos which have been tested on a relatively large test database.

Noise is an artifact found in images in the form of a random variation of brightness and color information (see Section 1.3.4 for more details on noise). An empirical formulation of the objective measure of image quality based on blur and noise has been proposed in [83]. The method is based on the level of image intensity variations around its edges. The authors argue that in modern digital cameras, the image signal processor (ISP) enhances the image by removing noise but in doing so, it may deteriorate the image texture. Hence, there is a need of finding a

trade-off between noise and blur and it provides a rationale for combining the estimation of noise and blur in the same method. Specifically, this method considers simulated conditions of white noise as source of the noise artifact in the test stimuli.

Another joint method for noise and blur estimation is found in [84]. It estimates the amount of degradations introduced by additive white noise, Gaussian blur, and defocus blur on the quality of an image. Given the fact that noise disturbs virtually all the spatial frequencies of an image and causes an adverse rise in the higher frequencies while blur has attenuation effect on them, it is justified to study the joint impact of noise and blur on the perceptual quality. The authors have evaluated the impact of noise in both spatial and frequency domain while only the frequency domain is used for blur estimation. The central idea is to influence the power spectra of the image in order to highlight the impact of the distortions on the spectrum properties. The source of noise in the test stimuli used in this work is also white noise. The proposed method has not been tested for its correlation with subjective assessment but it has a competitive performance in comparison with a contemporary method [85] of blind image quality evaluation.

In [86], a sharpness method is presented which is sensitive to the prevailing blur and noise in an image. The mathematical formulation of the method is based on image gradients computed through singular value decomposition (SVD) rather than edge detection as commonly found in contemporary pixel-based structure measures. However, it requires a prior estimate of noise variance. This issue has been resolved in the authors' later contribution [87]. Simulations on realistic noise data have substantiated the potential usage of this method in parameter optimization issues of image restoration such as applications for denoising. The support vector regression (SVR)-based method reported in [88] uses singular vectors from the SVD data instead of using singular values as in [87]. Various artifacts would modify the singular vectors, and hence the geometry of the distorted image will be changed leading to visual annoyance as perceived by humans. The usefulness of the method was tested on multiple image databases with a variety of artifacts. The results were found to be in accordance with subjective ratings.

Another quality method based on gradient statistics of JPEG and JPEG2000 images, degraded by blockiness and blur, is presented in [89]. This method differs from the methods given above in one way that it does not combine the estimated amount of artifacts to yield a single quality score. Instead, it uses the same approach of calculation of local features in gradient domain for both of JPEG and JPEG2000 images and then estimates the quality of the two sets separately. The obtained results lie in accordance with some contemporary methods of blocking estimation in JPEG images and blur estimation in JPEG2000 images. Further, an artificial neural network has been used in [90] to combine a blocking method, a blurring method, and a ringing method to estimate the overall quality of an image. Quality estimators targeted for images encoded by JPEG2000 usually quantify ringing only, but such images may contain blur as well. The method proposed in [91] first determines the type of distortion by using an ANN classifier and then, depending on these results, either uses a ringing [92] or blur [43] method for the quality assessment.

Different from the aforementioned IQA methods, another example of a composite method has been proposed for videos [93]. This method is based on blocking and flickering measure of H.264/AVC encoded videos. It correlates well with subjective quality assessment and also with the structural similarity (SSIM) index [94].

Most of the VQA methods are processed in the luminance plane only to simplify the computational complexity. However, the method proposed in [95] computes three artifacts both in the luminance and chrominance planes of a video. In this method, they compute the significance of the direction in which an artifact is calculated for determining its contribution to perceptual quality assessment. Hence, for example, the value of blur in vertical direction has been given more weighting than the same in horizontal direction. In this method, blocking is measured by computing boundary smoothness between 8×8 blocks and block visibility detection. The third impairment which is considered is jitter/jerkiness. Finally, a multiple regression scheme is employed for weighted integration of the six feature values towards the corresponding quality value. The suggested quality predictor bears competitive correlation with subjective MOS when compared with some contemporary methods as tested on standard-definition television (SDTV) sequences found in VQEG Phase 1 database.

A modular method of combining artifacts both from spatial and temporal domain for quality estimation has been proposed in [80]. The method accounts for frame freeze/jerkiness and clearness/sharpness in MPEG-4 encoded videos. It has been claimed that the combined model is an estimator of global visual quality.

1.4.1 Discussion

Given the fact that a certain type of processing, e.g., JPEG2000 coding, can introduce more than one kind of artifacts, it is imperative to have quality estimators that can assess the impact of more than one artifact. The application of the estimation of multiple artifacts becomes even more interesting when a certain processing that involves removal of an artifact, such as denoising, can produce another artifact due to its underlying methodology. The

popularity of digital cameras in the recent years increases the demand of a quality estimation mechanism to compute multiple artifacts that can be used as an aid to improve the photography experience. Global visual quality estimators such as in [80] are a useful contribution towards making an overall assessment of a video signal as it can be impaired by spatial artifacts like blurring and temporal artifacts like jerkiness at the same time. Table 2 presents a summary of some of the existing methods of quality assessment that are based on the estimation of multiple artifacts. Overall, it is noted that these methods should be tested on higher-resolution images/videos to account for the requirements of the new display devices with capability of presenting resolutions of HD and above.

1.5 Features measures-based methods

An image or video signal can be decomposed to obtain various features that may be used in the process of estimating the perceptual quality of an image or a video. Generally, such features can represent a particular aspect of the visual signal and its relation to the corresponding perceptual quality. Depending upon the nature of the feature with regards to its relation to perceptual quality, a certain feature can be a desired or an unwanted component of an image or video. For instance, the presence of sharpness in an image can be perceptually preferred in many cases and hence it may be considered as a wanted feature. On the other hand, an image with pixel distortions could be considered as of low quality. In addition, certain features represent different characteristics of an image or video and can be used as complementary information besides other features for making an estimate of quality. For example, the amount of spatio-temporal information content of a video can be used to characterize the masking effect on various artifacts that may be present in the signal. More examples of visual quality relevant features include local contrast, brightness, colorfulness, and structural activity [96,97].

Moreover, it has been described in [98] that natural images possess a common statistical behavior. This behavior has been termed as NSS, and it has been found to be a useful feature for the description of image quality. There have been numerous applications of NSS including image segmentation, denoising, and texture analysis and synthesis. Although it was concluded in [98] that the major usage of scene statistics would be in the investigation of visual sensory processing, these have recently been proved to be quite useful in the design of no-reference quality methods. It has been found that such common statistical characteristics get distorted by image processing applications like image compression, and a quantitative measure of this distortion can yield the relevant variations in the image quality. Thus, an NSS-driven NR quality assessment method would provide the measure of the

Table 2 Characteristic summary of multiple-artifacts-based and features measures-based metrics

Method	Reference	Processing	Resolution	Test data[a]	Performance[b]
Multiple artifacts NR-P-based	Liang et al. [19]	JPEG2000	768 × 512	LIVE image, TID2008	(LIVE) PC = 0.92, SC = 0.94
	Pastrana et al. [80]	MPEG-4	QCIF, CIF	6 SRCs	PC = 0.9, SC = 0.9
	Oelbaum et al. [82]	H.264/AVC	CIF	300 test videos	PC = 0.82, SC = 0.75
	Choi et al. [83]	JPEG2000, noise	768 × 512	LIVE image	PC = 0.91
	Cohen et al. [84]	Noise and blur	256 × 256	75 test images	-
	Zhu et al. [86]	JPEG2000	512 × 768	LIVE image	-
	Narwaria et al. [88]	Multiple	Multiple	Multiple	(LIVE) PC = 0.8894
	Liu et al. [89]	JPEG, JPEG2000	768 × 512	LIVE image	PC = 0.92
Natural scene statistics	Zhou et al. [99]	JPEG2000	768 × 512	LIVE image	-
	Lu et al. [100]	Multiple	768 × 512	LIVE image	Multiple
	Shen et al. [102]	Multiple	512 × 512	LIVE +26, 260 test images	Multiple
	Moorthy et al. [103]	Multiple	768 × 512, 512 × 384	LIVE image, TID2008	Multiple
Pixel-based features	Gastaldo et al. [111]	JPEG	480 × 720, 768 × 512	LIVE image	PC = 0.94
	Li et al. [112]	Multiple	768 × 512	LIVE image	PC = 0.87, SC = 0.87
	Zhang et al. [113]	JPEG2000	768 × 512	LIVE image	PC = 0.93, SC = 0.92
	Zhang et al. [97]	JPEG, JPEG2000	768 × 512	LIVE image	PC = 0.92, SC = 0.92
	Yao et al. [119]	-	-	VQEG phase 1	PC = 0.86, SC = 0.85
	Ries et al. [121]	H.264/AVC	SIF	10 SRCs	PC = 0.93
	Ries et al. [122]	H.264/AVC	SIF	10 SRCs	PC = 0.93
Pixel-based features and artifacts	Sazzad et al. [114]	JPEG2000	768 × 512	LIVE image	PC = 0.93, SC = 0.96
	Jiang et al. [127]	MPEG-2	HD	72 test images	PC = 0.91
	Keimel et al. [129]	H.264/AVC	HD	7 SRC videos	PC = 0.86, SC = 0.85
	Sazzad et al. [130]	JPEG	640 × 480	490 test image pairs	PC = 0.93

[a]The used test database; [b]performance denotes the correlation with subjective assessment, unless stated otherwise; SRC, source sequence; PC, Pearson's correlation coefficient; SC, Spearman's rank order correlation coefficient.

unnaturalness introduced into the natural scene statistics under the effect of image distortions. Figure 8 shows a basic schematic block diagram of feature-based methods. We have divided the review of such methods into three subsections: (i) Natural scene statistics, (ii) Pixel-based features, and (iii) Pixel-based features and artifacts.

1.5.1 Natural scene statistics

It has been claimed in [92] that the distortion introduced in the nonlinear dependencies found in natural images can be quantified for making an estimate of perceptual quality. Based on that notion, the authors presented an NSS-driven approach for quality assessment of images processed by wavelet-based compression standards like JPEG2000.

Similarly, the NSS-based image quality prediction approach presented in [99] is also limited to be applicable only to JPEG2000. The authors have used a neural

network to regress between inputs from NSS-based spectral amplitude fall-off curves in combination with positional similarity measure of wavelet coefficients and the corresponding quality value.

Harnessed by the measures to keep the model attributes unaffected by image content variations, the method proposed in [100] uses a contourlet transform [101] to quantify the degradations incurred on NSS. The authors show that wavelet transform does not completely exhibit the artifacts present in the image and the effect of degradations is visible in all the subbands of the contourlet domain. Hence, the contourlet domain can be more effective in image quality assessment. The proposed method has a clear advantage in precisely predicting the image quality while tested for images degraded by JPEG2000 and JPEG compression and distortions like Gaussian blur, fast fading channel, and white noise. Similarly, a statistical relationship between the characteristics of NSS in

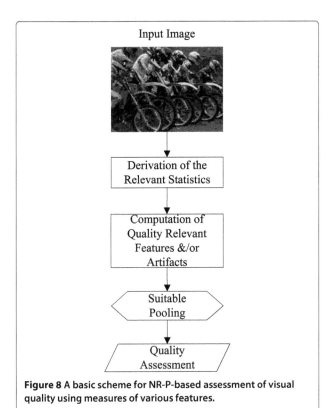

Input Image

↓

Derivation of the
Relevant Statistics

↓

Computation of
Quality Relevant
Features &/or
Artifacts

↓

Suitable
Pooling

↓

Quality
Assessment

Figure 8 A basic scheme for NR-P-based assessment of visual quality using measures of various features.

images and the corresponding quality values was studied in [102] to engineer a reference-free quality method. In order to provide the quality ranking of the filtered natural images, a histogram of a combination of image transforms, namely, curvelet, wavelet, and cosine transform is computed. The considered distortions include noise, blur, and artifacts introduced by compression using JPEG2000 and JPEG. As the authors pointed out, this is one of the few quality methods which can quantify the perceptual impact of such a broad range of degradation types. The additional advantage of this method is its ability to classify images on the basis of the presence of one or more of these artifacts. The proposed method was tested on a large set of images from the LIVE image database as well as authors' own test set of images. As a result, a promising level of correlation with subjective quality assessment was obtained.

The distortion identification-based image quality estimation method proposed in [103] offers an NSS-based approach of image quality prediction framework and algorithm. Firstly, the pertinent distortion is identified. Then, NSS features are used to quantify the relevant quality value which is largely independent of the distortion type present in the image. The used feature set describes (i) scale and orientation selective statistics, (ii) orientation selective statistics, (iii) correlations across scales, (iv) spatial correlation, and (v) across orientation statistics.

Support vector regression is used to train the model, and the proposed method is proved to be comparable in precision of assessment to full reference methods such as peak signal-to-noise ratio (PSNR) and SSIM. The method was evaluated on images found in TID2008 and LIVE databases. It was found quite closely correlated to subjective assessment of image quality and hence proved itself to be test-set independent.

The idea of the impact of distortions on NSS has been used in [104] for prediction of video quality where each frame of the video is decomposed into a Laplacian pyramid of a number of subbands. Intra-subband statistics including mean, variance, skewness, kurtosis, energy, entropy, and inter-subband statistics, namely, Jensen Shannon divergence, SSIM, and smoothness are computed. A Minkowski pooling scheme is adopted to yield a single value out of the aforementioned statistics. The proposed method is reported to perform better than some FR metrics while tested on the LIVE video quality database.

Similar to NSS, a basic model is presented in [105] to develop an NR quality method based on temporal statistics of videos called as natural motion statistics (NMS). The theory of independent component analysis (ICA) has been applied in order to compute NMS. The authors have shown that independent components calculated from the optical flow vectors of a video signal follow the Laplacian distribution. Consequently, it has been observed that the root mean square (RMS) error of the fit between the extracted independent components and Laplacian distribution can be used as an indicator of video quality.

Saad et al. have presented their DCT statistics-based image integrity index in [106]. The central idea is to track the change in particular statistics of an image while it traverses from being original to a distorted one. The proposed framework is mainly DCT based. Owing to the perceptual relevance, some features representing structural information and contrast of an image have been extracted from the DCT values at two levels of spatial sampling. An improved version of this approach is found in [107] where the impact of NSS features for various perceptual degrees of degradation has been added.

In contrast to most of the approaches mentioned before that involve transformation of an image into another domain such as DCT, the NSS-based quality estimator presented in [108] performs in the spatial domain. Locally normalized luminance and its products-based empirical distribution is used to compute quality relevant features for building a spatial NSS model. The performance of the proposed method has been found to be better than FR methods such as PSNR and SSIM. The authors have validated the NR application of this method by employing it in an image denoising system. A similar approach has been adopted in [109] to define latent quality factors that were used to estimate the image quality.

The idea of NSS features-based quality estimator has been used in the case of stereoscopic images as well. In reference [110], 2D- and 3D-based statistical features are extracted from stereopsis to estimate the image quality. A support vector machine model has been trained using these features, and the model has been tested using the LIVE 3D database.

1.5.2 Pixel-based features

There are some methods of no-reference quality estimation which rely on certain statistics, mainly spatial features, derived from pixels of an image or video to perform the corresponding perceptual quality evaluation. In [111], the authors present an example where they have used objective features related to energy, entropy, homogeneousness, and contrast from the color correlogram of an image. These features have been used to train an ANN which serves as a prediction model. Li et al. [112] have also deployed an ANN-based model to devise a quality estimation method using perceptually relevant image features including phase congruency, entropy of the degraded image, and gradient of the degraded image. The importance of phase of an image for its fidelity representation is well known, and the gradient of an image is an implication of changes in the luminance of an image. An ANN model is also used in the image semantic quality method presented in [96] where a variety of quality descriptive features have been used. The authors argue that the overall visual quality can be seen in terms of the usefulness and naturalness of an image. Sharpness and clarity are considered as the representatives of usefulness of an image, whereas brightness and colorfulness represent naturalness. These four representations of usefulness and brightness are further branched into a large set of pixel-based features; edge pixel distribution, contrast, mean brightness, and color dispersion are a few of the used 14 features. The advantage of using higher number of features has been shown by better performance of the predictor.

Compared to the aforementioned methods that rely on the process of training a particular model by using an extracted set of features, the pixel-activity-based method proposed in [113] does not use such methodology. The focus here is on the activity map of an image, essentially controlled by features, namely, monotone-changing, zero-crossing (ZC), and the existence of inactive pixels, which are calculated for non-overlapping image blocks. The concept of ZC has been used to refer to the places in the Laplacian of an image where the value of the Laplacian passes through zero, i.e., the points where the Laplacian changes sign. Such points often occur at edges in an image. The use of ZC as a constituent of an activity map

is justified as the method was proposed for JPEG2000 encoded images; and ringing, which can be caused by JPEG2000-based compression, has the potential of generating ZC around contours. Moreover, spatial features consisting of edge information and pixel distortion have been used to predict quality of JPEG2000 encoded images in [114]. Pixel distortion is computed using standard deviation of a central pixel and a measure of difference between central pixel and its closest neighbor pixels. Edge information relies on zero-crossing rate and a histogram measure. Particle swarm optimization has been employed to integrate these features into a single quality index. The authors have presented a similar method in their contribution [115].

The notion of quality estimation with regards to structural changes in images as a result of distortions has gained widespread attention. The FR method SSIM [94] is a commonly used representative method of this area. Zhang et al. [97] have put forward a similar approach of quality estimation based on structural changes. However, the nature of the particular distortion should be known beforehand. This method can be used to evaluate degradation caused by the following artifacts but one set at a time: (i) Gaussian blur and noise, (ii) blur and ringing, and (iii) blockiness. In a nutshell, local structural activity is taken in the form of direction spread whereas structural activity weight is computed through a measure of structural strength and zero-crossing activity.

Some feature-based methods make use of the properties of HVS to govern the performance of the method for better correlation with subjective assessment. A 3D multispectral wavelet transform-based method of NR quality estimation for color video has been given in [116]. Various channels of the HVS have been represented by wavelet decomposition of the video. To invoke the impact of the HVS, a perceptual mask of sensitivity with integrated impacts of spatio-temporal contrast and luminance has been applied to all wavelet bands. The final step is to draw a perceptual mask weighted flow tensor between successive frames to define the method. An ANN has been used in [117] with an extreme learning machine (ELM) algorithm for determining the relationship between spatial statistics of an image and its corresponding quality. These statistics are mainly HVS-inspired features, namely, edge amplitude, edge length, background activity, and background luminance of an image. As the proposed method is basically targeted at JPEG encoded images, some of the underlying methodologies which help calculate these features are focused on computation of blockiness. Since DCT coding is used in video coding also, the proposed algorithm can be generalized to be workable for video quality assessment.

In the experiments on determining the visual interest for different objects and locations inside an image, it has been found that HVS perception is not spatially uniform. Instead, there are specific areas called region of interest (ROI), which draw more attention and hence contribute more towards overall quality assessment of an image. Treisman et al. [118] observed that the visual system notices and codes different features in parallel channels before the observer actually recognizes the objects in an image. Features such as color, brightness, and orientation can be pooled together to form a unique entity to be observed. Based on this observation, there exist IQA methods which assess perceptual quality of an image by focusing mainly on those ROIs. One such method is proposed in [119] where the impact of importance of various ROIs in a video frame has been integrated into a wavelet-based just noticeable difference (JND) profile of visual perception. The proposed method works better than some contemporary methods when it was tested on the VQEG Phase I database.

In order to estimate the impact of packet loss impairments on video quality, a method based on edge strength around macroblock boundaries is proposed in [51]. Edge strength values are processed through a low-pass filter, and a threshold value is applied to compute the edge maps of adjacent rows. Finally, the impact of packet loss is computed through a difference between these edge maps.

In order to quantify the quality of enhanced images, the method given in [120] divides an image into smooth and textured areas. A JND formulation of perception is derived based on the local average brightness and local spatial frequency. The effect of enhancement is monitored through a comparison of local brightness and a JND threshold. The performance of the proposed method is reported to be better than that of conventional average local variance-based methods.

Features-based assessment of the content of an image or video can be used in the estimation of perceptual quality. Ries et al. have shown the relevance of the content class of videos in the process of determination of the visual quality in [121]. The authors classify a given set of videos into five groups based on the content. One of such group, called class here, contains videos which have a small moving ROI with a still scene in the background. Another content class has videos with huge spread of angle of movie capturing device and is called panorama. These content classes are created based on the statistics that are mainly related to motion dynamics of a video. Values of zero motion vector ratio, mean size of motion vector, uniformity of the movement, horizontalness of movement, and greenness are the classification parameters which are used to segregate the set of videos into different content classes. The central idea of the method is to first check the content class of a video and then estimate the visual quality based on bitrate and frame rate. The authors continued working on the same idea in their

contribution found in [122] where they have presented a method aimed at the most common content classes of videos for handheld devices. Khan et al. have proposed a content-based method to combine encoding and transmission level parameters to predict video quality in [123]. Based on spatio-temporal features, the videos are first divided into content-based groups using cluster analysis. Adaptive network-based fuzzy inference system (ANFIS) and a regression model have been used separately to estimate the quality score. As per their results, transmission parameters like packet error rate have more impact on the quality than the compression parameters such as frame rate etc. The underlying techniques of ANFIS model and content clustering have been used in the authors' other contributions as given in [124,125].

1.5.3 Pixel-based features and artifacts

Some of the existing no-reference perceptual quality assessment methods are composed of a set of spatial features combined with some measurement of artifacts. A set of spatial artifacts has been combined with some spatial image features to estimate perceptual image quality in [126]. An ANN model was trained with these features for the quality prediction. Working on a similar approach, the method presented in [127] integrates spatial features such as picture entropy (represents the amount of information of a picture) and frequency energy (distribution of frequency energy in images) with artifacts, namely, blur and blockiness. The proposed method seems prominent because of its use of the chrominance information also while most of the contemporary quality measures are based on statistics from the luminance channel only. In this contribution, it has been shown that extraction of these features from ROI further improves the value of correlation with subjective scores. Five features of quality significance have been used to model an ANN-based quality predictor in [128] where the features set constitutes a measure of artifacts such as blocking and ringing and spatial statistics such as zero-crossing rate, edge activity measure, and z-score. Another method built on similar principle is found in [129] where the amount of blurring and blocking has been combined with spatial activity in an image and predictability of an image. A partial least square regression (PLSR) approach has been used to determine the function between these features and the quality value.

The approach given in [130] uses local segmented features related to degradation and dissimilarity for quality estimation of 3D images. In fact, the essential methodology used in [114] for 2D images have been extended to be employed for 3D images in [130]. One of the key means used to check disparity in left and right images of a stereoscopic image is the block-based edge information measure.

The authors in [131] propose a method for the assessment of facial image quality. Eye-detection, sharpness, noise, contrast, and luminance values of a test image are calculated. A weighted sum of these quantities constitutes the value of the quality method. In view of the discussion presented in [132], relatively more weighting has been given to sharpness and eye-detection as they are more important for determining facial image quality.

In [133], a set of artifacts, namely, blocking, ringing, truncation of the number of bits for image values, and noise is combined with a set of features including contrast and sharpness for designing a video quality prediction method. Each of these parameters is fitted separately in a functional relationship with subjective assessment of quality such that the correlation between the parameter values and subjective scores is maximized. Subsequently, these individual fitting functions are merged together to form a joint relationship with the perceptual quality. The data used for training includes original videos as well as different combinations of sharpness-enhanced and noise-contaminated videos. The trained model is tested on another data set which reveals a promising correlation with subjective scores.

Unlike the aforementioned NR-P-based artifacts or features measures-based methods, the mean square error distortion due to network impairments for a H.264/AVC encoded video is computed in [134]. An estimate of MSE is computed using the pattern of lost macroblocks due to an erroneous transmission of the video. Information about the lost macroblocks is estimated through the traces of the error concealment process. The same methodology has been enhanced in [135] for more general application scenarios such as no assumption is done about a certain error concealment algorithm and it does not require the knowledge of exact slicing structure.

1.5.4 Discussion

From the review of the features measures-based methods, we can make some general observations. The approach of estimating visual quality by quantifying the impact of distortions on natural scene statistics has gained a wide interest to gauge degradations due to different image processing techniques including compression. However, more of such approaches should be tested in the case of videos as well. Moreover, assessment of quality degradation due to network impairments using NSS-based approaches could be useful. The pixel-based and features-based approaches can be seen as composed of techniques that rely on a variety of spatial features including those related to edges, contrast, and some measures of structural information. The performance of these approaches can be enhanced by adapting the computational procedure with regards to the input of HVS preferences. Additionally, including the impact of mostly occurring artifacts such as blurring,

blocking, or noise could be an advantage. We observe that most of the pixel domain features-based approaches have been designed for images and it is desirable to generalize the relevant methods for applications in the case of videos. Temporal pooling quality methods such as Minkowski summation or other methods such as adaptive to perceptual distortion [136] can be used for this purpose. Table 2 presents a summary of some of the methods discussed in this section. It is evident that most of the methods in this category exhibit very promising performance, with correlation coefficient values equal to or higher than 0.85.

1.6 Bitstream-based methods

An estimate of the quality of an encoded video can be made by parsing the coded bitstream to deliver readily available features such as encoding parameters and network quality of service (QoS)-related parameters. The methods that adopt the usage of the bitstream data for quality estimation avoid the computational complexity of processing the full video data, as full decoding of the input video is not usually required in the case of bitstream-based methods. Another advantage of this type of methods is the use of readily available information from the bitstream that is significant for the quality estimation, for example, the motion vectors, coding modes, and quantization parameter values. However, these methods are inherently coding standard specific as different encoders have different formats of bitstream. There is a range of quality relevant features that can be extracted by partial decoding or primary analysis of the bitstream data. The performance of such methods significantly depends upon the level of access to the bitstream [137]. A block diagram of general framework in bitstream-based methods is given in Figure 9. We have divided the discussion of these methods into three categories based on the level of information used for processing, in accordance with the standardized models recommended by telecommunication standardization sector of International Telecommunication Union (ITU-T), as discussed in [138,139]. This includes parametric models (parametric planning model and parametric packet-layer model) and bitstream layer model. In the former type, extrinsic features of a video that are of parametric nature such as bitrate, frame rate, and packet loss rate are used. Bitstream layer models have detailed access to the payload and intrinsic features related to a video such as coding modes, quantization parameter, and DCT coefficients. The standardization of these models includes the methods designed for estimation of audio quality as well, but our discussion is limited to video quality only.

1.6.1 Parametric planning model

The parametric planning models have rather low complexity as they do not access the bitstream and utilize

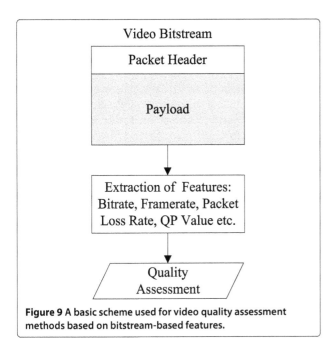

Figure 9 A basic scheme used for video quality assessment methods based on bitstream-based features.

bitrate, codec type, and packet loss rate for making a crude estimation of video quality. The work item related to this category in ITU-T is known as Opinion model for video-telephony applications, G.1070 [140]. ITU-T Recommendation G.1070 proposes a method for the assessment of videophone quality, based on speech and video parameters, that can be used by the network performance planners for ensuring the given level of end-to-end quality of the service. A quality prediction model for MPEG-2 and H.264/AVC encoded videos for IPTV is presented in [141]. The model takes some parameters related to encoding information, packet information and client information to assess the overall quality. In reference [142], a parametric model is proposed that is based on a simple method of estimating MSE that occurs due to a given pattern of packet loss. The authors derived a relationship between average motion vector length and MSE and this relation gives a fair estimate of the actual MSE.

1.6.2 Parametric packet-layer model

The packet layer models have access to the packet header of the bitstream and can extract a limited set of parameters including bitrate on sequence or frame level, frame rate and type, and packet loss rate. Parametric packet-layer models are also known as QoS-based methods. The work item related to this category in ITU-T is known as non-intrusive parametric model for the assessment of performance of multimedia streaming (P.NAMS) [143]. The visual quality estimation method proposed in [144] presents an approach where it is not required to decode the video at any level, suitable for situations where

the encoded video is encrypted. Given the observation that error concealment is more effective when there is less motion in the video, an estimation of the motion dynamics of a particular video is required to assess the effectiveness of an error concealment strategy. In this method, the ratio of the average of the B (bi-predictive coded) frame data size to the average of the size of all frames is compared with a predetermined threshold to adjust the value of the video quality score. The results obtained from the effectiveness of error concealment are refined by adjusting the values in accordance with the importance of the region in which the error has occurred.

The models in [141,145] are designed for H.264/AVC coded SD and HD videos where a support vector machine (SVM) classifier has been used to assess the video quality based on the visibility of packet loss. By the same research group, the packet layer model presented in [146] uses video resolution, bitrate, packet loss rate, and some information of the codec settings to design a quality estimator for H.264/AVC- and MPEG-2-based encoded videos. An improvement on such statistical parameters-based models is found in [147] where temporal and spatial characteristics of a video are estimated from the packet header to build a content-adaptive model for quality assessment. The no-reference method presented in [148] is based on a nonlinear relationship between an objective quality metric and the quality-related parameters. To make it computationally simple, the authors have used only two parameters, namely, packet loss rate and the value of the interval between intra-frames of a video.

In [149], the authors have presented preliminary results of their investigation into streamlining the impacts of different conditions of packet loss over visible degradation to classify packet loss as visible or invisible. The parameters used in the decision making are extracted from the encoded bitstream. This model was tested for SD resolution H.264/AVC coded videos. If 25% or less subjects perceived an artifact, such a packet loss event was classified as invisible. If 75% or more subjects perceived an artifact, the corresponding packet loss event was classified as visible. In this case, the artifacts perceived by subjects between 25% and 75% were not accounted for at all. This issue was addressed in the authors' later contribution [150] where all artifacts perceived by less than 75% subjects were classified as invisible. Moreover, they extended the model by including more quality-relevant parameters and generalized it by testing it on HD videos. The authors applied the same model for High Efficiency Video Coding (HEVC) encoded videos to examine its cross-standard performance, as reported in [151]. It was observed that the artifact visibility slightly increases while changing from H.264/AVC to HEVC-based video coding.

1.6.3   Bitstream layer model

In the bitstream-based methods, bitstream layer models have access to most of the data that can be used for the video quality estimation. The work item parametric non-intrusive bitstream assessment of video media streaming quality (P.NBAMS) [152] in its mode 1 (parsing mode) is related to the bitstream layer models. In this mode, it is allowed to do any kind of analysis of the bitstream except the usage of the pixel data. The input information includes parameters extracted from the packet header and payload. Besides the parameters included in the parametric models, this model uses QP, DCT coefficients of the coded video, and pixel information. This makes the model comparatively more complex but it generally offers better performance. A low-complexity solution of video quality prediction based on bitstream extracted parameters is found in [153]. The features used are mainly related to the encoding parameters and are taken on sequence level. Low complexity has been achieved by using a simple multilinear regression system for building the relationship between the parameters and quality values. An improvement of this approach is presented in [154] where the required number of parameters has been reduced for computational efficiency and the prediction accuracy has been improved by the virtue of the usage of an ANN. A further improvement is found in [155] where a larger features set is used and the prediction of subjective MOS is also performed. A set of 48 bitstream parameters related to slice coding type, coding modes, various statistics of motion vectors, and QP value was used in [156] to predict the quality of high-definition television (HDTV) video encoded by H.264/AVC. PLSR was used as tool for regression between the feature set and subjective assessment. This method outperformed the authors' earlier contribution [129] and some contemporary objective methods of visual quality assessment.

H.264/AVC employs an in-loop filter to suppress blocking, and this filter has a specific parameter called boundary strength (BS) assigned to transform blocks. Statistics of BS combined with QP and average bitrate has been used in [157] to predict quality of H.264/AVC encoded videos. The proposed method formulates a linear combination of these parameters and a linear regression was conducted to determine its relationship with the subjective assessment scores. A motion-based visual quality estimation method was proposed in [158] for H.264/AVC encoded videos. In this method, some statistical features related to motion vectors along with bitrate and frame rate are calculated. PCA is used to identify the parameters most influential in the estimation of video quality value. Finally, the selected set of features is fed to an equation of quality computation. The inclusion of motion features into the reference-free quality assessment

is justified by the fact that the reduction in visual quality is less for a certain level of compression when the motion is low, for example, the case of videos with static scenes.

A PSNR estimator for H.264/AVC encoded video is presented in [159] where bitrate, QP value, and coding mode are used as the features for quality prediction. The method given in [160] uses QP and block coding mode parameters for quality prediction of H.264/AVC encoded videos.

Based on an opinion model from ITU-T [140], an automatic QoE monitoring method is proposed in [161]. It depends on the network level information derived from packet loss pattern and loss rank of a frame in a group of pictures (GOP) and a measure of motion vectors to represent motion activity to train an ANN model against subjective scores of expert viewers.

In [162], the authors proposed a framework for quality estimation where a QoS parameter, packet loss rate, is combined with spatial and temporal complexities of a video. Usually, a complete decoding of the video is required to estimate its spatial and temporal complexity as these complexity values are generally obtained by an average measure of the pixel variance of codeblocks in a frame. However, the authors have proposed a method of estimating spatial and temporal complexity from the bitstream information only. Specifically, they have developed a rate-distortion model for QP value and bitrate which helps in estimating the complexity measure. Combining this complexity estimate with effects of packet loss delivers a measure of frame quality. Temporal domain quality degradation is computed through occurrences of frame freeze or frame loss. An overall estimate of the video quality is made by a pooling scheme which integrates the spatial and temporal quality indicators. The authors have argued that the suggested method can be used for real-time video services due to its fair accuracy and efficiency in computational cost.

In [163], the impact of compression on quality estimated through MSE prediction using DCT coefficients data [164] is combined with (i) a packet loss model similar to the one presented in ITU-T Recommendation G. 1070 [140], (ii) a frame type-dependent packet loss model, and (iii) a frame type- and error pattern-dependent model separately. It was concluded from the obtained results that a combination of [164] and (iii) offers the best prediction of visual quality of these three combinations.

Bitstream layer methods can also utilize the DCT coefficients data of the encoded image or video, as it can be obtained by partial decoding [138]. There are several such methods which make a quality estimate based on the statistics of the DCT coefficient values. Eden [165] has proposed an algorithm for estimation of PSNR using the assumption that the probability distribution function (pdf) of DCT coefficients follows Laplacian distribution for H.264/AVC encoded videos. A modified Laplacian model for estimation of DCT coefficients distribution has been presented in [166] for JPEG images. The authors proposed to use maximum likelihood with linear prediction estimates to compute the parameter λ (lambda) of the Laplacian pdf, where λ is a parameter of the distribution. Investigation of the correlation between distribution parameters at adjoining frequencies and integration of the prediction results using maximum-likelihood parameters are the key components of this method. They have also used Watson's model [167] for perceptual weighting of local error estimates in an image. The method given in [166] has been upgraded to be workable for videos in [168]. Here, the video quality predictor has a local error assessment unit, besides having statistics from motion vectors. These values are passed to a perceptual spatio-temporal model that incorporates the HVS sensitivity to produce the visual quality score. Two more methods based on the similar approach from these authors are PSNR estimation for H.264/AVC encoded videos [169] and PSNR estimation for MPEG-2 encoded videos as given in [170].

Contrary to the assumption of Laplacian distribution to model DCT coefficients, it has been argued in [171] that a Cauchy distribution better suits the H.264/AVC encoded data in the process of quality estimation. The proposed approach has been found to be better than the Laplacian distribution [165] in terms of bias between the actual and estimated values of PSNR.

The authors in [172] have used DCT basis functions to evaluate kurtosis measure of images for quality assessment. Three different kinds of kurtosis measures have been made, namely, 1D kurtosis based on frequency band, basis function-based 1D kurtosis, and 2D kurtosis. However, the proposed scheme is meant only for images degraded by blur and it has been tested on LIVE [14] data set JPEG2000 encoded images.

Nishikawa et al. presented a PSNR estimation method of JPEG2000 coded videos in [173] which is actually a no-reference version of their earlier article that needed reference information [174]. The method estimates the PSNR by using wavelet coefficients from the neighboring frames of the frame which has lost some compressed codeblocks. It is assumed that the effect of packet loss upon codeblocks is possible to compute at the receiver end, given that only packet loss occurs and no bit errors exist.

1.6.4 Discussion

Bitstream-based methods of VQA have recently received a significant attention for their computational simplicity and applications in the online quality monitoring. Potentially, the main advantage of these methods is the variety in choice of the features which can be used for quality estimation that in turn means the privilege of adapting to the desired level of complexity. As compared to pixel-based processing, the bitstream-based methods have special advantage of having access to readily available information such as bitrate, frame rate, QP, motion vectors, and various types of information regarding the impacts of network impairments. However, these methods are coding scheme specific that makes them less generally applicable. In the case of parametric planning models, the performance of quality estimation remains limited due to the constraints of the information that can be obtained from the allowed level of access to the bitstream. Packet layer models have better performance with popular application in intermediate nodes of a network as they do not need complex processing and decryption of the data. Bitstream layer models are superior in the performance and the complexity can be flexible depending upon the desired level of accuracy. For possible future works in this area, some comparative performance reports of various models, such as the ones presented in [139,175] would be useful to further accelerate the research in designing better bitstream-based VQA approaches. As we notice in the summary of bitstream-based methods in Table 3, the research community has mostly embraced H.264/AVC-based coding for the design of such methods. It would be advantageous to develop such methods for other popular coding standards as well. Moreover, analysis of the features relevant for quality estimation for the recently approved ITU-T standard of video coding, namely, H.265/HEVC [176] would be useful. For example, in [177], it has been shown that the existing methods of MSE estimation are not feasible for HEVC as it has significantly different coding structure as compared to the previous standards.

1.7 Hybrid of NR-P and NR-B methods

There are no-reference visual quality estimation methods which combine features from the coded bitstream and some statistics from the decoded media. This type of methods inherits the simplicity of computation from the bitstream-based approaches, and further accuracy in quality estimation is achieved by adding input from the pixel-based approaches. Therefore, such methods can avoid some of the difficulties involved in the pixel and bitstream-based methods [178]. One such example is the fusion of artifacts like blocking or blurring with parameters derived from motion vectors to build up a quality estimation method. The work item P.NBAMS [152] in its mode 2 (full decoding mode) is related to the hybrid models where the information from the coded bitstream as well as reconstructed video can be used. Figure 10 gives an overview of the methodology used in this type of methods. Essentially, the choice of the features for extraction from

Table 3 Characteristic summary of NR-B and hybrid metrics

Method	Reference	Processing	Resolution	Test data[a]	Performance[b]
Bitstream-based	Saad et al. [106]	Multiple	768 × 512	LIVE image	SC = 0.8
	Saad et al. [107]	Multiple	768 × 512	LIVE image	SC = 0.93, PC = 0.93
	Yamada et al. [144]	H.264/AVC	1,440 × 1,080	-	PC = 0.85
	Rossholm et al. [153]	H.264/AVC	QCIF	288 test videos	PC (PEVQ) = 0.95
	Shahid et al. [154]	H.264/AVC	QCIF	288 test videos	PC (PEVQ) = 0.98
	Shahid et al. [155]	H.264/AVC	QCIF, CIF	120 test videos	PC = 0.98
	Keimel et al. [156]	H.264/AVC	HD	-	PC = 0.93
	Lee [157]	H.264/AVC	QCIF	13 SRCs	PC = 0.9
	Ries et al. [158]	H.264/AVC	QCIF, SIF, CIF	-	PC = 0.80
	Yang et al. [162]	MPEG-4	QCIF	-	PC = 0.93, SC = 0.93
	Eden [165]	H.264/AVC	HD	5 SRCs	PC (PSNR) = 0.99
	Brandão et al. [166]	JPEG	768 × 512	LIVE image	PC = 0.97, SC = 0.97
	Brandão et al. [168]	H.264	-	50 test videos	PC = 0.93, SC = 0.95
	Zhang et al. [172]	JPEG2000	768 × 512	LIVE image	PC = 0.9
	Ichigaya et al. [191]	MPEG-2	SD, HD	26 test videos	PC (PSNR) = 0.95
Hybrid of NR-P and NR-B	Farias et al. [181]	H.264/AVC	CIF	5 SRCs	Regression (PSNR) = 0.79
	Shanableh [182]	MPEG-2	CIF	-	PC = 0.93
	Shanableh [183]	MPEG-2	CIF	-	NRMSE = 0.046
	Davis et al. [184]	H.264/AVC	-	18 test videos	PC = 0.91
	Yamada et al. [186]	H.264/AVC	SD	-	PC = 0.95
	Sugimoto et al. [189]	H.264/AVC	HD	14 SRCs	PC = 0.91

[a]The used test database; [b]performance denotes the correlation with subjective assessment, unless stated otherwise. SRC, source sequence; NRMSE, normalized root mean square error; PC, Pearson's correlation coefficient; SC, Spearman's rank order correlation coefficient.

bitstream or pixel domain depends on the design requirements of a method, the availability of a certain type of data for quality estimation, and the encoding scheme. The discussion on this class of methods is divided into two categories, namely, pixel-based and bitstream-based features or artifacts, and statistics of transform coefficients.

1.7.1 Pixel-based and bitstream-based features or artifacts
Video quality-related features and measures of artifacts can be computed both from the pixel and bitstream data and can be pooled for an overall quality estimate. One such method which focuses on quantifying the perceptual quality of H.264/AVC encoded videos degraded by loss of packets in the IP networks is presented in [179]. The error incurred due to packet loss becomes propagative due to the two types of coding predictions involved in H.264/AVC encoders, namely, intra-prediction (spatial) and inter-prediction (temporal) at the encoder end. Even more errors can be introduced while the decoder tries to conceal for the prediction residuals and/or motion vectors lost due to missing packets in the IP bitstream. For simulating the packet loss conditions, a packet loss rate in the range [0.1, 20]% with error patterns generated

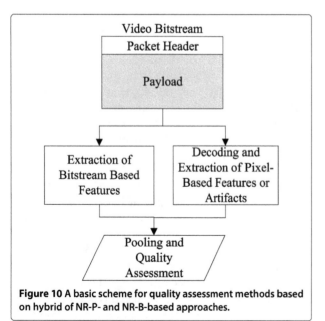

Figure 10 A basic scheme for quality assessment methods based on hybrid of NR-P- and NR-B-based approaches.

using a two-state Gilbert model set for average burst length of three packets was used. Quantitatively, the measures involved in the modeling of the proposed method encompass the impact of errors due to concealment, errors propagated due to loss of reference MBs, and the channel-induced degradation due to H.264/AVC-specific coding techniques. The calculations of these distortions are done on the macroblock level, and the resulting values are summed up to frame and sequence levels. It has been observed that the proposed method yields results which bear good correlation with SSIM [94]. Another method was presented by the same authors in their earlier published contribution [180] where the effects of loss of motion vector information and prediction residuals were incorporated for quality estimation. A method in which transmission and compression artifacts are integrated for VQA is presented in [181]. The constituents of the method are estimations of blockiness, blurring, and packet loss ratio.

Two MPEG-4 encoded video quality prediction methods based on several MB level statistics, derived from bitstream and reconstructed videos, are reported in [182] for PSNR and in [183] for SSIM. A plethora of bitstream-based and pixel-based features at macroblock level have been used in these two methods. One of the distinctive aspects of these two contributions is the usage of different models for system identification between the parameters and the corresponding quality index. In the method targeted for PSNR estimation, spectral regression and reduced model polynomial network have been employed. A multipass prediction system based on stepwise regression has been used in the estimation of SSIM method. The statistical features in both of the methods constitute mainly the coding information of an MB, some relative measures of motion vector of neighboring MBs, and some numerical values related to the texture of an MB.

Average QP values were combined with pixel difference contrast measure values to offer a visual quality method in [184]. The authors have shown that the method outperforms PSNR for a wide range of bitrates of H.264/AVC encoded videos. Similarly, two parametric models have been combined in [185] to design a hybrid model of perceptual quality for H.264/AVC encoded videos. This method uses average value of QP and an average measure of contrast from the decoded video, besides having input from noise masking property of the video content.

A hybrid of bitstream-based and pixel domain quality estimator is proposed in [186]. It has been argued that a video quality estimation merely based on the amount of impaired macroblocks could be erroneous as, in modern video decoders, some error concealment methods are applied to cure the impaired macroblocks and this concealment is not accounted for in such estimations. As the error concealment may not always be effective,

the proposed method uses motion intensity and luminance discontinuity measures to estimate the number of impaired macroblocks for which error concealment remains ineffective. In essence, the visual quality, in terms of MSE, is estimated directly based on the macroblocks for which the error concealment could not perform well. The same authors have generalized this approach for three methods of error concealment and a different value of packet length in [187].

In order to estimate the impact of transmission errors on the quality of H.264/AVC encoded videos, a saliency map-based method is proposed in [188]. Color, contrast, and luminance information has been used to compute spatial saliency map, while motion vector information, readily available in coded bitstream of a video, has been exploited for the computation of temporal saliency maps. A squared sum of spatial and temporal saliency maps has been used to pool them together for computing the overall spatio-temporal map. Accordingly, this map is used for weighting of an error map for each video frame to calculate the value of the proposed model.

Another hybrid method of perceptual quality measurement, which is based on information from the bitstream and spatio-temporal image features, is presented in [189]. The weighted Minkowski method is employed to integrate the average quantization scale with their proposed measures of flickering and blocking for H.264/AVC encoded videos.

A framework for a hybrid method for videos transmitted over long term evolution (LTE) networks is proposed in [190]. It suggests to include parameters from packet layer (packet loss rate, packet size), bitstream layer (frame error, frame duration), and media layer (blurring, blocking) for estimation of the quality. However, a suitable pooling scheme to integrate these parameters into a quality indication value remains as a future work.

1.7.2 Statistics of transform coefficients

In some cases, the transform coefficients can be obtained through partial decoding of the coded bitstream data and features from bitstream as well as pixel domain can be combined for the quality estimation. One such example is found in [191] where an estimate of PSNR has been computed for MPEG-2 coded videos using DCT coefficients. This is actually an improved version of the authors' earlier contribution [192] in which they modeled the distribution of DCT coefficients as a Laplacian pdf to calculate PSNR of the video frames one-by-one for all types, i.e., I, P, and B frames. However, it lacks in accuracy of assessment for B frames. Therefore, the authors conjectured that this happens as a result of fall in the amount of DCT coefficients information which is available for B frames due to processes of rate control and motion compensation. Henceforth, a hybrid approach to resolve this issue has been found in [191] where picture energy has also been used in addition to DCT coefficients. There is a significant improvement of correlation with estimated and actual PSNR, in the case when the proposed method was tested on SDTV and HDTV sequences.

1.7.3 Discussion

The hybrid methods use not only pixel-based information but also bitstream-based information, which in turn makes the hybrid framework having a potential of being the most accurate quality estimator as compared to the other approaches [193]. Thus, the importance of careful combination of the features from pixel and bitstream domains is evident. Further studies are needed to investigate the interaction among various types of artifacts due to compression and transmission and the joint impact towards the video quality.

Various approaches exist on how to combine the impact of various sources of degradation into one representative value for all the artifacts under consideration. In the recommendation ITU-T P.1202.1 that presents a complementary algorithm of NR quality assessment for the recommendation P.NBAMS [152], four types of degradations are sorted with respect to their impact on quality. The values of the two most significant artifact types are pooled together through a linear combination. A higher weighting is applied to the artifact value that is found to be the most significant out of the four types. As different artifact types can exist in different range of values, it is important that all of them are aligned to the same scale before the sorting is applied. Besides linear combination, some contributions [189] adopt the Minkowski metric [3] for pooling the values of different artifacts into a single quantity.

With regards to the preference on which a pooling strategy should be chosen it may depend on many factors including relative severity of different artifacts, spatio-temporal characteristics of the contents, and the presence of masking effects. Linear combination is more valid if the constituents can be related to the quality value through a linear regression. While combining different artifacts through a linear relation, different artifacts can be given different significance. For example, more weight is given to the impact of bitstream layer features than to media-layer features in the hybrid model given in [194]. On the other hand, the Minkowski metric of summation has its roots in additive properties of low-level vision. Therefore, it is required to find the suitable value of its exponent through measurements.

Most of the aforementioned hybrid methods make an assessment of quality in terms of MSE but this measure of quality is known to be rather inaccurate in representing the perceptual quality [195]. This fact necessitates the desire of enhancing such methods for better correlation

with subjective quality assessment. As can be seen from the summary of hybrid methods in Table 3, the main focus of the development of hybrid methods has been on videos.

2 Conclusions

Motivated by the growing interest in NR methods of quality assessment for images and videos, we have presented a classification and review of recent approaches proposed in this research area. The available contributions have been classified into different categories based on the methodologies used in the design. Recognized classifications and standardizations in the area have been extrapolated to introduce our approach of classification. The new classification enabled us to present a review of a large amount of recently published work. On the highest tier, three categories have been identified to group the existing NR methods. The NR methods that employ pixel domain approaches for quality assessment are called NR-P-based methods, and the methods that employ encoded bitstream and parametric information of the media signal are called NR-B-based methods. The third category is called hybrid methods which are designed by a composite of NR-P- and NR-B-based methods. A further subcategorization has been presented to organize the discussion of the review.

It is observed that the majority of the publications introduce methods that are processed in the pixel domain. This trend can be attributed to the rich heritage of work in the image processing area. In most cases, pixel-based methods require more processing power than bitstream-based methods. NR quality estimation is a widely adopted application in the area of online quality monitoring. It is thus required to employ computationally less complex methods. This fact necessitates to focus towards designing bitstream-based or hybrid methods. The distortions present in a network can introduce a variety of temporal perturbations in a video transmitted through it. Such perturbations have to be monitored by service providers to ensure a given threshold of visual quality at the end users' premises. This can be performed using NR metrics which estimate the impact of degradation in the temporal domain. Unfortunately, most of the existing methods are designed to account for a single or a limited set of degradations. Therefore, it is not easy to make an estimate of the overall loss of visual quality. Hence, methods which can make a complete assessment of the quality are desirable. Similarly, attention can be drawn towards designing less complex methods which are not application specific, such as the methods that are not limited to a particular coding standard.

In the context of the reviewed methods, it is interesting to compare the approaches adopted in case of IQA and VQA methods. In case of IQA, the main focus has been on addressing the most occurring spatial artifacts such as blocking, blurring, and ringing as a result of popular compression techniques such as JPEG and JPEG2000. Besides many methods that are specifically designed for particular artifacts and hence have limited application, it is exciting to see many methods that are not restricted to a specific artifact type and have a wider application area. In such methods of global application, the mostly adopted approach is based on computing the impact of distortions on natural scene statistics of natural images. This also suggests that such approaches may not be applied to artificial images (such as animations and cartoons). This issue can be considered as a challenge for future work in IQA. More focus has been seen on the development of bitstream-based approaches in the case of VQA methods. This is of advantage in the sense that bitstream-based approaches have relatively low computational complexity. However, they face the drawbacks of being coding scheme specific and sometimes less accurate. We believe that the development of more robust approaches based on hybrids of NR-P and NR-B methods may be beneficial to meet these challenges associated with the NR VQA area.

We observe that many of the existing contributions in NR IQA and VQA have reported the results of the proposed methods therein by doing the relevant performance tests on the publicly available test databases. This is useful for independent benchmarking and performance comparison tests of these methods by other researchers. Therefore, more variety in the content and resolution of the media available through public test databases would be of great value. On the other hand, one general drawback of many existing methods of NR quality assessment lies in the limited use of the test data, as the data used for the designing or training of a metric is often also used for its performance verification. This drawback actually does not allow to draw meaningful results from such studies. Also, it has been observed that most of the existing methods for video quality assessment are limited to one encoder implementation or rather one particular setting of an encoder. Hence, cross-encoder design of VQA metrics would be a useful contribution. Moreover, we enlist the following trends and directions towards future research in the area of NR quality assessment:

- The trend of contribution in the NR quality estimation has been settling towards finding approaches of lesser complexity as shown by the growing interest in the bitstream-based methods. However, bitstream-based methods face the challenge of being limited for a specific codec. Given the fact that such methods have been shown to have promising performance by having reasonable values of correlation with subjective quality assessment, it would be advantageous to generalize the methodologies of these methods for diverse coding schemes.

- The performance of the bitstream-based methods has been found to be largely content dependent, as the spatio-temporal perceptual complexities vary with varying content, and, in turn, the nature of the features used for quality estimation also changes. However, in the case of pixel-based methods, it is relatively easier to differentiate the content characteristics. Thus, it is required for bitstream-based models to be trained on a sufficiently high variety in content, enabling them to be used in practice. Future inventions can focus on the development of methods that can be applied in more general scenarios with the desired amount of variety in content.

- The existing NR methods are usually designed and tested for cases where the quality difference is beyond the threshold of perception of an artifact, i.e., rather clearly visible. However, attention needs to be paid to scenarios where the test stimuli may already be of high quality. Future developments should therefore envisage the degradations that are considered in the category of subthreshold artifacts. The need of such methods becomes even more important with regards to the newly approved HEVC standard that supports ultra-high definition video resolutions of 4K and beyond.

- It has been observed that emphasis is being put towards making the quality estimation more in line with the perceived quality by HVS. In the future, the NR quality assessment methods should continue to adapt for HVS parameters and further advancements in the understanding of HVS, such as attention-driven foveated quality assessment models [196] should be taken into consideration.

- A robust combination of audio-visual quality estimators can be devised for designing scenario-dependent models. For example, in quality monitoring of sports video, more emphasis can be put on the visual component than audio as the viewers might be interested more in video. For example, a video of a football match would draw more focus towards visual scene than audio, as compared to news or head and shoulder scenario. Moreover, audio-visual quality estimation is challenging due to the complex interplay of HVS preferences. In terms of the mutual impact of audio-visual subjective quality, some studies report an average cross-modal interaction level of 0.5 MOS [197] to above 2 MOS points [198] on a scale of 1 to 5 quality rating.

- Given the presented comprehensive literature review, it has been observed that developments of NR methods that consider visual attention are rather limited, especially, in the case of videos. As noted in [199], visual attention models can be integrated into existing NR methods to make them more robust. Generally, the advantage of including visual attention-based modeling appears to be larger for methods designed for video quality assessment than for image quality assessment methods. Visual attention becomes more significant in scenarios of audio-visual stimuli, as it is required to account for the cues from visual channels as well as auditory channels.

- To make the quality estimation closer to the subjective assessment, intelligent methods are needed that consider the content preference and expectations of humans in a given scenario. For example, the subjective quality assessment results mentioned in [200] indicate that desirable content is rated significantly higher than the undesirable and neutral contents.

- The task of finding the optimal trade-off between temporal and spatial resolution, and the level of quantization for its impacts on the perceptual quality in different scenarios of application, is challenging [201]. This issue should be taken into consideration for the future development of NR methods.

- In order to combine independent and isolated approaches for the development of hybrid NR VQA methods, a five-point agenda has been identified by joint effort group (JEG) at VQEG [202]. We believe that such collaborative works will be instrumental in paving the ways of NR VQA towards a measurable evolution.

We believe that our contribution in this article can be utilized and extended in various ways. One can use this review as a systematic literature review to perform comparisons on a class of NR methods using the same image or video test database to highlight the state-of-the-art. Furthermore, this review can be very useful for the beginner researchers in this area to achieve a concise yet comprehensive overview of the field. This way, we expect this contribution to be instrumental for future research and development in the area of NR visual quality assessment. Moreover, a possible future work is to survey the contributions for audio-visual quality assessment based on NR paradigm, similar to [203] that deals with FR methods of audio-visual quality assessment.

Competing interests
The authors declare that they have no competing interests.

Authors' contributions
MS prepared the database of the publications in the area, streamlined the publications to be reviewed in the paper, planned the structure of the paper in consultation with co-authors, and wrote the main draft of the paper. AR participated in writing some parts of the paper and involved in the discussions on improving the manuscript. BL took part in the initial discussions on the paper topic and gave feedback during the writing process on the structure, the content and its revisions, and wrote the first draft of the conclusions. HJZ helped with refining and structuring the content of the review; participated in drafting, correcting, and revising the article; and helped with assessing the reviewed approaches. All authors read and approved the final manuscript.

References
1. Cisco Visual Networking Index, Global mobile data traffic forecast update, 2013-2018. Cisco white paper (2014)
2. ITU, ITU-R Recommendation BT.500-13 Methodology for the subjective assessment of the quality of the television pictures. http://www.itu.int/rec/R-REC-BT.500-13-201201-I/en. Accessed 4 November 2013
3. HR Wu, KR Rao, *Digital Video Image Quality and Perceptual Coding (Signal Processing and Communications)*. (CRC, Boca Raton, 2005)
4. SS Hemami, AR Reibman, No-reference image and video quality estimation: applications and human-motivated design. Signal Process. Image Commun. **25**(7), 469–481 (2010)
5. Z Wang, AC Bovik, Reduced- and no-reference image quality assessment. IEEE Signal Process. Mag. **28**(6), 29–40 (2011)
6. W Lin, C-c Jay Kuo, Perceptual visual quality metrics: a survey. J. Vis. Commun. Image Representation **22**(4), 297–312 (2011)
7. M Vranješ, S Rimac-Drlje, K Grgić, Review of objective video quality metrics and performance comparison using different databases. Signal Process. Image Commun. **28**(1), 1–19 (2013)
8. S Chikkerur, V Sundaram, M Reisslein, LJ Karam, Objective video quality assessment methods: a classification, review, and performance comparison. IEEE Trans. Broadcasting **57**(2), 165–182 (2011)
9. R Soundararajan, A Bovik, Survey of information theory in visual quality assessment. Signal, Image Video Process. **7**(3), 391–401 (2013)
10. DM Chandler, Seven challenges in image quality assessment: past, present, and future research. ISRN Signal Processing 53 (2013). (doi:10.1155/2013/905685)
11. U Engelke, H-J Zepernick, Perceptual-based quality metrics for image and video services: a survey, in *EuroNGI Conference on Next Generation Internet Networks* (Trondheim, 21–23 May 2007), pp. 190–197
12. AR Reibman, S Sen, JV der Merwe, Analyzing the spatial quality of internet streaming video, in *International Workshop on Video Processing and Quality Metrics for Consumer Electronics* (Scottsdale, January 2005)
13. VQEG, Final report from the Video Quality Experts Group on the validation of objective models of multimedia quality assessment, phase I (2008). http://www.its.bldrdoc.gov/vqeg/projects/multimedia-phase-i/multimedia-phase-i.aspx. Accessed 11 April 2014
14. HR Sheikh, Z Wang, L Cormack, Bovik AC, LIVE Image Quality Assessment Database. http://live.ece.utexas.edu/research/quality. Accessed 11 April 2014
15. Video Quality Experts Group (VQEG). http://www.its.bldrdoc.gov/vqeg/downloads.aspx. Accessed 11 April 2014
16. N Ponomarenko, V Lukin, A Zelensky, K Egiazarian, M Carli, F Battisti, TID2008 - a database for evaluation of full reference visual quality assessment metrics. Adv. Modern Radioelectron. **10**, 30–45 (2009)
17. PL Callet, F Autrusseau, Subjective quality assessment IRCCyN/IVC database (2005). http://www.irccyn.ec-nantes.fr/ivcdb. Accessed 11 April 2014
18. ZMP Sazzad, Y Kawayoke, Horita Y, Image Quality Evaluation Database. http://mict.eng.u-toyama.ac.jp/mictdb.html. Accessed 11 April 2014
19. L Liang, S Wang, J Chen, S Ma, D Zhao, W Gao, No-reference perceptual image quality metric using gradient profiles for JPEG2000. Signal Process. Image Commun. **25**(7), 502–516 (2010)
20. S Winkler, *Digital Video Quality: Vision Models and Metrics.* (Wiley, Chichester, 2005)
21. N Narvekar, L Karam, A no-reference image blur metric based on the cumulative probability of blur detection (CPBD). IEEE Trans. Image Process. **20**(9), 2678–2683 (2011)
22. A Ciancio, ALNT da Costa, EAB da Silva, A Said, R Samadani, P Obrador, No-reference blur assessment of digital pictures based on multifeature classifiers. IEEE Trans. Image Process. **20**(1), 64–75 (2011)
23. X Marichal, W-Y Ma, H Zhang, Blur determination in the compressed domain using DCT information, in *IEEE International Conference on Image Processing*, vol. 2 (Kobe, 24–28 October 1999), pp. 386–390
24. H Tong, M Li, H Zhang, C Zhang, Blur detection for digital images using wavelet transform, in *IEEE International Conference on Multimedia and Expo*, vol. 1 (Taipei, 27–30 June 2004), pp. 17–20

25. P Marziliano, F Dufaux, S Winkler, T Ebrahimi, Perceptual blur and ringing metrics: application to JPEG2000. Signal Process. Image Commun. **19**(2), 163–172 (2004)

26. R Ferzli, LJ Karam, Human visual system based no-reference objective image sharpness metric, in *IEEE International Conference on Image Processing*, (2006), pp. 2949–2952

27. A Ciancio, ALN da Costa, EAB da Silva, A Said, R Samadani, P Obrador, Objective no-reference image blur metric based on local phase coherence. Electron. Lett. **45**(23), 1162–1163 (2009)

28. R Hassen, Z Wang, M Salama, No-reference image sharpness assessment based on local phase coherence measurement, in *IEEE International Conference on Acoustics Speech and Signal Processing* (Dallas, 14–19 March 2010), pp. 2434–2437

29. R Ferzli, LJ Karam, No-reference objective image sharpness metric based on the notion of just noticeable blur (JNB). IEEE Trans. Image Process. **18**(4), 717–728 (2009)

30. R Ferzli, LJ Karam, A no-reference objective image sharpness metric based on just-noticeable blur and probability summation, in *IEEE International Conference on Image Processing*, vol. 3 (San Antonio, TX, USA, 16–19 September 2007), pp. 445–448

31. NG Sadaka, LJ Karam, R Ferzli, GP Abousleman, A no-reference perceptual image sharpness metric based on saliency-weighted foveal pooling, in *15th IEEE International Conference on Image Processing* (San Diego, 12–15 October 2008), pp. 369–372

32. ND Narvekar, LJ Karam, A no-reference perceptual image sharpness metric based on a cumulative probability of blur detection, in *International Workshop on Quality of Multimedia Experience* (San Diego, 29–31 July 2009), pp. 87–91

33. N Narvekar, LJ Karam, An improved no-reference sharpness metric based on the probability of blur detection, in *Workshop on Video Processing and Quality Metrics* (Scottsdale, 13–15 January 2010)

34. S Varadarajan, LJ Karam, An improved perception-based no-reference objective image sharpness metric using iterative edge refinement, in *IEEE International Conference on Image Processing* (San Diego, 12–15 October 2008), pp. 401–404

35. L Debing, C Zhibo, M Huadong, X Feng, G Xiaodong, No reference block based blur detection, in *International Workshop on Quality of Multimedia Experience* (San Diego, 29–31 July 2009), pp. 75–80

36. P Marziliano, F Dufaux, S Winkler, T Ebrahimi, A no-reference perceptual blur metric, in *Proceedings of the International Conference on Image Processing 2002*, vol. 3 (Rochester, New York, 22–25 September 2002), pp. 57–60

37. A Maalouf, M-C Larabi, A no reference objective color image sharpness metric, in *The European Signal Processing Conference* (Aalborg, 23–27 August 2010), pp. 1019–1022

38. S Wu, W Lin, Z Lu, EP Ong, S Yao, Blind blur assessment for vision-based applications, in *IEEE International Conference on Multimedia and Expo* (Beijing, 2–5 July 2007), pp. 1639–1642

39. S Wu, W Lin, S Xie, Z Lu, EP Ong, S Yao, Blind blur assessment for vision-based applications. J. Vis. Commun. Image Representation **20**(4), 231–241 (2009)

40. C Chen, W Chen, JA Bloom, A universal reference-free blurriness measure. SPIE J. Image Q. Syst. Performance VIII **7867**, 78670–7867014 (2011)

41. M-J Chen, AC Bovik, No-reference image blur assessment using multiscale gradient, in *International Workshop on Quality of Multimedia Experience* (San Diego, 29–31 July 2009), pp. 70–74

42. R Ferzli, L Karam, A no reference objective sharpness metric using riemannian tensor, in *International Workshop on Video Processing and Quality Metrics for Consumer Electronics* (Scottsdale, 25–26 January 2007), pp. 25–26

43. A Chetouani, A Beghdadi, M Deriche, A new reference-free image quality index for blur estimation in the frequency domain, in *IEEE International Symposium on Signal Processing and Information Technology* (Ajman, 14–17 December 2009), pp. 155–159

44. Z Hua, Z Wei, C Yaowu, A no-reference perceptual blur metric by using OLS-RBF network, in *Pacific-Asia Workshop on Computational Intelligence and Industrial Application* (Wuhan, 19–20 December 2008), pp. 1007–1011

45. C Oprea, I Pirnog, C Paleologu, M Udrea, Perceptual video quality assessment based on salient region detection, in *Advanced International Conference on Telecommunications* (Venice, 24–28 May 2009), pp. 232–236

46. C Chen, JA Bloom, A blind reference-free blockiness measure, in *Proceedings of the Pacific Rim Conference on Advances in Multimedia Information Processing: part I* (Shanghai, 21–24 September 2010), pp. 112–123

47. H Liu, I Heynderickx, A no-reference perceptual blockiness metric, in *IEEE International Conference on Acoustics, Speech and Signal Processing* (Las Vegas, 31 March to 4 April 2008), pp. 865–868

48. H Liu, I Heynderickx, A perceptually relevant no-reference blockiness metric based on local image characteristics. EURASIP J. Adv. Signal Process. **2009**, 1–15 (2009)

49. G Zhai, W Zhang, X Yang, W Lin, Y Xu, No-reference noticeable blockiness estimation in images. Signal Process. Image Commun. **23**(6), 417–432 (2008)

50. RV Babu, S Suresh, A Perkis, No-reference JPEG-image quality assessment using GAP-RBF. Signal Process. **87**, 1493–1503 (2007)

51. RV Babu, AS Bopardikar, A Perkis, OI Hillestad, No-reference metrics for video streaming applications, in *International Workshop on Packet Video* (Irvine, 13–14 December 2004)

52. Z Zhang, H Shi, S Wan, A novel blind measurement of blocking artifacts for H.264/AVC video, in *International Conference on Image and Graphics* (Xian, 20–23 September 2009), pp. 262–265

53. Z Hua, Z Yiran, T Xiang, A weighted Sobel operator-based no-reference blockiness metric, in *Pacific-Asia Workshop on Computational Intelligence and Industrial Application*, vol. 1 (Wuhan, 19–20 December 2008), pp. 1002–1006

54. C-S Park, J-H Kim, S-J Ko, Fast blind measurement of blocking artifacts in both pixel and DCT domains. J. Math. Imaging Vis. **28**, 279–284 (2007)

55. S Suthaharan, No-reference visually significant blocking artifact metric for natural scene images. Signal Process. **89**(8), 1647–1652 (2009)

56. H Liu, N Klomp, I Heynderickx, A perceptually relevant approach to ringing region detection. IEEE Trans. Image Process. **19**(6), 1414–1426 (2010)

57. H Liu, N Klomp, I Heynderickx, A no-reference metric for perceived ringing artifacts in images. IEEE Trans. Circuits Syst. Video Technol. **20**(4), 529–539 (2010)

58. B-X Zuo, J-W Tian, D-L Ming, A no-reference ringing metrics for images deconvolution, in *International Conference on Wavelet Analysis and Pattern Recognition*, vol. 1 (Hong Kong, 30–31 August 2008), pp. 96–101

59. B-X Zuo, D-L Ming, J-W Tian, Perceptual ringing metric to evaluate the quality of images restored using blind deconvolution algorithms. SPIE J. Opt. Eng. **48**(3), 037004 (2009)

60. AC Bovik, Handbook of Image and Video Processing, 2nd edn. (Elsevier Academic, Burlington, 2005)

61. A Amer, E Dubois, Fast and reliable structure-oriented video noise estimation. IEEE Trans. Circuits Syst. Video Technol. **15**(1), 113–118 (2005)

62. J Tian, L Chen, Image noise estimation using a variation-adaptive evolutionary approach. IEEE Signal Process. Lett. **19**(7), 395–398 (2012)

63. SI Olsen, Estimation of noise in images: an evaluation. CVGIP: Graph. Models Image Process. **55**(4), 319–323 (1993)

64. K Rank, M Lendl, R Unbehauen, Estimation of image noise variance. IEE Proc. Vis. Image Signal Process. **146**(2), 80–84 (1999)

65. A Amer, E Dubois, Fast and reliable structure-oriented video noise estimation. IEEE Trans. Circuits Syst. Video Technol. **15**(1), 113–118 (2005)

66. M Ghazal, A Amer, Homogeneity localization using particle filters with application to noise estimation. IEEE Trans. Image Process. **20**(7), 1788–1796 (2011)

67. X Liu, M Tanaka, M Okutomi, Noise level estimation using weak textured patches of a single noisy image, in *19th IEEE International Conference on Image Processing (ICIP)* (Orlando, 30 September to 3 October 2012), pp. 665–668

68. X Liu, M Tanaka, M Okutomi, Single-image noise level estimation for blind denoising. IEEE Trans. Image Process. **22**(12), 5226–5237 (2013)

69. S Pyatykh, J Hesser, L Zheng, Image noise level estimation by principal component analysis. IEEE Trans. Image Process. **22**(2), 687–699 (2013)

70. Q Huynh-Thu, M Ghanbari, Temporal aspect of perceived quality in mobile video broadcasting. IEEE Trans. Broadcasting **54**(3), 641–651 (2008)

71. S Borer, A model of jerkiness for temporal impairments in video transmission, in *International Workshop on Quality of Multimedia Experience* (Trondheim, 21–23 June 2010), pp. 218–223

72. Q Huynh-Thu, M Ghanbari, No-reference temporal quality metric for video impaired by frame freezing artefacts, in *IEEE International Conference on Image Processing* (Cairo, 7–10 November 2009), pp. 2221–2224

73. ITU-T Recommendation J.247: objective perceptual multimedia video quality measurement in the presence of a full reference. http://www.itu.int/rec/T-REC-J.247/en. Accessed 4 November 2013

74. G Yammine, E Wige, F Simmet, D Niederkorn, A Kaup, Blind frame freeze detection in coded videos, in *Picture Coding Symposium* (Krakow, 7–9 May 2012), pp. 341–344

75. S Wolf, A no reference (NR) and reduced reference (RR) metric for detecting dropped video frames, in *International Workshop on Video Processing and Quality Metrics for Consumer Electronics* (Scottsdale, 15–16 January 2009)

76. K Watanabe, J Okamoto, T Kurita, Objective video quality assessment method for evaluating effects of freeze distortion in arbitrary video scenes. Proc. SPIE-Image Qual. Syst. Perform. IV **6494**, 64940–1649408 (2007)

77. K Watanabe, J Okamoto, T Kurita, Objective video quality assessment method for freeze distortion based on freeze aggregation. Proc. SPIE- Image Qual. Syst. Perform. III **6059**, 1–8 (2007)

78. K-C Yang, CC Guest, K El-Maleh, PK Das, Perceptual temporal quality metric for compressed video. IEEE Trans. Multimedia **9**(7), 1528–1535 (2007)

79. RR Pastrana-Vidal, J-C Gicquel, Automatic quality assessment of video fluidity impairments using a no-reference metric, in *International Workshop on Video Processing and Quality Metrics for Consumer Electronics* (Scottsdale, 22–24 January 2006)

80. RR Pastrana-Vidal, J-C Gicquel, A no-reference video quality metric based on a human assessment model, in *International Workshop on Video Processing and Quality Metrics for Consumer Electronics* (Scottsdale, 25–26 January 2007)

81. F Battisti, ANM Carli, No-reference quality metric for color video communication, in *International Workshop on Video Processing and Quality Metrics for Consumer Electronics* (Scottsdale, 19–20 January 2012)

82. T Oelbaum, C Keimel, K Diepold, Rule-based no-reference video quality evaluation using additionally coded videos. IEEE J. Select. Topics Signal Process. **3**(2), 294–303 (2009)

83. MG Choi, JH Jung, JW Jeon, No-reference image quality assessment using blur and noise. Int. J. Comput. Sci. Eng. **3**(2), 76–80 (2009)

84. E Cohen, Y Yitzhaky, No-reference assessment of blur and noise impacts on image quality. Signal, Image Video Process. **4**(3), 289–302 (2010)

85. S Gabarda, G Cristóbal, Blind image quality assessment through anisotropy. J. Opt. Soc. Am. A **24**(12), 42–51 (2007)

86. X Zhu, P Milanfar, A no-reference sharpness metric sensitive to blur and noise, in *International Workshop on Quality of Multimedia Experience* (San Diego, 29–31 July 2009), pp. 64–69

87. X Zhu, P Milanfar, A no-reference image content metric and its application to denoising, in *IEEE International Conference on Image Processing* (Hong Kong, 26–29 September 2010), pp. 1145–1148

88. M Narwaria, W Lin, Objective image quality assessment based on support vector regression. IEEE Trans. Neural Netw. **21**(3), 515–519 (2010)

89. H Liu, J Redi, H Alers, R Zunino, I Heynderickx, ed. by BE Rogowitz, TN Pappas, No-reference image quality assessment based on localized gradient statistics: application to JPEG and JPEG2000, in *SPIE Proceedings-Human Vision and Electronic Imaging*, vol. 7527, (2010), p. 75271

90. R Ferzli, L Karam, A novel free reference image quality metric using neural network approach, in *International Workshop on Video Processing and Quality Metrics for Consumer Electronics* (Scottsdale, 13–15 January 2010), pp. 1–4

91. A Chetouani, A Beghdadi, A new image quality estimation approach for JPEG2000 compressed images, in *IEEE International Symposium on Signal Processing and Information Technology* (Bilbao, 14–17 December 2011), pp. 581–584

92. HR Sheikh, AC Bovik, L Cormack, No-reference quality assessment using natural scene statistics: JPEG2000. IEEE Trans. Image Process. **14**(11), 1918–1927 (2005)

93. P Romaniak, L Janowski, MI Leszczuk, Z Papir, Perceptual quality assessment for H.264/AVC compression, in *IEEE International Workshop on Future Multimedia Networking* (Las Vegas, 14–17 January 2012)

94. Z Wang, AC Bovik, HR Sheikh, EP Simoncelli, Image quality assessment: from error visibility to structural similarity. IEEE Trans. Image Process. **13**(4), 600–612 (2004)

95. X Liu, M Chen, T Wan, C Yu, Hybrid no-reference video quality assessment focusing on codec effects. Korea Internet Inform. Soc. Trans. Internet Inform. Syst. **5**(3), 592–606 (2011)

96. S Ouni, E Zagrouba, M Chambah, M Herbin, No-reference image semantic quality approach using neural network, in *IEEE International Symposium on Signal Processing and Information Technology* (Bilbao, 14–17 December 2011), pp. 106–113

97. J Zhang, TM Le, SH Ong, TQ Nguyen, No-reference image quality assessment using structural activity. Signal Process. **91**(11), 2575–2588 (2011)

98. DL Ruderman, The statistics of natural images. Network: Comput. Neural Syst. **5**(4), 517–548 (1994)

99. J Zhou, B Xiao, Q Li, A no reference image quality assessment method for JPEG2000, in *IEEE International Joint Conference on Neural Networks* (Hong Kong, 1–8 June 2008), pp. 863–868

100. W Lu, K Zeng, D Tao, Y Yuan, X Gao, No-reference image quality assessment in contourlet domain. Neurocomputing **73**, 784–794 (2010)

101. MN Do, M Vetterli, The contourlet transform: an efficient directional multiresolution image representation. IEEE Trans. Image Process. **14**(12), 2091–2106 (2005)

102. J Shen, Q Li, G Erlebacher, Hybrid no-reference natural image quality assessment of noisy, blurry, JPEG2000, and JPEG images. IEEE Trans. Image Process. **20**(8), 2089–2098 (2011)

103. AK Moorthy, AC Bovik, Blind image quality assessment: from natural scene statistics to perceptual quality. IEEE Trans. Image Process. **20**(12), 3350–3364 (2011)

104. K Zhu, K Hirakawa, V Asari, D Saupe, A no-reference video quality assessment based on Laplacian pyramids, in *20th IEEE International Conference on Image Processing (ICIP)* (Melbourne, 15–18 September 2013), pp. 49–53

105. MA Saad, AC Bovik, Natural motion statistics for no-reference video quality assessment, in *International Workshop on Quality of Multimedia Experience* (San Diego, 29–31 July 2009), pp. 163–167

106. MA Saad, AC Bovik, C Charrier, A DCT statistics-based blind image quality index. IEEE Signal Process. Lett. **17**(6), 583–586 (2010)

107. MA Saad, AC Bovik, C Charrier, DCT statistics model-based blind image quality assessment, in *IEEE International Conference on Image Processing* (Brussels, 11–14 September 2011), pp. 3093–3096

108. A Mittal, A Moorthy, A Bovik, No-reference image quality assessment in the spatial domain. IEEE Trans. Image Process. **21**(12), 4695–4708 (2012)

109. A Mittal, GS Muralidhar, J Ghosh, AC Bovik, Blind image quality assessment without human training using latent quality factors. IEEE Signal Process. Lett. **19**(2), 75–78 (2012)

110. M-J Chen, LK Cormack, AC Bovik, No-reference quality assessment of natural stereopairs. IEEE Trans. Image Process. **22**(9), 3379–3391 (2013)

111. P Gastaldo, G Parodi, J Redi, R Zunino, No-reference quality assessment of JPEG images by using CBP neural networks, in *17th International Conference Artificial Neural Networks* (Porto, 9–13 September 2007). Lecture Notes in Computer Science, vol. 4669, (Springer, Heidelberg), pp. 564–572

112. C Li, AC Bovik, X Wu, Blind image quality assessment using a general regression neural network. IEEE Trans. Neural Netw. **22**(5), 793–799 (2011)

113. J Zhang, TM Le, A new no-reference quality metric for JPEG2000 images. IEEE Trans. Consumer Electron. **56**(2), 743–750 (2010)

114. ZMP Sazzad, Y Kawayoke, Y Horita, No reference image quality assessment for JPEG2000 based on spatial features. Image Commun. **23**, 257–268 (2008)

115. ZMP Sazzad, Y Kawayoke, Y Horita, Spatial features based no reference image quality assessment for JPEG2000, in *IEEE International Conference*

on Image Processing, vol. 3 (San Antonio, 16–19 September 2007), pp. 517–520

116. A Maalouf, M-C Larabi, A no-reference color video quality metric based on a 3D multispectral wavelet transform, in International Workshop on Quality of Multimedia Experience (Trondheim, 21–23 June 2010), pp. 11–16

117. S Suresh, R Venkatesh Babu, HJ Kim, No-reference image quality assessment using modified extreme learning machine classifier. Appl. Soft Comput. 9, 541–552 (2009)

118. AM Treisman, G Gelade, A feature-integration theory of attention. Cognit. Psychol. 12(1), 97–136 (1980)

119. S Yao, E Ong, MH Loke, Perceptual distortion metric based on wavelet frequency sensitivity and multiple visual fixations, in IEEE International Symposium on Circuits and Systems (Seattle, 18–21 May 2008), pp. 408–411

120. X-H Wang, Z Ming, A new metric for objectively assessing the quality of enhanced images based on human visual perception. J. Optoelectron. Laser 19(2), 254–262 (2008)

121. M Ries, C Crespi, O Nemethova, M Rupp, Content based video quality estimation for H.264/AVC video streaming, in IEEE Conference on Wireless Communications and Networking (Kowloon, 11–15 March 2007), pp. 2668–2673

122. M Ries, O Nemethova, M Rupp, Performance evaluation of mobile video quality estimators, in European Signal Processing Conference (Poznan, 3–7 September 2007)

123. A Khan, L Sun, E Ifeachor, Content-based video quality prediction for MPEG4 video streaming over wireless networks. J. Multimedia 4(4), 228–239 (2009)

124. A Khan, L Sun, E Ifeachor, An ANFIS-based hybrid video quality prediction model for video streaming over wireless networks, in International Conference on Next Generation Mobile Applications, Services and Technologies (Cardiff, 16–19 September 2008), pp. 357–362

125. A Khan, L Sun, E Ifeachor, Content clustering based video quality prediction model for MPEG4 video streaming over wireless networks, in IEEE International Conference on Communications (Dresden, 14–18 June 2009), pp. 1–5

126. U Engelke, H-J Zepernick, An artificial neural network for quality assessment in wireless imaging based on extraction of structural information, in IEEE International Conference on Acoustics, Speech and Signal Processing, vol. 1 (Honolulu, 15–20 April 2007), pp. 1249–1252

127. X Jiang, F Meng, J Xu, W Zhou, No-reference perceptual video quality measurement for high definition videos based on an artificial neural network, in International Conference on Computer and Electrical Engineering (Phuket, 20–22 December 2008), pp. 424–427

128. D Ćulibrk, D Kukolj, P Vasiljević, M Pokrić, V Zlokolica, Feature selection for neural-network based no-reference video quality assessment. Lecture Notes Comput. Sci. 5769, 633–642 (2009)

129. C Keimel, T Oelbaum, K Diepold, No-reference video quality evaluation for high-definition video, in IEEE International Conference on Acoustics, Speech and Signal Processing (Taipei, 19–24 April 2009), pp. 1145–1148

130. ZMP Sazzad, S Yamanaka, Y Kawayokeita, Y Horita, Stereoscopic image quality prediction, in International Workshop on Quality of Multimedia Experience, (2009), pp. 180–185

131. D Bhattacharjee, S Prakash, P Gupta, No-reference image quality assessment for facial images, in International Conference on Advanced Intelligent Computing Theories and Applications. With Aspects of Artificial Intelligence, Zhengzhou, vol. 6839 (Springer Heidelberg, Germany, 11–14 August 2011), pp. 594–601

132. OYG Castillo, Survey about facial image quality. Technical Report. Fraunhofer Institute for Computer Graphics Research (2007), Darmstadt, Germany, (2006)

133. JE Caviedes, F Oberti, No-reference quality metric for degraded and enhanced video, in Proceedings of SPIE 5150, Visual Communications and Image Processing, vol. 5150 (Lugano, 8 July 2003), pp. 621–632

134. G Valenzise, S Magni, M Tagliasacchi, S Tubaro, Estimating channel-induced distortion in H.264/AVC video without bitstream information, in Second International Workshop on Quality of Multimedia Experience (QoMEX) (Trondheim, 21–23 June 2010), pp. 100–105

135. G Valenzise, S Magni, M Tagliasacchi, S Tubaro, No-reference pixel video quality monitoring of channel-induced distortion. IEEE Trans. Circuits Syst. Video Technol. 22(4), 605–618 (2012)

136. J Park, K Seshadrinathan, S Lee, AC Bovik, Video quality pooling adaptive to perceptual distortion severity. IEEE Trans. Image Process. 22(2), 610–620 (2013)

137. AR Reibman, VA Vaishampayan, Y Sermadevi, Quality monitoring of video over a packet network. IEEE Trans. Multimedia 6(2), 327–334 (2004)

138. A Takahashi, D Hands, V Barriac, Standardization activities in the ITU for a QoE assessment of IPTV. IEEE Commun. Mag. 46(2), 78–84 (2008)

139. F Yang, S Wan, Bitstream-based quality assessment for networked video: a review. IEEE Commun. Mag. 50(11), 203–209 (2012)

140. ITU-T, ITU-T Recommendation G.1070: opinion model for video-telephony applications (2012). http://www.itu.int/rec/T-REC-G.1070. Accessed 11 April 2014

141. A Raake, MN Garcia, S Moller, J Berger, F Kling, P List, J Johann, C Heidemann, T-V-model: parameter-based prediction of IPTV quality, in IEEE International Conference on Acoustics, Speech and Signal Processing (Las Vegas, 31 March to 4 April 2008), pp. 1149–1152

142. J Han, Y-H Kim, J Jeong, J Shin, Video quality estimation for packet loss based on no-reference method, in IEEE International Conference on Advanced Communication Technology, vol. 1 (Phoenix Park, Dublin, 7–10 February 2010), pp. 418–421

143. ITU, ITU-T Recommendation P.1201: Parametric non-intrusive assessment of audiovisual media streaming quality (2012). http://handle.itu.int/11.1002/1000/11727. Accessed 11 April 2014

144. T Yamada, S Yachida, Y Senda, M Serizawa, Accurate video-quality estimation without video decoding, in IEEE International Conference on Acoustics Speech and Signal Processing (Dallas, 14–19 March 2010), pp. 2426–2429

145. S Argyropoulos, A Raake, M-N Garcia, P List, No-reference bit stream model for video quality assessment of H.264/AVC video based on packet loss visibility, in IEEE International Conference on Acoustics, Speech and Signal Processing (Prague, 22–27 May 2011), pp. 1169–1172

146. M-N Garcia, A Raake, Parametric packet-layer video quality model for IPTV, in 10th International Conference on Information Sciences Signal Processing and Their Applications (ISSPA) (Kuala Lumpur, 10–13 May 2010), pp. 349–352

147. F Yang, J Song, S Wan, HR Wu, Content-adaptive packet-layer model for quality assessment of networked video services. IEEE J. Select. Topics Signal Process. 6(6), 672–683 (2012)

148. I Sedano, K Brunnström, M Kihl, A Aurelius, Full-reference video quality metric assisted the development of no-reference bitstream video quality metrics for real-time network monitoring. EURASIP J. Image Video Process (2014). doi:10.1186/1687-5281-2014-4

149. N Staelens, N Vercammen, Y Dhondt, B Vermeulen, P Lambert, R Van de Walle, P Demeester, VIQID: a no-reference bit stream-based visual quality impairment detector, in International Workshop on Quality of Multimedia Experience (Trondheim, 21–23 June 2010), pp. 206–211

150. N Staelens, G Van Wallendael, K Crombecq, N Vercammen, J De Cock, B Vermeulen, R Van de Walle, T Dhaene, P Demeester, No-reference bitstream-based visual quality impairment detection for high definition H.264/AVC encoded video sequences. IEEE Trans. Broadcasting 58(2), 187–199 (2012)

151. G Van Wallendael, N Staelens, L Janowski, J De Cock, P Demeester, R Van de Walle, No-reference bitstream-based impairment detection for high efficiency video coding, in Fourth International Workshop on Quality of Multimedia Experience (Yarra Valley, 5–7 July 2012), pp. 7–12

152. ITU, ITU-T Recommendation P.1202: parametric non-intrusive bitstream assessment of video media streaming quality (2012). http://handle.itu.int/11.1002/1000/11730. Accessed 11 April 2014

153. A Rossholm, B Lövström, A new low complex reference free video quality predictor, in IEEE Workshop on Multimedia Signal Processing (Cairns, 8–10 October 2008), pp. 765–768

154. M Shahid, A Rossholm, B Lövström, A reduced complexity no-reference artificial neural network based video quality predictor, in International Congress on Image and Signal Processing, vol. 1 (Shanghai, 15–17 October 2011), pp. 517–521

155. M Shahid, A Rossholm, B Lövström, A no-reference machine learning based video quality predictor, in Fifth International Workshop on Quality of Multimedia Experience (QoMEX) (Klagenfurt, 3–5 July 2013), pp. 176–181

156. C Keimel, M Klimpke, J Habigt, K Diepold, No-reference video quality metric for HDTV based on H.264/AVC bitstream features, in IEEE

International Conference on Image Processing (Brussels, 11–14 September 2011), pp. 3325–3328

157. S-O Lee, K-S Jung, D-G Sim, Real-time objective quality assessment based on coding parameters extracted from H.264/AVC bitstream. IEEE Trans. Consumer Electron. **56**(2), 1071–1078 (2010)

158. M Ries, O Nemethova, M Rupp, Motion based reference-free quality estimation for H.264/AVC video streaming, in *International Symposium on Wireless Pervasive Computing* (San Juan, 5–7 February 2007)

159. M Slanina, V Ricny, R Forchheimer, A novel metric for H.264/AVC no-reference quality assessment, in *EURASIP Conference on Speech and Image Processing Multimedia Communications and Services* (Maribor, 27–30 June 2007), pp. 114–117

160. I Park, T Na, M Kim, A noble method on no-reference video quality assessment using block modes and quantization parameters of H.264/AVC, in *Proceedings of SPIE-Image Quality and System Performance VIII*, vol. 7867 (San Francisco Airport, 23 January 2011), pp. 78670–7867011

161. KD Singh, G Rubino, No-reference quality of experience monitoring in DVB-H networks, in *Wireless Telecommunications Symposium* (Tampa, 21–23 April 2010), pp. 1–6

162. F Yang, S Wan, Q Xie, HR Wu, No-reference quality assessment for networked video via primary analysis of bit stream. IEEE Trans. Circuits Syst. Video Technol. **20**(11), 1544–1554 (2010)

163. M Chin, T Brandão, MP Queluz, Bitstream-based quality metric for packetized transmission of H.264 encoded video, in *International Conference on Systems, Signals and Image Processing* (Vienna, 11–13 April 2012), pp. 312–315

164. T Brandão, M Chin, MP Queluz, From PSNR to perceived quality in H.264 encoded video sequences, in *Proceedings of EuroITV* (Lisbon, 29 June to 1 July 2011)

165. A Eden, No-reference estimation of the coding PSNR for H.264-coded sequences. IEEE Trans. Consumer Electron. **53**(2), 667–674 (2007)

166. T Brandão, PQ Maria, No-reference image quality assessment based on DCT domain statistics. Signal Process. **88**(4), 822–833 (2008)

167. AB Watson, DCT quantization matrices visually optimized for individual images, in *Proceedings of SPIE, Human Vision, Visual Processing, and Digital Display IV*, vol. 1913 (San Jose, 31 January 1993), pp. 202–216

168. T Brandão, PQ Maria, No-reference quality assessment of H.264/AVC encoded video. IEEE Trans. Circuits Syst. Video Technol. **20**(11), 1437–1447 (2010)

169. T Brandão, PQ Maria, No-reference PSNR estimation algorithm for H.264 encoded video sequences, in *European Signal Processing Conference* (Laussane, 25–29 August 2008)

170. T Brandão, PQ Maria, Blind PSNR estimation of video sequences using quantized DCT coefficient data, in *Picture Coding Symposium* (Lausanne, 12–13 November 2007)

171. S-Y Shim, J-H Moon, J-K Han, PSNR estimation scheme using coefficient distribution of frequency domain in H.264 decoder. Electron. Lett. **44**(2), 108–109 (2008)

172. J Zhang, SH Ong, TM Le, Kurtosis-based no-reference quality assessment of JPEG2000 images. Image Commun. **26**, 13–23 (2011)

173. K Nishikawa, K Munadi, H Kiya, No-reference PSNR estimation for quality monitoring of motion JPEG2000 video over lossy packet networks. IEEE Trans. Multimedia **10**(4), 637–645 (2008)

174. K Nishikawa, S Nagawara, H Kiya, QoS estimation method for JPEG2000 coded image at RTP layer. IEICE Trans. **E89-A**(8), 2119–2128 (2006). doi:10.1093/ietfec/e89-a.8.2119

175. J Joskowicz, R Sotelo, JCL Ardao, Towards a general parametric model for perceptual video quality estimation. IEEE Trans. Broadcasting **59**(4), 569–579 (2013)

176. ITU, ITU-T Recommendation H.265/high efficiency video coding. http://www.itu.int/rec/T-REC-H.265-201304-I. Accessed 11 April 2014

177. B Lee, M Kim, No-reference PSNR estimation for HEVC encoded video. IEEE Trans. Broadcasting **59**(1), 20–27 (2013)

178. S Winkler, P Mohandas, The evolution of video quality measurement: from PSNR to hybrid metrics. IEEE Trans. Broadcasting **54**(3), 660–668 (2008)

179. M Naccari, M Tagliasacchi, S Tubaro, No-reference video quality monitoring for H.264/AVC coded video. IEEE Trans. Multimedia **11**(5), 932–946 (2009)

180. M Naccari, M Tagliasacchi, F Pereira, S Tubaro, No-reference modeling of the channel induced distortion at the decoder for H.264/AVC video coding, in *IEEE International Conference on Image Processing* (San Diego, 12–15 October 2008), pp. 2324–2327

181. MCQ Farias, MM Carvalho, HTM Kussaba, BHA Noronha, A hybrid metric for digital video quality assessment, in *IEEE International Symposium on Broadband Multimedia Systems and Broadcasting* (Nuremberg, 8–10 June 2011), pp. 1–6

182. T Shanableh, No-reference PSNR identification of MPEG-4 video using spectral regression and reduced model polynomial networks. IEEE Signal Process. Lett. **17**(8), 735–738 (2010)

183. T Shanableh, Prediction of structural similarity index of compressed video at a macroblock level. IEEE Signal Process. Lett. **18**(5), 335–338 (2011)

184. AG Davis, D Bayart, DS Hands, Hybrid no-reference video quality prediction, in *IEEE International Symposium on Broadband Multimedia Systems and Broadcasting* (Bilbao, 13–15 May 2009), pp. 1–6

185. K Yamagishi, T Kawano, T Hayashi, Hybrid video-quality-estimation model for IPTV services, in *IEEE Global Telecommunications Conference, (GLOBECOM)* (Honolulu, 30 November to 4 December 2009), pp. 1–5

186. T Yamada, Y Miyamoto, M Serizawa, No-reference video quality estimation based on error-concealment effectiveness, in *International Workshop on Packet Video* (Lausanne, 12–13 November 2007), pp. 288–293

187. T Yamada, Y Miyamoto, T Nishitani, No-reference quality estimation for video-streaming services based on error-concealment effectiveness. IEICE Trans. Fundamentals Electron. Commun. Comput. Sci. **E95-A**(11), 2007–2014 (2012)

188. H Boujut, J Benois-Pineau, T Ahmed, O Hadar, P Bonnet, A metric for no-reference video quality assessment for HD TV delivery based on saliency maps, in *IEEE International Conference on Multimedia and Expo (ICME)* (Barcelona, 11–15 July 2011), pp. 1–5

189. O Sugimoto, S Naito, S Sakazawa, A Koike, Objective perceptual video quality measurement method based on hybrid no reference framework, in *IEEE International Conference on Image Processing* (Cairo, 7–10 November 2009), pp. 2237–2240

190. S Zhao, H Jiang, Q Cai, S Sherif, A Tarraf, Hybrid framework for no-reference video quality indication over LTE networks, in *23rd Wireless and Optical Communication Conference (WOCC)* (Newark, 9–10 May 2014), pp. 1–5

191. A Ichigaya, Y Nishida, E Nakasu, Nonreference method for estimating PSNR of MPEG-2 coded video by using DCT coefficients and picture energy. IEEE Trans. Circuits Syst. Video Technol. **18**(6), 817–826 (2008)

192. A Ichigaya, M Kurozumi, N Hara, Y Nishida, E Nakasu, A method of estimating coding PSNR using quantized DCT coefficients. IEEE Trans. Circuits Syst. Video Technol. **16**(2), 251–259 (2006)

193. VQEG, Draft VQEG Testplan: Hybrid Perceptual/Bitstream Group (2012). http://www.its.bldrdoc.gov/vqeg/projects/hybrid-perceptual-bitstream/hybrid-perceptual-bitstream.aspx. Accessed 11 April 2014

194. C Keimel, J Habigt, K Diepold, Hybrid no-reference video quality metric based on multiway PLSR, in *Proceedings of the 20th European Signal Processing Conference (EUSIPCO)* (Bucharest, 27–31 August 2012), pp. 1244–1248

195. Z Wang, AC Bovik, Mean squared error: love it or leave it? A new look at signal fidelity measures. IEEE Signal Process. Mag. **26**(1), 98–117 (2009)

196. J You, T Ebrahimi, A Perkis, Attention driven foveated video quality assessment. IEEE Trans. Image Process. **23**(1), 200–213 (2014)

197. B Belmudez, S Möller, Audiovisual quality integration for interactive communications. EURASIP J. Audio Speech Music Process. **2013**(1) (2013). 10.1186/1687-4722-2013-24

198. AN Rimell, MP Hollier, RM Voelcker, The influence of cross-modal interaction on audio-visual speech quality perception, in *Audio Engineering Society Convention 105* (San Francisco, 26–29 September 1998)

199. U Engelke, H Kaprykowsky, H-J Zepernick, P Ndjiki-Nya, Visual attention in quality assessment. IEEE Signal Process. Mag. **28**(6), 50–59 (2011)

200. P Kortum, M Sullivan, The effect of content desirability on subjective video quality ratings. Hum. Factors: J. Hum. Factors Ergonom. Soc. **52**, 105–118 (2010)

201. A Rossholm, M Shahid, B Lövström, Analysis of the impact of temporal, spatial, and quantization variations on perceptual video

quality, in *IEEE Network Operations and Management Symposium (NOMS)* (Krakow, 5–9 May 2014), pp. 1–5

202. M Barkowsky, I Sedano, K Brunnström, M Leszczuk, N Staelens, Hybrid video quality prediction: re-viewing video quality measurement for widening application scope. Multimedia Tools Appl (2014). doi:10.1007/s11042-014-1978-2

203. J You, U Reiter, MM Hannuksela, M Gabbouj, A Perkis, Perceptual-based quality assessment for audio-visual services: a survey. Signal Process. Image Commun. **25**(7), 482–501 (2010)

7

Error concealment algorithm using inter-view correlation for multi-view video

Yuan-Kai Kuan[1], Gwo-Long Li[2], Mei-Juan Chen[1*], Kuang-Han Tai[1] and Pin-Cheng Huang[1]

Abstract

This paper proposes an error concealment algorithm for whole frame loss for multi-view video decoding. In our proposal, the relationship between motion vectors and disparity vectors is exploited first. Based on the parallelogram-like motion relationship, the motion vectors of error frames can be indirectly derived by projecting the disparity vectors from the counterpart view. In addition, to further improve the concealing results, a joint sum of the absolute difference (SAD) minimization approach is also proposed to find the block for the purpose of concealing the current error block by jointly considering motion vectors and disparity vectors. Experimental results show that our proposed algorithm provides better video quality than previous work and reduces error propagation.

Keywords: Error concealment; Multi-view; MVC; Motion vector; Disparity vector

1. Introduction

As multimedia technology has advanced in recent years, the applications of three-dimensional (3D) television and free viewpoint video (FVV) have become more attractive. To support multi-view video coding, the multi-view video coding standard has been proposed [1,2] based on the motion-compensated prediction (MCP) technology adopted in H.264/AVC [3,4] by incorporating the disparity-compensated prediction (DCP) technology as shown in Figure 1, to eliminate inter-view redundancy.

In the error-prone network environment, packet errors or packet loss may occur very frequently due to the unpredictable interruption of noise sources, which leads to the decline of the received video quality as shown in Figure 2. Therefore, error recovering mechanisms have become an important research issue. To deal with the problem in multi-view applications, many studies have been proposed. In general, error recovery can be undertaken by two approaches called error resilience [5-9] and error concealment [10-18]. For multi-view error concealment, study [17] uses the intra-view difference, inter-view correlation, and difference of the inter-view disparity vector projections on the neighboring views

to conceal the error frames. However, this requires complex computations in terms of the temporal change detection, disparity estimation, and frame difference projection which results in difficulties for real-time applications. Study [18] compares the sum of the absolute difference (SAD) between the previous two frames and the SAD between adjacent views of the previous frame to achieve error concealment. However, useful information regarding disparity vectors has not been considered to help with the error concealment process. In [17], the authors prove that the disparity vectors could significantly improve the error concealment results.

To deal with error problem for multi-view video coding, we propose a whole frame error concealment algorithm which applies a predictive compensation approach as well as considering the inter-view correlation to conceal the error frame of the right view. By using the disparity vectors (DVs) in the previous frame as the reference prediction DVs, the motion vectors (MVs) inside the block, referred by the reference DVs, are collected to be the candidates for our error concealment process. Finally, the candidate MV with the smallest joint SAD is chosen as the best MV to conceal the error block, once the candidate MVs have been successfully collected.

The rest of this paper is organized as follows. In Section 2, the proposed algorithm is described in detail. Section 3 shows some simulation results to demonstrate

---

* Correspondence: cmj@mail.ndhu.edu.tw
[1]Department of Electrical Engineering, National Dong Hwa University, 97401 Hualien, Taiwan
Full list of author information is available at the end of the article

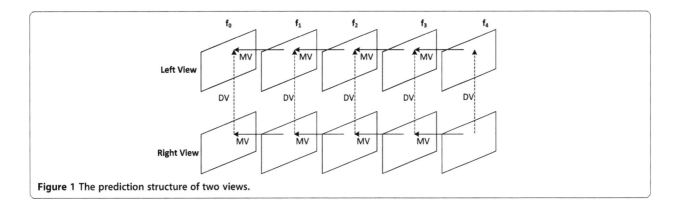

Figure 1 The prediction structure of two views.

the efficiency of our proposed error concealment algorithm. The conclusion is provided in Section 4.

2. Proposed algorithm

For the single-view error concealment approach, the error concealment algorithms are only considered using the information from the spatial and temporal domains. However, since we can have the information between coding views in the multi-view video coding, we can consider that the relationship between views achieves better error concealment results compared to the single-view error concealment. Therefore, we will first observe the relationship between views and propose our error concealment algorithm based on the observation.

2.1 Observation of multi-view characteristics

To create multi-view video sources, the cameras are usually placed along a horizontal line to capture the scene at the same time. In this case, the motion vectors between different views are very similar to each other due to the identical capturing target from the perspective of the time axis. However, when observing the target from the perspective of the view axis, we can observe that the distance between the placement of the cameras will cause the appearance of objects in the scene. Therefore, the inter-view disparity vectors are usually used to

describe the object relationship between views. Figure 3 gives an example to illustrate the movement between frames and views.

If we discover the multi-view sequences, we can investigate the following properties. First, for the quiescent regions which have almost zero motion behavior, the relationship between frames in single view is higher than that between views. Second, for the high-motion regions, the relationship between views is much higher than that between frames. Based on the above observation, study [17] proposes a parallelogram-like motion relationship to describe the correlation between motion vectors and disparity vectors as shown in Figure 4. From this figure, we can find that if an object has been moved from frame (f-1) to frame (f) in one view, we can also observe the same movement in another view. Similarly, if we obtain certain disparity vectors from frame (f-1), we can obtain the similar disparity vectors from frame (f) as well.

2.2 Proposed error concealment algorithm

From the above sub-section, we observe that the motion vectors between views and disparity vectors between frames have a high degree of similarity and a close relationship. The proposed error concealment algorithm is based on this observation. Figure 5 shows the flowchart of the proposed algorithm. First, a DV set is reconstructed

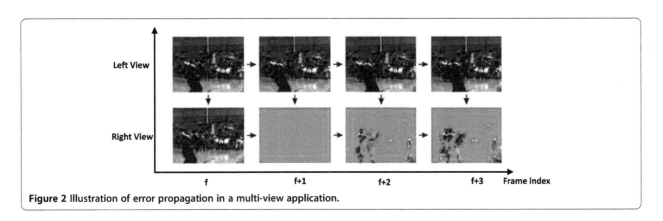

Figure 2 Illustration of error propagation in a multi-view application.

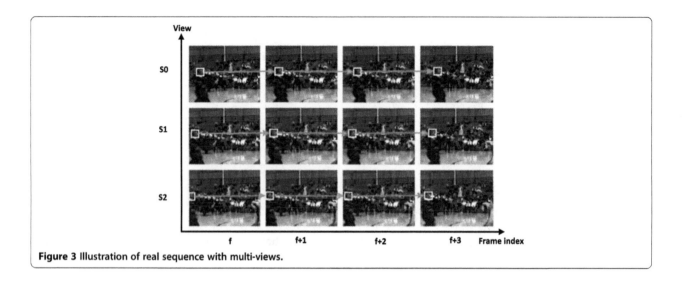

Figure 3 Illustration of real sequence with multi-views.

according to the extended window (EW). Once the EW has been decided, we check if there is any disparity vector within EW. If there is, the proposed DV-based error concealment algorithm will be applied for dealing with the error recover problem. Otherwise, the proposed MV-based error concealment algorithm will be used. The details of the proposed algorithm are described as follows:

1. EW construction

   In the proposed algorithm, the block size of B is adopted to conceal the erroneous frames. However, using 16 or 8 for B will obtain better concealment results since selecting 4 for B would result in a broken frame. After deciding on the block size, we extend B pixels all around the corresponding block in the previous frame to form a $3B \times 3B$-size EW as

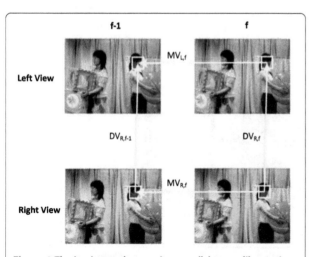

Figure 4 The in-view and cross-view parallelogram-like motion relationship ($DV_{R,f-1} \approx DV_{R,f}$, $MV_{R,f} \approx MV_{L,f}$).

shown in Figure 6. The derivation process of EW can be expressed as follows:

$$EW = \left\{ DV^i_{R,f-1} \middle| 0 \le i < N; \ DV^i_{R,f-1} \text{ covered by } 3B \times 3B \right\} \tag{1}$$

2. DV-based error concealment

   If the EW contains any DV, we will calculate the area covered by each disparity vector in the EW and check whether any covered area has exceeded a predefined threshold. In our proposed algorithm, the default of the threshold is set to half of the EW area. If all of the covered areas pointed to by DVs in the EW are less than a predefined threshold TH, the error concealment algorithm will switch to the MV-based error concealment. Otherwise, the covered area of each DV inside the EW will be calculated and the DV with the biggest area size in the EW will be selected to conceal the error block.

3. MV-based error concealment

   (a) Reconstruction of new extended window

   The proposed MV-based error concealment algorithm will be executed by two conditions. The first condition is the switching from DV-based error concealment while the second condition is the empty EW. Therefore, based on the condition, a new extended window (NEW) will be reconstructed as follows:

$$NEW = \begin{cases} \{DV^i_{R,f-1} | 0 \le i < N; \ DV^i_{R,f-1} \text{ covered by } W \times H\}, \\ \qquad\qquad \text{if EW is empty} \\ EW, \text{ if switched from DV-based EC} \end{cases} \tag{2}$$

where W and H mean the width and height, respectively, of the entire frame. In other words, if the MV-based

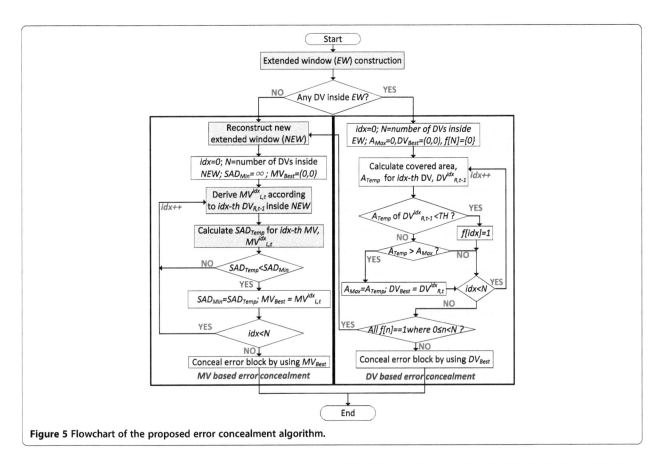

Figure 5 Flowchart of the proposed error concealment algorithm.

error concealment process is trigged by the empty EW, the NEW will be constructed by all DVs in the entire frame. Otherwise, the NEW will be the same as the EW.

(b) MV derivation process

Once the NEW has been constructed successfully, the DVs inside NEW will be considered to select the motion vectors from the left view. To derive the motion vectors corresponding to all DVs in NEW, the DVs inside NEW will be used to be projected onto the left view with a $B \times B$ window called a covered

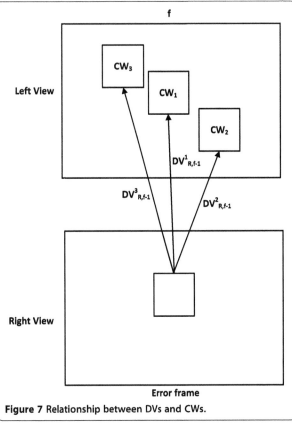

Figure 7 Relationship between DVs and CWs.

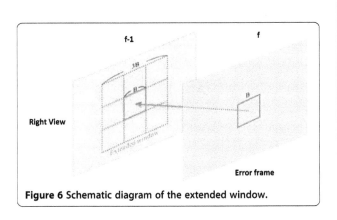

Figure 6 Schematic diagram of the extended window.

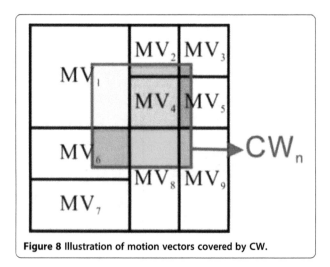

Figure 8 Illustration of motion vectors covered by CW.

window (CW) as shown in Figure 7. After the DV projection, we will face the problem that the CW would cover more than one motion vector as shown in Figure 8. Therefore, a simple mechanism that the motion vector with the largest covered area by CW will be selected as the final motion vector in the motion vector derivation process. The motion vectors can be selected as follows:

$$MV_{L,f}^i = \text{argmax}_{0 \le k < N}\{\text{Area}(MV_k)\}, \qquad (3)$$

where Area(.) is the function of the area calculation according to the specific target.

(c) SAD calculation according to selected MV

Based on the parallelogram-like motion relationship between inter-frame and inter-view correlation as shown in Figure 4, we can observe that the $DV_{R,f-1}^n$ will be very similar to the $DV_{R,f}^n$ and the $MV_{L,f}^n$ will be very similar to the $MV_{R,f}^n$ also. Therefore, when the fth frame of the right view has an error occurring, the MV obtained from the corresponding block in the left view shifted by the DV will be very similar to the original MV of the error frame if the corresponding DV in the previous frame is correct. Therefore, the SADs between B_1 and B_2 as shown in Figure 9 are calculated for all MVs covered by CW to determine the block for concealing the current erroneous block. However, the situation might be faced when the block has been shifted from the wrong DV and the luminance component difference between blocks pointed to by the wrong MVs is unnoticeable. To solve this problem, we further consider SADs between the left and right views in the previous frame ($F_{L,f-1}$). The step-by-step block selecting procedure for computing SADs is described below.

Step 1: The disparity vector $DV_{R,f-1}^n$ of erroneous block B_c has been selected and projected onto the left view to obtain the block B_1 pointed to by $DV_{R,f-1}^n$.

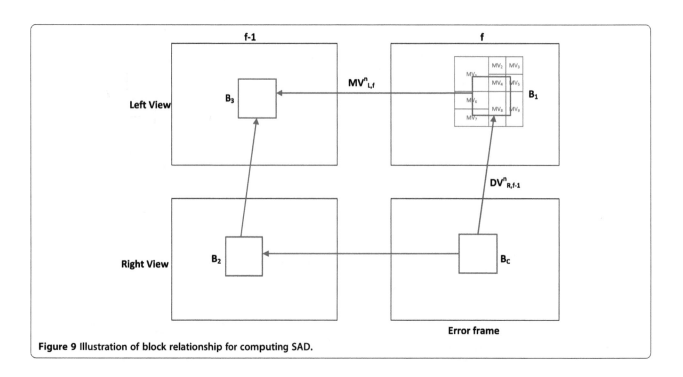

Figure 9 Illustration of block relationship for computing SAD.

Table 1 Simulation parameters

Parameter	Value
View	2
Reference software	JMVC8.5
Processor	Intel Core i7 870 2.93 GHz
GOP structure	IPPP...
Intra-refresh	Only the first frame
Frame rate	25
Frame number	100
Reference frame number	2
Coding order	$0 \rightarrow 1$
QP	32
PLR	5%, 10%, 15%, 20%

Step 2: The motion vector $MV_{L,f}^n$ with the largest area coverage by B_1 will be selected and projected onto the previous frame of the right view to obtain B_2.

Step 3: The corresponding block B_3 pointed by $DV_{R,f-1}^n$ from B_2 will be used to calculate the SAD between B_2 and B_3.

Step 4: Finally, the motion vector with minimum joint SADs will be derived by the following equations to conceal the error block B_c:

$$MV_{L,f}(i,j) = \arg\min_{MV_{L,f}^n \in MV_{L,f}} \sum_{a=0}^{B-1}\sum_{b=0}^{B-1} |F_{R,f-1} \tag{4}$$

$$\left(B \times i + MV_{L,f,x}^n + a, B \times j + MV_{L,f,y}^n + b \right)$$

$$-F_{L,f}\left(B \times i + DV_{R,f-1,x}^n + a, B \times j + DV_{R,f-1,y}^n + b \right)|$$

$$+\left| F_{R,f-1}\left(B \times i + MV_{L,f,x}^n + a, B \times j + MV_{L,f,y}^n + b \right)\right.$$

$$-F_{L,f-1}\left(B \times i + MV_{L,f,x}^n + DV_{R,f-1,x}^n + a, B \times j\right.$$

$$\left.+MV_{L,f,y}^n + DV_{R,f-1,y}^n + b) |$$

The notations of Equation 4 are listed as follows:
- i and j, the horizontal and vertical indexes of the $B \times B$ block in a frame
- a and b, the horizontal and vertical indexes of the pixel inside the block
- $F_{R,f}$, the lost frame of the right view
- $F_{R,f-1}$, the previous frame of the lost frame in the right view
- $F_{L,f}$, the current frame of the left view

Table 2 PSNR comparison of our proposed algorithm with other methods for entire frames ($B = 8$)

		Sequences						
		Ballroom	Vassar	Race1	Exit	AkkoKayo	Flamenco	Average
Error free		35.499	34.957	35.820	37.214	36.930	38.448	36.478
5%	FC	29.077	34.396	22.635	33.617	28.069	29.673	29.578
	MC	29.323	34.494	23.885	33.721	29.610	29.818	30.142
	[18]	29.292	34.388	22.780	33.614	28.184	29.743	29.667
	Proposed	30.241	34.541	26.926	33.608	31.232	30.239	31.131
	ΔPSNR	0.949	0.153	4.146	−0.006	3.048	0.496	1.464
10%	FC	25.463	33.525	19.551	30.748	23.431	26.445	26.527
	MC	25.445	33.579	21.189	31.083	26.098	26.325	27.287
	[18]	25.470	33.583	20.040	30.970	23.688	26.524	26.713
	Proposed	26.063	33.721	23.877	30.972	26.293	26.608	27.922
	ΔPSNR	0.593	0.138	3.837	0.002	2.6050	0.084	1.210
15%	FC	23.466	32.394	17.479	29.056	20.595	24.308	24.550
	MC	23.481	32.634	19.937	29.506	22.249	24.447	25.376
	[18]	23.666	32.480	18.336	29.114	20.762	24.557	24.819
	Proposed	24.399	33.114	21.557	28.902	23.547	24.917	26.073
	ΔPSNR	0.733	0.634	3.221	−0.212	2.785	0.360	1.254
20%	FC	22.117	31.900	16.568	27.301	19.939	22.948	23.462
	MC	22.220	31.747	19.048	28.247	22.089	23.095	24.408
	[18]	22.334	31.964	17.693	27.213	20.726	22.858	23.798
	Proposed	23.439	32.726	20.698	27.811	22.921	23.446	25.174
	ΔPSNR	1.105	0.762	3.005	0.598	2.195	0.588	1.376

Table 3 PSNR comparison of our proposed algorithm with [18] for error frames only (B = 8)

		Sequences						
		Ballroom	Vassar	Race1	Exit	AkkoKayo	Flamenco	Average
5%	Error free	35.520	34.991	35.792	37.275	36.906	38.505	36.498
	[18]	22.114	33.049	16.732	30.809	21.823	25.485	25.002
	Proposed	22.659	33.325	21.309	30.585	25.286	26.378	26.590
	ΔPSNR	0.545	0.276	4.577	−0.224	3.463	0.893	1.588
10%	Error free	35.519	34.970	35.772	37.225	36.953	38.480	36.487
	[18]	21.479	32.296	16.590	29.216	20.429	24.088	24.016
	Proposed	22.185	32.582	20.847	29.131	23.299	24.456	25.417
	ΔPSNR	0.706	0.286	4.257	−0.085	2.870	0.368	1.400
15%	Error free	35.513	34.973	35.762	37.224	36.972	38.439	36.481
	[18]	20.854	31.360	16.261	27.885	18.848	22.928	23.023
	Proposed	21.593	32.327	19.747	27.674	21.785	23.449	24.429
	ΔPSNR	0.739	0.967	3.486	−0.211	2.937	0.521	1.407
20%	Error free	35.513	34.965	35.790	37.219	36.950	38.462	36.483
	[18]	20.134	32.120	15.894	26.341	19.026	21.567	22.514
	Proposed	21.143	31.973	19.151	26.897	21.427	22.235	23.804
	ΔPSNR	1.009	−0.147	3.257	0.556	2.401	0.668	1.291

Table 4 PSNR comparison of our proposed algorithm with other methods for entire frames (B = 16)

		Sequences						
		Ballroom	Vassar	Race1	Exit	AkkoKayo	Flamenco	Average
Error free		35.499	34.957	35.820	37.214	36.930	38.448	36.478
5%	FC	29.077	34.396	22.635	33.617	28.069	29.673	29.578
	MC	29.323	34.494	23.885	33.721	29.610	29.818	30.142
	[18]	29.604	34.382	22.765	33.686	28.022	29.705	29.694
	Proposed	30.441	34.460	26.631	33.558	31.159	30.607	31.143
	ΔPSNR	0.837	0.078	3.866	−0.128	3.137	0.902	1.449
10%	FC	25.463	33.525	19.551	30.748	23.431	26.445	26.527
	MC	25.445	33.579	21.189	31.083	26.098	26.325	27.287
	[18]	25.782	33.509	20.141	30.769	23.870	26.468	26.757
	Proposed	26.668	33.831	23.684	31.445	25.872	26.509	28.002
	ΔPSNR	0.886	0.323	3.543	0.676	2.002	0.041	1.245
15%	FC	23.466	32.394	17.479	29.056	20.595	24.308	24.550
	MC	23.481	32.634	19.937	29.506	22.249	24.447	25.376
	[18]	23.933	32.458	18.515	28.960	20.719	24.541	24.854
	Proposed	25.131	33.075	21.264	29.478	22.781	25.209	26.156
	ΔPSNR	1.198	0.617	2.749	0.518	2.062	0.668	1.302
20%	FC	22.117	31.900	16.568	27.301	19.939	22.948	23.462
	MC	22.220	31.747	19.048	28.247	22.089	23.095	24.408
	[18]	22.506	31.942	17.867	27.220	20.881	23.016	23.905
	Proposed	24.040	32.996	20.741	28.031	22.787	23.167	25.294
	ΔPSNR	1.534	1.054	2.874	0.811	1.906	0.151	1.389

Table 5 PSNR comparison of our proposed algorithm with [18] for error frames only (B = 16)

		Sequences						
		Ballroom	Vassar	Race1	Exit	AkkoKayo	Flamenco	Average
5%	Error free	35.520	34.991	35.792	37.275	36.906	38.505	36.498
	[18]	22.229	33.039	16.674	31.007	21.862	25.495	25.051
	Proposed	23.965	33.759	21.246	31.382	26.274	26.474	27.183
	ΔPSNR	1.736	0.720	4.572	0.375	4.412	0.979	2.132
10%	Error free	35.519	34.970	35.772	37.225	36.953	38.480	36.487
	[18]	21.701	32.113	16.656	29.200	20.596	24.054	24.053
	Proposed	23.291	32.948	20.843	30.043	23.349	24.305	25.797
	ΔPSNR	1.590	0.835	4.187	0.843	2.753	0.251	1.743
15%	Error free	35.513	34.973	35.762	37.224	36.972	38.439	36.481
	[18]	20.993	31.330	16.401	27.757	18.831	22.916	23.038
	Proposed	22.603	32.306	19.633	28.399	21.351	23.715	24.668
	ΔPSNR	1.610	0.976	3.232	0.642	2.520	0.799	1.630
20%	Error free	35.513	34.965	35.790	37.219	36.950	38.462	36.483
	[18]	20.295	31.080	16.020	26.373	19.191	21.705	22.444
	Proposed	22.105	32.398	19.234	27.279	21.488	21.946	24.075
	ΔPSNR	1.810	1.318	3.214	0.906	2.297	0.241	1.631

- $F_{L,f-1}$, the previous frame of the lost frame in the left view
- $DV_{R,f-1,x}^n$, the horizontal component of the nth DV in the block of the previous frame of the right view
- $DV_{R,f-1,y}^n$, the vertical component of the nth DV in the block of the previous frame of the right view
- $MV_{L,f,x}^n$, the horizontal component of the nth MV in the block of the current frame of the left view
- $MV_{L,f,y}^n$, the vertical component of the nth MV in the block of the current frame of the left view

By jointly considering the SADs between views and frames, the concealing results can be further improved.

3. Simulation results

In this section, several simulation results are given to demonstrate the efficiency of our proposed MVC error concealment algorithm. The test sequences we used for simulation are Ballroom (640 × 480), Exit (640 × 480), Flamenco (640 × 480), Race1 (640 × 480), AkkoKayo (640 × 480), and Vassar (640 × 480). In our simulation, we assume that only the right view has the whole frame error while the left view has not. Study [18] is adopted for comparison in this paper, but we have made some modifications for [18] in order to allow the algorithm of [18] to be able to support whole frame loss error concealment. The simulation settings are summarized in Table 1, in which

the packet loss rate (PLR) is simulated by randomly dropping a certain number of frames. For example, the 5% PLR is simulated by randomly dropping 5 frames out of 100 frames.

Tables 2 and 3 tabulate the peak signal-to-noise ratio (PSNR) comparison for our proposed algorithm with other methods under different packet error rate conditions for entire frame and error frame only cases, respectively. Frame Copy (FC), Motion Copy (MC), and the algorithm of [18] are compared. In these tables, the ΔPSNR is calculated by the PSNR values of our proposal minus the PSNR values of [18] while B is set to 8, which means that the basic error concealing block size is 8. From these tables, we can observe that our proposed algorithm outperforms other methods. Quantitatively, our proposed algorithm can achieve about 4-dB PSNR improvement compared to [18] for the high-motion sequence Race1 under the 5% packet error rate condition. However, for other sequences such as Exit and Vassar, the PSNR improvement is less significant. This situation can be explained as follows. From [18], it can be found that the MB pixels at the same spatial position from the

Table 6 Average decoding time comparison of our proposed algorithm (Ballroom sequence) (ms/frame)

Packet loss rate	Error free	Proposed	Overhead (%)
5%	112.98	165.53	46.5
10%	112.98	231.22	104.7
15%	112.98	316.06	179.7
20%	112.98	362.59	220.9

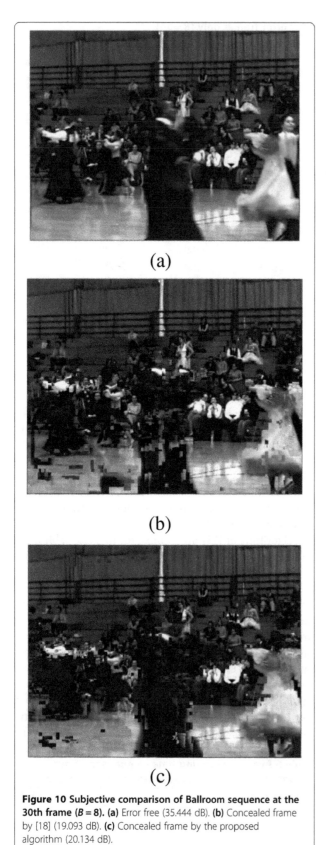

(a)

(b)

(c)

Figure 10 Subjective comparison of Ballroom sequence at the 30th frame ($B = 8$). (a) Error free (35.444 dB). **(b)** Concealed frame by [18] (19.093 dB). **(c)** Concealed frame by the proposed algorithm (20.134 dB).

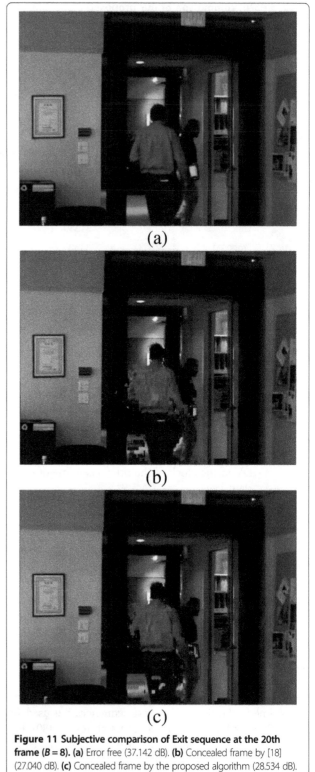

(a)

(b)

(c)

Figure 11 Subjective comparison of Exit sequence at the 20th frame ($B = 8$). (a) Error free (37.142 dB). **(b)** Concealed frame by [18] (27.040 dB). **(c)** Concealed frame by the proposed algorithm (28.534 dB).

temporal and inter-view directions are evaluated. In other words, [18] does not take the motion of the frame into account. This mechanism could be able to obtain good concealment results for low-motion sequences.

(a)

(b)

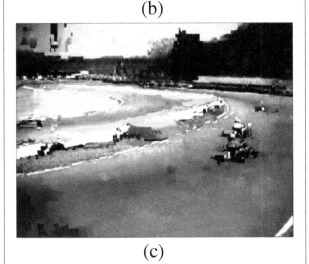

(c)

Figure 12 Subjective comparison of Race1 sequence at the 55th frame ($B = 8$). (a) Error free (36.016 dB). **(b)** Concealed frame by [18] (14.985 dB). **(c)** Concealed frame by the proposed algorithm (19.021 dB).

However, since our proposal takes both motion vector and disparity motion into account, the proposal can obtain better concealment results for high-motion sequences. On

average, our proposed algorithm can receive 1.326- and 1.421-dB PSNR improvement compared to [18] for entire frame and error frame only cases, respectively.

Tables 4 and 5 list the PSNR comparison for the case that B is 16. From these tables, we can observe that even though the basic error concealing block size has been extended to 16, our proposed algorithm can still achieve PSNR improvement when compared to [18]. On average, our proposed algorithm can receive 1.346- and 1.784-dB PSNR improvement compared to [18] for entire frame and error frame only cases, respectively. From Tables 2, 3, 4, and 5, we can observe that the PSNR improvement of smaller B is better than that of larger B. This situation can be explained as follows. In general, the larger B will contain more objects within a single block. Intuitively, it will not be easy to find a matching block from the temporal or inter-view directions which contains multiple objects. For smaller B, multiple objects can be possibly divided into multiple blocks and thus leads to the ease of finding matching blocks. Table 6 tabulates the decoding time of our proposed algorithm when compared to the error frame decoding.

Figures 10, 11, and 12 exhibit the subjective quality comparisons for our proposed algorithm with [18]. From these figures, it is very obvious that our proposed algorithm can significantly improve the subjective quality results. In general, our proposed algorithm can efficiently reduce the broken image effects.

4. Conclusions

To deal with entire frame loss problem in multi-view video decoding, this paper proposes an error concealment algorithm by considering the relationship between motion vectors and disparity vectors. Based on the parallelogram-like motion relationship, a joint SAD minimization approach is proposed to find the best block for concealing the current error block. Through the help of the proposal, the error propagation problem can thus be reduced. Simulation results demonstrate that our proposed algorithm outperforms previous work in terms of subject and objective quality measurements.

Competing interests
The authors declare that they have no competing interests.

Author details
[1]Department of Electrical Engineering, National Dong Hwa University, 97401 Hualien, Taiwan. [2]Department of Video Coding Core Technology, Industrial Technology Research Institute, 31040 Hsinchu, Taiwan.

References
1.   YS Ho, KJ Oh, Overview of multi-view video coding, in *Proceedings of International Workshop on Systems, Signals and Image Processing, 2007 and 6th EURASIP Conference focused on Speech and Image Processing, Multimedia Communications and Services* (Maribor, 2007), pp. 5–12

2. A Vetro, T Wiegand, GJ Sullivan, Overview of the stereo and multi-view video coding extensions of the H.264/MPEG-4 AVC standard. IEEE Proc. **99**(4), 626–642 (2011)

3. T Wiegand, GJ Sullivan, G Bjontegaard, A Luthra, Overview of the H.264/AVC video coding standard. IEEE Trans. Circ. Syst. Vid. Technol. **13**(7), 560–576 (2003)

4. T Wiegand, G Sullivan, Draft ITU-T recommendation and final draft international standard of joint video specification (ITU-T Rec. H.264/ISO/IEC 14496-10 AVC), in *Joint Video Team of ISO/IEC MPEG and ITU-T VCEG, JVT-G050* (Pattaya, 2003)

5. Y Wang, JY Tham, WS Lee, KH Goh, Pattern selection for error-resilient slice interleaving based on receiver error concealment technique, in *Proceedings of IEEE International Conference on Multimedia and Expo* (Barcelona, 2011)

6. BW Micallef, CJ Debono, An analysis on the effect of transmission errors in real-time H.264-MVC bit-streams, in *Proceedings of IEEE Mediterranean Electrotechnical Conference MELECON* (Valletta, 2010), pp. 1215–1220

7. MB Dissanayake, DVSX De Silva, ST Worrall, WAC Fernando, Error resilience technique for multi-view coding using redundant disparity vectors, in *Proceedings of IEEE International Conference on Multimedia and Expo* (Suntec, 2010), pp. 1712–1717

8. J Xiao, T Tillo, C Lin, Y Zhao, Joint redundant motion vector and intra macroblock refreshment for video transmission. EURASIP J. Image Vid. Process. **2011**(12), (2011). doi:10.1186/1687-5281-2011-12

9. S Ye, M Ouaret, F Dufaux, T Ebrahimi, Improved side information generation for distributed video coding by exploiting spatial and temporal correlations. EURASIP J. Image Vid. Process. **2009**, 683510 (2009). doi:10.1155/2009/683510

10. X Xiang, D Zhao, S Ma, W Gao, Auto-regressive model based error concealment scheme for stereoscopic video coding, in *Proceedings of IEEE International Conference on Acoustics, Speech and Signal Processing* (Prague, 2011), pp. 849–852

11. PJ Lee, KT Kuo, An adaptive error concealment method selection algorithm for multi-view video coding, in *Proceedings of IEEE International Conference on Consumer Electronics* (Las Vegas, 2013), pp. 474–475

12. O Stankiewicz, K Wegner, M Domanski, Error concealment for MVC and 3D video coding, in *Proceedings of Picture Coding Symposium* (Nagoya, 2010), pp. 498–501

13. SH Lee, SH Lee, NI Cho, JH Yang, A motion vector prediction method for multi-view video coding, in *Proceedings of International Conference on Intelligent Information Hiding and Multimedia Signal Processing* (Harbin, 2008), pp. 1247–1250

14. S Liu, Y Chen, YK Wang, M Gabbouj, MM Hannuksela, H Li, Frame loss error concealment for multi-view video coding, in *Proceedings of IEEE International Symposium on Circuits and Systems* (Seattle, 2008), pp. 3470–3473

15. L Liang, R Ma, P An, C Liu, An effective error concealment method used in multi-view video coding, in *Proceedings of International Congress on Image and Signal Processing* (Shanghai, 2011), pp. 76–79

16. TY Chung, S Sull, CS Kim, Frame loss concealment for stereoscopic video plus depth sequences. IEEE Trans. Consum. Electron. **57**(3), 1336–1344 (2011)

17. Y Chen, C Cai, KK Ma, Stereoscopic video error concealment for missing frame recovery using disparity-based frame difference projection, in *Proceedings of IEEE International Conference on Image Processing* (Cairo, 2009), pp. 4289–4292

18. Y Zhou, C Hou, R Pan, Z Yuan, L Yang, Distortion analysis and error concealment for multi-view video transmission, in *Proceedings of IEEE International Symposium on Broadband Multimedia Systems and Broadcasting* (Shanghai, 2010), pp. 1–5

8

Vehicle classification framework: a comparative study

Amol Ambardekar[*], Mircea Nicolescu, George Bebis and Monica Nicolescu

Abstract

Video surveillance has significant application prospects such as security, law enforcement, and traffic monitoring. Visual traffic surveillance using computer vision techniques can be non-invasive, cost effective, and automated. Detecting and recognizing the objects in a video is an important part of many video surveillance systems which can help in tracking of the detected objects and gathering important information. In case of traffic video surveillance, vehicle detection and classification is important as it can help in traffic control and gathering of traffic statistics that can be used in intelligent transportation systems. Vehicle classification poses a difficult problem as vehicles have high intra-class variation and relatively low inter-class variation. In this work, we investigate five different object recognition techniques: PCA + DFVS, PCA + DIVS, PCA + SVM, LDA, and constellation-based modeling applied to the problem of vehicle classification. We also compare them with the state-of-the-art techniques in vehicle classification. In case of the PCA-based approaches, we extend face detection using a PCA approach for the problem of vehicle classification to carry out multi-class classification. We also implement constellation model-based approach that uses the dense representation of scale-invariant feature transform (SIFT) features as presented in the work of Ma and Grimson (Edge-based rich representation for vehicle classification. Paper presented at the international conference on computer vision, 2006, pp. 1185–1192) with slight modification. We consider three classes: sedans, vans, and taxis, and record classification accuracy as high as 99.25% in case of *cars* vs *vans* and 97.57% in case of *sedans* vs *taxis*. We also present a fusion approach that uses both PCA + DFVS and PCA + DIVS and achieves a classification accuracy of 96.42% in case of *sedans* vs *vans* vs *taxis*.

Keywords: Computer vision; Video surveillance; Pattern recognition; Traffic monitoring; Vehicle classification; Machine vision and scene understanding; Image processing

MSC: 68T10; 68T45; 68U10

1 Introduction

Visual traffic surveillance has attracted significant interest in computer vision, because of its significant application prospects. Efficient and robust localization of vehicles from an image sequence (video) can lead to semantic results, such as 'Vehicle No. 3 stopped,' 'Vehicle No. 4 is moving faster than Vehicle No. 6.' However, such information can be more relevant if we not only can detect vehicles but also can classify them. Information such as gap, headway, stopped-vehicle detection, speeding vehicle, and class of a vehicle can be useful for intelligent transportation systems [1]. Monitoring vital assets using video surveillance has increased in recent years. The class of a detected vehicle can supply important information

that can be used to make sure that certain types of vehicles do not appear in certain areas under surveillance. Multi-camera systems such as the one used in [2] can benefit immensely if the information regarding the classes of vehicles is available, as vehicle classification can be used in matching objects detected in non-overlapping field of views from different cameras.

Object detection and tracking has achieved good accuracy in recent years. However, the same cannot be said about object classification. Object recognition in case of still images has the problem of dealing with the clutter in the scene and a large number of classes. Object recognition in video sequences has the benefit of using background segmentation to remove clutter [3]. However, images obtained from video surveillance cameras are generally of low resolution, and in case of traffic video surveillance,

* Correspondence: ambardek@cse.unr.edu
University of Nevada, 1664 N Virginia St., Reno, NV 89557, USA

the vehicles cover very small areas of these images, making the classification problem challenging. Vehicle classes such as *cars* and *vans* are difficult to differentiate as they have similar sizes. Therefore, classification techniques that use global features such as size and shape of the detected blob do not yield satisfactory results.

For this work, we consider three vehicle classes: *cars*, *vans*, and *taxis*. Classes like bus, semi, and motorcycle were not included because they are relatively easy to classify based on their size. We considered three different scenarios: *cars* vs *vans*, *sedans* vs *taxis*, and *sedans* vs *vans* vs *taxis*. *Taxis* and *sedans* are disjoint subsets of class *cars*. Therefore, results of *sedans* vs *taxis* will demonstrate the relevance of our approach when inter-class variability is low. For the purpose of this paper, we used a dataset provided in [4].

In [3], Ambardekar *et al.* presented a comprehensive traffic surveillance system that can detect, track, and classify the vehicles using a 3D model-based approach. The classification using the 3D model-based approach requires camera parameters and orientation of a vehicle which can be calculated using tracking results. When vehicle orientation information is available, the methods presented in this paper can be used in a traffic surveillance system such as [3] to improve the vehicle classification accuracy.

In this work, we present five different vehicle classification techniques that can be used in combination with a consideration to the requirements of the scenario and do not require camera calibration. The two main contributions of our work are the following: (1) We present several approaches (PCA + DFVS, PCA + DIVS, PCA + SVM, LDA, and constellation model) and improvements over the published results that used state-of-the-art techniques. (2) We perform a comparative study of these and other approaches in the literature for the purpose of vehicle classification.

There are similarities between the problem of face detection and vehicle recognition especially in the typical size of an image sample under consideration. In face detection, the problem is finding a face from non-face image samples. However, in case of vehicles, we have multiple classes, and we want to differentiate between them. Turk and Pentland used PCA to form eigenfaces that can reliably recognize faces [5]. We extend the face detection based on PCA and implement three different techniques: PCA + DFVS, PCA + DIVS, and PCA + SVM. In these approaches, we create a principal component space (PCS) using PCA which we call vehicle space. In case of PCA + DFVS, the decision is made by finding the distance from a separate vehicle space for each class, and therefore, it is named distance from vehicle space (DFVS). On the other hand, PCA + DIVS predicts the class of a test image after projecting a test image onto a combined vehicle space,

and distance from each class is calculated in vehicle space and hence named distance in vehicle space (DIVS). We achieved an overall accuracy as high as 95.85% in case of *sedans* vs *vans* vs *taxis* using PCA + DFVS. In the difficult case of *sedans* vs *taxis*, we achieved a 97.57% accuracy using PCA + DFVS which is higher than any published results using this dataset [6,7]. PCA + DIVS yielded 99.25% accuracy in case of *cars* vs *vans*. Our results match or surpass the results in all the cases considered in [4,8]. PCA depends upon most expressive features (MEFs) that can be different from most discriminant features (MDFs) [9]; therefore, we also implement LDA that relies on MDFs. We observed that PCA + DIVS approach works better when the classes have more inter-class variation, e.g., *cars* vs *vans*, and PCA + DFVS seems to work better even in the difficult case of *sedans* vs *taxis* when inter-class variation is low. Therefore, we devised a new fusion approach that combines the benefits of both the approaches to classify *sedans* vs *vans* vs *taxis*, and were able to achieve classification accuracy of 96.42%.

Constellation models [10,11] have been shown to be able to learn to recognize multiple objects using a training set of just a few examples. In [4], Ma and Grimson used a constellation model with mean-shift clustering of scale-invariant feature transform (SIFT) features to classify vehicles. However, the mean-shift clustering is considerably slow. In our implementation, we used K-means clustering. We also use an expectation maximization algorithm that considers up to 6 Gaussians and choose the number of Gaussians that maximizes the maximum likelihood for training data. We achieved similar accuracy with considerably less computation complexity compared to results achieved in [4]. In [4], Ma and Grimson dealt with only a two-class classification problem. We extend the approach by performing classification in the three class case of *sedans* vs *vans* vs *taxis*.

The rest of the paper is organized as follows: Section 2 discusses previous work. Section 3 gives details about the techniques compared in this paper, and Section 4 describes and compares the results obtained. Section 5 discusses the conclusions and future work.

2 Existing video annotation and retrieval systems

Object classification in general is a challenging field. Vehicle classification poses another challenge as inter-class variability is relatively smaller compared to intra-class variability. The approaches for vehicle classification can be broadly classified into four categories.

2.1 3D model-based approaches

3D model-based approaches have been proposed for the purpose of object detection and tracking in [3,12,13]. In [3], a region of interest (ROI) was extracted using statistical background modeling and extraction of foreground using background subtraction. Edges were detected using either the Sobel edge detector or the Canny edge detector. 3D wireframes of the models in the database are projected onto the image, and the best match is found based on the best matching pixel position [14], or mathematical morphology to match the model to the edge points [3]. All the models are subjected to the matching process, and the one with the highest matching score (i.e., lowest matching error) is selected as the model. These methods require camera parameters to be calibrated so that a 3D wireframe can be projected onto an image. They also need orientation of the vehicles which can be retrieved from optical flow calculation.

2.2 Global feature-based approaches

Gupte et al. [15] proposed a system for vehicle detection and classification. They classified the tracked vehicles into two categories: cars and non-cars. The classification is based on vehicle dimensions, where they compute the length and height of a vehicle and use them to distinguish cars from non-cars [15]. Avely et al. [16] used a similar approach, where the vehicles are classified on the basis of length using an uncalibrated camera. However, this method also classifies the vehicles into two coarse groups: short vehicles and long vehicles. In order to achieve a finer-level classification of vehicles, a more refined method needs to be devised that can detect and model the invariant characteristics for each vehicle category considered.

2.3 PCA-based approaches

Chunrui and Siyal developed a new segmentation technique for the classification of moving vehicles [17]. They used simple correlation to get the desired match. The results shown in the paper are for the lateral view of the vehicles, and no quantitative results were given. Towards this goal, a method is developed by Zhang et al. [18]. In their work, they used a PCA-based vehicle classification framework. They implemented two classification algorithms: eigenvehicle and PCA-SVM to classify vehicle objects into trucks, passenger cars, vans, and pickups. These two methods exploit the distinguishing power of principal component analysis (PCA) at different granularities with different learning mechanisms. Eigenvehicle approach used in [18] is similar to the proposed approach PCA + DIVS. However, we use distance from mean image in PCA space instead of finding distance from each image from each class as done in [18]. The performance of such algorithms also depends on the accuracy of vehicle normalization.

2.4 Local feature-based approaches

Local features have certain advantages over using global features as they are better suited to handle partial occlusion. In traffic surveillance, if the intersection monitoring is desired, then overlapping of passing vehicles will result in partial occlusion and errors in extracting ROIs. SIFT [19] has shown to outperform other local features in terms of repeatability [20].

Ma and Grimson developed a vehicle classification approach using modified SIFT descriptors [4]. They used SIFT features to train the constellation models that were used to classify the vehicles. They considered two cases: cars vs vans and sedans vs taxis. They reported good results for the difficult case of classifying sedans vs taxis. However, they do not report combined classification results for sedans vs vans vs taxis that will show the scalability of the approach. We used the same dataset provided by them. We implemented constellation model-based approach that differs slightly from [4], but we were able to achieve similar accuracy with better computational complexity.

2.5 Other approaches

Koch and Malone [21] used infrared video sequences and a multinomial pattern-matching algorithm [22] to match the signature to a database of learned signatures to do classification. They started with a single-look approach where they extract a signature consisting of a histogram of gradient orientations from a set of regions covering the moving object. They also implemented a multi-look fusion approach for improving the performance of a single-look system. They used the sequential probability ratio test to combine the match scores of multiple signatures from a single tracked object. Huang and Liao [23] used hierarchical coarse classification and fine classification. Ji et al. used a partial Gabor filter approach [24]. In [8], Wijnhoven and de With presented a patch-based approach that uses Gabor-filtered versions of the input images at several scales. The feature vectors were used to train a SVM classifier which was able to produce results better than those presented in [4] in cars vs vans case. However, this approach is global feature based; therefore, it is not best suited for cases with partial occlusion. Recently, Buch et al. presented a traffic video surveillance system which employs motion 3D extended histogram of oriented gradients (3DHOG) to classify road users [6].

3 Classification framework

The problem of face detection can be considered as a two-class classification when we deal with face vs non-face classification. In this research, we are interested in classifying vehicles in multiple classes, and we do so by extending the eigenface approach [5]. The components extracted from PCA are the MEFs, while LDA uses the MDFs. The constellation model is a generative model which models scale invariant features to distinguish between different classes of vehicles. As the constellation model is a part-based model, it can perform well even in the presence of partial occlusion.

3.1 Eigenvehicle approach (PCA + DFVS)

The images in the dataset have different sizes and therefore are not suitable for PCA directly. We normalize all the images to average width and height (74 × 43). In [5], PCA was used for single-class classification (i.e., face). We use it for up to three classes at the same time and therefore extend the approach by creating a separate PCS or vehicle space for each class. We define each eigenspace as eigenvehicle [18].

3.1.1 Training for eigenvehicles

For creating the principal component space for each class, i.e., creating eigenvehicle for each class, we normalize the images such that the width and height of all the images are the same. Since each sample image is a 2-D image, $A_i \in R^{m \times n}$, we create a vector from an image by concatenating rows to create a column vector $A'_i \in R^{1 \times mn}$. We consider $k = 50$ images for each class; then, we have a matrix of k columns $A' = [A'_1\ A'_2\ A'_3\ ...\ A'_k]$ that represents the set of training samples. The length of each column is $m \times n$. Then, we can compute the mean vector μ as below:

$$\mu = \frac{1}{k}\sum_{i=1}^{k} A'_i. \tag{1}$$

Let $\sigma_i = A'_i - \mu$, and $\sigma = [\sigma_1, \sigma_2, \sigma_3, ...\ \sigma_k]$. The covariance matrix of A' is

$$C = \frac{1}{k}\sum_{i=1}^{k} \sigma_i\sigma_i^T = \sigma\sigma^T \tag{2}$$

The eigenvectors of C are the principal components. The eigenvectors associated with the largest eigenvalues correspond to the dimensions in the space where the

data has the largest variance. In our training set, the size of C is $mn \times mn$ (3,182 × 3,182), which is not feasible to compute principal components. In [5], Turk and Pentland proposed a solution to this problem, where they find the eigenvectors and eigenvalues of $\sigma^T\sigma$, instead of $\sigma\sigma^T$. Suppose v^i is an eigenvector of $\sigma^T\sigma$, and λ_i is the associated eigenvalue. Then,

$$\sigma^T\sigma v_i = \lambda_i v_i \overset{\text{yields}}{\rightarrow} \sigma\sigma^T\sigma v_i = \lambda_i \sigma v_i \tag{3}$$

The above deduction shows that σv_i is an eigenvector of $\sigma\sigma^T$. This technique reduces the computation complexity since the dimension of $\sigma^T\sigma$ is only $k \times k$ (50 × 50). We are able to extract top k principal components of $\sigma\sigma^T$ by the following equation:

$$u_i = \sigma v_i \tag{4}$$

The eigenvectors corresponding to the biggest eigenvalue represent the most dominant dimensions or features of the images in a class. The length of each eigenvector is $m \times n$. Therefore, each of these eigenvectors can be re-arranged as an image that we call an eigenvehicle. As we use 50 sample images from each class during the creation of eigenvehicles, we have 50 eigenvehicles for each class. However, not all the eigenvehicles need to be used during the classification.

3.1.2 Classification using eigenvehicles

Classifying a new image in one of the classes is carried out in three steps. First, we reshape A_{new} into A'_{new}, such that the width and height of the image are normalized. We then obtain $\sigma_{\text{new}} = A'_{\text{new}} - \mu$. Second, we project σ_{new} onto an eigenvehicle space, i.e., the PCS created. Traditionally, this space has been called the face space. This process yields the k weights w_i where

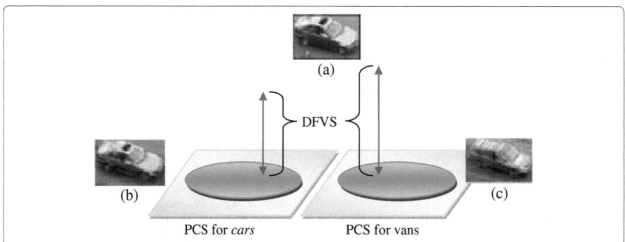

Figure 1 PCA-DFVS. (a) A test image showing an example from car class. **(b)** Back projection of the test image with respect to car PCS. **(c)** Back projection of the test image with respect to van PCS. The absolute difference (DFVS) between back-projected images and original image is calculated (red arrows).

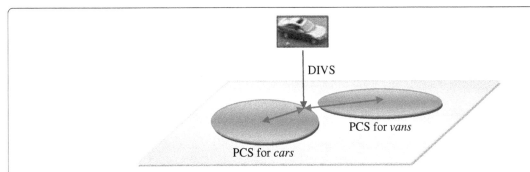

Figure 2 PCA-DIVS. A test image is projected on to the principal component space. The Euclidean distance (DIVS) between the projected image and mean projected image of each class is calculated (red arrows).

$$w_i = u_i^T \sigma_{\text{new}} \quad (5)$$

We choose the first l weights, where $l < k$ and back project to get an image A''_{new}:

$$A''_{\text{new}} = \sum_{i=1}^{l} w_i \sigma_i + \mu \quad (6)$$

The image A''_{new} is subtracted from the original test image A'_{new} to find the Euclidean distance, i.e., DFVS, which is essentially a back projection error:

$$DFFS = \sqrt[2]{\sum_{i=1}^{m \times n} (A''_{\text{new}i} - A_{\text{new}i})^2} \quad (7)$$

We do this for every class which yields a new A''_{new}. This process is described in Figure 1. The class related to the PCS that results in the smallest DFVS is assigned as the class of the test image. We tried to use a different number of principal eigenvectors to see the dependence of accuracy on the number of eigenvectors used. The detailed results are discussed in Section 4. This approach has an ability to perform well in the case of low inter-class variability (e.g., *sedans* vs *taxis*).

3.2 PCA + DIVS

In this approach, we start by employing PCA as described in eigenvehicle approach with a slight modification. We create a PCS or vehicle space for all the training samples irrespective of the class label. Therefore, there is only one PCS contrary to the previous approach, where we created a separate PCS for each class. All training images irrespective of class label are used to calculate a covariance matrix C whose eigenvectors define a single PCS. Then, all training images in a class c ($c \in \{1, 2\}$ in two class case) are projected onto the PCS and weights are calculated. The mean weight vector (principal component) w_{mean}^c for each class is calculated using the first l weights that belong to the eigenvectors with the largest eigenvalues ($l < k$, where k is the total number of training sample images in all the classes combined, k^c is the number of training samples in a class c, and l will be the dimension of w_{mean}^c).

$$w_{\text{mean}}^c = \frac{1}{k^c} \sum u^T \cdot \sigma_{\text{train}}^c \quad (8)$$

For testing, a test image is projected on the PCS to get the weight vector (principal component) w with l dimensions, where the components of w are calculated using

$$w_i = u_i^T \sigma_{\text{new}} \quad (9)$$

We calculate the Mahalanobis distance $d_{\text{Mahalanobis}}^c$ from the mean principal component w_{mean}^c of each class:

$$d_{\text{Mahalanobis}}^c = \sqrt{\left(w_i - w_{\text{mean}}^c\right)^T C^{-1} \left(w_i - w_{\text{mean}}^c\right)} \quad (10)$$

The smallest distance decides the class of the test image. This process is described in Figure 2. This approach works better when there is relatively high inter-class variability (e.g., *cars* vs *vans*).

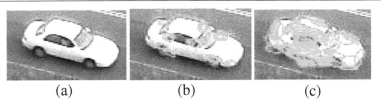

(a)	(b)	(c)

Figure 3 Interest point detection and respective affine regions. (a) Original image. **(b)** Detected Harris affine regions. **(c)** Detected LoG-affine regions.

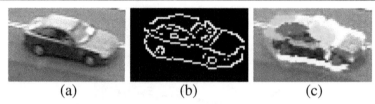

(a)   (b)   (c)

Figure 4 Clustering of feature descriptors. (a) Original image, **(b)** detected edge points after applying Canny edge detector, and **(c)** detected edge point groups are shown in different colors after clustering SIFT vectors using K-means.

3.3 PCA + SVM

In this approach, we used the approach described in Section 3.2 to create the PCS. However, instead of finding the distance from the mean principal component of each class, we train PCA vectors using a support vector machine (SVM) with a radial basis function (RBF) kernel [25]. The main objective of the support vector machine training is to find the largest possible classification margin, which indicates the minimum value of w in

$$\frac{1}{2}w^T w + E \sum \varepsilon_i \qquad (11)$$

where $\varepsilon_i \geq 0$ and E is the error tolerance level. The training vectors are grouped in labeled pairs $L_i (x_i, y_i)$ where x_i is a training vector and $y_i \in \{-1, 1\}$ is the class label of x_i and are used in training SVM that finds the hyperplane leaving the largest possible fraction of points of the same class on the same side, while maximizing the distance of either class from the hyperplane. We used four fold cross-validation and tried different values for bandwidth to find

the best parameters for SVM that minimize the cross-validation estimate of the test error.

For testing, a test image is projected on the PCS and then the corresponding principal component is classified using the trained SVM. The choice of kernel, the size of training set, and bandwidth selection plays a major role in the efficiency of SVM training and accuracy of the results.

3.4 LDA

Approaches based on PCA use the MEFs to classify novel images. However, MEFs are not always the MDFs. The linear discriminant analysis (LDA) automatically selects the features that provide an effective feature space to be used for classification [8].

To eliminate the problem of high dimensionality, we start by employing PCA as described in Section 3.2, where all the images irrespective of class label are projected onto a single PCS. The dimension of the PCS will be limited by the total number of training images minus the number of classes. The LDA involves calculating two matrices: the

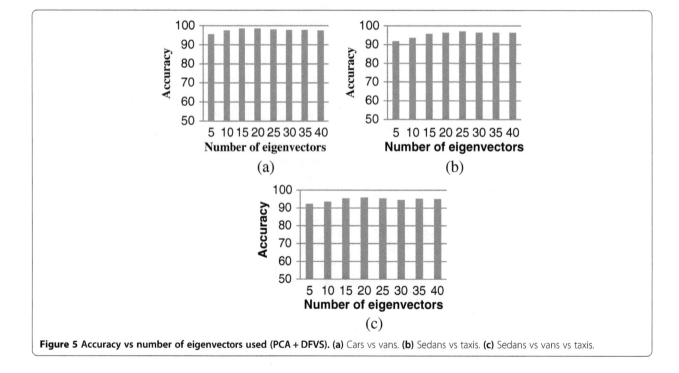

(a)   (b)

(c)

Figure 5 Accuracy vs number of eigenvectors used (PCA + DFVS). (a) Cars vs vans. **(b)** Sedans vs taxis. **(c)** Sedans vs vans vs taxis.

Table 1 Confusion matrices using PCA + DFVS: cars vs vans

	Cars	Vans
Cars	200	0
Vans	6	194

within-class scatter matrix E_{W} and the *between-class* scatter matrix S_{B}:

$$S_{\mathrm{W}} = \sum_{i=1}^{C}\sum_{j=1}^{M_i}\left(y_j-\mu_i\right)\left(y_j-\mu_i\right)^{T} \qquad (12)$$

$$S_{\mathrm{B}} = \sum_{i=1}^{C}(\mu_i-\mu)(\mu_i-\mu)^{T}, \qquad (13)$$

where C is the number of classes, μ_i is the mean vector of a class i, and M_i is the number of samples within class i. The mean of all the mean vectors is represented by μ and is calculated as

$$\mu = \frac{1}{C}\sum_{i=1}^{C}\mu_i \qquad (14)$$

LDA computes a transformation that maximizes the *between-class* scatter while minimizing the *within-class* scatter by maximizing the following ratio: $\det|S_{\mathrm{B}}|/\det|S_{\mathrm{W}}|$. The advantage of using this ratio is that it has been proven [26] that if S_{W} is a non-singular matrix, then this ratio is maximized when the column vectors of the projection matrix W are the eigenvectors of $S_{\mathrm{W}}^{-1}S_{\mathrm{B}}$. The W with dimension $C-1$ projects the training data onto a new space called fisherfaces. We use W to project all training samples onto the fisherfaces. The resulting vectors are used to create a KD-tree which is employed in finding the approximate nearest neighbors during the classification of a sample image. We use five nearest neighbors, and the class with the highest number of nearest neighbors is assigned as the class of the vehicle.

3.5 Constellation of SIFT features

Object recognition techniques that generally work well for object classification are not directly useful in the case of object categorization when inter-class variability is low. The problem of vehicle classification is different from many other object classification problems [10], where the difference between object classes is considerable (e.g., airplane vs motorcycle). Surveillance videos pose other problems, for example, surveillance image sizes

Table 2 Confusion matrices using PCA + DFVS: sedans vs taxis

	Sedans	Taxis
Sedans	193	7
Taxis	1	129

Table 3 Confusion matrices using PCA + DFVS: sedans vs vans vs taxis

	Sedans	Vans	Taxis
Sedans	189	1	10
Vans	8	190	2
Taxis	1	0	129

are generally small and captured images can have varying lighting conditions. Affine invariant detectors have shown to outperform simple corner detectors in the task of object classification [27]. We tried two interest point detectors: Harris-Laplace with affine invariance and LoG with affine invariance. Figure 3 shows the original image and the affine regions detected using the interest point detectors. The number of interest points detected using these techniques is small and may not provide enough information to classify an image successfully.

In this section, we present a constellation model-based approach that uses the same techniques as presented by [4] with a few modifications. In our implementation, we extend the approach to do the multi-class classification and use K-means clustering instead of mean-shift clustering to improve the computational complexity. Ma and Grimson [4] used a single Gaussian to model the features and a mixture of Gaussians (MoG) to model feature positions. However, in our implementation, we model both features and feature positions as independent MoGs that consider up to 6 Gaussians and choose the number of Gaussians that maximizes the maximum likelihood for training data.

3.51 Constellation of SIFT Features

In [19], Lowe used a corner detector to find interest points. The SIFT descriptors were calculated using image patches around the detected interest points. Therefore, there are two parts to SIFT feature detection: interest point detection and calculation of descriptor. In low-resolution images obtained using surveillance video, the number of corners detected is limited. Thus, we use a Canny edge detector [7] to detect the edge points which are used as interest points to improve robustness by using over-complete information. We adopt SIFT with some modifications as discussed in [4]. Lowe used eight orientations in the orientation histogram; we use only four orientations that reduce the size of the descriptor fourfold. Another modification that we use is instead of using 4×4 regions around interest points, we use 2×2 regions (24 pixels × 24 pixels determined experimentally), resulting in the length of SIFT descriptor to be 16 instead of 128 in Lowe's implementation. We use x^2 distance as the distance between SIFT vectors (descriptors) instead of Euclidean distance. This ensures that relative differences are taken instead of absolute differences as in the case of Euclidean distance.

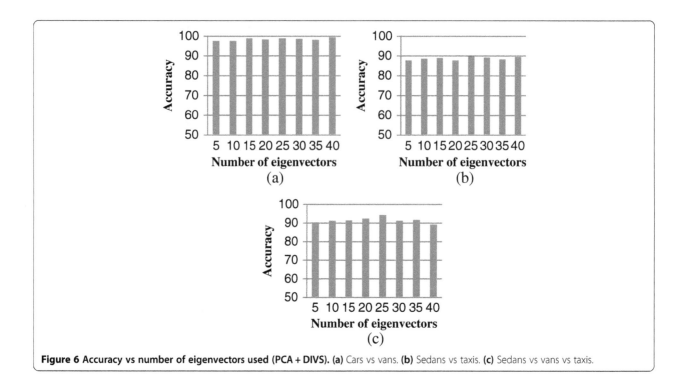

Figure 6 Accuracy vs number of eigenvectors used (PCA + DIVS). (a) Cars vs vans. **(b)** Sedans vs taxis. **(c)** Sedans vs vans vs taxis.

As a result of intra-class variation in appearance and low resolution of images, the individual edge points are not sufficient to model spatial repeatability. Therefore, we group the similar descriptors that results in edge point groups that are spatially repeatable. The other benefit of using edge point groups is that it results in concise models compared to using edge points directly. In [4], Ma and Grimson used mean-shift clustering to create the edge point groups. Although mean shift is a good technique to find the dominant modes, it is computationally intensive (time complexity: $O(Tn^2)$, where T is the number of iterations, and n is the number of features) and sensitive to parameters like the Gaussian kernel bandwidth. Thus, we use K-means clustering with $K = 10$ (time complexity: $O(KnT)$, where K is the number of clusters, T is the number of iterations, and n is the number of features). Figure 4 shows a sample image, detected edge points after applying the Canny edge detector, and edge point groups after applying K-means clustering.

After clustering the SIFT descriptors, we have edge points with their coordinates (pixel coordinates are normalized to (0.0, 1.0)) and respective SIFT descriptors. We denote the number of points in cluster (segment) i

as J_i, the 2D coordinates of the jth ($j = 1,...J_i$) point in segment i as $\vec{P}_{ij}$, and the SIFT vector of the point as $\vec{S}_{ij}$. A feature descriptor f_k ($k = 1,...N$, where N is the number of edge points in an image) is defined using the triplet $\left\{ \left\{ \vec{p}_{ij} \right\}, \left\{ \vec{s}_{ij} \right\}, \left\{ \vec{c}_i \right\} \right\}$, where $\vec{c}_i$ is the average of all $\vec{S}_{ij}$ of segment i. The feature descriptors obtained from an image are denoted by $F = \{f_i\}$. During the training phase, we extract all the feature descriptors of all the images related to a particular class and group them according to $\vec{c}_i$.

3.5.2 Constellation model

A constellation model is a probabilistic model of a set of characteristic parts with a variable appearance and spatial configuration [10,28]. Fergus *et al.* modeled the object as a constellation of parts where shape configuration of the parts was modeled as a joint Gaussian of object parts' coordinates, and the appearance of individual parts was modeled by independent Gaussians [10]. In [4], Ma and Grimson modified this constellation model to classify vehicles in two-class problem. We extend the approach

Table 4 Confusion matrices using PCA + DIVS: cars vs vans

	Cars	Vans
Cars	199	1
Vans	2	198

Table 5 Confusion matrices using PCA + DIVS: sedans vs taxis

	Sedans	Taxis
Sedans	167	34
Taxis	1	129

Table 6 Confusion matrices using PCA + DIVS: sedans vs vans vs taxis

	Sedans	Vans	Taxis
Sedans	186	2	12
Vans	7	193	0
Taxis	9	1	120

Table 8 Confusion matrices using PCA + SVM: sedans vs taxis

	Sedans	Taxis
Sedans	131	69
Taxis	78	122

to multi-class classification and use a mixture of Gaussians (up to 6) to fit the model parameters.

For c classes $\omega_1, \dots \omega_c$, a Bayesian decision is given by

$$C^* = \arg\max_c p(\omega_c|F) = \arg\max_c p(F|\omega_c)p(\omega_c) \quad (15)$$

where F contains the features of an observed object. By assuming constant priors, a hypothesis is defined as matching of detected features to parts. Then, the likelihood can be expanded as

$$p(F|\omega_c) = \sum_{h \in H} p(F, h|\omega_c)$$
$$= \sum_{h \in H} p(F|h, \omega_c)p(h|\omega_c), \quad (16)$$

where H is the set of all possible hypotheses. In [4], it was observed that over-segmentation of edge points of an observed object may result in several almost identical features that effectively produce many-to-one hypothesis mapping. Ma and Grimson [4] used an approximation, where only the most probable hypothesis is used instead of summing over the entire hypothesis space for all the combinations. Therefore, Equation 16 becomes

$$p(F|\omega_c) \cong p(F, h^*|\omega_c), \quad (17)$$

where h^* is the hypothesis, in which every $f_i(f_i \in F)$ is mapped to the most similar part in a model. We assume that features of an object are independent of each other, and for each feature, assume that its edge point coordinates $\{\vec{p_{ij}}\}$ and corresponding SIFT vectors $\{\vec{s_{ij}}\}$ are also independent. If we consider that there are N features, then Equation 16 can be written as

$$p(F|\omega_c) \cong \prod_{i=1}^{N} p\left(\left\{\vec{p_{ij}}\right\}|h^*, \omega_c\right) p\left(\left\{\vec{s_{ij}}\right\}|h^*, \omega_c\right) \quad (18)$$

We consider two variations of this model: implicit shape model and explicit shape model as discussed in [4]. In the implicit shape model, we do not model the position of the features. Therefore, Equation 18 becomes

$$p(F|\omega_c) \cong \prod_{i=1}^{N} p\left(\left\{\vec{s_{ij}}\right\}|h^*, \omega_c\right) \quad (19)$$

By assuming the independence of features, we can calculate $p\left(\left\{\vec{s_{ij}}\right\}|h^*, \omega_c\right)$ as

$$p\left(\left\{\vec{s_{ij}}\right\}|h^*, \omega_c\right) = \sum_{m=1}^{K^s_{h^*(i)}} \alpha^s_{h^*(i),m} \quad (20)$$
$$\times G\left(\left\{\vec{s_{ij}}\right\}|\mu^s_{h^*(i),m}, \Sigma^s_{h^*(i),m}\right),$$

where $h^*(i)$ is the index of the part that matches feature i of the observed object, $K^s_{h^*(i)}$ is the number of mixture components, $\alpha^s_{h^*(i),m}$ is the weight of the mth mixture component, and $\mu^s_{h^*(i),m}$ and $\Sigma^s_{h^*(i),m}$ are the mean vector and covariance matrix of the mth Gaussian component, respectively. We use a mixture of Gaussians instead of a single Gaussian as used in [4]. It allows us to handle problems in clustering such as undersegmentation.

In case of the explicit shape model, we use Equation 18, where $p\left(\left\{\vec{s_{ij}}\right\}|h^*, \omega_c\right)$ is defined by Equation 20, and $p\left(\left\{\vec{p_{ij}}\right\}|h^*, \omega_c\right)$ is given by

$$p\left(\left\{\vec{p_{ij}}\right\}|h^*, \omega_c\right) = \sum_{m=1}^{K^p_{h^*(i)}} \alpha^p_{h^*(i),m} \quad (21)$$
$$\times G\left(\left\{\vec{s_{ij}}\right\}|\mu^p_{h^*(i),m}, \Sigma^p_{h^*(i),m}\right),$$

where $h^*(i)$ is the index of the part that matches feature i of the observed object, $K^p_{h^*(i)}$ is the number of mixture components, $\alpha^p_{h^*(i),m}$ is the weight of the mth mixture component, and $\mu^p_{h^*(i),m}$ and $\Sigma^p_{h^*(i),m}$ are the mean vector and covariance matrix of the mth Gaussian component, respectively.

3.5.3 Learning and recognition
During the learning process, we have a choice of using all the features detected. However, it was observed by Ma and Grimson [4] that some features only appear in very few objects. Therefore, we can prune such features without losing the correctness of the model.

Table 7 Confusion matrices using PCA + SVM: cars vs vans

	Cars	Vans
Cars	200	0
Vans	147	53

Table 9 Confusion matrices using LDA: cars vs vans

	Cars	Vans
Cars	200	0
Vans	16	184

Table 10 Confusion matrices using LDA: sedans vs taxis

	Sedans	Taxis
Sedans	194	6
Taxis	10	120

We use a similar learning and recognition procedure as outlined in [4]. We start by computing the features of each training sample in a class first. Then, sequential clustering is carried out on all features to give a feature pool. For sequential clustering, we denote a pool of features for class c as F_q^c. To start, a training sample from class c with all its features $F = \{f_i\}$ is randomly selected and added to the feature pool. Then, another sample with all its features $F' = \{f'_i\}$ is added. For each f'_i, x^2-distance is calculated between the average SIFT feature vector c_i. Suppose f_{min} in the feature pool has the smallest distance to f'_i. If this smallest distance is less than a threshold, f'_i is merged with f_{min} in the feature pool by adding all its SIFT vectors and corresponding coordinates to f_{min}, and the mean SIFT vector of f_{min} is updated. Otherwise, f_i is added to F_q^c as a new feature. We repeat the same procedure for all training samples in class c to create the feature pool F_q^c. While creating feature pool, we also keep record of the percentage of sample images that contributed to feature f_i which is denoted by r_i. During the pruning process, any feature f_i with r_i less than some threshold is considered to be invalid and not considered in the future model learning process.

For the model structures established in the previous section, the parameters to be learned are $\{K_q^p, \alpha_{q,m}^p, \mu_{q,m}^p, \Sigma_{q,m}^p, K_q^s, \alpha_{q,m}^s, \mu_{q,m}^s, \Sigma_{q,m}^s\}$, where $m = 1, \ldots K_p$, $q = 1, \ldots Q$, where Q is the number of parts in the feature pool. The parameters of Gaussian mixture models are estimated using a typical EM algorithm.

In the recognition phase, the features of an observed object are computed, and class conditional likelihoods are evaluated using Equation 18 for explicit shape model or Equation 19 for implicit shape model. The Bayesian decision rule in Equation 16 gives the classification result.

3.6 A fusion of approaches

We presented five approaches that can be used in combination with each other and improve the classification

Table 11 Confusion matrices using LDA: sedans vs vans vs taxis

	Sedans	Vans	Taxis
Sedans	174	6	20
Vans	17	180	3
Taxis	7	0	123

Table 12 Confusion matrices using implicit shape model: cars vs vans

	Cars	Vans
Cars	191	9
Vans	6	194

accuracy. The fusion of approaches becomes more important when the number of classes increases. In Section 4, we present the results using all the approaches showing that certain approaches are better suited for a certain classification task, e.g., PCA + DIVS works well for the case of *cars* vs *vans*, while PCA + DFVS works well for the case of *sedans* vs *taxis*. As explained earlier, *sedans* and *taxis* are disjoint subsets of *cars*. Therefore, we train two classifiers where the first classifier uses PCA + DIVS and classifies a test image into *cars* and *vans*. The test images that were classified as *cars* are further classified into *sedans* and *taxis* using the second classifier which employs PCA + DFVS. The fusion of different methods is thus possible and yields better results than just using a single approach.

4 Results

In this work, we have considered five different approaches. This section provides details about the experimental setup used during testing, the effect of different parameter choices on the results, and the comparison between the different approaches.

4.1 Experimental setup

In our dataset, we have three types of vehicles: *cars*, *vans*, and *taxis*. Sedans and *taxis* are the disjoint subsets of class *cars*. The dataset provided in [4] has 50 images of each class for training and 200 images of *cars*, *vans*, and *sedans* each and 130 images of *taxis*. For the case of *cars* vs *vans*, we use 50 images from each class for training and 200 images of each class for testing. For the case of *sedans* vs *taxis*, we use 50 images from each class for training, while 200 images of sedans and 130 images of taxis are used for testing. We use the same experimental setup as that used in [6,7], so that a fair comparison is performed. In the case of *sedans* vs *vans* vs *taxis*, we use 50 images of each class for training and 200 images of sedans, and 200 images of vans and 130 images of taxis for testing. Previously published results do not consider such as a three-class case.

Table 13 Confusion matrices using implicit shape model: sedans vs taxis

	Sedans	Taxis
Sedans	183	17
Taxis	18	112

Table 14 Confusion matrices using implicit shape model: sedans vs vans vs taxis

	Sedans	Vans	Taxis
Sedans	137	22	41
Vans	3	190	7
Taxis	3	0	127

4.2 Eigenvehicle approach (PCA + DFVS)

As 50 images of each class were used for training, the dimension of the principal component space is limited to 50. The first principal component (eigen) vector is the most expressive vector, the second one is the second most expressive vector, and so on. We choose the first k principal components and perform the experiment. Figure 5 shows the accuracy vs number of eigenvectors used. We observed that changing the number of eigenvectors used does not change the accuracy greatly. For the case of *sedans* vs *vans* vs *taxis*, we achieved the accuracy of 95.85% when we used 20 eigenvectors. We got the accuracy of 98.5% in the case of *cars* vs *vans* by using 15 eigenvectors, while 97.57% in the case of *sedans* vs *taxis* by using 22 eigenvectors. Tables 1, 2 and 3 give the confusion matrices for the experiments performed while using optimal number of eigenvectors.

4.3 PCA + DIVS

In this approach, we create a single combined principal component space for all the classes. During recognition, we have to make a similar choice as in the previous approach to choose the number of eigenvectors that are used to calculate the Mahalanobis distance from the mean principal component vector of each class. We experimented with the choice of the number of eigenvectors. Figure 6 shows the bar graphs of the accuracy vs number of eigenvectors.

For the case of *sedans* vs *vans* vs *taxis*, we achieved an accuracy of 94.15% when we used 25 eigenvectors. Accuracy was 99.25% in the case of *cars* vs *vans* by using 40 eigenvectors, which is higher than any published results [6,7]. We achieved the accuracy of 89.69% in the case of *sedans* vs *taxis* by using 25 eigenvectors. Tables 4, 5 and 6 give the confusion matrices for the experiments performed while using optimal number of eigenvectors.

Table 15 Confusion matrices using explicit shape model: cars vs vans

	Cars	Vans
Cars	194	6
Vans	6	194

Table 16 Confusion matrices using explicit shape model: sedans vs taxis

	Sedans	Taxis
Sedans	183	17
Taxis	19	111

4.4 PCA + SVM

We used PCA + SVM to classify *cars* vs *vans* and *sedans* vs *taxis*. We achieved an accuracy of 63.25% in the case of *cars* vs *vans* and 76.67% in the case of *sedans* vs *taxis*. The accuracy achieved was low compared to other methods and therefore we did not perform the experiment on the more challenging case of *sedans* vs *vans* vs *taxis*. Tables 7 and 8 give the confusion matrices for the experiments performed.

4.5. LDA

LDA has shown to outperform PCA in the cases where there are many training samples [29]. In this algorithm, the number of nearest neighbors used k is the free variable. We experimentally chose [$k = 5$]. We observed an accuracy of 96% in the case of *cars* vs *vans* and 95.15% in the case of *sedans* vs *taxis*. In the difficult case of *sedans* vs *vans* vs *taxis*, we achieved an accuracy of 90.00%. Tables 9, 10 and 11 give the confusion matrices for the experiments performed.

4.6 Constellation model

We consider two types of constellation models: implicit and explicit. In the implicit shape constellation model, we do not model the positions of the features. Tables 12, 13 and 14 give the confusion matrix for all the cases considered using the implicit shape model.

Using the implicit shape model, we achieved an accuracy of 96.25% in the case of *cars* vs *vans*, 89.39% in the case of *sedans* vs *taxis*, and 85.66% in the case of *sedans* vs *vans* vs *taxis*. In the explicit shape model, we model the normalized position of the features along with the features themselves. We achieved slightly better results for *cars* vs *vans* and *sedans* vs *vans* vs *taxis*. However, the implicit shape model outperformed the explicit shape model in the case of *sedans* vs *taxis*. We achieved a 97% accuracy in the case of *cars* vs *vans* and 89.09% in the case of *sedans* vs *taxis* using the explicit shape model. In the difficult case when all three vehicle

Table 17 Confusion matrices using explicit shape model: sedans vs vans vs taxis

	Sedans	Vans	Taxis
Sedans	137	22	41
Vans	3	194	3
Taxis	5	0	125

Table 18 Confusion matrix using a fusion of approaches

	Sedans	Vans	Taxis
Sedans	189	3	8
Vans	4	194	2
Taxis	1	1	128

classes were considered, we achieved an accuracy of 86.04%. Tables 15, 16 and 17 give the confusion matrices for the experiments performed.

For both the implicit and explicit shape models, prior probabilities were considered to be the same. In the case of three class classification, we can observe that *sedans* are misclassified. We can alleviate this problem and improve the results by using higher prior probabilities for the sedan class.

4.7 A fusion of approaches

In this approach, we employ two classifiers: PCA + DIVS to classify between *cars* and *vans*, and PCA + DFVS to classify between *sedans* and *taxis*. For initial classification, we use the PCA + DIVS as explained in Section 3.2. To classify the images that are classified as *cars*, we use the PCA + DFVS as discussed in Section 3.1. We use this combined approach to classify vehicles in case of *sedans* vs *vans* vs *taxis* and achieve an accuracy of 96.42%. The fusion approach works better than using any individual approach. Table 18 gives the confusion matrix for the experiment performed.

4.8 Comparison of approaches

In this paper, we used six different approaches to classify vehicles. The dataset that we used contains the images of vehicles taken from a surveillance video camera and segmented using a tracking algorithm [30]. The images were taken such that vehicles are captured in a more general oblique view instead of side or top view. We compare our approaches with the approaches presented in [4] and [8] that use the same dataset. We observe that our PCA + DFVS outperforms all other approaches in

the case *sedans* vs *taxis*, while our PCA + DIVS outperforms the rest in the case of *cars* vs *vans*. In the case of *sedans* vs *vans* vs *taxis*, the proposed fusion of approaches (PCA + DIVS and PCA + DFVS) gives the best results.

The constellation model-based approach presented in this paper gives performance benefits by using K-means clustering over mean shift. It also has an advantage over all other approaches presented in this work that it has an ability to handle partial occlusions, owing to its reliance of local features rather than global features. Our constellation model-based approach gives comparable results to the constellation model-based approach presented in [4] for the cases of *cars* vs *vans* and *sedans* vs *taxis*. In this work, we extended the constellation model-based approach to handle multi-class case. We can observe that the accuracy decreases while doing multi-class classification which can be attributed to increased number of common features as the number of classes increases.

Table 19 provides the accuracy achieved using each approach, and the approaches that yielded the best results are italicized. The first seven rows of Table 19 provide the results obtained using techniques investigated in this paper. The last two rows of the Table 19 give the results obtained by the state-of-the-art techniques in vehicle classification when applied to the same dataset. They are copied from [4] and [8] respectively and use the same experimental setup as presented in this paper. However, these techniques do not extend to perform multi-class classification.

5 Conclusion

In this work, we investigated and compared five different approaches for vehicle classification. Using the PCA + DFVS (eigenvehicle) approach, we were able to achieve an accuracy of 97.57% in the challenging case of *sedans* vs *taxis* which is higher than any published results using this dataset. PCA + DIVS outperformed all other approaches investigated in this paper in the case of *cars* vs *vans*. We also extended the constellation model approach [4] for classifying all three vehicle classes at the same time. LDA

Table 19 Comparison of approaches

	Cars vs vans (%)	Sedans vs taxis (%)	Sedans vs vans vs taxis (%)
PCA + DFVS (eigenvehicle)	98.5	*97.57*	95.85
PCA + DIVS	*99.25*	89.69	94.15
PCA + SVM	63.25	76.67	
LDA	96	95.15	90.00
Constellation model (implicit shape)	96.25	89.39	85.66
Constellation model (explicit shape)	97	89.09	86.04
A fusion of approaches			*96.42*
Constellation model [4]	98.5	95.86	
Patch-based object classification [8]	*99.25*	95.25	

performed reliably but did not produce the best results in any of the cases we experimented on. PCA + SVM did not perform satisfactorily, but more experimentation with the choice of kernel and parameters might improve the results. Overall, PCA + DFVS approach achieves good results. However, the constellation model-based approach can be configured to work better in the presence of partial occlusion and minor rotations. We also presented an approach that combines two approaches and achieves improvements over using just one approach. We report accuracy of 96.42% in case of *sedans* vs *vans* vs *taxis* using a fusion of approaches. We can use the SIFT-PCA features to train the constellation models. Also, features other than SIFT, such as LoG affine regions can be used for modeling. The performance of the constellation model deteriorates as we extend it to multiple classes. A boosting algorithm can be used to choose the appropriate features for training.

In this paper, we used the images extracted from surveillance video captured using a fixed-angle camera. In the real traffic surveillance videos, vehicles can have different orientations and different view angles and sizes. The problem of orientation can be solved using camera self-calibration and the result of a tracking algorithm. Appearance-based algorithms have limited ability to model different view angles. A 3D model-based approach with strong thresholds (low false positives) can be used to train an appearance-based approach for better accuracy.

Competing interests
The authors declare that they have no competing interests.

Acknowledgements
This work has been supported by the Office of Naval Research, under grant number N00014-09-1-1121.

References
1. USDOT, USDOT intelligent transportation systems research. (2011). http://www.fhwa.dot.gov/research/. Accessed 22 Jan 2013
2. D Ang, Y Shen, P Duraisamy, *Video analytics for multi-camera traffic surveillance* (Paper presented at the second international workshop on computational transportation science, Seattle, WA, USA, 2009), pp. 25–30
3. A Ambardekar, M Nicolescu, G Bebis, *Efficient vehicle tracking and classification for an automated traffic surveillance system* (Paper presented at the international conference on signal and image processing, Kailua-Kona, HI, USA, 2008), pp. 1–6
4. X Ma, W Grimson, *Edge-based rich representation for vehicle classification* (Paper presented at the international conference on computer vision, New York, NY, USA, 2006), pp. 1185–1192
5. M Turk, A Pentland, Eigenfaces for recognition. J. Cogn. Neurosci. **3**(1), 71–86 (1991)
6. N Buch, J Orwell, S Velastin, *Three-dimensional extended histograms of oriented gradients (3-DHOG) for classification of road users in urban scenes* (Paper presented at the British machine vision conference, London, UK, 2009)
7. J Canny, Computational approach to edge detection. IEEE Trans. Pattern Anal. Machine Intell. **PAMI-8**, 679–698 (1986)
8. R Wijnhoven, P de With, *Experiments with patch-based object classification* (Paper presented at the IEEE conference on advanced video and signal based surveillance, London, U.K, 2007), pp. 105–110
9. D Swets, J Weng, Using discriminant eigenfeatures for image retrieval. IEEE Trans. Pattern Anal. Machine Intell. **18**(8), 831–836 (1996)
10. R Fergus, P Perona, A Zisserman, *Object class recognition by unsupervised scale-invariant learning* (Paper presented at the IEEE conference on computer vision and pattern recognition, Madison, WI, USA, 2003), pp. 264–271
11. L Fei-Fei, R Fergus, P Perona, *Learning generative visual models from few training examples: an incremental Bayesian approach tested on 101 object categories* (Paper presented at the IEEE conference on computer vision and pattern recognition, Washington D.C., USA, 2004)
12. H Kollnig, H Nagel, 3D pose estimation by directly matching polyhedral models to gray value gradients. Int. J Comput. Vision **23**(3), 283–302 (1997)
13. J Lou, T Tan, W Hu, H Yang, S Maybank, 3-D model-based vehicle tracking. IEEE Trans. Image Processing **14**(10), 1561–1569 (2005)
14. R Wijnhoven, P de With, *3D wire-frame object modeling experiments for video surveillance* (Paper presented at the international symposium on information theory, Seattle, WA, USA, 2006), pp. 101–108
15. S Gupte, O Masoud, RFK Martin, N Papanikolopoulos, Detection and classification of vehicles. IEEE Trans. Intell. Transport. Syst. **3**(1), 37–47 (2002)
16. R Avely, Y Wang, G Rutherford, *Length-based vehicle classification using images from uncalibrated video cameras* (Paper presented at the intelligent transportation systems conference, Washington, WA, USA, 2004)
17. Z Chunrui, M Siyal, *A new segmentation technique for classification of moving vehicles* (Paper presented at the vehicular technology conference, Boston, MA, USA, 2000), pp. 323–326
18. C Zhang, X Chen, W Chen, *A PCA-based vehicle classification framework* (Paper presented at the international conference on data engineering workshops, Atlanta, GA, USA, 2006), pp. 17–17
19. D Lowe, Distinctive image features from scale-invariant keypoints. Int. J. Comput. Vis. **60**(2), 91–110 (2004)
20. K Mikolajczyk, C Schmid, *A performance evaluation of local descriptors* (Paper presented at the computer vision and pattern recognition, Madison, WI, USA, 2003), pp. 257–263
21. M Koch, K Malone, *A sequential vehicle classifier for infrared video using multinomial pattern matching* (Paper presented at the conference on computer vision and pattern recognition workshop, New York, NY, USA, 2006), pp. 127–133
22. K Simonson, *Multinomial Pattern Matching: A Robust Algorithm for Target Identification* (Automatic Target Recognizer Working Group, Huntsville, 1997)
23. C Huang, W Liao, *A vision-based vehicle identification system* (Paper presented at the international conference on pattern recognition, Cambridge, UK, 2004), pp. 364–367
24. P Ji, L Jin, X Li, *Vision-based vehicle type classification using partial Gabor filter bank* (Paper presented at the international conference on automation and logistics, Jinan, China, 2007), pp. 1037–1040
25. B Schölkopf, J Platt, J Shawe-Taylor, A Smola, R Williamson, Estimating the support of a high-dimensional distribution. Neural Comput. **13**(7), 1443–1471 (2001)
26. R Fisher, The statistical utilization of multiple measurements. Annals of Eugenics **8**(4), 376–386 (1938)
27. K Mikolajczyk, T Tuytelaars, C Schmid, A Zisserman, J Matas, F Schaffalitzky, T Kadir, L Van Gool, A comparison of affine region detectors. Int. J. Comput. Vis. **65**(1–2), 43–72 (2005)
28. M Burl, M Weber, P Perona, *A probabilistic approach to object recognition using local photometry and global geometry* (Paper presented at the European conference on computer vision, Freiburg, Germany, 1998), pp. 628–641
29. AM Martinez, AC Kak, PCA vs LDA. IEEE Trans. Pattern Anal. Machine Intell. **23**(2), 228–233 (2001)
30. J Migdal, W Grimson, *Background subtraction using Markov thresholds* (Paper presented at the IEEE workshop on motion and video computing, Breckenridge, CO, USA, 2005), pp. 58–65

9

High-performance hardware architectures for multi-level lifting-based discrete wavelet transform

Anand D Darji[1*], Shailendra Singh Kushwah[2], Shabbir N Merchant[1] and Arun N Chandorkar[1]

Abstract

In this paper, three hardware efficient architectures to perform multi-level 2-D discrete wavelet transform (DWT) using lifting (5, 3) and (9, 7) filters are presented. They are classified as folded multi-level architecture (FMA), pipelined multi-level architecture (PMA), and recursive multi-level architecture (RMA). Efficient FMA is proposed using dual-input Z-scan block (*B1*) with 100% hardware utilization efficiency (HUE). Modular PMA is proposed with the help of block (*B1*) and dual-input raster scan block (*B2*) with 60% to 75% HUE. Block *B1* and *B2* are micro-pipelined to achieve critical path as single adder and single multiplier for lifting (5, 3) and (9, 7) filters, respectively. The clock gating technique is used in PMA to save power and area. Hardware-efficient RMA is proposed with the help of block (*B1*) and single-input recursive block (*B3*). Block (*B3*) uses only single processing element to compute both predict and update; thus, 50% multipliers and adders are saved. Dual-input per clock cycle minimizes total frame computing cycles, latency, and on-chip line buffers. PMA for five-level 2-D wavelet decomposition is synthesized using Xilinx ISE 10.1 for Virtex-5 XC5VLX110T field-programmable gate array (FPGA) target device (Xilinx, Inc., San Jose, CA, USA). The proposed PMA is very much efficient in terms of operating frequency due to pipelining. Moreover, this approach reduces and totals computing cycles significantly as compared to the existing multi-level architectures. RMA for three-level 2-D wavelet decomposition is synthesized using Xilinx ISE 10.1 for Virtex-4 VFX100 FPGA target device.

Keywords: Clock gating; DWT; Dual-scan architecture; Folding; FPGA; Lifting

1 Introduction

In recent years, multi-level two-dimensional discrete wavelet transform (2-D DWT) is used in many applications, such as image and video compression (JPEG 2000 and MPEG-4), implantable neuroprosthetics, biometrics, image processing, and signal analysis. due to good energy compaction in higher-level DWT coefficients. To meet application constraint such as speed, power, and area, there is a huge demand of hardware-efficient VLSI architectures in recent years. DWT provides high compression ratio without any blocking artifact that deprives reconstructed image of desired smoothness and continuity. However, implementation of convolution-based DWT has many practical obstacles, such as higher computational complexity and more memory requirement. Therefore, Swelden et al. [1] proposed lifting wavelet, which is also known as second-generation wavelet. DWT can be implemented using convolution scheme as well as lifting scheme. The computational complexity and memory requirement of lifting scheme is very less as compared to convolution. Several architectures have been proposed to perform lifting-based DWT, which differ in terms of numbers of multipliers, adders, register, line buffers requirement, and scanning scheme adopted. 2-D DWT can be computed by applying 1-D DWT row-wise, which produces low-frequency (L) and high-frequency (H) sub-bands and then process these sub-bands column-wise to compute one approximate (LL) and three detail (LH, HL, HH) coefficients.

Jou et al. have proposed architecture with straightforward implementation of the lifting steps and therefore this

*Correspondence: anand@ee.iitb.ac.in
[1] Department of Electrical Engineering, Indian Institute of Technology Bombay, Powai, Mumbai 400076, India
Full list of author information is available at the end of the article

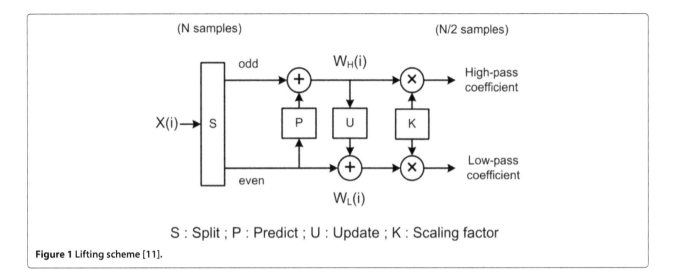

(N samples)   (N/2 samples)

S : Split ; P : Predict ; U : Update ; K : Scaling factor

Figure 1 Lifting scheme [11].

architecture has long critical path [2]. An efficient pipeline architecture having critical path of only one multiplier has been proposed by merging predict and update stages by Wu and Lin [3]. Lai et al. have implemented dual-scan 2-D DWT design based on the algorithm proposed by Wu et al. with critical path delay of one multiplier and throughput of 2-input/2-output at the cost of more pipeline registers [4]. Dual-scan architecture with one multiplier as a critical path has also been proposed by Zhang et al. at the cost of complex control path [5]. Hsia et al. [6] have proposed a memory-efficient dual-scan 2-D lifting DWT architecture with temporal buffer 4N and critical path of two multipliers and four adders. Recently, a dual-scan parallel flipping architecture is introduced with the critical path of one multiplier, less pipeline registers, and simple control path [7].

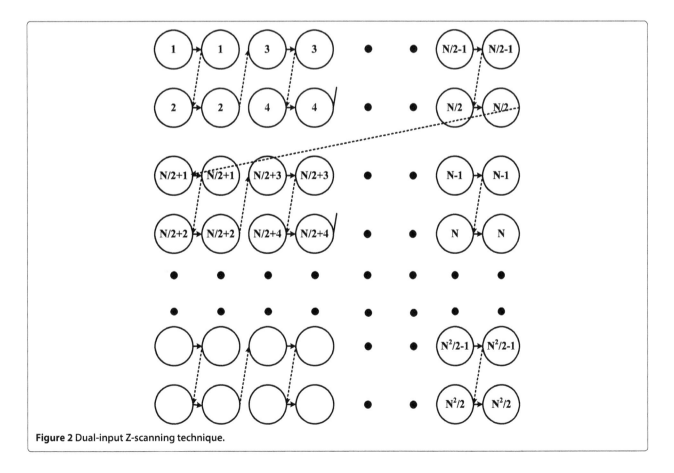

Figure 2 Dual-input Z-scanning technique.

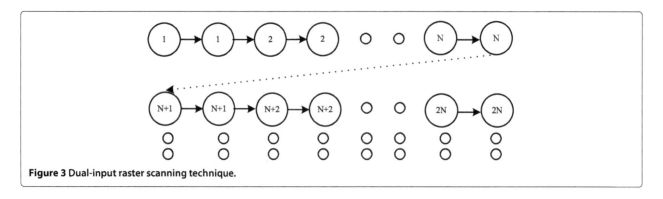

Figure 3 Dual-input raster scanning technique.

Several lifting-based 2-D DWT multi-level architectures have been suggested for efficient VLSI implementation [3,8-15] that take into consideration various aspects like memory, power, and speed. These architectures can be classified as folded architectures [8], parallel architectures [14], and recursive architectures [16]. Andra et al. [8] proposed simple folded architecture to perform several stages of 2-D DWT with the help of memory. Systolic architecture is proposed by Huang et al. [9] for a DWT filter with finite length. Multi-level 2-D DWT decomposition is implemented by recursive architecture (RA) [10,16], but these approaches demand large amount of frame buffers to store the intermediate LL output and also require complex control path. Wu and Lin [3] proposed folded scheme, where multi-level DWT computation is performed level by level, with memory and single processing element. Unlike RA, folded architecture uses simple control circuitry, and it has 100% hardware utilization efficiency (HUE). Folded architectures consist of memory and a pair of 1-D DWT modules, a row processing unit (RPU) and a column processing unit (CPU). Mohanty and Meher [12] proposed a multi-level architecture for high throughput with more number of adders and multipliers. Xiong et al. [13] proposed two line-based high-speed architectures by employing parallel and

pipelining techniques, which can perform j-level decomposition for $N \times N$ image in approximate $2(1 - 4^{-j})N^2/3$ and $(1 - 4^{-j})N^2/3$ clock cycles. Hsia et al. [17] have proposed a symmetric mask-based scheme to compute 2-D integer lifting DWT, where the separate mask is used for each sub-band. Mask-based algorithms do not require temporal buffers, but they are not suitable for area efficient implementation due to a large number of adder and multiplier requirement. A memory efficient architecture is proposed by Lai et al. [4] with low latency. Al-Sulaifanie et al. [18] designed an architecture, which is independent of input image size with moderate speed and HUE. Recently, Aziz and Pham [15] have proposed parallel architecture for lifting (5, 3) multi-level 2-D DWT with a single processing unit to calculate both predict and update values. But this architecture requires $4N$ line buffers for single-level decomposition and has less HUE due to the wastage of the alternate clock cycle. Memory management is key to design multi-level 2-D DWT architectures. The lifting-based multi-level 2-D DWT architecture is suggested using overlapped stripe-based scanning method [19].

Three types of memory buffer are generally used in any 2-D DWT architecture, i.e., frame, transposition, and temporal memory. Frame memory is required to

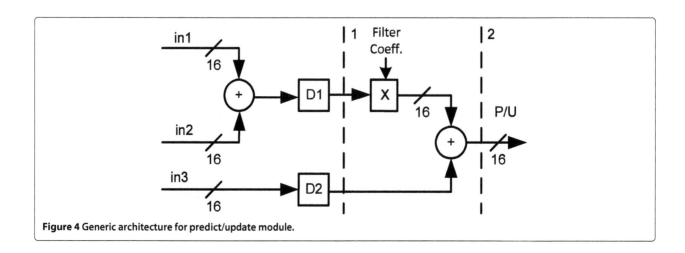

Figure 4 Generic architecture for predict/update module.

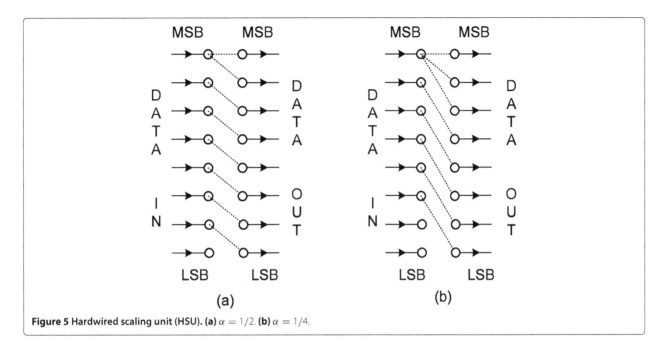

Figure 5 Hardwired scaling unit (HSU). **(a)** $\alpha = 1/2$. **(b)** $\alpha = 1/4$.

store intermediate LL coefficients, transposition memory is mainly required for storing row processor output, and temporal memory is required to store partial results during column processing. Temporal and transposition memories are on-chip, while the frame memory is on or off-chip, depending upon the architecture. Size of transposition memory is limited by the method adopted to scan external memory. Different scanning techniques have been proposed, such as line-based, block-based, and stripe-based [14,19-21].

This paper is organized as follows. Section 2 provides a brief overview of lifting scheme. In Section 3, design of three efficient multi-level architectures and their modules are discussed. Performance comparison, field-programmable gate array (FPGA) implementation and timing analysis are described in Section 4. Conclusions are presented in Section 5.

2 Lifting scheme
The lifting scheme is a hardware-efficient technique to perform DWT. Lifting scheme entirely relies on spatial domain and it has many advantages as compared to the convolution method of calculating DWT such as in-place

Table 1 Data flow of predict/update module

Clock	Input	D1	D2	P/U
1	$X_{1,1} : X_{1,3} : X_{1,2}$			
2	$X_{1,3} : X_{1,5} : X_{1,4}$	$X_{1,1} + X_{1,3}$	$X_{1,2}$	
3	$X_{1,5} : X_{1,7} : X_{1,6}$	$X_{1,3} + X_{1,5}$	$X_{1,4}$	$P/U_{1,1}$
4	$X_{1,7} : X_{1,9} : X_{1,8}$	$X_{1,5} + X_{1,7}$	$X_{1,6}$	$P/U_{1,2}$

computation, symmetric forward and inverse transforms, and perfect reconstruction. The basic principle of lifting scheme is to factorize the polyphase matrix of a wavelet filter into a sequence of alternating upper and lower triangular matrices and a diagonal matrix and convert the filter implementation into banded matrices multiplications [1] as shown by (1) and (2). Where, $h_e(z)$ and $g_e(z)$ ($h_o(z)$ and $g_o(z)$) represent the even parts (odd part) of the low-pass and high-pass filters, respectively. $s_i(z)$ and $t_i(z)$ are denoted as predict lifting and update lifting polynomials. K and $1/K$ are scale normalization factors. Factorization of classical wavelet filter into lifting steps reduces the computational complexity up to 50%.

$$P(z) = \begin{bmatrix} h_e(z) h_o(z) \\ g_e(z) g_o(z) \end{bmatrix} \tag{1}$$

$$P(z) = \prod_{i=1}^{m} \begin{bmatrix} 1 & s_i(z) \\ 0 & 1 \end{bmatrix} \begin{bmatrix} 1 & 0 \\ t_i(z) & 1 \end{bmatrix} \begin{bmatrix} K & 0 \\ 0 & 1/K \end{bmatrix} \tag{2}$$

Every reconstructible filter bank can be expressed in terms of lifting steps in general. Figure 1 shows a block diagram of a forward lifting scheme to compute 1-D DWT. It is composed of three stages: split, predict, and update. In split stage, input sequence is divided into two subsets, an even indexed sequence and an odd indexed sequence. During the second stage, the even indexed sequence is used to predict odd sequence. Two consecutive even and one odd indexed input sequences $X(i)$ are used to calculate high-pass coefficient $W_H(i)$ (detail coefficients), as given by (3). Two consecutive high-pass coefficients (present and previous) and one even indexed

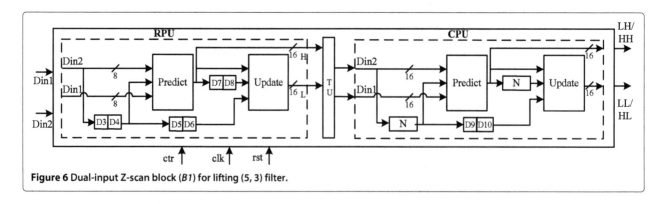

Figure 6 Dual-input Z-scan block (*B1*) for lifting (5, 3) filter.

input sequence are used to calculate low-pass coefficients $W_L(i)$ (approximate coefficients), as given by (4).

$$W_H(i) = X(2i-1) + \alpha[X(2i) + X(2i-2)] \qquad (3)$$

$$W_L(i) = X(2i-2) + \beta[W_H(i) + W_H(i-1)] \qquad (4)$$

3 Proposed architectures

In this section, the proposed dual-input Z-scan architecture (*B1*), dual-input raster scan module (*B2*), and single-input block *B3* are discussed. All these blocks are designed with consideration of lifting wavelet to perform single-level 2-D DWT. Blocks *B1* and *B2* are designed to process two inputs and generate two outputs at every clock cycle. The total clock cycles required to perform one-level decomposition of a $N \times N$ image is $N^2/2$ without considering latency. Then, three novel architectures for multi-level

Table 2 Data flow of block (*B1*): image size 256 × 256

Clk	Input	1-D DWT output	2-D DWT output
1	$X_{1,1} : X_{1,2}$		
2	$X_{2,1} : X_{2,2}$		
3	$X_{1,3} : X_{1,4}$		
4	$X_{2,3} : X_{2,4}$		
5	$X_{1,5} : X_{1,6}$		
6	$X_{2,3} : X_{2,4}$	$L_{1,1} : H_{1,2}$	
7	$X_{1,5} : X_{1,6}$	$L_{2,1} : H_{2,2}$	
8	$X_{2,5} : X_{2,6}$	$L_{1,2} : H_{1,3}$	
9	$X_{1,7} : X_{1,8}$	$L_{2,2} : H_{2,3}$	
10	$X_{2,7} : X_{2,8}$	$L_{1,3} : H_{1,4}$	
...	...	...	
257	$X_{3,1} : X_{3,2}$	$L_{1,254} : H_{1,255}$	
258	$X_{4,1} : X_{4,2}$	$L_{2,254} : H_{2,255}$	
...	...	...	
268	$X_{4,11} : X_{4,12}$	$L_{3,3} : H_{3,4}$	$LL_{1,1} : LH_{1,2}$
269	$X_{3,13} : X_{3,14}$	$L_{4,3} : H_{4,4}$	$HL_{2,1} : HH_{2,2}$
269	$X_{4,13} : X_{4,14}$	$L_{3,4} : H_{3,5}$	$LL_{1,2} : LH_{1,3}$

2-D DWT are presented, i.e., folded multi-level architecture (FMA), pipelined multi-level architecture (PMA), and recursive multi-level architecture (RMA). The FMA is composed of a block (*B1*) and $N^2/4$ off-chip memory, where as the PMA is composed of a block (*B1*) to perform first-level decomposition and block (*B2*) for higher levels of decompositions. The RMA is composed of block (*B1*) and block (*B3*) to compute first-level and higher-level decomposition.

Three different architectures are suggested based on different VLSI optimization criteria such as area, power, speed, throughput, and memory. FMA is a straight forward design which requires simple control but has lower throughput and it demands $N^2/4$ memory. PMA is designed to satisfy the need of high throughput at the cost of area, whereas RMA gives moderate throughput and utilizes moderate area. RMA gives throughput higher than FMA but lower than PMA. Therefore, for the application which demands high throughput, PMA can be deployed. In applications with no memory constraint but need simple control, we can go for FMA design. RMA can be deployed where we have constraints of area and power but need to achieve high throughput.

3.1 Scanning schemes

Pixels are accessed by architecture *B1* in dual-input Z-scan manner as shown in Figure 2. In this method, data scanning is optimized for simultaneous operation on two rows which produces coefficients required for vertical filtering such that the latency involved in calculating 2-D DWT coefficients with boundary treatment is decreased and become independent of image size. Two pixel values are read from the first row in a single clock and processed by 1-D DWT architecture in the next clock. During the same clock, two values are read from the next row. Architecture *B2* accesses pixels in dual-input raster scan manner as shown in Figure 3.

3.2 Predict/update module

The main processing element in the blocks *B1*, *B2*, and *B3* is predict/update. Both RPU and CPU consist of pipelined

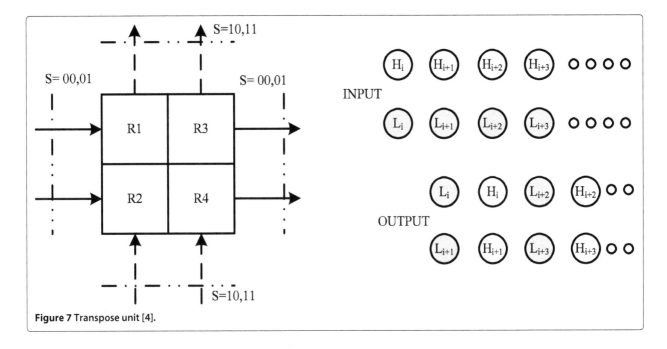

Figure 7 Transpose unit [4].

predict and update blocks to reduce the critical path. Both the predict and update have the same data path, so it can be designed as one generic processing element, as shown in Figure 4. 1-D DWT using lifting (5, 3) filter requires multiplication of two filter coefficients, α and β, whose values are $-1/2$ and $1/4$, respectively. Coefficient multiplication is designed using logical left shift operation by one and two bits, respectively. We have used simple and power efficient hardwired scaling unit (HSU), in which shifters are replaced by hardwired connections. This operation optimizes the speed without compromising power and area. The HSU to perform divide by two and divide by four operations on signed input is shown in Figure 5. In

case of (9, 7) lifting, multipliers are used to reduce quantization noise generated due to fractional value of filter coefficients.

Both predict and update consist of two adders, two delay registers and one multiplier or HSU. Predict/update module takes three inputs and produces two outputs per clock cycle. Entire predict/update operation is divided into two stages. In the first pipeline stage, $in1$ and $in2$ are added and stored in $D1$ register and at the same time $in3$ is stored in $D2$. In the second stage, data of $D2$ and shifted or multiplied value of $D1$ are added to compute predict value as shown in Table 1. $D1$ and $D2$ registers are used to pipeline the predict/update module. Thus, predict/update

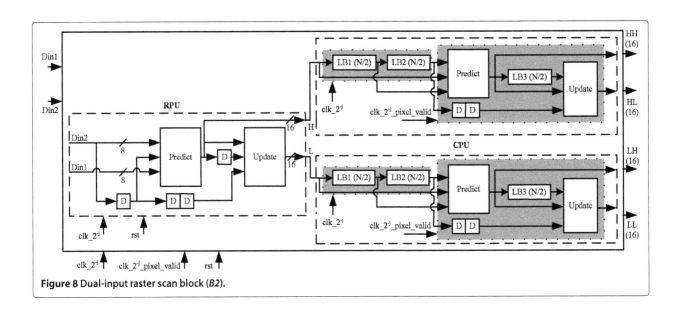

Figure 8 Dual-input raster scan block (*B2*).

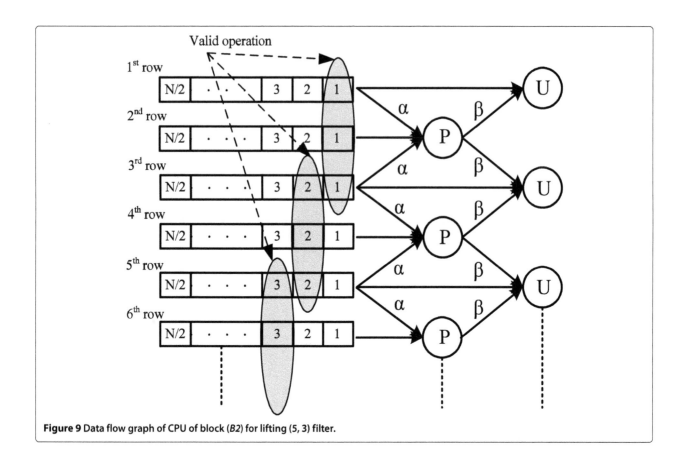

Figure 9 Data flow graph of CPU of block (*B2*) for lifting (5, 3) filter.

module takes two clock cycles to compute predict/update coefficients.

3.3   Dual-input Z-scan block (*B1*)

The proposed Z-scan-based block (*B1*) for lifting (5, 3) is composed of RPU, transpose unit (TU), and CPU as shown in Figure 6. Each RPU and CPU uses two processor elements for predict and update operations. This block uses $2N$ line buffers and 8 registers for temporary storage. Structure of CPU is identical to RPU, except temporal buffers. Two buffers of length N are used in the CPU.

These buffers are initialized to zero for zero boundary extension technique for boundary treatment. Pixels are accessed in Z-scan manner as shown in Figure 2 and processed by RPU to produce high-pass (H) and low-pass (L) 1-D coefficients in a single clock. The 1-D coefficients are then given to TU for transposition, so that the CPU can process them in order to produce 2-D DWT coefficient. Block (*B1*) takes two inputs and produces two 2-D DWT coefficients (LL,LH) and (HL,HH) at alternate clock cycle. Predict module of RPU uses three input *Din*1, *Din*2 and a delayed version of *Din*2. Delay registers *D*5 and *D*6 are

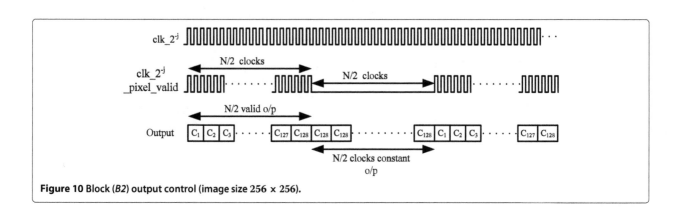

Figure 10 Block (*B2*) output control (image size 256 x 256).

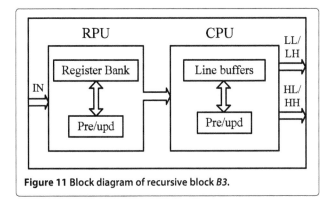

Figure 11 Block diagram of recursive block *B3*.

used to synchronize the predict output and *Din2* (input signal of update module) because predict operation consumes two clocks as shown in Table 1. So, the RPU and CPU takes 6 and $N + 4$ clock cycle, respectively, and TU consumes two clocks; hence, latency of block (*B1*) to compute 2-D DWT is $N + 12$ clock cycle as shown in Table 2. The latency is reduced to only 12 clock cycles if the output is considered with boundary treatment. The advantage of Z-scan is 100% HUE and the simple control path as compared to [10] and [13] to achieve 100% HUE. The simple control path of architecture further reduces the power and area requirement.

CPU accepts column-wise data, which is managed through efficient TU architecture described in [4]. TU exploits the decimation characteristic of lifting scheme. TU is composed of four registers and two 4 × 2 multiplexers. Input/output sequences and block diagram of TU are shown in Figure 7, where *S* is select input of multiplexer. Block (*B1*) for lifting (9, 7) filter can be extended by using

two instances of the predict and update modules with 4*N* memory buffers.

3.4   Dual-input raster scan block (*B2*)

A novel architecture block (*B2*) with dual-input raster scan is proposed for lifting (5, 3) DWT operation as shown in Figure 8. Block (*B2*) is composed of one RPU and two CPUs. Block (*B2*) takes two inputs at the rising edge of clk_2^{-j} in raster scan manner and produces four outputs at every clock cycle. TU is not required because of the two dedicated 1-D CPUs. RPU of block (*B2*) works in the same manner as of block (*B1*) and produces two 1-D DWT coefficient (L and H). The 1-D coefficients are then given to two independent CPU blocks to produce 2-D DWT coefficients as shown in Figure 8. CPU constitutes of three line buffers *LB1*, *LB2*, and *LB3* of length $N/2$ to process $N \times N$ image. Predict operation of the CPU is managed by two previous rows of 1-D coefficient stored in *LB1* and *LB2* along with one current on-line coefficient as third-row input from RPU. Past predict values are stored in *LB3* to compute update operation. Therefore, line buffers used for one CPU is $1.5 \times N$, and since block (*B2*) uses two instances of CPU, a total of $3 \times N$ line buffers are required. Block (*B2*) for *j*th-level calculation uses two clock signals, clk_2^{-j} and clk_2^{-j}_pixel_valid. RPU of block (*B2*) uses only clk_2^{-j}, while CPU uses both the clock signals. RPU remains busy in each clock to process two incoming pixels/clock; this justifies 100% HUE for RPU. The CPU uses three rows of 1-D coefficient to produce one row of valid 2-D coefficients as shown in Figure 9. But the RPU of block (*B2*) produces two rows of 1-D high and low coefficients, respectively, so the CPU has to wait for $N/2$ clock to save required 1-D coefficient in line buffers

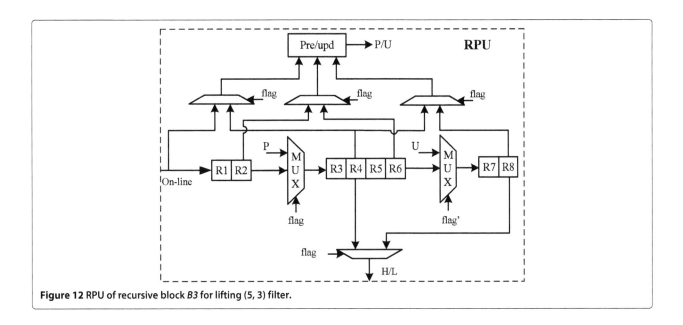

Figure 12 RPU of recursive block *B3* for lifting (5, 3) filter.

Table 3 Mapping of register bank and predict/update module

Flag	Operation	Predict/update module		
		in1	in2	in3
0	Predict	On-line	R4	R2
1	Update	R4	R8	R6

*LB*1 and *LB*2 to start predict operation. Due to this fact, output from the CPU of block (*B2*) is valid for $N/2$ clock cycles and remains constant for next $N/2$ clock cycles as shown in Figure 10. Gated clock clk_2^{-j}_pixel_valid is used to save an extra $N/2$ buffer, otherwise is required as *LB*3, when the CPU does not produce valid coefficients.

3.5 Single-input recursive block (*B3*)

Single-input recursive block (*B3*) consists of RPU and CPU is shown in Figure 11. RPU and CPU use only single processing unit (pre/upd) to compute predict and update alternately. RPU is shown in Figure 12; it consists of a register bank with eight registers and a predict/update module. Data of register bank are right shifted at every clock cycle. The predict/update receives inputs from the register bank and performs predict and update operations alternately, i.e., for two clock cycles predict and for the next two clock cycles update. Mapping of the register bank with inputs of predict/update module is shown in Table 3. Flag input is used to determine predict or update operation. The flag remains '0' for two clock cycles and '1' for next two clock cycles. Input pixel (on-line) is given to register *R*1, and output is taken from register *R*4 and *R*8. The output of predict/update module is written in register *R*3

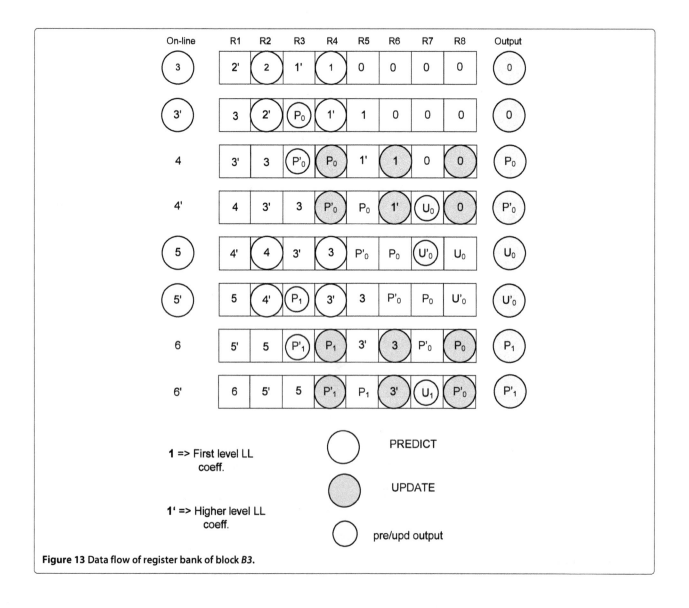

Figure 13 Data flow of register bank of block *B3*.

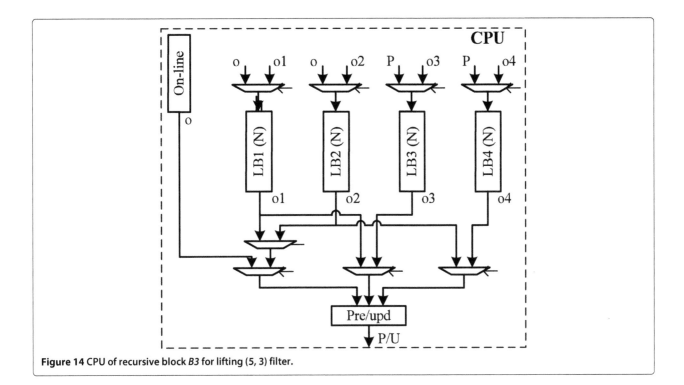

Figure 14 CPU of recursive block *B3* for lifting (5, 3) filter.

and *R7*. Complete data flow of register bank of RPU is shown Figure 13.

CPU consists of line buffers and a predict/update module as shown in Figure 14 and works in a similar manner to the RPU. The CPU consists of four line buffers of size N to store 1-D coefficients and intermediate predict values. Data flow of memory bank is similar to register bank. 1-D coefficients for first and second rows of input (1st and 2nd) are stored in line buffer LB1 and LB2, respectively. Then, when the first 1-D coefficient for the

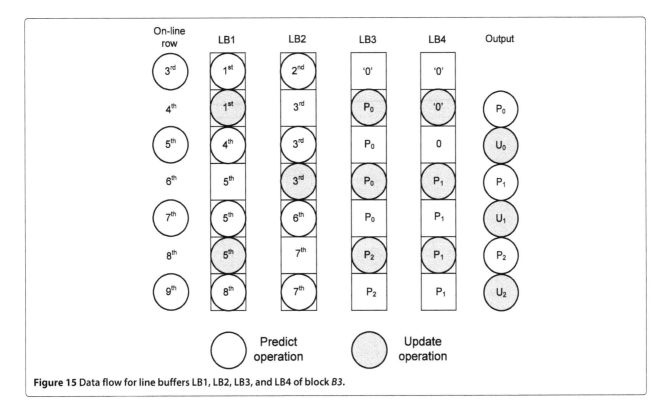

Figure 15 Data flow for line buffers LB1, LB2, LB3, and LB4 of block *B3*.

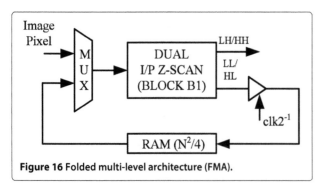

Figure 16 Folded multi-level architecture (FMA).

Table 4 Function of control pin in PMA

Control (ctr)	Level of decomposition
000	1
001	2
010	3
011	4
100	5

3.6 Multi-level design

3.6.1 Folded multi-level architecture

Block diagram of the proposed folded multi-level architecture is shown in Figure 16. It is composed of dual-input Z-scan block (*B1*), multiplexer and memory module (RAM). The multiplexer either selects input data from the image for the first-level decomposition or from RAM for higher-level decompositions. Block (*B1*) takes two inputs and produces two outputs. Since LL coefficient is produced alternately, the output of block (*B1*) is saved in RAM at half clock rate. Complete data flow is shown in Table 2. RAM of length $N^2/4$ is used to store *j*th-level LL coefficients to obtain *j*th+1 level of decomposition. In this scheme, next level decomposition can start only after completion of previous level decomposition, known as level-by-level decomposition. This procedure is repeated until the desired level of decomposition is obtained. FMA for lifting (9, 7) filter is implemented by replicating predict and update modules in block (*B1*).

3.6.2 Pipelined multi-level architecture (PMA)

The proposed PMA to perform 5-level lifting (5,3)-based 2-D DWT is shown in Figure 17. The proposed architecture is composed of one instance of dual-input Z-scan

third row (3rd) comes, the predict/update module starts operation on third row (on-line) with data of LB1 and LB2 as shown in Figure 15. Predict/update module computes predict value and stores it in the first location of LB3, at the same time CPU stores third row of 1-D coefficient in LB2, whose current content value in 2nd row is no longer needed. Then onward, when CPU stores 1-D coefficient for third row in LB2, predict value is stored in the LB3, moving from left to right, until all columns are processed. When the 4th row is on-line, predict/update module computes update value from output of LB1, LB3, and LB4, at the same time the 4th row of 1-D coefficient is stored in LB1, whose current content value 1st row is no longer needed. The process continues until all 2-D coefficients are generated for the input image. The proposed memory organization is extremely efficient such that four line buffers are used to store all intermediate 1-D coefficients and predict values. RMA for lifting (9, 7) can be designed using two instances of RPU and CPU in block (*B3*).

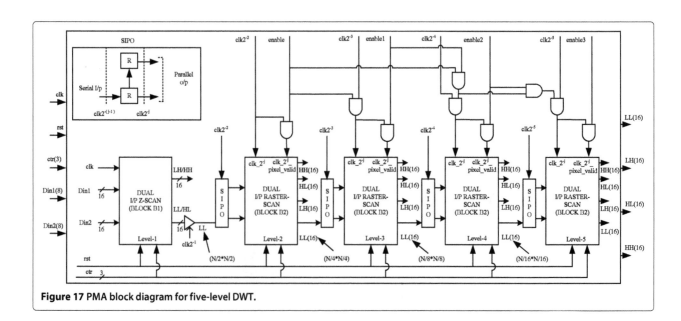

Figure 17 PMA block diagram for five-level DWT.

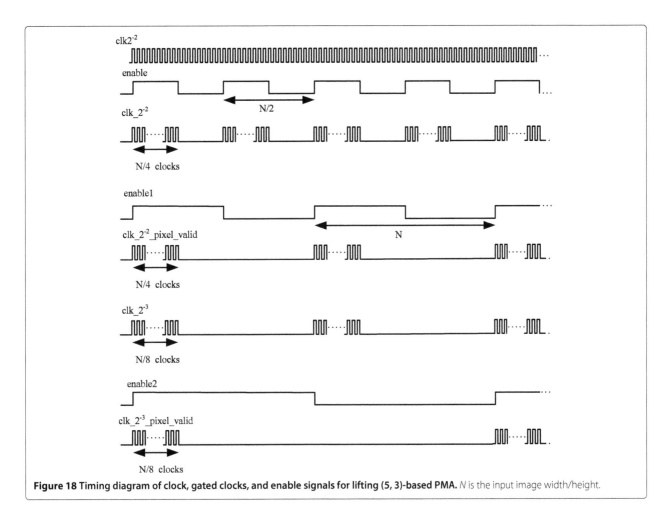

Figure 18 Timing diagram of clock, gated clocks, and enable signals for lifting (5, 3)-based PMA. N is the input image width/height.

block ($B1$) and four instances of dual-input raster scan block ($B2$). Here, the blocks ($B1$) and ($B2$) perform first-level and higher-level 2-D DWT decomposition, respectively. In the proposed PMA, all 2-D DWT modules operate parallel with dual input. Each single-level processor computes 2-D DWT independently and outputs the low-frequency (LL) coefficient to the next level. The proposed architecture takes two 8-bit inputs and produces four 16-bit output coefficients. Designed control path is responsible to decide the number of decomposition level as per

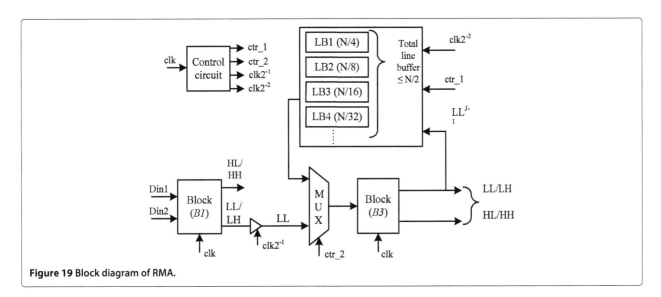

Figure 19 Block diagram of RMA.

Table 5 Performance comparison of 2-D DWT architectures

Architecture	Mul.	Add.	Buff.	C.P.	Thr.	C.C.	HUE (%)
DSA [10]	12	16	4N	$4T_m + 8T_a$	1	$N^2/2$	100
Wu [3]	6	8	4N	T_m	1	N^2	100
FA [13]	10	16	5.5N	$T_m + 2T_a$	2	$N^2/2$	100
HA [13]	18	32	5.5N	$T_m + 2T_a$	4	$N^2/4$	100
Lai [4]	10	16	4N	T_m	2	$N^2/2$	100
Zhang [5]	10	16	4N	T_m	2	$N^2/2$	—
Hsia [6]	0	16	4N	$2T_m + 4T_a$	2	$3N^2/4$	—
Darji [7]	10	16	4N	T_m	2	$N^2/2$	100

Mul., multipliers; Add., adders; Buff., buffers; C.P., critical path; Thr., throughput; C.C., computational cycle; P, parallel factor; HUE, hardware utilization efficiency.

Table 6 Hardware and time complexity comparison of the proposed FMA for lifting (5, 3) filter

Architecture	Multipliers/ shifters	Adders/ subtractors	Memory On-chip	Memory Off-chip	Computing time for j level	Output latency	Critical path delay	HUE (%)
Andra [8]	4	8	$N^2 + 4N$	0	$2N^2(1 - 4^{-j})/3$	2N	$2Ta + 2Ts$	100
Wu [3]	4	8	5N	$N^2/4$	$2N^2(1 - 4^{-j})/3$	2N	$2Ta + Tm$	100
Barua [22]	4	8	5N	$N^2/4$	$2N^2(1 - 4^{-j})/3$	5N	Tm	100
Xiong [13] FA	4	8	3.5N	$N^2/4$	$2N^2(1 - 4^{-j})/3$	N	$2Ta + Tm$	100
Xiong [13] HA	8	16	3.5N	$N^2/4$	$N^2(1 - 4^{-j})/3$	N	$2Ta + Tm$	100
FMA	4	8	2N	$N^2/4$	$2N^2(1 - 4^{-j})/3$	N	$Ta + Ts$	100

Input image size $N \times N$ and $j \geq 1$. Ta, adder delay; Tm, multiplier delay; Ts, shifter delay.

Table 7 Comparison of hardware and time complexity of the proposed FMA for lifting (9, 7) filter

Architecture	Multipliers/ shifters	Adders/ subtractors	Memory On-chip	Memory Off-chip	Output latency	Computing time for j level	Critical path delay	HUE (%)
Andra [8]	32	32	N^2	0	$N^2/2$	$4N^2(1 - 4^{-j})/3$	$4Ta + 2Tm$	100
Wu [3]	6	8	5.5N	$N^2/4$	$\sim$	$2N^2(1 - 4^{-j})/3$	Tm	100
Barua [22]	12	16	7N	$N^2/4$	7N	$2N^2(1 - 4^{-j})/3$	$2Ta + Tm$	100
Xiong [13] FA	10	16	5.5N	$N^2/4$	2N	$2N^2(1 - 4^{-j})/3$	$2Ta + Tm$	100
Xiong [13] HA	18	32	5.5N	$N^2/4$	N	$N^2(1 - 4^{-j})/3$	$2Ta + Tm$	100
FMA	10	16	4N	$N^2/4$	N	$2N^2(1 - 4^{-j})/3$	$Ta + Tm$	100

Input image size $N \times N$ and $j \geq 1$. Ta, adder delay; Tm, multiplier delay; Ts, shifter delay; $\sim$, not available.

Table 8 Comparison of hardware and time complexity of the proposed PMA for lifting (5, 3) filter

Architecture	Multipliers/ shifters	Adders/ subtractors	Memory $j = 1$ On-chip	Memory $j = 1$ Off-chip	Computing cycle for j level	Latency $j = 1$	Critical path delay	HUE (%)
Hasan [23]	$2j$	j	3N	0	$O(N^2)$	3N	$2Ta + Ts$	100
Aziz [15]	$2j$	$4j$	4N	0	$\sum_{m=1}^{j}\left(1 + \frac{3N}{2^{m-1}} + \frac{N^2}{2^{2(m-1)}}\right)$	$3N+1$	$2Ta$	50 to 60
PMA	$4 + 6(j-1)$	$8 + 12(j-1)$	2N	0	$2 + \sum_{m=1}^{j}\left(10 + \frac{N}{2^{m-1}} + \frac{N^2}{2^{2m-1}}\right)$	$N + 12$	$Ta + Ts$	60 to 75

Input image size $N \times N$ and $j \geq 1$. Ta, adder delay; Tm, multiplier delay; Ts, shifter delay; j, level of decomposition.

Table 9 Line buffer comparison for PMA for lifting (5, 3) filter

Architecture	Memory	
	For $j = 1$	For $j = 5$
Aziz [15]	4N	$4N + 2N + N + \frac{N}{2} + \frac{N}{4} \approx 7.7N$
PMA	2N	$2N + \frac{3N}{2} + \frac{3N}{4} + \frac{3N}{8} + \frac{3N}{16} \approx 4.8N$

Input image size $N \times N$.

the need of application as described in Table 4. Due to decimation property of wavelet transform, at each level, total computation is reduced to 1/4 than the preceding stage. To maintain a dual-input processing at every level of decomposition, the clock rate is set as 1/2 than the preceding stage through a timing control circuit. Serial input and parallel output (SIPO) is used in between 2-D DWT modules for pipelining as shown in Figure 17. SIPO block is composed of two registers, which are filled with serial input coming from the previous pipelined stage at the rising edge of clock $(clk2^{-(j-1)})$ and output is taken at half clock rate $(clk2^{-j})$ as shown in Figure 17. PMA for lifting (9, 7) filter can be implemented by replicating predict and update modules twice in blocks $(B1)$ and $(B2)$.

Clock gating is a well-known method to reduce dynamic power dissipation in synchronous digital circuits by adding more logic to a circuit to prune the clock tree (clock distribution network). Pruning the clock disables portions of the circuitry and thus saves the power. Clock gating also saves significant die area, as it removes a large number of multiplexers and replaces them with clock gating logic. Mainly, five clock signals are generated $clk2^{-1}, clk2^{-2}, clk2^{-3}, clk2^{-4}, clk2^{-5}$ from clk. Clock $clk2^{-j}$ is $1/2^{-j}$ rate of clk, where j indicates decomposition level. Period of enable signal is $N/2$ and signals enable1, enable2, and enable3 are generated from it with period $N, 2N, 4N$, respectively. clk_2^{-2} is generated by logical AND operation of $clk2^{-2}$ and enable signal. clk_2^{-3} is generated by logical AND operation of $clk2^{-3}$, enable,

and enable1, and in the same way, clk_2^{-4} and clk_2^{-5} are generated. clk_2^{-2}_pixel_valid is generated from logical AND of $clk2^{-2}$, enable, and enable1; in the same way, clk_2^{-3}_pixel_valid is generated from $clk2^{-3}$, enable, enable1, and enable2 as shown in Figure 18. Clocks and enable used by second-level and third-level block $(B2)$ are shown in Figure 17. Every block $(B2)$ operates on two gated clocks signals, clk_2^{j} and clk_2^{j}_pixel_valid.

3.6.3 Recursive multi-level architecture

The proposed RMA is composed of blocks $(B1)$ and $(B3)$ as shown in Figure 19. Block $(B1)$ is employed to process the input image to get first-level 2-D DWT coefficients, and block $(B3)$ works recursively for computing multi-level coefficients. RMA requires line buffer for temporary storage of coefficients generated from the block $(B3)$. A multiplexer is used at the input of block $(B3)$ to select the input sample either from block $(B1)$ or from line buffers. Careful management of the switching of this multiplexer utilizes the idle interleaved clock cycles of block $(B3)$ to process higher-level coefficients such that maximum hardware utilization is achieved.

Block $(B1)$ produces LL coefficient at alternate clock cycle, which is fed to block $(B3)$ for multi-level processing. Block $(B3)$ is designed such that it operates one sample per clock cycle. The block $(B3)$ also has a feedback mechanism that brings the higher-level LL coefficients at the input to compute next higher-level coefficients. A buffer of size less than $N/2$ is used to store intermediate LL coefficients. This buffer is divided into different lengths, such as $N/4, N/8, N/16 \ldots$ to store one row of LL coefficients. These buffered LL coefficients are serially provided to block $(B3)$ to get next higher-level DWT coefficients. Here, a multiplexer is used, which is operated on the control signal ctr_2 and provides first- and higher-level LL coefficients at alternate clock cycle. Thus, every clock cycle is utilized to process the first- and higher-level LL coefficients alternatively. Valid multi-level coefficients are available at every fourth clock cycle. The depth of

Table 10 Comparison of hardware and time complexity of the proposed PMA for lifting (9, 7) filter

Architecture	Mohanty [14]	Mohanty [21]	Hu [19]	Proposed PMA
Scheme	LT	CV	LT	LT
Multiplier	$6Px_3$	189	$\frac{105S}{8} + 6$	32
Adder	$32Px_3/3$	294	$21S+12$	64
Registers	$N(11x_2 + 10x_5)$	$\frac{21N}{4} + 443$	$3N + \frac{341S}{8}$	48
Line buffers	0	0	0	$4N + 24N$
ACT	$\frac{N^2}{P}$	$\frac{N^2}{16}$	$\frac{N^2}{2S}$	$\frac{N^2}{2} + \sum \frac{N}{2^2}$
Critical path delay	$2Ta + Tm$	$\approx Tm$	$Ta + Tm$	$Ta + Tm$

Input image size $N \times N$ and $j = 3$. L.B., line buffer; P, number of samples processed per clock cycle; S, strip size; Ta, adder delay; Tm, multiplier delay; $J = \min(\log_2 M, \log_2 N)$; $x_1 = 2/3 \times (1 - 4^{-L})$; $x_2 = (1 - 2^{-L})$; $x_3 = (1 - 2^{-2L})$.

Table 11 Hardware and time complexity of the proposed RMA

Architecture	Mult./ shift.	Add./ sub.	Memory j = 1		Output latency	Critical path delay	HUE (%)
			On-chip	Off-chip			
RMA (5, 3)	6	12	6.5N	0	2N	$2Ta + Tm$	75
RMA (9, 7)	16	24	12.5N	0	4N	$2Ta + Tm$	75

Input image size $N \times N$ and $j \geq 1$. Ta, adder delay; Tm, multiplier delay; Ts, shifter delay.

the data is decreased fourfold at each level of operation, i.e., first-level data depth is decreased from N^2 to $N^2/4$, second level to $N^2/16$, and so on. This property of inherent compression is utilized for pushing the higher-level coefficients into buffers.

4 Performance analysis and comparison

In this section, architecture performance is evaluated based on following parameters: HUE, speed, computing time, output latency, line buffers, complexity of control circuit, number of adders and multipliers, system power consumption, configurable logic block (CLB) slices, critical path delay, memory, and maximum frequency of operation. The % HUE is defined by (5).

$$\%HUE = \frac{\text{Number of block in use}}{\text{Total number of blocks}} \times 100 \quad (5)$$

Pipelining is done between predict and update stages in FMA, PMA, and RMA to reduce the critical path delay from conventional $4Ta + 2Tm$ to only $Ta + Ts$ for lifting (5, 3) and Tm for lifting (9, 7) at the cost of latency of few clock cycles. Total $2N$ on-chip line buffers are required in the proposed FMA and PMA for lifting (5, 3) and $j = 1$ level, which is lowest among existing architectures. The latency of the proposed scheme is N cycles (without boundary treatment). The proposed RMA utilizes only one processing element to calculate both predict and update, resulting into 50% reduction in number of adders and multipliers.

4.1 Hardware complexity and timing analysis

Hardware complexity is mainly sensitive to number of adders, multipliers, on-chip buffers, and control path. Performance comparison of 2-D DWT architecture is given in Table 5. Hardware complexity of folded multi-level

structure is reported in literature as [3,8,10,13,22] is compared in Table 6 and Table 7, respectively, for the j-level of decomposition. HA structure in [13] appears to be the best in terms of computing cycles, but it requires 8 multipliers and 16 adders. The proposed FMA has only half-area requirement in terms of on-chip memory buffers, adders/subtractors, and multiplier/shifter required as compared to HA. Moreover, the critical path delay of the proposed FMA for lifting (5, 3) is $Ta + Ts$, which is lowest among similar architectures. Structure in Wu and Lin [3] appears to be the best for lifting (9, 7) in terms adder, multiplier and critical path delay but requires $5.5N$ on-chip buffers for processing as compared to the proposed FMA. The critical path delay of the proposed FMA for (9, 7) is $Ta + Tm$, and it requires only $4N$ on-chip buffers. Hardware and time complexity of the proposed PMA for lifting (5, 3) filter are compared in Table 8 with the architectures described in literature with similar specifications, such as [15] and [23]. The proposed PMA has not only the lowest critical path but it also requires less computing cycles as shown in Table 8. The extra two cycles in the total computing cycle are added due to transposition in block (B1). It must be also observed that the architecture proposed by Hasan et al. [23] utilizes less number of multipliers and adders but requires more line buffers to compute multi-level 2-D DWT. It is evident from Table 9 that the PMA uses $4.8N$ line buffers, while the architecture given [15] required $7.7N$ line buffers for five-level DWT decomposition using lifting (5,3) filter.

$$\left(\frac{N^2}{2} + 10\right) + \left[\left(\frac{N}{2} + 8\right) + \left(\frac{N}{4} + 8\right) + \left(\frac{N}{8} + 8\right) + \left(\frac{N}{16} + 8\right)\right] = \frac{N^2}{2} + \frac{15N}{16} + 42 \quad (6)$$

Table 12 Comparison of hardware and time complexity of the proposed RMA for (9, 7) with existing architectures

Arch.	Mult.	Add.	Line buffers	Control complexity	Computing time
Liao [10]	12	16	$10N(1 - 2^{-j})$	Medium	$N^2/2$
Xiong [16]	28	48	$10N(1 - 2^{-j}) + 0.5N$	Medium	$N^2/4$
RMA	16	24	$12.5N$	Simple	$N^2/2$

Image size $N \times N$ and $j \geq 1$. j, level of decomposition.

Table 13 FPGA synthesis results for FMA: image size 256 × 256

Architecture	FMA (5, 3)	FMA (9, 7)
FPGA	Virtex-5	Virtex-5
Device	5VLX110TFF1136-3	5VLX110TFF1136-3
Slice LUTs	494 (0%)	1008 (1%)
Slice registers	633 (0%)	1091 (1%)
MUF (MHz)	537	210

MUF, maximum utilization frequency.

A total computing cycle required by PMA for five-level decomposition of an image (size $N \times N$) is shown in (6). All single-level processors (*B1* and *B2*) work in a parallel fashion in PMA. Block (*B1*) utilizes $\left(\frac{N^2}{2} + 10\right)$, and remaining clocks are consumed in consecutive four blocks of (*B2*). So, most of the processing is done within $N^2/2$ clock cycles and very small additional cycles, i.e., (N/2+8), (N/4+8), (N/8+8), and (N/16+8) are needed to compute further levels.

Architecture comparison of the proposed PMA with [14,19,21] for three-level 2-D DWT using lifting (9, 7) filter is shown in Table 10. The proposed architecture uses lowest number of multipliers and adders as compared to other architectures. Architectures [14,19,21] do not use any line buffers at the cost of more computation logic and complex control path.

The hardware complexity of the proposed RMA for lifting (5, 3) and (9, 7) is shown in Table 11. The RMA for lifting (5, 3) uses a total of six multipliers, out of which four are used in block (*B1*) and two are used in block (*B3*). In case of RMA for lifting (9, 7) filter, a total of 16 multipliers are required, out of which 10 are utilized in block (*B1*) and 6 are used in block (*B3*). The additional two multipliers are required to scale output coefficients. Block (*B1*) uses a total $2N$ and $4N$ line buffers for lifting (5, 3) and lifting (9, 7) filters, respectively. The number of buffers and multipliers required for (9, 7) filter is double than that for (5, 3). HUE of block (*B1*) is 100%, but block (*B2*) has some interleaved clock cycles that results into 75% HUE of all over RMA.

Hardware and time complexity of the proposed RMA for lifting (9, 7) are compared with architectures proposed by [10] and [16] in Table 12. The proposed RMA uses a total of 16 multipliers, out of which block (*B1*) uses 10 and block (*B3*) uses 6. Numbers of adder utilized by blocks (*B1*) and (*B3*) are 16 and 8, respectively. $4N$ line buffers are used by block (*B1*), $8N$ are consumed by block (*B3*), and $0.5N$ are used in storing intermediate-level coefficient, which resulted in a total of $12.5N$ line buffers in the design of RMA. The proposed RMA is simple and reuses same processing element to compute predict and update values. The proposed architecture requires less multipliers, adders, and computing time as compared to [16]. Liao et al. [10] require the lowest number of multipliers and adders because it uses only one 2-D DWT block, but require more complex control path as compared to the proposed RMA.

4.2 FPGA Implementation

The proposed FMA for lifting (5, 3) and (9, 7) filters is implemented on Xilinx Virtex-5 XC5VLX110T FPGA target device (Xilinx, Inc., San Jose, CA, USA), and the results are reported in Table 13. The maximum utilization frequency (MUF) for FMA is very high as a result of very low critical path delay, i.e., $Ta + Ts$ and $Ta + Tm$ for lifting (5, 3) and (9, 7) filters, respectively.

The proposed PMA for five-level lifting (5, 3) is synthesized using Xilinx ISE 10.1 for Xilinx Virtex-5 XC5VLX110T FPGA target device, and the results are reported in Table 14. Sixteen-bit word length is used in the proposed scheme for higher-level decomposition without overflow. Since the pipelined processor element is used in the design, 537-MHz frequency of operation is obtained. The CLB count reported in [15] is less than that in the proposed scheme because of folded processor element, but this approach leads to lower throughput. Throughput is calculated by (7). The proposed PMA utilizes 1,178 slices and provides throughput rate of 4,080 frames/s for lifting (5, 3) for 512 × 512 frame resolution. This is almost five times more than [15]. Power is estimated using Xilinx X-power at a 100-MHz frequency and reported in Table 14. It is apparent from this comparison that the proposed scheme consumes lower power as compared

Table 14 FPGA synthesis results of the proposed PMA for lifting (5, 3) 2-D DWT

Architecture	Power for $j = 1$ (mW)			Frequency	CLB slice count		Throughput frames/s
	Dynamic	Quiescent	Total		For $j = 1$	For $j = 5$	
Aziz [15]	33.85	1,186.94	1,220.79	221.44	206	1,052	835
PMA without clk gating	29.6	980.8	1,010.6	539	412	1,329	4,080
PMA with clk gating	28	980.8	1,008.2	539	342	1,178	4,080

Virtex-5 XC5VLX110T FPGA at 100 MHz. Image size 512 × 512.

Table 15 Comparison of FPGA synthesis results for RMA: image size 256 × 256 and $j = 3$

Arch.	Liao [10]	Xiong [16]	RMA (5, 3)	RMA (9, 7)
FPGA	Virtex-4	Virtex-4	Virtex-4	Virtex-4
Device	4VFX100FF1152-12	4VFX100FF1152-12	4VFX100FF1152-12	4VFX100FF1152-12
LE/slices	1,180	2,532	1,040	1,822

LE, logic elements or cells.

to [15] because of dual-scan technique and lower line buffers are used in design implementation.

$$\text{Throughput} = F_{\max}/\text{Total clocks required for a frame transform} \tag{7}$$

The proposed RMA is synthesized for lifting (5, 3) and (9, 7) filters using Xilinx ISE 10.1 for Xilinx Virtex-4 XC4VFX100 FPGA target device, and the results are reported in Table 15. The RMA implementation uses 1,822 (4%) and 1,040 (2%) slices for lifting (9, 7) and (5, 3) filters, respectively. The output of FMA using lifting (9, 7) filter with $j = 1$ and RMA using lifting (9, 7) filter with $j = 3$ is shown in Figure 20. Output of PMA for lifting (5, 3) filter with $j = 1$ to $j = 5$ levels for input image Cameraman (256 × 256) is shown in Figure 21.

5   Conclusions

In this paper, we have proposed high-performance FMA, PMA and RMA with dual-pixel scanning method for computing multi-level 2-D DWT. The architectures are compared on the basis of resources utilized and speed. Micro-pipelining is employed in predict/update processor element to reduce the critical path to $Ta + Ts$ and $Ta + Tm$ for lifting (5, 3) and (9, 7) filters, respectively. Optimized single-level 2-D DWT blocks (B1), (B2), and (B3) are proposed to design multi-level architecture. The

proposed FMA for lifting (5, 3) and lifting (9, 7) uses only $2N$ and $4N$ line buffers, respectively. The proposed PMA is simple, regular, modular, and can be cascaded for n-level decomposition. The PMA for lifting (5, 3) has a critical path delay of $Ta + Ts$. Moreover, it requires only $4.8N$ line buffers for five-level decomposition, thus reduces line buffer approximately 50% than other similar designs. The proposed RMA uses 16 multipliers and 24 adders for n-level decomposition. Moreover, a requirement of line buffers is independent of level of decomposition. The proposed architectures are implemented on Xilinx Virtex family devices. The proposed FMA and PMA operate with frequency of 537 MHz, which is sufficient to handle 518 full-HD frames with $1,920 \times 1,080$ resolution. The proposed PMA, when implemented on FPGA for five-level DWT, utilizes 1,178 slices and provides a throughput rate of 4,080 frames (512 × 512) per second, which is almost five times than that of the existing design. The proposed RMA uses unique buffer management and only single processing element for computing predict and update to save area and power. The Xilinx Virtex-4 implementation of RMA uses 1,822 (4%) and 1,040 (2%) slices for lifting (9, 7) and (5, 3) filters, respectively.

FPGA implementation of the proposed schemes show higher operating frequency, low latency, and lower power as compared to other architectures with the same specifications. The proposed designs can be used for

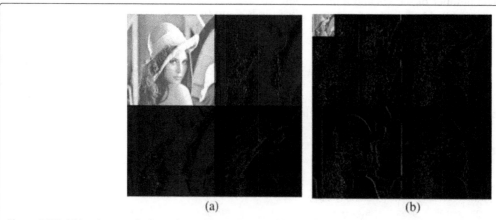

Figure 20 Multi-level output for input image size 256 × 256. (a) FMA lifting (9, 7) and $j = 1$. **(b)** RMA lifting (9, 7) and $j = 3$.

Figure 21 PMA output. (a) Original image. **(b)** One-level, **(c)** two-level, **(d)** three-level, **(e)** four-level, and **(f)** five-level lifting (5, 3) 2-D DWT decomposition of image size 256 × 256.

practical applications with power, area, and speed constrains. The proposed architectures are suitable for high-speed real-time systems such as image de-noising, on-line video streaming, watermarking, compression, and multi-resolution analysis.

Competing interests
The authors declare that they have no competing interests.

Author details
[1]Department of Electrical Engineering, Indian Institute of Technology Bombay, Powai, Mumbai 400076, India. [2]Electronics Engineering Department, S. V. National Institute of Technology, Surat, Gujarat 395007, India.

References
1. I Daubecies, W Sweldens, Factoring wavelet transforms into lifting steps. J. Fourier Anal. Appl. **4**, 247–269 (1998)
2. J-M Jou, Y-H Shiau, C-C Liu, Efficient VLSI architectures for the bi-orthogonal wavelet transform by filter bank and lifting scheme, in *Proc. IEEE International Symposium on Circuits Systems (ISCAS)*, vol. 2 (Sydney, New South Wales, 06–09 May 2001), pp. 529–532
3. B Wu, C Lin, A high-performance and memory-efficient pipeline architecture for the 5/3 and 9/7 discrete wavelet transform of JPEG2000 codec. IEEE Trans. Circuits Syst. Video Technol. **15**(12), 1615–1628 (2005)
4. Y-K Lai, L-F Chen, Y-C Shih, A high-performance and memory-efficient VLSI architecture with parallel scanning method for 2-D lifting-based discrete wavelet transform. IEEE Trans. Consum. Electron. **55**(2), 400–407 (2009)
5. W Zhang, Z Jiang, Z Gao, Y Liu, An efficient VLSI architecture for lifting-based discrete wavelet transform. IEEE Trans. Circuits Syst. II. **59**(3), 158–162 (2012)
6. C-H Hsia, J-S Chiang, J-M Guo, Memory-efficient hardware architecture of 2-D dual-mode lifting-based discrete wavelet transform. IEEE Trans. Circuits Syst. Video Technol. **25**(4), 671–683 (2013)
7. A Darji, S Agrawal, A Oza, V Sinha, A Verma, SN Merchant, A Chandorkar, Dual-scan parallel flipping architecture for a lifting-based 2-D discrete wavelet transform. IEEE Trans. Circuits Syst. II, Exp. Briefs. **61**(6), 433–437 (2014)
8. K Andra, C Chakrabarti, T Acharya, A VLSI architecture for lifting-based forward and inverse wavelet transform. IEEE Trans. Signal Process. **50**(4), 966–977 (2002)
9. C-T Huang, P-C Tseng, L-G Chen, Efficient VLSI architectures of lifting-based discrete wavelet transform by systematic design method, in *Proceedings of the IEEE International Symposium on Circuits and Systems*, vol. 5 (Scottsdale, Arizona, 26–29 May 2002), pp. 565–568
10. H Liao, MK Mandal, BF Cockburn, Efficient architectures for 1-D and 2-D lifting-based wavelet transforms. IEEE Trans. Signal Process. **52**(5), 1315–1326 (2004)
11. P-Y Chen, VLSI implementation for one-dimensional multilevel lifting-based wavelet transform. IEEE Trans. Comput. **53**(4), 386–398 (2004)
12. BK Mohanty, PK Meher, VLSI architecture for high-speed / low-power implementation of multilevel lifting, DWT, in *Proceedings of the IEEE Asia Pacific Conference on Circuits and Systems* (Singapore, 4–7 Dec 2006), pp. 458–461
13. C Xiong, J Tian, J Liu, Efficient architectures for two-dimensional discrete wavelet transform using lifting scheme. IEEE Trans. Image Process. **16**(3), 607–614 (2007)
14. BK Mohanty, PK Meher, Memory efficient modular VLSI architecture for highthroughput and low-latency implementation of multilevel lifting 2-D DWT. IEEE Trans. Signal Process. **59**(5), 2072–2084 (2011)
15. SM Aziz, DM Pham, Efficient parallel architecture for multi-level forward discrete wavelet transform processors. J. Comp. Elect. Eng. **38**, 1325–1335 (2012)
16. C-Y Xiong, J-W Tian, J Liu, Efficient high-speed/low-power line-based architecture for two-dimensional discrete wavelet transform using lifting scheme. IEEE Trans. Circuits Syst. Video Technol. **16**(2), 309–316 (2006)
17. C-H Hsia, J-M Guo, J-S Chiang, Improved low-complexity algorithm for 2-D integer lifting-based discrete wavelet transform using symmetric mask-based scheme. IEEE Trans. Circuits Syst. Video Technol. **19**(8), 1202–1208 (2009)
18. AK Al-Sulaifanie, A Ahmadi, M Zwolinski, Very large scale integration architecture for integer wavelet transform. J. IET Comp. Digital Tech. **4**(6), 471–483 (2010)

19. Y Hu, CC Jong, A memory-efficient high-throughput architecture for lifting-based multi-level 2-D DWT. IEEE Trans. Signal Process. **61**(20), 4975–4987 (2013)

20. ME Angelopoulou, K Masselos, PY Cheung, Y Andreopoulos, Implementation and comparison of the 5/3 lifting 2-D discrete wavelet transform computation schedules on FPGAs. J. Signal Process. Syst. **51**(1), 3–21 (2008)

21. BK Mohanty, PK Meher, Memory-efficient high-speed convolution-based generic structure for multilevel 2-D DWT. IEEE Trans. Circuits Syst. Video Technol. **23**(2), 353–363 (2013)

22. S Barua, JE Carletta, KA Kotteri, AE Bell, An efficient architecture for lifting-based two-dimensional discrete wavelet transforms. J. Integration, VLSI J. **38**(3), 341–352 (2005)

23. H Varshney, M Hasan, S Jain, Energy efficient novel architectures for the lifting-based discrete wavelet transform. IET Image Process. **1**(3), 305–310 (2007)

10

Modeling of SSIM-based end-to-end distortion for error-resilient video coding

Qiang Peng[1], Lei Zhang[1,2*], Xiao Wu[1] and Qionghua Wang[3]

Abstract

Conventional end-to-end distortion models for videos measure the overall distortion based on independent estimations of the source distortion and the channel distortion. However, they are not correlating well with the perceptual characteristics where there is a strong inter-relationship among the source distortion, the channel distortion, and the video content. As most compressed videos are represented to human users, perception-based end-to-end distortion model should be developed for error-resilient video coding. In this paper, we propose a structural similarity (SSIM)-based end-to-end distortion model to optimally estimate the content-dependent perceptual distortion due to quantization, error concealment, and error propagation. Experiments show that the proposed model brings a better visual quality for H.264/AVC video coding over packet-switched networks.

Keywords: End-to-end distortion model; Structural similarity; Error resilience

1 Introduction

Most video coding standards achieve high compression using transform coding and motion-compensated prediction, which creates a strong spatial-temporal dependency in compressed videos. Thus, transmitting highly compressed video streams over packet-switched networks may suffer from spatial-temporal error propagation and may lead to severe quality degradation at the decoder side [1]. To protect compressed videos from packet loss, error-resilient video coding becomes a crucial requirement. Given transmission conditions, such as bit rate and packet loss ratio, the target of error resilient video coding is to minimize the distortion at the receiver [2]:

$$\min\{D\} \quad \text{s.t.} \quad R \le R_T \quad \text{and} \quad \rho \qquad (1)$$

where D and R denote the distortion at the receiver and the bit rate, respectively. R_T is the target bit rate and ρ is the packet loss ratio. Note that we assume the transmission conditions are available at the encoder throughout this paper. This can be either specified as part of the initial negotiations or adaptively calculated from information provided by the transmission protocol [3].

Assume packet containing video data is lost in the channel and the decoder performs error concealment. Clearly, the resulting reconstruction at the decoder is different from the reconstruction at the encoder and the difference will propagate to the following frames due to the prediction chain. Therefore, the key challenge of the error-resilient video coding is to estimate at the encoder the reconstruction error and error propagation of the decoder, which is useful to optimize the coding options to solve the above minimization problem.

A number of end-to-end distortion models (also known as joint source-channel distortion models) for video transmission over lossy channels have been proposed in the literature. In [4,5], several low-complexity estimation models were presented for low error rate applications. For a more accurate distortion estimation model, the work in [2] developed a frame-level recursion distortion model, which relates to the channel-induced distortion due to bit errors. Another efficient approach is the well-known recursive optimal pixel estimation (ROPE) model [3] and its extensions [6-10], which estimate the overall distortion due to quantization, error concealment, and error propagation. Recently, several novel source-channel distortion models were developed for distributed video coding [11], generic multi-view video transmission [12], and error-resilient schemes based on forward error correction [13].

* Correspondence: zl.swjtu@gmail.com
[1]School of Information Science and Technology, Southwest Jiaotong University, Chengdu, China
[2]Institution of Academia Sinica, Jiuzhou Electric Group, Sichuan, China
Full list of author information is available at the end of the article

However, these models are derived in terms of mean squared error (MSE), which has been criticized for weak correlation with perceptual characteristics. As most compressed videos are presented to humans, it is meaningful to incorporate visual features into the error-resilient video coding to protect important visual information of compressed videos from packet loss. Thus, several region-of-interest (ROI)-based approaches were presented to better evaluate the visual quality [14,15]. However, ROI-based approaches do not provide accurate distortion estimation, and ROI determination may be difficult for most videos, especially for videos with natural scenes. Therefore, it is expected that a perception-based end-to-end distortion model could provide a more general and accurate perceptual distortion estimation.

In [16], the structural similarity (SSIM)-based end-to-end distortion was predicted by several factors extracted from the encoder. Although the variation trend is very similar at the block level, the estimated SSIM cannot reach the peak points of the actual SSIM. In [17], a parametric model was proposed to accurately estimate the degradation of SSIM over error-prone networks, in which the content, encoding, and network parameters are considered. However, the encoding parameters only included the number of slices per frame and the GOP length. The proposed model cannot estimate the relative quality of a block given different coding modes. In our earlier work [18], we introduced a block-level SSIM-based distortion model into the error-resilient video coding to minimize the perceptual distortion. In [19], improved SSIM-based distortion model and Lagrange multiplier decision method are proposed for better coding performance. In [18] and [19], the expected SSIM scores were estimated by the expected decoded frames. Due to the nonlinear variation of SSIM, the estimated SSIM scores may be less accurate, especially at high bit rate.

In this paper, we develop an SSIM-based end-to-end distortion model to estimate the overall perceptual distortion for H.264/AVC coded video transmission over packet-switched networks. Unlike the traditional end-to-end distortion model, the perceptual quantization distortion and the perceptual error propagation distortion are dependent on the video content, which makes the end-to-end distortion become complex or difficult to estimate at the encoder. Therefore, this paper provides two major contributions: 1) a SSIM-based reconstruction quality model; 2) a SSIM-based error propagation model. Both models are useful to estimate the content-dependent perceptual distortion at the encoder. Our extensive experimental results demonstrate that the proposed end-to-end distortion model can bring visual quality improvement for H.264/AVC video coding over packet-switched networks. We would like to mention that the scheme presented in this paper is an enhanced approach based on our

preliminary work in [20]. Different settings are considered in this paper, including additional descriptions of related works, technical and implementation details, and comparison experiment results to better evaluate the efficiency of the proposed scheme.

The rest of the paper is organized as follows. Section 2 states the problem and motivation. Section 3 describes the proposed SSIM-based end-to-end distortion model. Section 4 introduces the distortion model into the error-resilient video coding. Section 5 provides the simulation results and Section 6 concludes the paper.

2 Problem and motivation

For H.264/AVC coded video transmission over packet-switched networks, the general formulation of the widely used MSE-based end-to-end distortion can be defined as

$$D = (1-\rho) \cdot D_Q + \rho \cdot D_C + (1-\rho) \cdot D_{P\_f} + \rho \cdot D_{P\_c} \quad (2)$$

where ρ is the packet loss ratio. D is the estimated overall distortion. D_Q denotes the source distortion due to the quantization. D_c, D_{P_f} and D_{P_c} represent the channel distortion due to the error concealment, error propagation from the reference frames, and error propagation from the concealment frames, respectively.

With such a model in Equation 2, the end-to-end distortion can be individually and independently estimated by the quantization distortion, error concealment distortion, and error propagation distortion. This model is appealing because it is easy to calculate and has clear physical meanings. However, since the perceptual distortion is dependent on the video content, the individual and independent objective distortion estimation does not correspond well with human perceptual characteristics. For instance, as shown in Figure 1, since ten compressed or lossy transmitted videos (Live video quality database [21,22]) have different perceptual characteristics, a similar objective distortion may result in different levels of perceptual quantization distortion or transmission distortion. Therefore, we aim to propose a perception-based end-to-end distortion model for more accurate estimation of the overall perceptual distortion in the following section.

3 SSIM-based end-to-end distortion model

To estimate the overall perceptual distortion of decoded videos, we adopt the SSIM index [23] as the perceptual distortion metric due to its best trade-off among simplicity and efficiency [24]. Three important perceptual components, luminance, contrast, and structure, are combined as an overall similarity measure. For two images x and y, the SSIM index is defined as follows:

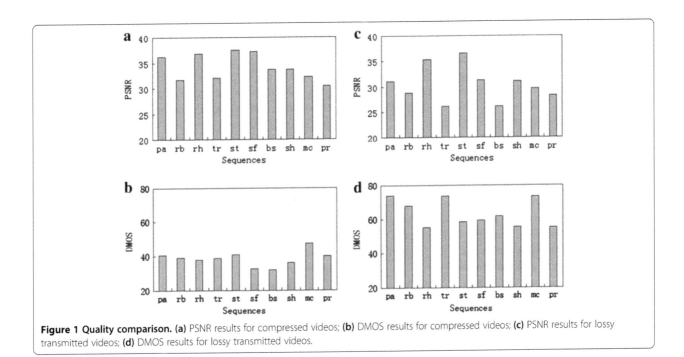

Figure 1 Quality comparison. (a) PSNR results for compressed videos; (b) DMOS results for compressed videos; (c) PSNR results for lossy transmitted videos; (d) DMOS results for lossy transmitted videos.

$$\text{SSIM}(x,y) = l(x,y) \cdot c(x,y) \cdot s(x,y)$$
$$= \frac{2\mu_x\mu_y + c_1}{\mu_x^2 + \mu_y^2 + c_1} \cdot \frac{2\sigma_{xy} + c_2}{\sigma_x^2 + \sigma_y^2 + c_2} \qquad (3)$$

where $l(x,y)$, $c(x,y)$, and $s(x,y)$ represent the luminance, contrast and structure perceptual components, respectively. μ, σ^2, and σ_{xy} are the mean, variance, and cross covariance, respectively. c_1 and c_2 are used to avoid the instability when means or variances are close to zero.

Based on the perceptual distortion metric, we develop a novel end-to-end distortion model as follows. In Figure 2, b denotes the original block and $\tilde{b}$ is the corresponding reconstruction block at the decoder. $\hat{r}$ and $\tilde{r}$ represent the prediction block of b at the encoder and at the decoder, respectively. e denotes the prediction residual and its reconstruction value is $\hat{e}$. If the block is received correctly, $\tilde{b} = \tilde{r} + \hat{e}$. When the block is lost, an error concealment technique is used to estimate the missing content. Let $\hat{c}$ and $\tilde{c}$ represent the concealment block of b at the encoder

and at the decoder, respectively. In this case, $\tilde{b} = \tilde{c}$. For a given packet loss ratio ρ, the general SSIM-based end-to-end distortion can be expressed as

$$D_{\text{SSIM}}(b,\tilde{b}) = (1-\rho) \cdot E\{1-\text{SSIM}(b,\tilde{r}+\hat{e})\} \qquad (4)$$
$$+\rho \cdot E\{1-\text{SSIM}(b,\tilde{c})\}$$

with

$$E\{1-\text{SSIM}(b,\tilde{r}+\hat{e})\} = 1-E\{\text{SSIM}(b,\tilde{r}+\hat{e})\}$$
$$= 1-\Phi_r \cdot E(b,\hat{r}+\hat{e}) \qquad (5)$$

$$E\{1-\text{SSIM}(b,\tilde{c})\} = 1-E\{\text{SSIM}(b,\tilde{c})\}$$
$$= 1-\Phi_c \cdot \text{SSIM}(b,\hat{c}) \qquad (6)$$

where $E\{\}$ is the expectation operator. Φ is the error propagation factor. It indicates how the transmission errors from prediction block or concealment block influence the quality of current block. $\text{SSIM}(b,\tilde{r}+\hat{e})$ and $\text{SSIM}(b,\tilde{c})$ denote the quality of prediction coding and error concealment at the decoder, respectively. SSIM

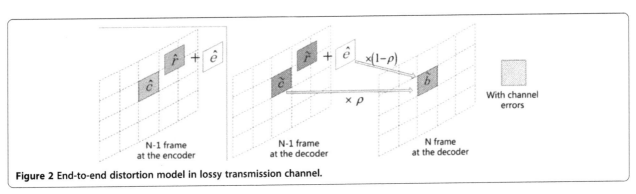

Figure 2 End-to-end distortion model in lossy transmission channel.

$(b, \tilde{r} + \hat{e})$ and $\mathrm{SSIM}(b, \hat{c})$ are the quality of prediction coding and error concealment at the encoder, respectively.

With this formula, the reconstruction quality $\mathrm{SSIM}(b, \hat{r} + \hat{e})$ and error propagation factor Φ are the key terms of the SSIM-based end-to-end distortion model. In the following section, we will make a development of the two terms based on content dependency.

3.1 Development of reconstruction quality model

In this section, we aim to estimate the content-dependent reconstruction quality $\mathrm{SSIM}(b, \hat{r} + \hat{e})$ at the block level (the 4×4 transform and quantization unit is used throughout this paper). Since the accurate reconstruction quality can only be obtained after de-quantization, the proposed quality estimation reduces the computational complexity of de-quantization process for each candidate modes.

According to the SSIM index, the reconstruction quality is derived as

$$\mathrm{SSIM}(b, \hat{r} + \hat{e}) = l(b, \hat{r} + \hat{e}) \cdot c(b, \hat{r} + \hat{e}) \cdot s(b, \hat{r} + \hat{e}) \quad (7)$$

with

$$l(b, \hat{r} + \hat{e}) = \frac{2\mu_b \mu_{\hat{r}} + 2\mu_b \mu_{\hat{e}} + c_1}{\mu_b^2 + \mu_{\hat{r}}^2 + \mu_{\hat{e}}^2 + 2\mu_{\hat{r}}\mu_{\hat{e}} + c_1} \quad (8)$$

$$c(b, \hat{r} + \hat{e}) \cdot s(b, \hat{r} + \hat{e}) = \frac{2\sigma_{b\hat{r}} + 2\sigma_{b\hat{e}} + c_2}{\sigma_b^2 + \sigma_{\hat{r}}^2 + \sigma_{\hat{e}}^2 + 2\sigma_{\hat{r}\hat{e}} + c_2} \quad (9)$$

From Equations 8 and 9, we can see that the estimation of content-dependent reconstruction quality is converted to the estimation problem of three content-independent parameters: 1) the variance of reconstructed prediction residual; 2) the cross-covariance between the reconstructed prediction residual and current block; 3) the cross-covariance between the reconstructed prediction residual and prediction block.

It is reported that the DCT coefficients of prediction residual closely follows a zero-mean Laplacian distribution [25]. Based on this phenomenon, the work in [26] proved that the reconstruction distortion from the prediction residual can be estimated by the Laplacian parameter and the quantization step. Extending the derivation in [26] into pixel-domain, we establish the following two estimation models for above parameters:

$$\sigma_{\hat{e}}^2 = M_{\mathrm{var}}(\alpha, QP) \cdot \sigma_e^2, \quad \alpha = \sqrt{2/\sigma_e^2} \quad (10)$$

$$\sigma_{b\hat{e}} = M_{\mathrm{cov}}(\beta, QP) \cdot \sigma_{be}, \quad \beta = \sqrt{2/\sigma_{be}} \quad (11)$$

where α and β denote the Laplacian parameters. QP is the quantization parameter in H.264/AVC. M_{var} and M_{cov} indicate the scaling maps, which vary from 0 to 1.

The scaling maps M_{var} and M_{cov} are modeled based on four video sequences [27]: 'Crow_run', 'In_to_tree', 'Ducks_take_off', and 'Old_town_cross', which have abundant and various structural information. Each sequence is coded as intra-frame (I frame) and inter-frame (P frame), respectively. To cover various reconstruction variances, 11 different QP values are tested, ranging from 15 to 45 uniformly with the step size of 3.

Firstly, we calculate the variance of initial and reconstructed prediction residual with different QP values. Secondly, we obtain the scaling curve by doing statistics analysis for each test QP. Finally, we interpolate the eleven scaling curves to establish the scaling map. Based on the simulations, the fitted scaling map M_{var} and M_{cov} are shown in Figure 3, which can be constructed as look-up tables.

To demonstrate the accuracy of the proposed reconstruction quality models, 250 frames of each sequence are coded with constant quantization parameters: 20, 25, 30, and 35, respectively. Table 1 shows the average mean absolute deviation (MAD) between the actual and estimated variance, cross covariance, and reconstruction quality. The first two terms denote the accuracy of the fitted models (10) and (11), respectively. The following three terms show the accuracy of the final estimated SSIM scores. It can be seen that the proposed models are valid to predict the reconstruction quality.

3.2 Development of error propagation model

The error propagation is the key component of the end-to-end distortion model. Different from the independent estimation in conventional MSE-based end-to-end distortion model, the perceptual error propagation depends on the source distortion or the concealment distortion. In this section, our primary goal is to develop the error propagation models to estimate the overall perceptual quality for given transmission errors of prediction block or concealment block.

The error propagation models are motivated by three observations. The first observation is related to the impact of error propagation on the three components of SSIM. Let Q_{att} denote the quality attenuation of a given block b due to the error propagation.

$$Q_{\mathrm{att}}(b) = \mathrm{SSIM}(b, \tilde{b}) / \mathrm{SSIM}\left(b, \hat{b}\right) \quad (12)$$

To illustrate the fact, Q_{att} is measured by three different similarity metrics: 1) luminance component of SSIM, 2) the contrast and structure components of SSIM, 3) SSIM index. Figure 4 illustrates an example where the quality attenuation is calculated by Equation 12 for each frame suffering from random transmission errors. As shown, the contrast and structure components have the similar

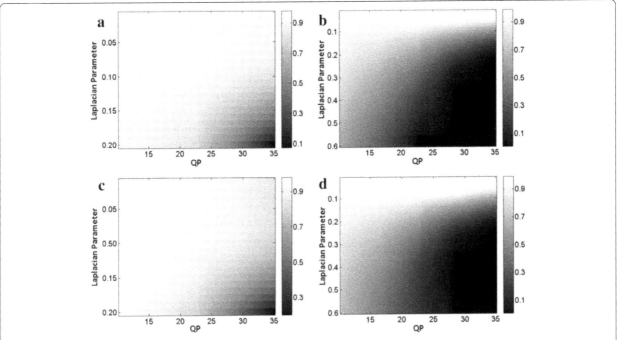

Figure 3 The scaling maps. (a) For residual variance by intra-coding; **(b)** for residual variance by inter-coding; **(c)** for residual cross covariance by intra-coding; **(d)** for residual cross covariance by inter-coding.

changes with SSIM. On the other hand, the impact of error propagation on the luminance component is limited.

The second observation is made on the relationship f_p between the quality attenuation of block b and the quality attenuation of its compensation block p. p indicates the compensation block of b, which may contain the transmission errors. Thus, p can be used to represent the prediction block r or concealment block c of b.

$$f_p = Q_{att}(b_p)/Q_{att}(p) = \frac{\mathrm{SSIM}(b,\tilde{p})}{\mathrm{SSIM}(b,\hat{p})} \Big/ \frac{\mathrm{SSIM}(p,\tilde{p})}{\mathrm{SSIM}(p,\hat{p})} \quad (13)$$

Usually, the quality attenuation of block b correlates with the quality attenuation of its compensation block p. In addition, the structural similarity between current block and its compensation block may be another factor in estimation of f_p. x_p is defined as follows to explore the effect of quality attenuation and structural similarity on f_p.

$$x_p = Q_{att}(p) \cdot \mathrm{SSIM}(b,\hat{p}) \quad (14)$$

The simulation results are carried out on the same four sequences as Section 3.1. Each sequence is coded with

four different QPs: 15, 25, 35, and 45. One I frame followed by all inter frames (IPPP). To cover various error propagation, each block is tested with random transmission errors propagated from prediction block and concealment block, respectively. Note that the prediction residuals of block b are not included in this observation.

Figure 5a displays the simulation results. The mean of each test frame is recorded as one blue sample, and the fitted curve of f_p (x_p) is shown as the red line. It shows that the quality attenuation of block, in terms of SSIM, is

Table 1 MAD between actual and estimated scores

Test terms	$\sigma\hat{e}^2$	$\sigma_{b\hat{e}}$	l	$c \cdot s$	D_{SSIM}
MAD (Intra-coding)	5.8118	3.4852	0.0001	0.0067	0.0067
MAD (Inter-coding)	2.4700	3.0642	0.00004	0.0056	0.0056

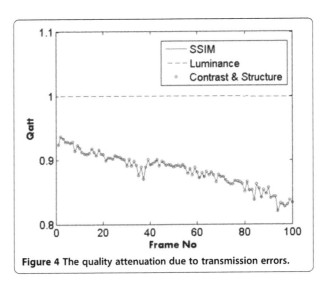

Figure 4 The quality attenuation due to transmission errors.

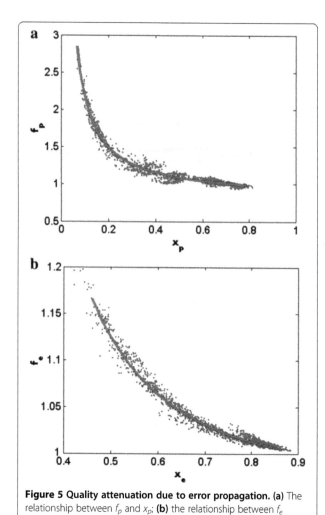

Figure 5 Quality attenuation due to error propagation. (a) The relationship between f_p and x_p; **(b)** the relationship between f_e and x_e.

related with the quality attenuation of its compensation block and the structural similarity. Moreover, it demonstrates that less quality attenuation of compensation block or less structural similarity between current block and compensation block leads to less quality attenuation.

The third observation is related to the impact of prediction residual on the decoded quality. Let Q_{enh} denote the quality enhancement of a given block b due to its prediction residuals e. f_e represents the relationship between the quality attenuation of block b with and without the prediction residual.

$$Q_{enh}(b_{p,e}) = SSIM(b, p + e)/SSIM(b, p) \quad (15)$$

$$f_e = Q_{att}(b_{p,e})/Q_{att}(b_p)^{att} = \frac{SSIM(b, \tilde{p} + \hat{e})}{SSIM(b, \hat{p} + \hat{e})} / \frac{SSIM(b, \tilde{p})}{SSIM(b, \hat{p})} \quad (16)$$

In this observation, the quality attenuation of block b may link with the quality attenuation of its compensation block p and the quality enhancement of its prediction

residuals e. x_e is defined as follows to explore the effect of quality attenuation and quality enhancement on f_p:

$$x_e = Q_{att}(b_p)/Q_{enh}(b_{\hat{p},\hat{e}}) \quad (17)$$

The simulation set-up is the same as that in the second observation. In this observation, each block including the prediction residuals is tested with random transmission errors propagated from its prediction blocks. Figure 5b shows the simulation results. The mean of each test frame is recorded as one blue sample, and the fitted curve of $f_e(x_e)$ is shown as the red line. The results show that a larger prediction residual leads to a better decoded quality of current block, and the influence of error propagation from prediction blocks will be smaller.

According to Equations 13 and 16, the effective approximation of $SSIM(b, \tilde{r} + \hat{e})$ and $SSIM(b, \tilde{c})$ can be developed as

$$SSIM(b, \tilde{r} + \hat{e}) \approx f_e(x_e) \cdot SSIM(b, \hat{r} + \hat{e}) \cdot \frac{SSIM(b, \tilde{r})}{SSIM(b, \hat{r})}$$

$$\approx f_e(x_e) \cdot SSIM(b, \hat{r} + \hat{e}) f_p(x_r) \cdot \frac{SSIM(r, \tilde{r})}{SSIM(r, \hat{r})}$$

$$\approx Q_{att}(r) \cdot f_e(x_e) \cdot f_p(x_r) \cdot SSIM(b, \hat{r} + \hat{e}) \quad (18)$$

$$SSIM(b, \tilde{c}) \approx f_p(x_c) \cdot SSIM(b, \hat{c}) \cdot \frac{SSIM(c, \tilde{c})}{SSIM(c, \hat{c})} \quad (19)$$

$$\approx Q_{att}(c) \cdot f_p(x_c) \cdot SSIM(b, \hat{c})$$

Where $SSIM(r, \tilde{r})$ and $SSIM(c, \tilde{c})$ represent the end-to-end distortion of prediction block and concealment block, respectively. The approximations used in the equations represent the estimation of f_p and f_e.

Based on Equations 18 and 19, the error propagation factors in Equations 5 and 6 can be obtained by

$$\Phi_r = Q_{att}(r) \cdot f_p(x_r) \cdot f_e(x_e) \quad (20)$$

$$\Phi_c = Q_{att}(c) \cdot f_p(x_c) \quad (21)$$

To better demonstrate the accuracy of the proposed error propagation models, Table 2 shows the average MAD between the actual and estimated SSIM of the four test sequences. It indicates that video quality at the

Table 2 MAD between actual and estimated SSIM

Test sequences	Error propagation from concealment block	Error propagation from prediction block
Crow_run	0.0213	0.0238
In_to_tree	0.0112	0.0137
Ducks_take_off	0.0126	0.0140
Old_town_cross	0.0153	0.0173
Average	0.0151	0.0172

Table 3 MAD between actual and estimated end-to-end distortion

Test sequences	[16]	[19]	Proposed
Park_joy	0.15784	0.01182	0.00880
Blue sky	0.09282	0.00779	0.00780
Mobile calendar	0.12679	0.01444	0.01209
Pedestrian area	0.24684	0.02055	0.01561
Park run	0.19973	0.02865	0.04162
River bed	0.09601	0.00797	0.00560
Rush hour	0.14633	0.01719	0.00762
Sunflower	0.17936	0.01888	0.01078
Shields	0.10850	0.01320	0.00790
Station	0.18221	0.02256	0.01231
Average	0.153643	0.016305	0.013013

decoder, in terms of SSIM, can be approximately calculated by the fitted models (20) and (21) at the encoder.

4 Error-resilient video coding

It is widely recognized that intra-update is an effective approach for error-resilient video coding because decoding of an intra-coding block does not require information from its previous frames. To better evaluate the performance of our proposed model, we incorporate the proposed SSIM-based end-to-end distortion model into the mode selection to improve the RD performance over packet-switched networks. Thus, the optimization problem in Equation 1 can be converted to the problem of mode selection between intra-coding and inter-coding as follows:

$$\min\{J(\text{mode})\} = \min\{D_{\text{SSIM}}(\text{mode}|\rho, \text{QP}) \qquad (22)$$
$$+\lambda_{\text{SSIM}} \cdot R(\text{mode}|\text{QP})\}$$

where D_{SSIM} and R denote the end-to-end distortion and bit-rate of current coding block. ρ is the packet loss ratio. mode denotes the coding mode. QP is the quantization parameter, which is determined by the target bit rate. According to [8,28,29], the Lagrange multiplier λ_{SSIM} is determined as follows:

$$\lambda_{\text{SSIM}} = (1-\rho) \cdot \overline{D_{\text{SSIM}}} \cdot f(R_T) \qquad (23)$$

where $\overline{D_{\text{SSIM}}}$ denotes the average distortion of previous coding units. $f(R_T)$ is an look-up experimental function [20], which is inversely proportional to the target bit rate R_T.

5 Experimental results

5.1 Evaluation of end-to-end distortion model

To validate the effectiveness of our proposed models, the end-to-end distortion models proposed in [16] and [19] are used as comparison. In [17], the SSIM-based

Table 4 Detail information of the test sequences

Test sequences	Resolution	Frame rate (fps)	Target bit rates (Kbps)			
Flower	352 × 288	30	2,000	1,300	700	400
Football	352 × 288	30	1,400	840	500	300
Mobile	352 × 288	30	2,800	1,600	800	380
Stefan	352 × 288	30	1,700	1,000	500	270
Bus	352 × 288	30	1,700	1,000	560	310
Crow_run	640 × 360	25	7,500	4,500	2,500	1,500
Park_joy	640 × 360	25	8,000	5,000	2,600	1,500
Ducks_take_off	640 × 360	25	7,000	4,500	2,400	1,200
In_to_tree	640 × 360	25	1,000	480	220	120
Old_town_cross	640 × 360	25	1,400	620	270	140
Blue sky	768 × 432	25	2,800	1,400	630	320
Mobile calendar	768 × 432	50	7,400	3,400	1,300	560
Pedestrian area	768 × 432	25	1,800	1,100	600	400
Park run	768 × 432	50	15,200	8,800	4,600	2,400
River bed	768 × 432	25	8,700	5,500	3,200	1,800
Rush hour	768 × 432	25	1,500	850	470	280
Sunflower	768 × 432	25	1,200	650	380	220
Shields	768 × 432	50	5,000	2,400	1,100	560
Station	768 × 432	25	850	440	250	160
Tractor	768 × 432	25	4,100	2,200	1,200	690

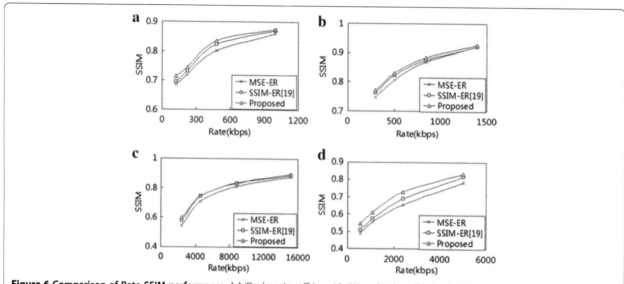

Figure 6 Comparison of Rate-SSIM performance. (a) 'Ducks_take_off' by with 5% packet loss. **(b)** 'Football' by with 10% packet loss. **(c)** 'Park run' by with 10% packet loss. **(d)** 'Shields' by with 20% packet loss.

estimation model is not suitable for a block given different coding modes. Thus, we did not compare the performance with the proposed model in [17].

We performed the simulation with ten LIVE sequences [21,22]. First 100 frames of each sequence are encoded by

four different QPs: 24, 28, 32, and 36, respectively. Random packet losses (10% and 20%) are used. Each experiment is repeated 200 times and the results are averaged. Table 3 shows the average MAD between the actual and estimated end-to-end distortion, in terms of

Table 5 Simulation results of SSIM again with different packet loss ratios and bit rates

Test sequences	Packet loss ratio: 20%		Packet loss ratio: 10%		Packet loss ratio: 5%	
	[19]	Proposed	[19]	Proposed	[19]	Proposed
Flower	0.0234	0.0255	0.0143	0.0182	0.0054	0.0154
Football	0.0093	0.0171	0.0132	0.0167	0.0173	0.0174
Mobile	0.0185	0.0210	0.0128	0.0279	0.0112	0.0198
Stefan	0.0192	0.0294	0.0233	0.0334	0.0220	0.0299
Bus	0.0312	0.0319	0.0387	0.0428	0.0384	0.0447
Crow_run	0.0134	0.0174	0.0109	0.0168	0.0091	0.0141
Park_joy	0.0229	0.0241	0.0212	0.0240	0.0148	0.0213
Ducks_take_off	0.0056	0.0042	0.0001	0.0039	−0.0038	0.0026
In_to_tree	0.0200	0.0280	0.0163	0.0266	0.0129	0.0248
Old_town_cross	0.0072	0.0170	0.0038	0.0142	0.0026	0.0120
Blue sky	0.0131	0.0309	0.0197	0.0366	0.0121	0.0311
Mobile calendar	0.0272	0.0239	0.0222	0.0138	0.0231	0.0125
Pedestrian area	0.0040	−0.0029	0.0055	−0.0025	0.0060	0.0013
Park run	0.0318	0.0375	0.0242	0.0332	0.0129	0.0213
River bed	0.0069	0.0062	0.0058	0.0065	0.0049	0.0061
Rush hour	0.0083	0.0043	0.0062	0.0046	0.0050	0.0045
Sunflower	0.0363	0.0554	0.0258	0.0560	0.0292	0.0566
Shields	0.0262	0.0589	0.0295	0.0512	0.0278	0.0313
Station	0.0039	0.0097	−0.0004	0.0076	0.0007	0.0198
Tractor	0.0147	0.0179	0.0088	0.0166	0.0037	0.0157
Average	0.01715	0.02287	0.01509	0.02240	0.01276	0.02011

Figure 7 Subjective quality comparison of one CIF sequence. (a) Original frame of 'Stefan'; **(b)** 'Stefan' by 'MSE-ER' (SSIM 0.913); **(c)** 'Stefan' by SSIM-ER [19] (SSIM 0.917); **(d)** 'Stefan' by our proposed (SSIM 0.929).

SSIM. It is obvious that our proposed model achieves better performance for most sequences.

5.2 Evaluation of RD performance
To validate the RD performance of error-resilient video coding, the MSE-based error resilient video coding scheme (MSE-ER) and the SSIM-based error-resilient video coding scheme (SSIM-ER) in [19] are used as the comparison schemes. For MSE-ER, the end-to-end distortion is estimated by the ROPE model [3], which is well studied and regarded as an advanced MSE-based distortion model, and the

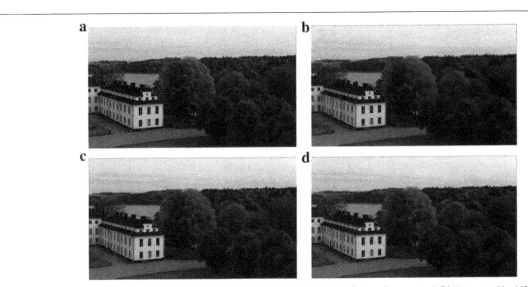

Figure 8 Subjective quality comparison of one 640 × 360 sequence. (a) Original frame of 'In_to_tree'; **(b)** 'In_to_tree' by MSE-ER (SSIM 0.833); **(c)** 'In_to_tree' by SSIM-ER [19] (SSIM 0.860); **(d)** 'In_to_tree' by our proposed (SSIM 0.873).

Figure 9 Subjective quality comparison of one LIVE sequence. (a) Original frame of 'Station'; **(b)** 'Station' by MSE-ER (SSIM 0.826); **(c)** 'Station' by SSIM-ER [19] (SSIM 0.851); **(d)** 'Station' by our proposed (SSIM 0.869).

Lagrange multiplier is calculated by the model presented in [8].

We evaluate the performance on the platform of JM 15.1 [30], in which the SSIM index is adopted as an optimal quality metric. Five CIF sequences [27], five 640 × 360 sequences [27] and ten LIVE sequences [21,22] are tested in the experiments. The first frame is coded as I frame and the rest are coded as P frames. The rate control is turned on. Table 4 shows the detail information of target bit rates for test sequences. Corresponding to four different target bit rates, the initial QP is equal to 24, 28, 32, and 36 for the first I frame and P frame. Frames are partitioned into one or more slices (each slice contains no more than 1,200 bytes), and the slices are organized in packets for transmission where each slice is packed into one packet. The test sequences are encoded with 5%, 10%, and 20% random packet loss ratio, respectively. For each packet loss ratio, four different target bit rates are tested in the experiments. Each experiment is repeated by 200

times, and the results are averaged, which are used as the final result.

Figure 6 illustrates the results of Rate-SSIM performance comparison for four test sequences. Moreover, we choose the MSE-ER scheme as the baseline and calculate all the simulation results of average SSIM gain with different bit rates and packet loss ratios, which are tabulated in Table 5.

It can be seen that the proposed model yields consistent gains over the MSE-ER for all sequences except 'Pedestrian area'. Our proposed scheme achieves an average SSIM gain of 0.0218 or equivalently a bit rate saving of 15.7%. Comparing to the SSIM-ER [19], our proposed scheme has better performance of most sequences and obtains an average gain of 0.0068. For some sequences, such as 'Mobile calendar' and 'Pedestrian area', although our proposed scheme cannot achieve the best performance, the quality of the two SSIM-ER schemes is similar.

Table 6 Average encoding time ratio of SSIM-ER [19] and proposed scheme to MSE-ER, respectively

Test sequences	[19]	Proposed	Test sequences	[19]	Proposed
Flower	2.77%	4.63%	Blue sky	4.09%	6.97%
Football	3.70%	4.99%	Mobile calendar	6.23%	9.77%
Mobile	4.37%	6.95%	Pedestrian area	3.89%	3.66%
Stefan	3.60%	4.78%	Park run	2.72%	4.85%
Bus	5.33%	7.13%	River bed	2.64%	2.21%
Crow_run	1.39%	3.98%	Rush hour	3.99%	4.46%
Park_joy	2.24%	3.22%	Sunflower	6.33%	7.54%
Ducks_take_off	2.40%	2.76%	Shields	5.19%	7.43%
In_to_tree	1.91%	6.57%	Station	3.70%	7.70%
Old_town_cross	3.45%	6.90%	Tractor	2.98%	5.23%
Average	3.12%	5.19%	-	4.18%	5.98%

5.3 Evaluation of subjective quality

Finally, we show the visual quality comparison of reconstructed images by different error-resilient video coding schemes. Figure 7 compares the subjective quality of the 25th frame of 'Stefan' encoded at 1.7 Mbps with 10% packet loss. Figure 8 shows the comparison on visual quality of the 38th frame of 'In_to_tree' encoded at 1 Mbps with 20% packet loss. Figure 9 represents the visual quality of the 29th frame of 'Station' encoded at 0.85 Mbps with 5% packet loss.

For the similar bit rate, the reconstructed images based on the SSIM-based error-resilient video coding can provide a better visual quality due to more image details being protected from transmission errors. On the other side, the reconstructed images based on the conventional MSE-based error-resilient video coding suffer from larger perceptual distortion. Compared to SSIM-ER [19], our proposed scheme obtains similar or better visual quality.

5.4 Evaluation of coding complexity

Our proposed SSIM-based error resilient video coding scheme improves the RD performance for lossy transmission over packet-switched network. However, the computational complexity of codec is increased due to SSIM-based distortion calculation and mode selection.

We compare the coding efficiency with different bit rates and packet loss ratios. Table 6 shows the average encoding time ratio of SSIM-ER [19] and proposed scheme to MSE-ER, respectively. The experiments are performed on a laptop with 3.4 GHz Intel Core i7-3770 CPU and 4G memory running on Microsoft Windows 7 professional platform. Each experiment is repeated 100 times and the results are averaged.

Comparing to MSE-ER, the average computation of SSIM-ER [19] and proposed scheme increase by 3.65% and 5.58%, respectively. In addition, different sequences have inconsistent degree of encoding time, as can be seen in Table 6. That is because the computation complexity is also affected by the characteristics of video content and the results of mode selection. The SSIM-based schemes may take more time to code the image details, such as 'Sunflower' and 'Mobile'.

6 Conclusions

In this paper, we propose an SSIM-based end-to-end distortion model for H.264/AVC video coding over packet-switched networks. This model is useful to estimate the content-dependent perceptual distortion of quantization, error concealment, and error propagation. We integrate the proposed end-to-end distortion model into the error-resilient video coding framework to optimally select the coding mode. Simulation results show that the proposed scheme outperforms the state-of-the-art schemes in terms of SSIM.

Competing interests
The authors declare that they have no competing interests.

Acknowledgements
The work described in this paper was supported by the National Natural Science Foundation of China (No. 60972111, 61036008, 61071184, 61373121), Research Funds for the Doctoral Program of Higher Education of China (No. 20100184120009, 20120184110001), Program for Sichuan Provincial Science Fund for Distinguished Young Scholars (No. 2012JQ0029, 13QNJJ0149), the Fundamental Research Funds for the Central Universities (Project no. SWJTU09CX032, SWJTU10CX08, SWJTU11ZT08), and Open Project Program of the National Laboratory of Pattern Recognition (NLPR).

Author details
[1]School of Information Science and Technology, Southwest Jiaotong University, Chengdu, China. [2]Institution of Academia Sinica, Jiuzhou Electric Group, Sichuan, China. [3]School of Electronics and Information Engineering, Sichuan University, Chengdu, China.

References
1. S Wenger, H.264/AVC over IP. IEEE Transact Circ Syst Video Technol **13**, 645–656 (2003)
2. ZH He, JF Cai, CW Chen, Joint source channel rate-distortion analysis for adaptive mode selection and rate control in wireless video coding. IEEE Transact Circ Syst Video Technol **12**, 511–523 (2002)
3. R Zhang, SL Regunathan, K Rose, Video coding with optimal inter/intra-mode switching for packet loss resilience. IEEE J Selected Areas Commun **18**, 966–976 (2000)
4. XK Yang, C Zhu, ZG Li, X Lin, GN Feng, S Wu, N Ling, Unequal loss protection for robust transmission of motion compensated video over the Internet. Signal Process. Image Commun. **18**, 157–167 (2003)
5. CY Zhang, H Yang, SY Yu, XK Yang, GOP-level transmission distortion modeling for mobile streaming video. Signal Process. Image Commun. **23**, 116–126 (2008)
6. Y Wang, ZY Wu, JM Boyce, Modeling of transmission-loss-induced distortion in decoded video. IEEE Transact Circ Syst Video Technol **16**, 716–732 (2006)
7. H Yang, K Rose, Advances in recursive per-pixel end-to-end distortion estimation for robust video coding in H.264/AVC. IEEE Transact Circ Syst Video Technol **17**, 845–856 (2007)
8. Y Zhang, W Gao, Y Lu, Q Huang, D Zhao, Joint source-channel rate-distortion optimization for H.264 video coding over error-prone networks. IEEE Transact Multimed **9**, 445–454 (2007)
9. H Yang, K Rose, Optimizing motion compensated prediction for error resilient video coding. EURASIP J Image Video Process **19**, 108–118 (2010)
10. JM Xiao, T Tillo, CY Lin, Y Zhao, Joint redundant motion vector and intra macroblock refreshment for video transmission. EURASIP J Image Video Process **12**, (2011). doi: 10.1186/1687-5281-2011-12
11. YX Zhang, C Zhu, KH Yap, A joint source-channel video coding scheme based on distributed source coding. IEEE Transact Multimed **10**, 1648–1656 (2008)
12. Y Zhou, CP Hou, W Xiang, F Wu, Channel distortion modeling for multiview video transmission over packet-switched networks. IEEE Transact Circ Syst Video Technol **21**, 1679–1692 (2011)
13. JM Xiao, T Tillo, CY Lin, Y Zhao, Dynamic sub-GOP forward error correction code for real-time video applications. IEEE Transact Multimed **14**, 1298–1308 (2012)
14. Z Xue, KK Loo, J Cosmas, M Tun, PY Yip, Error-resilient scheme for wavelet video coding using automatic ROI detection and Wyner-Ziv coding over packet erasure channel. IEEE Transact Broadcast **56**, 481–493 (2010)
15. MB Dissanayake, S Worrall, WAC Fernando, Error resilience for multi-view video using redundant macroblock coding, in *Proceedings of the IEEE International Conference on Industrial Information Systems (ICIIS)* (University of Peradeniya, Kandy, 2011), pp. 472–476
16. YX Wang, Y Zhang, R Lu, PC Cosman, SSIM-Based End-to-End Distortion Modeling for H.264 Video Coding, in *Proceedings of the Pacific-Rim Conference on Multimedia (PCM)* (Singapore, 2012), pp. 117–128

17. YJ Kwon, J-S Lee, Parametric estimation of structural similarity degradation for video transmission over error-prone networks. Electron. Lett. **49**, 1147–1148 (2013)

18. L Zhang, Q Peng, X Wu, SSIM-based Error-resilient video coding over packet-switched, in *Proceedings of the Pacific-Rim Conference on Multimedia (PCM)* (Singapore, 2012), pp. 263–272

19. PH Zhao, YW Liu, JX Liu, S Li, RX Yao, SSIM-based error-resilient rate-distortion optimization of H.264/AVC video coding for wireless streaming. Signal Process. Image Commun. **29**, 303–315 (2014)

20. L Zhang, Q Peng, X Wu, SSIM-based end-to-end distortion model for error resilient video coding over packet-switched networks, in *Proceedings of the International Conference on Multimedia Modeling (MMM)* (Huangshan, 2013), pp. 307–317

21. K Seshadrinathan, R Soundararajan, AC Bovik, LK Cormack, Study of subjective and objective quality assessment of video. IEEE Transact Image Process **19**, 1427–1441 (2010)

22. *Live Video Quality Database*, 2012. http://www.utexas.edu/ece/research/live/vqdatabase/

23. Z Wang, AC Bovik, HR Sheikh, EP Simoncelli, Image quality assessment: from error visibility to structural similarity. IEEE Transact Image Process **13**, 600–612 (2004)

24. WS Lin, CCJ Kuo, Perceptual visual quality metrics: a survey. J Visual Commun Image Represent **22**, 297–312 (2011)

25. E Lam, J Goodman, A mathematic analysis of the DCT coefficient distribution for images. IEEE Transact Image Process **9**, 1661–1666 (2000)

26. TW Yang, C Zhu, XJ Fan, Q Peng, Source distortion temporal propagation model for motion compensated video coding optimization, in *Proceedings of the IEEE International Conference on Multimedia and Expo (ICME)* (Melbourne, 2012), pp. 85–90

27. *Xiph.org Video Test Media*, 2010. http://media.xiph.org/video/derf/

28. TS Ou, YH Huang, HH Chen, SSIM-based perceptual rate control for video coding. IEEE Transact Circ Syst Video Technol **21**, 682–691 (2011)

29. T Wiegand, B Girod, Lagrange multiplier selection in hybrid video coder control, in *Proceedings of the IEEE International Conference on Image Processing (ICIP)* (Thessaloniki, Thessaloniki, 2001), pp. 542–545

30. *JVT Reference Software*, 2011. http://iphome.hhi.de/suehring/tml/

11

Robust fuzzy scheme for Gaussian denoising of 3D color video

Alberto Jorge Rosales-Silva*, Francisco Javier Gallegos-Funes, Ivonne Bazan Trujillo and Alfredo Ramírez García

Abstract

We propose a three-dimensional Gaussian denoising scheme for application to color video frames. The time is selected as a third dimension. The algorithm is developed using fuzzy rules and directional techniques. A fuzzy parameter is used for characterization of the difference among pixels, based on gradients and angle of deviations, as well as for motion detection and noise estimation. By using only two frames of a video sequence, it is possible to efficiently decrease Gaussian noise. This filter uses a noise estimator that is spatio-temporally adapted in a local manner, in a novel way using techniques mentioned herein, and proposing a fuzzy methodology that enhances capabilities in noise suppression when compared to other methods employed. We provide simulation results that show the effectiveness of the novel color video denoising algorithm.

Keywords: Fuzzy theory; Video frames; Motion detection; Directional processing; Gaussian noise

1. Introduction

All pixels in digital color video frames are commonly affected by Gaussian-type noise due to the behavior of the image acquisition sensor; in accordance with this, we make the following assumptions as to the noise:

$$G(x_\beta) = N(0, \sigma) = \frac{1}{\sqrt{2\pi} \cdot \sigma} \exp\left(\frac{-x_\beta{}^2}{2 \cdot \sigma^2}\right), \qquad (1)$$

where x_β represents the original pixel component value, $\beta = \{Red, Green, Blue\}$ are the notations on each pixel color component (or channel), and σ is the standard deviation of the noise. In our case, the Gaussian function is independently used on the pixel component of each channel of the frame in order to obtain the corrupted video sequence.

A pre-processing procedure to reduce noise effect is the main stage of any computer vision application. It should include procedures to reduce the noise impact in a video without degrading the quality, edges, fine detail, and color properties.

The current proposal is an attempt to enhance the quality while processing the color video sequences corrupted by Gaussian noise; *this methodology is an extension of the method proposed for impulsive noise removal* [1]. There exist numerous algorithms that perform the processing of 3D signals using only the spatial information [2]. Other applications use only the temporal information [3,4]; an example is one that uses wavelet procedures to reduce the delay in video coding [5]. There exist also some interesting applications that use spatio-temporal information [6-13]. The disadvantage of these 3D solutions is that they often require large memory and may introduce a significant time delay in cases where there is a need for more than one frame to be processed. This is undesirable in interactive applications such as infrared camera-assisted driving or videoconferencing. Moreover, full 3D techniques tend to require more computation than separable ones, and their optimal performance can be very difficult to determine. For example, integrating video coding and denoising is a novel processing paradigm and brings mutual benefits to both video processing tools. In Jovanov et al. [14], the main idea is the reuse of motion estimation resources from the video coding module for the purpose of video denoising. Some disadvantages of the work done by Dai et al. [15] is that they use a number of reference frames that increases the computational charge; the algorithm MHMCF was originally applied to grayscale video signal; and in the paper referenced [14], it was adapted to color video denoising, transforming the RGB video in a luminance color difference space proposed by the authors.

* Correspondence: arosaless@ipn.mx
School of Advanced Mechanical and Electrical Engineering, U.P.A.L.M, Av. Instituto Politécnico Nacional S/N, ESIME Zacatenco, Col. Lindavista, México D.F. 07738, Mexico

Other state-of-the-art algorithms found in literature work in the same manner; for example in Liu and Freeman [16], a framework that integrates robust optical flow into a non-local means framework with noise level estimation is used, and the temporal coherence is taken into account in removing structured noise. In the paper by Dabov et al. [17], it is interesting to see how they propose a method based on highly sparse signal representation in local 3D transform domain; a noisy video is processed in blockwise manner, and for each processed block, they form data array by stacking together blocks found to be similar to the currently processed one. In [18], Mairal et al. presented a framework for learning multiscale sparse representations of color images and video with overcomplete dictionaries. They propose a multiscaled learned representation obtained by using an efficient quadtree decomposition of the learned dictionary and overlapping image patches. This provides an alternative to predefined dictionaries such as wavelets.

The effectiveness of the algorithm designed is justified by comparing it with four other state-of-the-art approaches: 'Fuzzy Logic Recursive Spatio-Temporal Filter' (FLRSTF), where a fuzzy logic recursive scheme is proposed for motion detection and spatio-temporal filtering capable of dealing with Gaussian noise and unsteady illumination conditions in both the temporal and the spatial directions [19]. Another algorithm used for comparison is the 'Fuzzy Logic Recursive Spatio-Temporal Filter using Angles' (FLRSTF_ANGLE). This algorithm uses the angle deviations instead of gradients as a difference between pixels in the FLRSTF algorithm. The 'Video Generalized Vector Directional Filtering in Gaussian Denoising' (VGVDF_G) [20] is a directional technique that computes the angle deviations between pixels as a difference criterion among them. As a consequence, the vector directional filters (VDF) do not take into account the image brightness when processing the image vectors. Finally, the 'Video Median M-type K-Nearest Neighbor in Gaussian Denoising' filter (VMMKNN_G) [21,22] uses order statistics techniques to characterize the pixel differences.

The proposed algorithm employs only two frames in order to reduce the computational processing charge and memory requirements, permitting one to produce an efficient denoising framework. Additionally, it applies the relationship that the neighboring pixels have to the central one in *magnitude* and *angle deviation*, connecting them by fuzzy logic rules designed to estimate the motion and noise parameters. The effectiveness of the present approach is justified by comparing it with four state-of-the-art algorithms found in literature as explained before.

The digital video database is formed by the *Miss America*, *Flowers*, and *Chair* color video sequences; this database is well known in scientific literature [23]. Frames were manipulated to be 24 bits in depth to form true-color images with 176 × 144 pixels, in order to work with the Quarter Common Intermediate Format (QCIF). These video sequences were selected because of their different natures and textures. The database was contaminated by Gaussian noise at different levels of intensity for each channel in an independent manner. This was used to characterize the performance, permitting the justification of the robustness of the novel framework.

2. Proposed fuzzy design

The first frame of the color video sequence is processed as follows. First, the histogram and the mean value $(\bar{x}_\beta)$ for each pixel component are calculated, using a 3 × 3 processing window. Then, an angle deviation between two vectors $(\bar{x}$ and $x_c)$ containing components in the Red, Green, and Blue channels is computed as $\theta_c = A(\bar{x}, x_c)$, where $\theta_c = \cos^{-1}\left\{\frac{\bar{x} \cdot x_c}{|\bar{x}| \cdot |x_c|}\right\}$ is the angle deviation of the mean value vector $(\bar{x})$ with respect to the central pixel vector (x_c) in a 3 × 3 processing window. Color-image processing has traditionally been approached in a component-wise manner, that is, by processing the image channels separately. These approaches fail to consider the inherent correlation that exists between the different channels, and they may result in pixel output values that are different from the input values with possible shifts in chromaticity [24]. Thus, it is desirable to employ vector approaches in color image processing to obtain the angle deviations.

The angle interval [0, 1] is used to determine the histogram. The pixel intensity takes values from 0 to 255 in each channel; the angle deviation θ_c for any given pixel with respect to another one falls within the interval $[0, \frac{\pi}{2}]$. The angle deviations outside the proposed interval ([0, 1]) are not taken into account in forming the histogram. Therefore, the noise estimator is obtained using only values inside this interval; this is to avoid the smoothness of some details and improve the criteria results.

It is common practice to normalize a histogram by dividing each of its components by the total number of pixels in the image; this is an estimate of the probability of occurrence of intensity levels in the image. Using this same principle, we propose the use of a normalized histogram based on angle deviations; this normalized histogram being an estimate of the probability of occurrence of the angle deviations between pixels. The procedure used to obtain the histogram is that of using the vectorial values: if $[(F - 1)/255] \le \theta_c \le [F/255]$, the histogram is increased by '1' in the F position; the parameter F increases from 1 to 255; if the aforementioned condition does not hold for the range of F, the histogram remains unchanged for F, where θ_c is the angle deviation of the central pixel with respect to one of its neighboring pixel. The parameter F is proposed only to determine to which value of pixel intensity in a histogram the angle deviation belongs.

After obtaining the histogram, the probability of occurrence for each one of the elements of the histogram must be calculated. After the mean value $\mu = \sum_{j=0}^{255} j \cdot p_j$ is computed (where p_j is the probability of occurrence of each element in the histogram), the variance $\sigma_\beta^2 = \sum_{j=0}^{255} (j-\mu)^2 \cdot \left(p_j \right)$ (where j represents each element inside the histogram) and the *general standard deviation (SD)* $\sigma'_\beta = \sqrt{\sigma_\beta^2}$ are determined. The SD parameter is used as the noise estimator for the purpose of decreasing Gaussian noise only for the first frame of the video sequence. In this step of the algorithm, σ'_β is the same for all three channels of a color image for the general process of the Gaussian denoising algorithm, as Figure 1 indicates. The SD parameter is used to find the deviations representing the data in its distribution from the arithmetic mean. This is in order to present them more realistically when it comes to describing and interpreting them for decision-making purposes. We estimate the SD parameter of the Gaussian noise from the input video sequence only for the first frame ($t = 0$) and subsequently try to adapt the SD to the input video and noise changes by spatio-temporal adaptation of the noise estimator SD.

To summarize, we use the SD parameter as an estimate of the noise to be applied in the *spatial algorithm*, which will be renewed on a temporary adaptive filter in order to ultimately generate an adaptive spatio-temporal noise estimator.

2.1. Spatial algorithm

The spatial algorithm allows one to estimate the angle deviation of the neighboring pixels with respect to the central one. The results are adjusted according to the processing windows used (see Figure 2b). This methodology was developed to effectively identify uniform areas within the image to be processed with a fast processing algorithm, like the 'Mean Weighted Filtering Algorithm' described below.

The proposed fast filtering procedure is carried out using the following methodology under an '*IF-OR-THEN-ELSE*' condition: IF ($\theta_1 \text{AND} \theta_3 \text{AND} \theta_4 \text{AND} \theta_6 \geq \tau_1$) OR ($\theta_0 \text{AND} \theta_2 \text{AND} \theta_5 \text{AND} \theta_7 \geq \tau_1$) THEN the Mean Weighted Filtering Algorithm, ELSE the *Spatial Filtering Algorithm* (where τ_1 is a threshold defined as 0.1). All parameter values were proposed according to the best results of the *peak signal-to-noise ratio (PSNR)* and *mean absolute error (MAE)* criteria obtained after numerous experiments. If the Mean Weighted Filtering Algorithm [25] is selected, one processes the pixel's intensity components of the 3×3 window sample using Equation 2. This procedure is used because the angle deviation between the pixels is very small, which could indicate a uniform region where it is likely that there are no edges and details which may be softened. Thus, the use of the Mean Weighted Filtering Algorithm is proposed. Taking into account the fact that the relationship between a distance measure (angle deviation) is generally exponential, a sigmoidal linear membership function is suggested and a fuzzy weight

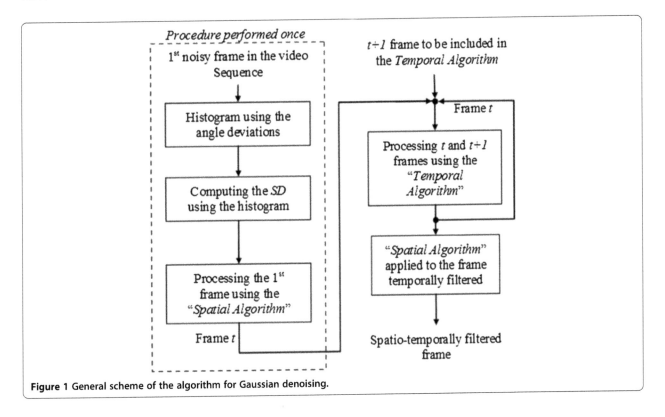

Figure 1 General scheme of the algorithm for Gaussian denoising.

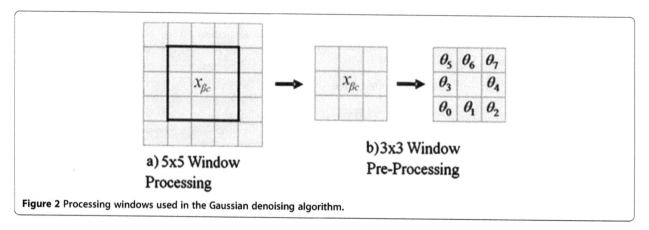

Figure 2 Processing windows used in the Gaussian denoising algorithm.

$\left(2/\left(1+e^{\theta_i}\right)\right)$ associated with the vector $x_{\beta i}$ can be used in the following equation:

$$y_{\beta out} = \left[\sum_{\substack{i=0 \\ j \neq c}}^{N-1} x_{\beta i} \cdot \left(\frac{2}{(1+e^{\theta_i})}\right) + x_{\beta c}\right] \Bigg/ \left[\sum_{i=0}^{N-1}\left[\frac{2}{(1+e^{\theta_i})}\right] + 1\right],$$

(2)

where $N = 8$ represents the number of data samples to be taken into account and it is in agreement with Figure 2; the fuzzy weight computed will produce an output in the interval [0,1], and it corresponds to each angle deviation value computed excluding the central angle deviation.

If the Spatial Filtering Algorithm was selected, it probably means that the sample contained edges and/or fine details. To implement this filter, the following methodology is proposed. The procedure consists of computing a new *locally adapted SD* (σ_β) for each plane of the color image, using a 5×5 processing window (see Figure 2a). In addition, the local updating of the SD should be undertaken according to the following condition: if $\sigma_\beta = \sigma'_\beta$, then $\sigma_\beta = \sigma'_\beta$; otherwise $\sigma'_\beta = \sigma_\beta$, where σ'_β was previously defined. This is most likely because the sample has edges and details, presenting a large value of dispersion among the pixels, so the largest SD value describes best this fact.

To provide a parameter indicating the similarity between the central and neighboring pixels, a gradient (∇) was defined. This parameter describes the magnitude differences between pixels, and the gradient is applied to each β component of the noisy color frame independently, as follows: $\nabla_{(k,l)\beta}(i,j) = |\nabla_\beta(i+k, j+l) - \nabla_\beta(i,j)| = \nabla_{\gamma\beta}$, where the pair (k, l) (with $k, l \in \{-1, 0, 1\}$) represents each of the eight cardinal directions, and (i, j) is the center of the gradient. This leads to the *main values* (see Figure 3) [19]. The eight gradient values according to the eight different directions (or neighbors) are called *main gradient values*. To provide more robustness to the algorithm, and avoid image blurring, the use of two *related gradient values* in the same direction is proposed. We assume that

in case an edge like image structure extends in a certain direction $\gamma = \{N, S, E, W, SE, SW, NE, NW\}$, it leads to large derivative values perpendicular to the direction γ at the current pixel position (i, j) and at the neighboring pixels as well, in other words; these values are determined making use of a right angle with the direction of the main gradient. For example (see Figure 3a), in the SE direction (for $(k, l) = (1, 1)$ and $(i, j) = (0, 0)$), we calculate the main gradient value $\nabla_{(1,1)\beta}(i, j) = |\nabla_\beta(i+1, j+1) - \nabla_\beta(i, j)| = \nabla_{\gamma\beta M}$ and two related gradient values: $\nabla_{(2,0)\beta}(i+1, j-1) = |\nabla_\beta(i+2, j) - \nabla_\beta(i+1, j-1)| = \nabla_{\gamma\beta D1}$ and $\nabla_{(0,2)\beta}(i-1, j+1) = |\nabla_\beta(i, j+2) - \nabla_\beta(i-1, j+1)| = \nabla_{\gamma\beta D2}$. In such a manner, by taking into account those three derivative values for each direction (and combining them in a fuzzy logic manner), we distinguish local variations due to noise from those due to the edge-like image structures. The two *derived gradient values* are used to distinguish noisy pixels from edge pixels; when all of these gradients are larger than a predefined threshold T_β, (i, j) is considered to be a noisy pixel and must be filtered out.

Subsequently, the following condition should be verified: IF $\nabla_{\gamma\beta(M,D1,D2)} < T_\beta$ (where $T_\beta = 2 \cdot \sigma_\beta$), THEN a membership value using $\nabla_{\gamma\beta(M,D1,D2)}$ is computed; otherwise, the membership value is 0. The threshold value T_β is obtained experimentally according to the PSNR and MAE criteria: γ represents each of the eight cardinal points, and $\nabla_{\gamma\beta(M,D1,D2)}$ represents each of the values computed for each of the neighboring pixels with respect to the central one, within a sliding window. These gradients are called 'main gradient values'. Two 'derived gradient values' are employed, avoiding the blurring of the image in the presence of an edge instead of a noisy pixel.

The detailed methodological procedures used to compute the main and derived gradient values for the eight cardinal directions are described by Zlokolica et al. [19]. If $\nabla_{\gamma\beta(M,D1,D2)} < T_\beta$ for each of the three gradient values (the main and derived according to Figure 3a), then the angle deviation is calculated in the corresponding direction (γ). This means that if the main and derived gradient values are of a lower value than the threshold (T_β), one

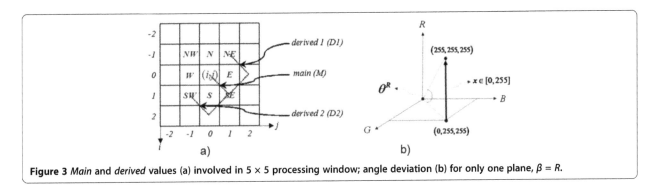

Figure 3 *Main* and *derived* values (a) involved in 5 × 5 processing window; angle deviation (b) for only one plane, $\beta = R$.

gets the angle deviations from the values for the three gradients; however, if any of these values do not satisfy the condition, the angle deviation is set to 0 for the values that do not comply.

Another way to characterize the difference between pixels is by calculating the angle deviation from the central pixel and its neighbors; this is called the *main* and *derived vectorial values*. Calculated angle deviations in the cardinal directions are taken as the weight values for each color plane of an image (Equation 3). These weights provide a relationship between pixels in a single plane at a given angle deviation. Equation 3 illustrates the calculation of the angle deviation to obtain the weight values, where

$$\theta^\beta = \cos^{-1}\left\{\frac{2(255)^2 + x_{\gamma\beta(M,D1,D2)} \cdot x'_{\gamma\beta(M,D1,D2)}}{\sqrt{2\cdot(255)^2 + \left(x_{\gamma\beta(M,D1,D2)}\right)^2} \cdot \sqrt{2\cdot(255)^2 + \left(x'_{\gamma\beta(M,D1,D2)}\right)^2}}\right\};$$

these values range from 0 to 1 according to Figure 3b.

$$\alpha_{\gamma\beta} = \frac{2}{\left(1 + \exp\left[\theta^\beta\right]\right)}, \qquad (3)$$

where $x_{\gamma\beta(M,D1,D2)}$ is the pixel component in the associated direction. For example, for the $x_{\gamma\beta M}$ component of the pixel, the coordinate is (0, 0) as shown in Figure 3a. Therefore, for component $x'_{\gamma\beta M}$, the coordinate should be (1, 1) for the 'SE' cardinal direction, and so on. This parameter indicates that the smaller the difference in angle between the pixels involved, the greater the weight value of the pixel in the associated direction.

Finally, the main and derived vectorial gradient values are used to find a degree of membership using membership functions, which are functions that return a value between 0 and 1, indicating the degree of membership of an element with respect to a set (in our case, we define a BIG fuzzy set). Then, we can characterize the level of proximity of the components of the central pixel with respect to its neighbors, and see if it is a noisy or in motion component, or free of motion and/or low noise.

As mentioned above, we have defined a BIG fuzzy set; it will feature the presence of noise in the sample to be processed. The values that belong to this fuzzy set, in whole or in part, will represent the level of noise present in the pixel.

The membership function used to characterize the 'main and derived vectorial gradient values' is defined by:

$$\mu_{\text{BIG}} = \begin{cases} \max\left\{\left(1-\left[\nabla_{\gamma\beta(M,D1,D2)}/T_\beta\right]\right), \alpha_{\gamma\beta(M,D1,D2)}\right\}, & if \ \nabla_{\gamma\beta} < T_\beta \\ 0 & , \ \text{otherwise} \end{cases},$$

$$(4)$$

A *fuzzy rule* is created from this membership function, which is simply the application of the membership function by fuzzy operators. In this case, fuzzy operator *OR* is defined as $OR(f_1, f_2) = \max(f_1, f_2)$.

Each pixel has one returned value defined by the level of corruption present in the pixel. That is, one says 'the pixel is corrupted' if its BIG membership value is 1, and 'the pixel is low-noise corrupted' when its BIG membership value is 0. The linguistics 'the pixel is corrupted' and 'the pixel is low-noise corrupted' indicate the degree of belonging to each of the possible states in which the pixel can be found.

From the fuzzy rules, we obtain outputs, which are used to make decisions. The function defined by Equation 4 returns values between 0 and 1. It indicates how the parameter behaved with respect to the proposed fuzzy set. Finally, the following fuzzy rule is designed to connect gradient values with angle deviations, thus forming the 'fuzzy vectorial-gradient values'.

Fuzzy rule 1 helps to detect the edges and fine details using the membership values of the BIG fuzzy set obtained by Equation 4. The fuzzy values obtained by this rule are taken as fuzzy weights and used in a fast processing algorithm to improve the computational load. This fast processing algorithm is defined by means of Equation 5.

Fuzzy rule 1: the fuzzy vectorial-gradient value is defined as $\nabla_{\gamma\beta}\alpha_{\gamma\beta}$, so: IF (($\nabla_{\gamma\beta M}$, $\alpha_{\gamma\beta}$) is BIG AND ($\nabla_{\gamma\beta D1}$, $\alpha_{\gamma\beta D1}$) is BIG) OR (($\nabla_{\gamma\beta M}$, $\alpha_{\gamma\beta}$) is BIG AND ($\nabla_{\gamma\beta D2}$, $\alpha_{\gamma\beta D2}$) is BIG), THEN $\nabla_{\gamma\beta}\alpha_{\gamma\beta}$ is BIG. In this fuzzy rule, the 'AND' and 'OR' operators are defined as algebraic operations, consequently: AND $= A \cdot B$, and OR $= A + B - A \cdot B$.

The fuzzy weights are used in the fast algorithm as a final step in the noise suppression of the spatial algorithm; the fast algorithm is defined as an averaging procedure with weights as follows:

$$y_{\beta\text{out}} = \frac{\sum\limits_{\gamma} \left(\nabla_{\gamma\beta} \alpha_{\gamma\beta} \right) \cdot x_{\gamma\beta}}{\sum\limits_{\gamma} \left(\nabla_{\gamma\beta} \alpha_{\gamma\beta} \right)}, \tag{5}$$

where $x_{\gamma\beta}$ represents each component magnitude of the neighboring pixels around the central pixel within the pre-processing window (Figure 2b) in the respective cardinal direction, and $y_{\beta\text{out}}$ is the output of the spatial algorithm applied to the first frame of the video sequence. From this, we obtain the first spatially filtered t frame which is then passed to the temporal algorithm, joined to the $t + 1$ frame according to the scheme described in Figure 1.

2.2. Temporal algorithm

The outlined spatial algorithm smoothes Gaussian noise efficiently but still loses some of the image's fine details and edges. To avoid these undesirable outputs, a temporal algorithm is proposed. To design such an algorithm, only two frames of the video sequence are used. The spatially filtered t frame obtained with the methodology developed in Section 2 is used once in order to provide the temporal algorithm of a filtered t frame to be used for reference to enhance the capabilities of the temporal algorithm from the first frame of the video stream without losing significant results, and the corrupted $t + 1$ frame of the video sequence.

The temporal algorithm, like the spatial algorithm, is governed by fuzzy rules to help detect the noise and motion present between pixels of two frames (t and $t + 1$), thus avoiding the loss of important features of video frames. The proposed fuzzy rules are used for each color plane of the two frames (t and $t + 1$) independently. In the same way as the spatial algorithm, the gradient and the angle deviation values are calculated in order to characterize the difference between pixels in the two frames of the video sequence. These values are related to the central pixel $x_{\beta c}^{t+1}$ with respect to its neighbors in frames t and $t + 1$ and are computed as follows:

$$\theta_{\beta ic}^1 = A\left(x_{\beta i}^t, x_{\beta c}^{t+1} \right), \quad \nabla_{\beta ic}^1 = \left| x_{\beta i}^t - x_{\beta c}^{t+1} \right|, \tag{6}$$

$$i, j = 0, \ldots, N; \text{ where } N = 8,$$

$$\theta_{\beta ij}^2 = A\left(x_{\beta i}^t, x_{\beta j}^{t+1} \right), \quad \nabla_{\beta ij}^2 = \left| x_{\beta i}^t - x_{\beta j}^{t+1} \right|, \tag{7}$$

$$\theta_{\beta jc}^3 = A\left(x_{\beta j}^{t+1}, x_{\beta c}^{t+1} \right), \quad \nabla_{\beta j}^3 = \left| x_{\beta j}^{t+1} - x_{\beta c}^{t+1} \right|.$$

This is better understood with an example, as illustrated in Figure 4, for the case where β = Red (R), and $i = j = 2$.

Similarly defined as was the BIG fuzzy set, this set is defined as the SMALL fuzzy set. The same meanings for the expressions 'the pixel is corrupted' and the 'the pixel is low-noise corrupted' apply, but in the opposite direction. Assuming that a fuzzy set is totally characterized by a membership function, the membership function μ_{SMALL} (in the SMALL fuzzy set) is introduced to characterize the values associated with no movement and low-noise presence. By doing this, one can have a value between [0, 1] in order to measure the membership value with respect to the SMALL fuzzy set, where the value of 1 implies that the sample has no movement and low noise presence, and the value of 0 implies the opposite.

Thus, two fuzzy sets separately defined as BIG and SMALL are used to characterize the level of noise and/or movement in the sample processing. The membership functions μ_{BIG} and μ_{SMALL}, for gradients and angle deviations used by the temporal algorithm, are defined by the following expressions [25]:

$$\mu_{\text{SMALL}}(\chi) = \begin{cases} 1 & \text{if } \chi < \mu_1 \\ \exp\left\{ -\left((\chi - \mu_1)^2 / (2 \cdot \sigma^2) \right) \right\} & \text{otherwise} \end{cases}, \tag{8}$$

$$\mu_{\text{BIG}}(\chi) = \begin{cases} 1 & \text{if } \chi > \mu_2 \\ \exp\left\{ -\left((\chi - \mu_2)^2 / (2 \cdot \sigma^2) \right) \right\} & \text{otherwise} \end{cases}, \tag{9}$$

when $\chi = \theta_{\beta\gamma}$ for angle deviations, one has to select the parameters, standard deviation $\sigma = 0.3163$, mean $\mu_1 = 0.2$, and mean $\mu_2 = 0.615$; when $\chi = \nabla_{\beta\gamma}$ for gradient values, select the parameters, standard deviation $\sigma = 31.63$, mean $\mu_1 = 60$, and mean $\mu_2 = 140$. The parameter values were obtained through extensive simulations carried out on the color video sequences used in this study. The idea was to find the optimal parameter values according to the PSNR and MAE criteria. The procedure used to compute the optimal values of the parameters in the event that $\chi = \theta_{\beta\gamma}$ is selected was the beginning and variation of standard deviation starting with the value 0.1, so the PSNR and MAE criteria could reach their optimal values while maintaining the fixed values of $\mu_1 = 0.1$ and $\mu_2 = 0.1$. Once we have the optimal values of PSNR and MAE, the parameter of standard deviation is fixed and μ_1 subsequently increases until it reaches the optimal values for the PSNR and MAE criteria. Finally, upon the fixing of the standard deviation and μ_1, the μ_2 is varied until it again reaches the optimal values for the PSNR and MAE criteria. The same approach is used to calculate the values of the parameters when the event $\chi = \nabla_{\beta\gamma}$ is selected, based on the PSNR and MAE criteria. These experimental results were obtained using the well-known Miss America and Flowers color video sequences.

The fuzzy rules illustrated in Figure 5 are designed to detect, pixel by pixel, the presence of motion. First, the

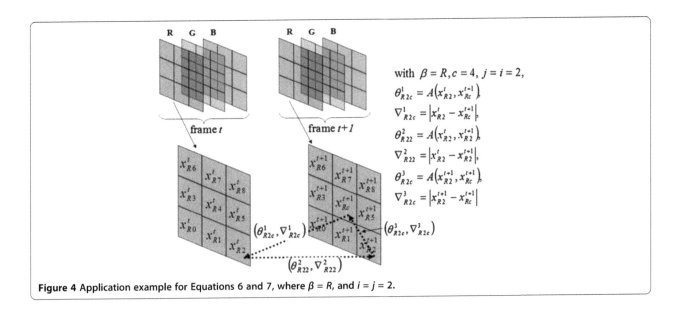

Figure 4 Application example for Equations 6 and 7, where $\beta = R$, and $i = j = 2$.

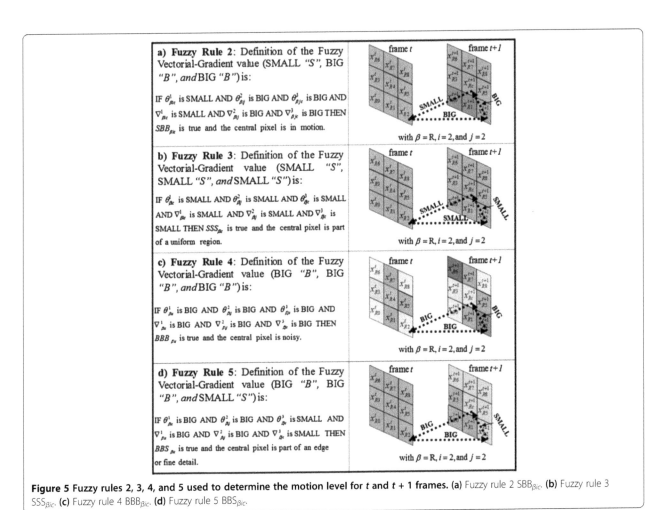

Figure 5 Fuzzy rules 2, 3, 4, and 5 used to determine the motion level for t and $t + 1$ frames. (a) Fuzzy rule 2 $SBB_{\beta ic}$. **(b)** Fuzzy rule 3 $SSS_{\beta ic}$. **(c)** Fuzzy rule 4 $BBB_{\beta ic}$. **(d)** Fuzzy rule 5 $BBS_{\beta ic}$.

motion relative to the central pixel in the $t + 1$ frame is detected, using the pixels in the t frame; then, motion detection is performed on a pixel basis in both frames; and finally, this procedure applies only to the pixels of the $t + 1$ frame. Following this, the procedure for the proposed fuzzy rules is described in Figure 5; these fuzzy rules allow the analyst to characterize the presence of motion and/or noise in the sample in order to determine which procedure to utilize during the image processing.

The fuzzy rules of Figure 5 were designed to characterize, in a fuzzy directional manner, the relationship between pixels in a sliding window using two frames. Hence, the movement and the noise level presence in the central pixel of the sample are found. To understand the meaning of these fuzzy rules, the following situation is assumed: if the fuzzy directional values obtained by the membership function for the SMALL fuzzy set are close to one, then there is neither motion nor low-noise presence in the central pixel component. Conversely, if the values of the membership function are close to one for the BIG fuzzy set, the central pixel component is noisy and/or presents motion. Thus, for fuzzy rule 2, the values SMALL, BIG, and BIG (SBB) characterize a pixel in motion, in such a way that the first value characterizes the closeness of a SMALL component to the central pixel in the $t + 1$ frame with the pixel component of a neighbor in the t frame; the first BIG value indicates that the component of the pixel in the t frame and the component of the pixel in the $t + 1$ frame are unrelated; and the second BIG conveys that the value of the component of the pixel of the $t + 1$ frame, with respect to the component of the central pixel of the $t + 1$ frame shows some difference, therefore this pixel is highly likely to belong to an edge and/or is in motion. These findings reinforce the correctness of the parameters obtained for other neighboring component pixels. In this way, the relationship of proximity between the central pixel of the $t + 1$ frame with respect to the neighboring pixels of the t and $t + 1$ frames is obtained.

This study also aims at improving performance over computational resources of the algorithm making the distinction among different areas, especially, finding areas of an image that could be processed by a magnitude filter without affecting the fine image details and other image characteristics. The procedure to accomplish this is as follows: the sample standard deviation that includes the $3 \times 3 \times 2$ pre-processing window for each color channel in the t and $t + 1$ frames is calculated, thereby obtaining the parameter σ_β''. This is described as the temporal SD because it is calculated over two frames (t and $t + 1$) of the video sequence. The procedure to calculate σ_β'' is similar to that used in Section 2 but applied

to a $3 \times 3 \times 2$ sample consisting of both frames. Then, it is compared with the SD σ_β'' obtained for the spatial algorithm in Subsection 2.1, as follows: IF $\{ (\sigma_{red}'' \geq 0.4 \sigma_{red}')$ AND $(\sigma_{green}'' \geq 0.4 \sigma_{green}')$ AND $(\sigma_{blue}'' \geq 0.4 \sigma_{blue}') \}$, THEN fuzzy rules 2, 3, 4, and 5 are employed; otherwise, the *Mean Filter* is utilized. The AND operator therein is the 'logical AND'. Here, the value 0.4 in the condition sentence is selected to distinguish different areas containing fine details from those showing a uniform pattern. This value was found experimentally, according to the optimal PSNR and MAE values. Therefore, the application of the Mean Filter Algorithm implies that the uniform area is under processing:

$$\bar{y}_{\beta out} = \sum_{i=0}^{N} x_{\beta i}/N, \quad N = 17, \tag{10}$$

where $x_{\beta i}$ represents each one of the pixels in a $3 \times 3 \times 2$ pre-processing window, $N = 17$ is selected to take into account all pixel components in the two frames to be processed.

The general standard deviation used in this stage of the algorithm was adapted locally according to the pixels that agree with Figure 5 in the current sample. To acquire a new locally adapted SD, which will be used in the next frame of video sequence, a sensitive parameter α must be introduced describing the current distribution of the pixels and featuring a measure of temporal relationship between the t and $t + 1$ frames. The main idea of the sensitive parameter is to control the amount of filtering; this parameter modifies its value on its own to agree with the locally adapted SD. The same parameter allows the upgrading of the SD that helps to describe the relationship in the frames t and $t + 1$, producing a temporal parameter. When the Mean Filter is applied, the sensitivity parameter value is $\alpha = 0.125$.

In case there is a drastic change in the fine details, edges, and movements in the current samples, these will be reflected in their parameter values - such as the membership functions, the SD, and the sensitivity parameters, as well as in their fuzzy vectorial-gradient values. The consequences, which are applied for each fuzzy rule, are based on the different conditions present in the sample.

The updating of the general standard deviation that should be used in the processing of the next frame is performed according to the expression:

$$\sigma_\beta' = \left(\alpha \cdot \left(\sigma_{total}'' / 5 \right) \right) + (1-\alpha) \cdot \left(\sigma_\beta' \right). \tag{11}$$

The aim of this equation is to control the locally adapted spatial SD and, in the same manner, control the temporal SD which will, on its turn, control the amount of filtering modifying the T_β threshold as will be shown later.

Parameters σ_β', σ_β'', and σ_{total} describe how the pixels in the t and $t+1$ frames are related to each other in a spatial $\left(\sigma_\beta'\right)$ and temporal $\left(\sigma_\beta'', \text{ and } \sigma_{total}\right)$ way. The SD updating of σ_{total} is achieved through: $\sigma_{total} = \left(\sigma_{Red}'' + \sigma_{Green}'' + \sigma_{Blue}''\right)\Big/3$; this is the average value of the temporal SD using the three color planes of the images. This relationship is designed to have the other color components of the image contribute to the sensitivity parameter.

The structure of Equation 11 can be illustrated using an example: if the Mean Filter Algorithm was selected for application instead of fuzzy rules 2, 3, 4, and 5, the sensitive parameter $\alpha = 0.125$ used for the algorithm describes that the t and $t+1$ frames are closely related. This means that the pixels in the t frame bear low noise due to the fact that the spatial algorithm was applied to this frame (see Subsection 2.1) and that the pixels in the $t+1$ frame are probably low-noise too. However, at this time, because the t frame has only been filtered by the spatial algorithm (see Subsection 2.1), it seems better to increase the weight obtained by the t frame in the spatial SD $\left(\sigma_\beta'\right)$, rather than using that obtained by the $t+1$ frame $\left(\text{temporal SD} \left(\sigma_\beta''\right)\right)$. That is why the weights of σ_{total} multiplied by $\alpha = 0.125$, and the weight of σ_β' multiplied by $(1-\alpha) = 0.875$ are used.

The application of fuzzy rules to pixels allows a better preservation of the inherent characteristics of the color images. The following methodology is based on these concepts, using the pixels indicated by each fuzzy rule in the process of noise suppression. That is: if the number of pixels presented in the next condition, (1) IF {(# pixels$_{SBB}$ > # pixels$_{SSS}$)AND(# pixels$_{SBB}$ > # pixels$_{BBB}$)AND(# pixels$_{SBB}$ > # pixels$_{BBS}$)}, is the biggest as compared to the other ones in the following IF conditions: (2) IF {(# pixels$_{SSS}$ > # pixels$_{SBB}$)AND(# pixels$_{SSS}$ > # pixels$_{BBB}$)AND(# pixels$_{SSS}$ > # pixels$_{BBS}$)}, (3) IF {(# pixels$_{BBS}$ > # pixels$_{SBB}$)AND(# pixels$_{BBS}$ > # pixels$_{SSS}$)AND(# pixels$_{BBS}$ > # pixels$_{BBB}$)}, and (4) IF {(# pixels$_{BBB}$ > # pixels$_{SBB}$)AND(# pixels$_{BBB}$ > # pixels$_{SSS}$)AND(# pixels$_{BBB}$ > # pixels$_{BBS}$)}, the following methodology is applied to only those pixels that fulfill the condition:

$$y_{\beta out} = \sum_{i=1}^{\#pixels} x_{\beta i}^{t-1} \cdot SBB_{\beta i} \Big/ \sum_{i=1}^{\#pixels} SBB_{\beta i}, \quad (12)$$

where $x_{\beta i}^t$, and $x_{\beta i}^{t+1}$ represent each pixel in the t and $t+1$ frames that fulfills the assumed fuzzy rule conditions, respectively, with $\alpha = 0.875$. For a better understanding of the use of fuzzy rules, see Figure 6. The following equations are used in cases where the largest number of

pixels compared to the others is, for example, in case of the second condition (if #pixels$_{SSS}$ is the biggest, that means: # pixels$_{SSS}$ > # pixels$_{SBB}$ > # pixels$_{BBB}$ > # pixels$_{BBS}$) we perform:

$$y_{\beta out} = \sum_{i=1}^{\#pixels} \left(x_{\beta i}^{t-1} \cdot 0.5 + x_{\beta i}^t \cdot 0.5\right) \cdot SSS_{\beta i} \Big/ \sum_{i=1}^{\#pixels} SSS_{\beta i}, \quad (13)$$

where $\alpha = 0.125$; or for the third condition (# pixels$_{BBS}$ is the biggest):

$$y_{\beta out} = \sum_{i=1}^{\#pixels} x_{\beta i}^t \cdot \left(1 - BBS_{\beta i}\right) \Big/ \sum_{i=1}^{\#pixels} \left(1 - BBS_{\beta i}\right) \quad (14)$$

where $\alpha = 0.875$. Finally, for the fourth condition (# pixels$_{BBB}$ is the biggest), when the number of pixels (# pixels) with BBB$_{\beta i}$ value is the biggest, the next algorithm is performed:

Procedure 1: consider the nine fuzzy vectorial-gradient values obtained from the BBB$_{\beta i}$ values. The central value is selected along with the three neighboring fuzzy values in order to detect the motion. The conjunction of the four subfacts is performed, which are combined by a triangular norm [19]. The intersection of all possible combinations of BBB$_{\beta i}$ and three different neighboring membership degrees gives 56 values to be obtained: $C_{N-1}^K = \binom{N-1}{K} = 56$, where $N = 9$, and with $K = 3$ elements are to be included in the intersection process. The values are added using an algebraic equation (sum $= A + B - A \cdot B$) [19] of all instances in order to obtain the *motion-noise* confidence parameter.

The motion-noise confidence parameter is used to update the SD and to obtain the output pixel by means of the next algorithm: $y_{\beta out} = (1-\alpha) \cdot x_{\beta c}^{t+1} + \alpha \cdot x_{\beta c}^t$, (where $\alpha = 0.875$ if the motion-noise $= 1$; and $\alpha = 0.125$ when the motion-noise $= 0$. If there is no majority in the number of pixels to any of the fuzzy rules, then the output pixel is computed as follows: $y_{\beta out} = 0.5 \cdot x_{\beta c}^{t+1} + 0.5 \cdot x_{\beta c}^t$, where $\alpha = 0.5$.

Finally, the algorithm employs the above-outlined spatial algorithm for smoothing the non-stationary noise remaining after application of the temporal filter, with the only modification in its threshold value of $T_\beta = 0.25\sigma_\beta'$, in agreement with Figure 1.

In summary, all parameters and their optimal values used in the development of this algorithm is given in the Table 1. All the optimum parameters were found under numerous simulations using different video color sequences with different levels of Gaussian noise and with different criteria to characterize noise suppression (PSNR), details and edges preservation (MAE), and

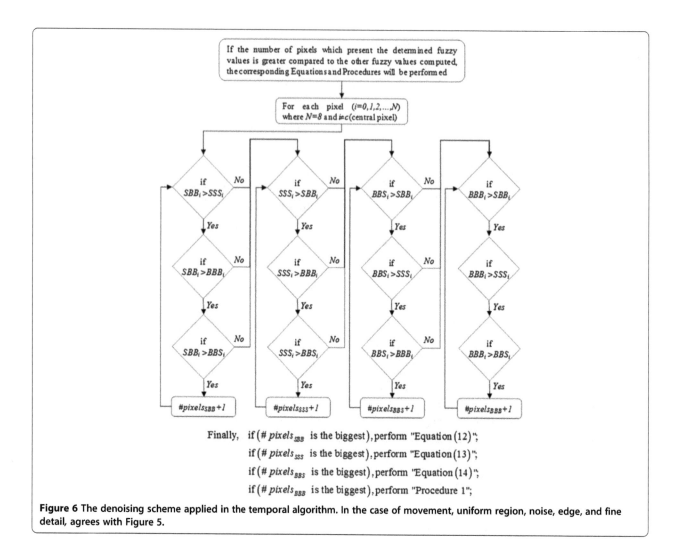

Figure 6 The denoising scheme applied in the temporal algorithm. In the case of movement, uniform region, noise, edge, and fine detail, agrees with Figure 5.

chromaticity preservation (normalized chromaticity deviation (NCD)).

All the other parameters used in the algorithm are locally updated in agreement with the adaptive method; this means that these parameters change locally in all the sequences of the video frames.

3. Simulation results

The results presented show the effectiveness of the proposed algorithm against others used for comparison.

Table 1 All parameters used in the algorithm and their optimal values

Parameters with optimal values used in the algorithm

$\tau_1 = 0.1$ (threshold used in the 'Spatial Filtering Algorithm' used only once)

$\tau_\beta = 0.25\sigma'_\beta$ (threshold value used in the whole video sequence)

when $\chi = \theta_{\beta\gamma}$	$\sigma = 0.3163$	$\mu_1 = 0.2$	$\mu_2 = 0.615$
when $\chi = \nabla_{\beta\gamma}$	$\sigma = 31.63$	$\mu_1 = 60$	$\mu_2 = 140$

$a = 0.125$ (sensitivity parameter)

$1 - a = 0.875$ (complement of the sensitive parameter)

To accomplish this, video sequences containing different features and textures were used: Miss America, Flowers, and Chair sequences; all of them contaminated by Gaussian noise with a variance (VAR) 0.0 to 0.05. The color video sequences processed for this work were 24-bit true color and 176×144 pixels (QCIF format).

Figure 7 shows the frames of the original video sequences subjectively used to characterize the noise suppression, detail and edge preservation, and the chromaticity. The filtered frames and complete video sequences were quantitatively evaluated according to the following criteria: PSNR was used to characterize the noise suppression capabilities (a larger PSNR reflects a better preservation of the characteristics of video frames); the MAE was used to numerically measure the level of preservation of edges and fine details; and the NCD was used to characterize the perceptual error between two color vectors, according to the human perception of color [22,26]. These criteria were applied to the proposed framework and compared with several algorithms that have demonstrated beneficial properties in video denoising.

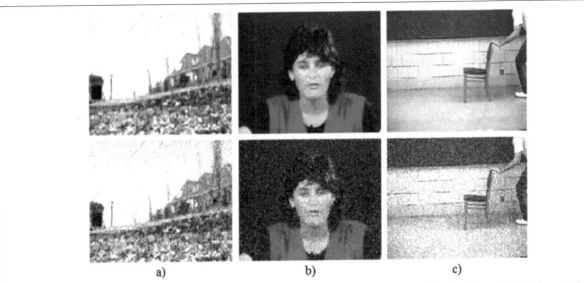

Figure 7 Original and corrupted images used to subjectively evaluate proposed and comparative algorithms. (a) 10th Flowers video sequence frame, **(b)** 10th Miss America video sequence frame, and **(c)** 10th Chair video sequence frame. Frames are corrupted with VAR = 0.01.

The proposed 'Fuzzy Directional Adaptive Recursive Temporal Filter for Gaussian Denoising' algorithm, referred to as FDARTF_G, was compared with others, the FLRSTF algorithm that uses similar fuzzy techniques [19], the FLRSTF_ANGLE, the VGVDF_G, and the VMMKNN_G [21,22] algorithm that uses order statistics techniques for the removal of Gaussian noise.

Figure 8 illustrates the denoising capability and preservation ability of all mentioned filters for the 10th frame of the Miss America and Flowers video sequences. This figure shows that the designed framework produces the best results. The criteria applied are the PSNR and MAE. Here, one can observe that the performance of our design

is the best for the Miss America frame; on the other hand, for the Flowers frame, the best results are generated by the PSNR criterion for the majority of the noise levels, while for the MAE criterion, the best results are for low-noise levels.

The processing results in the cases of the 20th and 30th frames for the three video sequences with corruption levels of VAR = 0.005 and VAR =0.01 have shown that the best performances in the MAE, PSNR, and NCD criteria are most of the times achieved through applying the proposed algorithm, as shown in Table 2.

A more sophisticated filter used as a comparison is the CBM3D [17]; this filter works in other domain, which

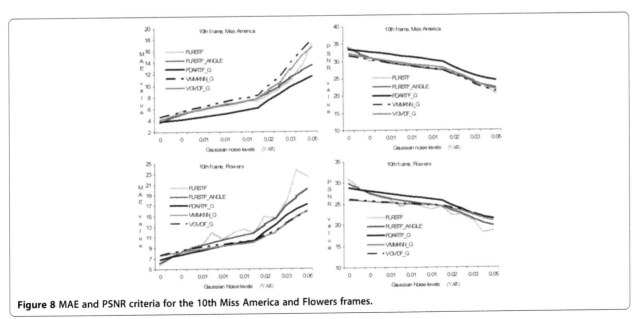

Figure 8 MAE and PSNR criteria for the 10th Miss America and Flowers frames.

Table 2 Comparative restoration results agree with the MAE, PSNR, and NCD criteria

| Algorithm | Criteria | Gaussian noise VAR = 0.005 | | | | | | Gaussian noise VAR = 0.01 | | | | | |
| | | Chair | | Miss America | | Flowers | | Chair | | Miss America | | Flowers | |
		Frame 20	Frame 30	Frame 20	Frame 30	Frame 20	Frame 30	Frame 20	Frame 30	Frame 20	Frame 30	Frame 20	Frame 30
FLRSTF	MAE	6.375	6.613	5.818	5.622	9.628	9.551	8.400	8.325	7.477	7.362	11.932	11.652
	PSNR	28.979	28.720	29.926	30.157	26.192	26.263	26.701	26.589	27.686	27.720	24.363	24.559
	NCD	0.0110	0.0112	0.0263	0.0261	0.0167	0.0168	0.0140	0.0137	0.0257	0.0260	0.0205	0.0203
FLRSTF_ANGLE	MAE	6.374	6.620	5.826	5.629	9.825	9.643	8.458	8.319	7.500	7.386	11.971	11.661
	PSNR	28.968	28.716	29.905	30.133	26.007	26.164	26.638	26.605	27.681	27.687	24.340	24.556
	NCD	0.0110	0.0112	0.0263	0.0262	0.0175	0.0171	0.0140	0.0137	0.0258	0.0259	0.0205	0.0203
FDARTF_G	MAE	5.501	5.603	4.459	4.279	8.503	8.281	7.416	7.245	6.069	5.909	10.438	10.056
	PSNR	29.170	29.291	32.510	32.917	27.309	27.611	27.454	27.391	30.059	30.300	25.717	26.054
	NCD	0.0105	0.0106	0.0219	0.0216	0.0155	0.0151	0.0135	0.0128	0.0220	0.0216	0.0185	0.0182
VMMKNN_G	MAE	7.987	7.886	6.178	6.103	8.777	8.459	9.250	9.677	8.143	8.081	9.916	9.634
	PSNR	25.368	25.607	29.799	29.826	25.348	25.801	25.159	24.427	27.612	27.683	24.629	24.978
	NCD	0.0146	0.0141	0.0286	0.0285	0.0153	0.0147	0.0174	0.0164	0.0287	0.0282	0.0167	0.0167
CBM3D	MAE	*4.863*	*4.854*	*3.512*	*3.509*	*7.821*	*7.795*	*7.712*	*7.729*	*4.518*	*4.526*	*9.934*	*9.896*
	PSNR	*33.185*	*33.193*	*33.658*	*33.931*	*30.790*	*30.670*	*32.1*	*32.06*	*32.58*	*32.87*	*29.45*	*29.363*
	NCD	–	–	–	–	–	–	–	–	–	–	–	–

For the 20th and 30th frames of the video sequences used. Numbers in italics indicate best results which agreed with the method and criteria implemented.

consists of two steps in which blocks are grouped by spatio-temporal predictive blockmatching and each 3D group is filtered by a 3D transform domain shrinkage, and the complex *3D wavelet transform method 3DWF* shows better results in terms of PSNR and MAE criteria than our proposed filter. For the Flowers sequence, the received results for our algorithm are worse because the performance of the additional time-recursive filtering in pixels where no motion is detected will be reduced for a moving camera. Advantages to take into account in our filtering method are the prevention/avoidance of spatiotemporal blur; one should only consider neighboring pixels from the current frame in case of detected motion. Other advantage is in preserving the details in the frame content; the filtering should not be as strong when large spatial activity e.g., a large variance, is detected in the current filtering window. As a consequence, more noise will be left, but large spatial activity corresponds to high spatial frequencies, where the eye is not sensitive enough to detect this. In the case of homogeneous areas, strong filtering should be performed to remove as much noise as possible.

The performance of our methodology is similar to the achieved in the paper of Mélange et al. [27], and it was outperformed by CBM3D method too.

Table 3 presents average results for all of the proposed criteria from all of the frames that form the video sequences used. Based on these results, one can state that the best performance response is by the proposed filtering algorithm (FDARTF_G) for all the Gaussian noise levels for the Miss America video sequence. In the Flowers video sequence, the best results are achieved by the PSNR criterion for the majority of the noise levels. Additionally, the use of the MAE and NCD criteria achieves very good results in the preservation of details and chromatic properties.

In Figure 9, we see that for the Chair video sequence, the best performance is given by our proposed method for every frame forming the video at medium and high noise levels. The best results were obtained for all of the criteria used (PSNR, MAE, and NCD). Evidently, the CVBM3D version, to process video color images, [17] filtering method will deliver better results against our

Table 3 The *PSNR, MAE,* and *NCD* criteria averaged results

Gaussian noise (VAR)			0.001	0.005	0.01	0.015	0.02	0.03	0.04	0.05
Miss America	MAE	FLRSTF	3.624	5.967	7.625	8.853	9.847	11.414	12.999	14.477
		FDARTF_G	*3.549*	*4.542*	*6.126*	*7.453*	*8.465*	*9.832*	*10.822*	*11.694*
		VMMKNN_G	4.377	6.217	8.198	9.871	11.372	13.934	16.072	17.921
		VGVDF_G	3.71	5.685	7.419	8.92	10.253	12.563	14.609	16.441
	PSNR	FLRSTF	34.303	29.73	27.573	26.267	25.328	23.998	22.827	21.888
		FDARTF_G	*34.013*	*32.303*	*29.929*	*28.258*	*27.127*	*25.811*	*25.02*	*24.404*
		VMMKNN_G	32.057	29.689	27.55	26.045	24.887	23.23	22.083	21.213
		VGVDF_G	33.048	30.384	28.383	26.921	25.789	24.111	22.847	21.85
	NCD	FLRSTF	0.013	0.021	0.027	0.031	0.034	0.039	0.044	0.049
		FDARTF_G	*0.013*	*0.016*	*0.022*	*0.027*	*0.031*	*0.036*	*0.04*	*0.042*
		VMMKNN_G	0.015	0.022	0.029	0.034	0.04	0.049	0.058	0.066
		VGVDF_G	0.013	0.021	0.027	0.033	0.037	0.046	0.053	0.06
Flowers	MAE	FLRSTF	*6.011*	9.866	12.013	13.823	14.911	17.142	20.408	20.664
		FDARTF_G	7.295	*8.847*	10.647	12.262	13.539	15.288	16.464	17.39
		VMMKNN_G	7.754	9.07	*10.31*	*11.357*	*12.258*	*13.896*	15.346	16.642
		VGVDF_G	8.04	9.588	10.786	11.736	12.571	14.036	*15.331*	*16.459*
	PSNR	FLRSTF	*30.289*	25.969	24.289	23.052	22.411	21.182	19.569	19.525
		FDARTF_G	28.139	*26.906*	*25.427*	*24.255*	*23.424*	*22.375*	*21.722*	*21.24*
		VMMKNN_G	26.128	25.324	24.523	23.858	23.303	22.347	21.564	20.907
		VGVDF_G	25.765	24.835	24.135	23.602	23.139	22.358	21.693	21.127
	NCD	FLRSTF	*0.011*	0.018	0.021	0.025	0.026	0.03	0.033	0.036
		FDARTF_G	0.014	0.017	0.02	0.023	0.025	0.028	0.03	0.032
		VMMKNN_G	0.014	*0.016*	*0.018*	*0.02*	*0.021*	*0.023*	*0.025*	*0.027*
		VGVDF_G	0.017	0.019	0.021	0.023	0.024	0.026	0.028	0.03

For the frames of the *Miss America* and *Flowers* video sequences corrupted by different Gaussian Noise levels. Numbers in italics indicate best results which agreed with the method and criteria implemented.

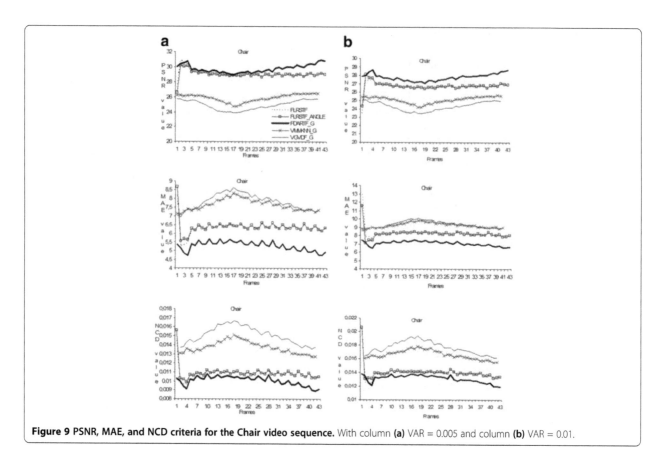

Figure 9 PSNR, MAE, and NCD criteria for the Chair video sequence. With column **(a)** VAR = 0.005 and column **(b)** VAR = 0.01.

suggestion, since 5 dB through 8 dB in the PSNR criterion, because it is more sophisticated and works in different domain and uses complex 3D wavelet transform method 3DWF that makes it powerful even though, until now, algorithms are not more powerful as those suggested in [17], as the methods proposed by Yu et al. [28], by

Priyam Chatterjee and Milanfar [29], by Zuo et al. [30], and by Li et al. [31].

Finally, in Figure 10, one can see the filtered frames after different algorithms were used to estimate the quality of the subjective vision perception. From the results of the proposed algorithm, it is easy to corroborate that

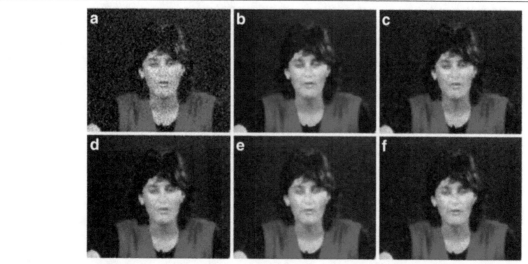

Figure 10 The filtered 10th frames of the Miss America video sequence. (a) Frame corrupted by Gaussian noise, VAR = 0.005, **(b)** FDARTF_G, **(c)** FLRSTF, **(d)** FLRSTF_ANGLE, **(e)** VGVDF_G, and **(f)** VMMKNN_G.

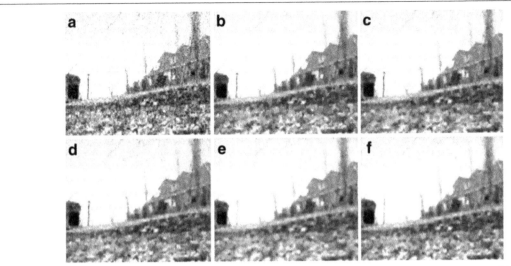

Figure 11 The filtered 10th frames of the Flowers video sequence. (a) Image corrupted by Gaussian noise, VAR = 0.01, **(b)** FDARTF_G, **(c)** FLRSTF, **(d)** FLRSTF_ANGLE, **(e)** VGVDF_G, and **(f)** VMMKNN_G.

this filter has the best performance in detail preservation and noise suppression. In the FDARTF_G filtered image, one can observe cleaner regions with better preservation of fine details and edges, as compared to other algorithms.

In Figure 11 below, the proposed framework produces the best results in the areas of detail preservation and noise suppression. One can perceive (in the vicinity of the tree) that in the case of the FDARTF_G filtering, the resulting image is less influenced by noise compared to the image produced by other filters. In addition, the new

filter preserves more details of the features displayed in the background environment.

From Figure 12, one can see that the proposed framework achieves the best results in details, edges, and preservation of chromaticity. We can observe that the uniform regions are free from noise influence in the case of the FDARTF_G filtering than with the other filters implemented. Also, the new filter preserves more details in the features seen in the background environment.

Since the proposed algorithm is adaptive, it is difficult to obtain computational information related to how many

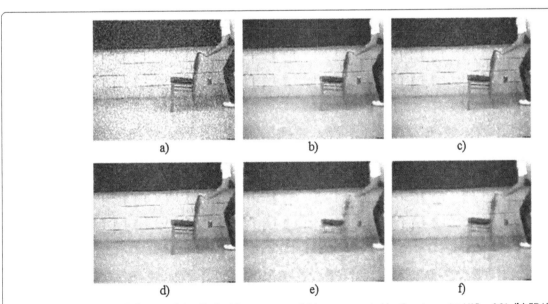

Figure 12 The filtered 10th frames of the Chair video sequence. (a) Image corrupted by Gaussian noise, VAR = 0.01, **(b)** FDARTF_G, **(c)** FLRSTF, **(d)** FLRSTF_ANGLE, **(e)** VGVDF_G, and **(f)** VMMKNN_G.

adds, multiplies, or divisions among other operations like trigonometrical ones were carried out; we provide real-time performance using a DSP from Texas Instruments, Dallas, TX, USA; this was the DM642 [32] giving the following results: for our proposed FDARTF_G, it spent an average time of 17.78 s per frame, but in a complete directional (VGVDF_G) processing algorithm, it spent an average time of 25.6 s per frame, both in a QCIF format.

4. Conclusions

The fuzzy and directional techniques working together have proven to be a powerful framework for image filtering applied in color video denoising in QCIF sequences. This robust algorithm performs motion detection and local noise standard deviation estimation. These proper video-sequence characteristics have been obtained and converted into parameters to be used as thresholds in different stages of the novel proposed filter. This algorithm permits the processing of t and $t + 1$ video frames, producing an appreciable savings of time and resources expended in computational filtering.

Using the advantages of both techniques (directional and diffuse), it was possible to design an algorithm that can preserve edges and fine details of video frames besides maintaining their inherent color, improving the preservation of the texture of the colors versus results obtained by the comparative algorithms. Other important conclusion is that for sequences obtained by a still camera, our method has a better performance in terms of PSNR than other multiresolution filters of a *similar complexity*, but it is outperformed by some more sophisticated methods (CBM3D).

The simulation results under the proposed criteria PSNR, MAE, and NCD were used to characterize an algorithm's efficiency in noise suppression, fine details, edges, and chromatic properties preservation. The perceptual errors have demonstrated the advantages of the proposed filtering approach.

Competing interests
The authors declare that they have no competing interest.

Acknowledgements
The authors thank the Instituto Politécnico Nacional de México (National Polytechnic Institute of Mexico) and CONACYT for their financial support.

References

1. AJ Rosales-Silva, FJ Gallegos-Funes, V Ponomaryov, Fuzzy Directional (FD) Filter for impulsive noise reduction in colour video sequences. J. Vis. Commun. Image Represent. 23(1), 143–149 (2012)
2. A Amer, H Schrerder, A new video noise reduction algorithm using spatial subbands. Int. Conf. on Electronic Circuits and Systems 1, 45–48 (13-16 October 1996)
3. G De Haan, IC for motion-compensated deinterlacing, noise reduction, and picture rate conversion. IEEE Trans. On Consumers Electronics 45(3), 617–624 (1999)
4. R Rajagopalan, M Orchard, Synthesizing processed video by filtering temporal relationships. IEEE Trans. Image Process. 11(1), 26–36 (2002)
5. V Seran, LP Kondi, New temporal filtering scheme to reduce delay in wavelet-based video coding. IEEE Trans. Image Process. 16(12), 2927–2935 (2007)
6. V Zlokolica, M De Geyter, S Schulte, A Pizurica, W Philips, E Kerre, Fuzzy logic recursive change detection for tracking and denoising of video sequences, in Paper presented at the IS&T/SPIE Symposium on Electronic Imaging, San Jose, California, USA, 14 March 2005. doi: 10.1117/12.585854
7. A Pizurica, V Zlokolica, W Philips, Noise reduction in video sequences using wavelet-domain and temporal filtering, in Paper presented at the SPIE Conference on Wavelet Applications in Industrial Processing, USA, 27 February 2004. doi:10.1117/12.516069
8. W Selesnick, K Li, Video denoising using 2d and 3d dual-tree complex wavelet transforms, in Paper presented at the Proc. SPIE on Wavelet Applications in Signal and Image Processing, USA, volume 5207, pp. 607-618; 14 November 2003. doi: 10.1117/12.504896
9. N Rajpoot, Z Yao, R Wilson, Adaptive wavelet restoration of noisy video sequences, in Paper presented at the IEEE International Conference on Image Processing, pp. 957-960, October 2004. doi: 10.1109/ICIP.2004.1419459
10. C Ercole, A Foi, V Katkovnik, K Egiazarian, Spatio-temporal pointwise adaptive denoising of video: 3d nonparametric regression approach (Paper presented at the First Workshop on Video Processing and Quality Metrics for Consumer Electronics, January, 2005)
11. D Rusanovskyy, K Egiazarian, Video denoising algorithm in sliding 3D DCT domain. Lecture Notes in Computer Science 3708 (Springer Verlag, Advanced Concepts for Intelligent Vision Systems, 2005), pp. 618–625
12. V Ponomaryov, A Rosales-Silva, F Gallegos-Funes, Paper presented at the Proc. of SPIE-IS&T, Published in SPIE Proceedings Vol. 6811: Real-Time Image Processing 2008, 4 March 2008. doi:10.1117/12.758659
13. G Varghese, Z Wang, Video denoising based on a spatio-temporal Gaussian scale mixture model. IEEE Trans. Circ. Syst. Video. Tech. 20(7), 1032–1040 (2010)
14. L Jovanov, A Pizurica, S Schulte, P Schelkens, A Munteanu, E Kerre, W Philips, Combined wavelet-domain and motion-compensated video denoising based on video codec motion estimation methods. IEEE Trans. Circ. Syst. Video. Tech. 19(3), 417–421 (2009)
15. J Dai, C Oscar, W Yang, C Pang, F Zou, X Wen, Color video denoising based on adaptive color space conversion, in Proceedings of 2010 IEEE International Symposium on Circuits and Systems (ISCAS), June 2010, pp. 2992-2995. doi: 10.1109/ISCAS.2010.5538013
16. C Liu, WT Freeman, A high-quality video denoising algorithm based on reliable motion estimation, in Paper presented at the Proceedings of the 11th European conference on computer vision conference on Computer vision: Part III (Springer-Verlag, Heraklion, Crete, Greece, 2010), pp. 706–719
17. K Dabov, A Foi, K Egiazarian, Video denoising by sparse 3D transform-domain collaborative filtering, in Proc. 15th European Signal Processing Conference, EUSIPCO 2007 (, Poznan, Poland, September 2007)
18. J Mairal, G Sapiro, M Elad, Learning multiscale sparse representations for image and video restoration. SIAM Multiscale Modeling and Simulation 7(1), 214–241 (2008)
19. V Zlokolica, S Schulte, A Pizurica, W Philips, E Kerre, Fuzzy logic recursive motion detection and denoising of video sequences. J. Electron. Imag. 15(2), 1–13 (2006). doi:10.1117/1.2201548
20. PE Trahanias, D Karakos, AN Venetsanopoulos, Directional processing of color images: theory and experimental results. IEEE Trans. Image Process. 5(6), 868–880 (1996)
21. VI Ponomaryov, Real-time 2D-3D filtering using order statistics based algorithms. J. Real-Time Image Proc. 1(3), 173–194 (2007)
22. V Ponomaryov, A Rosales-Silva, V Golikov, Adaptive and vector directional processing applied to video color images. Electron. Lett. 42(11), 1–2 (2006)
23. Arizona State University, http://trace.eas.asu.edu/yuv/, October-2010
24. J Zheng, KP Valavanis, JM Gauch, Noise removal from color images. J. Intell. Robot. Syst. 7, 3 (1993)
25. KN Plataniotis, AN Venetsanopoulos, Color Image Processing and Applications (Springer-Verlag, 26 May 2000)
26. A Pearson, Fuzzy Logic Fundamentals. Chapter 3, 2001, pp. 61–103. www.informit.com/content/images/0135705991/samplechapter/0135705991.pdf. August 2008
27. T Mélange, M Nachtegael, EE Kerre, V Zlokolica, S Schulte, VD Witte, A Pizurica, W Philips, Video denoising by fuzzy motion and detail adaptive

averaging. J. Electron. Imag. **17**(4), 043005-1–043005-19 (2008). http://dx.doi. org/10.1117/1.2992065

28. S Yu, O Ahmad, MNS Swamy, Video denoising using motion compensated 3-D wavelet transform with integrated recursive temporal filtering. IEEE Trans. Circ. Syst. Video. Tech. **20**(6), 780–791 (2010)

29. P Chatterjee, P Milanfar, Clustering-based denoising with locally learned dictionaries. IEEE Trans. Image Process. **18**(7), 1438–1451 (2009)

30. C Zuo, Y Liu, X Tan, W Wang, M Zhang, Video denoising based on a spatiotemporal Kalman-bilateral mixture model. Scientific World Journal (Hindawi) (2013)

31. S Li, H Yin, L Fang, Group-sparse representation with dictionary learning for medial image denoising and fusion. IEEE Transaction on Biomedical Engineering **59**(12) (2012)

32. Texas Instruments. http://www.ti.com/tool/tmdsevm642, January 2008

12

Distributed video coding supporting hierarchical GOP structures with transmitted motion vectors

Kyung-Yeon Min[1], Woong Lim[1], Junghak Nam[1], Donggyu Sim[1*] and Ivan V Bajić[2]

Abstract

In this paper, we propose a new distributed video coding (DVC) method, with hierarchical group of picture (GOP) structure. Coding gain of DVC can be significantly improved by enlarging GOP size for slow-moving frames. The proposed DVC decoder estimates a side information (SI) frame and transmits motion vectors (MVs) of the SI to the proposed encoder. Using the received MVs from the decoder, the proposed encoder can generate a predicted SI (PSI), which is the same as the SI in the decoder, and estimate the quality of PSI with minimal computational complexity. The proposed method decides the best coding mode among key, Wyner-Ziv (WZ), and skip modes, by estimating rate-distortion costs. Based on the selected best coding mode, the best GOP size can be automatically determined. As the GOP size is adaptively decided depending on the SI quality, entropy and parity bits can be effectively consumed. Experimental results show that the proposed algorithm is around 0.80 dB better in Bjøntegaard delta (BD) bitrate than an existing conventional DVC system.

Keywords: Video coding; Distributed video coding; Side information; GOP; RD competition

1 Introduction

As many portable multimedia devices have been developed, such as mobile phones, electronic pads, and laptops, many people enjoy using them to take videos, transmit them to friends or web-sites such as YouTube and Facebook, and in turn, view them. These days, video sensor networks are also used to monitor very large outdoor areas for environment surveillance and safety. Therefore, demands for low cost and powerful encoders are continuously increasing. However, conventional video coding standards, such as MPEG-x and H.26x, cannot satisfy these requirements, because those encoders have high computational complexity, while their decoders require low complexity. Distributed video coding (DVC) methods have been researched to meet these requirements. DVC technology is based on migration of computational complexity from encoders to decoders and can achieve coding gain with regard to prediction on the decoder side.

DVC was developed as a new video-coding paradigm derived from Slepian-Wolf information theory [1]. They proved that the DVC can perform encoding by disregarding

correlation between two input signals and the coding performance of the decoder side by exploiting the correlation can come close to the efficiency of the conventional coding systems that employs the correlation at the encoder side. Wyner-Ziv [2] presented the extended work to show information theoretic bounds for lossy compression by side information at the decoder. Based on the Wyner-Ziv theory, several lossy DVC approaches which do not perform motion estimation have been proposed in order to reduce computational complexity of the DVC encoder [3-6]. To reduce temporal redundancy, motion estimation is performed on the DVC decoder side, not in the encoder. For DVC based on the Wyner-Ziv approach, the original input frames are coded by two different modes [3-6]. One mode is to code with the conventional intra coding technique and the coding mode is called the key-frame mode. The other mode is performed by a channel coder after preprocessing, and the coding mode is called the Wyner-Ziv (WZ) mode. While the outputs of the channel coder are parity bits and original data, only a part of parity bits are sent to the DVC decoder for compression performance. The reconstructed WZ frame is reconstructed by a channel decoder with the transmitted parity bits for a side information (SI) frame. The SI frame is generated the same as possible as the original frame with the reconstructed

* Correspondence: dgsim@kw.ac.kr
[1]Department of Computer Engineering, Kwangwoon University, Wolgye-dong, Seoul 447-1, Nowon-gu, South Korea
Full list of author information is available at the end of the article

key frames in the decoder when the size of the group of picture (GOP) is small, e.g., the size is equal to 2. The error of SI frame is assumed to be transmission error caused by a variable channel. SI frame is regarded as the predicted frame of the original frame (WZ frame), degraded by channel errors. Therefore, the errors are corrected by a channel decoder. A low density parity check accumulate (LDPCA) coder and Turbo coder are often used for DVC systems [7-12].

In general, conventional codecs, such as h.26x and MPEG-x, set GOP size from 8 to 30, as the increasing number of intra-frame degrades compression rate. However, a lot of the conventional DVC systems set the GOP size to the minimum of two, because performance of DVC is directly related to accuracies of SI frames. Accuracies of SI frames cannot be known at both the encoder and decoder sides, and accuracies of SI frames are generally the best with GOP size set as two. In addition, since accuracies of SI frames vary, depending on the features of a sequence, they cannot be correctly predicted. However, SI frames are generated well for slow-moving cases. For these cases, GOP size can be prolonged, to reduce the entropy bits and/or parity bits. Therefore, some conventional DVC algorithms are proposed to predict accuracies of SI frames on the encoder side and increase GOP size [13,14]. Since the purpose of DVC is to reduce computational complexity of the encoder, they should generate a predicted SI (PSI) with low delay, though an SI frame which is generated using several motion estimation algorithms and filters, for high quality of an SI on the decoder side. Therefore, although the encoder generates a PSI frame by using the estimated MVs and key frames in its own, the PSI frame is not the same as the SI frame on the decoder side. As a result, the estimated accuracies of PSI frames are different from those of SI frames and lead to a decrease in compression performance.

The proposed DVC performs motion estimation at the decoder side, and the estimated motion vectors (MVs) are transmitted to the corresponding DVC encoder. The proposed encoder can generate a PSI that is identical to the SI frame of the decoder side with minimal computation load, because motion compensation is performed with the received MVs and reference key frames. Therefore, the proposed encoder can correctly estimate the quality of the SI frames. Based on the accuracies of the SI frames, the best coding mode is selected based on rate-distortion (RD) optimization; thus, the GOP size can be adaptively and hierarchically set. In this paper, each frame is coded as one among key, WZ, and skip modes. In order to assess the RD cost of the key mode with minimum computational complexity, the proposed method estimates it with a weighted linear interpolation of RD costs of neighboring key frames. Distortion of a

frame coded by WZ mode can be estimated with the original frame, and the PSI frame and rates of the frame can be estimated with the number of errors. Therefore, the proposed method assesses the RD cost of WZ mode with the compensated frame. The RD cost of skip mode can be estimated with the PSI frame on the encoder side. Based on RD competition, the proposed method can select the best coding mode and GOP size prior to actual encoding. The RD competition estimates rates and distortions for each coding modes in advance. Therefore, the proposed method improves coding performance by enlarging the GOP size for slow-moving frames. Note that the WZ frame is coded in frequency domain with LDPCA.

The rest of this paper is organized as follows. Section 'Conventional DVC algorithms' introduces several conventional DVC algorithms. Section 'Proposed DVC for hierarchical GOP structure' presents details of the proposed method. In Section 'Experimental results', experimental results are given and discussed. Finally, Section 'Conclusions' concludes this paper and gives further work items.

2 Conventional DVC algorithms

DVC is a new video-coding paradigm that allows us to shift complexity from an encoder to a decoder, for distribution of computation complexity. While the conventional video codecs employ motion estimation at the encoder side, motion estimation can be performed on the decoder side of DVC. Therefore, the DVC encoder can be suitable for portable devices, unlikely conventional encoders. Figure 1 shows the block diagram of conventional WZ DVC systems [2-12,15-37]. Original input frames are divided into two types according to coding methods, as shown in Figure 1. Input frames are coded by key mode or WZ mode. Key mode is the same as the conventional intra coding method, such as H.264/ AVC intra mode. WZ frames are coded with three main modules: pre-processing which can be regarded as transform and/or quantization, channel coding, and key frame coder. For DVC, motion estimation is conducted on the decoder side, and a predicted frame is generated. The estimated frame is called SI. The SI has some prediction errors, and the errors can be corrected with transmitted parity bits from a channel encoder. For the channel coder, LDPCA and Turbo channel coders are generally used in the DVC system [32-37].

The quality of SI frames directly impacts the performance of DVC systems, since the required number of parity bits is proportional to the errors of SIs. Most conventional DVC systems set their key frame interval to minimum, since it is much easier to estimate accurate SI frames with closer key frames. However, because the amount of motion activities varies over time, even in a sequence, the

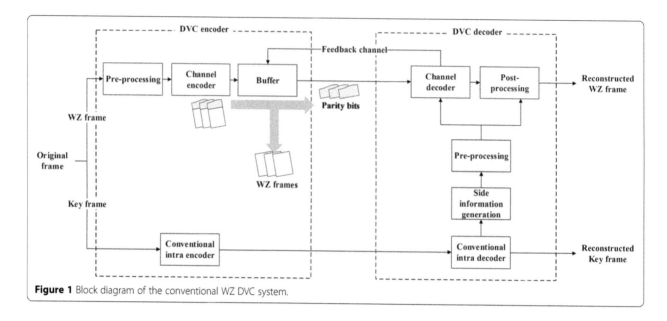

Figure 1 Block diagram of the conventional WZ DVC system.

quality of SI frames also varies from frame to frame, and sequence to sequence. Table 1 shows the average peak signal-to-noise ratio (PSNR) of SI frames in terms of the key frame intervals, for six sequences. To obtain the PSNR of SI, we employed the existing algorithm [23]. Figure 2 shows a PSNR graph of SI frames over time in terms of the key frame intervals for the 'Race' sequence. As shown in Figure 2, PSNR values of the 90th to 100th SI frames with GOP size of 8 are slightly better than those with GOP size of 4. Thus, the RD performance of DVC can be improved with the adaptive GOP size depending on frames characteristics. However, the encoder should estimate the quality of the SI, to determine the best size of GOP. It is not easy to estimate the quality of SI frames at the encoder side, due to non-availability of SI. Therefore, several conventional algorithms were proposed to assess the quality of SI frames [7-9,24-27]. Since the purpose of the DVC encoder is to encode videos with low computation complexity, the conventional algorithms generate PSIs with minimum computational complexity, by repetition, temporal linear interpolation, or rough block matching algorithms [7-9,24-27]. Ahmad et al. proposed a DVC supporting adaptive GOP size, so that the GOP size is

determined by the rate of the previous WZ frame at the encoder side [25]. They can improve performance of DVC with additional minimum complexity of the encoder. However, the method of SI frame generation at an encoder is different from that of a decoder. Even though the estimated rates are correct, the RD for the current frame might not be appropriate for the consecutive future frames, because of scene change and/or moving objects. For higher performance, Yaacoub et al. proposed a hierarchical decision of the GOP size, based on RD competition [26]. Two successive frames, the first and the last frames, for a given GOP size are coded as key frames. A target frame in between two given frames is coded as either WZ or key frame, based on RD competition. This procedure is hierarchically repeated for decision of the best GOP size. However, the encoder requires high computational complexity for GOP size decision in hierarchically evaluating the RD costs of key and WZ modes. The predicted SI at the encoder side is different from that at the decoder side, thus, the RD cost of the WZ mode is not the same to the original one. As a result, the amount of parity bits would not be accurate to correct the errors of SI frames.

3 Proposed DVC for hierarchical GOP structure

Since videos generally include not only fast-motion but also slow-motion performance of DVC, systems can be improved by adaptively modifying the GOP size. When the accuracies of SI frames are quite high, the encoder is not likely to send parity bits, and can reduce the number of key frames. Therefore, the proposed method adaptively modifies hierarchical GOP size based on RD competition, for compression performance of DVC systems.

Table 1 Average PSNRs of SI frames in terms of key frame intervals

Test sequence	Key frame interval						
	2	3	4	5	6	7	8
Akko	33.81	31.19	29.24	27.59	25.79	25.67	24.67
Ballroom	28.97	26.44	24.32	22.79	21.70	21.85	21.11
Flamenco2	31.35	28.96	27.44	26.40	25.55	25.53	24.91
Race1	23.85	22.07	20.46	19.83	18.84	20.94	19.53

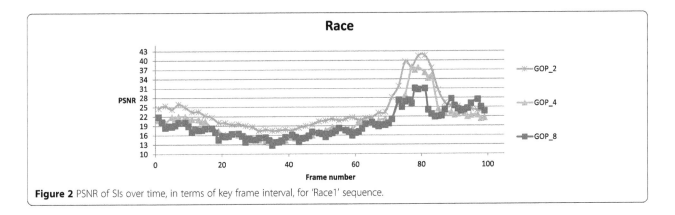

Figure 2 PSNR of SIs over time, in terms of key frame interval, for 'Race1' sequence.

3.1 Proposed DVC encoder and decoder supporting hierarchical GOP structure

The proposed method sets the initial GOP size (S) and encodes the first frame at t and the last frame at $t + S$ in a GOP range as the key mode. Coded bitstreams of the key frames are sent and reconstructed in the decoder side. The SI frame at $t + S/2$ that is located at the inter-position between two key frames is generated with the key frames, and then MVs are estimated from the SI frame at $t + S/2$ to the key frames, and the compressed MVs in a lossless mode are sent to the encoder side. As the encoder generates a PSI frame at $t + S/2$ with the received MVs and the key frames, the PSI can be the same as the SI in the decoder, without high computational complexity. Based on the PSI frame, the proposed encoder assesses the RD costs of key, WZ, and skip modes and selects one of them. The frame at $t + S/2$ is coded by the selected mode, and its associated data are sent to the decoder side. Hierarchically, the SI frame at $t + S/4$ ($t + 3S/4$) is generated with the frame t and the frame at $t + S/2$ (frame at $t + S/2$ and frame at $t + S$).

Figure 3 shows the flowchart of the proposed DVC encoder. The first frame (frame[t]) and the last frame (frame[$t + S$]) are coded as a key-frame coding and H.264/AVC intra-frame coding is employed for our implementation. The other frames between two key frames are hierarchically and recursively coded, as shown in the flowchart. Given two reconstructed frames, the encoder receives the MVM (MVM[$t + S/2$]) that includes MVs and their compensation directions for all the blocks of the target frame (frame[$t + S/2$]). With the received MVs, the proposed DVC encoder can generate the PSI (PSI[$t + S/2$]), and then decide RD competition candidates, according to the modes of the two input frames. When either input frame (Rec[t] and Rec[$t + S$]) is coded by 'Skip' mode, the target frame (frame[$t + S/2$]) is coded by skip mode, and only one 'Skip' indication bit is transmitted. In addition, recursive processing is not required, since all the frames between the two input frames (Rec[t] and Rec[$t + S$]) are coded by skip mode.

If either input frames of the reconstructed frames (Rec[t] and Rec[$t + S$]) is coded by 'WZ' mode, RD competition candidates for the target frame are skip and WZ modes. Based on the RD competition, the frame is encoded by a selected mode, and the associated indication bit is sent to the decoder side. When both input frames are coded by the key mode, the candidates are key, WZ, and skip modes for RD competition. The target frame is encoded by one of the candidate modes, and the mode bits are sent to the decoder side. This recursive encoding keeps running, until all the frames between two key frames are coded. Note that the WZ frames are coded in frequency domain with the LDPCA channel coder. Because the proposed DVC encoder requires motion compensation with the received motion vectors, the encoder computing time could slightly increase. However, the proposed hierarchical DVC encoder can skip several frames in a GOP structure. As a result, we found that the proposed DVC encoder complexity is almost same to the conventional DVC encoders. In our evaluation, the proposed algorithm is up to 5% slower than the DISCOVER coder, depending on sequences.

Figure 4 shows the flowchart of the proposed DVC decoder. First, two key frames are decoded by the corresponding intra decoder with a received bitstream. The other frames are hierarchically and recursively decoded in the proposed method. With two reconstructed frames (Rec[t] and Rec[$t + S$]), an SI frame (SI[$t + S/2$]) and MVM (MVM[$t + S/2$]) are generated in the proposed method, as shown in the flowchart. If two input frames are decoded by the skip mode, all the frames between them will be regarded as skip mode, and reconstructed by the SI generation algorithm, without any additional data. Otherwise, the SI frame is decoded depending on following syntax elements. MVM (MVM[$t + S/2$]) is not sent to the encoder for all the frames between two input frames. When neither of two input frames is coded by the skip mode, MVM (MVM[$t + S/2$]) should be sent to the encoder and the target frames are decoded depending on the coding mode. Note that the motion vectors

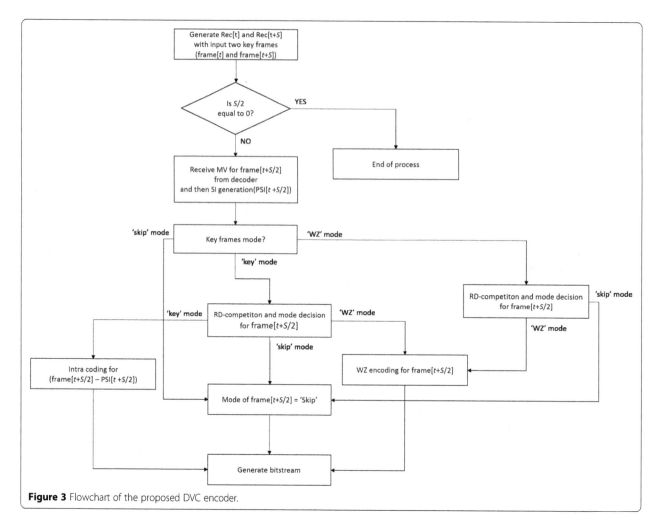

Figure 3 Flowchart of the proposed DVC encoder.

are predicted with median filtering of the neighboring motion vectors and motion vector difference is coded with the Exp-Golomb code for better compression.

3.2 SI frame generation and PSI frames compensation

The quality of an SI frame directly impacts on the performance of a DVC system. For the proposed algorithm, it is also important to generate a PSI frame that is the same as the SI frame, for proper decisions of coding modes on the encoder side. In order to make sure that PSI frames are the same as SI frames, SI frames in the proposed algorithm are generated with the existing two-stage algorithm [38]. In the first stage, an initial SI (ISI) frame is estimated with key frames [23] for a target frame, however; any SI frame generation (SIG) algorithms with a gap-filling algorithm can be employed. At the second stage, the proposed DVC decoder performs motion estimation from the ISI frame to the neighboring key frames, and then the final SI frame is reconstructed with the key frames and the estimated MVs [38]. The motion vectors are sent to the decoder side. Regardless of the first stage motion estimation algorithm, we can

guarantee that the SI of the decoder side can be reconstructed with the transmitted MVs and related data at the encoder side, because the motion vectors are defined from the target frame to key frames. In addition, the proposed DVC encoder does not require any hole-filling algorithms and blending of two over-lapped blocks. As a result, the SI frame can be generated with minimum computational load. Note that the first stage motion estimation is conducted with a conventional algorithm, based on adaptive search range for DVC [23].

Figure 5 shows the flowchart of the proposed ISI algorithm. The proposed method performs hierarchical ME in descending order of block variance values with adaptive search range. Search range is adaptively determined according to MVs of neighboring blocks. Then, the hole regions are compensated with uni-directional ME and a linear interpolation.

3.3 RD competition

Conventional codecs such as H.264/AVC calculate RD cost for all cases and select the best mode having the

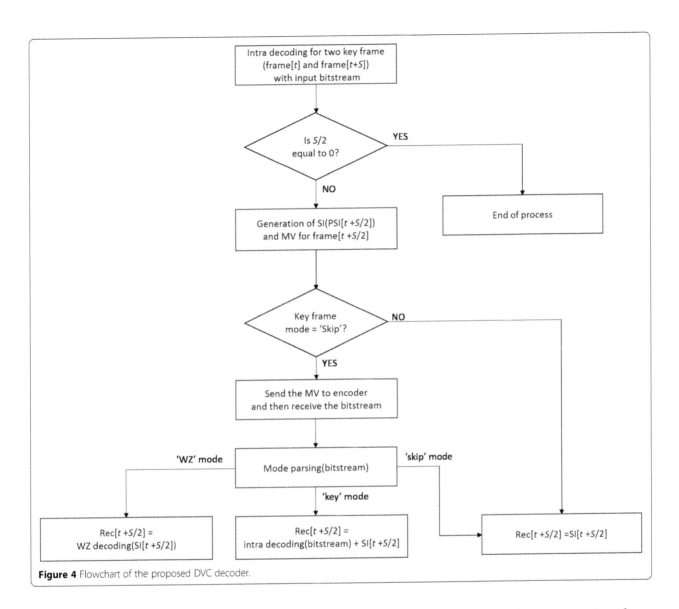

Figure 4 Flowchart of the proposed DVC decoder.

smallest RD cost for the best RD performance. The RD cost is defined by:

$$RD = \lambda \cdot rate + distortion \qquad (1)$$

where λ is a scaling factor. Conventional encoders, such as H.264/AVC, conduct pre-encoding and calculate rates and distortions for multiple modes. Then they select the best coding mode jointly having minimum rate and distortion. Therefore, they require high computational complexity, although they can select the best coding mode. However, since the purpose of the proposed DVC is to encode videos with low computational complexity, conventional methods to compute RD costs are not suitable for the best mode selection in the DVC encoder.

The key feature of DVC codecs is to encode videos with low computational complexity. In the conventional codecs, RD competition generally increases RD performance with high computational complexity. However, conventional DVC encoders do not employ RD competition, due to the computational complexity and nonavailability of the reconstructed frames. In the proposed DVC, we employ RD competition for high RD performance with minimum computational complexity. In addition, to reduce encoding computational time, the proposed method determines the candidate modes to conduct RD competition among key, WZ, and skip modes, depending on the coding mode of a previous coded frame. As input frames are hierarchically coded in the proposed method, we can predict which modes are suitable for the consecutive frames, based on the coding mode of the previous frame. In the proposed algorithm, approximate RD costs are computed. To perform RD competition, the proposed method estimates RD costs of the selected candidates

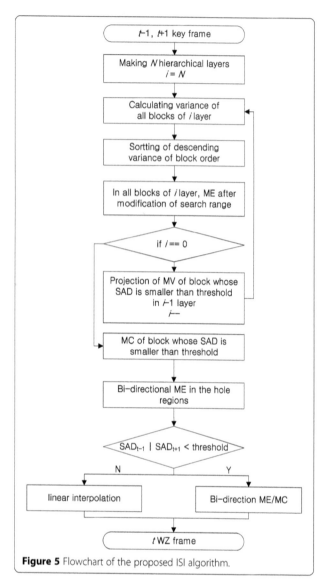

Figure 5 Flowchart of the proposed ISI algorithm.

depending on the conditions, as shown in the encoder flowchart. However, we need to note that the quality of a frame coded by WZ (skip) mode could be reasonably good, even when the rate is 0. The distortion of the frame is the same as that of the associated SI frame, because SI frames are generated from reference key frames without any explicit data. Therefore, WZ or skip mode is likely to be selected with low rate and high distortion by RD competition. However, a video quality that is too low is not suitable for commercial video applications. For quality control, the best mode is decided not only by RD competition but also by a quality threshold.

When an accurate objective visual quality and its bitrate are known, we can perform accurate RD competition. For the competition, actual encoding and decoding should be conducted at the encoder side. However, DVC-based encoders have the philosophy of

low complexity at the encoder side. In the proposed algorithm, the PSI can be reconstructed with the received motion vectors; thus, it is helpful to estimate more accurate objective visual quality. However, we cannot reconstruct the decoded frames at the encoder side due to low complexity constraint. Nevertheless, the proposed algorithm is better than the exiting algorithms with better prediction in estimating approximated RD competition.

3.3.1 Approximate RD cost of key frame mode
In this work, we propose an approximate RD cost of key frame modes before actual encoding for low computational complexity. Since the conventional RD costs require high computational complexity, DVC encoders cannot conduct pre-encoding of all the modes for RD competition. In addition, it is hard to correctly estimate rate and distortion of a frame before actual encoding. Figure 6 shows the actual data rate and distortion values for 100 intra-coded frames of the 'Akko' sequence. However, we found that rate and distortion are likely to slowly change for a short period of time, as shown in Figure 6a,b. Note that the key frames are coded by H.264/AVC intra coding. We assume that one rate for a key frame can be estimated by a linear relationship of those of adjacent key frames for low complexity. Thus, we propose the approximately estimated RD value with weighted linear interpolation by:

$$R_{L_{l,t}}{}^K = w_i \cdot R_{L_{\alpha,\beta}}{}^K + w_j \cdot R_{L_{i,j}}{}^K \qquad (2)$$

$$D_{L_{l,t}}{}^K = w_i \cdot D_{L_{\alpha,\beta}}{}^K + w_j \cdot D_{L_{i,j}}{}^K \qquad (3)$$

where R, D, and L denote rate of a key mode, its distortion, and hierarchical layer, respectively. l, α, and i are layer indexes ($\alpha < l$ and $i > l$). t, β, and j are display indexes ($\beta < t$ and $j > t$). The weight values (w_i, w_j) are determined by distance ratio between the key frames to the target frame with the condition, $w_i + w_j = 0$. The RD cost of the key mode is estimated by:

$$\mathrm{RD}_{L_{l,t}}{}^K = \lambda_K \cdot R_{L_{\alpha,\beta}}{}^K + D_{L_{i,j}}{}^K \qquad (4)$$

where λ_K is a scaling factor between rate and distortion.

3.3.2 Approximate RD cost of WZ mode
WZ frames are reconstructed from the SI frame with error correction via a channel decoder. Since channel decoding operation is one of the main sources of computational load, it is not proper to perform the channel decoding on the encoder side for low complexity encoding. Therefore, the proposed method estimates approximate RD costs, by predicting the reconstructed WZ

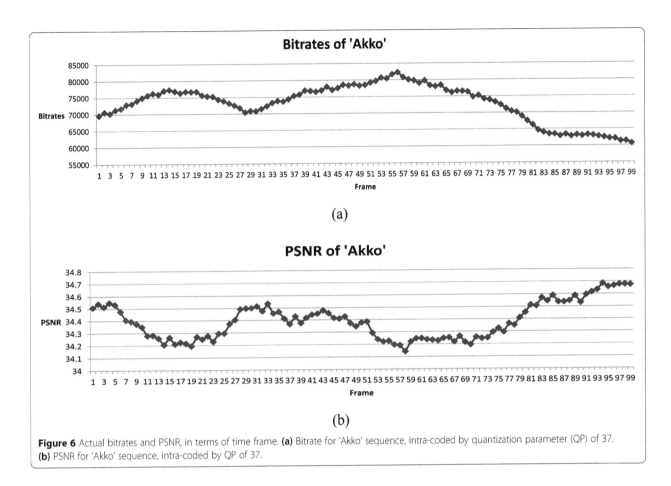

Figure 6 Actual bitrates and PSNR, in terms of time frame. **(a)** Bitrate for 'Akko' sequence, intra-coded by quantization parameter (QP) of 37. **(b)** PSNR for 'Akko' sequence, intra-coded by QP of 37.

frame with low computation complexity, before actual WZ encoding.

Conventional DVC encoders quantize discrete cosine transform (DCT) coefficients and generate parity bits for pre-determined frequency components in a DCT block, in order to correct all of the errors in the pre-determined regions. Therefore, we can assume that the pre-determined DCT regions of a WZ frame have no errors, and other regions have errors as much as those of the corresponding parts of an SI frame, as shown in Figure 7. Figure 7a,b shows blocks of an SI frame and a reconstructed WZ frame in the DCT domain, respectively. In Figure 7a, the light gray region is the pre-determined region by a quantization, and the region will be coded by a channel coder. Therefore, after conducting of channel decoding, the light gray part will be corrected. The white region in Figure 7b represents the no-error region, because all errors are corrected by a channel decoder with the received parity bits from an encoder. This means that the part is the same as the corresponding part of an original frame. The dark-gray parts that exist in Figure 7a,b depict the regions not to be corrected by a channel coder for coding efficiency. Therefore, the region of an SI frame is the same as the corresponding part of a WZ frame. Therefore, the proposed method can

generate the predicted reconstructed WZ (PRW) frame without high computational complexity, as the white part and dark-gray part are reconstructed by the original frame and the PSI, respectively, with minimal complexity.

With the PRW frame, the proposed method can predict the approximate rate and distortion of the WZ mode without high computational complexity. In the proposed method, the rate of the PRW frame is predicted with the correction capability of a channel coder and error rates of the PRW frame. The correction capability of a channel coder is generally related to the quantity of parity bits, and the amount of parity bits depends on the number of errors, as shown in Figure 8. Figure 8 shows the number of bits to correct the error in the triangular pyramid of the DCT bitplane in terms of the error rate of the PSI for several test sequences. Therefore, as the proposed method accounts for the number of errors of a PSI frame, the rate of the WZ mode can be approximately assessed. For each block, the demand bit is determined based on the rate of the WZ mode. Therefore, as the proposed method accounts for the number of errors of a PSI frame, the rate of the WZ mode can be approximately assessed. Since error correction by a channel coder is conducted in the frequency domain, the original and PSI frames are transformed with DCT by:

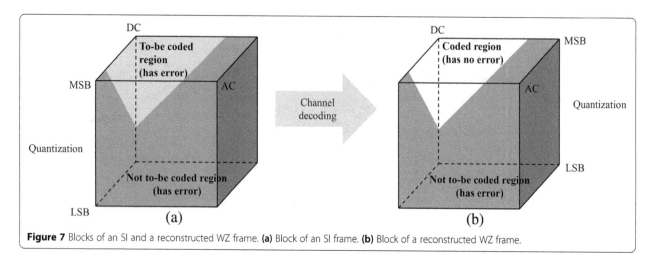

Figure 7 Blocks of an SI and a reconstructed WZ frame. **(a)** Block of an SI frame. **(b)** Block of a reconstructed WZ frame.

$$PSI_{L_{l,t}}{}^{DCT} = FD(PSI_{L_{l,t}}) \qquad (5)$$

$$ORI_{L_{l,t}}{}^{DCT} = FD(ORI_{L_{l,t}}) \qquad (6)$$

where FD is a function of forward DCT transform. After the transformation, the proposed method calculates the amount of errors of a PSI frame by:

$$NE_{L_{l,t}} = \sum_{b}^{B} \sum_{c}^{C} \sum_{p}^{P} |ORI_{L_{l,t}}{}^{DCT}[b,c,p] - PSI_{L_{l,t}}{}^{DCT}[b,c,p]| \qquad (7)$$

where (b, c, p) indicates block, coefficient, and bitplane parameters, respectively. (B, C) means the number of blocks in a frame and coefficients in a block, respectively. P represents the number of bitplanes. The error rate $(E_{LL,t})$ of the frame is estimated by:

$$E_{L_{l,t}} = \frac{NE_{L_{l,t}}}{NT_{L_{l,t}}} \times 100 \qquad (8)$$

where $NT_{Ll,t}$ indicates the number of total bits in a frame. Based on the computed error rate, the proposed method estimates the approximate rate of the WZ mode, as shown in Figure 8. In order to compute the distortion of the PRW frame, we need to generate the PRW frame. With the transformed original and PSI frames, the PRW frame is compensated for by:

$$PRW_{L_{l,t}}{}^{DCT}[b,c,p] = f(p)ORI_{L_{l,t}}{}^{DCT}[b,c,p]$$
$$+ (1-f(p))PSI_{L_{l,t}}{}^{DCT}[b,c,p] \qquad (9)$$

$$f(p) = \begin{cases} 1 & p < P_Q \\ 0 & \text{otherwise} \end{cases}$$

Note that P_Q is a quantization parameter in defined in bitplane. In order to assess a distortion, the sum of squared error (SSE) is computed after inverse transformation and is denoted by:

$$PRW_{L_{l,t}} = ID(PRW_{L_{l,t}}{}^{DCT}) \qquad (10)$$

$$D_{L_t}{}^W = \sum_{x=0}^{X} \sum_{y=0}^{Y} (ORI_{L_{l,t}}[x,y] - PRW_{L_{l,t}}[x,y])^2 \qquad (11)$$

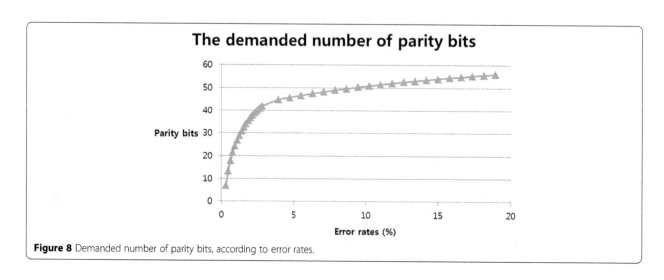

Figure 8 Demanded number of parity bits, according to error rates.

where ID represents a function of inverse DCT. With the estimated rate and distortion, the proposed method computes the RD cost of the WZ mode by:

$$\mathrm{RD}_{L_{l,t}}{}^{W} = \lambda_K\left(1 + R_{L_{i,j}}{}^{W}\right) + D_{L_{i,j}}{}^{W} \qquad (12)$$

When a frame is selected to encode by WZ mode, the proposed method sends as many parity bits by accounting for the number of DCT blocks and the number of the demanded bit for the block, as shown in Figure 8. Therefore, the proposed method does not need feedback iteration and reduces time delay. If the demanded number of parity bits for error correction is different from the computed value, the performance of the proposed method could decrease. Once a frame is to be coded as the WZ mode, each block is evaluated whether its quality is enough good or not. Parity bits for the well-predicted one with the PSI could be not sent to the decoder side. For other blocks, the proper amount of bits given by Figure 8 is supposed to be sent.

3.3.3 Approximate RD cost of skip mode

For the proposed skip mode, the proposed method estimates the RD values with the PSI frames that are generated in the previous step. Since a skip indication bit is sent to the decoder side, the rate is one bit for skip mode. The distortion is calculated with the SSE between an original and PSI frames, instead of SI frames, and the distortion is represented by:

$$D_{L_t}{}^{S} = \sum_{x=0}^{X}\sum_{y=0}^{Y}\left(\mathrm{ORI}_{L_{l,t}}[x,y] - \mathrm{PSI}_{L_{l,t}}[x,y]\right)^2 \qquad (13)$$

For the skip RD cost, the proposed method computes a skip RD cost with a distortion of skip by:

$$\mathrm{RD}_{L_{l,t}}{}^{S} = 1\cdot\lambda_K + D_{L_{i,j}}{}^{S} \qquad (14)$$

Note that λ_K is empirically computed with six sequences ('Akko', 'Ballroom', 'Exit', Flamenco2', 'Race1', and 'Rena' sequences). The parameter is set to (1,518, 3,824, 9,636, 24,281, and 61,185) as a function of QPs (33, 37, 41, 45, and 49).

4 Experimental results

For performance evaluation of the proposed algorithm, the RD performance of the proposed and conventional algorithms was evaluated. Four test sequences ('Akko', 'Ballroom', 'Flamenco2', and 'Race1') were used with the format and size of 4:0:0 YUV and 640 × 480, respectively. Key frames were coded using JM 17.2, and five QP points (33, 37, 41, 45, and 49) were used. Note that the

'Akko', 'Ballroom', 'Flamenco2', and 'Race1' sequences consist of 300, 250, 250, and 250 frames, respectively. The conventional algorithm employs every other frame as the key frame, while the number of key frames are determined depending on GOP size. The SI frames are reconstructed based on an adaptive search range [24] and an LDPCA channel coder with a matrix length of 6,336 [5].

Table 2 shows errors of the estimated rate and PSNR of the proposed algorithm in terms of GOP size for four test sequences. The accuracies are shown in differences of rates and PSNRs for all the frames between the key frames given by intra periods of 8, 4, and 2. The proposed algorithm has three estimators for three modes. The figures in the table are average errors for the three modes of the proposed algorithm. For the case of GOP size of two, the proposed accuracy is quite high. As the GOP increases, estimated errors become larger. As shown in the table, although computed rates and PSNRs for 'GOP8' are less accurate than those for 'GOP2', we can say that the overall accuracy is high, with minimal computational load. In any cases, accuracies of the computed values are less than 2%. 'Ballroom' and 'Race1'

Table 2 Estimated errors of rates and PSNRs with the proposed algorithm in terms of GOP sizes

Sequence	QP	Rate (%)			PSNR (%)		
		Average rate difference			Average PSNR difference		
		GOP8	GOP4	GOP2	GOP8	GOP4	GOP2
Akko	33	0.725	0.328	0.219	0.078	0.063	0.033
	37	0.814	0.423	0.257	0.088	0.072	0.035
	41	0.993	0.519	0.310	0.115	0.076	0.046
	45	0.939	0.654	0.390	0.151	0.111	0.055
	49	1.057	0.696	0.399	0.168	0.124	0.061
Ballroom	33	1.027	0.434	0.222	0.111	0.065	0.025
	37	1.116	0.526	0.326	0.132	0.081	0.036
	41	1.186	0.609	0.313	0.155	0.100	0.046
	45	1.308	0.696	0.405	0.163	0.109	0.045
	49	1.156	0.622	0.360	0.216	0.155	0.065
Flamenco2	33	0.596	0.376	0.202	0.099	0.077	0.036
	37	0.509	0.373	0.245	0.100	0.074	0.031
	41	0.683	0.518	0.294	0.123	0.102	0.055
	45	1.075	0.692	0.405	0.128	0.106	0.049
	49	0.857	0.628	0.362	0.212	0.168	0.084
Race1	33	0.910	0.361	0.168	0.095	0.067	0.025
	37	0.788	0.411	0.214	0.120	0.079	0.032
	41	0.940	0.465	0.265	0.152	0.107	0.040
	45	0.986	0.629	0.344	0.175	0.115	0.054
	49	1.270	0.684	0.404	0.282	0.153	0.083
Average		0.944	0.577	0.320	0.143	0.104	0.049

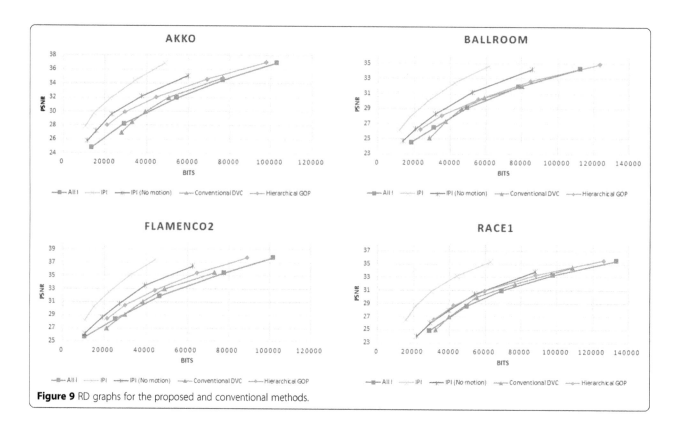

Figure 9 RD graphs for the proposed and conventional methods.

sequences have relatively high motion activity over the other sequences. Thus, the estimated errors are obtained to be somehow larger.

Figure 9 shows RD graphs of the exiting [24] and the proposed methods. 'All I' means that all the frames in a video are coded by intra mode. 'IPI' indicates that even frames are coded by inter mode, and odd frames are encoded by intra mode. 'IPI(No motion)' represents that even frames are coded by intra mode, and the other frames are coded by inter mode with zero motion vectors. 'Conventional DVC' means that each sequence is coded by DISCOVER [29]. The accuracies of SI frames are likely to be high, when motion is linear and/or slow in a video. The proposed method can exactly compute the SI quality without high computational complexity, using the PSI frames in the proposed DVC encoder. Therefore, we can reduce the number of key frames to increase RD performance. This means that the proposed method yields higher performance than the existing DVC and the all intra-coded cases, as shown in Figure 9. For the existing DVC cases, a lot of parity bits are required to correct the error in SI frames for large motion pictures. However, the proposed method evaluates the accuracies of SI frames, and it can prevent excessive parity bits, by balancing the rate and distortion at the encoder side. In addition, the proposed method influences the current coding mode on the decision of coding mode of nest frames for low computational complexity.

Since the proposed method hierarchically determines coding modes, the best coding mode for each frame is effectively decided with low computational complexity. Experimental results show that the proposed algorithm yields BD bitrate reduction of around −11.42% on the top of the existing DVC system. However, the DVC-based coders do not outperform the exiting video coders based on hybrid transform coding such as H.264/AVC and others. DVC is employed to improve predicted frames by channel coders. Any channel coders cannot perfectly guarantee error corrections, however; they can statically achieve error correction. The conventional video coders (H.264/AVC, HEVC, and other international standards) guarantee matching between encoder and decoder sides, while DVC-based coders cannot in general guarantee the encoder-decoder matching. The encoder cannot know the exact decoded pictures and vice versa. Thus, at any sides, we cannot make sure whether the correction is proper or not. Parity bits from channel coders could make errors corrected; however, they could also make corrected prediction wrong. That is one of critical reasons that DVC-based coders have difficulty in outperforming the H.264/AVC, HEVC, and so on.

Figure 10 shows the bitrates and PSNR of the proposed algorithm with respect to frame index for 'Ballroom' sequence. The bitrates and PSNR were obtained with QP of 33. As shown in the figure, high bitrates are observed periodically with GOP size of 8 due to intra-frame coding.

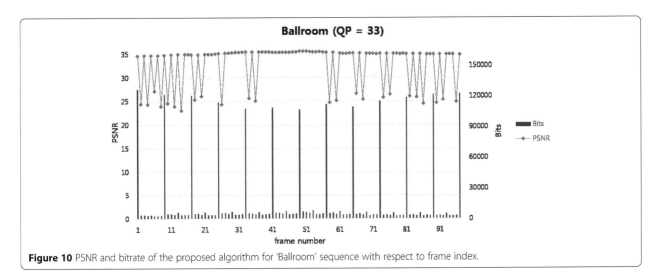

Figure 10 PSNR and bitrate of the proposed algorithm for 'Ballroom' sequence with respect to frame index.

In between two intra frames, low bitrates are seen for parity bits, motion vectors, and additional syntaxes. High quality coding is achieved for the frames between 40th and 55th indexes because motion activity is relatively low. For several frames, prediction accuracy is not so high thus error correction does not work well because the error rates exceed the correction rate of the channel coder.

Due to the proposed hierarchical GOP structure, a delay should be involved, like conventional video coding having GOPs. Figure 11 shows a delay diagram of the proposed method. The first and last frames for the initial GOP structure are encoded and sent to the decoder side in parallel. The decoder reconstructs the frames with the received bitstreams. With the reconstructed frames, the SI frame located in between the frames is generated, and the motion vectors for the SI frame are transmitted to the encoder.

The encoder generates the PSI with the received motion vectors and performs the proposed RD competition. With the decided best mode, the proposed encoder codes the target frame. This processing is repeated until half of the initial GOP structure has been reached. The processing delay of the proposed method can be denoted by:

$$\text{Delay} = \frac{S}{2}(\alpha + \varepsilon) + (S-1)\beta + \left(\frac{S}{2} - 1\right)(\gamma + \delta + \zeta) \quad (15)$$

where S means the time interval for the initial GOP size (=8). α, ε, β, γ, δ, and ξ indicate encoding, decoding, transmission, PSI generation, RD competition, and SI generation times, respectively. Through the experiment for estimation of the delay, the encoding, decoding, transmission, PSI generation, RD competition, and SI

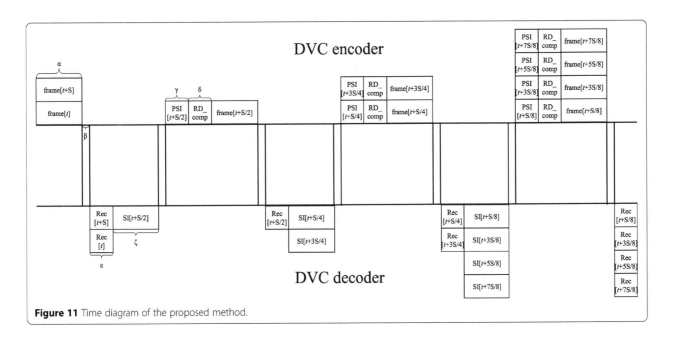

Figure 11 Time diagram of the proposed method.

generation time are 600, 14, 5, 14, 400, and 3,500 ms, respectively. We found in the experiment that the proposed DVC requires 14,233 ms for a GOP structure. Note that the proposed system was implemented on Intel i5 (2,53 GHz) with 4 GB over Window 7. The proposed feedback-based DVC requires the delay, and it makes the proposed algorithm applied for high frame-rate video applications. However, the proposed algorithm is considered to be a trade-off between no-feedback DVC and iterative feedback DVC algorithms. Note that RD performance of the proposed algorithm is better than the no-feedback algorithms. This evaluation and assessment would be not practical for practical scenarios and conditions. The network delay can vary depending on traffics. In addition, we employed JM reference encoding software and SIG having large computational complexity in the evaluation. Hardwired logics or fast computing platforms can be employed to implement practical applications based on the proposed DVC system. Extensive further research should be performed for practical applications and services in the future.

5 Conclusions

In this paper, a new adaptive distributed video coder has been proposed, with hierarchical GOP structure. In the proposed algorithm, the PSI can be reconstructed in the encoder, using reference key frames and MVs without motion estimation. Therefore, we can estimate the exact accuracies of SI frames with the PSI frames. With the PSI frames, the proposed method performs RD competition and selects the best coding mode. Based on the decided coding mode, the best GOP structure is automatically decided in the proposed method. As the proposed method reduces the number of key frames when a video has little and/or linear motion, the performance of the proposed method improves. In addition, the proposed method reduces the number of WZ frames, if large motion between consecutive frames occurs, because an SI frame of low accuracy requires many parity bits for error correction. Therefore, the proposed method has higher performance than the several existing methods. However, the proposed method requires high computational complexity, according to the initial GOP size. For further work, we would optimize the encoding, decoding, and SI generation modules, for reduction of the delay.

Competing interests
The authors declare that they have no competing interests.

Acknowledgements
This research was partly supported by Basic Science Research Program through the National Research Foundation of Korea (NRF) funded by the Ministry of Science, ICT & Future Planning (NRF-2014R1A2A1A11052210) and the MSIP (Ministry of Science, ICT & Future Planning), Republic of Korea, under the ITRC (Information Technology Research Center) support program supervised by the NIPA (National IT Industry Promotion Agency) (NIPA-2014-H0301-14-1018).

Author details
[1]Department of Computer Engineering, Kwangwoon University, Wolgye-dong, Seoul 447-1, Nowon-gu, South Korea. [2]School of Engineering Science, Simon Fraser University, 8888 University Drive, Burnaby, BC, Canada.

References

1. D Slepian, J Wolf, Noiseless coding of correlated information sources. IEEE Trans Inf Theory **19**(4), 471–480 (1973)
2. A Wyner, J Ziv, The rate-distortion function for source coding with side information at the decoder. IEEE Trans Inf Theory **22**(1), 1–10 (1976)
3. J Micallef, JR Farrugia, C Debono, *Low-density parity-check codes for asymmetric distributed source coding. Paper presented at the 2010 1st IEEE International Conference on Information Theory and Information Security* (IEEE, Beijing, China, 2010)
4. Q Linbo, H Xiaohai, L Rui, D Xiewei, *Application of punctured turbo codes in distributed video coding. Paper presented at the 2007 4th IEEE International Conference on Image and Graphics* (IEEE, Sichuan, China, 2007)
5. A Aaron, R Zhang, B Girod, *Wyner-Ziv coding of motion video. Paper presented at the 2002 37th Asilomar Conference on Signals and Systems* (IEEE, Grove, CA, 2002)
6. D Varodayan, A Aaron, B Girod, Rate-adaptive codes for distributed source coding. EURASIP Signal Process J Spec Sect Distributed Source Coding **86**(11), 3123–3130 (2006)
7. C Brites, F Pereira, *Encoder rate control for transform domain Wyner-Ziv video coding. Paper presented at the 2007 14th IEEE International Conference on Image Processing* (IEEE, San Antonio, TX, 2007)
8. F Zhai, IJ Fair, Techniques for early stopping and error detection in turbo decoding. IEEE Trans Commun **51**(10), 1617–1623 (2003)
9. WJ Chien, LJ Karam, GP Abousleman, *Rate-distortion based selective decoding for pixel-domain distributed video coding. Paper presented at the 2008 15th IEEE International Conference on Image Processing* (IEEE, San Diego, CA, 2008)
10. J Skorupa, J Slowack, S Mys, P Lambert, R Van de Walle, C Grecos, *Stopping criterions for turbo coding in a Wyner-Ziv video codec. Paper presented at the 2009 27th IEEE Picture Coding Symposium* (IEEE, Chicago, IL, 2009)
11. JL Martinez, C Holder, GE Fernandez, H Kalva, F Quiles, *DVC using a half-feedback based approach. Paper presented at the 2008 9th IEEE International Conference on Multimedia and Expo* (IEEE, Hannover, Germany, 2008)
12. B Du, H Shen, *Encoder rate control for pixel-domain distributed video coding without feedback channel. Paper presented at the 2009 3rd IEEE International Conference on Multimedia and Ubiquitous Engineering* (IEEE, Qingdao, China, 2009)
13. C Yaacoub, J Farah, B Pesquet-Popescu, *Content adaptive gop size control with feedback channel suppression in distributed video coding. Paper presented at the 2009 16th IEEE International Conference on Image Processing* (IEEE, Cairo, Egypt, 2009)
14. J Ascenso, C Brites, F Pereira, *Content adaptive Wyner-Ziv video coding driven by motion activity. Paper presented at the 2006 13th IEEE International Conference on Image Processing* (IEEE, Atlanta, GA, 2006)
15. M Morbee, J Prades-Nebot, A Pizurica, W Philips, *Rate allocation algorithm for pixel-domain distributed video coding without feedback channel. Paper presented at the 2007 32nd IEEE International Conference on Acoustic, Speech, and Signal Processing* (IEEE, Honolulu, HI, 2007)
16. J Kubasov, K Lajnef, C Guillemot, *A hybrid encoder/decoder rate control for a Wyner-Ziv video codec with a feedback channel. Paper presented at the 2007 9th IEEE Workshop on Multimedia Signal Processing* (IEEE, Crete, Greece, 2007)
17. WJ Chien, LJ Karam, GP Abousleman, *Block-adaptive Wyner-Ziv coding for transform-domain distributed video coding. Paper presented at the 2007 32nd IEEE International Conference on Acoustic, Speech, and Signal Processing* (IEEE, Honolulu, HI, 2007)
18. L Limin, L Zhen, EJ Delp, *Backward channel aware Wyner-Ziv video coding. Paper presented at the 2006 13th IEEE International Conference on Image Processing* (IEEE, Atlanta, GA, 2006)
19. W Jia, W Xiaolin, Y Songyu, S Jun, New results on multiple descriptions in the Wyner-Ziv setting. IEEE Trans Inf Theory **55**(4), 1708–1710 (2009)
20. R Liu, Z Yue, C Chen, Side information generation based on hierarchical motion estimation in distributed video coding. J Aeronaut **22**(2), 167–173 (2009)

21. Y Shuiming, M Ouaret, F Dufaux, T Ebrahimi, *Improved side information generation with iterative decoding and frame interpolation for distributed video coding. Paper presented at the 2008 15th IEEE International Conference on Image Processing* (IEEE, San Diego, CA, 2008)

22. H Xin, S Forchhammer, *Improved side information generation for distributed video coding. Paper presented at the 2008 10th IEEE Workshop on Multimedia Signal Processing* (IEEE, Cairns, Australia, 2008)

23. KY Min, SN Park, DG Sim, *Side information generation using adaptive search range for distributed video coding. Paper presented at the 2009 11th IEEE Pacific Rim Conference on Communications, Computers and Signal Processing* (IEEE, B.C., Canada, 2009)

24. KY Min, SN Park, JH Nam, DG Sim, SH Kim, Distributed video coding based on adaptive block quantization using received motion vectors. KICS J **35**(2), 172–181 (2010)

25. I Ahmad, Z Ahmad, I Abou-Faycal, *Delay-efficient GOP size control algorithm in Wyner-Ziv video coding, Paper presented at the 2009 7th IEEE International Symposium on Signal Processing and Information Technology* (IEEE, Ajman, UAE, 2009)

26. C Yaacoub, J Farah, B Pesquet-Popescu, New adaptive algorithms for GOP size control with return channel suppression in Wyner-Ziv video coding. Int J Digit Multimedia Broadcasting **2009**, 319021 (2009)

27. G Huchet, W Demin, *Distributed video coding without channel codes. Paper presented at the 2010 3rd IEEE International Symposium on Broadband Multimedia Systems and Broadcasting* (IEEE, Shanghai, China, 2010)

28. JL Martinez, G Fernandez-Escribano, H Kalva, WARJ Weerakkody, *Feedback-free DVC architecture using machine learning. Paper presented at the 2008 15th IEEE International Conference on Image Processing* (IEEE, San Diego, CA, 2008)

29. X Artigas, J Ascenso, M Dalai, S Klomp, D Kubasov, M Ouaret, *The discover codec, architecture, techniques and evaluation. Paper presented at the 2007 IEEE Picture Coding Symposium* (IEEE, Lisbon, Portugal, 2007)

30. M Jang, JW Kang, and SH Kim, A design of rate-adaptive LDPC codes for distributed source coding using PEG algorithm. Paper presented at the 2010 IEEE Military Communications Conference, San Joes, CA, 31 October-3 November 2010

31. SY Shin, M Jang, JW Kang, SH Kim, *New distributed source coding scheme based on LDPC codes with source revealing rate-adaptation. Paper presented at the 2011 12th IEEE Pacific Rim Conference on Communications, Computers and Signal Processing* (IEEE, Victoria, Canada, 2011)

32. CK Kim, DY Suh, *Channel adaptive rate control for loss resiliency of distributed video coding. Paper presented at the 2010 International Conference on Electronics, Information, and Communication* (IEEK, Cebu, Philippine, 2010)

33. JA Park, DY Suh, GH Park, Distributed video coding with multiple side information sets. IEICE Trans Inf Syst **E93-D**(3), 654–657 (2010)

34. JY Lee, CW Seo, DG Sim, JK Han, *Efficient ME/MD schemes for Wyner-Ziv codec to VC-1 transcoder. Paper presented at the 2011 International Technical Conference on Circuits/Systems, Computers and Communications* (IEEK, Gyeongju, Korea, 2011)

35. SY Shim, JK Han, J Bae, Adaptive reconstruction scheme using neighbour pixels in PDWZ coding. Electron Lett **46**(9), 626–628 (2010)

36. R Oh, JB Park, BW Jeon, Fast implementation of Wyner-Ziv video codec using GPGPU, in *Symposium on IEEE BMSB*, 2010, pp. 1–5

37. X Van Hoang, BW Jeon, Flexible complexity control solution for transform domain Wyner-Ziv video coding. IEEE Trans Broadcasting **58**(2), 209–220 (2012)

38. KY Min, DG Sim, Adaptive distributed video coding with motion vectors through a back channel. EURASIP J Image Video Process **22**, 1–12 (2013)

13

Low-complexity depth map compression in HEVC-based 3D video coding

Qiuwen Zhang[1][*], Ming Chen[2], Xinpeng Huang[1], Nana Li[1] and Yong Gan[1]

Abstract

In this paper, a low-complexity algorithm is proposed to reduce the complexity of depth map compression in the high-efficiency video coding (HEVC)-based 3D video coding (3D-HEVC). Since the depth map and the corresponding texture video represent the same scene in a 3D video, there is a high correlation among the coding information from depth map and texture video. An experimental analysis is performed to study depth map and texture video correlation in the coding information such as the motion vector and prediction mode. Based on the correlation, we propose three efficient low-complexity approaches, including early termination mode decision, adaptive search range motion estimation (ME), and fast disparity estimation (DE). Experimental results show that the proposed algorithm can reduce about 66% computational complexity with negligible rate-distortion (RD) performance loss in comparison with the original 3D-HEVC encoder.

Keywords: 3D video; 3D-HEVC; Depth coding; Low complexity

1 Introduction

Three-dimensional video standard has been recently finalized by the Joint Collaborative Team on 3D Video Coding (JCT-3V), and the high-efficiency video coding (HEVC)-based 3D video coding (3D-HEVC) is developed as an extension of HEVC [1-3]. For the efficient compression of 3D video data with multiview texture video and depth map, a number of coding tools are investigated to exploit in 3D-HEVC such as inter-view motion prediction and disparity-compensated prediction [4]. This technique achieves the highest possible coding efficiency in multiview texture video compression, but it results in extremely large encoding time with small increase of depth coding efficiency which obstructs it from 3D-HEVC practical use. Therefore, it is necessary to develop a fast algorithm that can reduce the complexity of multiview depth map compression with minimal loss of coding efficiency in a 3D-HEVC encoder.

Recently, a number of approaches have been made to explore fast algorithms in depth map coding. A motion vector (MV) sharing algorithm is proposed in [5] to reduce the complexity of depth map coding. An early termination algorithm for depth coding is introduced in [6] based on the detection of the differences between the current macroblock (MB) and the co-located MBs in texture video. An intra prediction algorithm for depth coding is presented in [7] to reduce the number of candidate prediction directions for smooth regions. A low-complexity mode decision and motion estimation algorithm is proposed in [8] to take advantage of the texture motion information which may be usefully exploited in the encoding of the corresponding depth map. A novel depth and depth-color codec is proposed in [9] based on a shape-adaptive wavelet transform and an explicit encoding of the locations of major depth edges. A depth map compression algorithm [10] uses the corresponding texture video as side information to improve the coding performance. A fast motion search and mode decision algorithm is proposed in [11] to speed up the motion estimation (ME) stages of the depth coding process, and a fast depth map method is proposed in our previous work [12] based on sharing motion vector and SKIP mode from the texture video to reduce complexity of depth coding. All these algorithms are efficient in reducing computational complexity with acceptable quality degradation in coding performance for previous video coding standards. However, these algorithms are not directly applicable to the new standard 3D-HEVC, where high

* Correspondence: zhangqwen@126.com
[1]College of Computer and Communication Engineering, Zhengzhou University of Light Industry, No. 5 Dongfeng Road, Zhengzhou 450002, China
Full list of author information is available at the end of the article

computational complexity is intrinsically related to the use of new prediction coding structures for the 3D-HEVC encoder.

To this end, several fast algorithms [13-16] have been proposed for the 3D-HEVC encoder to reduce the complexity of depth map coding. A fast mode decision algorithm is proposed in [13] to early terminate the unnecessary prediction modes full rate-distortion (RD) cost calculation in 3D-HEVC. A low-complexity depth map coding algorithm based on the associated texture video is introduced in [14] to reduce the number of wedgelet candidates. A fast wedgelet partitioning algorithm is proposed in [15] to simplify the intra mode decision in 3D-HEVC depth map coding. A content adaptive complexity reduction algorithm is proposed in [16] to reduce the 3D-HEVC coding complexity by utilizing the correlations between the base view and the dependent view. The aforementioned algorithms are well developed for depth map coding achieving significant time savings in 3D-HEVC. However, the coding information correlations between the depth map and the texture video are not fully studied. This situation results in a limited time saving. There is still some room for further reduction of computational complexity of the 3D-HEVC depth map compression.

The depth map represents a 3D scene information, which has the same content with similar characteristic of the texture video. Therefore, there is a high correlation among motion information from depth map and texture video. In this paper, we propose a low-complexity depth compression algorithm using the correlation among motion information from depth map and texture video. The proposed algorithm consists of three approaches: early termination mode decision, adaptive search range ME, and fast disparity estimation (DE) for depth map coding. Experimental results illustrate that the proposed algorithm can significantly reduce the computational complexity of depth map compression while maintaining almost the same coding performance in comparison with the original 3D-HEVC encoder.

The rest of the paper is organized as follows. Section 2 analyzes the property of depth map and the correlation among motion information from depth map and texture video. A low-complexity depth coding algorithm base on adaptive search range ME and fast DE is presented in Section 3. Experimental results and conclusions are given in Sections 4 and 5, respectively.

2 Observations and analysis

In the test model of 3D-HEVC, the variable sizes the ME and DE to exploit both temporal and view correlation within temporally successive pictures and neighboring views. The coding unit (CU) is the basic unit of region splitting used for 3D-HEVC similar to macroblock in H.264/AVC, which has a hierarchical quadtree structure having variable sizes from 64×64 to 8×8. The partition unit (PU) is the basic unit used for 3D-HEVC inter/intra prediction processes. At each treeblock, 3D-HEVC performs ME and DE with different PU sizes including $2N \times 2N$, $2N \times N$, $N \times 2N$, and $N \times N$.

Similar to HEVC for a treeblock, the mode decision process in 3D-HEVC is performed using all the possible prediction modes to find the one with the least RD cost using a Lagrange multiplier. The RD cost function (J) used in 3D-HEVC is defined as follows:

$$J = D + \lambda \cdot SSE \tag{1}$$

where D specifies the bit cost to be considered for the 3D-HEVC mode decision, SSE is the average difference between the current treeblock and the matching treeblock, and λ is the Lagrange multiplier. However, calculation of the RD cost needs to execute both the ME and DE processes in 3D-HEVC, and these 'try all and select the best' method will result in high computational complexity and limit the use of 3D-HEVC encoders in practical applications. Therefore, low-complexity algorithms, which can reduce the complexity of the ME and DE processes with negligible loss of coding efficiency, are extremely necessary for real-time implementation of 3D-HEVC encoders.

Since the depth map and its associated texture video are both projections of the same scenery from the same viewpoint at the same time instant, the motion characteristics (i.e., block partitioning and corresponding motion vectors) of the depth map and its associated texture video are typically similar. Therefore, a new coding mode motion parameter inheritance (MPI) [4,17], where the data that are already transmitted for the texture video picture can be reused for efficient encoding of the depth map, has been introduced in the 3D-HEVC encoder. This achieves the highest coding efficiency but requires a very high computational complexity. Since the motion vectors of the texture video have quarter-sample accuracy, whereas for the depth map only full-sample accuracy is used, in the inheritance process, the motion vectors are quantized to their nearest full-sample position. In addition, the inherited reference picture shall be the one with the same picture order count (POC) and viewpoint as the reference picture of the co-located block in the texture video picture. If there is no reference picture in the reference lists that satisfies this condition, such a candidate is treated as invalid and it is not inserted to the merge candidate list. However, the coding information correlations between the depth map and texture video are not fully studied. The coding information includes the reference picture, prediction mode, and motion vector.

Therefore, the prediction mode of the depth map tree-block is similar to that of the corresponding texture video treeblock. Meanwhile, the homogeneous regions in the depth map have a strong spatial correlation, and thus, spatially neighboring depth map treeblocks have similar coding information. The relationship among the current depth map treeblock, co-located texture video treeblock, and spatially neighboring treeblock is shown in Figure 1. The reference picture in the co-located texture view has the same POC value as the reference picture of current depth map view.

On the basis of these observations, we propose to analyze the depth intra prediction mode using the coding information from the spatial neighboring depth map and the co-located texture video treeblock. The neighboring depth map and the co-located texture video treeblock are described as in Figure 2. D_c denotes the current depth map treeblock, D_l, D_u, D_{ul}, and D_{ur} denote the neighboring treeblocks in the depth map. C_{col} denotes the co-located treeblock in the texture video and C_l, C_u, C_{ul}, and C_{ur} its left treeblock, up treeblock, upleft treeblock, and upright treeblock, respectively, as shown in Figure 2.

According to the coding information correlation with the mode maps of encoded frames, we define a set of intra mode predictors (P) for depth map treeblock as follows:

$$P = \{D_l, D_u, D_{ul}, D_{ur}, C_{col}, C_l, C_u, C_{ul}, C_{ur}\} \qquad (2)$$

Based on this predictor set, a mode complexity (C) parameter is defined according to the mode context of the spatial neighboring depth map and the co-located texture video treeblock, and then, the mode characteristic of a depth map treeblock is estimated. The mode complexity of a depth map treeblock is described as follows:

$$C = \sum_{i \in P} \beta_i \cdot \eta_i \qquad (3)$$

where i is the related treeblock in predictors P, β_i is the treeblock weight factor of each predictor in Equation 2, and η_i is the treeblock mode factor of each predictor. Only the prediction modes of those available neighboring treeblocks in predictors P will be used. In 3D-HEVC, various prediction mode sizes are used in the mode decision process. The mode factor of each predictor η_i can be assigned based on the complexity of each mode as follows: when the predictor i is SKIP mode, merge mode, inter $2N \times 2N$, and intra $2N \times 2N$ mode, η_i is assigned with a small value '1;' when the predictor i is inter $2N \times N$, inter $N \times 2N$ mode, η_i is assigned with a medium value '2;' when the predictor i is small-size inter modes, intra $N \times N$ mode (depth modeling modes (DMM) and region boundary chain (RBC) mode in the neighboring depth map treeblocks), and DE mode, η_i is assigned with a large value '3.' The treeblock weight factors of these nine predictors have an additional property, $\sum_i \beta_i = 1$. β_i is defined according to the effect of related treeblocks on current treeblock. Since treeblocks in the horizontal and vertical directions have a large effect on the current treeblock compared to treeblocks in the diagonal direction, the weight factors β_i for the horizontal

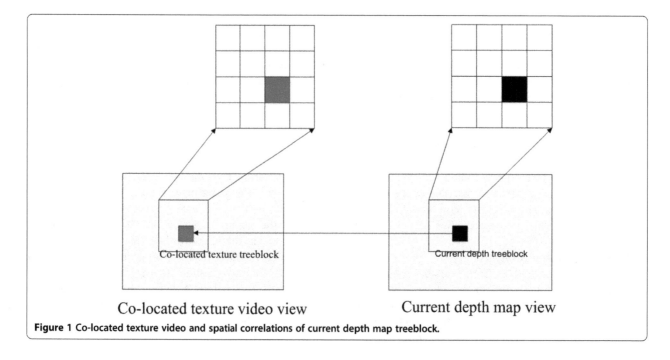

Co-located texture treeblock   Current depth treeblock

Co-located texture video view   Current depth map view

Figure 1 Co-located texture video and spatial correlations of current depth map treeblock.

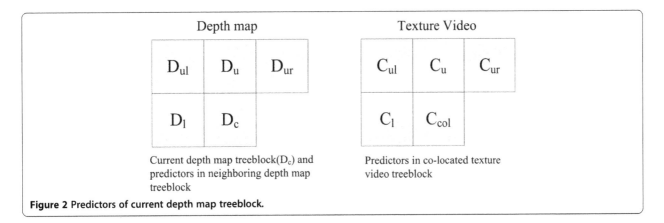

Current depth map treeblock(D_c) and predictors in neighboring depth map treeblock

Predictors in co-located texture video treeblock

Figure 2 Predictors of current depth map treeblock.

and vertical treeblocks (D_l, D_u, C_l, and C_u) are set to 0.1, and that of the diagonal direction treeblocks (D_{ul}, D_{ur}, C_{ul}, and C_{ur}) are set to 0.05. In the case of the co-located texture video treeblock, the treeblock weight factor β_{Ccol} is set to 0.4.

Generally, the larger the mode factor, the more complex the treeblock is. According to the value of C, each treeblock can be divided into three types. T_1 and T_2 are set to determine whether a treeblock belongs to the region with the simple mode, normal mode, or complex mode. The criterion is defined as follows:

$$
\begin{cases}
C \leq T_1 & \textbf{Treeblock} \in \textbf{simple mode region} \\
T_1 < C < T_2 & \textbf{Treeblock} \in \textbf{normal mode region} \\
C \geq T_2 & \textbf{Treeblock} \in \textbf{complex mode region}
\end{cases}
$$

$$(4)$$

where T_1 and T_2 are mode-weight factors. Those threshold settings are crucial for effective depth map compression, and it is always a tradeoff between depth map coding quality and computational complexity reduction. From simulations on various test sequences, it can be found that the optimal threshold for each sequence depends on the sequence content. In order to cope with different texture characteristics of test sequences, extensive simulations have been conducted on eight video sequences to analyze the thresholds for three types of treeblocks. Among these test sequences, *Kendo*, *Balloons*, and *Newspaper* are in $1{,}024 \times 768$ resolution, while *Undo_Dancer*, *GT_Fly*, *Poznan_Street*, *Poznan_-Hall2*, and *Shark* are in $1{,}920 \times 1{,}088$ resolution, and the 'Shark' and 'Undo_Dancer' sequences are with a large global motion or rich texture, the 'Kendo', 'Balloons', 'Newspaper', and 'Poznan_Street' sequences are with a medium local motion or a smooth texture, and 'Poznan_-Hall2' is a small global motion or a homogeneous texture sequence. The test conditions are as follows: I-B-P view structure; test full-length frames for each sequence; quantization parameter (QP) is chosen with 34, 39, 42, and 45; group of pictures (GOP) size = 8; treeblock size =

64; search range of ME is configured with 64; and context-adaptive binary arithmetic coding (CABAC) is used for entropy coding. Then, we calculated the average thresholds of those eight test sequences.

Table 1 shows the accuracies of the proposed algorithm using various thresholds. The accuracies here are defined as the ratio of the number of the simple mode, normal mode, and complex mode, which select the same best modes using the 3D-HEVC encoder as well as the proposed algorithm. It can be seen from Table 1 that when the threshold values are $T_1 = 0.8$, $T_2 = 1.2$, the average accuracy of the proposed algorithm achieves more than 93% with a maximum of 97% in the 'Shark' sequence. Based on extensive experiments, T_1 and T_2 are set to 0.8 and 1.2, respectively, which achieve a good and consistent performance on a variety of test sequences with different texture characteristics and motion activities and fixed for each treeblock QP level in 3D-HEVC encoder.

3 Proposed low-complexity depth map compression algorithm

3.1 Early termination mode decision

The depth map is usually not the ground truth because existing depth map estimation methods still have difficulties to generate accurate depths at object edges or in areas with less texture. Distortion may occur during depth map estimation, which will result in a noisy depth map (caused by occlusion and areas of low texture), such that it would be inefficient to spend more bits to achieve an accurate representation of the depth map in 3D-HEVC coding. To overcome this problem, this paper proposes an early termination mode decision for 3D-HEVC, which takes into account the correlations between coding information from texture videos and depth maps to speed up the coding process.

The depth map content is similar with that of texture video, and thus, the coding modes of texture and depth map are similar. By utilizing the information of the corresponding treeblock in the texture video, the coding

Table 1 Statistical analysis of accuracy for proposed algorithm using various thresholds

Sequences	$T_1 = 0.6$, $T_2 = 1.0$ (%)	$T_1 = 0.7$, $T_2 = 1.1$ (%)	$T_1 = 0.8$, $T_2 = 1.2$ (%)	$T_1 = 0.9$, $T_2 = 1.3$ (%)
Kendo	84	86	93	91
Balloons	76	83	91	92
Newspaper	81	85	94	92
Shark	85	89	97	95
Undo_Dancer	82	88	93	91
GT_Fly	80	84	91	87
Poznan_Street	81	85	89	90
Poznan_Hall2	82	86	95	93
Average	81	86	93	91

information of previously encoded texture images at the same view can be effectively shared and reused. Such that we propose a novel early termination mode decision considering a co-located texture video. The merge/skip mode provides good coding performance and requires little complexity in the 3D-HEVC encoder, where the motion vector predictor (MVP) is adopted for the current treeblock to generate a compensated block. Meanwhile, the merge/skip mode is the dominant mode at low bitrates (high QPs) in the 3D-HEVC encoder, and the distribution is similar to that in the previous video coding standard, H.264/AVC. Once the merge/skip mode can be predecided, variable size ME and DE computation for a treeblock can be entirely saved. Usually, the decision to use merge/skip mode is delayed until the RD costs of all other modes (inter-, intra-, and DE-modes) have been calculated and merge/skip mode is found to have the minimum RD cost. Thus, if we can exploit previously encoded texture coding information to determine that those depth map treeblocks are encoded in merge/skip mode (this mode along with CU partition inherited to encode forcefully the depth treeblock without going further in depth quadtree level), we can skip the time-consuming process of computing RD costs on smaller block sizes for a high percentage of treeblocks and, thus, significantly reduce the computation complexity of the 3D-HEVC mode decision process.

Based on this consideration, the proposed algorithm introduces an early termination mode decision to skip checking unnecessary ME and DE by utilizing the co-located texture video prediction mode information. In our approach, we first take advantage of the relations of previously encoded texture images at the same view for early merge/skip mode decision. Since both depth map and texture video are generally captured at the same time, it is likely for each treeblock to have the same motion and block partition information. So when a

treeblock of depth map is encoded, we consider how the corresponding texture video treeblock (C_{col} in Figure 2) was encoded. When the merge/skip mode is selected as the best prediction mode on the texture treeblock in the 3D-HEVC mode decision, it indicates that the current texture treeblock is located in a low-motion or static region. The motion of the texture treeblock can be predicted well using the merge/skip mode, which results in a lower energy residual after motion compensation compared to other prediction modes such as inter $2N \times 2N$, $2N \times N$, $N \times 2N$, and $N \times N$. Thus, no further processing of variable size ME and DE computation is necessary.

However, the proposed early termination mode decision algorithm has a few strong assumptions: depth map content is not always similar to the color content, e.g., in a planar highly textured area, there is a high-color variance but depth is constant. Depth acquisition can be unreliable but the assumption that information can be discarded for this reason is questionable. Finally, if motion estimation on color data is wrong with the proposed approach, errors can propagate to depth data even if the estimation from depth could be correct. Based on this observation, we investigate the effectiveness of the proposed early termination mode decision algorithm. By exploiting the exhaustive mode decision in the 3D-HEVC encoder under the aforementioned test conditions in Section 2, extensive simulations have been conducted on a set of test sequences as listed in Table 2. Table 2 shows the hit rate of the early termination mode decision algorithm. This hit rate is defined as the ratio of the number of depth map treeblocks, which selects the same best prediction mode using the 3D-HEVC encoder as well as the proposed algorithm, to the total number of depth map treeblocks. The average hit rate of the proposed algorithm is larger than 93% with a maximum of 95% in 'QP = 45' and a minimum of 91% in 'QP = 34'. The

Table 2 Hit rate of the proposed early termination mode decision algorithm

Sequences	QP = 34 (%)	QP = 39 (%)	QP = 42 (%)	QP = 45 (%)
Kendo	92	93	94	95
Balloons	86	89	91	93
Newspaper	92	93	95	96
Shark	93	95	96	97
Undo_Dancer	91	92	93	95
GT_Fly	87	90	92	93
Poznan_Street	92	94	95	96
Poznan_Hall2	94	95	97	98
Average	91	93	94	95

Table 3 Statistical analysis of motion vector distribution for three types of treeblocks

Sequences	Treeblocks in simple mode region			Treeblocks in normal mode region			Treeblocks in complex mode region		
	S1 (%)	S2 (%)	S3 (%)	S1 (%)	S2 (%)	S3 (%)	S1 (%)	S2 (%)	S3 (%)
Kendo	87.3	98.1	98.9	81.8	92.1	97.2	59.4	76.8	84.3
Balloons	85.5	96.3	97.1	79.6	91.3	96.1	47.2	69.2	79.8
Newspaper	86.2	97.4	98.3	78.9	90.8	96.5	49.8	71.3	81.6
Shark	89.2	97.9	99.4	82.1	92.5	97.3	51.5	73.4	86.2
Undo_Dancer	90.1	98.3	99.7	83.8	92.8	98.2	57.2	76.6	87.3
GT_Fly	91.2	99.2	100	84.1	93.2	99.4	59.3	78.2	90.2
Poznan_Street	88.6	96.5	98.2	77.5	90.3	96.5	43.2	69.3	81.4
Poznan_Hall2	86.3	96.8	97.6	76.3	91.1	95.7	39.8	64.7	78.2
Average	88.1	97.6	98.7	80.5	91.8	97.1	50.9	72.4	83.6

'S1', 'S2', and 'S3', respectively, represent the motion search windows of [SR/16 × SR/16], [SR/8 × SR/8], and [SR/4 × SR/4].

simulation results shown in Table 2 indicate that the proposed early termination mode decision algorithm can accurately reduce the unnecessary depth map CU mode by utilizing the information of the corresponding treeblock in texture video.

Based on this statistical tendency, the proposed depth map early termination algorithm checks the prediction modes from the co-located texture video: if texture treeblock (C_{col}) has no motion, corresponding depth map treeblock (D_c) has motion due to unreliable depth estimation; therefore, the motion in the depth map can be ignored. When the texture video treeblock selects merge/skip as the best mode, it indicates that the motion can be efficiently represented using the current depth

map treeblock, and the variable size ME and DE computation for a depth map treeblock can be skipped in the 3D-HEVC mode decision.

3.2 Adaptive search range motion estimation

ME is the most computationally expensive task in the 3D-HEVC encoder, which is defined as the search of the best matched treeblock within a predefined region in the reference frame. The larger ME search range produces higher computational load, and a very small ME search range may reduce the coding performance due to poor matching results. A suitable ME search range can reduce the computational complexity of 3D-HEVC and also maintain the good RD performance.

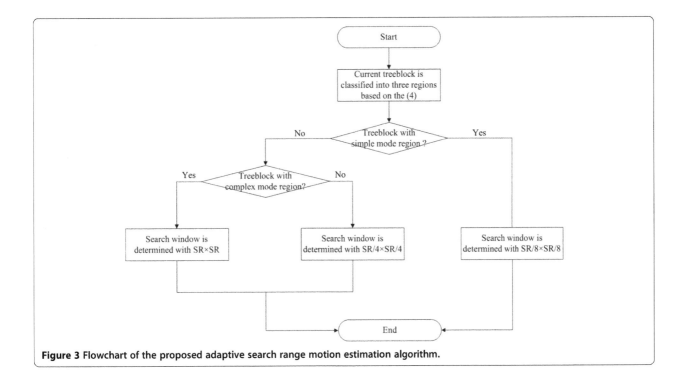

Figure 3 Flowchart of the proposed adaptive search range motion estimation algorithm.

Table 4 Analysis of view prediction and temporal prediction distributions for three treeblock types

Sequences	Treeblocks in simple mode region		Treeblocks in normal mode region		Treeblocks in complex mode region	
	T (%)	V (%)	T (%)	V (%)	T (%)	V (%)
Kendo	98.9	1.1	88.2	11.8	60.2	39.7
Balloons	97.5	2.5	84.1	15.9	68.6	31.4
Newspaper	99.7	0.3	92.3	7.8	71.3	29.7
Shark	98.2	1.8	85.2	14.8	64.2	35.9
Undo_Dancer	97.7	2.2	92.7	7.3	58.9	41.1
GT_Fly	95.8	4.2	89.9	10.1	54.7	45.3
Poznan_Street	97.9	2.1	88.4	11.6	61.5	38.5
Poznan_Hall2	96.2	3.7	91.7	8.3	70.1	30.0
Average	97.7	2.2	89.1	11.0	63.7	36.4

'T' and 'V' represent temporal prediction and view prediction, respectively.

In 3D video coding, since both depth map and texture video represent the same scene, it is likely for the depth map and texture video treeblock to have similar motion information. Based on this observation, we propose to use the mode complexity parameter (C) defined in Equation 3 to speed up the procedure of depth map coding DE search range computational complexity. According to the motion complexity of a depth map treeblock (based on Equation 3), we first classify the depth map treeblock to different categories in terms of DE search range as follows:

$$\text{Search range}_{depth} = \begin{cases} SR/8 \times SR/8 & \text{Treeblock} \in \text{simple mode region} \\ SR/4 \times SR/4 & \text{Treeblock} \in \text{normal mode region} \\ SR \times SR & \text{Treeblock} \in \text{complex mode region} \end{cases}$$

$$(5)$$

where SR represents the search range defined in the configuration file of the 3D-HEVC, and Search

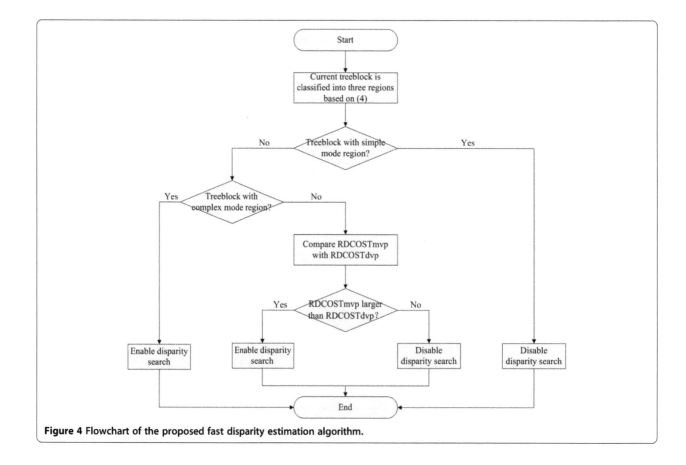

Figure 4 Flowchart of the proposed fast disparity estimation algorithm.

Table 5 Test sequence information

Sequence	Resolution	Frames	Two-view case	Three-view case
Kendo	1,024 × 768	300	1-3	1-3-5
Balloons	1,024 × 768	300	1-3	1-3-5
Newspaper	1,024 × 768	300	2-4	2-4-6
Shark	1,920 × 1,088	300	1-5	1-5-9
Undo_Dancer	1,920 × 1,088	250	1-5	1-5-9
GT_Fly	1,920 × 1,088	250	9-5	9-5-1
Poznan_Street	1,920 × 1,088	250	5-4	5-4-3
Poznan_Hall2	1,920 × 1,088	200	7-6	7-6-5

$range_{depth}$ is the adjusted search range of the corresponding treeblock in the depth map.

To verify legitimacy of the proposed adaptive search range motion estimation algorithm, extensive simulations have been conducted on eight video sequences to analyze the motion vector distribution for these three types of treeblocks. By exploiting the exhaustive mode decision in 3D-HEVC under the aforementioned test conditions, we investigate the motion vector distribution for these three types of treeblocks.

Table 3 shows the motion vector distribution for each type of treeblocks. It can be seen from Table 3 that for treeblocks in the simple mode region, more than 97% of all motion vectors lie in the [SR/8 × SR/8] window. In other words, if the maximum search range is set to SR/8, it will most likely cover about 97% of all motion vectors. For the treeblocks in normal mode region, about 97% of all motion vectors lie in the [SR/4 × SR/4] window. If the maximum search range is set to be SR/4, it will most likely cover about 97% of motion vectors. For the treeblocks in the complex mode region, the percentage of all motion vectors that lie in the [SR/16 × SR/16], [SR/8 × SR/8], and [SR/4 × SR/4] windows are relatively low, only about 51%, 72%, and 84%, respectively, and thus, 3D-HEVC motion vector search range cannot be reduced. The results shown in Table 3 demonstrate that the proposed adaptive search range motion estimation algorithm can accurately reduce the unnecessary ME search range in 3D-HEVC. A flowchart of the proposed adaptive search range motion estimation algorithm is given in Figure 3.

3.3 Fast disparity estimation for depth map coding

In the test model of 3D-HEVC, when coding the dependent views, the HEVC codec is modified by including some high-level syntax changes and the disparity-compensated prediction (DCP) techniques, similar to the inter-view prediction in the MVC extension of H.264/AVC [4]. In addition, different from coding dependent texture view, depth map is characterized by sharp edges and large regions with nearly constant values. The eight-tap interpolation filters that are used for ME interpolation in HEVC can produce ringing artifacts at sharp edges in the depth map, which are visible as disturbing components in synthesized intermediate views. For avoiding this issue and for decreasing the encoder and decoder complexity, the ME as well as the DE has been modified in a way that no interpolation is used. That means, for depth map, the inter-picture prediction is always performed with full-sample accuracy. For the actual DE, a block of samples in the reference picture is directly used as the prediction signal without interpolating any intermediate samples. In order to avoid the transmission of motion and disparity vectors with an unnecessary accuracy, full-sample accurate motion and disparity vectors are used for coding the depth map. The transmitted motion vector differences are coded using full-sample instead of quarter-sample precision. This modified technique achieves the highest possible depth map coding efficiency, but it results in extremely large encoding time which obstructs 3D-HEVC from practical application. In this paper, a fast DE algorithm for depth map coding is proposed to reduce 3D-HEVC computational complexity.

Table 6 Results of each individual algorithm compared to 3D-HEVC encoder in two-view case

Sequences	ETMD			ASRME			FDE		
	BDBR (%)	BDPSNR (dB)	Dtime (%)	BDBR (%)	BDPSNR (dB)	Dtime (%)	BDBR (%)	BDPSNR (dB)	Dtime (%)
Kendo	0.02	−0.01	−20.1	0.13	−0.03	−32.4	0.02	−0.00	−18.2
Balloons	0.01	−0.01	−17.3	0.09	−0.02	−36.8	0.02	−0.00	−22.7
Newspaper	0.00	−0.02	−26.8	0.21	−0.02	−42.1	0.04	−0.01	−15.6
Shark	−0.07	0.00	−9.8	0.07	−0.01	−61.2	0.75	−0.06	−30.8
Undo_Dancer	−0.12	0.01	−12.1	0.05	−0.01	−55.8	0.63	−0.05	−38.2
GT_Fly	−0.08	0.00	−7.6	0.08	−0.01	−63.2	0.82	−0.07	−36.9
Poznan_Street	0.01	−0.01	−26.5	0.21	−0.03	−43.9	0.06	−0.00	−16.5
Poznan_Hall2	0.02	−0.02	−31.2	0.16	−0.02	−42.6	0.09	−0.01	−24.3
Average	−0.03	−0.01	−18.9	0.13	−0.02	−47.3	0.30	−0.03	−25.4

Table 7 Results of each individual algorithm compared to 3D-HEVC encoder in three-view case

Sequences	ETMD			ASRME			FDE		
	BDBR (%)	BDPSNR (dB)	Dtime (%)	BDBR (%)	BDPSNR (dB)	Dtime (%)	BDBR (%)	BDPSNR (dB)	Dtime (%)
Kendo	0.01	−0.01	−20.9	0.10	−0.02	−33.1	0.02	−0.00	−18.7
Balloons	0.01	−0.00	−18.1	0.07	−0.02	−37.3	0.02	−0.00	−23.6
Newspaper	0.00	−0.02	−27.8	0.19	−0.02	−42.7	0.03	−0.01	−15.9
Shark	−0.05	0.00	−10.4	0.07	−0.01	−63.4	0.68	−0.05	−32.3
Undo_Dancer	−0.09	0.01	−12.7	0.05	−0.01	−56.7	0.57	−0.04	−39.7
GT_Fly	−0.07	0.00	−7.9	0.07	−0.01	−64.5	0.71	−0.05	−38.5
Poznan_Street	0.01	−0.01	−28.3	0.18	−0.03	−44.1	0.05	−0.00	−17.1
Poznan_Hall2	0.02	−0.01	−32.7	0.15	−0.02	−43.6	0.07	−0.01	−25.4
Average	−0.02	−0.01	−19.9	0.11	−0.02	−48.2	0.27	−0.02	−26.4

As mentioned in the above, disparity prediction is used to search the best matched block in frames from neighbor views. Although temporal prediction is generally the most efficient prediction mode in 3D-HEVC, it is sometimes necessary to use both DE and ME rather than only use ME to achieve better predictions. In general, temporal motion cannot be characterized adequately, especially for regions with non-rigid motion and regions with motion boundaries. For the former, ME based on simple translation movement usually fails and, thus, produces a poor prediction. For the latter, regions with motion boundaries are usually predicted using small mode sizes with a larger magnitude of motion vectors and higher residual energy [18]. Thus, the treeblocks with a simple mode region are more likely to choose temporal prediction (ME), and treeblocks with a complex mode region are more likely to choose inter-view prediction (DE).

By exploiting the exhaustive mode decision in the 3D-HEVC encoder under the aforementioned test experimental conditions in Section 3.2, we investigate the probabilities of choosing inter-view prediction and temporal prediction for each type of treeblocks in Table 4. For treeblocks with a simple mode region, the average probabilities of choosing temporal prediction and inter-view prediction are 97.7% and 2.2%, respectively. For treeblocks with a normal mode region, they are 89.1% and 11.0%, respectively. For treeblocks with a complex mode region, the probabilities are 63.7% and 36.4%, respectively. We can see from Table 4 that treeblocks with a simple mode region are much more likely to choose temporal prediction. Thus, for a simple mode region, the procedure of the inter-view prediction can be skipped with only a very low miss detection ratio by using the optimal prediction mode chosen by the full inter-view and temporal prediction modes. But for complex mode region treeblocks and treeblocks with a normal mode region, the average probabilities of choosing inter-view prediction are 36.4% and 11.0%, respectively. Although the test sequences such as 'Poznan_Hall2' and 'Newspaper' contain a large area of the homogeneous textures and low-activity motion, which are more likely to be encoded with temporal prediction, the probability of inter-view prediction for a treeblock with a normal mode region and complex mode region is still highest. Thus, if we disable inter-view prediction in the normal mode region and complex mode region, the coding efficiency loss is not negligible.

Table 8 Comparing the proposed overall algorithm compared with 3D-HEVC encoder

Sequences	Two-view case			Three-view case		
	BDBR (%)	BDPSNR (dB)	Dtime (%)	BDBR (%)	BDPSNR (dB)	Dtime (%)
Kendo	0.19	−0.03	−47.3	0.17	−0.03	−49.8
Balloons	0.13	−0.04	−51.9	0.11	−0.03	−53.2
Newspaper	0.24	−0.05	−54.2	0.19	−0.05	−56.8
Shark	0.79	−0.06	−83.4	0.72	−0.05	−84.9
Undo_Dancer	0.68	−0.07	−80.7	0.63	−0.06	−82.1
GT_Fly	0.83	−0.05	−86.3	0.79	−0.05	−87.5
Poznan_Street	0.31	−0.04	−53.1	0.26	−0.04	−56.7
Poznan_Hall2	0.27	−0.04	−57.6	0.23	−0.03	−59.3
Average	0.43	−0.05	−64.3	0.39	−0.04	−66.3

Table 9 Comparing the proposed overall algorithm compared with CACRS algorithm [16]

Sequences	Two-view case			Three-view case		
	BDBR (%)	BDPSNR (dB)	Dtime (%)	BDBR (%)	BDPSNR (dB)	Dtime (%)
Kendo	−1.52	0.08	−14.7	−1.87	0.09	−15.1
Balloons	−1.21	0.06	−21.4	−1.58	0.07	−22.8
Newspaper	−0.81	0.03	−19.3	−0.92	0.04	−19.7
Shark	−0.21	0.01	−33.9	−0.31	0.02	−35.2
Undo_Dancer	−0.47	0.02	−29.2	−0.56	0.02	−31.1
GT_Fly	−0.28	0.01	−36.2	−0.32	0.01	−38.6
Poznan_Street	−0.96	0.07	−19.8	−1.26	0.08	−20.2
Poznan_Hall2	−2.12	0.11	−21.8	−2.87	0.13	−22.6
Average	−0.95	0.05	−24.5	−1.21	0.06	−25.7

Based on the aforementioned analysis, we propose a fast disparity estimation algorithm in which a disparity search is selectively enabled. For treeblocks with a simple mode region, disparity search is skipped (only the RD cost of the MVP is used); while for treeblocks with a normal mode region, the RD cost of the MVP is compared with that of the disparity vector predictor (DVP). If the RD cost of MVP is larger than that of DVP, the disparity search is enabled; otherwise, it is disabled. For treeblocks with a complex mode region, disparity search is enabled (all the RD cost of MVP and DVP are used). A flowchart of the scheme is given in Figure 4.

3.4 Overall algorithm

Based on the aforementioned analysis, including the approaches of early termination mode decision, adaptive search range ME and fast DE for depth map coding, we propose a low-complexity depth map compression algorithm for 3D-HEVC as follows.

Step 1: start mode decision for a depth map treeblock.
Step 2: locate the spatial neighboring depth map treeblock and its co-located texture video treeblocks (shown in Figure 2) at the previously coded data. Derive the coding information from predictors in the depth map and texture video.
Step 3: derive the prediction mode of the co-located texture video treeblocks; if texture treeblock has no motion, perform early merge/skip mode decision and go to Step 7, else go to Step 4.
Step 4: compute C based on Equation 3 and T_1 and T_2 based on Equation 4; classify the current depth map treeblock into the simple mode region, normal mode region, and complex mode region.
Step 5: perform adaptive search range ME determination: for the treeblocks in a simple mode region, the search range window is reconfigured with [SR/8 × SR/8]; for the treeblock in a normal mode

region, the search range window is with [SR/4 × SR/4]; otherwise, the search range window is unchanged.
Step 6: perform variable size DE: for treeblocks with a simple mode region, disparity search is skipped, while for treeblocks with a complex mode region, disparity search is enabled. For treeblocks with a normal mode region, the RD cost of the MVP is compared with that of the DVP.
Step 7: determine the best prediction mode. Go to step 1 and proceed with next depth map treeblock.

4 Experimental results

In order to confirm the performance of the proposed low-complexity depth map compression algorithm, which is implemented on the recent 3D-HEVC Test Model (HTM ver.5.1), we show the results obtained in the test on eight sequences released by the JCT-3V Group. The detailed information of the test sequences is provided in Table 5. All the experiments are defined under the common test conditions (CTC) [19] required by JCT-3V. The encoder configuration is as follows: two-view case (coding order: left-right) and three-view case (coding order: center-left-right); GOP length 8 with an intra period of 24; HEVC codecs are configured with 8-bit internal processing; the coding treeblock has a fixed size of 64 × 64 pixels and a maximum CU depth level of 4, resulting in a minimum CU size of 8 × 8 pixels; search range of the ME is configured with 64, inter-view motion prediction mode on, P-I-P inter-view prediction; and CABAC is used as the entropy coder. The proposed algorithm is evaluated with QP combinations for texture video and depth map (25, 34), (30, 39), (35, 42), and (40, 45) (the first number is the texture video QP, the second number gives the depth map QP). The experiments test full-length frames for each sequence. After encoding, the intermediate rendered views were synthesized between each view. The intermediate rendered views are generated at the receiver using view

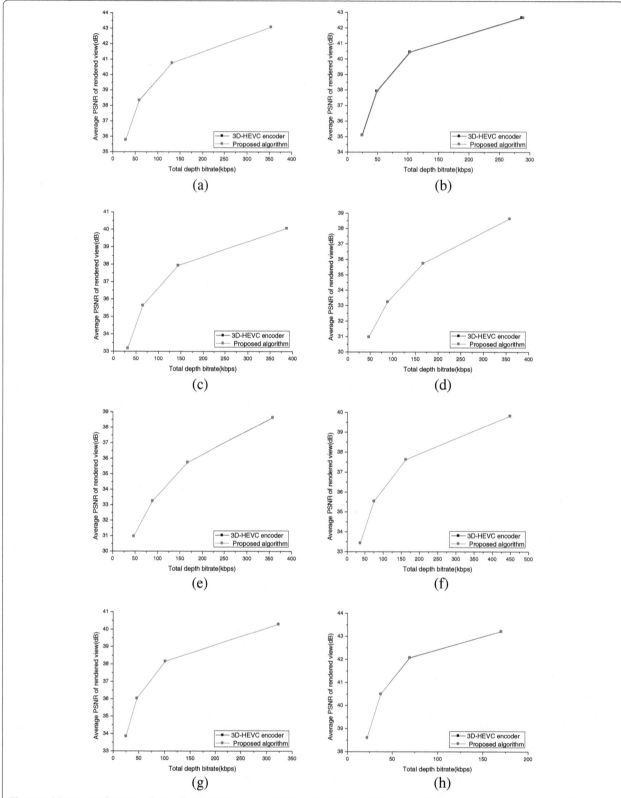

Figure 5 RD curves of proposed overall algorithm and 3D-HEVC under different QP combinations. RD curves of proposed overall algorithm and 3D-HEVC under different QP combinations for texture video and depth map (25, 34), (30, 39), (35, 42), and (40, 45). **(a)** Kendo, **(b)** Balloons, **(c)** Newspaper, **(d)** Shark, **(e)** Undo_Dancer, **(f)** GT_Fly, **(g)** Poznan_Street, **(h)** Poznan_Hall2.

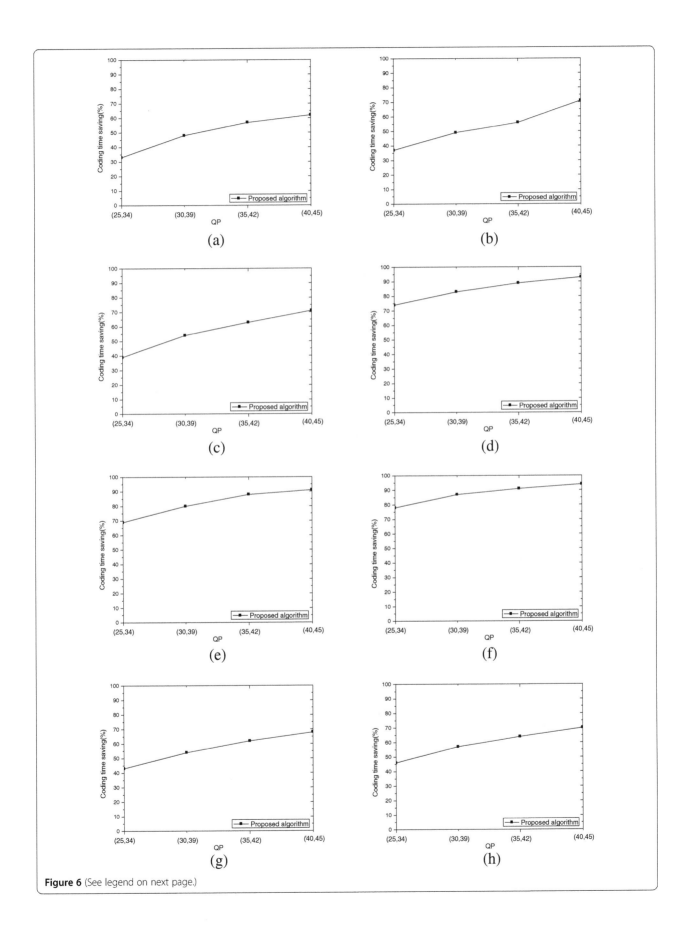

Figure 6 (See legend on next page.)

(See figure on previous page.)

Figure 6 Time-saving curves of proposed overall algorithm compared to 3D-HEVC under different QP combinations. Time-saving curves of proposed overall algorithm compared to 3D-HEVC under different QP combinations for texture video and depth map (25, 34), (30, 39), (35, 42), and (40, 45). **(a)** Kendo, **(b)** Balloons, **(c)** Newspaper, **(d)** Shark, **(e)** Undo_Dancer, **(f)** GT_Fly, **(g)** Poznan_Street, **(h)** Poznan_Hall2.

synthesis reference software (VSRS) algorithm provided by MPEG [20]. Since the depth map sequences are used for rendering instead of being viewed directly, we only compute the peak signal-to-noise ratio (PSNR) between the synthesized views using compressed depth map sequences and the synthesized views using uncompressed depth map sequences. The experimental results are presented in Tables 6, 7, 8, and 9 in which coding efficiency is measured with rendered PSNR and total bitrate (depth map), and computational complexity is measured with the consumed coding time. Since the proposed approaches affect only depth map intra coding, results for texture video coding are identical; thus, the texture video results are not included in the table. The Bjontegaard Delta PSNR (BDPSNR) [21] represents the average texture quality for synthesized views PSNR gain, Bjontegaard Delta Bitrate (BDBR) represents the improvement of total bitrates for depth map coding, and 'Dtime (%)' represents the entire depth map coding time change in percentage.

4.1 Individual performance results of the proposed algorithms

Tables 6 and 7 give individual evaluation results of the proposed algorithms compared with the original 3D-HEVC encoder (Table 6 in two-view case, Table 7 in three-view case), i.e., early termination mode decision (ETMD), adaptive search range motion estimation (ASRME), and fast disparity estimation (FDE), when they are applied alone. The proposed three algorithms can greatly reduce the encoding time with similar encoding efficiency for all sequences. For the ETMD algorithm, about 18.9% and 19.9% coding time has been reduced in the two-view and three-view conditions, respectively, with the highest gain of 32.7% in 'Poznan_Hall2' (two-view case) and the lowest gain of 7.6% in 'GT_Fly' (three-view case). It can be also observed that a consistent gain is obtained over all sequences under both conditions. The average PSNR drop for all the test sequences is 0.01 dB, which is negligible, and bitrate has been reduced by 0.02% to 0.03% on average, which indicates that the proposed ETMD algorithm can improve the bitrate performance for depth map compression in 3D-HEVC. For the proposed ASRME algorithm, 32.4% encoding time has been reduced with the maximum of 64.5% in two-view and three-view conditions. The coding efficiency loss is very negligible with a 0.02-dB PSNR drop or 0.11% to 0.13% bitrate increase. This result indicates that ASRME can efficiently skip unnecessary ME search

range computation in 3D-HEVC depth map coding. As far as the FDE algorithm, 25.4% and 26.4% coding time has been reduced in the two-view and three-view conditions, respectively; the average PSNR drop for all the test sequences is 0.02 to 0.03 dB, and the average increase of bitrate is 0.27% to 0.3%, which is negligible. The foregoing result analysis indicates that the FDE algorithm can efficiently reduce unnecessary DE computation time while maintaining nearly similar coding efficiency as the original 3D-HEVC encoder.

4.2 Combined results

In the following, we will analyze the experimental result of the proposed overall algorithm, which incorporates ETMD, ASRME, and FDE. The comparison result of the overall algorithm is shown in Table 8. The proposed overall algorithm reduces 64.3% and 66.3% encoding time on average under the two-view and three-view case, respectively, and achieves the better gain in coding speed among all the test sequence approaches compared to 3D-HEVC. Also shown is a consistent gain in coding speed for depth map compression with a minimum of 47.3% in 'Kendo' (two-view case) and the maximum of 87.5% in 'GT_Fly' (two-view case). For sequences with ground-truth depth map like 'Shark', 'Undo_Dancer', and 'GT_Fly', the proposed algorithm saves more than 80% coding time. The computation reduction is particularly high because the variable size ME and DE decision process of a significant number of depth map treeblocks are reasonably skipped. Meanwhile, the coding efficiency loss is negligible, where the average PSNR drop for the entire test sequences is 0.04 to 0.05 dB or the average increase of bitrate is 0.39% to 0.43%. Therefore, the proposed overall algorithm can reduce more than 64% depth map coding time with the same RD performance of the original 3D-HEVC encoder.

In addition to the 3D-HEVC encoder, we also compare the proposed overall algorithm with a state-of-the-art fast algorithm for 3D-HEVC (content adaptive complexity reduction scheme (CACRS) [16]) in Table 9. Compared with CACRS, the proposed overall algorithm performs better on all the sequences and achieves more than 24.5% coding time saving, with a minimum of 14.7% in 'Kendo' (two-view case) and the maximum of 38.6% in 'GT_Fly' (three-view case). Meanwhile, the proposed overall algorithm achieves a better depth map coding performance, with 0.05- to 0.06-dB PSNR increase or 0.95% to 1.21% bitrate decrease for all the test sequences compared to CACRS.

Figures 5 and 6 gives more detailed experiment results (RD and time-saving curves) of the proposed overall algorithm compared to 3D-HEVC in the three-view case. As shown in Figures 5 and 6, the proposed low-complexity depth map compression algorithm can achieve a consistent time saving over a large bitrate range with almost negligible loss in PSNR and increment in bitrate.

5 Conclusions

This paper presents a low-complexity depth map compression algorithm to reduce the computational complexity of the 3D-HEVC encoder by exploiting three fast approaches, i.e., early termination mode decision, adaptive search range motion estimation, and fast disparity estimation for depth map coding. The recent 3D-HEVC test model is applied to evaluate the proposed algorithm. The experimental results show that the proposed algorithm can significantly reduce the computational complexity of depth map compression and maintain almost the same RD performances as the 3D-HEVC encoder.

Competing interests
The authors declare that they have no competing interests.

Acknowledgements
The authors would like to thank the editors and anonymous reviewers for their valuable comments. This work was supported in part by the National Natural Science Foundation of China under grant No. 61302118, 61401404, 61340059, and 61272038; the Scientific and Technological Project of Zhengzhou under Grant No.141PPTGG360; and in part by the Doctorate Research Funding of Zhengzhou University of Light Industry, under grant No. 2013BSJJ047.

Author details
[1]College of Computer and Communication Engineering, Zhengzhou University of Light Industry, No. 5 Dongfeng Road, Zhengzhou 450002, China. [2]Software Engineering College, Zhengzhou University of Light Industry, Zhengzhou 450002, China.

References
1. GJ Sullivan, JM Boyce, C Ying, J-R Ohm, CA Segall, A Vetro, Standardized extensions of high efficiency video coding (HEVC). IEEE J. Sel. Top. Sign. Proces. **7**(6), 1001–1016 (2013)
2. GJ Sullivan, J-R Ohm, W-J Han, T Wiegand, Overview of the high efficiency video coding (HEVC) standard. IEEE Trans. Circuits Syst. Video Technol. **22**(12), 1649–1668 (2012)
3. K Müller, H Schwarz, D Marpe, C Bartnik, S Bosse, H Brust, T Hinz, H Lakshman, P Merkle, H Rhee, G Tech, M Winken, T Wiegand, 3D high efficiency video coding for multi-view video and depth data. IEEE Trans. Image Process. **22**(9), 3366–3378 (2013)
4. L Zhang, G Tech, K Wegner, S Yea, in *Joint Collaborative Team on 3D Video Coding Extensions (JCT-3V) Document JCT3V-E1005, 5th Meeting*, 3D-HEVC test model 5 (Vienna, Austria 2013).
5. H Oh, YS Ho, in *Proc. The Pacific-Rim Symposium on Image and Video Technology*, H.264-based depth map sequence coding using motion information of corresponding texture video (LNCS 2006), **4319**, 898–907
6. M Wang, X Jin, S Goto, in *Proc. 28th Picture Coding Symp.*, Difference detection based early mode termination for depth map coding in MVC (2010), pp. 502–505
7. S Tsang, Y Chan, W Siu, Efficient intra prediction algorithm for smooth regions in depth coding. Electron. Lett. **48**(18), 1117–1119 (2012)
8. G Cernigliaro, F Jaureguizar, J Cabrera, N García, Low complexity mode decision and motion estimation for H.264/AVC based depth maps encoding in free viewpoint video. IEEE Trans. Circuits Syst. Video Techn. **23**(5), 769–783 (2013)
9. M Maitrea, MN Do, Depth and depth–color coding using shape-adaptive wavelets. J. Vis. Commun. Image **21**(5–6), 513–522 (2010)
10. S Milani, P Zanuttigh, M Zamarin, S Forchhammer, in *Proc. IEEE Int. Conf. Multimedia and Expo(ICME)*, Efficient depth map compression exploiting segmented color data (Barcelona, 2011), pp.1–6
11. L Shen, P An, Z Liu, Z Zhang, Low complexity depth coding assisted by coding information from color video. IEEE Trans. Broadcasting **60**(1), 128–133 (2014)
12. Q Zhang, P An, Y Zhang, L Shen, Z Zhang, Low complexity multiview video plus depth coding. IEEE Trans. Consumer Electron. **57**(4), 1857–1865 (2011)
13. Z Gu, J Zheng, N Ling P Zhang, in *Proc. 2013 IEEE International Conference on Multimedia and Expo Workshops*, Fast depth modeling mode selection for 3D HEVC depth intra coding (2013), pp. 1–4
14. Y Song, Y Ho, in *Proc. IEEE 11th IVMSP Workshop*, Simplified inter-component depth modeling in 3D-HEVC, (2013), pp. 1–4
15. M Zhang, C Zhao, J Xu, H Bai, in *Proc. IEEE International Symposium on Circuits and Systems(ISCAS)*, A fast depth-map wedgelet partitioning scheme for intra prediction in 3D video coding (2013), pp.2852–2855
16. HRTohidypour, MT Pourazad, P Nasiopoulos, V Leung, in *Proc. 18th International Conference on Digital Signal Processing (DSP 2013)*, A Content Adaptive Complexity Reduction Scheme for HEVC-Based 3D Video Coding (2013), pp.1–5
17. M Winken, H Schwarz, T Wiegand, in *Proc. Picture Coding Symp.*, Motion vector inheritance for high efficiency 3D video plus depth coding (Krakow, Poland 2012), pp. 53–56
18. L Shen, Z Liu, T Yan, Z Zhang, P An, View-adaptive motion estimation and disparity estimation for low complexity multiview video coding. IEEE Trans. Circuits Syst. Video Technol. **20**(6), 925–930 (2010)
19. D Rusanovskyy, K Mueller, A Vetro, *Common test conditions of 3DV core experiments* (Joint Collaborative Team on 3D Video Coding Extensions (JCT-3V) document JCT3V-E1100, 5th Meeting, Vienna, AT, 2013)
20. M Tanimoto, T Fujii, K Suzuki, View Synthesis Algorithm in View Synthesis Reference Software 2.0 (VSRS 2.0), (Lausanne, Switzerland, ISO/IEC JTC1/SC29/WG11 M16090, Feb. 2008).
21. G Bjontegaard, *Calculation of average PSNR difference between RD-curves* (13th VCEG-M33 Meeting, Austin, TX, 2001)

14

Vehicle color classification using manifold learning methods from urban surveillance videos

Yu-Chen Wang[1*], Chin-Chuan Han[2], Chen-Ta Hsieh[1] and Kuo-Chin Fan[1]

Abstract

Color identification of vehicles plays a significant role in crime detection. In this study, a novel scheme for the color identification of vehicles is proposed using the locating algorithm of regions of interest (ROIs) as well as the color histogram features from still images. A coarse-to-fine strategy was adopted to efficiently locate the ROIs for various vehicle types. Red patch labeling, geometrical-rule filtering, and a texture-based classifier were cascaded to locate the valid ROIs. A color space fusion together with a dimension reduction scheme was designed for color classification. Color histograms in ROIs were extracted and classified by a trained classifier. Seven different classes of color were identified in this work. Experiments were conducted to show the performance of the proposed method. The average rates of ROI location and color classification were 98.45% and 88.18%, respectively. Moreover, the classification efficiency of the proposed method was up to 18 frames per second.

Keywords: Color classification; Manifold learning; Dimension reduction; Coarse-to-fine strategy; Nearest feature line

1. Introduction

Recently, vehicle color identification has been widely in demand for video surveillance on urban roads. When an accident occurs, license plate (LP) numbers are an intuitive and direct cue for the escaping vehicle. However, these cues are ineffective because small LPs can be missed due to view angle or distance. Witnesses only tend to remember the escape vehicle's color or type. Moreover, the government has installed cameras on roads for traffic monitoring or crime prevention. The color identification from video data can assist police both in crime prevention and later investigation.

Earlier, color feature descriptors have been widely used in content-based image retrieval (CBIR) [1,2]. High quality images with less illumination impact were required in their studies. However, the color identification of vehicles from outdoor video clips is sensitive to camera installation and environmental factors. First, the sequential images captured from outdoor cameras are distorted by chromatic polarization and white balance functions. Second, the performance is influenced by illumination and weather conditions. As illustrated in Figure 1, classification errors

always occur because the mixed sample distributions of colors cannot be clearly separated in various color spaces. Many researchers try to reduce illumination impacts in classification by two approaches: *discriminative feature extraction* and *image-based color calibration*. Basically, discriminative features are extracted from the color histogram of an individual color space or the fused spaces. Histogram is the widely used object representation in color classification or image retrieval. In MPEG-7 standard, color channels are encoded and quantized to generate the color histogram, e.g., scalable color descriptor (SCD). Baek et al. [3] extracted the two-dimensional histogram features on the hue (H) and saturation (S) plane. Kim et al. [4] quantized color features on channels H, S, and intensity (I) and found the best combination of features. In [5], the color histograms on channels H and S are classified to determine the red, yellow, green, and blue colors, while the normalized features on channels RGB are classified to determine the black, gray, and white colors. The choice of a color space is a critical issue in identifying color objects. Tsai et al. [6] and Chen et al. [7] used the principal component analysis (PCA)-based technique to calculate the eigenvectors and the corresponding eigenvalues from the training samples in color space RGB. After the transformations of color spaces, the classifiers, e.g., multi-class support vector machine (SVM) [3], k-nearest neighbor (KNN) [4], Bayesian

---

* Correspondence: m09502062@chu.edu.tw
[1]Department of Computer Science and Information Engineering, National Central University, Taoyuan, Taiwan
Full list of author information is available at the end of the article

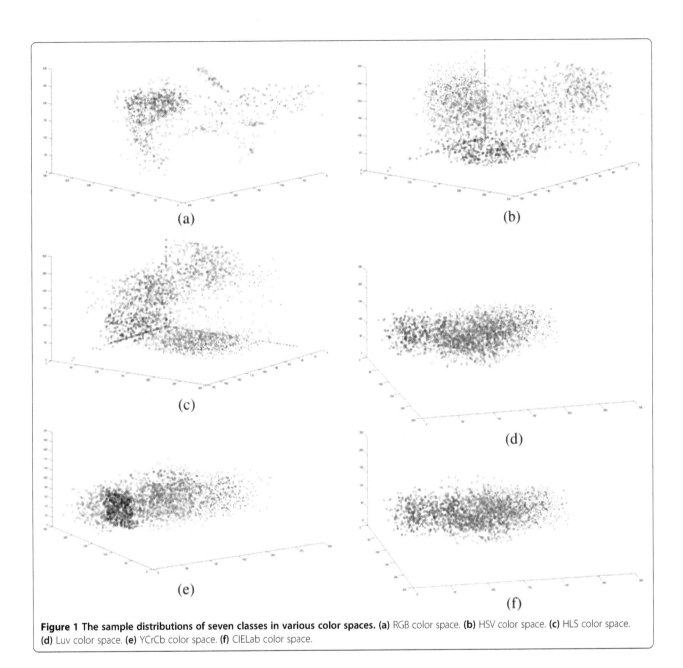

Figure 1 The sample distributions of seven classes in various color spaces. (a) RGB color space. **(b)** HSV color space. **(c)** HLS color space. **(d)** Luv color space. **(e)** YCrCb color space. **(f)** CIELab color space.

classifier [6], or the multiple instance learning (MIL) [7], were trained to identify vehicles' colors. Furthermore, Brown [8] evaluates four color feature descriptors: *standard color histogram, weighted color histogram, variable bin size color histogram,* and *color correlogram.*

On the other hand, image-based color calibration is an enhancement method on image quality to reduce illumination variation. Li et al. [9] propose a classification method using the template-matching strategy. Before the identification process, a color calibration procedure is executed to adjust the image colors [10]. The relative error distances in color space *HSI* are calculated to identify vehicle colors. Similarly, color compensation is performed for

color calibration in [11]. Shen et al. [12] present an image correction algorithm which combines synthesized texture information to recover color information in overexposure regions. Guo et al. [13] separately recover the color and lightness of overexposure regions from a single image. The lightness in channel L is recovered using the exposure likelihood, and the colors in channels a and b are corrected by the weighted summation of neighborhoods. However, their methods [12,13] cannot be used in a real-time surveillance system because of the high computational loading.

In color histogram-based classification, images with similar colors are represented in the same color histogram because similar colors fall into the same bins due to the quantization. The original color components should be represented by more bits to keep more details, e.g., 8 bits of 256 levels. In addition, various color spaces represent different meanings. It is a hard work to accurately choose the color space for the classification on various applications. Stokman et al. [14] propose a fusion scheme to integrate several color spaces. Twelve color components are weighted and summarized by a linear programming method [15]. In this study, six color spaces of 18 components, *RGB*, *CIELab*, *YCrCb*, *HSV*, *Luv*, and *HLS*, were catenated to generate a color histogram. However, the dimensionality of this histogram-based descriptor is very high, and samples of the same color are distributed in a manifold structure. Recently, many manifold learning and dimensional reduction (DR) approaches are proposed for face recognition, image classification, image retrieval, etc. Local linear embedding (LLE) [16], locality preservation projection (LPP) [17], nearest feature space embedding (NFSE) [18], ISOMAP [19], and Laplacian eigenmap (LE) [20] try to preserve the structural locality of samples which are distributed in a manifold structure. Even though the objective functions in these methods are different, the goal, preserving the manifold structure, is the same.

In traffic surveillance systems, cameras are frequently set up on islands or shoulders of roads. They capture vehicle images from the front or back view. The safety cameras commonly set on highways or urban roads face the lanes and capture the vehicle images of back view. In this study, vehicle color in multi-lanes was identified outdoors from the back. The identification procedure consisted of two modules as shown in Figure 2: The location of a valid ROI and the color classification. Unlike the traditional background subtraction methods, which need video sequences and are very sensitive to illumination changes, the taillight detection algorithm has been designed to obtain the valid ROI from video frames. The valid regions of interest (ROIs)

were determined by the detected red patches (e.g., vehicle taillights) and their corresponding pairs. The unfeasible taillight pairs were pre-filtered out and eliminated using geometric rules. It is necessary to identify the vehicle types because the locations of ROI are different for different vehicle types. Before the second module, non-panel regions, e.g., vehicle windows or other reflecting area, were eliminated. Second, the color histograms in an ROI were classified using a trained classifier. A manifold learning algorithm, called nearest feature line embedding (NFLE) [18], reduces the dimensionality of color features for reducing the illumination impacts. NFLE discovers the intrinsic manifold structure from the data by considering the relationship among samples. Not only the dimensions are reduced, but also the illumination impacts are reduced. Finally, the vehicle colors were determined by the dominant colors in the ROI. Seven colors, e.g., red, yellow, blue, green, black, white, and gray, were identified in this study.

The contributions of this work are twofold and briefly summarized in the following: The taillight detection and pairing algorithms fast locate ROI candidates from video frames. Foreground objects are found without the construction of background model in various urban roads. Furthermore, vehicle types are identified to correctly locate ROI regions. Second, the proposed manifold learning method, NFLE, preserves the local structures among samples in manifold distributions. The uncollected color prototypes are linearly approximated from collected prototypes by the NFL strategy in feature spaces. Both the high dimensionality and illumination impacts are reduced under various weather conditions. Comparing with our previous work in [21], four problems have been solved in this work. First, the proposed method locates multiple valid ROIs from video frames in multi-lane. Second, the vehicle types are identified by an SVM classifier instead of a heuristic rule for accurately locating ROI. The type identification also reduces the taillight pairing errors.

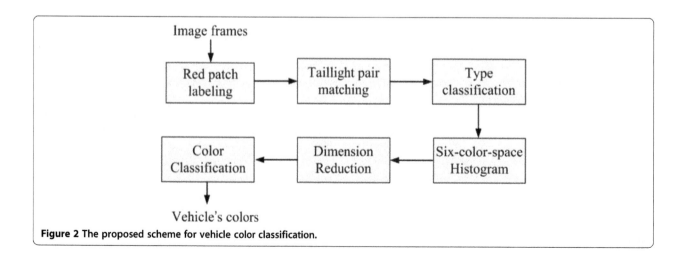

Figure 2 The proposed scheme for vehicle color classification.

Third, the fused color descriptors in multiple color spaces are adopted rather than a single descriptor in a specified color space. Illumination impacts are reduced by generating the virtual prototypes from the linear combination of collected prototypes. Fourth, manifold learning algorithm reduces the high feature dimensions to find the discriminative features. In addition, the NFL strategy is embedded into the transformation. Instead of the template matching strategy in [21], an SVM classifier has been trained for classification. The proposed method is executed on the large-scale surveillance videos in various weather conditions and the color classification performance is significantly enhanced.

The rest of this paper is organized as follows: The location of valid ROIs is presented in Section 2. Vehicle color identification using a trained classifier is given in Section 3. Some experimental results to show the validity of the proposed method are presented in Section 4. Some conclusions are given in Section 5.

2. Location of region of interest (ROI)

Object detection is widely used in many computer vision applications. A detector is trained from the collected training samples, and a window slides an image from left to right and top to bottom in multi-scales to identify the objects. Homogenous objects, e.g., license plates and faces, are frequently detected by a trained detector. It is a challenge to locate the ROI from various vehicle shapes using the window-based detection approach. In addition, much time is needed to check a large number of sliding windows using brute force searching. Dule et al. [22] manually assigned the ROIs on vehicle hoods from the detected foreground objects. However, automatic ROI finding is a critical issue in surveillance systems. Wu et al. [23] find the ROIs by integrating the results of background subtraction and color segmentation. An SVM-based classifier in a two-layer structure is then applied to classify the pixels in ROI. Yang et al. [5] find the ROIs by using the geometric rule-based scheme. In this study, a coarse-to-fine strategy was adopted for efficiently identifying the ROIs from various types of vehicles. Three steps, *red patch labeling, taillight pair matching*, and *shape feature verification*, were performed to locate the ROIs from still images. First, red patches were detected for finding possible taillight candidates using several simple thresholding rules. Then, possible ROIs were generated from the taillight pairs, and geometric rules filtered out improbable taillight pairs to determine the valid ROI areas. Compared with the positions of taillight pairs, three vehicle types, e.g., sedan type (sedan, coupe, or Hatchback), SUV type (sport utility vehicles or recreational vehicles), and truck type (caravan, pickup truck, or autotruck), were defined for color classification. After that, shape features in a specified mask were verified to identify the exact ROI.

2.1 Red patch labeling

Since the sunlight shines vertically on the vehicle hoods, these are prone to reflect white in image frames. These overexposure regions generated incorrect results in color classification. Therefore, the valid color regions were obtained from the back view of vehicles. The ROI identification reduced overexposure during color classification.

In our previous work [24], the red pixels of taillights were detected using color features. The Cr component of pixels possesses more discriminant power than the other components in red pixel labeling. Image pixels in color space RGB were transformed to space $YCbCr$ using Eq. (1). Each pixel $I(x, y)$ in space $YCbCr$ was next classified as a red pixel if satisfying the conditions in Eq. (2):

$$\begin{bmatrix} Y \\ Cr \\ Cb \end{bmatrix} = \begin{bmatrix} 0.257 & 0.504 & 0.098 \\ -0.148 & -0.291 & 0.439 \\ 0.439 & -0.368 & -0.071 \end{bmatrix} \begin{bmatrix} R \\ G \\ B \end{bmatrix} + \begin{bmatrix} 16 \\ 128 \\ 128 \end{bmatrix} \quad (1)$$

$$I(x, y) = \begin{cases} 255 & \text{if } \theta_{Cr} \le Cr(x, y) \text{ and,} \\ & \theta_{Cb1} \le Cb(x, y) \le \theta_{Cb2}; \\ 0 & \text{otherwise.} \end{cases} \quad (2)$$

Here, threshold values θ_{Cr} and $[\theta_{Cb1}, \theta_{Cb2}]$ were manually assigned for channels Cr and Cb, respectively. Since yellow and red pixels in space $YCbCr$ possess similar features, yellow pixels can frequently be misclassified as red pixels using the simple rules, i.e., the loose criteria in Eq. (2) and the pre-defined thresholds. Since yellow and red pixels were mixed on the $CbCr$ plan, false alarms were frequently generated (see Figure 3b). When a yellow taxi was checked, a lot of yellow pixels were misclassified as red pixels. An SVM-based classifier was further trained to eliminate the false alarms as shown in Figure 3c.

The coarse-to-fine strategy was adopted in red patch labeling for efficiency. First, image pixels in space RGB were converted to space $YCbCr$. Pixels with features (Cr and Cb) were checked using the simple criteria. If they satisfied the simple criteria, eight neighbors around them were further extracted and encoded to generate the 18-dimensional vectors in the SVM-based classification [25]. Based on the coarse-to-fine strategy, a large number of non-red pixels were filtered out using the simple criteria, and few patches of 3 by 3 were verified with the complex SVM-classifier.

2.2 Taillight pair matching

A binary image was obtained from the previous step, and red patches were labeled from the binary image. Three geometrical rules were tested for selecting the candidate pairs. The first one was to filter out too small or too large regions from the labeled results. Two thresholds θ_{s1} and θ_{s2} were manually set to reserve the red patches whose sizes fell within the range $[\theta_{s1}, \theta_{s2}]$. Furthermore, if a labeled patch was larger than θ_{s2} and its compactness was high, a red vehicle was identified. The density of labeled

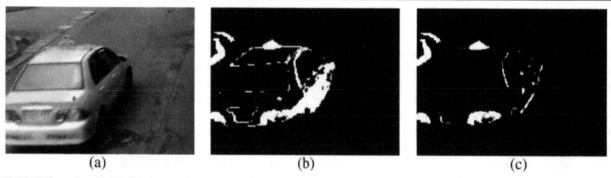

Figure 3 The red patch labeling for a taxi. (a) A taxi image. **(b)** The misdetected red pixels using simple rules. **(c)** The labeled results verified by an SVM classifier.

points within a bounded box was calculated for a specified patch P in the second rule. If the density of a bounded box was greater than θ_d, patch P was reserved; otherwise, it was eliminated. The last rule considered the angle of taillight pairs. C_2^N possible pairs were checked, where N was the number of red patches surviving from the first two rules. The impossible taillight pairs were filtered out by the line angle and length criteria. The line angle of two patch centers $C_i(x_i, y_i)$ and $C_j(x_j, y_j)$ was calculated, i.e., $\theta = \tan^{-1}(y_j - y_i/x_j - x_i)$. A taillight pair was chosen; if its length was within a range $[l_1, l_2] = [50, 150]$ and its line angle was close to zero, e.g., within $-5°$ to $+5°$. As abovementioned, the candidate red patches are detected by Section 2.1; then, each candidate red path can be paired as taillight pair by using geometric rules which is described in this section. Thus, the valid ROI region in the image frame is set with a fix region according to taillight pair.

2.3 Type classification using shape features

Using the geometrical rules in the previous section, the remaining pairs were regarded as the taillight pairs. However, two problems occurred especially in the multi-lane cases. First, the left taillight of a vehicle matched the right taillight of another vehicle as shown in Figure 4a,b. The second problem was that a fixed ROI locating rule was not suitable for all vehicle types. Different vehicle types need different ROIs for color classification. Figure 4c,d illustrates the improper ROI problems for trucks and SUVs using the generation rule for sedans. In Figure 4c, the invalid ROI, the chassis shadow and the partial ground, was generated using the same rule of sedans. On the other hand, the windshield of SUV was located for the ROI as shown in Figure 4d. Thereafter, vehicle type classification is needed for locating the valid ROIs. Thus, vehicle type identification was needed to generate the desired ROIs using complex features, e.g., shape features. Three issues were considered for vehicle type identification: *checked region determination*, *feature representation*, and *classifier design*.

The checked window for type classification was determined by the taillight pair. The reference length of one taillight pair d determined the size of a verified region $d \times d$ as shown in Figure 5. This region was normalized to a fixed size of 64 by 64. On average, fewer than ten pairs were checked in an image frame. This region was next represented by the histogram of oriented gradients (HOG) [26]. The HOG features of 1,764 in a verified ROI were extracted for classification. An SVM classifier of multiclass was trained using HOG features for vehicle type classification. One thousand two hundred image samples of four classes, i.e., sedan type, SUV type, truck type, and non-vehicle type, were collected for training. Figure 6a shows several illustrations for training the multi-class SVM classifier. In the training set, sedans, coupes, or Hatchbacks are classified as the 'sedan' type. Similarly, sport-utility vehicles and recreational vehicles are classified as the 'SUV' type; and caravans, pickup trucks, and autotrucks are classified as the 'truck' type. Moreover, the samples of 'non-vehicle' type are also collected for training. After the vehicle type classification, the ROI for a specified vehicle type was determined by its corresponding rule. For example, the ROIs of SUVs were located at the bottom of taillight pairs, while the ROIs of trucks were located at the top of taillight pairs. The ROIs of sedan type, SUV type, and truck type were determined, drawn by the blue rectangles as shown in Figure 6b-d. The color features in these ROIs are classified in the color classification below.

3. Eigenspace-based color classification

As is generally known, the classification process is composed of three steps in pattern recognition (PR): feature representation, feature discriminant analysis, and classifier design. In this study, a color space fusion plus dimension reduction scheme was designed for color classification. Color histograms in ROIs were extracted, reduced, and classified by a multi-class SVM classifier.

Figure 4 Mismatched taillight pairs and invalid ROIs. (a) and **(b)** is the mismatched taillight pairs. **(c)** and **(d)** is the invalid ROIs using the rules for sedans.

3.1 Feature representation: linear color feature combination

Many color spaces [27], e.g., *RGB, HSV, HLS, CIELab, YCrCb,* ..., etc., were explored in color classification. The choice of a color space was critical in identifying vehicle colors. Though color spaces were interpreted in many different models, no color space could be regarded as a universal space. A selection and fusion scheme proposed by Stokman et al. [14] combines many color spaces, and the better results are achieved. Twelve color components were weighted and summarized with a linear programming method in [15]. In this study, a color histogram was extracted from the color pixels in an ROI

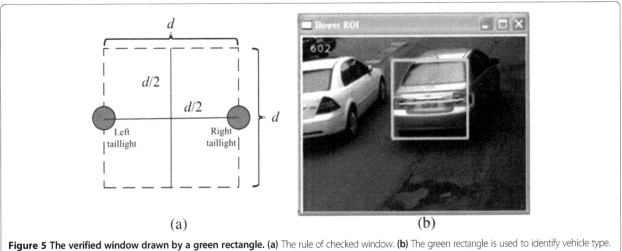

Figure 5 The verified window drawn by a green rectangle. (a) The rule of checked window. **(b)** The green rectangle is used to identify vehicle type.

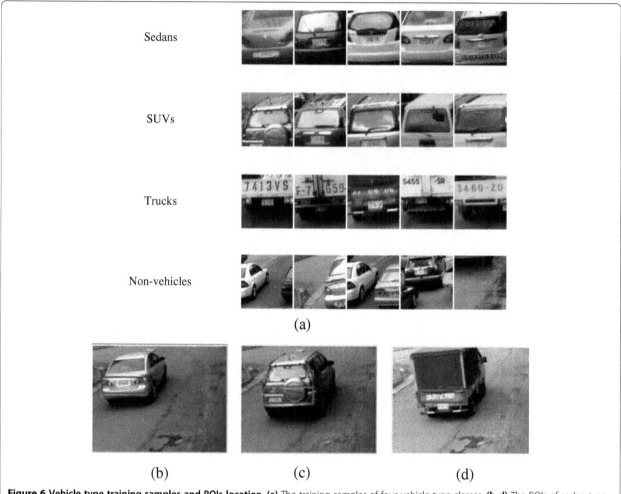

Sedans

SUVs

Trucks

Non-vehicles

(a)

(b)   (c)   (d)

Figure 6 Vehicle type training samples and ROIs location. (a) The training samples of four vehicle type classes. **(b-d)** The ROIs of sedan type, SUV type, and truck type drawn by the blue rectangles.

for feature representation. A window of w by w slides the ROI from left to right and top to bottom; here, $w = 20$. The color component for each pixel was quantized into 256 levels. The statistical histogram of length 256 was obtained. Eighteen histograms of six color spaces, i. e., *RGB*, *CIELab*, *YCrCb*, *HSV*, *Luv*, and *HLS* were combined to represent the ROI's color. The feature vector of length $4,608 = 256 \times 6 \times 3$ in this window was extracted as shown in Figure 7. This descriptor with high dimensions was reduced to a lower dimensional space for reducing illumination impacts.

A toy example is given in the following. In order to show the reconstruction of intrinsic manifold structure using eigenspace approaches, 1,400 patches of size 20 by 20 of seven color classes are collected for training. These patches are drawn by their corresponding colors in six color spaces *RGB*, *YCrCb*, *HSV*, *HLS*, *Luv*, and *CIELab* as shown in Figure 1a-f, respectively. In these figures, cross marks represent the samples of white color due to the white papers, and circle marks of pink color represent the

samples of gray color for the clear representation. These samples of seven classes are heavily mixed due to the illumination factors. The features in six color spaces are catenated to generate a new vector of length 4,608. The same class patches under various illumination conditions are represented in different colors, e.g., the ROI templates of dark yellow, general yellow, and bright yellow colors as shown in Figure 8. They are classified as 'class yellow'. According to the consequences in Li's approach for face recognition [28], they claimed that 'the feature line approximates variants of the two prototypes under variations in pose, illumination, and expression'. A linear model virtually interpolates an infinite number of prototypes of the class in feature spaces. Similarly, the features of general yellow color are obtained from the linear combination of features of dark yellow and bright yellow features.

3.2 Feature discriminant analysis: dimension reduction (DR)
LPP [17] and LLE [16] are two popular manifold learning algorithms which are applied to keep the manifold

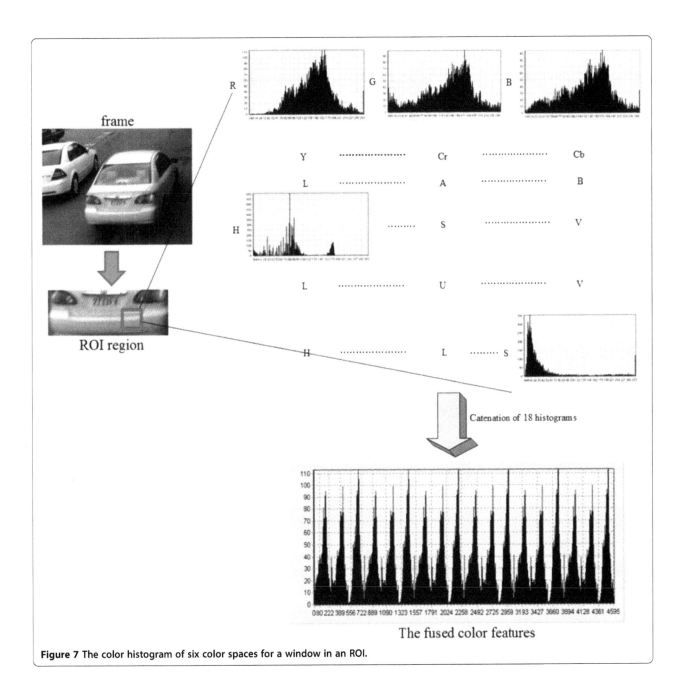

The fused color features

Figure 7 The color histogram of six color spaces for a window in an ROI.

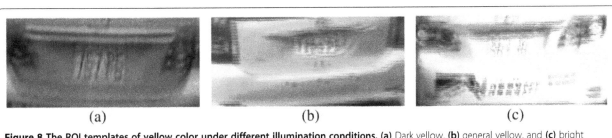

Figure 8 The ROI templates of yellow color under different illumination conditions. (a) Dark yellow, **(b)** general yellow, and **(c)** bright yellow samples.

structure of samples. They try to minimize the objective functions to obtain the best transformation for DR. Though their objective functions are represented in different forms, their goals are the same. Moreover, the two objective functions have been proved to be equivalent in [29]. Both of them were represented in a Laplacian matrix form. The best transformation matrix was composed of the eigenvectors with the smallest corresponding eigenvalues by solving the general eigenvalue decomposition problem. Two neighboring samples in a high-dimensional space were neighbors in a low-dimensional space in the LPP-based minimization.

The NFLE transformation [18] was a new manifold learning method based on the point-to-line (p-2-l) distance measurement which was originated from the nearest linear combination (NLC) approach [28]. The NFLE method tried to find a discriminative subspace for reducing the histogram dimensions of six color spaces for feature extraction. The reduced subspace had more discriminative power than any one specified color space. Before the classifier training, the PCA and NFL processes were used to reduce the feature dimensions. The NFLE transformation is briefly described below.

Given N training samples $x_1, x_2 \ldots x_N \in R^D$ constituting C classes, new samples $y_1, y_2 \ldots y_N \in R^d$, $m << M$, were obtained in a low-dimensional space with a linear projection $y_i = W^T x_i$. Consider a specified point y_i in the transformed space; the distance from point y_i to a feature line was defined as $||y_i - f_{m,n}(y_i)||$, in which $f_{m,n}(y_i)$ was the projected point of line $L_{m,n}$. Point $f_{m,n}(y_i)$ is a virtually constructed point which is generated by points y_m and y_n. In the training phase, it is a hard task to collect all possible prototypes in various outdoor illuminations. The NFL strategy creates more virtual points to efficiently represent the vehicle colors. For example, y_m and y_n can be regarded as the samples of bright yellow and dark yellow, respectively. Point $f_{m,n}(y_i)$ is considered as the general yellow sample by linearly weighting samples y_m and y_n.

The scatter computation of feature points to feature lines were calculated and embedded during the discriminant analysis phase. C_2^{N-1} possible generated lines for point y_i were more than $N-1$ points in the conventional point-to-point (p-2-p) methods, e.g., LPP and LLE. Thus, the p-2-l method retained much more scatter information than the conventional p-2-p-based methods. In addition, the NFL metric was embedded into the transformation through the discriminant analysis phase instead of in the matching phase [22]. The objective function of NFLE is defined as follows:

$$W^* = \arg \min_{W} \sum_{i} \sum_{m \neq n} \left\| y_i - f_{m,n}(y_i) \right\|^2 w_{m,n}(y_i) \qquad (3)$$

Here, weight $w_{m,n}(y_i)$ represents the connectivity strength for point y_i and line $L_{m,n}$. Since the objective function in

Eq. (3) was represented as a Laplacian matrix, the topology of samples could be preserved. Furthermore, the within-class scatter matrix S_w was calculated as follows:

$$S_w = \sum_{p=1}^{C} \left(\sum_{\substack{x_i \in C_p \\ L_{m,n} \in F_{K_1}(x_i, C_p)}} \left(x_i - f_{m,n}(x_i) \right) \left(x_i - f_{m,n}(x_i) \right)^T \right), \text{ and}$$

$$(4)$$

where $F_{K_1}(x_i, C_p)$ represents the K_1 nearest feature lines within the same class C_p of point x_i. The within-class scatter matrix S_w was minimized to obtain the projection matrix W^*, which consisted of the eigenvectors with the corresponding smallest eigenvalues. In general, since the NFL metric generalized the representative capacity of prototypes during the discriminant analysis phase, the NFLE preserved much more information than the conventional p-2-p-based methods. More details are given in [18].

One thousand four hundred feature points are reduced to a new space of dimension 3 after the projecting transformations, e.g., PCA, PCA plus LDA, PCA plus LPP, and PCA plus NFLE. Similar to Figure 1, 1,400 transformed samples of seven classes are drawn in Figure 9 by their corresponding colors. In this figure, red stars denote the patch windows (red rectangles) of an ROI which are projected onto the new spaces by the transformations. In Figure 9c,d, a specified sample could be represented by the linear combination of other samples of the same class in the transformed space. For example, the sample of general yellow color is represented by the linear combination of samples with the dark and bright yellow colors. Points of the same class are as close as possible, while samples of different classes should be separated as far as possible. In summary, manifold learning methods, LPP or NFLE, discover the more intrinsic manifold structure than the global eigenspace methods, PCA and LDA. Besides, manifold learning algorithms not only reduce the feature dimensions but also preserve the sample relationship of the same classes under various illumination conditions.

3.3 Classifier design: 1-NN, SVM, and SRC

When discriminant features in an ROI were extracted by the DR process, the classifier was trained to classify the ROI's colors. In this study, the nearest neighbor classifier (1-NN), one-vs-all SVM classifier, and sparse representation classifier (SRC) [30] are adopted for color classification. The seven most used different classes of color in commercial vehicles were chosen for classification. They included red, yellow, blue, green, black, white, and gray. Classified with the trained classifiers, the vehicle colors were determined in the following steps. A valid ROI was obtained for color classification in Section 2. A window of 20 by 20

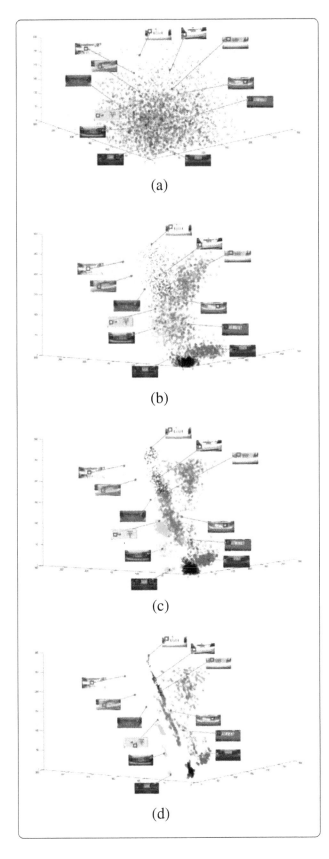

Figure 9 The sample distributions of seven color classes after various eigenspace transformations. (a) PCA transformation, **(b)** PCA + LDA transformation, **(c)** PCA + LPP transformation, and **(d)** PCA + NFLE transformation.

slides the ROI from left to right and top to bottom. The color histogram of six color spaces in this window was generated and reduced to a lower dimensional vector in feature discriminant analysis. This reduced vector was classified with the trained SVM classifier or the 1-NN classifier to determine the color class. Finally, the classification results of sliding windows in an ROI were counted, and the ROI color was determined using the voting strategy.

SRC is a discriminative nature of sparse representation for classification. The designed SRC classifier in this study is briefly described as following: (1) Similar to the SVM classifier, a window of 20 by 20 slides the ROI from left to right and top to bottom. The color histograms of each sliding window in six color spaces are generated. The reduced features in the low-dimensional space are obtained by the eigenspace transformation. (2) After feature extraction, the N training samples $A = [A_1, A_2, ..., A_7]$ are collected for seven color classes, in which $A_i = [a_{i,1}, a_{i,2}, ..., a_{i,n_i}] \in R^{d \times n_i}$ is the sample of class i and $N = \sum_{i=1}^{7} n_i$. The columns of A are normalized to be unit ℓ^2 norm. (3) When a test sample $y \in R^d$, a reduced vector of fusing color histogram on a sliding window, is verified, solve the ℓ^1-minimization problem via a primal-dual algorithm for linear programming based on [31,32]: $\hat{x}_1 = \arg \min_x \|x\|_1$, subject to $Ax = y$. The residual errors for each class are calculated: $r_i(y) = \|y - A\delta_i(\hat{x}_1)\|_2, i = 1, 2, ..., 7$, where δ_i is the characteristic function which selects the coefficient associated with the i-th class. The test sample y is classified as the i-th class, if the residual error $r_i(y)$ is the smallest. Finally, the color classification results of sliding windows in an ROI were counted, and the ROI color was determined using the voting strategy.

4. Experimental results

In this section, the experiments conducted to show the performance of the proposed method are discussed. A stationary CCD camera was set up on the shoulder of roads. Eighteen video clips were captured in various weather conditions, e.g., in sunny, cloudy, or rainy. Due to the varied outdoor illumination from different weather conditions, the captured images are illustrated as shown in Figure 10.

Fifteen video clips of 320 by 240 were grabbed from the scenes in a single lane as shown in Figure 10a-j. On the other hand, three clips of an image of 720 by 480 were also grabbed from the senses in multi-lanes as shown in Figure 10k-n. The ROIs of the vehicles were incomplete when a vehicle moved in or out of the image frame. Two lines were set to obtain the complete rear view of vehicles.

Figure 10 The vehicle color classification results in single and multiple lanes. (a-j) The classification results in a single lane. **(k-n)** The classification results in multiple lanes.

The data set consisted of 18 clips for evaluation. More than 42,000 vehicles were segmented from the clips. The ground truths (GTs) of taillight locations, vehicle types, and color classes were manually labeled in the data set. In this study, the locations of ROIs in a still image were first identified. The color histograms of blocks in an ROI were next classified for color classification. For a specified block in a valid ROI, a histogram-based feature vector of length 4,608 was extracted from the 20 by 20 window in six color spaces. This vector with high dimensionality was reduced to the lower dimensional subspace by PCA plus NFLE. The block color was classified by an SVM classifier. The ROI's color was determined using voting of the classification results. Two experiments were conducted to evaluate the performance of ROI location and color classification. The proposed method was implemented in a PC-based machine with a CPU model i7-920 in 2.67 GHz using the Microsoft Visual C++ 2008 and OpenCV 2.1 tool kits.

4.1 ROI location

Before color classification, the ROI for each vehicle had to be accurately located. To achieve this goal, a coarse-to-fine strategy was adopted to locate the valid ROIs from still images. In the first experiment, three results were reported showing the performance of ROI location.

Table 2 The confusion matrix of classification using texture features

	Sedan	SUV	Truck	Non-vehicle	Accuracy rates (%)
Sedan	31,509	712	0	0	97.8
SUV	245	5,796	0	0	95.9
Truck	0	0	4,179	204	95.3
Non-vehicle	863	587	2,547	257,657	98.5

First, simple rules in Eq. (2) were employed to label the red patches. An SVM classifier was further trained to classify the confused pixels: yellow and red. Initially, the GT regions were manually labeled. The accuracy rates of red patch labeling were calculated by comparing the detected regions with the GT ones. When the overlapping region was larger than 1/10 of the corresponding GT region, the detected red patch successfully hit the taillight. The average hit rate of red patch labeling was more than 98% for 18 evaluation clips, as shown in Table 1. Using the simple rules with loose thresholds, taillight patches were labeled with high accuracy rates. In video clip 14, a low labeling rate was achieved because images were captured in the gradually dimming light of dusk. A lot of noise was generated in image frames due to the white balance function of cameras.

Table 1 The correct rates of taillight pairs for the evaluation data set (%)

Video clips	Times	Weather[a]	Number of red patches (ground truth)	Number of hit patches	Hit rates (%)	The average numbers of taillight pairs
1	8:00–10:30	Sun: through cloud/haze	424	424	100.00	3.91
2	13:30–15:00	Overcast sky	476	476	100.00	4.68
3	7:30–9:00	Overcast sky	468	468	100.00	3.05
4	9:30–11:00	Overcast sky	182	182	100.00	4.82
5	15:30–17:00	Partly cloudy sky	1,144	1,144	100.00	4.42
6	14:30–16:30	Sun: through cloud/haze	1,104	1,104	100.00	4.53
7	9:30–14:30	Outdoor shade areas	1,762	1,762	100.00	2.79
8	10:00–15:00	Outdoor shade areas	3,222	3,094	96.02	2.67
9	13:30–16:00	Outdoor shade areas	2,790	2,772	99.35	2.46
10	15:00–17:00	Sun: through cloud/haze	894	894	100.00	2.60
11	16:00–17:00	Partly cloudy sky	188	188	100.00	4.17
12	13:00–15:30	Sun: through cloud/haze	2,318	2,300	99.27	2.74
13	15:00–17:00	Overcast sky	2,038	2,038	100.00	2.54
14	15:30–18:00	Sun: through cloud/haze	1,810	1,620	89.5	3.54
15	9:00–16:00	Rainy day	10,600	10,452	98.60	3.86
16 (multi-lanes)	8:00–15:00	Daylight(sun + sky) and partly cloudy sky	17,094	16,924	99	6.89
17 (multi-lanes)	8:00–15:00	Daylight(sun + sky) and partly cloudy sky	18,850	18,556	98.45	8.03
18 (multi-lanes)	10:00–17:00	Daylight(sun + sky) and partly cloudy sky	21,160	20,892	98.73	11.45
Total			86,524	85,290	98.57	—

[a]http://www.3drender.com/glossary/colortemp.htm.

Figure 11 The vehicle type misclassified examples. (a) Sedans were misclassified as type 'SUV'. **(b)** SUVs were misclassified as type 'sedan'. **(c)** Trucks were misclassified as the 'non-vehicle' regions. **(d)** The non-vehicle regions were misclassified as type 'sedan'. **(e)** The non-vehicle regions were misclassified as type 'SUV'. **(f)** The non-vehicle regions were misclassified as type 'truck'.

The geometric rule-based filter was then employed to determine the taillight pair candidates. All taillight pairs were reserved in the second results. On average, less than five pairs in a single lane and less than 12 pairs in multi-lanes were needed for the further process as listed in the last column of Table 1.

The third results were the ROI verification using HOG features. HOG is an efficient feature descriptor for object representation because it is robust to illumination and geometric distortion. Not only were both the vehicle and non-vehicle regions verified, but the vehicle types were also classified. Four classes, sedan, SUV, truck, and non-vehicle, were identified for vehicle type verification and classification. Three hundred images for each class were collected for training. A multi-class SVM classifier was trained using HOG features for vehicle type classification. In testing, more than 300,000 ROIs, including 32,221 sedans, 6,041 SUVs, 4,383 trucks, and 261,654 non-vehicle regions, were classified to determine the vehicle types.

The accuracy rates and confusion matrix are tabulated in Table 2 for 18 video clips. The correct rates for classes, sedan, SUV, truck, and non-vehicle region, were 97.8%, 95.9%, 95.3%, and 98.5%, respectively. The proposed method could effectively identify the valid vehicle ROIs in different types and multi-lanes. In addition, the proposed method is robust to the weather conditions. For an example, the reflected regions of taillights, the dark red regions in Figure 10b-e, are efficiently filtered out by the proposed method in rainy days.

In addition, some misclassification results are also given in Figure 11. In Table 2, the regions of sedan and SUV were misclassified due to the similar shapes as shown in Figure 11a,b. The regions of trucks were misclassified as the non-vehicle regions because the planar plates of the truck were similar to the ground regions as shown in Figure 11c. Similarly, the non-vehicle regions were frequently misclassified as the truck class, as shown in Figure 11d. On the other hand, the non-vehicle regions, the

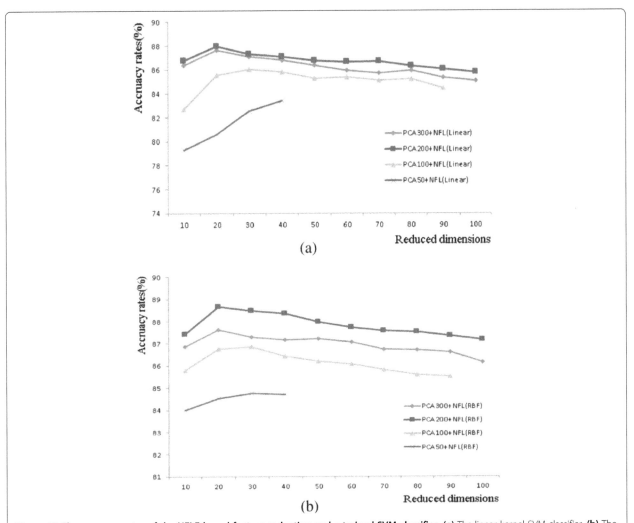

Figure 12 The accuracy rates of the NFLE-based feature reduction and a trained SVM classifier. (a) The linear kernel SVM classifier. **(b)** The RBF kernel SVM classifier.

false alarms, were misclassified as the regions of sedan and SUV were generated due to cluttered backgrounds as shown in Figure 11e,f. From the experimental results, more than 98.3% accuracy rate was achieved using HOG features and SVM classifiers. Therefore, 42,645 vehicles' ROIs survived from 43,262 vehicles after the ROI location step.

4.2 Color classification

After the ROIs of vehicles in the rear view were located, seven most used color classes were classified, including red, yellow, blue, green, black, white, and gray. The color histograms of blocks of 20 by 20 were extracted from an ROI. Since the dimensionality of the color histogram was very high, i.e., 4,608, PCA was performed to find the best representation for avoiding the small-sample-size problem. The best discriminative projections were next found by the NFLE method. The color histograms of 4,608 were reduced to the vectors of dimensions D_{PCA} and D_{NFLE} by PCA and NFLE, respectively. Two thousand one hundred samples of seven classes were collected to train the multi-class SVM classifiers, and the linear and RBF kernel functions are used during the training. Each block was classified to determine its color. All classification results of blocks in an ROI were counted and the ROI's color was determined by a voting strategy. To evaluate the proposed method, more than 42,000 vehicles from 18 video clips were identified according to color features. Figure 10 shows the classification results of the testing video clips in a single-lane and in the multi-lane cases, respectively. The red patches and ROIs were drawn by the green and blue rectangular boxes. They also show that the proposed method was effectively performed on urban roads in various weather conditions. Moreover, the classification rates for various reduced dimensions are shown in Figure 12. Three curves represent the classification results in which D_{PCA} is the reduced dimensions of 300, 200, and 100 by PCA, and D_{NFLE} is the reduced dimension from 10 to 100 by NFLE. From the results in Figure 12, the classification results were very similar for these three curves. After DR, the SVM classifiers with a linear kernel function and an RBF kernel function were trained for color classification. The best classification rates are 87.93% and 88.67% for the linear SVM classifier and the RBF kernel SVM classifier, respectively. The RBF kernel SVM classifier with 1,594 support vectors obtains the best classification rate which D_{PCA} is 200 and D_{NFLE} is 20. Two parameters (c and γ) are 2.0 and 0.0078125 which were obtained from the LIBSVM tool kit [25]. The other parameters were initialized as the default values for training the classifier. The best accuracy rates for each video clip are tabulated in Table 3, and the average classification rate for the 18 clips was 88.67% by the SVM classifier with a RBF kernel function.

To show the performance of color space fusion plus the DR scheme, two experiments were implemented for comparison. First, the original histograms of color spaces RGB, LAB, HSV, and fused space were fed to the SVM classifier for training and testing. According to the results in Table 4, the fused space outperformed the other color spaces. In the second experiment, the original histograms were reduced to new vectors of dimensions 200 and 20 by PCA and NFLE before the SVM training. The reduced vectors were classified by the trained classifier. The accuracy for all color spaces was improved. These implied the discriminative features had been extracted from feature discriminant analysis.

Similarly, the confusion matrix of color classification is tabulated in Table 5 for the testing video clips. The correct rates for color classes, red, yellow, blue, green, black, white, and gray, are 91.34%, 93.73%, 90.34%, 91.62%, 90.17%, 85.22%, and 87.8%, respectively. Illumination impacted the classification performance is given in Table 5, especially with classes 'black', 'white', and 'gray'. The worst results occurred at class 'white' in Table 5. The samples in class 'white' were misclassified as classes 'gray' and 'black' at nightfall. Similarly, the samples in class 'black' were misclassified as classes 'gray' and 'white' due to the sunlight. Several misclassification cases are given in Figure 13. The vehicle in Figure 13a was misclassified as 'black' due to the dark red pixels. The misclassification for Figure 13b,c occurred

Table 3 The classification rates using the SVM classifier

Video clips	Correct classification	Number of vehicles	Accuracy rates (%)
1	191	212	90.01
2	209	238	87.82
3	196	234	83.76
4	78	91	85.71
5	501	572	87.59
6	498	552	90.22
7	779	881	88.42
8	1,355	1,547	87.59
9	1,155	1,386	83.33
10	391	447	87.47
11	94	94	1
12	956	1,150	83.13
13	835	1,019	81.94
14	749	810	92.47
15	4,551	5,226	87.08
16 (multi-lane)	7,583	8,462	89.61
17 (multi-lane)	8,266	9,278	89.09
18 (multi-lane)	9,428	10,446	90.25
Average accuracy rate		88.67	

Table 4 The comparison of accuracy rates for various color spaces

Experiments	Color space	Histogram dimensions	Reduced dimensions (PCA/NFL)	Accuracy rates (%)
I	RGB	768	Nil	73.88
	LAB	768	Nil	77.79
	HSV	768	Nil	79.31
	Six color spaces	4,608	Nil	81.98
II	RGB	768	200/20	75.66
	LAB	768	200/20	82.15
	HSV	768	200/20	81.63
	Six color spaces	4,608	200/20	88.67

because of the bumper color. The misclassification results as given in Figure 13g,h. These were generated from the illumination impacts. Most misclassification occurred at classes 'white' and 'gray'. In addition, the performance of this system was 18 frames per second.

In order to show the effectiveness of the proposed method, several state-of-the-art algorithms [3-5,22,23] are implemented for the comparison. Color histogram-based features are widely used in color classification. Bin quantization is the simplest skill for DR in many papers. Kim et al. [3,4] quantize the color bins in space *HSI*. The color histograms of lengths 360 and 128 are next classified by an SVM classifier and the 1-NN classifier. Dule et al. [22] list ten possible histograms for classification. These ten histograms are evaluated and randomly fused to find the best combination, i.e., *HS-SV-ab-La-Lb*-gray. The combined histogram of length 328 is classified by a neural-network classifier. Yang et al. [5] designed a two-layer classifier: *HS* color histogram for color classification in layer one and normalized *RGB* features for the block-gray-white classification in layer two. A two-stage classifier is proposed for color classification in [11,23]. Color (i.e., red, yellow, blue, and green) and monochrome (i.e., black, gray, and white) classes are first classified in the first stage. In stage two, different features are classified by two SVM-based classifiers for color and monochrome classes, respectively. Wu et al. [23] use color features on channels *HS* in stage 1. The features on channels *HV* and *SV* are respectively classified for the four color and

the three monochrome classes in stage two. On the other hand, Hsieh et al. [11] construct a Gaussian mixed model (GMM) for color/monochrome classification in stage one. Four color classes and three monochrome classes are identified by two trained SVM classifiers. Features in color space *Lab* plus features in normalized space *RGB* are classified for four color classes, and features in normalized space *RGB* are classified for three monochrome classes. The configurations for the compared algorithms are tabulated in Table 6. The quantized bin numbers are written in the parentheses. Two thousand one hundred samples of seven classes, 300 samples per class, were collected to train the classifier, and 42,645 vehicle ROIs from 18 video clips were collected for performance evaluation in this comparison. The training and testing sets are two disjoint datasets which were independently collected[a]. The training samples are also collected from video clips which are captured in different locations and time of testing ones. In order to show the effectiveness, the same evaluation process has been run five times, where $2,100 \times 5$ patches were randomly selected for training and 42,645 ROIs were evaluated by five trained classifiers. The average accuracy rates and the standard derivations are listed in Table 6. From the compared results, the proposed method outperforms the other methods.

On the other hand, several eigenspace methods for DR have been implemented for comparison. After DR, three classifiers are trained for evaluation, e.g., *k*-NN classifier,

Table 5 The confusion matrix of color classification

	Red	Yellow	Blue	Green	Black	White	Gray	Accuracy rates (%)
red	1,677	38	0	0	121	0	0	91.34
yellow	81	3,168	0	0	0	69	62	93.73
blue	0	0	1,357	21	57	27	40	90.34
green	0	22	13	1,312	51	0	34	91.62
black	0	0	0	0	10,232	483	632	90.17
white	0	0	0	0	68	8,399	1,389	85.22
gray	0	0	0	0	691	931	11,670	87.8

Figure 13 The color misclassified examples. (a) Red cars were classified as black ones. **(b)** Yellow taxis were classified as white ones. **(c)** Blue cars were classified as gray ones. **(d)** Green cars were classified as white ones. **(e)** Black cars were classified as white ones. **(f)** Black cars were classified as gray ones. **(g)** White cars were classified as gray ones. **(h)** Gray cars were classified as white ones.

SRC, and SVM classifier with an RBF kernel function. The recognition results of three classifiers are compared as shown in Figure 14. In this experiment, the parameters for each classifier are set in the following: Value k is set as 1 in classifier k-NN, and the RBF kernel is applied in the SVM classifier. The reduced feature dimensions are set from 10 to 100 for the DR methods PCA, PCA + LDA, PCA + LPP, and PCA + NFLE. The reduced dimension of PCA is set to be 200 for preserving more than 99% information of training samples. Since the reduced

Table 6 The accuracy rates for the proposed method and the state-of-the-art algorithms (%)

Methods	Features	Classifiers	Average accuracy rates	Computational time (ms)
Baek [3]	H (36)*S (10)	SVM	73.88 (±1.0)	18
Kim [4]	H (8)*S (4)*I (4)	1-NN	71.04 (±1.12)	824
Yang [5]	Layer 1: H (16) + S (8)	Two-layer rule-based classifier	64.03 (±1.3)	34
	Layer 2: normalized RGB			
Hsieh [11]	Lab + transformed RGB	GMM + two-stage SVM	84.77 (±0.83)	58
Dule [21]	HS (64) + SV (64) + ab (64)	Neural network	76.12 (±1.41)	1,210
	+La (64) + Lb (64) + Gray(8)			
Wu [22]	HS (256) + HV (256) + SV (256)	Two-stage SVM	80.66 (±1.5)	33
The proposed method	Six color spaces (4,608)	NFL (20) + SVM (RBF-kernel function)	88.18 (±0.89)	18
	PCA reduction (200)			

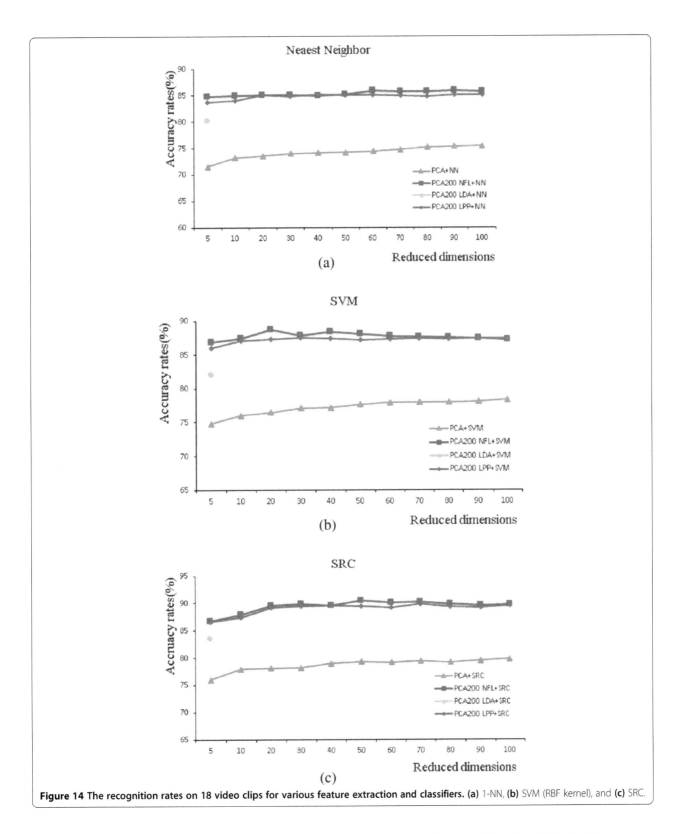

Figure 14 The recognition rates on 18 video clips for various feature extraction and classifiers. **(a)** 1-NN, **(b)** SVM (RBF kernel), and **(c)** SRC.

dimensions of LDA depend on the class number, the recognition results of LDA method only show the results of dimension 5 in the experiments. The best recognition rates and average processing time for three classifier and four DR methods are tabulated in Table 7. The numbers in the parentheses are the reduced dimensions of the best recognition rates. The best recognition rates of classifier 1-NN for DR methods PCA, PCA + LDA, PCA +

LPP, and PCA + NFLE are 75.36%, 80.23%, 85.07%, and 85.84%, respectively. Similarly, the best recognition rates for classifiers SVM and SRC are tabulated in Table 7. From this figure, manifold learning-based DRs (LPP or NFLE) outperform the global learning-based methods (PCA and LDA). Though the recognition rates of SRC are higher than those of SVM classifier a little bit, the classification time of SRC is more expensive than SVM classifier. Practically, classifier SVM is adopted instead of SRC in designing a real-time surveillance system.

5. Conclusions

In this paper, a novel method is proposed for real-time vehicle color classification. Two modules: ROI location and color classification constituted the classification process. Unlike the traditional background subtraction methods which are sensitive to illumination change and the background models, the ROIs of vehicles taken from the back were located/determined using still images. To meet real-time requirements, the coarse-to-fine strategy was used in classifying from the simple pixel level to the complex region level. Six color spaces were fused to generate a histogram-based feature vector for the representation of ROI color. High-dimensional feature vectors were reduced to the lower ones in feature discriminant analysis. The best recognition rate in Table 7 is 90.51% by using PCA + NFL for DR and SRC for classification. Though the best performance is achieved by the SRC, it needs much computational time. Practically, the SVM-based method, PCA + NFL for DR and SVM for classification, is recommended for color classification. A multi-class SVM classifier was trained for color classification in a real-time surveillance system. Experimental results have shown that the vehicles' colors were effectively identified using the proposed method.

Table 7 The best recognition rates and average time for three classifiers and four DR methods

Classifiers	DR methods	Rates (%)	Time (seconds)
1-NN	PCA	75.36 (100)	0.8141
	PCA + LDA	80.23 (5)	
	PCA + LPP	85.07 (60)	
	PCA + NFLE	85.84 (60)	
SVM	PCA	78.34 (100)	0.0176
	PCA + LDA	82.01 (5)	
	PCA + LPP	87.45 (30)	
	PCA + NFLE	88.67 (20)	
SRC	PCA	79.71 (100)	4.0561
	PCA + LDA	83.43 (5)	
	PCA + LPP	89.78 (70)	
	PCA + NFLE	*90.51 (50)*	

Endnote

[a]The color features are available in a website http://www.csie.nuu.edu.tw/#/personal/labadd/lab404.

Competing interests

The authors declare that they have no competing interests.

Acknowledgements

The work was supported by the National Science Council under grant nos. NSC 101-2221-E-239-034 and 102-2221-E-239 -023.

Author details

[1]Department of Computer Science and Information Engineering, National Central University, Taoyuan, Taiwan. [2]Department of Computer Science and Information Engineering, National United University, Miaoli, Taiwan.

References

1. G. Qiu, Embedded colour image coding for content-based retrieval. J. Visual Commun. Image Repres. **15**, 507–521 (2004)
2. L.V. Tran, R. Lenz, Compact colour descriptors for colour-based image retrieval. Signal Process **85**, 233–246 (2005)
3. N. Baek, S.M. Park, KJ. Kim, S.B. Park, Vehicle color classification based on the support vector machine method. Proc. Commun. Comput. Inf. Sci. **2**, 1133–1139 (2007)
4. KJ. Kim, S.M. Park, Y.J. Choi, Deciding the number of color histogram bins for vehicle color recognition. Proc. IEEE Asia-Pacific Services Computing Conference, 134–138 (2007)
5. MJ. Yang, G. Han, X.F. Li, X.C. Zhu, L. Li, Vehicle color recognition using monocular camera. Proc. IEEE Int. Conf. on Wireless Communications and Signal Processing, 1–5 (2011)
6. L.W. Tsai, J.W. Hsieh, K.C. Fan, Vehicle detection using normalized color and edge map. IEEE Trans. Image Process. **16**, 850–864 (2007)
7. S.Y. Chen, J.W. Hsieh, J.C. Wu, Y.S. Chen, Vehicle retrieval using eigen color and multiple instance learning. Proc. Int. Conf. Int. Information Hiding and Multimedia Signal Process, 657–660 (2009)
8. L.M. Brown, Example-based color vehicle retrieval for surveillance. Proc. IEEE Int. Conf. Advanced Video and Signal Based Surveillance, 91–96 (2010)
9. X. Li, G. Zhang, J. Fang, J. Wu, Z. Cui, Vehicle color recognition using vector matching of template. Proc. Int. Symp. Electronic Commerce and Security, 189–193 (2010)
10. G.D. Finlayson, B. Schiele, J.L. Crowley, Comprehensive color image normalization. Proc. 5th European Conference on Computer Vision **1**, 475–490 (1998)
11. J.W. Hsieh, L.C. Chen, S.Y. Chen, S.C. Lin, D.Y. Chen, Vehicle color classification under different lighting conditions through color correction. Proc IEEE Int Symp Circuits and Systems, 1859–1862 (2012)
12. Y. Shen, R. Mo, Y. Zhu, L. Wei, W. Gao, Z. Peng, Over-exposure image correction with automatic texture synthesis. Proc. Int. Congress on Image and Signal Process, 794–797 (2011)
13. D. Guo, Y. Cheng, S. Zhuo, T. Sim, Correcting over-exposure in photographs. Proc. IEEE Int. Conference on Computer Vision and Pattern Recognition, 515–521 (2010)
14. H. Stokman, T. Gevers, Selection and fusion of color models for image feature detection. IEEE Trans. Pattern Anal. Mach. Intell. **29**(3), 371–381 (2007)
15. P. Wolfe, The simplex method for quadratic programming. Econometric **27**(3), 382–398 (1959)
16. S.T. Roweis, L.K. Saul, Nonlinear dimensionality reduction by locally linear embedding. Science **290**(22), 2323–2326 (2000)
17. X. He, S. Yan, Y. Ho, P. Niyogi, H.J. Zhang, Face recognition using Laplacianfaces. IEEE Trans. Pattern Anal. Mach. Intell. **27**(3), 328–340 (2005)
18. Y.N. Chen, C.C. Han, C.T. Wang, K.C. Fan, Face recognition using nearest feature space embedding. IEEE Trans. Pattern Anal. Mach. Intell. **33**(6), 1073–1086 (2011)
19. J. Tenenbaum, V. de Silva, J. Langford, A global geometric framework for nonlinear dimensionality reduction. Science **290**(5500), 2319–2323 (2000)

20. M. Belkin, P. Niyogi, Laplacian eigenmaps and spectral techniques for embedding and clustering. Proc Advances in Neural Information Processing Systems (MIT Press) **14**, 585–591 (2001)
21. Y.C. Wang, C.T. Hsieh, C.C. Han, K.C. Fan, The color identification of automobiles for video surveillance. Proc. IEEE Int. Carnahan Conference on Security Technology (ICCST), 1–5 (2011)
22. E. Dule, M. Gokmen, M.S. Beratoglu, A convenient feature vector construction for vehicle color recognition. Proc11th WSEAS International Conference on Neural Networks, Evolutionary Computing and Fuzzy systems, 250–255 (2010)
23. Y.T. Wu, J.H. Kao, M.Y. Shih, A vehicle color classification method for video surveillance system concerning model-based background subtraction. Proc. Pacific-Rim Conference on Multimedia **6297**, 369–380 (2010)
24. Y.Y. Lu, C.C. Han, M.C. Lu, K.C. Fan, A vision-based system for the prevention of car collisions at night. Mach. Vision Appl. **22**, 117–127 (2011)
25. R.E. Fan, P.H. Chen, C.J. Lin, Working set selection using second order information for training SVM. J. Mach. Learn. Res. **6**, 1889–1918 (2005)
26. N. Dalal, B. Triggs, Histograms of oriented gradients for human detection. Proc. IEEE Int. Conf. Computer Vision and pattern Recognition **1**, 886–893 (2005)
27. G. Wyszecki, W.S. Stiles, *Color Science: Concepts and Methods, Quantitative Data and Formulae*, 2nd edn. (Wiley, New York, 1982)
28. S.Z. Li, Face recognition based on nearest linear combinations. Proc. IEEE Int. Conf. Computer Vision and Pattern Recognition, 839–844 (1998)
29. S. Yan, D. Xu, B. Zhang, H.J. Zhang, Q. Yang, S. Lin, Graph embedding and extensions: general framework for dimensionality reduction. IEEE Trans. Pattern Anal. Mach. Intell. **29**(1), 40–51 (2007)
30. J. Wright, A.Y. Yang, A. Ganesh, S.S. Sastry, Y. Ma, Robust face recognition via sparse representation. IEEE Trans. Pattern Anal. Mach. Intell. **31**(2), 210–227 (2009)
31. S. Boyd, L. Vandenberghe, *Convex Optimization* (Cambridge University Press, Cambridge, 2004)
32. E. Candes, J. Romberg, ℓ^1-magic: Recovery of sparse signals via convex programming. (2005). http://www.acm.caltech.edu/l1magic/

15

A novel framework for semantic analysis of an illumination-variant soccer video

Devang S Pandya[1*] and Mukesh A Zaveri[2]

Abstract

This paper presents an effective, novel and robust framework for semantic analysis of a soccer video possessing varying illumination conditions. The proposed algorithm works in two phases. The proposed framework effectively detects and gathers important events in the first phase, and a later phase carries out the task of event classification. The proposed system aims to identify high-level semantics of a soccer video like card event, goal event, goal attack and other classes of events. The proposed framework effectively exploits optical flow and colour features to detect and classify the events. The use of event filtration and categorization features successfully makes the system effective over various conditions. Simulations have been performed on a large number of video datasets of different conditions of various soccer leagues. Simulation results reflect the efficiency and robustness of the proposed framework.

Keywords: High-level semantics; Optical flow; Event filtration; Event categorization

1 Introduction

Rapid revolution in digital video has brought many applications at home in affordable cost. The volume of digital data has been increasing rapidly due to the wide usage of multimedia applications in the areas of education, entertainment, business, medicine etc. One of the major applications is sports video analysis. Sports videos attract majority of people due to their capability of producing thrill as well as uncertainty of results. Hence, there has been an enormous increase of such video contents on the Internet. Video summarization helps to address these needs by developing a condensed version of full-length videos [1-3]. Extraction of important events and creation of summaries do not only make the video compact but also make it possible to deliver over low-bandwidth networks.

A raw video is an unstructured data stream, physically consisting of a sequence of video shots. A video shot is composed of a number of frames, and its visual content can be represented by key frames. Most of the video summarization techniques may be categorized into two classes, segmentation-based video summarization and event-based video summarization. The former is defined as a collection of key frames extracted from a video. This type of technique is applicable to uniformly informative video content where all parts of the programme may be equally important for the user. Examples of such contents are presentation videos, documentaries and home movies. This summary can be a sequence of stationary images or moving images (video skims). In general, content-based video summarization can be thought as a two-step process. The first step is partitioning the video into shots, called video segmentation or video shot boundary detection. The second step is to find such representative frames from every shot that can well describe the video. Thus, the video can be considered as a collection of shots and every shot consists of key frames. Event-based video summarization techniques are applicable to video contents that contain easily identifiable video units that form either a sequence of different events and non-events. Such kind of summary is usually presented as an organized sequence of interesting events. The best example of this type of video content is sports highlights. In sports highlights, exciting events such as wicket fall, hitting a six in cricket, goal, issuing a card in soccer etc. are included and dull segments are eliminated. Other examples are surveillance videos, talk shows and news programmes. The past several years have observed significant research to the event-based

---

* Correspondence: devang.pandya@ganpatuniversity.ac.in
[1]U V Patel College of Engineering, Ganpat University, Kherva 384012, Mehsana, India
Full list of author information is available at the end of the article

video summarization of various kinds of sports such as soccer, baseball, tennis, cricket etc.

Event-based video summarization extracts the highest meaningful contents of the video which is the most favourable in the end-user perspective. In [4], different solutions to video summarization have been described in detail. Low-level features such as colour, motion and textures are important and widely used features for such video processing. There exist different colour histogram-based approaches in which consecutive frames are compared to decide key frames. In [5,6], HSV colour space is used to measure interframe difference. It has been shown that the HSV (hue, saturation, value) colour space has outperformed the RGB (red, green, blue) colour space due to its perceptual uniformity. RGB mutual information and joint entropy of adjacent two frames have been used in [7] for marking key frames. A colour histogram is insensitive to camera and object motion. Therefore, colour-based key frame selection may not be able to deliver the visual content of the shot. Motion is an important clue about camera zooming and panning. To address camera motion, optical flow components are extracted and the motion function is computed between two frames in [8-10].

Object motion trajectories and interactions have been used for soccer play classification and for soccer event detection [11-13]. However, both [11] and [12] rely on pre-extracted precise object trajectories, which were generated manually in [11] and are not useful for real-time applications. For a soccer video, rule-based classification has been used in [12]. Xie et al. have carried out classification by defining mutually exclusive states of the game, namely, play and break [14]. A combination of cinematic and object descriptors has been used in [15]. A superimposed caption embedded in the video has been used in [16] to detect the scoreboard of the baseball videos. Semantic features along with replays and audio energy have been applied for soccer video summarization in [17]. In [18], rule-based approaches have been used for the detection of events in sports videos.

Several approaches use stochastic methods that employ self-learning capability to extract knowledge such as hidden Markov models (HMM). HMM has been extensively used to detect events of the different types of sports videos [19-22]. A knowledge-based semantic inference has been applied for event recognition in sports videos in [23]. A combination of speech-band energy and pattern recognition based on dominant colour provides important clues for event detection in soccer videos [24]. Researchers have also attempted dynamic Bayesian network (DBN) which is based on the Bayesian network (BN) and its extension [25]. Learning through DBN has been applied to many real applications [26,27].

In [27], the Bayesian belief network has been used for the analysis of goal attack events of soccer videos. In the last recent years, machine learning-based approaches have dragged attention. A machine learning system that learns to predict video transitions based on feature information derived from the frames is developed. In supervised learning, low-level features are employed to train the system that can predict transitions on unseen data [28,29]. Various unsupervised learning approaches have been attempted in the literature to extract key frames and found faster as they do not require training [30]. An adaptive neuro-fuzzy system has been proposed in [31]. Literature study reveals that stochastic and machine learning approaches have drawn the major attention of researchers. Sports videos experience huge motion so it is a natural cue, and we exploit the motion as a low-level feature for our proposed framework. The rest of the paper is organized as follows. The proposed framework is described in Section 2. Section 3 discusses experimental results and Section 4 concludes the paper.

2 Proposed framework

Semantic video analysis involves the inclusion or identification of the major events of the video. We propose a robust and efficient framework for semantic analysis of a soccer video possessing highly varying illumination conditions. It is robust in the sense that it succeeds to achieve favourable results even under various conditions of the soccer video with minimal assumptions. It is also efficient as we apply low-level features like colour and motion to detect the important events while neglecting object-based features which are computationally expensive. The proposed framework of semantic analysis of a soccer video is shown in Figure 1. The proposed framework is fully automatic. The entire video is processed frame by frame. The block diagram of the framework is briefly described below.

1) The first step of our framework is to carry out event segmentation. We propose a novel algorithm for event segmentation based on change in optical flow between the successive frames of the video. Change in the horizontal component of optical flow is found very successful to segment the video. At the end of event segmentation, we have a set of events. There are many dull events which are not important to the end users. A block diagram trifurcates after the event segmentation. Each process is carried out independently than the others which is subsequently described.

2) We propose a novel and robust card event detection algorithm. The algorithm understands the caption and exploits this domain knowledge effectively to detect the card event. After event segmentation, the card detection algorithm is applied on the obtained set of events.

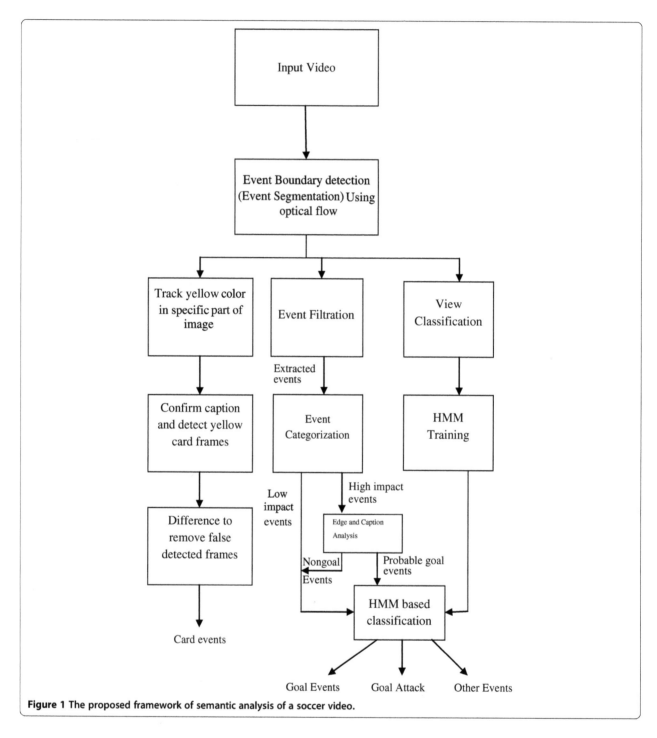

Figure 1 The proposed framework of semantic analysis of a soccer video.

3) Event filtration is applied to remove dull events like just passing the ball on the ground, audience views etc. After obtaining meaningful events, event categorization is applied to separate out high-impact and low-impact classes of events. High-impact class of events is lengthy as well as involve more view transitions. High-impact class consists of events like goal, injury, player exchange etc. while low-impact class consists of events like goal

attacks or corner and other events like throw in, offside etc.

4) View classification is carried out for all the detected event segments. This algorithm heavily depends on the dominant colour and edges. The algorithm is robust to the varying conditions of the ground which extremely affect the grass colour. Grass colour exhibits different brightness in flood light condition compared to the daylight condition. Based on this

view classification, HMM models are generated for the goal, corner/goal attack and other types of events.

5) Event classification is carried out on the low-impact and probable goal class of events using the obtained HMM models.

All the above-mentioned steps of the framework are described in detail in the subsequent Section 2 of the paper.

2.1 Event segmentation

Event segmentation is carried out by computing optical flow between consecutive frames of the video. As sports videos are very dynamic in nature and involve huge motion, optical flow becomes the most appropriate choice. We apply the Lukas and Kanade optical flow technique [9], which is a widely used differential method for optical flow estimation in computer vision. It is also less sensitive to image noise and also fast. The Lucas and Kanade method assumes that displacement of the image contents is approximately constant within a neighbourhood (window) of the pixel under consideration. The velocity vector (V_x, V_y) must satisfy:

$$Av = b \tag{1}$$

where:

$$A = \begin{bmatrix} I_x(q_1) & I_y(q_1) \\ I_x(q_2) & I_y(q_2) \\ \cdot & \cdot \\ I_x(q_n) & I_y(q_n) \end{bmatrix}, \quad b = \begin{bmatrix} -I_t(q_1) \\ -I_t(q_2) \\ \cdot \\ -I_t(q_n) \end{bmatrix}, \quad v = \begin{bmatrix} V_x \\ V_y \end{bmatrix}$$

$q_1, q_2, ..., q_n$ are pixels inside the window, and $I_x(q_i)$, $I_y(q_i)$ and $I_t(q_i)$ are the partial derivatives of image I with respect to positions x, y and t evaluated at pixel q_i and at the current time. The solution of Equation 1 is obtained by the least squares method. It is computed as:

$$v = \begin{bmatrix} \sum_i I_x(q_i)^2 & \sum_i I_x(q_i)I_y(q_i) \\ \sum_i I_x(q_i)I_y(q_i) & \sum_i I_y(q_i)^2 \end{bmatrix}^{-1} \begin{bmatrix} -\sum_i I_x(q_i)I_t(q_i) \\ -\sum_i I_x(q_i)I_t(q_i) \end{bmatrix}$$

In the experiments, the neighbourhood (window) size is set to 3. For the group of $N+1$ frame, N optical fields (F_1, $F_2, ..., F_n$) will be computed by the algorithm. Before applying the optical flow computation algorithm, the resolution of the frames is down-sampled by a factor of 2 to speed up the computation. After obtaining the optical flow component, the optical flow magnitude is computed using Equation 2. It is observed that optical flow components V_x and V_y are quite sensitive to the shot transition also. This is natural due to global camera motion.

$$M(i) = \sum_{(x,y) \in F_i} \sqrt{V_x^2(x,y) + V_y^2(x,y)} \tag{2}$$

Occurrence of any major event in soccer involves gathering of players, audience feelings and a rapid change in views. The camera undergoes huge motion during the occurrences of all major events in soccer. Camera motion is well and effectively observed by the optical flow components. We have emphasized on change in the horizontal component V_y as cameras track the soccer ball which has a more horizontal movement. We propose a novel feature to measure optical flow variation. For this, we differentiate Equation 2 with respect to V_y. The obtained equation is described below:

$$M_y'(i) = \frac{\sum_{(x,y) \in F_i} \sqrt{V_y^2(x,y)}}{\sum_{(x,y) \in F_i} \sqrt{V_x^2(x,y) + V_y^2(x,y)}} \tag{3}$$

The above equation is found very efficient to exhibit a noticeable change at the beginning or at the end of an event period. As the event occupies the time span in the video, it is necessary to demarcate the event boundary. However, this task is very challenging to identify such candidate frames which mark the beginning and ending of an event. Figure 2 clearly reflects the occurrences of major events in soccer by showing a larger fluctuation in M_y'. We can easily understand that in the case of a goal event, M_y' undergoes a rapid and large change due to frequent shot transition and rapid camera motion. Threshold is decided automatically to detect important events by using the following min-max normalization equation:

$$T = \frac{\overline{M}' - \min_{M'}}{\max_{M'} - \min_{M'}} (\text{new\_max}_{M'} - \text{new\_min}_{M'}) + \text{new\_min}_{M'} \tag{4}$$

where $\overline{M}'$ is the average value of M_y', $\min_{M'}$ is the minimum value of M_y', $\max_{M'}$ is the maximum value of M_y'. new_max and new_min values have been set to 0.5 and 0.8, respectively. After performing a large number of experiments on various video datasets, it has been observed that the minimum value of the M' is 0.5 for the detection of any event. Based on a newly determined threshold (T), significant events are demarcated. Important events like card, corner and goal continue over a certain minimum time span.

Using this fact, we consider only those events which sustain more than 5 s. This fact helps to reduce false detections. In Figure 2, the horizontal line is the threshold which is calculated using Equation 3. The computed M_y' value is varying over time (frames). As shown in Figure 2, it consists of multiple peaks corresponding to a significant soccer event. Figure 3a,b shows the corner and goal event sequences, respectively. These sequences are the series of various views like goal post views, close-up,

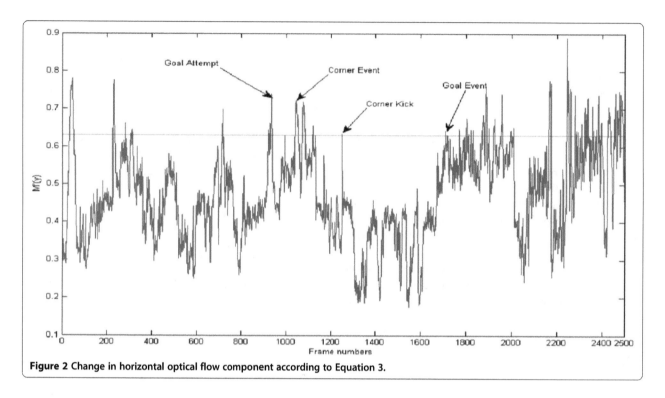

Figure 2 Change in horizontal optical flow component according to Equation 3.

player gathering etc. As the goal event shows a large number of continuous higher peaks above the threshold, it clearly exhibits more fluctuations compared to the corner event and it also continues longer than the corner event. Any M_y' which is higher than the obtained threshold marks the candidate frames which indicate the presence of an event. To separate out two events, there is at least a gap of 6 s between two peaks of M_y'; otherwise, the next

peak also contributes to the first event. This is valid because the corner event lasts at least for 5 s while the card and goal events are much longer than the corner event.

2.2 Yellow card event detection
Soccer is an eventful sport. Any unfair behaviour or some foul may cause the issue of a yellow card to the player. The yellow card itself is a very important event because it

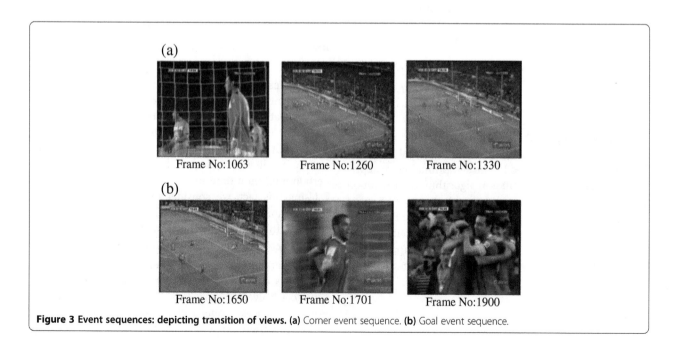

Figure 3 Event sequences: depicting transition of views. (a) Corner event sequence. (b) Goal event sequence.

is like a warning to the issued player. Issuing a second yellow card to the player (red card) compels the player to discontinue the game. This event itself gains very high importance; if the yellow card has been issued in the penalty area, then the opponent may be offered a penalty kick which may eventually end in scoring a goal by the opponent. Hence, it may generate a series of events. An algorithm to detect a yellow card by examining every frame of the segments obtained after event segmentation is described below.

Normally, a yellow card caption stays 2 to 4 s on the screen while the whole event lasts longer. The caption remains on display for the duration of almost 50 to 100 frames. A novel algorithm to detect a yellow card frame is proposed, which is described below. Generally, the yellow card is displayed as a caption with the player information at the bottom part of the image. It is observed that in most broadcast soccer videos, the caption appears on the bottom of the screen. We process an input frame below the centre of an image and that is also not exactly at the bottom area as it is very difficult to have an idea of the caption placement and its size and height variations. This domain knowledge helps us to detect this event easily rather than classifying this event from a set of events like goal, corner and even other types of events.

Yellow card frame detection algorithm
Phase I

1. Divide the image horizontally into three equal parts and choose the bottom part where the caption is located.
2. Convert the input frame from the RGB image into a grey image.
3. Apply a canny edge detection operator on the grey image to detect horizontal lines of the rectangular box.
4. Erode the horizontal lines which have a length shorter than the threshold.
5. Extract the connected components.
6. If number components >1, then
   a. Convert the image from the RGB image into an HSV image.
   b. Set the pixels with the highest grey level values (255) which have the hue, saturation and value range as per empirically defined values. Set the rest of the pixels to grey value 0.
   c. Convert the image in binary.
   d. Extract the connected components.
      i. If any connected component is found which has the number of pixels in a specified range,
         1. Declare a probable yellow card frame.
      ii. Otherwise, neglect and proceed to the next frame.

   e. Otherwise, neglect and proceed to the next frame.
7. Collect probable yellow card frames.
8. Keep those frames as yellow card frames if the minimum number of frames within that segment meets the defined criteria.

Phase II

9. Compute the edge pixel ratio of the cropped image. Apply the Sobel operator to find edges.
10. If the edge pixel ratio (EPR) is within the threshold, declare that segment as a yellow card event.

Phase III

11. Perform steps 1 to 6d on two chosen yellow card frames of every segment.
12. Find the absolute distance between the detected connected component.
13. If the distance is less than the threshold.
    a. Declare a yellow frame and accept the segment.
    b. Else, discard the segment.

The entire algorithm involves three phases. The first phase consists of one to eight steps which find probable yellow card frames based on the presence of yellow colour. Steps 1 to 3 are straightforward. Step 4 involves erosion which uses a horizontal structuring element of size 20 which removes all lines shorter than a length of 20. In step 6, we first check for connected components because their absence indicates a smooth or constant-intensity image. The display of a yellow card in the caption exhibits various colours, hence gives rise to a number of edges. After steps 3 and 4, we still have few longer edges left which eventually contribute to connected components. Step 6a does the conversion of the RGB image to HSV as an HSV model is considered perceptually uniform. We deal with yellow cards of largely varying shades, so HSV becomes the most appropriate model. The pure yellow colour is represented at 60° in HSV; this defines a range of hue for yellow colour at 0.16 (60°/360°). But there may be variation in the intensity of yellow colour in different league videos. It is observed that the hue range for yellow colour at 0.14 to 0.22 is found to be satisfactory for detecting yellow card frames. From an empirical study, the threshold values of the saturation and value components of HSV are set greater than or equal to 0.8 and 0.6, respectively. These thresholds are set in step 6b of the algorithm. At the end of step 6b, we confirm the presence of yellow colour and we set the yellow region with the highest grey level intensity while the rest of the pixels are set with the lowest intensity. In step 6c, the binary threshold has been set to 0.8 because a strict threshold removes all the unnecessary components. From observation of different broadcast videos of standard league matches, the area of the yellow card is fixed between 20 to 450 number of pixels (step 6d) which represent a smaller to wider size of yellow card at a different tilt.

As the yellow card stays for 2 to 4 s, step 8 uses this knowledge to identify the yellow card frames. The minimum number of frames which is required to declare a yellow card event is set to 15. Various types of yellow cards are shown in Figure 4. Figure 4 clearly depicts the largely varying size, intensity as well as location of the yellow card. Figure 5 shows various intermediate steps of the yellow card event detection algorithm. Few leagues display a yellow card whose intensity keeps varying. The second phase attempts to mark the presence of caption in these detected probable yellow card frames. In soccer videos, there are misleading frames like a player wearing a yellow t-shirt or yellow socks and even a yellow ball. We compute the edge pixel ratio of the cropped image to confirm the presence of a caption showing a yellow card. The edge pixel ratio is computed using following equation:

$$EPR = \frac{\text{Total number of edge pixels}}{\text{Total number of pixels in the frame}} \qquad (5)$$

The range of EPR is set between 0.38 and 0.55. However, every event is narrated with the support of the caption, so there could be misleading cases where the frame shows a player wearing a yellow t-shirt along with the caption which conveys the information of a goal event. Phase III takes care of misleading frames that have a caption which coincides with a yellow t-shirt or some

yellow logos of the t-shirt. This type of typical case is shown in Figure 6. In the case of wrong yellow event frames, due to the movements of the player, the player's t-shirt of these frames experiences motion. Step 11 selects two frames at some specific interval of the detected yellow event segment. If these are genuine yellow event frames, then after applying steps 1 to 6d, almost similar images are produced consisting of one connected component at the place of the yellow card. We find the city block distance between the top left coordinates of the connected components of both images. Absolute distance is the sum of x and y differences of the top left coordinate of connected components. Due to motion, the city block distance between both images will be high.

2.3 Event filtration

After event segmentation of the video, we obtain the set of events. The change in optical flow is a key parameter for demarcation of events in an input video. As we are processing a broadcast video, there is no control over capturing of video content, i.e. the camera is moved over the ground from one angle to another and it results into a change in optical flow and leads to an event segmentation which does not actually represent any event. We apply event filtration on this set to filter out certain events which are not significant and dull according to the interest of the end user. In order to carry out this task, we apply Fourier transform on M_y'. Every event is characterized by the mean of the magnitude of the Fourier transform. Fourier transform and the magnitude can be found using the following formula. If the event is short and not important and there are smooth and

Figure 4 Various types of yellow cards. (a) Video 13, frame no. 11053. **(b)** Video 9, frame no. 48230. **(c)** Video 11, frame no. 35620. **(d)** Video 3, frame no. 18680. **(e)** Video 7, frame no. 5968. **(f)** Video 5, frame no. 2580.

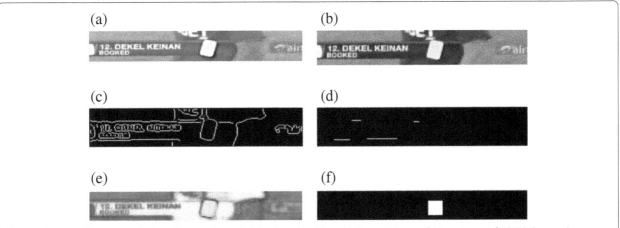

(a) (b)

(c) (d)

(e) (f)

Figure 5 Intermediate steps of the yellow card event detection algorithm. **(a)** Cropped image. **(b)** Gray image of **(a)**. **(c)** Canny edge detection. **(d)** Erosion of image **(c)**. **(e)** HSV image of **(a)**. **(f)** Binary image of **(e)** after step 6c.

fewer fluctuations within the event, it has a smaller magnitude of Fourier transform. Even if the event is short in time duration but consists of many views like far, goal post, audience etc. and transitions among these views, then it gives rise to the magnitude of high-frequency components. This can be very well captured using Fourier transform magnitude. We choose only 10% of frequency coefficients and extremely high-frequency components.

$$\Im\left(M_y^{'}(u)\right) = \frac{1}{N}\sum_{x=0}^{N-1}M^{'}(x)e^{-j2\pi ux/N}$$

$$|\Im(M^{'})| = \sqrt[2]{R^2(u) + I^2(u)} \tag{6}$$

However, shorter events can also be an important event, so every event can be further analysed by how many frames of an event experience the change in average motion magnitude $(M_y^{'})$ above the threshold. This is

Figure 6 Caption along with yellow colour in the background.

a useful descriptor because goal and player exchange events last longer and also involve frames which have a greater change in motion than the threshold. This can easily be found by the formula given in Equation 7.

Most goal events are followed by a celebration which involves gathering of players and cheering in the audience, so one can easily look out for this feature. However, there are goal events which are shorter and may not be followed by the much more cheering and celebration, but still due to more camera movements, they involve more frames undergoing a larger change in motion. We successfully think to use the product of the two features: Fourier transform and the ratio of frames having a change in motion greater than the threshold to total frames of an event. This product feature itself carries the neutral effect of Fourier transform and change in motion greater than the threshold. We introduce this product as an event filtration feature (EFF). This product feature enhances the capability to filter out insignificant events. We compute the mean of the EFF of every event. Events which succeed to satisfy the following criteria will be selected as filtered events:

$$\Pr\left(M_y^{'} > T\right) = \frac{\text{Number of frames whose } M_y^{'} > T}{\text{Total number of frames in an event}} \tag{7}$$

$$EFF_i > \alpha_1 \times \overline{EFF} \tag{8}$$

where $\overline{EFF}$ is the average value of the EFF of every event while α_1 is the empirical parameter which can be set between 0 and 1. We have set the value of α_1 to 0.7. EFF_i corresponds to the EFF value of event i. Next, we proceed to the event categorization phase.

2.3.1 Event categorization
The event categorization phase splits the set of events into low-impact and high-impact sets. The high-impact set

consists of events like goal, player exchange, injury etc. while the low-impact set includes events like goal attack, corner, foul, cheering in audience etc. Broadly, high-impact events are longer in span while low-impact events are shorter. Goal event is the most valuable event for the end users as well as for the game itself. For each event, the following features will be computed. Each event is characterized by the n number of M_y' values. Using these values, the first kurtosis is computed for every event. It is a descriptor of the shape of a probability distribution. Higher kurtosis means more of the variance is the result of infrequent extreme deviations. Goal event produces more deviations which can be frequent or infrequent. We can conclude that for the goal event, the value of kurtosis cannot be low but the values will be more than average or high. Kurtosis is computed using the following equation:

$$K_i = \frac{E\left(M_y' - \mu\right)^2}{\sigma^4} \tag{9}$$

where μ is the mean and σ is the standard deviation of the M_y' values. Second, we compute the energy for each event i using the following sum of squared formula:

$$e_i = \sum M'y^2 \tag{10}$$

The above equation has quite good capacity to realize the event which is longer over time span and having higher M_y' values. In soccer, goal and player exchange types of event can be easily identified by this parameter. To address this issue, we formulated an event categorization feature (ECF), which is a product of kurtosis and the energy of an event:

$$\text{ECF}_i = K_i \times e_i \tag{11}$$

High-impact events are selected using following equation:

$$\text{High\_impact} = \begin{matrix}\left(F_{\text{EVENT}} > \alpha_2 \times \overline{\text{ECF}}\right) \\ \text{and } \left(F_{\text{EVENT}} > \alpha_3 \times \overline{\text{EFF}}\right)\end{matrix} \tag{12}$$

where α_2 and α_3 are empirically set to 1.1 and 0.85. F_{EVENT} corresponds to the filtered events after event filtration. $\overline{\text{ECF}}$ and $\overline{\text{EFF}}$ indicate the average value of the event categorization feature and event filtration feature, respectively. Events which satisfy Equation 12 are referred as high-impact events while the rest of the events are put in low-impact class of events. At the end of the event categorization stage, we obtain high-impact and low-impact sets of events. Other events may remain present in both these classes because player clash, foul and injury are such events which may exist for a longer span or shorter span.

2.4 Edge and caption analysis

After obtaining the high-impact events, we analyse them using the edge pixel ratio and contents of the caption. Goal event is mostly followed by cheering in the audience view as well as gathering of players as well as goal post views which may give rise to edges in the frames. After the occurrence of goal events, every broadcaster displays the caption about the goal information. Broadcasters display the caption containing the information of players who has scored the goal and his team name just after the occurrence of an event as shown in Figure 7a. This caption almost stays for 4 to 8 s. After the completion of an event, the broadcaster displays the caption of team score information at the bottom part of the frame (image) as shown in Figure 7b. Generally, it is observed that the goal score caption is displayed within 55 s after the goal event. The presence of such views and detailed caption becomes a very important clue for the confirmation of the goal event. We do not consider initial frames up to 4 s (100 frames) of an event for EPR computation, and we continue to compute EPR for another 55 s (1,250 frames) even after the end of an event for the inclusion of the goal score caption.

We apply the following steps to carry out edge analysis of high-impact events:

1. Divide the image horizontally into three equal parts and choose the bottom part where the caption is located.
2. Convert the image in grey and apply the Sobel operator to detect horizontal edges.
3. Compute EPR.

EPR is computed using the formula mentioned in Equation 5.

The EPR of every frame of an event is computed, and then we compute the average value of the EPR of an event and also the average EPR of all high-impact events. Finally, we select such events whose EPR value is greater than the threshold. The threshold is empirically set to 0.97 times the

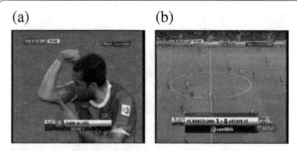

Figure 7 Goal caption displaying the player and team information. (a) Goal caption displaying the player's name. **(b)** Goal score caption displaying team names.

mean of the EPR of high-impact events. Events which have a higher EPR also include player exchange events. Player exchange events experience huge motion as the players are replaced on the ground. Many times, it involves transitions among far (ground), close-up and audience views similar to the goal event. The caption is also displayed for a longer duration while the player is leaving and a new player is entering. When the player leaves the ground, a red triangular symbol is displayed within the caption, and a green triangular symbol is displayed within the caption while a new player is entering the ground. This caption contains the important triangular shape of either red or green colour. These types of captions and the results of the below

mentioned algorithm are shown in Figure 8a,b, respectively. Now, we analyse the high EPR events based on the nature of their caption. A brief algorithm has been described below to separate the player exchange events from the high EPR events. The algorithm process is much more similar to the yellow card detection algorithm.

1. Divide the image horizontally into three and vertically two equal parts and choose the bottom right part where the caption is located.
2. Resize the bottom right image by a factor of 2.
3. Obtain the HSV image and search for the triangle symbol made of red/green pixels in the HSV image.

(a)

(b)

Resized HSV image of bottom right of original image showing player leaving and entering the ground

Exactly hitting the Red and Green spot indicating Player Exchange Events

Figure 8 Player exchange events and detected symbols. (a) Various images of player exchange events and divided into six regions. **(b)** Detected symbols of player exchange events.

4. Obtain the connected components of the image which has an area within the specified range.
5. Keep those frames as player exchange frames if the minimum number of frames within that segment meets the defined criteria.
6. Find the distance between the red and the green spot of the selected images; if the distance is less than threshold, then declare a player exchange event.

We resize the image by a factor of 2 to have enough large area of red/green triangle for proper detection. The hue range for red has been set to more than 0.90, and for green, it has been set between 0.30 and 0.40, while saturation and value for both red and green colours are set more than 0.80 and 0.60, respectively, in step 3. This region is smaller; hence, we cannot exactly search for the triangular shape or symbol, but we only search for pixels which belong to the above specified range of hue, saturation and value. The threshold for the area of the symbol is set between 10 and 150 in step 4 after observing various sizes of the symbol of player exchange events. The minimum number of frames which are required to declare a player exchange event is set to 15 for both the red and green symbols. The threshold for the city block distance between the top left coordinates of the red and green spots is empirically set less than 20. Detected player exchange events are removed from the set of events which have high EPR, and we refer to the remaining set of events as probable goal events.

2.5 View classification

After edge analysis, two sets of probable goal and low-impact events. In order to appropriately classify or label these events, it is necessary to realize the temporal pattern of the frames of an event. To furnish this task, it is necessary to label every frame of the event of the video. This process is referred to as view classification. Since this process is entirely independent of event filtration and categorization, it can be applied in parallel. In order to carry out view classification, we extract visual features from the frames and classify them into one of the predefined views. Characteristics of different views are described below:

- *Far field view*: A far field view displays a global view of the game field. It is captured by a camera at a long distance. It is often used to show the play status, such as play position and long passes. In this view, the ratio of the field area to the whole image is high, and the size of players within the field is small.
- *Goal post view*: A goal post view displays a goal post area. It is shown when players are attempting to get a goal. If the goal post is captured from a long

distance, the ratio of the field area is high; otherwise, the field ratio is medium to low. The goal post view is partially dominated by audience view.

- *Medium field view*: A medium view is a zoom-in view of a specific part of the field. It usually shows players and referees with the field as a background. In a medium view, the size of players in the playfield is bigger than that in a long view and the field ratio is in the medium range.
- *Close-up view*: An outfield view displays close-up of players, coach or players gathering with non-field background. It often focuses on the leading actor of current event. In this view, the field ratio is very low.
- *Audience view*: An outfield view displays the audience, as an indication of a break caused by highlights, such as an audience cheer view after a goal. In the audience view, the field ratio is extremely low and generally texture is dominant and complex.

The view classification system is shown in Figure 9. At the first level of classification, algorithm I is applied on all the frames of an event of the video for far field view and non-far field view classifications.

Algorithm I: field view detection

1. Convert the input frame from an RGB image into an HSV image.
2. Get the hue histogram of the image.
3. Define the hue range, which covers the different variations of the playfield's green colour, as a green window.
4. Compute the grass pixel ratio (GPR).
5. Apply the K-means algorithm on GPR to cluster frames into two clusters, one with high GPR values and the other with low GPR values.

The playfield usually has a distinct tone of green that may vary from stadium to stadium of different leagues of soccer. Matches that are played under floodlight exhibit different tones of green than sunlight. Even the shadow effect is also observed on the playfield many times under sunlight which also affects the intensity of green colour. So, hue range, which can cover different playfields' green colour, is carefully decided and identified as green range. The range of hue for the identification of various shades of green is set between 0.23 and 0.38 which we can refer to as a green window. We also involve the saturation and value components by setting them greater than 0.40. Due to varying green tones, the grass pixel ratio differs largely on various datasets; hence, it is not wise to set the threshold statically for the separation of far field and non-far field views. Instead, in step 5, we apply k-means to separately cluster these views. Algorithm I classifies

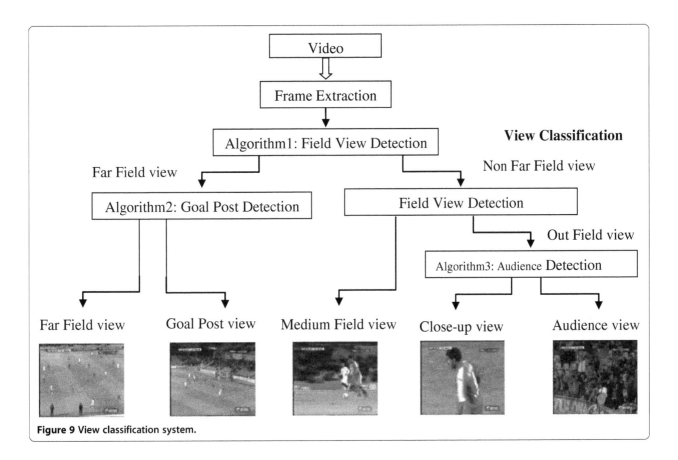

Figure 9 View classification system.

each frame in either far field view or non-far field view. The proposed goal post view detection method is mentioned below.

Algorithm II: goal post detection

1. Convert the input RGB image into a grey scale image.
2. Apply the Sobel edge detection operator on the grey image to detect vertical edges.
3. Erode the image with a vertical structuring element.
4. Apply a canny edge detection operator on the grey image to detect field lines near the goal post.
5. Apply Hough transformation.
6. If vertical parallel lines and parallel lines on the field are detected, then the frame belongs to a goal post view.

The Sobel edge detection operator is applied on the image to detect vertical lines. The resultant image exhibits vertical lines of the goal post as well as many other vertical lines, whose length is less than that of goal post lines. To remove such unimportant lines, erosion operation with a vertical structuring element is applied on the resultant image. We have used a vertical structuring element of length 5.

The output of edge detection operation is an image described by a set of pixels having vertical edges. This set of pixels rarely characterizes an edge completely because of noise and breaks in the edge. So, edge detection operation is followed by edge linking technique to assemble edge pixels into meaningful edges. We apply the Hough transform to detect linked vertical edges. If parallel vertical lines of the goal post and parallel field lines are detected, then we can conclude that the frame is having a goal post view. Figure 10c shows the detected two vertical poles of the goal post; however, these edges may be broken or noisy. Hence, results of the Hough transformation in Figure 10c are shown in Figure 10d. For the detection of parallel field lines near the goal post which are partially horizontal, the canny edge detection method is applied. Canny is a good candidate for thin as well as dull edges; we opt canny detection for these horizontal edges. Figure 10e depicts the existence of field lines near the goal post, and Figure 10f shows the result of the Hough transformation. Figure 11a,b,c,d,e,f shows the results of the goal post detection method of a left-oriented goal post.

2.6 Audience view detection

Classification of audience view and close-up view is based on finding EPR. Edge images generated using

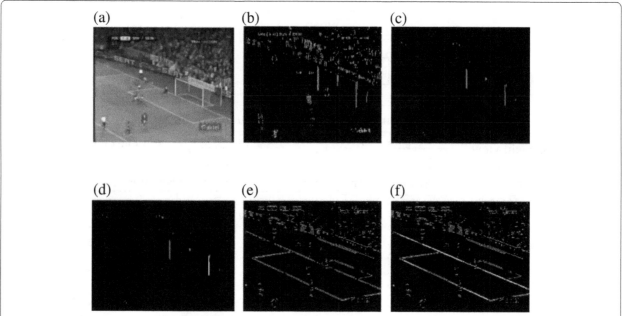

Figure 10 Goal post view (right-oriented) detection algorithm results. (a) Goal post view. **(b)** Vertical edge detection result of **(a)** using Sobel. **(c)** Erosion of image **(b)**. **(d)** Hougth transformation result of **(c)**. **(e)** Horizontal edge detection result of **(a)** using canny. **(f)** Hough transformation result of **(e)**.

canny edge detection are shown in Figure 12b,d along with their EPR values. The EPR value of audience view is quite higher than that of close-up view. EPR is statically set to 4.5 by experimenting on a large number of frames of different condition videos. The audience view detection algorithm has been described below.

Algorithm III: audience view detection

1. Convert the input RGB image into a grey image.
2. Convert the grey image into a binary image using canny edge detection operator.
3. Compute EPR as shown in Equation 5.

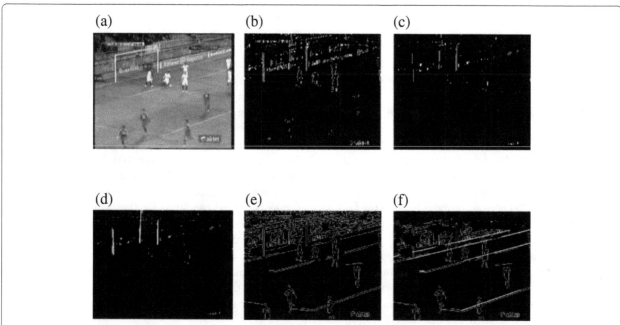

Figure 11 Goal post view (left-oriented) detection algorithm results. (a) Goal post view. **(b)** Vertical edge detection result of **(a)** using Sobel. **(c)** Erosion of image **(b)**. **(d)** Hougth transformation result of **(c)**. **(e)** Horizontal edge detection result of **(a)** using canny. **(f)** Hough transformation result of **(e)**.

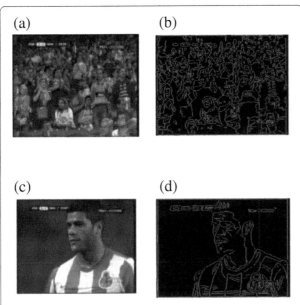

Figure 12 Audience and close-up views. (a) Audience view: frame no. 42723, video 10. **(b)** Edge image of left EPR: 6.18. **(c)** Close-up view, frame no. 33718, video 10. **(d)** Edge image of left EPR: 2.29.

4. Define the edge pixel threshold (EP_{th}) for audience view classification.
5. If $EPR > EP_{th}$, then
   i. The frame is classified as audience view.
6. Else
   i. The frame is classified as close-up view.

3 Event classification using HMM

At the end of the view classification phase, we end up with classification of every frame of an event in one of the above-mentioned views. To recognize certain interesting events from sports videos, temporal transition patterns among the frames (views) within the event can be utilized. To formulate the pattern of an event, it is necessary to map low-level features into high-level semantic. For example, to detect a goal scoring event, there are temporal patterns such as more transitions that happen among goal post, close-up and audience views because every goal event is followed by gathering of players and cheers in the audience. If these patterns can be recognized for the event sequence, the corresponding events can be identified. To boost up the efficiency of the event classification, it takes low-impact and high-impact classes of events as inputs which are produced by the event categorization phase. Since card events are already detected using the yellow card event detection algorithm, card event segments are removed from the high- or low-impact class of events. The event classification system proposed here uses the hidden Markov model to classify goal event, goal attack and other events in a soccer video. High-impact events are classified into either a goal event or

other events using a trained goal event model and other event models. Similarly, low-impact events are classified into goal attack or other events using a trained goal attack event model and other event models. HMM is described in following section.

3.1 Hidden Markov model

HMM is a statistical model for dealing with hidden states and observations. A video semantic event forms a Markov process, so the HMM is adopted as a powerful tool for video content analysis.

A HMM is defined by

- a set of states, Q
- a set of transitions, where transition probability $a_{kl} = P(\pi_i = l \mid \pi_{i-1} = k)$ is the probability of transitioning from state k to state l for $k, l \in Q$
- an emission probability, $e_k(b) = P(x_i = b \mid \pi_i = k)$, for each state, k, and each symbol, b, where $e_k(b)$ is the probability of seeing symbol b in state k. The sum of all emission probabilities at a given state must equal 1, that is, $\Sigma_b e_k = 1$ for each state, k.

There are basically three problems which can be solved using HMM.

Evaluation: Given an observation sequence x, and model parameters, determine the probability, $P(x)$, of obtaining sequence x in the model. The solution to this is the forward-backward algorithm.
Decoding: Given an observation sequence and model parameters, determine the corresponding optimal state sequence. This problem solution is the Viterbi algorithm.
Learning: Given a model and a set of training sequences, find the model parameters (transition and emission probabilities) that explain the training sequences with relatively high probability. The Baum-Welch algorithm is used for this purpose.

The steps of the event detection process are briefly described below.

3.2 Event detection using HMM

1. Each event corresponds to one model. In classification, we generated three models corresponding to goal, goal attack/corner and other events. Other event classes include events like foul, free pass, player exchange etc. which do not produce much impact on the nature of the game.
2. Given an observation sequence $O = O_1, O_2,..., O_n$ produced from a shot sequence, the probability $P(O|\lambda_i)$ relative to each model λ_i is calculated by using

the Viterbi algorithm. Thus, this sequence belongs to event$_j$ where $j = \arg \max_{i\,=\,1\,\ldots\,N} P(O/\lambda_i)$.

To achieve a higher recognition rate of the events correctly, at the end of the event categorization stage, we successfully separate the low-impact and high-impact events. Training the model also poses several questions like with how many events should we train the model to obtain highly accurate recognition. Normally, a goal event consists of transitions among the far, goal post, close-up and audience views in which close-up and audience views are dominating. A general observation infers that every goal is followed by cheering in the audience; however, in several goal events, the camera is not much more focused to the audience and their cheering. Prior to the goal event, occurrence of penalty kick types of events can also change the general pattern of the goal event. This situation applies to every rest event of soccer. Models of goal and other events are applied to the high-impact class while goal attack and other event models are applied to the low-impact class.

4 Simulation results and discussions

We have experimented with soccer videos of total length almost 6 h. We have conducted experiments on 13 video datasets from seven well-known soccer leagues like Barclays Premier League, La Liga, Serie A Premier League, FIFA EURO CUP, Europa, England 2 and Champions League. All these videos possess varying ground and illumination conditions, e.g. daylight, floodlight, rainy as well as shadow. Video datasets have a 352 × 288 resolution. Video dataset information is shown in Table 1 along with the video illumination condition. Date information of the match is shown in DD/MM/YYYY format. Varying ground and illumination conditions are clearly depicted in Figure 13 where we have depicted the far view images of different videos

used in the experiments. We can easily observe that every far view is highly different than the far view of other videos as this is natural because videos belong to different leagues and different illumination conditions. Datasets used in the experiments are available on the web at http://dspinnovations.blogspot.in/. We aim to propose a novel framework for a large number of various leagues and every type of illumination conditions. Table 2 reflects the average variance of the red, green and blue components of far-view-classified images of videos. Each video exhibits a large amount of difference in the average variance of the green component with the other one. Due to this fact, it is also observed that every video also differs largely in the number of far views which are classified by view classification. Soccer is a highly eventful game in which events like card, penalty kick, corner, foul, throw in, off side, goal attempts, goal etc. usually happen frequently, but card, goal and goal attack/corner types of events attract user's attention. We do not consider the repeated segments (replay) of an event because after the occurrence of the event replay is played, we only classify the original event.

Experimental results are evaluated using standard parameters: precision and recall. Precision quantifies what proportion of the detected events is correct while recall quantifies what proportion of the correct events is detected. If we denote D the events correctly detected by the algorithm, D_m the number of missed detections (the events that should have been detected but were not) and D_f the number of false detections (the events that should not have been detected but were), we have:

$$Recall = \frac{D}{D + D_m}$$

$$Precision = \frac{D}{D + D_f}$$

Table 1 Soccer video information

Serial number	Match information (team name, league name, date information, condition)	Duration in minutes
1	Getafe vs Sevilla, 1st half, April 2012, La Liga 2012 16/4/2012, floodlight	16:00
2	FC Barcelona vs Getafe, 1st half, March 2011, La Liga 2011, 19/3/2011, floodlight	10:00
3	FC Barcelona vs Almeria, 2nd half, La Liga 2011, 19/3/2011, floodlight	14:05
4	Real Sociadad vs Athletic Club, 2nd half, La Liga, 2011 29/9/2012, floodlight	33:00
5	Real Madrid vs Deportivo, 1st half, La Liga, 2011 30/9/2012, floodlight	22:00
6	Celta Vigo vs RCD Mallorca, 2nd half, La Liga, 2011 18/11/2012, daylight, shadow	20:00
7	Udinese vs Bologna, Serie A, 2nd half, 2/10/2011, daylight, shadow	16:10
8	Catania vs Intermilan, Serie A, 1st half, 15/10/2011, floodlight, rainy	16:00
9	Cardiff vs Middlesbrough, 1st half, England 2, 2/5/2011, daylight, shadow	35:00
10	Porto-Spartak Moscow, 2nd half, Europa League 7/4/2011, floodlight	40:00
11	Germany vs Greece, 2nd half, FIFA WC 2012, 21/6/2012, floodlight	38:00
12	Southampton vs Spurs, 1st half, Barclays Premier League, 22/12/2013, daylight, shadow	48:00
13	Arsenal vs Montpellier, 2nd half, Champions League, 21/11/2012, floodlight	46:00

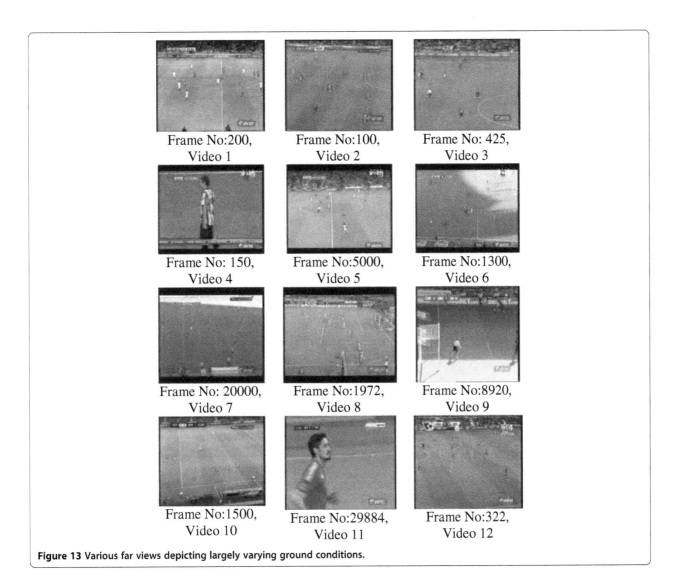

Frame No:200, Video 1

Frame No:100, Video 2

Frame No: 425, Video 3

Frame No: 150, Video 4

Frame No:5000, Video 5

Frame No:1300, Video 6

Frame No: 20000, Video 7

Frame No:1972, Video 8

Frame No:8920, Video 9

Frame No:1500, Video 10

Frame No:29884, Video 11

Frame No:322, Video 12

Figure 13 Various far views depicting largely varying ground conditions.

Table 2 Average variance of far views of videos

Dataset	Number of far views detected	Average variance of RGB of far views		
		R	G	B
La Liga 1	8,745	926.50	1,188	1,969
La Liga 2	9,533	963.99	813.23	1,213
La Liga 3	14,653	810.81	765.11	1,232
La Liga 4	9,374	1,711	2,063	2,148
La Liga 5	18,968	1,661	2,774	2,018
La Liga 6	13,333	1,325	2,059	1,602
Serie A 1	1,949	2,998	3,125	2,132
Serie A 2	365	2,267	2,773	2,946
England 2	1,477	2,088	1,741	1,713
Europa	37,831	808.22	1,245	1,254
EURO CUP	182	3,379	2,388	3,473
Barclays	345	184,637	195,797	299,013
Champions	5,981	88,651	120,522	159,864

Table 3 shows the performance of the card event detection algorithm. Results are very encouraging and achievement of 100% recall also sustains excellent precision of more than 95% in spite of having different types of cards like tilted, smaller or larger in size and varying shades of yellow. Our framework does not have any constraints, for example, in [32], for card event detection, the approach relies on the detection of the referee wearing a black t-shirt. Also, very limited types of soccer leagues have been experimented in [11,32] which possess almost similar types of ground and illumination conditions. The proposed yellow card event detection algorithm is found generic as it overcomes all such mentioned limitations. Our proposed algorithm succeeds and does not detect the yellow card event in the soccer dataset which does not contain the card event. Table 4 shows the number of events (shots) detected in every video and also the number of

Table 3 Performance of the yellow card detection algorithm

League name	Total yellow cards	Detected	Precision (%)	Recall (%)
La Liga 1	1	1	100	100
La Liga 2	1	1	100	100
La Liga 3	2	2	100	100
La Liga 4	2	2	100	100
La Liga 5	2	2	100	100
La Liga 6	1	1	100	100
Serie A 1	1	1	100	100
Serie A 2	0	0	100	100
England 2	3	3	100	100
Europa	3	4	75	100
EURO CUP	1	1	100	100
Barclays	1	1	100	100
Champions	3	3	100	100
Total	21	22	95.4	100

low- and high-impact events detected after event filtration and event categorization.

Every goal event has much more similarity to the other goal events while goal attack events may differ slightly because goal attack can happen from the frontal side of the goal post or from the corner (corner event). There is no specific criterion about the number of samples (events) required to accurately train the system, even overtraining can also result in poor classification accuracy. The corner/goal attack event has been trained using seven event shots

Table 4 Number of events detected as low/high-impact events after various stages

Soccer league	Number of events detected after threshold T (Equation 5)	Number of events after event filtration	Number of events after event categorization	
			Low-impact	High-impact
La Liga 1	12	7	6	1
La Liga 2	11	6	4	2
La Liga 3	22	11	8	3
La Liga 4	44	22	17	5
La Liga 5	24	11	9	2
La Liga 6	30	11	7	4
Serie A 1	23	11	6	5
Serie A 2	22	13	10	3
England 2	43	27	19	8
Europa	54	32	22	10
EURO CUP	36	23	18	5
Barclays	59	36	30	6
Champions	47	19	15	4

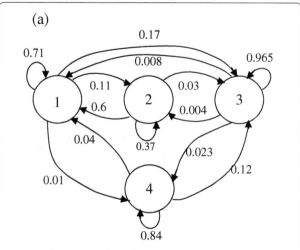

(a)

State transition diagram, Goal Attack Model

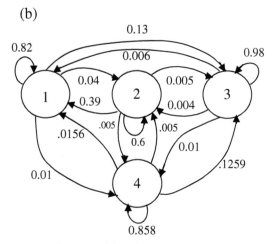

(b)

State transition diagram, Goal Model

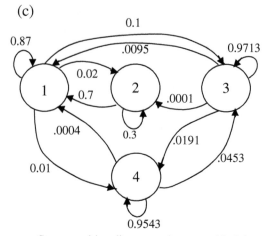

(c)

State transition diagram, other event Model

Figure 14 State transition diagrams. (a) Goal attack model. **(b)** Goal model. **(c)** Other event model.

Table 5 Goal event classification results

Soccer league	Total goals	Detected	Correct	False	Missed	Precision (%)	Recall (%)
La Liga 1	1	1	1	0	0	100	100
La Liga 2	1	1	1	0	0	100	100
La Liga 3	2	2	2	0	0	100	100
La Liga 4	2	2	2	0	0	100	100
La Liga 5	2	2	2	0	0	100	100
La Liga 6	1	1	1	0	0	100	100
Serie A 1	1	1	1	0	0	100	100
Serie A 2	1	2	1	1	0	50	100
England 2	4	4	2	2	2	50	50
Europa	5	6	5	1	0	83.33	100
EURO CUP	6	6	5	1	1	83.33	83.33
Barclays	3	3	2	1	0	66.67	100
Champions	2	1	1	0	1	100	50
Total	31	32	26	6	4	81.25	86.7

while goal and other event models are trained using eight and ten event shots, respectively. As a result of training, the generated state transition diagrams to classify goal attack, goal and other events are shown in Figure 14. Numbers 1, 2, 3 and 4 indicate far view, goal post view, close-up/mid-field view and audience view, respectively. Since goal events are lengthy events, they exhibit interrelationships between every state. Other events include foul, throw in and player injury types of events. It is natural to realize that transitions between goal post to audience and between goal post to close-up are not observed in the other event models. The goal attack event model exhibits high transition probabilities between goal post view and close-up view compared to other event models as the

event has the dominance of goal post view and its associated transitions.

Results of the event classification stage are shown in Tables 5, 6 and 7. For the goal event, we achieve a very good recall rate of 86.7% and precision of 81.25% in spite of various leagues. Several genuine goal attacks are also misclassified as goal events because many times goal attacks are followed by a player's disappointment and disgust of the audience which also create similar kinds of transition patterns among states like goal events. There are also goal events in which the camera is not focused on the audience or even does not follow more celebration by the players. Such events are misclassified due to the change in their pattern. We achieve a very

Table 6 Goal attack/corner event classification results

Video	Total	Detected	Correct	False	Missed	Precision (%)	Recall (%)
La Liga 1	5	5	5	0	0	100	100
La Liga 2	1	3	1	2	0	33.33	100
La Liga 3	4	5	4	1	0	80	100
La Liga 4	6	4	4	0	2	100	66.67
La Liga 5	3	5	3	2	0	60	100
La Liga 6	5	6	5	1	0	83.33	100
Serie A 1	3	4	3	0	0	100	100
Serie A 2	2	3	1	2	1	33.3	50
England 2	9	10	8	2	1	80	88.89
Europa	13	11	11	0	2	100	84.6
EURO CUP	8	10	6	4	2	60	75
Barclays	9	17	8	9	1	47.05882	88.89
Champions	8	11	8	3	0	72.72727	100
Total	76	94	67	26	9	72.04	88.15

Table 7 Other (throw in, offside, injury etc.) event classification results

Video	Total	Detected	Correct	False	Missed	Precision (%)	Recall (%)
La Liga 1	0	0	0	0	0	100	100
La Liga 2	3	0	0	0	3	100	0
La Liga 3	2	1	1	0	1	100	50
La Liga 4	11	13	11	2	0	84.6	100
La Liga 5	2	0	0	0	2	0	0
La Liga 6	6	4	4	0	2	100	66.7
Serie A 1	3	2	2	0	1	100	66.7
Serie A 2	8	5	4	1	4	80	50
England 2	7	4	2	2	5	50	28.5
Europa	7	8	7	1	1	87.5	87.5
EURO CUP	9	6	5	1	5	83.3	50
Barclays	23	10	9	1	14	90	39.1
Champions	5	0	0	0	5	0	0
Total	86	53	45	8	43	84.9	51.1

good precision for other events of 84.9% and a recall of 51%. Goal attack is also well recognized with a high recall of 88.1% as well as a quite good precision of 72%. Many times, other types of events which happen near goal posts are wrongly classified as goal attack due to the presence of the goal post in many views, so this reduces the precision of the goal attack event and recall of other events. Other events themselves consist of many events like foul and injury where each could even have different transition patterns. In spite of this fact, the framework achieves very good precision. There is no labelled and accurate dataset that is available for soccer videos. Hence, comparison cannot be considered fair, but we have compared our results with the results of [32]. Comparative performance is shown in Figure 15. The proposed approach proves its soundness as it outperforms in precision. Also, in [32], the authors have experimented with only two types of leagues while we have used seven various types of leagues.

We have analysed our proposed framework with different conditions like floodlight, daylight, shadow and dim illumination, and rainy condition. These conditions lead to major variation in illumination, and in this context, it is our major achievement to have a framework which successfully works in the presence of such conditions. However, we obtain little less recall in goal and corner/goal attack events. There are two clear reasons for this: 1) every league has its intrinsic characteristics of movement of cameras during the entire match as well as after the occurrence of an event. This pattern slightly differs in other leagues, e.g. a corner event is shown with more close-up views in one league while in another same event with more far views in another league. Hence, it is difficult to obtain precise view classification

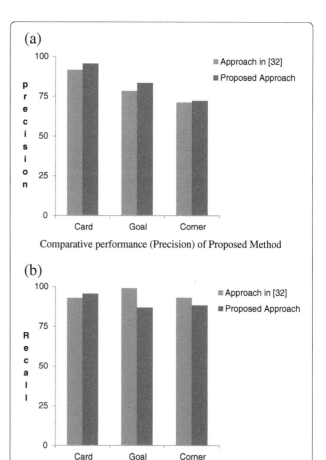

(a)

Comparative performance (Precision) of Proposed Method

(b)

Comparative performance (Recall) of Proposed Method

Figure 15 Comparative performance. (a) Precision of the proposed method. **(b)** Recall of the proposed method.

over different leagues. 2) There is no labelled dataset in soccer, and there is no ground truth available for the beginning and ending marks of various events within the match, so one cannot say exactly which are the beginning and ending frames of an event. We carry out the task of event segmentation automatically by our proposed method, but no method can be accurate to mark exactly this span of an event. It is important to note that our framework is not tuned to any specific broadcast video. Our framework needs only an input video and each video will be converted into a set of images for further processing. The input videos to our framework are broadcast ones, and hence, it is worth to mention that there is no control over the type of input video. Our framework does not have any constraints on frames per second.

5 Conclusions

In this paper, a novel, effective, robust fully automatic framework is proposed to detect and classify the important events of the soccer videos of various leagues under various illumination conditions. The proposed framework effectively uses the optical flow to demarcate the event. The proposed algorithm for card event detection achieves very high accuracy and found invariant to scale, tilt and varying yellow shades of the card. In order to improve the classification accuracy of the system, event filtration and event categorization processes are applied. These processes do not only contribute in improving the efficiency but also make the framework robust to the varying condition datasets. Event classification is successfully carried out by hidden Markov models after obtaining low-impact and high-impact classes of events. HMM can be easily adopted because every event has its own transition pattern. The generated results clearly reflect the efficiency and efficacy of the framework with different kinds of leagues. It is also important to note that our approach is fully automatic in the sense that our framework is able to classify all the detected events with high precision. Experimentation and investigations are still under progress to develop a framework which can be applicable to a large number of various soccer leagues.

Competing interests
The authors declare that they have no competing interests.

Author details
[1]U V Patel College of Engineering, Ganpat University, Kherva 384012, Mehsana, India. [2]Sardar Vallabhbhai National Institute of Technology, Surat 395007, India.

References

1. L Ying, Z Tong, T Daniel, *An Overview of Video Abstraction Techniques*. Technical Report. HP-2001-191 (HP Laboratories, Palo Alto, 2001)
2. M Roach, J Mason, L-Q Xu, F Stentiford, Recent trends in video analysis: a taxonomy of video classification problems, in *Proceedings of the 6th International Conference on Internet and Multimedia Systems and Applications (IASTED)* (Hawaii, 2002), pp. 348–353
3. S Carrato, I Koprinska, Temporal video segmentation: a survey. Signal Process. Image Commun. **16**(5), 477–500 (2001)
4. AG Money, A Harry, Video summarization: a conceptual framework and survey of the state of the art. J Visual. Commun. Image. Represent **19**(2), 121–143 (2008). doi:10.1016/j.jvcir.2007.04.002
5. G Yue, D Hai, Shot based similarity measure for content based video summarization, in *Proceedings of 15th IEEE International Conference on Image Processing (ICIP)* (San Diego, 2008), pp. 2512–2515
6. H Chen, L Zeng, Indexing and matching of video shots based on motion and color analysis, in *Proceedings of 9th IEEE International Conference on Control, Automation, Robotics and Vision (ICARCV)* (Singapore, 2006), pp. 1–6
7. S Wei, Jiang, A novel algorithm for video retrieval using video metadata information, in *Proceedings of IEEE International Workshop on Education Technology and Computer Science (ETCS)*, vol. 2 (Wuhan, 2009), pp. 1059–1062
8. W Wolf, Key frame selection by motion analysis, in *Proceedings of IEEE International Conference on Acoustics, Speech, and Signal Processing (ICASSP)* (Atlanta, 1996), pp. 1228–1231
9. B Lucas, T Kanade, An iterative image registration technique with an application to stereo vision, in *Proceedings of Seventh International Joint Conference on Artificial Intelligence (IJCAI)* (Vancouver, 1981), pp. 674–679
10. S Ling, J Ling, Motion histogram analysis based key frame extraction for human activity representation, in *Proceedings of Canadian Conference on Computer and Robot Vision (CRV)* (Kelowna, 2009), pp. 88–92
11. B Li, MI Sezan, Event detection and summarization in American football broadcast video. Proc. SPIE **4676**, 202–213 (2002)
12. R Leonardi, P Migliorati, Semantic indexing of multimedia documents. Proc IEEE. Multimedia **9**, 44–51 (2002)
13. J Liu, X Tong, W Li, T Wang, Y Zhang, H Wang, Automatic player detection, labeling and tracking in broadcast soccer video, in *Proceedings of British Machine Vision Conference (BMVC)* (Warwick, 2007), pp. 1–10
14. X Lexing, SF Chang, A Divakaran, S Huifang, Structure analysis of soccer video with hidden Markov models, in *Proceedings of International Conference Acoustics, Speech and Signal Processing (ICASSP)* (Orlando, 2002), pp. 4096–4099
15. W Zhou, A Vellaikal, C-CJ. Kuo, Rule-based video classification system for basketball video indexing, in *Proceedings of ACM Multimedia Conference* (Los Angeles, 2000), pp. 213–216
16. D Zhang, S-F Chang, Event detection in baseball video using superimposed caption recognition, in *Proceedings of 10th ACM of International Conference Multimedia* (Juan Les Pins, 2002), pp. 315–318
17. V Kiani, HR Pourreza, Flexible soccer video summarization in compressed domain, in *Proceedings of International Conference on Computer and Knowledge Engineering (ICCKE)* (Mashhad, 2013), pp. 213–218
18. DW Tjondronegoro, YP Chen, Knowledge discounted event detection in sport video. IEEE Sys. Man. Cybern Part A: Syst. Hum **40**(5), 1009–1024 (2010). doi:10.1109/TSMCA.2010.2046729
19. H Chung-Lin, C Chih-Yu, Video summarization using hidden Markov model, in *Proceedings of International Conference on Information Technology: Coding and Computing (ITCC)* (Las Vegas, 2001), pp. 473–477
20. W Jinjun, X Changsheng, C Engsiong, T Qi, Sports highlight detection from keyword sequences using HMM, in *Proceedings of IEEE International Conference on Multimedia and Expo (ICME)* (Taipei, 2004), pp. 599–602
21. J Assfalg, M Bertini, A Del Bimbo, W Nunziati, P Pala, Soccer highlights detection and recognition using HMMs, in *Proceedings of IEEE International Conference on Multimedia and Expo (ICME)* (Lausanne, 2002), pp. 825–828
22. G Xu, YF Ma, HJ Zhang, SQ Yang, An HMM-based framework for video semantic analysis. IEEE Trans. Circuits. Syst. Video. Technol **15**(11), 1422–1433 (2005). doi:10.1109/TCSVT.2005.856903
23. C Wu, Y-F Ma, H-J Zhang, Y-Z Zhong, Events recognition by semantic inference for sports video, in *Proceedings of IEEE International Conference on Multimedia and Expo (ICME)*, vol. 1 (Lausanne, 2002), pp. 805–808
24. DA Sadlier, N O'Connor, S Marlow, N Murphy, A combined audio-visual contribution to event detection in field sports broadcast video, in *Proceedings of IEEE Symposium on Signal Processing and Information Technology (ISSPIT)* (Darmstadt, 2003), pp. 552–555
25. M Petkovic, V Mihajlovic, W Jonker, S Kajan, Multi-model extraction of highlights from formula 1 programs, in *Proceedings of IEEE International Conference on Multimedia and Expo (ICME)*, vol. 1 (Lausanne, 2002), pp. 817–820

26. V Mihajlovic, M Pekovic, *Dynamic Bayesian Networks: A State of the Art* (CS Dept. Univ. Twente, Enschede, 2001)

27. S Alipour, P Oskouie, AM Moghadam, Bayesian belief based tactic analysis of attack events in broadcast soccer video, in *Proceedings of International Conference on Informatics, Electronics and Vision (ICIEV)* (Dhaka, 2012), pp. 612–617

28. Ren, Z Yuesheng, A Video Summarization approach based on machine learning, in *Proceedings of International Conference on Intelligent Information Hiding and Multimedia Signal Processing (IIHMSP)* (Harbin, 2008), pp. 450–453

29. J Basak, V Luthra, S Chaudhury, Video summarization with supervised learning, in *Proceedings of 19th International Conference on Pattern Recognition (ICPR)* (Tampa, 2008), pp. 1–4

30. K Ren, WAC Fernando, J Calic, Optimising video summaries using unsupervised clustering, in *Proceedings of 50th International Symposium (ELMAR)*, vol. 2 (Zadar, 2008), pp. 451–454

31. MS Hosseini, AM Moghadam, An adaptive neuro-fuzzy approach for semantic analysis of broadcast soccer video, in *Proceedings of International Conference on Development and Learning and Epigenetic Robotics (ICDL)* (San Diego, 2013), pp. 1–6

32. C Huang, H Shih, CY Chao, Semantic analysis of soccer video using dynamic Bayesian network. IEEE Trans Multimedia **8**(4), 749–759 (2006). doi:10.1109/TMM.2006.876289

16

No reference quality assessment for MPEG video delivery over IP

Federica Battisti[*], Marco Carli and Alessandro Neri

Abstract

Video delivering over Internet protocol (IP)-based communication networks is widely used in the actual information sharing scenario. As well known, the best-effort Internet architecture cannot guarantee an errorless data delivering. In this paper, an objective no-reference video quality metric for assessing the impact of the degradations introduced by video transmission over heterogeneous IP networks is presented. The proposed approach is based on the analysis of the inter-frame correlation measured at the output of the rendering application. It does not require any information on errors, delays, and latencies affecting the links and on the countermeasures introduced by decoders in order to face the potential quality loss. Experimental results show the effectiveness of the proposed algorithm in approximating the assessments obtained by using human visual system (HVS)-inspired full reference metrics.

1 Introduction

In the last decade, a fast market penetration of new multimedia services has been experienced. UMTS/CDMA2000-based videotelephony, multimedia messaging, video on demand over Internet, and digital video broadcasting are a growing share of nowadays' economy. The large-scale spreading of portable media players indicates the increasing end user demand for portability and mobility. At the same time, media sharing portals and social networks are mostly based on user-contributed video content, showing a different perspective of user relation with digital media: from being media consumers to being part of content creation, distribution, and sharing. This information sharing evolution presents many challenges; in particular, Internet protocol (IP)-based multimedia services require a transparent delivery of media resources to end users that has to be independent on the network access, type of connectivity, or current network conditions [1]. Furthermore, the quality of the rendered media should be adapted to the end users' system capabilities and preferences. An overview of the future challenges of video communication are addressed in [2] and in [3]. As can be noted, there are many factors that can prejudice the quality of the delivered video.

For this reason, the effectiveness of each video service must be monitored and measured for verifying its compliance with the system performance requirements, for benchmarking competing service providers, for service monitoring and automatic parameters setting, network optimization, evaluation of customer satisfaction, and adequate price policies setting.

To this aim, *ad hoc* designed tools have to be employed. In fact, the systems adopted for assessing the performances of traditional voice-based transmission systems are usually inadequate for evaluating the quality of multimedia data. In fact, a single training sequence comparison or the bit-wise error collection, which is used for measuring the quality of the received signal in the voice-based communication model, is not able to catch the dynamic feature of a video stream and its correlation with the overall experience of the final user.

To cope with this task, the research on video quality assessment has mainly been focused on the development of objective video quality metrics able to mimic the average subjective judgment. This task is of difficult solution being dependent on many factors as:

- Video characteristics and content: size, smoothness, amount of motion, of sharp details, and the spatial and temporal resolution
- Actual network conditions: congestion, packet loss, bit error rate, time delay, time delay variation

*Correspondence: federica.battisti@uniroma3.it
Department of Engineering, Universita' degli Studi Roma TRE, Rome 00146, Italy

- Viewer's condition: display size and contrast, processing power, available memory, viewing distance
- Viewer's status: feeling, expectations, experience, involvement

These factors are often difficult or impossible to be measured, especially in real-time communication services. Furthermore, each factor has a different impact on the overall perceived distortion whose visibility strongly depends on the content (e.g., salt and pepper noise can be not noticeable in highly textured areas of a frame while it can become highly visible in the next uniform frame).

In this contribution, a no-reference metric for assessing the degradations introduced by transmission of an original video, encapsulated in a MPEG2 TS, over a heterogeneous IP network is presented. Variable channel conditions may cause both isolated and clustered packet losses resulting in data and temporal integrity loss at the decoder side. This could lead to the impossibility of decoding isolated or clustered blocks, tiles, and even entire frames. Considering the continuous increase of computing power of both mobile and wired terminals, a wide spread of error concealment techniques aimed at increasing the perceived quality can be expected. The proposed system can be considered blind with respect to errors, such as delays and latencies that affected the link, and to the concealment strategies implemented at the decoders to face the potential quality loss. The proposed method is based on the evaluation of perceived quality of video delivered by a packet switched network. These networks are characterized by loss, delayed, or out-of-sequence delivery of packets. The proposed metric is therefore valid for mobile networks exploiting IP, i.e., UMTS, long-term evolution (LTE), and LTE Advanced.

The rest of the paper is organized as follows. In Section 2, the state-of-the-art research addressing video quality metrics is addressed, while in Section 3, the model of the proposed metric is presented. In Section 4, the evaluation of the video distortion is described. In Section 5, the results of the performed experiments are presented based on two types of evaluation: comparison with the National Telecommunications and Information Administration (NTIA) scores and comparison with subjective tests. Finally, in Section 6, the conclusions are drawn.

2 State of the art

A set of parameters describing the possible distortion in a video has been defined and classified in 'ITU-T SG9 for RRNR project' [4]. Here, temporal distortion, temporal complexity, blockiness, blurring, image properties, activity, and structure distortion are independently evaluated and then linearly combined with the aim of reliably fitting the measured mean opinion score (MOS) with the calculated MOS. This general model has been

recently improved in [5] taking into account the dynamic range distortion. Objective quality metrics can be classified according to different criteria [6-8]. One of this is the amount of side information required to compute a given quality measurement; depending on this, three classes of objective metrics can be described:

- *Full reference metrics (FR)*: the evaluation system has access to the original media. Therefore, a reliable measure for video fidelity is usually provided. A drawback presented by these metrics is that they require the knowledge of the original signal at the receiver side.
- *Reduced reference metrics (RR)*: the evaluation system has access to a small amount of side information regarding the original media. In general, certain features or physical measures are extracted from the reference and transmitted to the receiver as side information to help the evaluation of the video quality. The metrics belonging to this class may be less accurate than the FR metrics, but they are also less complex, and make real-time implementations more affordable.
- *No-reference metrics (NR)*: the evaluation system has no knowledge of the original media. This class of metrics is the most promising in the context of video broadcast scenario since the original images or videos are in practice not accessible to end users.

The FR class includes all methods based on pixel-wise comparison between the original and the received frame. Among them, the most relevant example of objective metric is the peak signal-to-noise ratio (PSNR), which is widely used to perform a fast and simple quality evaluation. It is based on the computation of the ratio between the mean square error (MSE) between the image to be evaluated and the reference image, and the maximum range of pixel values. Even if the metrics belonging to this class are easy to compute, they do not always well correlate with quality as perceived by human observers. In fact, these metrics do not consider the masking effects of the human visual system (HVS) and each pixel degradation contributes to the overall error score even if the error is not perceived by a human subject.

A novel and effective approach has been proposed in [9] with the NTIA-video quality metric (VQM) which combines in a single score the perceptual impact of different video artifacts (block distortion, noise, jerkiness, blurring, and color modifications). The NTIA-VQM is a general purpose video quality model designed and tested in a wide range of quality and bit rates. It is based on a preprocessing consisting in spatial and temporal alignment of reference and impaired sequences, region extractions, gain, and offset correction. Following, feature extraction, spatio-temporal parameter estimation, and local indexes polling are performed for computing the overall quality score. The features considered in VQM are extracted from the spatial gradients of the luminance and chrominance components and from measuring contrast and temporal information extracted from the luminance component only. It has been validated by exploiting extensive subjective and objective tests. The high correlation with MOS shown in the performed subjective tests is the reason for the wide use of this metric as a standard tool (ANSI) for FR video assessment[10].

Similarly, moving picture quality metric (MPQM) [11] and its colored version color moving picture quality metric [12] are based on the assumption that the degradation of the quality of a video is strictly related to the visibility of the artifacts. In more detail, it is based on the decomposition of the original and of the impaired videos in visual channel, and on the distortion computation performed by considering the masking effect and the sensitivity contrast function. The main limitation of this, and similar methods based on error sensitivity model, is in the simple (often linear) model adopted for the HVS, which badly approximates the complex, non-linear, and still partially disclosed vision system.

A different approach is based on the hypothesis that the human brain is very efficient in extracting the structural information of the scene rather than the error information. Therefore, as proposed by Wang et al. in [13], a perceptual-based metric should be able to extract information about structural distortions. The SSIM metric, proposed in [13], shows a good correlation with the subjective scores obtained by campaigns of subjective tests. Other classical FR metrics inspired by the HVS are in the works by Wolf et al. [14] and Watson et al. [15], while a survey of available FR video quality metrics can be found in [16]. It is worth noticing that for an effective frame-to-frame comparison, both the original video and the one under test must be synchronized.

Recently, Shnayderman et al. [17] compared the singular value decomposition coefficients of the original and the coded signal, while in [18], the authors computed the correlation between the original and the impaired images after a 2D Gabor-based filter bank, based on the consideration that the cell of the visual cortex can be modeled as 2D Gabor functions. As can be noticed, these metrics can also be applied to videos by computing a frame by frame quality evaluation.

As previously stated, the usability of FR metrics is often limited in real scenarios due to the need for availability of the original video. Nevertheless, being the perceived quality dependent on the content, it cannot be directly inferred from the knowledge of parameters such as channel reliability and temporal integrity. To partially overcome this problem, RR and NR quality metrics have been devised.

With respect to FR metrics, only few attempts of RR and NR metrics have been presented in literature. Among RR ones, Carnec et al. in [19] present a still image metric based on color perception and masking effects, resulting in a small overhead. Blocking, blurring, ringing, masking, and lost blocks are linearly combined in [20] for a frame by frame comparison. Wang and Simoncelli in [21], based on the frequency distribution characteristics of natural images, proposed to use the statistics of the coded image to predict the visual quality.

Different approaches are proposed by Kanumuri et al. in [22]: the RR metric is based on a two-step approach. The information gathered from the original, received, and decoded video are used in a classifier whose output will be used in the evaluation of artifact visibility performed on a decision tree trained by subjective tests. Similarly, in [23], a general linear model (GLM) is adopted for estimating the visibility threshold of packet loss in H.264 video streaming. In [24], GLM is modified by computing a saliency map, for weighting the pixel-wise errors, and by taking into account the influence of the temporal variation of saliency map and packet loss. The results show that if the HVS features are considered, the prediction of subjective scores is improved.

Finally, a novel approach is represented using different communication systems for delivering information on the original media. In this classification are, for example, the data hiding-based RR metrics. In these approaches, a thumbnail of the original frame [25-28], a perceptually weight watermark [29], or a particular image projection [30] are used in the quality evaluation as fingerprint of the original frame quality. The main vulnerability of these methods is in the robustness of the watermarking method. In fact, any alteration, wanted or not, of the inserted data may strongly affect the objective assessment.

The need for the reference video or for partial information about it is a considerable drawback in many real-time applications. For this reason, the design of effective NR metrics is a big challenge. In fact, although human observers are able to assess the quality of a video without using the reference, the creation of a metric that could mimic such a task is difficult and, most frequently, it results in a loss of performances in comparison to the FR/RR approaches. To achieve effective evaluations, many existing NR metrics estimate the annoyance by detecting and estimating the strength of common artifacts (e.g., blocking and ringing).

NR techniques are the most promising because their final score can be considered, for an ideally perfect metric, as an absolute quality value, independent from the knowledge of the original content. Few metrics have been designed for the evaluation of impairments due to single artifacts as blockiness [31], blurriness [32], and jerkiness [33].

Different strategies have been proposed to evaluate the impact of impairments caused by compression algorithms and transmission over noisy channels. These can be classified according to the parts of the communication channel that are involved:

- Source coder errors: MSE estimation due to compression [34], example-based objective reference in [35], motion-compensation edge artifacts in [36];
- Variable delay [37,38];
- Packet loss effects [39-41]. In [41], the NR metric is based on the estimation of mean square error propagation among the group of picture (GOP) in motion compensation-based encoded videos. The idea is to consider the motion activity in the block as initial guess of the distortion caused by the initial packet loss;
- Bitstream-based video quality metric: in these systems, several bitstream parameters, such as motion vector length or number of slice losses, are used for predicting the impairments visibility in MPEG-2, SVC [42], or H.264 [43,44] and HD H.264 [45] videos. Recently, the bitstream metric proposed in [46] has been modified with pixel-based features to cope with HDTV stream [47];
- Rendering system errors: [48-50].

Other examples include the works presented by Webster et al. [51] and Brétillon et al. [52]. The estimation of the pattern of lost macroblocks based on the knowledge of the decoded pixels is used as input to a no-reference quality metrics for noisy channel transmission. The metrics by Wu and Yuen and Wang et al. estimate quality based on blockiness measurements [31,53], while the metric by Caviedes and Jung takes into account measurements of five types of artifacts [54]. Recently, in [55], a methodology for fusing metrics feature for assessing video quality has been presented. This work has also been adopted in the ITU-T Recommendation P.1202.2.

3 The NR procedure
In the following, the motivations behind each step of the NR procedure are briefly described and then detailed in Subsections 3.1 to 3.4. As previously stated, channel errors and end-to-end jitter delays can produce different artifacts on the received video. The effect of these errors can have a dramatic impact on the quality perceived by users since the loss of a single packet can result in a corrupted macroblock. Corrupted information can affect both spatial (to neighboring blocks) and temporal (over adjacent frames) quality due to the predictive, motion-compensated coding scheme adopted by most of existing video coders. The visual impact of these errors strictly depends on the effectiveness of the decoder scheme and on the concealment strategy that is adopted.

In order to recover transmission errors, decoders can exploit several strategies depending on the error resilience or concealment techniques adopted in the communication scheme. Error resilience is based on the addition of redundant information at the encoder side for allowing the decoder to recover some transmission errors: the drawback is the increase in the amount of transmitted data. On the other hand, error concealment is a post-processing technique in which the decoder tries to mask the impairments caused by packet losses and bit stream errors that have been detected but not corrected. In this case, even if the quality of the recovered data is usually lower than the original one, the system does not require encoder/decoder modification or extra information delivering. Several concealment techniques have been proposed in literature whose effectiveness increases with complexity. The simplest proposed strategy consists in filling the missing areas with a constant value or with information extrapolated by considering the last correctly decoded block. More sophisticated techniques apply prediction/interpolation of the lost block(s) by exploiting spatial and temporal redundancy [28]. Concealment effectiveness is largely affected by the spatial and temporal extension of the missing information, with best performances obtained in the case of small clusters and isolated blocks. An example of visual artifacts on a test sequence 'Brick', when transmitted on a noisy channel affected by a 15% packet loss, is shown in Figure 1. When an error affects the entire frame or a large part of it, the decoder may decide to completely drop the corrupted frame and to *freeze* the last error-free video frame until a new valid frame is correctly decoded. In this case, the perceived quality of the played video will depend on the dynamics of the scene. In fact, although only error-free frames are played, the motion of objects composing the scene may appear unnatural, due to its stepwise behavior (jerkiness effect). The dropping mechanism can also be caused by a playback system that is not fast enough to decode and display each video frame at full nominal speed. It is worth noticing that the same experience is perceived in the presence of *frame freezing* artifacts or by repetition of the same frame.

The NR metric proposed in this paper is independent from the error concealment techniques implemented in the video player; however, since frame repetition is a very common concealment method, here, the assessment of the quality loss produced by *freezing* the video in correspondence of frame losses is specifically addressed. More in details, before applying the NR jerkiness metric proposed by the authors in [56], the played sequence is analyzed in order to detect the presence of repeated frames.

To this aim, the rendered sequence is first partitioned into static and dynamical shots, on the basis of the amount

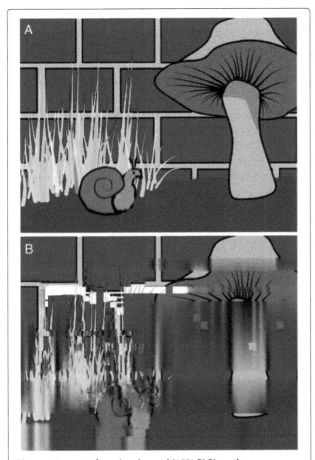

Figure 1 Impact of a noisy channel (15% PLR) on the transmission of a test video sequence. In particular, by considering the rendered frame **(A)** versus the original one **(B)**, several artifacts can be noted: isolated blocks, repeated lines, blurring and wrong color reconstruction.

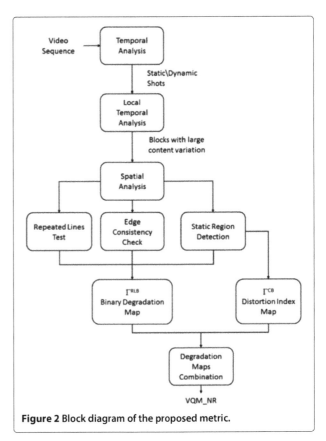

Figure 2 Block diagram of the proposed metric.

of changes between consecutive frames. Next, the shots classified as static are evaluated in order to detect if the identified small amount of changes corresponds to a real static scene or to the freeze of entire frames or part of them. At the same time, the dynamical shots are tested to verify the presence of isolated and clustered corrupted blocks. These analyses result in temporal variability and spatial degradation maps that are used to assess the video quality by evaluating the overall distortion as shown in Figure 2. In the following, the details of the proposed system are presented.

3.1 Frame segmentation in dynamic and static shots based on a global temporal analysis

As previously described, the first step of the NR procedure is the grouping of frames in dynamic or static shots based on a temporal analysis.

Let $\mathbf{F} = \{\mathbf{F}_k, k = 1, \ldots, L\}$ denote a video sequence composed by L frames of $m \times n$ pixels.

The generic kth frame can be partitioned in $N_r \times N_c$ blocks $\mathbf{B}_k^{(i,j)}$ of $r \times c$ pixels with top left corner located in (i, j). Let $\bar{\mathbf{F}}_k$ be the mean luminance value for the kth frame and $\bar{\mathbf{B}}_k^{(i,j)}$ the mean luminance value of block $\mathbf{B}_k^{(i,j)}$. Let $\Delta \mathbf{F}_k = \mathbf{F}_k - \bar{\mathbf{F}}_k$ and $\Delta \mathbf{B}_k^{(i,j)} = \mathbf{B}_k^{(i,j)} - \bar{\mathbf{B}}_k^{(i,j)}$ denote the deviation of the luminance of the kth frame and of the block $\mathbf{B}_k^{(i,j)}$ from the corresponding mean values.

The normalized inter-frame correlation coefficient ρ_k between the kth and the $(k-1)$th frames is defined as:

$$\rho_k = \frac{\left\langle \Delta \mathbf{F}_k, \Delta \mathbf{F}_{k-1} \right\rangle}{\|\Delta \mathbf{F}_k\|_{L_2} \|\Delta \mathbf{F}_{k-1}\|_{L_2}}, \tag{1}$$

where $< \bullet, \bullet >$ denotes the inner product and $\|\bullet\|_{L_2}$ the L_2 norm. Similarly, the inter-block correlation $\rho_k^{\mathbf{B}(i,j)}$ can be computed as:

$$\rho_k^{\mathbf{B}(i,j)} = \frac{\left\langle \Delta \mathbf{B}_k^{(i,j)}, \Delta \mathbf{B}_{k-1}^{(i,j)} \right\rangle}{\left\|\Delta \mathbf{B}_k^{(i,j)}\right\|_{L_2} \left\|\Delta \mathbf{B}_{k-1}^{(i,j)}\right\|_{L_2}}. \tag{2}$$

It is possible to group the frames into static and dynamical shots by comparing the inter-frame correlation $\rho_k, k = 1, \ldots, L$, with a threshold λ_s:

$$\begin{cases} \rho_k < \lambda_S : \text{dynamical shot} \\ \rho_k > \lambda_S : \quad \text{static shot} \end{cases} \tag{3}$$

where the threshold λ_s is set to the equal error rate (EER) between the classification of a static block as *dynamic* and vice versa.

As illustrated in Figure 3, the inter-frame correlation presents a spiky behavior with values close to one in correspondence of *frozen* frames. It is important to underline that the detection of such a behavior is not sufficient to identify a partial or total frame loss. In fact, in the case of static scenes, consecutive frames present a high inter-frame correlation.

Therefore, it is important to be able to distinguish between frames that are affected by errors and the ones belonging to a static scene. This can be achieved by using a system for assessing the presence of jerkiness. In fact,

jerkiness is the phenomenon that leads to perceive a video as consisting of a sequence of individual still images. In this contribution, we adopt the approach that has been presented in [56].

After the segmentation into dynamic and static shots, the task of quality evaluation gets easier. In fact, for static shot sequences, it is possible to evaluate the quality of the first frame and to extend the obtained score to the frames belonging to the static cluster. In this way, a degradation map is computed for the first frame (that can still be affected by artifacts) and is inherited by the frames belonging to the same static shot. When dealing with the distortion associated to isolated and clustered impaired blocks, it is estimated by means of a two-step procedure

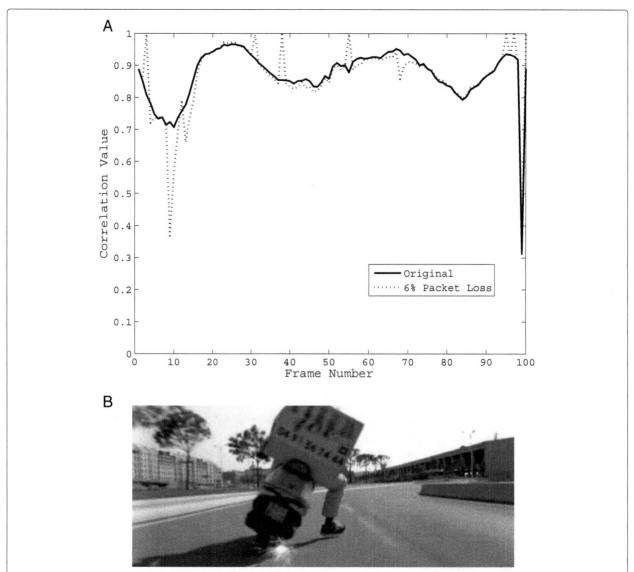

Figure 3 Test video sequence affected by 6% packet loss. (A) The normalized interframe correlation among the first 100 frames extracted from the original video sequence *Taxi* and the first 100 frames extracted from the same sequence affected by 6% packet loss. **(B)** One frame extracted by the video sequence.

based on temporal and spatial degradation analysis. In the following, this will be referred to as 'degradation map' computation.

3.2 Local temporal analysis

The local temporal analysis is performed in two stages. The aim of the first one is to identify and to extract from each frame the blocks that are potentially affected by artifacts. This analysis is performed by classifying the blocks as:

- With medium content variations
- Affected by large temporal variations
- With small content variations

depending on their temporal correlation $\rho_k^{B^{(i,j)}}$.

The corresponding temporal variability map $\Gamma_k^V = \{\Gamma_k^{VB^{(i,j)}}\}$ is computed by comparing the inter-frame correlation of each block with two thresholds θ_l and θ_h:

$$\Gamma_k^{VB^{(i,j)}} = \begin{cases} 1, & if \ \rho_k^{B^{(i,j)}} < \theta_l \\ 0, & if \ \theta_l \leq \rho_k^{B^{(i,j)}} \leq \theta_h \\ 2, & if \ \rho_k^{B^{(i,j)}} > \theta_h \end{cases} \quad (4)$$

The selection of the two thresholds, θ_l and θ_h, is performed based on the assumption that:

- The correlation, between corresponding blocks belonging to consecutive frames, is close to one in the presence of a repeated block or of a block belonging to a static region.
- The correlation value is close to zero in case of a sudden content change (usually occurring after shot boundaries) or in the presence of an error.

For this reason, as can be noted in Equation 4, the highest temporal variability index is assigned to blocks considered as *unchanged* from the previous frame, while zero distortion index is assigned to blocks with *medium* content variation. In more details, let us define with probability of false alarm (P_{fa}) the probability of detecting the repeated blocks as affected by errors in the absence of distortion and with probability of miss detection (P_{md}) the probability of considering as unaltered a frame in the presence of errors. The two thresholds, θ_l and θ_h have been selected in order to grant

$$|P_{fa} - P_{md}| < \varepsilon_1$$

where ε_1 has been experimentally determined, during the training phase, by comparing the performances achieved by the temporal analysis algorithm with the scores provided by a group of video quality experts in an informal subjective test.

3.3 Spatial analysis

The blocks classified as potentially affected by packet loss during the temporal analysis phase undergo a spatial analysis. The spatial analysis is performed in several steps:

- Static regions detection: it aims at verifying whether a high correlation between the current block $\mathbf{B}_k^{(i,j)}$ and the previous one $\mathbf{B}_{k-1}^{(i,j)}$ is due to the loss of a single or multiple blocks or to a static region. To perform this task, for each block with $\Gamma_k^{VB^{(i,j)}} = 2$, it is checked if at least v among the surrounding blocks present a strong temporal correlation. In case of positive result, the block is classified as belonging to a static region and its potential distortion index $\Gamma_k^{CB^{(i,j)}}$ is set to zero. The parameter v has been identified by experimental test. Practically, a set of expert viewers has been presented with a set of short videos presenting different content situations affected by increasing blocking artifacts. The parameter v has been selected as the one resulting in the highest correlation between the people score and the algorithmically performed spatial analysis block. That is:

$$\Gamma_k^{CB^{(i,j)}} = \begin{cases} 0 & if \ |\{(p,q)| \ (p,q) \in N(i,j), and \ \Gamma_k^{VB^{(p,q)}} = 2\}| > v \\ \Gamma_k^{VB^{(i,j)}}: & otherwise \end{cases}$$

$$(5)$$

- Edge consistency check: the presence of edge discontinuities in block boundaries can be used as an evidence of distortions. For the sake of simplicity, we detail the procedure for the case of gray scale images. It can be easily extended to the color case by evaluating separately the edge consistency for each color component. Let E_l and E_r be the L_1 norms of the vertical edges, respectively, on the left and on the right boundary of the block, and with A_c, A_l and A_r the average values of the L_1 norms of the vertical edges inside the current block and of the left and right adjacent blocks. A block with $\Gamma_k^{CB^{(i,j)}} \neq 0$ is classified as affected by visible distortion if:

$$\left| E_l - \frac{(A_c + A_l)}{2} \right| > \theta \quad or \quad \left| E_r - \frac{(A_c + A_r)}{2} \right| > \theta$$

$$(6)$$

where the threshold θ has been defined on the basis of experimental trials. In particular, it corresponds to just noticeable distortion collected evaluated for the 90% of subjects. The same procedure is then applied to the horizontal direction. If the block edges are consistent (i.e., no visible distortion has been detected along horizontal and vertical directions), $\Gamma_k^{CB^{(i,j)}}$ is reset to 0.

- Repeated lines test: it is performed to detect frames that have been partially correctly decoded. A very common concealment strategy is based on the fact that when the packet loss affects an intra-frame encoded image, and a portion of the frame is properly decoded, the remaining part is replaced with the last row correctly decoded. As can be noted in Figure 4, the procedure results in a region containing vertical stripes.

Let $f_k[i]$ be the ith row of the kth frame. Starting from the mth line of the frame, the L_1 norm of the horizontal gradient component is computed and compared to a threshold λ_H. If

$$\left\| \Delta f_k[i] \right\|_{L_1} > \lambda_H, \tag{7}$$

the procedure is repeated on the previous line $(i-1)$ to check if consecutive lines are identical by comparing the L_1 norm of their difference with a threshold λ_V

$$\left\| f_k[i] - f_k[i-1] \right\|_{L_1} < \lambda_V. \tag{8}$$

This procedure is iterated until the test fails, thus meaning that there is a different information carried out by consecutive lines. After the repeated lines test has been performed, a binary spatial degradation map, $\Gamma_k^{RLB^{(i,j)}}$ of $[0,1]$ entries, is created where '1' corresponds to a block belonging to a vertical stripes region and '0' otherwise. The two thresholds, λ_V and λ_H have been set after a training process with a pool of experts trying to match the subjective impression of repeated lines.

3.4 Reference frame detection

The previous procedure allows to assess the presence of blocks belonging to the current frame which are affected by distortions caused by packet loss. Nevertheless, due to error propagation, the impairment can propagate until an intra-frame encoded image (I-frame), is received. Figure 5 shows the normalized inter-frame correlation of a sequence extracted from an action movie. As can be noted, an I-frame is usually characterized by a low correlation with the previous frame and a high correlation with the next frame. This behavior is always verified unless the same scene is shown for a long period.

Let us denote with v_k^{CB} the number of corrupted blocks, i.e.,

$$v_k^{CB} = |\{\Gamma_k^{CB^{(i,j)}} \neq 0\}|. \tag{9}$$

Then, the kth frame is classified as an I-frame if

$$\rho_{k-1} - \rho_k > 2\eta_P \quad \text{and} \quad \rho_{k+1} - \rho_k > 2\eta_S \tag{10}$$

and no more than P_p out of the Q_p previous frames and no more than P_n out of the Q_n following frames are characterized by a number v_k^{CB} of blocks with inconsistent edges exceeding a threshold λ_I.

The decision thresholds are adapted to the current video content. In particular, η_P and η_S are proportional to the mean absolute differences of the correlation coefficients in the intervals $[k - M_l, k]$ and $[k, k + M_h]$, i.e.:

$$\eta_P = \frac{1}{M_l} \sum_{h=k-M_l+1}^{k} |\rho_h - \rho_{h-1}| \tag{11}$$

and

$$\eta_S = \frac{1}{M_h} \sum_{n=k+1}^{k+M_h} |\rho_n - \rho_{n-1}|. \tag{12}$$

The value M_l is selected to guarantee that the time interval needed for the adaptation of η_P starts at the frame following the last correctly detected I-frame. When processing the kth frame, no information about location of next I-frames is available and the length of the interval employed for the adaptation of η_S is considered to be constant. When the time interval between two I-frames is less than M_h, only the I-frame with the lowest correlation with the previous frame is retained.

4 Distortion map evaluation

The evaluation of the video quality metric VQM$_{NR}$ is based on the degradation index maps $\Gamma_k^{RLB^{(i,j)}}$ and $\Gamma_k^{CB^{(i,j)}}$

Figure 4 Frame affected by vertical stripes.

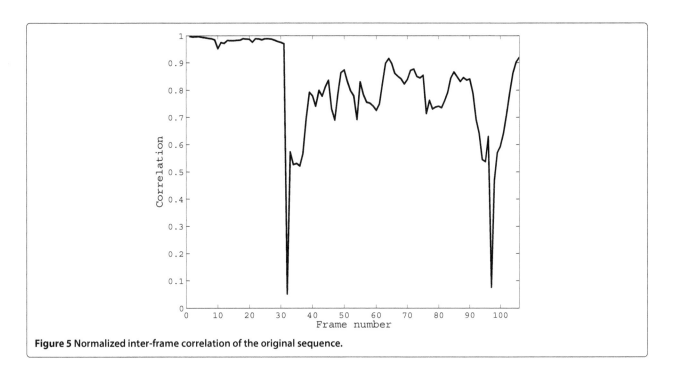

Figure 5 Normalized inter-frame correlation of the original sequence.

whose computation has been illustrated in the previous section. To account for the error propagation induced by predictive coding, a low-pass temporal filtering is applied to the degradation index maps. To this aim, let D_{k-1} denote the generic distortion map at time $(k-1)$; at time k, the distortion map D_k of frames belonging to dynamical shots is evaluated as follows:

$$\mathbf{D}_k^{CB} = \mu \left[\Gamma_k^{CB} + \varphi\left(\rho_k\right) \mathbf{D}_{k-1}^{CB} \right]; \tag{13}$$

$$\mathbf{D}_k^{RLB} = \mu \left[\Gamma_k^{RLB} + \varphi\left(\rho_k\right) \mathbf{D}_{k-1}^{RLB} \right] \tag{14}$$

where $\mu(x)$ is a non-linearity shown in Figure 6 and defined as follows:

$$\mu(x) = \begin{cases} 0 & x < \gamma \\ x & \gamma \le x < 2 \\ 2 & x \ge 2 \end{cases} \tag{15}$$

This non-linearity shrinks small distortions and allows to account for saturation in case of consecutive degradations of the same block through an operation of hard limiting.

The number of frames to be low-pass filtered is determined by the inter-frame correlation and in the following it will be indicated as φ.

More in details:

- For a given block $b(i,j)$, φ is set to zero if the corresponding block in the previous frame is affected by repeated line distortion and the inter-block correlation is below a predefined threshold (i.e., $\rho_k^{B^{(i,j)}} < \lambda_{RLB}$) indicating that the block has been updated by I-frame coding.

- φ is set to zero when processing I-frames.
- φ is set to one for frames belonging to static shots.

In order to evaluate the overall distortion index, the map $\mathbf{D}_k^{CB}$ of corrupted blocks is decomposed into two groups: the first one, denoted in the following with $\mathbf{D}_k^{CCB}$, contains the entries of $\mathbf{D}_k^{CB}$ associated to clustered corrupted blocks, while the second one, denoted in the following with $\mathbf{D}_k^{ICB}$, contains the contributions corresponding to the remaining, isolated, blocks. A block $b(i,j)$ for which $D_k^{CB}[i,j] > 0$ is considered member of a cluster if at least for one of its eight surrounding neighbors, $b(p,q)$, the condition $D_k^{CB^{(p,q)}} > 0$ holds. Let

- $\mathbf{N}_k^{CCB} = \left\| \mathbf{D}_k^{CCB} \right\|_{L_1}$ be the the L_1 norm of clustered corrupted block map
- $\mathbf{N}_k^{ICB} = \eta^{ICB}\left(\left\| \mathbf{D}_k^{ICB} \right\|_{L_1} \right)$ be the L_1 norm of isolated corrupted blocks where

$$\eta^{ICB}(x) = \begin{cases} 0 & x \le \lambda_{ICB} \\ x & \text{otherwise} \end{cases} \tag{16}$$

- $\mathbf{N}_k^{RL} = \left\| \mathbf{D}_k^{RLB} \right\|_{L_1}$ be the column vector of the number of repeated lines for each image color component
- ρ^{LOSS} the packet loss rate

Then, denoting with $\boldsymbol{\xi}$ is the column vector

$$\boldsymbol{\xi} = \left[1 \ \overline{N}^{CCB} \ \overline{N}^{ICB} \ \overline{N}^{RL} \ \rho^{LOSS} \right]^T \tag{17}$$

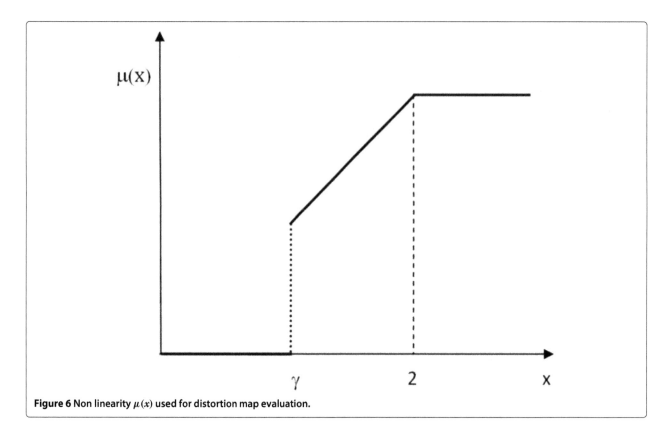

Figure 6 Non linearity $\mu(x)$ used for distortion map evaluation.

where

$$\overline{N}^{\mathrm{CCB}} = \frac{1}{L}\sum_{k=1}^{L} N_k^{\mathrm{CCB}}, \tag{18}$$

$$\overline{N}^{\mathrm{ICB}} = \frac{1}{L}\sum_{k=1}^{L} N_k^{\mathrm{ICB}}, \tag{19}$$

$$\overline{N}^{\mathrm{RL}} = \frac{1}{L}\sum_{k=1}^{L} N_k^{\mathrm{RL}}, \tag{20}$$

are the average values of the corresponding L_1 norms and L is the length of the video sequence, the NR metric $\mathrm{VQM}_{\mathrm{NR}}^{(Y)}$ based on the luminance component can be computed as follows:

$$\mathrm{VQM}_{\mathrm{NR}}^{(Y)} = \alpha \left[\boldsymbol{\xi}^T Q^{(Y)} \boldsymbol{\xi} \right]^{1/2} + \beta. \tag{21}$$

The weighting matrix $Q^{(Y)}$ (Table 1) and the regression coefficients α and β can be estimated by fitting subjective experiments, as illustrated in the next section.

We remark that, since $\boldsymbol{\xi}_1 = 1$, the quadratic form includes both linear and quadratic terms.

The above relationships can be directly extended to color images by building a degradation map for each color component. Therefore, assuming that each frame is represented by the luminance Y and color difference components C_b, C_r, the proposed video quality metric specifies as follows

$$\mathrm{VQM}_{\mathrm{NR}}^{(Y,C_b,C_r)} = \alpha_c \left[\boldsymbol{\zeta}^T Q^{(Y,C_b,C_r)} \boldsymbol{\zeta} \right]^{1/2} + \beta_c. \tag{22}$$

where $\boldsymbol{\zeta}$ is the column vector:

$$\boldsymbol{\zeta} = \left[1\ \ \overline{N}_Y^{\mathrm{CCB}}\ \ \overline{N}_Y^{\mathrm{ICB}}\ \ \overline{N}_Y^{\mathrm{RL}}\ \ \overline{N}_{C_b}^{\mathrm{CCB}}\ \ \overline{N}_{C_b}^{\mathrm{ICB}} \right. $$
$$\left. \overline{N}_{C_b}^{\mathrm{RL}}\ \ \overline{N}_{C_r}^{\mathrm{CCB}}\ \ \overline{N}_{C_r}^{\mathrm{ICB}}\ \ \overline{N}_{C_r}^{\mathrm{RL}}\ \ \rho^{\mathrm{LOSS}} \right]^T \tag{23}$$

having demoted with

- $\overline{N}_Y^{\mathrm{CCB}}, \overline{N}_{C_b}^{\mathrm{CCB}}, \overline{N}_{C_r}^{\mathrm{CCB}}$ the average numbers of clustered corrupted blocks for the three color components,
- $\overline{N}_Y^{\mathrm{ICB}}, \overline{N}_{C_b}^{\mathrm{ICB}}, \overline{N}_{C_r}^{\mathrm{ICB}}$ the average numbers of isolated corrupted blocks for the three color components,
- $\overline{N}_Y^{\mathrm{RL}}, \overline{N}_{C_b}^{\mathrm{RL}}, \overline{N}_{C_r}^{\mathrm{RL}}$ the average numbers of repeated lines for the three color components.

Table 1 Weighting matrix $Q^{(Y)}$

$Q_{i,j}^{(Y)}$	$i = 1$	$i = 2$	$i = 3$	$i = 4$	$i = 5$
$j = 1$	-0.0328	-0.0740	-0.0074	0.1138	0.0383
$j = 2$	-0.0740	0.0072	0.0007	0.0392	-0.0006
$j = 3$	-0.0074	0.0007	0.0006	0.0137	-0.0000
$j = 4$	0.1138	0.0392	0.0137	-0.1077	-0.0099
$j = 5$	0.0383	-0.0006	-0.0000	-0.0099	-0.0012

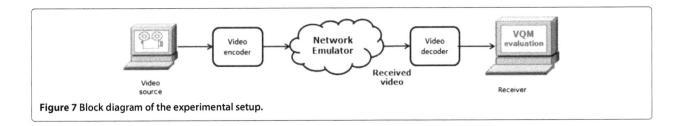

Figure 7 Block diagram of the experimental setup.

It is important to notice that the reduction of the impact of isolated corrupted blocks allows to mitigate the effects produced by misclassifications and to account for the lower sensitivity to artifacts in small areas compared to those in wider areas.

5 Experimental results

To identify the parameters specifying a NR metric and to verify its effectiveness, experiments involving human subjects should be performed. As already stated, this procedure is expensive, time-consuming, and often impossible to be performed. The alternative is to compare, under the same testing conditions, the gathered results with those provided by reliable full reference metrics. In the performed test, the NTIA video quality metric (VQM_{NTIA}) whose software implementation is publicly available and freely downloadable at the URL http://www.its.bldrdoc. gov/vqm, has been adopted.

5.1 Experimental setup

The experimental setup is shown in Figure 7, and it is composed by a streaming source, a network segment, and a receiver. The video server consists of a personal computer equipped with the open source VideoLAN server [57] and the FFmpeg tool [58]. The original video is encapsulated in a MPEG2 TS, packetized in the RTP/UDP/IP protocol stack and transmitted on a 100/1000Base-T Ethernet interface. The network segment has been accounted for by means of an open source network emulator: NETwork EMulator (NETEM) [59]. The emulator has been used for introducing packet losses in the incoming stream, in accordance to the statistics of real networks based on the best-effort paradigm.

Each considered media stream has been processed in order to simulate a set of increasing packet loss rates (PLRs). The selected PLRs are: 0.1%, 0.5%, 0.7%, 0.9%, 1.1%, 1.3%, 1.5%, 2.0%, 3.0%, 5.0%, 10%, 15%, and 20%. At the receiver side, the VLC client receives the media packets and uses concealment techniques for reconstructing the original video.

To evaluate the increase in VQM_{NR} performance achievable when full color information is employed with respect to the use of the luminance alone, the parameter identification and the performance assessment have been performed for both gray scale and color videos. Two sets of sequences have been used in our tests. The first one (*test set 1*) is composed by eight video sequences and it has been used for calibrating the $VQM_{NR}^{(Y)}$ metric parameters. The sequences are of different content and characterized by still scenes and slow or fast motion rates. The second one (*test set 2*) has been used for evaluating the effectiveness of the proposed metric. The sequences have been extracted from the online database 'The Consumer Digital Video Library' [60]. All analyzed videos have a VGA resolution (640 × 480 pixels, progressive) and a frame rate equal to 30 fps and they are composed by 360 frames. The test set 2 video dataset characteristics are reported in Table 2 while sample frames from the videos are shown in Figure 8.

Table 2 Video dataset characteristics

Video name	Chroma sampling	File size (Mb)	Run time (s)
NTIA Bells: man directing handbell choir	4:2:2	223.5	0:12
NTIA Cargas: car pulls into a gas station	4:2:2	223.5	0:12
NTIA Cartalk: boy complains about sister	4:2:2	223.5	0:12
NTIA Catjoke: a man tells a joke	4:2:2	221.2	0:12
NTIA Diner: young man talks in a diner	4:2:0	223.5	0:12
NTIA Drmset: young man plays on a drum set	4:2:2	223.5	0:12
NTIA Fish: goldfish pond with fades	4:2:2	331.8	0:18
NTIA Guitar: man plays guitar using finger picking style	4:2:2	223.5	0:12
NTIA Magic: girl performs magic trick	4:2:2	223.5	0:12
NTIA Music: a man playing banjo	4:2:2	223.5	0:12
NTIA Rfdev: RF device	4:2:2	221.2	0:12
NTIA Schart: school art	4:2:2	221.2	0:12
NTIA Wboard: man draws a chart on a whiteboard	4:2:2	1.663,4	1:30

Figure 8 Sample frames extracted from the videos in the dataset used in the experimental tests. (A) Bells. **(B)** Cargas. **(C)** Cartalk. **(D)** Catjoke. **(E)** Diner. **(F)** Drmset. **(G)** Fish. **(H)** Guitar. **(I)** Magic. **(J)** Music. **(K)** Rfdev. **(L)** Schart. **(M)** Wboard.

5.2 Gray scale video tests

The luminance component of a the test set 1 training set has been used for calibrating the $\text{VQM}_{\text{NR}}^{(Y)}$ metric parameters. In this phase, the goal has been to mimic the VQM_{NTIA} score computed on the training sequences as much as possible. Based on the achieved results, the thresholds θ_l and θ_h in Equation 4 have been set to 0.3 and 0.9, respectively. The parameters λ_H and λ_V, defined in Equation 7 and 8 have been set to 5 and 1, respectively. From the performed test, it can be noticed that λ_V, although small, is not null to account for small variations induced by partial decoding of a tile affected by errors. The length of the interval employed for the adaptation of

η_S (as in Equation 12) is considered constant and $M_h = 7$ has been employed in the reported results. The parameters λ_I, P, and Q, as defined in Equation 10 have been set to 0.25, 2, and 5, respectively.

The capability of the proposed metric to mimic the behavior of the VQM_{NTIA} for the training set is illustrated in Figures 9, 10, and 11. In more details, in Figure 9, the results concerning the *Taxi* sequence affected by three packet loss rates (1.9% top row, 3% middle row, and 6.7% bottom row) are reported. As can be noticed from the plots, the proposed metric scores are coherent with the VQM_{NTIA} ones, especially for the PLR $= 3\%$ and PLR $= 6.7\%$ cases.

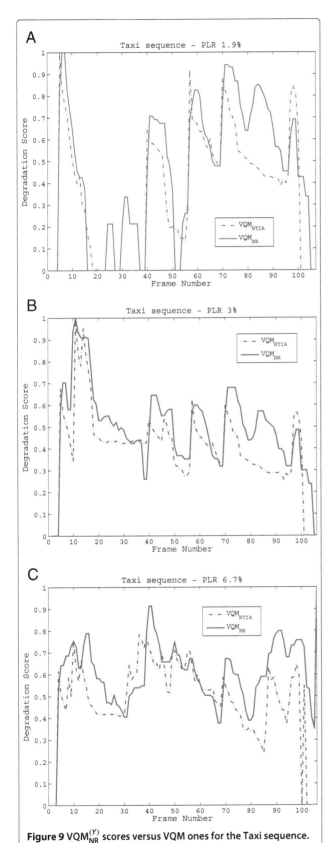

Figure 9 VQM$_{NR}^{(Y)}$ scores versus VQM ones for the Taxi sequence. **(A)** PLR = 1.9%. **(B)** PLR = 3%. **(C)** PLR = 7%.

It is worth noticing that in Figure 9A, around frame 85, the VQM$_{NR}$ presents a peak not corresponding to a similar quality variation detected by the VQM$_{NTIA}$. This behavior highlights the differences between the two metrics. As can be easily noticed by a visual inspection of the considered frames in the Taxi sequence and in its degraded version in Figure 10, there are errors resulting in block artifacts affecting both the main object and the road curbs. In this case, the proposed metric is able to cope with the masking effect of textures and with the perceived impact of silhouette definition and text readability.

The same behavior can be noticed for the sequence Field as reported in Figure 11. For almost the whole sequence, the two indexes show the same behavior. There is a slight tendency in overestimating the video artifacts by the VQM$_{NR}^{(Y)}$ index. Only for a few frames, the quality assessments provided by the two metrics are opposite: the value is over or below the quality threshold.

In the sequence Horse ride, the overlapping between the two curves is not homogeneous, as shown in Figure 12. Moreover, if the average behavior is compared, among the 25th and the 38th frame, the VQM$_{NR}^{(Y)}$ indicator shows high degradation while VQM$_{NTIA}$ only shows a slight degradation. The same different degradation rate can also be noticed in the last part of the sequence.

In order to evaluate the performances of the gray scale VQM$_{NR}^{(Y)}$ with respect to the quality estimation provided by the full color VQM$_{NTIA}$ metric, the test set 2 has been employed.

For comparing the performance achieved with the proposed gray scale and full color no-reference metrics, a Monte Carlo simulation of the transmission of the set of full color videos over an IP channel affected by packet losses for several packet loss rates has been performed. Then, only the luminance component of the decoded videos has been employed for computing VQM$_{NR}^{(Y)}$ while both luminance and color differences have been employed for computing both VQM$_{NR}^{(Y,c_b,C_r)}$ and VQM$_{NTIA}$.

In Figure 13, the results obtained for each sequence with the VQM$_{NR}^{(Y)}$ have been plotted versus VQM$_{NTIA}$ ones. As can be noticed, there is good matching between the two metrics and the root mean square error (RMSE) value is 0.14. The regression value is 0.86.

5.3   Color video tests

To verify the gain achieved when chrominance is employed, the multivariate regression procedure has then been applied to the full reference metric and to the packet loss rate, the average numbers of clustered corrupted blocks, isolated corrupted blocks, and repeated lines extracted from Y, C_b, and C_r decoded components, thus, obtaining the regression coefficients $\alpha_c = 1.0419$ and

Figure 10 Degraded version of the *Taxi* sequence. Original **(A)** and impaired **(B)** version of the frame number 85 of the *Taxi* sequence.

$\beta_c = -0.0465$. The weighting matrix is reported in Table 3.

In Figure 14, the plot of $\text{VQM}_{\text{NR}}^{(Y,C_b,C_r)}$ versus the VQM_{NTIA} is reported for the selected videos. The plot shows improved performances of the proposed metric in matching the full reference score. In fact, the use of color information increases the fitting performances resulting

in a regression value of 0.91 and on a RMSE value equal to 0.11.

By analyzing the results, a few issues are open for future investigation. First of all, from the performed experiments for both metric parameters tuning and metric performance effectiveness assessment, a key factor for a successful comparison of NR and FR metrics is

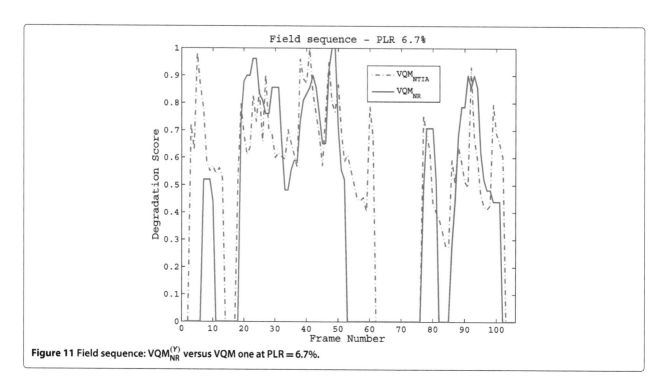

Figure 11 Field sequence: $\text{VQM}_{\text{NR}}^{(Y)}$ versus VQM one at PLR = 6.7%.

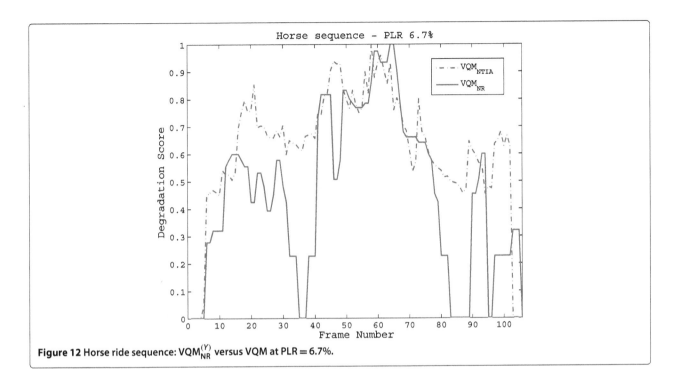

Figure 12 Horse ride sequence: VQM$_{NR}^{(Y)}$ versus VQM at PLR $= 6.7\%$.

represented by the temporal realignment algorithm. In the presence of highly textured backgrounds, severe frame losses, and medium to high compression ratios, at least our implementation of the VQM$_{NTIA}$ algorithm does not provide reliable estimates of the variable delay between the original and decoded videos. This implies a potential bias in the estimated NR metrics induced by the wrong selection of the reference frame to be used for the comparison. Furthermore, we noticed that the adopted key-frame detection algorithm has an impact on overall distortion evaluation, since many elements, considered in the proposed metric, depend on the shot boundaries detection.

5.4 Subjective experiment

Finally, in order to further verify the effectiveness of the proposed metric, a subjective experiment has been performed.

Sixteen test subjects drawn from a pool of students of the University of Roma TRE have participated to the test. The students are thought to be relatively naive concerning video artifacts and the associated terminology. They were asked to wear any vision correcting devices (glasses or contact lenses) they normally wear to watch television. The subjects were asked to rate the quality of the videos in the test database (listed in Table 2) through a single stimulus quality evaluation method [61].

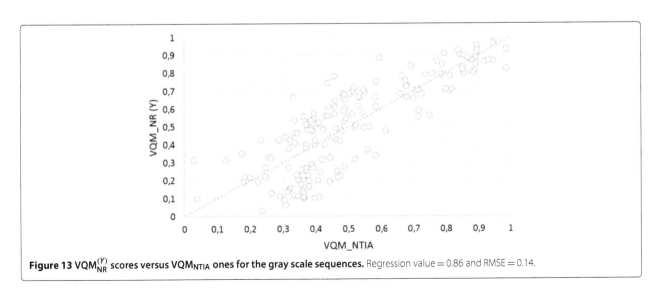

Figure 13 VQM$_{NR}^{(Y)}$ scores versus VQM$_{NTIA}$ ones for the gray scale sequences. Regression value $= 0.86$ and RMSE $= 0.14$.

Table 3 Weighting matrix Q

$Q_{i,j}$	i = 1	i = 2	i = 3	i = 4	i = 5	i = 6	i = 7	i = 8	i = 9	i = 10	i = 11
j = 1	0.0094	0.0728	0.0101	0.0099	-0.0202	-0.0003	0.0768	0.1929	-0.0065	0.0195	0.0266
j = 2	0.0728	-0.0085	-0.0011	-0.0520	-0.0633	0.0013	0.0071	0	-0.0245	0.2121	-0.0022
j = 3	0.0101	-0.0011	-0.0009	0.0039	-0.0119	0.0007	0.0041	0	-0.0043	0.0071	0.0001
j = 4	0.0099	-0.0520	0.0039	-0.0052	0.0855	-0.0016	-0.0524	0	-0.0254	0.0329	0.0008
j = 5	-0.0202	-0.0633	-0.0119	0.0855	-0.0242	-0.0456	0.1776	0	0.2104	-0.4598	0.0080
j = 6	-0.0003	0.0013	0.0007	-0.0016	-0.0456	-0.0005	-0.0030	-0.0094	0.0012	-0.0013	0.0004
j = 7	0.0768	0.0071	0.0041	-0.0524	0.1776	-0.0030	-0.1082	-0.1023	-0.0038	0.1061	-0.0007
j = 8	0.1929	0	0	0	0	-0.0094	-0.1023	-0.0120	0.0224	-0.3094	0.0109
j = 9	-0.0065	-0.0245	-0.0043	-0.0254	0.2104	0.0012	-0.0038	0.0224	0.0091	0.0220	-0.0006
j = 10	0.0195	0.2121	0.0071	0.0329	-0.4598	-0.0013	0.1061	-0.3094	0.0220	-0.1038	-0.0078
j = 11	0.0266	-0.0022	0.0001	0.0008	0.0080	0.0004	-0.0007	0.0109	-0.0006	-0.0078	-0.0011

A Panasonic Viera monitor (46") is used to display the test video sequences. The experiment is run with one subject at a time. Each subject was seated straight ahead in front of the monitor, located at or slightly below eye height for most subjects. The subjects are positioned at a distance of four screen heights (80 cm) from the video monitor in a controlled light environment. The experimental session consisted of four stages. In the first stage, the subject was verbally given instructions for performing the test. In the second stage, training sequences were shown to the subject. The training sequences represent the impairment extremes for the experiment and are used to establish the annoyance value range. In the third stage, the test subjects run through several practice trials. The practice trials are identical to the experimental trials and are used to familiarize the test subject with the experiment. Finally, the experiment is performed on the complete set of test sequences. After each video was displayed, the subject was asked to enter his/her judgment in a scale from 1 to 5, where 5 corresponds to best quality and 1 to worst quality.

In Figure 15, the comparison between the collected MOS and the two objective metrics are reported. The MOS has been normalized in the range 0 (best quality) to 1 (worst quality). The RMS is 0.10 for the $VQM_{NR}^{(Y,C_b,C_r)}$ metric and 0.16 for VQM_{NTIA} metric, respectively. As can be noticed, the proposed metric is able to predict the subjective judgment.

6 Conclusions

In this paper, a no-reference metric for assessing the quality of MPEG-based video transmissions over IP-based networks is presented. The proposed approach is based on the analysis of the inter-frame correlation measured at the receiver side. Several tests have been performed for tuning and evaluating the performances of the proposed metric. The scores collected by this tool in evaluating

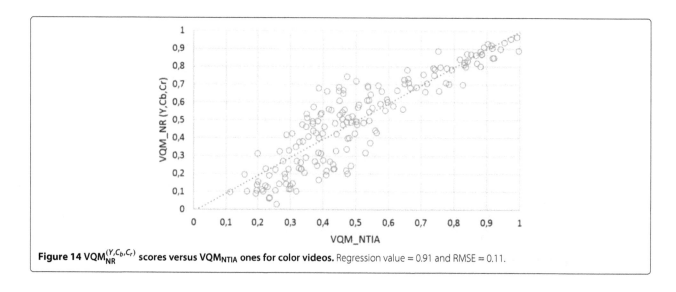

Figure 14 $VQM_{NR}^{(Y,C_b,C_r)}$ **scores versus VQM_{NTIA} ones for color videos.** Regression value = 0.91 and RMSE = 0.11.

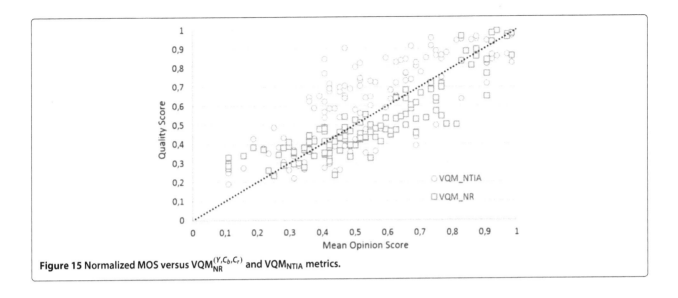

Figure 15 Normalized MOS versus $VQM_{NR}^{(Y,C_b,C_r)}$ and VQM_{NTIA} metrics.

impaired videos have been compared with the ones gathered with the full reference VQM_{NTIA} metrics and with the MOS collected by means of a subjective experiment. The overall analysis demonstrates the effectiveness of the VQM_{NR}. Current investigation is devoted to solve the problems arising when using evaluation methods that are not based on reference signals. In particular, for the temporal realignment algorithm that is needed for the FR metrics in order to correctly estimate the NR parameters, we plan to test a novel re-synchronization procedure. Recently, the NTIA group announced the release of a new version of VQM metrics especially tuned for variable packet loss rate. Even if the problem of realignment is still to be solved, the use of such a metric could probably be used for a more effective parameters tuning. As a general remark, the influence of the adopted key-frame detection algorithm should be investigated. In fact, if a fake key-frame is selected due to estimation errors, the quality metric immediately decreases. Another issue is related to the amount of motion characterizing the sequences. We noticed a difference in the scores when slow or almost null motion rate is present. The choice of the parameter λ_s should be based on the consideration, confirmed by many studies, that human attention is attracted by objects whose movement is relevant with respect to the other elements in the scene. Therefore, λ_s should probably be adapted to the relative motion of the surrounding areas. Finally, a key issue to be further investigated is the influence of the adopted error concealment technique implemented in the decoder. With the improving of error concealment masking techniques, the concealed video may present different error patterns from the ones we are experiencing at the moment. For example, we noticed that the latest version of VLC is able to mask, in a more effective way, some transmission errors like the presence of

isolated blocks. This means that in the future, the weight of such parameters may be different depending on the improvements achieved in the field of error concealment techniques.

Competing interests

The authors declare that they have no competing interests.

References

1. F Battisti, M Carli, E Mammi, A Neri, A study on the impact of AL-FEC techniques on TV over IP quality of experience. EURASIP J. Adv. Signal Process. **2011**, 86 (2011). http://asp.eurasipjournals.com/content/2011/1/86.
2. A Perkis, Y Abdeljaoued, C Christopoulos, T Ebrahimi, JF Chicharo, Universal multimedia access from wired and wireless systems. Circuits, Syst., Signal Process. Special Issue Multimedia Commun. **20**(3), 387–402 (2001)
3. F Pereira, I Burnett, Universal multimedia experiences for tomorrow. IEEE Signal Process. Mag. **20**(2), 63–73 (2003)
4. Psytechnics Ltd, Psytechnics no-reference video quality assessment model, in *ITU-T SG9 Meeting, COM9-C190-E: Geneva, 5 May 2008* (Psytechnics Ltd., Ipswitch, 2008)
5. YH Kim, J Han, H Kim, J Shin, Novel no-reference video quality assessment metric with estimation of dynamic range distortion, in *Proceedings of the 12th International Conference on Advanced Communication Technology (ICACT): 7–10 Feb 2010; Phoenix Park*, vol. 2 (IEEE, Piscataway, 2010), pp. 1689–1692
6. S Chikkerur, V Sundaram, M Reisslein, LJ Karam, Objective video quality assessment methods: a classification, review, and performance comparison. IEEE Trans. Broadcasting. **57**(2), 165–182 (2011)
7. M Vranješ, S Rimac-Drlje, K Grgić, Review of objective video quality metrics and performance comparison using different databases. Image Commun. **28**, 1–19 (2013)
8. S Winkler, Video quality measurement standards—current status and trends, in *Proceedings of the Seventh International Conference Information, Communications and Signal Processing: 8–10 Dec 2009; Macau* (IEEE, Piscataway, 2009), pp. 1–5
9. M Pinson, S Wolf, A new standardized method for objectively measuring video quality. IEEE Trans. Broadcasting. **50**(3), 312–322 (2004)
10. ITU-T, *Recommendation J.144, objective perceptual video quality measurement techniques for digital cable television in the presence of a full reference* (ITU, Geneva, 2004)

11. A Basso, I Dalgic, FA Tobagi, CJ van den Branden Lambrecht, Feedback-control scheme for low-latency constant-quality MPEG-2 video encoding, in *SPIE:16 Sept 1996; Berlin*, vol. 2952 (SPIE, Berlin, 1996), pp. 460–471

12. CJ van den Branden Lambrecht, Color moving pictures quality metric, in *Proceedings of the International Conference on Image Processing (ICIP): 16–19 Sept 1996; Lausanne*, vol. 1 (IEEE, Piscataway, 1996), pp. 885–888

13. Z Wang, A Bovik, H Sheikh, EP Simoncelli, Image quality assessment: from error visibility to structural similarity. IEEE Trans. Image Process. **13**, 600–612 (2004). citeseer.ist.psu.edu/article/wang04image.html

14. S Wolf, MH Pinson, SD Voran, AA Webster, Objective quality assessment of digitally transmitted video, in *Proceedings of the IEEE Pacific Rim Conference on Communications, Computers and Signal Processing: 9–10 May 1991; Victoria* (IEEE, Piscataway, 1991), pp. 477–482

15. AB Watson, QJ Hu, JFM Gowan, Digital video quality metric based on human vision. J. Electron. Imaging **10**, 20–29 (2001)

16. S Winkler, Issues in vision modeling for perceptual video quality assessment. Signal Process. **78**(2) (1999). citeseer.ist.psu.edu/winkler99issues.html

17. A Shnayderman, A Gusev, AM Eskicioglu, An SVD-based grayscale image quality measure for local and global assessment. IEEE Trans. Image Process. **15**(2), 422–429 (2006)

18. G Zhai, W Zhang, X Yang, S Yao, Y Xu, GES: a new image quality assessment metric based on energy features in Gabor transform domain, in *Proceedings of the IEEE International Symposium on Circuits and Systems (ISCAS): 21–24 may 2006; Island of Kos* (IEEE, Piscataway, 2006), p. 4

19. M Carnec, P Le Callet, D Barba, Full reference and reduced reference metrics for image quality assessment, in *Proceedings of the 7th International Symposium on Signal Processing and its Applications (ISSPA):1–4 Jul 2003; Paris*, vol. 1 (IEEE, Piscataway, 2003), pp. 477–480

20. TM Kusuma, HJ Zepernick, M Caldera, On the development of a reduced-reference perceptual image quality metric, in *Proceedings on Systems Communications: 14–17 Aug 2005* (IEEE, Piscataway, 2005), pp. 178–184

21. Z Wang, EP Simoncelli, Reduced-reference image quality assessment using a wavelet-domain natural image statistic model, in *Proceedings of SPIE Human Vision and Electronic Imaging X: San Jose*, vol. 5666 (SPIE, Berlin, 2005)

22. S Kanumuri, SG Subramanian, PC Cosman, AR Reibman, Predicting H.264 packet loss visibility using a generalized linear model, in *Proceedings of the IEEE International Conference on Image Processing (ICIP): 8–11 Oct 2006; Atlanta* (IEEE, Piscataway, 2006), pp. 2245–2248

23. S Kanumuri, PC Cosman, AR Reibman, VA Vaishampayan, Modeling packet-loss visibility in MPEG-2 video. IEEE Trans. Multimedia **8**(2), 341–355 (2006)

24. T Liu, X Feng, AR Reibman, Y Wang, Saliency inspired modeling of packet-loss visibility in decoded videos, in *Proceedings of the 4th International workshop on Video Processing and Quality Metrics for Consumer Electronics (VPQM): 14–16 Jan 2009; Scottsdale*. Online: www.vpqm.org

25. P Campisi, M Carli, G Giunta, A Neri, Blind quality assessment system for multimedia communications using tracing watermarking. Signal Process., IEEE Trans. **51**(4), 996–1002 (2003)

26. M Farias, M Carli, S Mitra, Objective video quality metric based on data hiding. IEEE Trans. Consum. Electron. **51**, 983–992 (2005)

27. M Carli, M Farias, E Drelie Gelasca, R Tedesco, A Neri, Quality assessment using data hiding on perceptually important areas, in *IEEE International Conference on Image Processing: 11–14 Sept 2005; Genoa*, vol. 3 (IEEE, Piscataway, 2005), pp. 1200–1203

28. F Battisti, M Carli, A Neri, Video error concealment based on data hiding in the 3D wavelet domain, in *Proceedings of the 2nd European Workshop on Visual Information Processing (EUVIP): 5–6 Jul 2010; Paris* (IEEE, Piscataway, 2010), pp. 134–139

29. A Ninassi, PL Callet, F Autrusseau, Pseudo no reference image quality metric using perceptual data hiding, in *Proceedings of the SPIE Human Vision and Electronic Imaging XI* (SPIE, Berlin, 2006)

30. A Phadikar, P Maity, C Delpha, Data hiding for quality access control and error concealment in digital images, in *Proceedings of the 2011 IEEE International Conference on Multimedia and Expo (ICME): 11–15 Jul 2011; Barcelona* (IEEE, Piscataway, 2011), pp. 1–6

31. HR Wu, M Yuen, A generalized block edge impairment metric for video coding. Signal Process. Lett. **4**(11), 317–320 (1997)

32. P Marziliano, F Dufaux, S Winkler, T Ebrahimi, A no-reference perceptual blur metric, in *Proceedings of the IEEE International Conference on Image Processing*, vol. 3 (IEEE, Piscataway, 2002)

33. M Carli, D Guida, A Neri, No-reference jerkiness evaluation method for multimedia communications. Procs. SPIE Image Qual. Syst. Perform. III. **6059**, 350–359 (2006)

34. DS Turaga, Y Chen, J Caviedes, No reference PSNR estimation for compressed pictures. Proc. Elsevier Signal Process. Image Commun. **19**, 173–184 (2004)

35. W Ci, H Dong, Z Wu, Y Tan, Example-based objective quality estimation for compressed images. IEEE Multimedia. **99** (2009)

36. A Leontaris, PC Cosman, AR Reibman, Quality evaluation of motion-compensated edge artifacts in compressed video. IEEE Trans. Image Process. **16**(4), 943–956 (2007)

37. A Leontaris, PC Cosman, Compression efficiency and delay trade-offs for hierarchical B-Pictures and pulsed-quality frames. IEEE Trans. Image Process. **16**(7), 1726–1740 (2007)

38. J Gustafsson, G Heikkila, M Pettersson, Measuring multimedia quality in mobile networks with an objective parametric model, in *Proceedings of the 15th IEEE International Conference on Image Processing (ICIP): 12–15 Oct 2008; San Diego* (IEEE, Piscataway, 2008), pp. 405–408

39. M Naccari, M Tagliasacchi, F Pereira, S Tubaro, No-reference modeling of the channel induced distortion at the decoder for H.264/AVC video coding, in *Proceedings of the 15th IEEE International Conference on Image Processing (ICIP): 12–15 Oct 2008; San Diego* (IEEE, Piscataway, 2008), pp. 2324–2327

40. Y Liu, Y Zhang, M Sun, W Li, Full-reference quality diagnosis for video summary, in *Proceedings of the IEEE International Conference on Multimedia and Expo: 23 Jun–26 Apr 2008; Hannover* (IEEE, Piscataway, 2008), pp. 1489–1492

41. J Han, YH Kim, J Jeong, J Shin, Video quality estimation for packet loss based on no-reference method, in *Proceedings of the 12th International Conference on Advanced Communication Technology: 7–10 Feb 2010; Phoenix Park* (IEEE, Piscataway, 2010), pp. 418–421

42. SO Lee, DG Sim, Hybrid bitstream-based video quality assessment method for scalable video coding. Opt. Eng. **51**(6) (2012)

43. N Staelens, N Vercammen, Y Dhondt, B Vermeulen, P Lambert, R Van de Walle, P Demeester, ViQID: a no-reference bit stream-based visual quality impairment detector, in *2010 Second International Workshop on Quality of Multimedia Experience (QoMEX)* (IEEE, Piscataway, 2010), pp. 206–211

44. N Staelens, D Deschrijver, E Vladislavleva, B Vermeulen, Constructing a no-reference H.264/AVC bitstream-based video quality metric using genetic programming-based symbolic regression, in *2010 Second International Workshop on Quality of Multimedia Experience (QoMEX), Klagenfurt*, vol. 23 (IEEE, Piscataway, 2013), pp. 1322–1333

45. N Staelens, GV Wallendael, K Crombecq, N Vercammen, *No-reference bitstream-based visual quality impairment detection for high definition H.264/AVC encoded video sequences*, vol. 58 (IEEE, Piscataway, 2012), pp. 187–199

46. C Keimel, J Habigt, M Klimpke, K Diepold, Design of no-reference video quality metrics with multiway partial least squares regression, in *2011 Third International Workshop on Quality of Multimedia Experience (QoMEX): 7–9 Sep 2011; Mechelen* (IEEE, Piscataway, 2011), pp. 1322–1333

47. C Keimel, J Habigt, K Diepold, Hybrid no-reference video quality metric based on multiway PLSR, in *2012 Proceedings of the 20th European Signal Processing Conference (EUSIPCO): 27–31 Aug 2012; Bucharest* (IEEE, Piscataway, 2012), pp. 1244–1248

48. S Shi, K Nahrstedt, R Campbell, Distortion over latency: novel metric for measuring interactive performance in remote rendering systems, in *2011 IEEE International Conference on Multimedia and Expo (ICME): 11–15 July 2011; Barcelona* (IEEE, Piscataway, 2011), pp. 1–6

49. E Bosc, F Battisti, M Carli, P Le Callet, A wavelet-based image quality metric for the assessment of 3D synthesized views, in *2011 IEEE International Conference on Multimedia and Expo (ICME)*, vol. 8648 (IEEE, Piscataway, 2013)

50. L Azzari, F Battisti, A Gotchev, M Carli, K Egiazarian, A modified non-local mean inpainting technique for occlusion filling in depth-image-based rendering, in *2011 IEEE International Conference on Multimedia and Expo (ICME)*, vol. 7863 (IEEE, Piscataway, 2011)

51. AA Webster, CT Jones, MH Pinson, SD Voran, S Wolf, An objective video quality assessment system based on human perception, in *Proceedings of SPIE Human Vision, Visual Processing, and Digital Display IV*, vol. 1913 (SPIE, Berlin, 1993), pp. 15–26

52. P Bretillon, J Baina, M Jourlin, G Goudezeune, Method for image quality monitoring on digital television networks, in *Proceedings of the SPIE Multimedia Systems and Applications II*, vol. 3845 (SPIE, Berlin, 1999), pp. 298–306

53. Z Wang, A Bovik, B Evans, Blind measurement of blocking artifacts in images. Proc. IEEE Int. Conf. Image Process. **3**, 981–984 (2000)

54. J Caviedes, J Jung, No-reference metric for a video quality control loop, in *Proceedings of the 5th World Multiconference on Systemics, Cybernetics, and Informatics* (IIIS, Orlando, 2001), pp. 290–295

55. F Zhang, W Lin, Z Chen, KN Ngan, Additive log-logistic model for networked video quality assessment. Image Process., IEEE Trans. **22**(4), 1536–1547 (2013)

56. M Montenovo, A Perot, M Carli, P Cicchetti, A Neri, Objective quality evaluation of video services, in *Procs. of the 1st International Workshop on Video Processing and Quality Metrics for Consumer Electronic (VPQM)*, (2006). www.vpqm.org

57. VideoLan team, VideoLAN - VLC media player. http://www.videolan.org/. Accessed 3 Feb 2014

58. FFmpeg team, FFmpeg. http://www.ffmpeg.org/. Accessed 3 Feb 2014

59. NetEm team, Network Emulation with NetEm (2005). http://www.linuxfoundation.org/. Accessed 3 Feb 2014

60. CDVL Team, The consumer digital video library (2011). http://www.cdvl.org. Accessed 3 Feb 2014

61. ITU-T, *Recommendation BT.500-11, methodology for the subjective assessment of the quality of television pictures* (ITU, Geneva, 2002). www.itu.org

Permissions

The contributors of this book come from diverse backgrounds, making this book a truly international effort. This book will bring forth new frontiers with its revolutionizing research information and detailed analysis of the nascent developments around the world.

We would like to thank all the contributing authors for lending their expertise to make the book truly unique. They have played a crucial role in the development of this book. Without their invaluable contributions this book wouldn't have been possible. They have made vital efforts to compile up to date information on the varied aspects of this subject to make this book a valuable addition to the collection of many professionals and students.

This book was conceptualized with the vision of imparting up-to-date information and advanced data in this field. To ensure the same, a matchless editorial board was set up. Every individual on the board went through rigorous rounds of assessment to prove their worth. After which they invested a large part of their time researching and compiling the most relevant data for our readers.

The editorial board has been involved in producing this book since its inception. They have spent rigorous hours researching and exploring the diverse topics which have resulted in the successful publishing of this book. They have passed on their knowledge of decades through this book. To expedite this challenging task, the publisher supported the team at every step. A small team of assistant editors was also appointed to further simplify the editing procedure and attain best results for the readers.

Apart from the editorial board, the designing team has also invested a significant amount of their time in understanding the subject and creating the most relevant covers. They scrutinized every image to scout for the most suitable representation of the subject and create an appropriate cover for the book.

The publishing team has been an ardent support to the editorial, designing and production team. Their endless efforts to recruit the best for this project, has resulted in the accomplishment of this book. They are a veteran in the field of academics and their pool of knowledge is as vast as their experience in printing. Their expertise and guidance has proved useful at every step. Their uncompromising quality standards have made this book an exceptional effort. Their encouragement from time to time has been an inspiration for everyone.

The publisher and the editorial board hope that this book will prove to be a valuable piece of knowledge for researchers, students, practitioners and scholars across the globe.

List of Contributors

Iñigo Sedano
TECNALIA, ICT - European Software Institute, Parque Tecnológico de Bizkaia, Edificio 202, Zamudio E-48170, Spain

Kjell Brunnström
Acreo Swedish ICT AB, NETLAB: Visual Media Quality, Box 1070, Kista SE-164 25, Sweden.
Department of Information Technology and Media, Mid Sweden, University, Holmgatan 10, Sundsvall SE-851 70, Sweden

Maria Kihl
Deptartment of Electrical and Information Technology, Lund University, Box 117, Lund SE-221 00, Sweden

Andreas Aurelius
Acreo Swedish ICT AB, NETLAB: Visual Media Quality, Box 1070, Kista SE-164 25, Sweden
Deptartment of Electrical and Information Technology, Lund University, Box 117, Lund SE-221 00, Sweden

Yong-Jo Ahn
Department of Computer Engineering, Kwangwoon University, Wolgye-dong, Nowon-gu, Seoul 447-1, South Korea

Tae-Jin Hwang
Department of Computer Engineering, Kwangwoon University, Wolgye-dong, Nowon-gu, Seoul 447-1, South Korea

Dong-Gyu Sim
Department of Computer Engineering, Kwangwoon University, Wolgye-dong, Nowon-gu, Seoul 447-1, South Korea

Woo-Jin Han
Department of Software Design and Management, Gachon University, Seongnam, Gyeonggi 461-701, South Korea

Elham Kermani
Electrical Engineering Faculty, K.N. Toosi University of Technology, Tehran 1431714191, Iran

Davud Asemani
Electrical Engineering Faculty, K.N. Toosi University of Technology, Tehran 1431714191, Iran

Epameinondas Antonakos
Department of Electrical and Computer Engineering, National Technical University of Athens, Athens 15773, Greece
Department of Computing, Imperial College London, 180 Queen's Gate, London SW7 2AZ, UK

Vassilis Pitsikalis
Department of Electrical and Computer Engineering, National Technical University of Athens, Athens 15773, Greece

Petros Maragos
Department of Electrical and Computer Engineering, National Technical University of Athens, Athens 15773, Greece

Wilbert G Aguilar
Automatic Control Department, UPC-BarcelonaTech, Pau Gargallo Street 5, 08028 Barcelona, Spain

Cecilio Angulo
Automatic Control Department, UPC-BarcelonaTech, Pau Gargallo Street 5, 08028 Barcelona, Spain

Muhammad Shahid
Blekinge Institute of Technology, Karlskrona SE-37179, Sweden

Andreas Rossholm
Blekinge Institute of Technology, Karlskrona SE-37179, Sweden

Benny Lövström
Blekinge Institute of Technology, Karlskrona SE-37179, Sweden

Hans-Jürgen Zepernick
Blekinge Institute of Technology, Karlskrona SE-37179, Sweden

Yuan-Kai Kuan
Department of Electrical Engineering, National Dong Hwa University, 97401Hualien, Taiwan

Gwo-Long Li
Department of Video Coding Core Technology, Industrial Technology Research Institute, 31040 Hsinchu, Taiwan

Mei-Juan Chen
Department of Electrical Engineering, National Dong Hwa University, 97401Hualien, Taiwan

Kuang-Han Tai
Department of Electrical Engineering, National Dong Hwa University, 97401Hualien, Taiwan

Pin-Cheng Huang
Department of Electrical Engineering, National Dong Hwa University, 97401Hualien, Taiwan

Amol Ambardekar
University of Nevada, 1664 N Virginia St., Reno, NV 89557, USA

Mircea Nicolescu
University of Nevada, 1664 N Virginia St., Reno, NV 89557, USA

George Bebis
University of Nevada, 1664 N Virginia St., Reno, NV 89557, USA

Monica Nicolescu
University of Nevada, 1664 N Virginia St., Reno, NV 89557, USA

Anand D Darji
Department of Electrical Engineering, Indian Institute of Technology Bombay, Powai, Mumbai 400076, India

Shailendra Singh Kushwah
Electronics Engineering Department, S. V. National Institute of Technology, Surat, Gujarat 395007, India

Shabbir N Merchant
Department of Electrical Engineering, Indian Institute of Technology Bombay, Powai, Mumbai 400076, India

Arun N Chandorkar
Department of Electrical Engineering, Indian Institute of Technology Bombay, Powai, Mumbai 400076, India

Qiang Peng
School of Information Science and Technology, Southwest Jiaotong University, Chengdu, China

Lei Zhang
School of Information Science and Technology, Southwest Jiaotong University, Chengdu, China
Institution of Academia Sinica, Jiuzhou Electric Group, Sichuan, China

Xiao Wu
School of Information Science and Technology, Southwest Jiaotong University, Chengdu, China

Qionghua Wang
School of Electronics and Information Engineering, Sichuan University, Chengdu, China

Alberto Jorge Rosales-Silva
School of Advanced Mechanical and Electrical Engineering, U.P.A.L.M, Av. Instituto Politécnico Nacional S/N, ESIME catenco, Col. Lindavista, México D.F. 07738, Mexico

Francisco Javier Gallegos-Funes
School of Advanced Mechanical and Electrical Engineering, U.P.A.L.M, Av. Instituto Politécnico Nacional S/N, ESIME catenco, Col. Lindavista, México D.F. 07738, Mexico

Ivonne Bazan Trujillo
School of Advanced Mechanical and Electrical Engineering, U.P.A.L.M, Av. Instituto Politécnico Nacional S/N, ESIME catenco, Col. Lindavista, México D.F. 07738, Mexico

Alfredo Ramírez García
School of Advanced Mechanical and Electrical Engineering, U.P.A.L.M, Av. Instituto Politécnico Nacional S/N, ESIME catenco, Col. Lindavista, México D.F. 07738, Mexico

Kyung-Yeon Min
Department of Computer Engineering, Kwangwoon University, Wolgye-dong, Seoul 447-1, Nowon-gu, South Korea

Woong Lim
Department of Computer Engineering, Kwangwoon University, Wolgye-dong, Seoul 447-1, Nowon-gu, South Korea

Junghak Nam
Department of Computer Engineering, Kwangwoon University, Wolgye-dong, Seoul 447-1, Nowon-gu, South Korea

Donggyu Sim
Department of Computer Engineering, Kwangwoon University, Wolgye-dong, Seoul 447-1, Nowon-gu, South Korea

Ivan V Bajić
School of Engineering Science, Simon Fraser University, 8888 University Drive, Burnaby, BC, Canada

Qiuwen Zhang
College of Computer and Communication Engineering, Zhengzhou University of Light Industry, No. 5 Dongfeng Road, Zhengzhou 450002, China

Ming Chen
Software Engineering College, Zhengzhou University of Light Industry, Zhengzhou 450002, China

Xinpeng Huang
College of Computer and Communication Engineering, Zhengzhou University of Light Industry, No. 5 Dongfeng Road, Zhengzhou 450002, China

Nana Li
College of Computer and Communication Engineering, Zhengzhou University of Light Industry, No. 5 Dongfeng Road, Zhengzhou 450002, China

Yong Gan
College of Computer and Communication Engineering, Zhengzhou University of Light Industry, No. 5 Dongfeng Road, Zhengzhou 450002, China

Yu-Chen Wang
Department of Computer Science and Information Engineering, National Central University, Taoyuan, Taiwan

Chin-Chuan Han
Department of Computer Science and Information Engineering, National United University, Miaoli, Taiwan

Chen-Ta Hsieh
Department of Computer Science and Information Engineering, National Central University, Taoyuan, Taiwan

Kuo-Chin Fan
Department of Computer Science and Information Engineering, National Central University, Taoyuan, Taiwan

Devang S Pandya
U V Patel College of Engineering, Ganpat University, Kherva 384012, Mehsana, India

Mukesh A Zaveri
Sardar Vallabhbhai National Institute of Technology, Surat 395007, India

Federica Battisti
Department of Engineering, Universita' degli Studi Roma TRE, Rome 00146, Italy

Marco Carli
Department of Engineering, Universita' degli Studi Roma TRE, Rome 00146, Italy

Alessandro Neri
Department of Engineering, Universita' degli Studi Roma TRE, Rome 00146, Italy

Printed in the USA
CPSIA information can be obtained
at www.ICGtesting.com
JSHW051428221024
72173JS00006B/1408